Wiltshire Record Society

(formerly the Records Branch of the Wiltshire Archaeological and Natural History Society)

VOLUME 66

Sarah, duchess of Somerset, died 1692

THE MINUTE BOOKS OF FROXFIELD ALMSHOUSE 1714–1866

edited by

DOUGLAS CROWLEY

CHIPPENHAM

2013

c/o Wiltshire and Swindon History Centre,
Cocklebury Road, Chippenham SN15 3QN

ISBN 978-0-901333-43-8

The Wiltshire Record Society gratefully acknowledges the continued financial support of Wiltshire Council.

Typeset by John Chandler
Produced for the Society by
Salisbury Printing Company Ltd, Salisbury
Printed in Great Britain

CONTENTS

LIST OF ILLUSTRATIONS

PREFACE

The documents edited below are listed and described on pages 109–11 of the introduction to the text. Most of them are among the muniments of the Duchess of Somerset's Hospital at Froxfield and are kept in the Wiltshire and Swindon History Centre. The society is very grateful to the steward of the hospital's trustees for making them available.

The editor of the volume again expresses his thanks to all the staff of the Archive Service for their unfailing helpfulness, patience, and efficiency, and in particular to Jane Silcocks who made the digital images from which the edition was prepared. He also thanks Dr. John Chandler who has again been more than generous with his time and expertise.

Steven Hobbs

ABBREVIATIONS AND NOTANDA

a. acre(s)
Alum. Oxon. *Alumni Oxonienses*, ed. J. Foster
Aubrey, *Topog. Colln.* ed. Jackson *The Topographical Collections of John Aubrey*, edited by J. E. Jackson (Devizes, 1862)
Burke, *Commoners* J. Burke and others, *A History of the Commoners* (London, 1833–8)
Burke, *Ext. and Dorm. Baronetcies* J. Burke and others, *Extinct and Dormant Baronetcies*
Burke, *Landed Gentry* J. Burke and others, *Landed Gentry*
Burke, *Peerage* J. Burke and others, *A Dictionary of the Peerage*
Christmas, old Christmas 25 December, 5 January
Complete Peerage G. E. C[ockayne] and others, *The Complete Peerage* (2nd edition, 1910–59)
cwt. hundredweight
D.L. deputy lieutenant
DNB *Dictionary of National Biography*. Online version
drock channel or culvert in which water might flow
Endowed Charities of Wiltshire *Endowed Charities of Wiltshire*, H.C. 273 (1908), lxxx (northern division); H.C. 273–i (1908), lxxxi (southern division)
GEC *Baronetage* G. E. C[ockayne], *Complete Baronetage* (1900–9)
gn(s). guinea(s)
GWR Great Western Railway
Hist. Parl. *The History of Parliament*
Hoare, *Modern Wilts.* Sir Richard Colt Hoare and others, *The History of Modern Wiltshire* (London, 1822–44)
Lady day, Lady day old style 25 March, 5 April
Le Neve, *Fasti* J. Le Neve, *Fasti Ecclesiae Anglicanae* (revised edition issued by the Institute of Historical Research)
lug area roughly equal to 1 pole (160th part of 1 acre)
Michaelmas (the feast day of St. Michael the Archangel), Michaelmas old style (old Michaelmas) 29 September, 10 October
Midsummer, old Midsummer 24 June, 5 July
p. pole(s) (160th part of 1 acre)
Phillipps, *Wiltshire Institutions* *Institutiones Clericorum in Comitatu Wiltoniae*, edited by Sir Thomas Phillipps (privately printed 1825)
qr(s). quarter(s) (of a hundredweight)
r. rood(s) (¼ acre)

rectius more correctly
St. Thomas's day, old St. Thomas's day 21 December, 1 January
S.L. ?sergeant at law
TNA The National Archives
VCH *Victoria History of the Counties of England*
WAM *Wiltshire Archaeological and Natural History Magazine*
WANHS Wiltshire Archaeological and Natural History Society
Ward, *Somerset Hospital* J. Ward, *Somerset Hospital* (Marlborough, 1888 edition; copy in Wiltshire and Swindon Archives 2037/9)
WRS Wiltshire Record Society
WSA Wiltshire and Swindon Archives
yds. yards

INTRODUCTION

FROXFIELD ALMSHOUSE, also called the duchess of Somerset's hospital at Froxfield and sometimes referred to locally as the college, is a Wiltshire success story. Opened in the 1690s, and still open in 2013, it has provided homes for widows for over 300 years and pensions for them for most of that time. The building is large and a landmark on what until 1971 was the main road from London to Bath and Bristol. The minute books and other documents edited below give an insight into how it prospered in the 17th, 18th, and 19th centuries. They show how a trust could be set up and perpetuated, how an estate could be successfully managed in a changing world, and how life in the almshouse was regulated benignly according to the standards of the day. Not only do the minute books show how the almshouse thrived over the centuries but they also provide a window on the kind of everyday decision making which was always necessary.

FOUNDATION

Sarah, duchess of Somerset, who founded Froxfield almshouse, was born in 1632. Her father was Edward Alston and her mother was Susan, the daughter of Christopher Hudson of Norwich and, when she married Edward, the relict of Jasper Hussey. Alston was a London physician and a leading Presbyterian, and he grew rich. He was president of the College of Physicians 1655–66, welcomed the Restoration, and was knighted in 1660. He died in 1669. One of his patients was Sir Harbottle Grimston, bt. (d. 1685), a politician and lawyer, and in 1652 Sarah married Sir Harbottle's son George. Sarah and George had two sons, both of whom died in infancy, and in 1655 George himself died.[1] In 1661 Sarah married John Seymour, who in 1671 succeeded his nephew as duke of Somerset. In 1675 John died, and in 1682 Sarah married Henry Hare, Baron Coleraine (d. 1708). Sarah died in 1692, wealthy, separated from her husband, and with no surviving issue. She did have more distant relatives, her sister Mary (d. 1660) having married and having had a daughter and five grandchildren. By her will Sarah made gifts to a cousin and second cousins, to her

1 *DNB*, s.vv. Edward Alston, Harbottle Grimston; N. King, *Grimstons of Gorhambury* (1983), 35.

niece's relict, to her grandnephews and grandnieces, and to relatives of her first two husbands.[1]

On her marriage to George Grimston Sarah's dower was £6,000, from his death she held a jointure, her father gave her £10,000 on her marriage to Seymour, and, as his only surviving child, she inherited much of her father's wealth. By 1672 she had separated from her husband,[2] who in that year, partly in consideration of the £10,000, settled an estate to enhance her jointure. The settlement was unusual. John settled Froxfield manor, the estate called the manor of Huish and Shaw, land in Clench, seven other manors, and other lands on himself for life, on Sarah if she survived him, and without limitation on the heirs of the survivor.[3] From 1675 the estate was thus Sarah's to dispose of as she would. She added to it in 1678 by purchasing land in Chirton[4] and in 1680 by purchasing land in Milton Lilbourne and Fyfield.[5] In 1682, when she was too old to bear a child and immediately before her marriage to Lord Coleraine, she took steps to safeguard her social standing and fiscal autonomy. She procured a royal warrant to enjoy the precedence of a duchess whomever she might marry thereafter[6] and, with Lord Coleraine's consent, placed her property in the hands of trustees. She gave the land of which she was seised in fee to Sir Harbottle Grimston and his son Samuel, her rights as a mortgagee to Sir Harbottle and Sir William Gregory, and her ready money, jewels, plate, and other personal possessions to Sir Harbottle, Sir William, and Samuel, all in trust to do with as she directed. She gave her directions in a will made in 1686, when Sir Harbottle was dead, and she appointed Samuel, then Sir Samuel Grimston, bt., Sir William, and her niece's husband Henry Booth, Baron Delamere, her executors. She gave further directions in a codicil annexed to the will in 1692, by which time Henry had been created earl of Warrington.[7]

By her will the duchess made many charitable gifts.[8] The largest was to found the almshouse at Froxfield. Others were to found apprenticing and educational charities. She appointed her executors as trustees for the almshouse charity and gave them £1,700 to build the almshouse on a site at Froxfield which had already been chosen. The almshouse was to be built of brick around a square quadrangle in which a brick chapel was to stand. It was to accommodate 30 poor

1 *Complete Peerage*, iii. 366; xii (1), 75–6; xii (2), 355; Burke, *Peerage* (1908), 1008; TNA PROB 11/474, ff. 176–93.

2 King, *Grimstons of Gorhambury*, 34–6; A. D. Briscoe, *Stuart Benefactress* (Lavenham, 1973), 106–10; *DNB*, s.vv. Edward Alston; TNA PROB 11/332, ff. 9v.–10.

4 WSA 1300/290.

4 *VCH Wiltshire*, x. 63.

5 Ibid. xiv. 170, 173.

6 Briscoe, *Stuart Benefactress*, 172.

7 TNA PROB 11/474, ff. 176–93 (below, pp. 115–21).

8 This and the following 3 paragraphs are based on TNA PROB 11/474, ff. 176–93.

widows and each widow was to have her own house.[1] The houses and the chapel were to be furnished, and the duchess gave £200 for the furniture. The first 30 widows to live in the houses were to be chosen by the duchess's trustees: 15 were to be widows of clergymen, 15 the widows of laymen. Of the clergy widows 10 should have been from Wiltshire, Berkshire, or Somerset and 5 from London or Westminster. Of the lay widows 10 or more should have been from the duchess's manors in Wiltshire and 5 or less from elsewhere in the three counties. The choice of widows to fill future vacancies was to be made so as to keep the prescribed number in each class. The duchess declared that widows with an income of £20 or more a year from property should be debarred from the almshouse.[2]

Besides a house the duchess provided a pension for each widow, and each widow was to be paid the same as the others.[3] So that the pensions might be paid in perpetuity out of the income from land the duchess directed Sir Samuel Grimston, as the surviving trustee for her lands, to settle Froxfield manor, the manor of Huish and Shaw, and the lands in Milton Lilbourne and Fyfield in such a way as to achieve that end. So that the pensions might be paid regularly, and so as to achieve that end by ensuring an even flow of money, she directed her trustees to lease property at improved rents for short periods and to change the way in which income was derived from copyholds.[4] Because time had to pass before such policies could take effect, and in the meantime annual income from the estate would be depressed, the duchess made special arrangements for the first 10 years in which widows were to live in the almshouse. She directed that the net income from the estate from the date of her death to the date on which the almshouse was finished, and £500 from her personal estate, should be added together and that a tenth of the total should be shared equally among the widows in each of the 10 years as an addition to what they would otherwise have been paid.[5]

Except for the special payments for the first 10 years the duchess required that three uses of the income from the estate should be satisfied before any pension was paid. First, a cloth gown was to be bought for each widow once a year.[6] Secondly, the almshouse was to be kept in good repair. Thirdly, the minister or curate who served Froxfield church was to be paid £10 a year to read prayers with the widows and

1 For more details, below, almshouse buildings (houses).
2 For more details, below, almshouse life (the poor widows); for other comment, below, philanthropy *in excelsis*?
3 For details, below, almshouse life (pensions).
4 For more details, below, estate (preamble; tenures).
5 For details, below, Attorney General *v* Grimston (1697–8); almshouse life (pensions).
6 For details, below, almshouse life (gowns).

to visit those of them who were sick.[1] The rest of the income was to be shared among the 30 widows. Any widow who married was to be foreclosed from her house and pension. The duchess expected the income to rise and she directed that the additional money should be spent in three ways. When annual income exceeded £300 the £10 a year to the minister or curate was to be replaced by a payment of £30 a year to a chaplain chosen for the almshouse, and when the annual income from rents exceeded £400 the almshouse was to be enlarged by the building of 20 more houses. Of the 20 additional widows 5 were to have been living in or about London or Westminster and 15 anywhere in England, except Wiltshire, Berkshire, or Somerset, no more than 150 miles from London. Any 5 of the 20 were to be the widows of clergymen.[2] After 50 gowns had been bought, the almshouse maintained, and the chaplain paid, the rest of the income was to be shared equally among the 50 widows.

In a codicil dated 10 February 1692 the duchess directed Sir Samuel Grimston, still the surviving trustee for her lands, to convey the advowson of Huish church to the end that, when the rectory of Huish should become vacant, the chaplain of the almshouse would be presented as rector and the payment of £30 a year to him would cease.[3] The duchess also added her land at Chirton to the endowment of the almshouse and gave an additional £500 for building the almshouse and the chapel and an additional £100 for furnishing them.

Sarah, dowager duchess of Somerset, died on 25 October 1692[4] leaving the task of building the almshouse at Froxfield to her trustees. She allowed them their expenses and, from the estate with which she endowed it, the salaries and allowances of their officers.[5] The work of commissioning the almshouse was undertaken by Sir William Gregory. Sir Samuel Grimston declined to act[6] and the earl of Warrington died in 1694.[7] Sir William had practical experience of estate management and was in 1692 a judge of the King's Bench.[8] He appointed William Bailey to receive the income from the estate, the almshouse had been built under his aegis by 1694, and 30 widows of his choice had been installed by 1695. In view of the arrangement made for the disposal of the income from the estate from the date of the duchess's death to the date at which the almshouse was finished it was necessary to certify a

1 For details, below, officers (chaplain).
2 For details, below, almshouse buildings (houses); almshouse life (the poor widows); officers (chaplain).
3 For details, below, officers (chaplain).
4 *Complete Peerage*, xii (1), 76.
5 TNA PROB 11/474, ff. 176–93 (below, pp. 116–21).
6 Ibid. C 33/289, ff. 250–2 (below, pp. 122–4).
7 *Complete Peerage*, xii (2), 355.
8 *DNB*.

completion date. The date was set as June 1695. Sir William died in May 1696 from when Sir Samuel Grimston, who still held the estate as the trustee for the duchess's lands, was the sole surviving trustee for the almshouse. On Sir William's death the £500 due to the widows out of the duchess's personal estate, and what was left of the income from the estate between October 1692 and June 1695, passed from his hands to those of his daughter-in-law and executrix Elizabeth Gregory. By 1697 no pension had been paid.[1]

South-west view of Froxfield almshouse, 1806

ATTORNEY GENERAL *v* GRIMSTON

1697–8

In 1696, on the death of Sir William Gregory, the widows claimed their pensions from Sir Samuel Grimston, the trustee for the almshouse, and Elizabeth Gregory, who held the money with which the first 10 years' pensions were to be enhanced. By an action in which they through the Attorney General were the plaintiffs, and Sir Samuel Grimston, Elizabeth Gregory, and William Gregory were the defendants, they submitted their claim to the High Court of Chancery. On 21 December 1697 the cause was debated in front of the Lord Chancellor, who took immediate action to protect the widows and referred all the affairs of the almshouse to a master in Chancery for a report. He ordered Sir Samuel to appoint a steward to replace Bailey. The new steward was to be approved of by the master, Sir Richard Holford, be given Sir

1 Ward, *Somerset Hospital*, 29; TNA C 33/289, ff. 250–2 (below, pp. 122–5); ibid. C 38/260 (below, pp. 125–8); ibid. PROB 11/474, ff. 176–93 (below, p. 120).

Samuel's authority to receive the charity's income, and make payments to the widows. The Lord Chancellor ruled that for Sir Samuel to give that authority would not be for him to accept the trust or to become liable for its income.[1] Sir Samuel appointed Alexander Thistlethwaite and executed the required authority, and Thistlethwaite and his sureties entered into a recognizance. On 22 February 1698 Sir Richard gave his approval to the appointment and allowed the authority,[2] in obedience to an order made by the court on 2 March the title deeds of the estate with which the duchess had endowed the almshouse were delivered to him by Elizabeth Gregory, and on 1 June he presented his report.[3]

The cause begun in 1697 was probably not contentious and the court followed what was apparently an agreed course. The duchess seems to have envisaged that her trustees would appoint new governors of the almshouse, before his death Sir William Gregory had drafted deeds by which the endowments would have been transferred to local trustees, Sir Samuel Grimston could hardly have been expected to manage the almshouse from his home in Hertfordshire, and all the defendants were willing to give up their interest in the almshouse and its estate if the court of Chancery would discharge them from the trust and indemnify them. On 3 June 1698 the Lord Chancellor ordered that Sir Richard Holford's report should be given effect. The court appointed as trustees nine laymen whose homes lay near Froxfield, perhaps the men put forward by Sir William. Sir Samuel conveyed the almshouse's endowments to them and was thereupon discharged from the trust and indemnified. William Gregory, Sir William's grandson and heir, signified his consent to the conveyance by being a party to it and he too was discharged and indemnified. It was agreed that Elizabeth Gregory retained the £500 given by the duchess for pensions and £404 0*s.* 3*d.* remaining from the income from the estate which had accrued between October 1692 and June 1695. The court ordered that the plaintiffs' and defendants' costs, £183 11*s.* 6*d.*, should be paid out of the £404 0*s.* 3*d.* It confirmed Thistlethwaite as the new steward and ordered Elizabeth Gregory to transfer to him the rest of the money, £720 8*s.* 9*d.*, whereupon she would be discharged and indemnified. It ordered Bailey to transfer to Thistlethwaite the net income received from the estate since June 1695, whereupon he too would be discharged.[4] Bailey's accounts showed him liable for £65 6*s.* 7*d.*[5]

1 TNA C 33/289, ff. 250–2 (below, pp. 122–5). In Attorney General *v* Grimston the officer here called the steward was usually called the receiver: for the name of the office, below, officers (steward).

2 TNA C 38/257.

3 Ibid. C 38/260 (below, pp. 125–8).

4 Ibid. (below, pp. 125–8); C 33/289, ff. 250–2 (below, pp. 122–5), 563v.–564 (below, pp. 128–30); ibid. PROB 11/474, ff. 176–93 (below, p. 119); WSA 2037/2, deed, Gregory to Popham, 1698.

5 WSA 2037/26.

The court made detailed arrangements for the disposal of the £720 8*s.* 9*d.* That sum was divided into 10 equal parts, and one thirtieth of one part was to be given to each surviving widow as a pension for each of the 3 years since June 1695, a total of £7 4*s.* 0¾*d.* The remainder, £504 6*s.* 1½*d.*, and any of the sums of £7 4*s.* 0¾*d.* of which the death of a widow had prevented payment, was to be invested, and in each of the following 7 years the interest and one tenth of the capital was to be shared among the widows.[1] In 1699, when Elizabeth Gregory still held the £504 6*s.* 1½*d.*, the court ordered her to give £200 of it immediately to the new trustees to enable them to repair the almshouse, the trustees having assured the court that they had sufficient income to pay the widows' pensions without it.[2]

The court of Chancery thus transferred the almshouse and its endowments to the new trustees. It gave them the power to choose widows to fill vacancies, to make contracts and leases, to appoint officers and pay salaries, and to make rules for the better government of the almshouse. In all those matters, however, the trustees remained subject to the directions of the court, and the court of Chancery, acting in the cause Attorney General *v* Grimston, retained ultimate control of the almshouse's affairs.

1699–1729

In November 1698 the trustees promulgated regulations to govern certain aspects of the widows' behaviour.[3] The decree of June 1698, however, had given them no express power to compel obedience or punish contempt and, although common sense might have decreed that a gift of the power to make rules carried with it such a further gift, lawyers decreed otherwise and it took the trustees 30 years to acquire it unequivocally. The trustees alleged that some of the widows, most notably Susannah Cherry, dissented to the rules made in 1698, disregarded them, and by public affronts lessened their authority. They withheld money due to Mrs. Cherry and another widow and in May 1699 petitioned the court of Chancery for the power to expel offending widows or to suspend their pensions.[4] Affidavits to prove the allegations were taken in June, and the court heard the petition in July. On 27 October the trustees ordered Alexander Thistlethwaite to expel Mrs. Cherry and to stop her pension and the pensions of two other widows. In November Mrs. Cherry herself petitioned the

1 TNA C 33/289, ff. 563v.–564 (below, p. 129); C 38/260 (below, pp. 126–7).

2 Ibid. C 33/291, ff. 116, 211v.

3 Ibid. C 38/267; the regulations are set out below, p. 132, and are discussed below, almshouse life (regulations, rules).

4 TNA C 33/291, f. 540; WSA 2037/26.

court and in December made an affidavit to support a claim that her pension should be restored. Both petitions were referred to Sir Richard Holford. In the meantime Mrs. Cherry was not to be expelled, her pension and arrears were to be paid in full, and she was to submit to the authority of the trustees. New affidavits were made on both sides.[1]

The master reported on 1 December 1700. He made no recommendation and his report was not considered by the court until 17 February 1702. At the hearing on that date the court ordered that only when the regulations promulgated in November 1698 had been considered and settled by both the Solicitor General and the master would the court confirm them and make them part of the decree of June 1698. It recommended that new rules should be added and ordered the trustees to appoint a matron for the almshouse. It required Thistlethwaite to give a new security and the trustees to pay him a salary. The question of Mrs. Cherry had become vexed. She had been paid the money withheld from her before 27 October 1699 but nothing for the time since then. The court ordered her to subscribe to all present and future rules, but it also ordered that four fifths of her unpaid pension should be paid forthwith and one fifth when she had shown herself to behave well, and that all her legal costs should be paid from the almshouse's funds.[2] The trustees could hardly have been happy that Mrs. Cherry, whose conduct they much deplored, remained unscathed, and by their direction Thistlethwaite paid neither her pension nor her costs. In November 1703 Mrs. Cherry petitioned the court for the money and on 11 December the court gave Thistlethwaite 10 days to pay her.[3] He did not pay, and the Lord Chancellor invited counsel for him and Mrs. Cherry, such trustees as happened to be in London, and Sir Richard Holford to attend him in the matter. The trustees failed to persuade him that Mrs. Cherry should be expelled and paid nothing: as a consequence they resigned the trust and Thistlethwaite, who had been replaced as steward at Michaelmas, asked to be discharged from the stewardship. At a hearing on 2 February 1704 the court discharged the trustees, discharged Thistlethwaite, and ordered that Mrs. Cherry should be paid the four fifths of her pension and her legal costs and should submit. The terms of her submission were to be settled by the Solicitor General and, when she had signed it, she was to be paid the one fifth.[4] On 6 July 1704 the master named new trustees and, in Joseph Wall, a new steward. He declared that if laymen of considerable estates refused to act in the trust he would name

1 TNA C 33/293, ff. 65v., 111v.; C 38/267 (below, pp. 130–2).
2 Ibid. C 33/297, f. 126 and v.; C 38/267 (below, pp. 130–3); WSA 2037/26.
3 TNA C 33/301, ff. 73v.–74.
4 Ibid. ff. 259v.–260; ibid. C 38/308.

clergymen, and he nominated seven clerics. Despite claims on the charity's funds made by Thistlethwaite and the old trustees remaining unsettled he recommended that the court should direct the new trustees to act, and on 22 July the widows petitioned for the court to confirm the new trustees and the new steward. At a hearing on 3 August the court ordered that the new trustees and the new steward should act: counsel for neither the old trustees nor Thistlethwaite attended the hearing.[1]

Having thus lost to Mrs. Cherry the trustees still lacked the power to enforce their own rules. They tried again in 1710. New trustees were needed, one of the seven appointed in 1704 having not accepted the trust and one having died, and on 6 May, in response to a petition from the existing trustees, the court asked Sir Richard Holford to name three or four new ones. Sir Richard was also asked to propose new regulations for the governance of the almshouse. He did as he was asked, nominated four more clerics, and reported on 18 August 1710. The regulations which he proposed may have been drafted in consultation with the trustees. They were more comprehensive than those promulgated in 1698 and included new rules as recommended in 1702, a rule for the appointment of a matron as ordered then, and sanctions which the trustees might invoke against those who broke the rules. On 6 February 1711 the trustees petitioned for the report to be confirmed so that the regulations could be adopted and enforced, but on 10 November 1711 the Lord Chancellor ordered that the regulations should first be laid before the Attorney General, presumably for his comments on behalf of the widows. Moreover, by then Fleetwood Dormer had succeeded Sir Richard as the master to whom the cause Attorney General *v* Grimston stood referred and the request to name the new trustees was transferred to him. Only when the new trustees had been appointed and the new regulations approved of by the Attorney General would the court confirm the regulations.[2] More complications dogged the trustees. In 1712 the steward died,[3] presumably to protect themselves from liability while they lacked a steward the existing trustees declined to act, the regulations proposed in 1710 were not laid before the Attorney General, and the proposal of new trustees to the new master was delayed. On 6 January 1713 the trustees said that they would resign if their number were not added to, and soon afterwards eight laymen proposed themselves to Dormer as trustees. They had probably been asked to do so by the existing

1 Ibid. C 33/301, ff. 521v.–522; ibid. C 38/283.

2 TNA C 33/317, f. 407 and v.; C 38/308; WSA 2037/8, orders proposed 1710; for the regulations and the matron, below, almshouse life. The regulations differed little from those confirmed in 1729, for which, below, pp. 134–6.

3 TNA PROB 11/530, ff. 208v.–209.

clerical trustees; two of them had been trustees 1698–1704. On 15 June Dormer nominated them, on 17 July they explained to the court that for lack of a steward the widows were not being paid, and they stated that, if the court were to appoint them, they would nominate a steward for the master to approve and lay the proposed regulations before the Attorney General. On 23 July the Lord Chancellor gave the nominated trustees what they asked for. He ordered that they should act with the old, that the master should appoint a new steward, and that the executor of the old steward should immediately give £40 for the new trustees to pay the widows. The executor's accounts were to be laid before the master, who would offer them to the solicitor of the new trustees for scrutiny and acceptance: on acceptance the executor was to be indemnified. At last, the proposed regulations were to be laid before the Attorney General and, if approved, to be presented to the court for confirmation.[1] Alas, no presentation or confirmation ensued.

In 1727 the trustees ordered the steward to expel Grace Gibbs, a widow who had misbehaved, having previously ordered him to stop her pension.[2] They claimed to think that the regulations proposed in 1710 entitled them to take such actions and to have been informed only *post factum* that the court of Chancery had not confirmed them. Mrs. Gibbs took legal advice and declined to be expelled, in 1728 the trustees petitioned the court to give them the power to 'enforce a proper behaviour' by confirming the regulations proposed in 1710, and in February 1729 the court referred the matter to Robert Holford, the master to whom Attorney General *v* Grimston then stood referred. On 7 June 1729 the master stated that rules were necessary for the good of the almshouse and incorporated in his report regulations differing little from those proposed in 1710. On 25 July the court confirmed the regulations and made them part of the decree of 1698 so that they might remain on record and be obeyed. At last the trustees might legitimately invoke sanctions against those who broke their rules. Mrs. Gibbs was spared and the trustees paid her legal costs.[3]

The right to appoint their own successors came to the trustees more quickly than the power to enforce their own rules. In 1698, 1704, and 1713 the master nominated new trustees, and the court of Chancery appointed them and ordered the old or existing trustees to convey the almshouse and its assets to them.[4] Each conveyance

1 Ibid. C 33/319, f. 629 and v.; C 38/322.

2 Below, pp. 154–5, 157–8; for Mrs. Gibbs's misbehaviour, below, almshouse life (troublesome widows).

3 TNA C 33/351, ff. 97, 175, 391v.–392 (below, pp. 133–7); C 38/395; below, pp. 159–60. The regulations are set out below, pp. 134–6.

4 TNA C 33/289, ff. 563v.–564 (below, p. 128); C 33/301, ff. 521v.–522; C 33/319, f. 629 and v.; C 38/260 (below, p. 126); C 38/322.

imposed a trust on all the trustees of following the directions of the duchess of Somerset, and that of 1698 imposed on them the further trust of nominating new trustees when two had died. Before 1713 there had been no need to observe that further trust, and it was not re-imposed in the conveyances which followed the nominations of 1704 and 1713.[1] The trustees appointed in 1713, however, may have thought that the process by which a master nominated new trustees was undesirable. In 1717 they ordered their steward to ask Christopher Appleby, the solicitor in Chancery who had acted for them in 1713, for the three decrees which related to the conveyance of the almshouse to the trustees, and in 1718 and 1722 they asked for copies of them.[2] Whether or not copies were obtained, in 1725 the existing trustees conveyed the almshouse and its assets to themselves and new trustees whom they had themselves nominated. They claimed to have derived the authority to do so from the duchess's will, the decree of 1697, and the deed by which Sir Samuel Grimston had conveyed the almshouse to the trustees appointed in 1698. The conveyance of 1725 re-imposed the trust on all the trustees of nominating new ones when two had died.[3] It evidently went unchallenged and from then the existing trustees nominated new trustees and executed conveyances to them without reference to the court of Chancery.[4]

1729–85

One of the rules confirmed in 1729 imposed a pecuniary penalty on any widow who was absent from the almshouse for 1 week or more without good cause. That cause was to be certified by the chaplain and the matron.[5] By 1747 the trustees had become dissatisfied with that rule because it gave them no power to expel widows who had long been absent, to repossess their houses, and to install new widows, and in March 1748 they petitioned the court of Chancery to permit them to declare houses vacant after 1 week of a widow's unauthorized absence. Again, common sense might have decreed that the trustees should have what they asked for, but the court uncovered an anomaly and the widows objected. No matron had been in office since 1735, and therefore good causes for absence could not have been certified. The trustees had a cash reserve but would not increase pensions, thus exposing themselves to the argument that poverty was a good cause for

1 WSA 2037/2, deeds, Gregory to Popham, 1698; Popham to Yate, 1704; Yate to Seymour, 1714.
2 Below, pp. 141, 145–6, 151; for Appleby, cf. TNA C 33/319, f. 629 and v.
3 WSA 2037/2, deed, Pocock to Popham, 1725; below, p. 153.
4 The deeds are preserved in WSA 2037/2.
5 TNA C 33/351, ff. 391v.–392 (below, p. 135); absenteeism and the rules against it are discussed below, almshouse life.

widows to be absent. At a hearing in April 1748 the court ordered the trustees to meet at Whitsuntide, appoint a matron, prepare a new rule to oblige widows to reside in the almshouse and to expel them if they did not, and prepare a rule for how their cash reserves should be spent. The trustees met on 3 June. As ordered, they appointed a new matron and drafted a new rule on absenteeism, but they declined to make a rule for the application of the charity's present or future reserves of cash. At a hearing on 20 July they asked the court to confirm the new rule, which was more lenient than that proposed in March, and they explained that they were required to enlarge the almshouse and that therefore they must keep their existing reserves and increase them. On 3 August the widows petitioned the court. They complained of their poverty, asked for the pensions withheld from absentees to be divided among those who remained, and asked for the rule on absenteeism to be even more lenient. This time the court acted promptly and unconditionally. On 5 August it dismissed the widows' petition and confirmed the trustees' new rule.[1] In 1781 the trustees made a more elaborate rule on absenteeism,[2] and in 1783 the Lord Chancellor asked for that, and some of the orders and resolutions previously made by the trustees on other subjects, to be considered by Peter Holford, the master to whom Attorney General *v* Grimston then stood referred. Holford consulted the widows' solicitor, the trustees' solicitor, the steward, and the porter, and on 14 June 1784 reported his approval of all the orders and resolutions. The court sanctioned them on 29 June.[3] Later rules were made and enforced without reference to Chancery.

The duchess of Somerset directed that, after certain uses had been satisfied, the almshouse's income should be divided equally among the widows. She also directed that, when rents exceeded £400 a year, the amount by which rents and fines exceeded that sum should be used to enlarge the almshouse.[4] Those directions were potentially difficult to reconcile with each other because money set aside for the enlargement might be claimed by the widows. Grounds for such a claim might be that some of that money came not from rents and fines but from exceptional sources such as withheld pensions or the sale of timber, that it might never be enough for the enlargement, and that the ends of the charity would be defeated if the widows

1 TNA C 33/389, ff. 285v.–286, 445 and v., 674–5; for the trustees' dissatisfaction, below, p. 176; for the meeting of 3 June 1748, the minutes of which contain less information about it than do the Chancery records, below, p. 177; for pensions and the matron, below, almshouse life.

2 Below, pp. 219–21, 225.

3 Ward, *Somerset Hospital*, 21; TNA C 38/713; for the steward and the porter, below, officers.

4 TNA PROB 11/474, ff. 176–93 (below, pp. 119–20); cf. above, foundation.

became indigent while there was money available to increase their pensions. The trustees were aware of the difficulty in 1739, when they resolved to petition the Lord Chancellor for directions on how they should dispose of their excess income.[1] Apparently no petition was preferred but, by dismissing the widows' petition of 3 August 1748, the court of Chancery tacitly acknowledged that the trustees might save money to pay for the enlargement.[2] In 1753 the trustees nevertheless did prefer such a petition, in 1754 the master to whom Attorney General *v* Grimston stood referred was asked to consider how surplus income should be used, and the trustees then proposed to him that it should be invested in government securities until it was needed for the enlargement. The master approved of the scheme and in 1755 the court ordered that it should be implemented.[3] In 1765 and 1769 the trustees proposed to apply to the court to direct them to spend their savings on the enlargement.[4] It seems that no application was made, and the almshouse was enlarged in 1772–3 at a cost of '£2,977 and upwards' without such direction.[5]

Although the court of Chancery had allowed the trustees to save money to enlarge the almshouse and the trustees had used the money to enlarge it, that did not mean that the court approved of how the money had been spent. A difficulty arose because the steward was required not only to present his accounts to the trustees for approval but also to pass them before a master.[6] By the time of his death in 1775 the steward had made no statement of his accounts for 1772–5, presumably the period in which many of the bills for the enlargement were paid, and the trustees asked counsel what they should do. In 1776 accounts for that period were produced by the attorney of the administrator of the will of the deceased steward, the trustees approved of them, and the new steward presented them to Peter Holford, the master. Holford, however, declined to pass them until the court had ordered that so large an expenditure on the building work should be allowed. In 1777 the court heard the trustees' requests that Holford should allow the sums paid on the enlargement, pass the accounts, and allow the sums paid on building works and repairs since 1775. The Lord Chancellor granted those requests.[7] The master continued to pass the steward's accounts until 1785. The steward appointed in that year applied to the court for the practice to be discontinued and, much to

1 Below, p. 169.
2 TNA C 33/389, ff. 674–5.
3 Ibid. C 33/403, f. 564; below, p. 182.
4 Below, pp. 198, 200–1.
5 TNA C 33/447, ff. 471v.–472; cf. below, almshouse buildings (houses).
6 Below, officers (steward).
7 TNA C 33/447, ff. 471v.–472; below, pp. 209–12.

his relief, his application was successful. Thenceforward the court no longer scrutinized the annual accounts.[1]

By 1785 the trustees had acquired the right to make rules for the governance of the almshouse, impose appropriate sanctions on those who broke them, appoint their own successors, and save and spend the almshouse's money as they wished. The cause Attorney General *v* Grimston ceased to be relevant.

TRUSTEES

Appointment

The first trustees for the almshouse, Henry, earl of Warrington (d. 1694), Sir Samuel Grimston, and Sir William Gregory, were appointed by the duchess of Somerset in her will. On the death of one of them the trust was to reside in the other two, on the death of a second in the survivor, and on the survivor's death in his executors. New governors of the almshouse were evidently envisaged by the duchess,[2] Sir William put forward the names of certain men to succeed Sir Samuel and him as trustees, and in 1698, 1704, and 1713 the court of Chancery appointed new trustees. From 1725 all new trustees were appointed by the existing ones.[3]

Numbers

There were nine trustees 1698–1704, seven from 1704.[4] In 1713, when eight were added to the five existing trustees, one of whom was inactive, it was evidently intended that thenceforward there should be a complement of 12 active trustees.[5] That intention was frequently frustrated.[6] One of those appointed in 1713 never acted in the trust and in 1725, after five active trustees had died, only two were appointed.[7] In 1729, when there were seven active trustees and two inactive, five new ones were appointed,[8] but one of the new ones failed to act after 1730. No trustee is known to have been intentionally inactive after 1751, and thereafter whenever new trustees were appointed the complement was restored to 12. The further trust imposed by the

1 Ward, *Somerset Hospital*, 28; WSA 2037/27.

2 TNA PROB 11/474, ff. 176–93 (below, pp. 116, 119).

3 Above, Attorney General *v* Grimston (1697–8; 1699–1729).

4 TNA C 33/289, ff. 563v.–564 (below, p. 128); C 38/260 (below, p. 126); WSA 2037/2, deed, Popham to Yate, 1704.

5 TNA C 33/301, ff. 521v.–522; C 33/319, f. 629 and v.; WSA 2037/2, deed, Yate to Seymour, 1714.

6 The remainder of this paragraph is based on the list of trustees printed below, pp. 392–401; also on appointments of trustees recorded in the minute books, below, *passim*.

7 Below, p. 153.

8 Below, p. 158.

trustees on themselves that when two of them had died they would nominate two replacements[1] was designed to prevent their number remaining long below 11. Sometimes, however, it did because there was a delay before new appointments were made. For example, in the 1760s no trustee was appointed for 3 years after two had died.

Personnel, status, rank

The earl of Warrington, Sir Samuel Grimston, and Sir William Gregory, the trustees appointed by the duchess of Somerset, were men well versed in public affairs and among them had knowledge of the law and estate management. Those who replaced them as trustees were men of high status locally. The laymen appointed in 1698 lived near Froxfield and nearly every one was the lord of a manor, the clerics appointed in 1704 all held livings, and probably lived, not far from Froxfield, and the laymen appointed in 1713 were again local landowners most of whom lived in manor houses.[2] If the status of those early local trustees was already high, later in the 18th century and in the 19th it was higher still. Thomas Brudenell Bruce, earl of Ailesbury, was a trustee from 1789 and successive marquesses of Ailesbury were trustees. Some trustees, T. H. S. Sotheron Estcourt, Henry Petty-Fitzmaurice, marquess of Lansdowne, and Sidney Herbert, were men of great wealth who held office in various governments, and others, such as Sir John Dugdale Astley of Everleigh, successive Goddards of Swindon, and Sir James Tylney Long of Draycot Cerne, were wealthy landowners and M.P.s. John Pearse, a trustee from 1807, was governor of the Bank of England, and Henry Manvers Pierrepont, a trustee from 1839, was a privy counsellor. Several trustees were senior officers in the regular army, and others, such as H. N. Goddard and Sir John Wither Awdry, were prominent public figures in Wiltshire. The clerics lived in parsonage houses, many of them held cathedral stalls, and Edward Goddard, D.D. and John Ashfordby Trenchard, D.D., held rich livings which, as lords of the relevant manors and owners of the advowson, they gave to themselves.

Throughout the period 1698–1866 to act as a trustee for Froxfield almshouse seems to have been a duty which descended informally with certain estates.[3] Nearly all the owners of the Littlecote estate, the Pophams and Leyborne Pophams, were trustees in that period. Five Goddards were successive lords of Swindon manor, and the earls and marquesses of Ailesbury were successive owners of the Savernake

1 Above, Attorney General *v* Grimston (1699–1729).

2 Brief notes on each trustee appointed before 1866 are printed below, pp. 392–401.

3 The lay trustees' estates, and the clerical trustees' estates and livings, are referred to below, pp. 392–401.

estate. Successive Ernles of Brimslade, Seymours of Easton, Joneses of Ramsbury, Penruddockes of Compton Chamberlayne, and Walker Heneages of Compton Bassett were trustees. Three Stonehouses and Thomas Michell, each of South Standen (then in Wiltshire), were trustees, as were three Awdrys of Notton and three Goddards of Clyffe Pypard. James Sutton, T. G. Bucknall Estcourt, and T. H. S. Sotheron Estcourt were successive owners of New Park, Devizes. Three successive rectors of Mildenhall and three rectors of Chilton Foliat were all trustees.

Three of the nine trustees appointed in 1698 lived on their estates in Berkshire, but all the clerics appointed in 1704 held Wiltshire livings and all the trustees appointed thereafter lived in Wiltshire. In 1698 and from 1725 the trustees imposed the further trust upon themselves of filling future vacancies among them with men living within 10 miles of the almshouse,[1] and in the 1750s three trustees resigned because they were removing to places far away.[2] The terms of that trust, however, were often honoured in the breach. For example, John Ashfordby Trenchard of Stanton Fitzwarren, Sidney Herbert of Wilton House, the Goddards of Swindon, Henry, marquess of Lansdowne, of Bowood House, and Robert Wilsonn of Purton all lived more than 10 miles from Froxfield. Likewise, although not a breach of the trust, no Berkshire man was appointed although many places in Berkshire lay within 10 miles of Froxfield. If the purpose of the 10-mile rule was to ensure that trustees had local knowledge and that they would attend meetings regularly it may not have been defeated by the breaches or the absence of Berkshire men.

Even though the almshouse was founded and endowed by a woman to benefit other women, in the period 1698–1866 there was of course no woman trustee. Each of the men who accepted the trust was, so far as can be judged and in the understanding of the time, a wealthy gentleman.[3] Most of the clerics and some of the laymen were graduates, and many of the laymen occupied positions in which general competence was probably essential.[4] There may have been a sense of class loyalty to the duchess who founded the almshouse, the almshouse may have seemed a worthwhile cause because of its large scale and generous endowment, men may have been flattered to be asked to attend meetings with social equals or superiors, and the right to nominate widows for vacant houses may have had its attractions,[5] but

1 WSA 2037/2, deeds, Gregory to Popham, 1698; Pocock to Popham, 1725.
2 Ward, *Somerset Hospital*, 16.
3 Cf. *Endowed Charities of Wiltshire* (southern division), 982.
4 All the trustees in the period are named below, pp. 392–401.
5 Cf. below, meetings; for nominations, below, this section (exercise of patronage).

none of that seems quite enough to explain why busy and wealthy men became trustees. It can only be surmised that the trust was accepted as a routine obligation by wealthy, competent, energetic, and conscientious men out of a sense of public duty. All the trustees gave all their services to the almshouse entirely gratuitously.[1]

Period of trusteeship

After 1704 most men who accepted the trust were trustees for life.[2] In some cases that meant for many years. Charles Brudenell Bruce, earl and marquess of Ailesbury, was a trustee 1798–1856, and several other men, including George, marquess of Ailesbury, were trustees for over 40 years. The average time served as a trustee was about 20 years. Few resigned. The most notable resignation was that of Edward Seymour, duke of Somerset, who as Edward Seymour of Easton was appointed a trustee in 1729. Seymour attended no meeting after 1730, moved to Maiden Bradley probably about 1740, and in 1747 was invited to resign: his resignation was recorded in 1751.[3]

Functions

Subject to the directions given by the duchess of Somerset and the court of Chancery[4] the trustees' functions were to perpetuate the trust, to own and manage the estate with which the almshouse had been endowed, and to own and manage the almshouse itself. To perpetuate the trust the existing trustees from time to time conveyed the estate and the almshouse to themselves and the new trustees who, from 1725, they themselves chose.[5] Being thus owners of the estate they sought to derive an income from it sufficient to give permanent effect to the duchess's intentions for the almshouse,[6] and as owners of the almshouse they chose the widows to occupy it, maintained the building, and made rules for everyday life in it.[7] Regulations confirmed in 1729 gave the trustees the right to examine the steward's accounts whenever they saw fit[8] and, although until 1785 the accounts were still passed by a master in Chancery,[9] to scrutinize and pass them yearly was one of the trustees' routine functions.[10]

1 *Endowed Charities of Wiltshire* (southern division), 982; TNA C 33/389, ff. 674–5; WSA 2037/26–8.
2 The period for which each man was a trustee is given below, pp. 392–401.
3 For Seymour, below, pp. 158, 161, 175, 179.
4 Above, foundation; Attorney General *v* Grimston (1697–8).
5 Above, Attorney General *v* Grimston (1699–1729); this section (appointment).
6 Below, estate.
7 Below, this section (exercise of patronage); almshouse buildings; almshouse life (regulations, rules).
8 TNA C 33/351, ff. 391v.–392 (below, p. 134).
9 Below, officers (steward).
10 WSA 2037/27–8; below, p. 227 sqq.

Committees, delegation

Sometimes the trustees committed particular questions to one, two, three, or four of their number, and in each case the committee was expected to investigate and report to the trustees as a whole. For example, in 1717 various estate matters were committed to three trustees whose report was acted on in 1718,[1] and in 1857 the question how the chapel was to be served was committed to four trustees.[2] Sometimes the trustees went further and delegated items of business for a decision to be made by one trustee or more. In the 18th century they did so only occasionally. For example, in 1724 four trustees settled a dispute over a seat in Chirton church and in 1791 two or three trustees were empowered to reach agreement with the trustees of the turnpike road through Froxfield.[3] In the 19th century it apparently became routine to delegate decisions on minor matters. Examples of delegated estate business include the authorization in 1839 of three trustees to decide what to do about an old brewhouse and the appointment in 1860 of three trustees to make decisions on matters arising from the extension of the Berks. & Hants railway.[4] From 1843 items of estate business were regularly referred for a decision to G. W. Wroughton, one of the trustees, who was often to make it in conjunction with the steward. Examples of delegated almshouse business include questions whether individual widows should be allowed leave of absence, whether absent widows should receive their pensions, whether sick or aged widows should be nursed at the almshouse's expense, and whether individual widows should be allowed to share their houses with an inmate.[5]

Professional services

The trustees often paid for professional services besides those provided routinely by their steward, their other officers, builders, and other tradesmen. They were represented by counsel in the cause Attorney General *v* Grimston, employed a solicitor in the court of Chancery in 1713,[6] and from time to time consulted counsel on how to proceed in Chancery and how they might best manage the almshouse.[7] Most other consultations with counsel were on estate business. The trustees asked for opinions in disputes over tithes and cottages, on how to proceed

1 Below, pp. 146–7. 2 Below, p. 360.

3 Below, pp. 152–3, 236-7; for the road, below, estate (road, canal, railways).

4 Below, pp. 321, 372–3; for the brewhouse and the railway, below, estate (other assets; road, canal, railways).

5 Below, pp. 254, 281, 329, 331, 358–9; for all those questions, below, almshouse life (nursing; regulations, rules; absenteeism; children, inmates, men).

6 e.g. TNA C 33/291, f. 116; C 33/297, f. 126 and v.; C 33/319, f. 629 and v.; C 33/351, ff. 391v.–392 (below, p. 134); C 33/389, ff. 674–5; C 33/447, ff. 471v.–472. 7 Below, pp. 151, 200, 210.

against troublesome tenants, and as to the rateability of the widows' houses.[1] On almshouse business they asked for an opinion in 1791 on what to do about a troublesome widow, in 1803 on what to do about a deserted house, and in 1845 on who might enter the chapel.[2] Besides lawyers, the trustees often employed land surveyors and valuers on estate business. Such business included proposed inclosure, exchange, or sale of land and the assessment of fair rents, and a mapmaker was employed in 1753. A report on the almshouse or the chapel was occasionally sought from a buildings surveyor or an architect.[3] An architect designed a new chapel and changes to the almshouse, and a surveyor designed a pair of cottages at Froxfield.[4]

Exercise of patronage

The duchess of Somerset directed that her trustees should choose which widows were to live in the almshouse, and the first 30 were chosen by Sir William Gregory.[5] The decree of 1698 directed the new trustees to fill vacancies but did not specify how they were to do so.[6] Vacancies were filled between 1698 and about 1709–10, none between then and 1714.[7] On 19 October 1714 the trustees decided that, except for London and Westminster vacancies, a single trustee would nominate a properly qualified widow for a vacant house, and on that day nine individually nominated widows were admitted. The order in which the trustees were to make nominations was that in which their names appeared in the current trust deed, and the steward was to tell each trustee when it was his turn. If when his turn came a trustee had not attended a meeting of the trustees for a year he forfeited that turn and presumably went to the back of the queue; the nomination passed to the next in turn. London and Westminster widows were to be recommended by Cornelius Yate, then a trustee and vicar of Islington St. Mary, and his recommendations would interrupt, but not otherwise vary, the regular nominations by individual trustees.[8] The special arrangement for London and Westminster was reaffirmed in 1717 but there is no evidence that it survived Yate, who died in 1720. From 1717 the time available to a trustee to nominate a widow was limited to 6 months.[9]

1 Below, pp. 144, 146, 152, 169, 213, 326, 382, 384.
2 Below, pp. 238, 258, 334; those matters are discussed below, almshouse life (religious worship; absenteeism; troublesome widows).
3 Below, pp. 181, 219, 259–62, 281, 309, 311, 315, 317, 329, 349, 364, 373.
4 WSA 2037/87; below, pp. 281, 375.
5 Above, foundation.
6 TNA C 33/289, ff. 563v.–564 (below, pp. 128–9).
7 Below, almshouse life (occupancy).
8 Below, pp. 138–41.
9 Below, p. 145; for Yate, below, p. 401.

In 1715 it was noticed that one of the duchess's directions was not being followed. Of the 15 laymen's widows living in the almshouse only 5 were manor widows whereas there should have been at least 10, and 10 were three-counties widows whereas there should have been no more than 5. The trustees then agreed to tailor future nominations to comply with the direction.[1] In 1737, when only one three-counties widow remained to be replaced by a manor widow, the trustees decided that he next in turn to nominate should be informed in writing by the steward what class of widow should be nominated. The qualification of a nominated widow, if there was any doubt or dispute about it, was to be judged by the trustees at their next meeting.[2] Doubt did arise, as in 1763 when two widows were given notice to quit because they were not in the same class as those whom they had been nominated to replace:[3] both lived in the almshouse until each died in 1776.[4]

In 1779, when clergy houses were vacant and no widow had applied for one, the trustees ordered the steward to advertize the vacancies, and in 1783 they resolved that, when a clergy house had been vacant for 1 month, the vacancy would be advertized in a London evening paper if it was for a London or Westminster widow or in the *Salisbury Journal* if for a widow from elsewhere. In June 1783 they ordered that any clergy house vacant for 1 year might be occupied by a lay widow,[5] and in October they varied that order. Thenceforward, if no clergy widow of the relevant district had applied for a vacant house within 1 year of the advertisement it would be offered to clergy widows of the other districts, and if no clergy widow had applied within 2 years it would be offered to a qualified lay widow of the district from which the widow who had left the house vacant had come.[6] Also in 1783, because there were many applications for each vacant house for a manor widow, the trustees decided to forgo their individual rights to nominate manor widows and to choose a successful applicant collectively at a general meeting.[7] It is thus likely that by 1786, when the trustees condemned that procedure for choosing manor widows because it might delay admittance to a vacant house, no manor or clergy widow had been nominated by an individual trustee for several years but that the nomination of other widows by individual trustees in turn had continued. Therefore, when in 1786 the trustees decided that future nominations of manor and clergy widows should again be made by individual trustees in turn, they also decided that the turns

1 Below, p. 138.
2 Below, pp. 167–8.
3 Below, pp. 194, 196–7.
4 WSA 1635/2.
5 Below, pp. 217, 222, 225–6.
6 Below, pp. 225–6. The period of 1 month was extended to 3 months in the regulations of 1834: below, p. 314.
7 Below, p. 222.

should be separated from the turns by which they nominated the other widows.[1] In 1786 two lists of trustees were compiled. One, at the head of which was the first, and at the foot the last, of the living trustees to have been appointed, was used for the nomination of manor and clergy widows. The other, at the head of which was the trustee who had made the least recent nomination, and at the foot the trustee who had made the most recent, was used for the nomination of the other widows. In each case the right to nominate a widow for a vacant house proceeded down the list and back to the top, and when a trustee died or resigned his replacement became the last of the existing trustees to have the right to nominate.[2]

The right to nominate probably passed down the first list more quickly than down the second because, after the enlargement of the 1770s, there were more houses for manor and clergy widows than for other widows.[3] The general speed of the passing was affected in several ways. It was reduced in the 1790s and early 1800s when the trustees again experimented with joint nomination: the trustees themselves objected to the delay to the turns, and the experiment was abandoned in 1803.[4] It was increased whenever a trustee forfeited his right to nominate. The rule under which a trustee did so was amended in 1783, from when any who had been absent from two consecutive general meetings would forfeit his right until he had attended a future meeting.[5] The absenter trustee was evidently entitled to take the first turn to nominate after he had attended a meeting,[6] and from 1786 it was thus a matter of chance how many turns in any one list he would miss. The process was sometimes further complicated by a place on a list being given in exchange by one trustee to another.[7]

By her will the duchess of Somerset defined the classes of widows to be placed in the almshouse, but she did not define exactly how a widow was qualified for inclusion in a class.[8] The trustees thrice interpreted and made precise her intentions. In 1716 they declared that widows of Fyfield and Milton Lilbourne, where the duchess held estates which she had given to the almshouse, would no longer be deemed manor widows,[9] and the same evidently applied to Chirton

1 Below, pp. 230–1.
2 Ward, *Somerset Hospital*, 31; for John Whitelock, at the head of the first list, below, meetings (chairmen); for entry at the foot, below, p. 278.
3 For the enlargement and the classes of new widows admitted, below, almshouse buildings (houses); almshouse life (poor widows).
4 Below, pp. 240–1, 252.
5 Below, pp. 222–3. Some absences were excused: below, meetings (attendance).
6 Cf. below, p. 314.
7 WSA 2037/80 (below, p. 419); 2037/119, ff. 152, 171, 174.
8 TNA PROB 11/474, ff. 176–93 (below, pp. 117–18, 120).
9 Below, p. 144.

widows. In 1786 the steward defined the duchess's manors as Froxfield, Broad Town, Huish and Shaw, Wootton Rivers, and Thornhill, all of which she had devised for charitable purposes, and in 1800 the trustees confirmed that definition.[1] Estates which were less than manors were excluded as, perhaps less rationally, were manors such as Pewsey which the duchess had held but did not devise for charitable purposes.[2] Secondly, the trustees found it necessary to define what was meant by in or about the cities of London and Westminster, and in 1845 they resolved that any widow deriving her qualification from any place within 10 miles of Temple Bar could be counted a London or Westminster widow.[3] That definition was objected to in 1892 by the trustees of the charities of St. John's and St. Margaret's parishes, Westminster, on the grounds that those living so far outside the bounds of the cities as they were when the duchess made her will should not benefit from it.[4] Thirdly, to define how a widow might successfully claim to live in any of the areas from which qualified widows were drawn, from 1785 the trustees required that every widow must have been legally settled in a district from which a house was to be filled or to have lived there for the 40 days immediately preceding the occurrence of the vacancy.[5]

From 1714 to 1785 the usual procedure for admitting a widow to the almshouse was apparently for the nominating trustee to send a written order to the steward to admit his nominee, for the widow to take the order from the steward to the porter, and for the porter to admit the widow. In 1785 that procedure was said to cause expense and inconvenience to the widows and was altered. Thenceforward the trustee sent his order directly to the porter,[6] and in 1786 forms on which such an order might be sent were printed.[7] In the 1830s the practice was for the steward to send a printed form to the trustee whose turn it was to nominate, having entered on it the number of the house which was vacant, the reason for the vacancy, and the class of widow to be nominated. The trustee entered on it the name of his nominated widow and the name and address of her late husband, dated and signed it, and returned it to the steward, who sent it to the widow. The widow took the form and certificates to prove her marriage and

1 Ward, *Somerset Hospital*, 31; below, p. 252.
2 For Pewsey, *VCH Wiltshire*, xvi. 193.
3 Below, p. 332.
4 p. 4 of a printed report by the trustees of the parochial charities of St. Margaret and St. John, Westminster, 1892, part of which survives in WSA 2037/1.
5 Below, p. 228; the requirement is discussed below, almshouse life (the poor widows).
6 Below, pp. 140–1, 228.
7 WSA 2037/27.

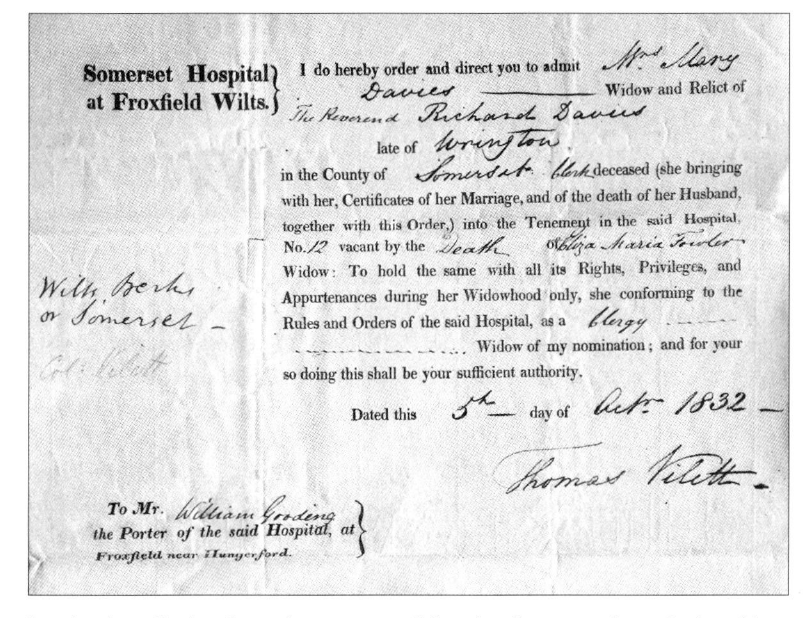
Somerset Hospital at Froxfield Wilts. I do hereby order and direct you to admit Mrs. Mary Davies ———— Widow and Relict of The Reverend Richard Davies late of Wrington in the County of Somerset Clerk deceased (she bringing with her, Certificates of her Marriage, and of the death of her Husband, together with this Order,) into the Tenement in the said Hospital, No. 12 vacant by the Death of Eliza Maria Fowler Widow: To hold the same with all its Rights, Privileges, and Appurtenances during her Widowhood only, she conforming to the Rules and Orders of the said Hospital, as a Clergy Widow of my nomination; and for your so doing this shall be your sufficient authority.

Wilts, Berks or Somerset –

Col: Vilett

Dated this 5th — day of Octr. 1832 —

Thomas Vilett.

To Mr. William Groding the Porter of the said Hospital, at Froxfield near Hungerford.

her husband's death to the porter of the almshouse, who admitted her to the vacant house.[1]

MEETINGS

The trustees held three kinds of meeting, one to do the general business of the almshouse, a view meeting at which some of the trustees visited the almshouse and met some of the widows, and one which was special *ad hoc*. The minute books to 1866 contain the records of the general and special meetings and of a few of the view meetings.

The subsections below, except the last three, relate only to the general meetings. The view meetings and the special meetings are discussed in two of the last three.

Notice, next meeting, adjournment

General meetings were held either pursuant to notice or by adjournment. Pursuant to notice seems to have meant that the steward convened the meeting on his own initiative and gave notice of it to the trustees. In 1781 it was decided that meetings would be held on the same day each year, but in 1791 the trustees nevertheless resolved that the steward should, using his own authority, give a month's notice of them to all the trustees.[2] The notice was given in writing, and

1 Ibid. 2037/80 (below, pp. 418–32).
2 Below, pp. 218, 236.

the steward sent what was called a circular letter to each trustee.[1] In the 18th century the letters were sent by messenger,[2] and in the 19th presumably by post.

By adjournment seems to have meant that the trustees at a general meeting themselves called for a future meeting on a certain day. They did so either by setting a date for the next meeting or by declaring a meeting to be adjourned to a future day. Between 1714 and 1781 there was little difference between the two methods because to record that a meeting was adjourned then seems to have meant not that it was broken off for later resumption but that a new meeting would be held on the given date. Sometimes in that period the future meeting was called so that particular business might be transacted,[3] and sometimes it was a view meeting.[4] The future date was rarely more than 3 months away, and a meeting usually took place on it. After 1781, when they knew that a meeting would be held on the same day each year, the trustees at a general meeting who appointed the day for a future meeting were in effect calling for an additional meeting. They did so in the same two ways, in the 1780s by setting a date for the next meeting and in the period 1795–1814 by declaring their current meeting adjourned to a future date. Most of the appointed dates were 2–3 months ahead, with one exception a meeting was held on each appointed day,[5] and most meetings were evidently called to deal with an important item of business which was carried over. The steward presumably gave the trustees notice of meetings to be held by adjournment as he did of those to be held pursuant to notice. No general meeting was held by adjournment in the period 1814–66. One appointed to be held thus in 1853 was found to be unnecessary and was not attended.[6]

One annual meeting was adjourned in the 21st-century sense of being broken off for later resumption. It met in Marlborough on 21 October 1818, first at the town hall and afterwards at the steward's house.[7]

Date, frequency

In the regulations drafted in 1710 it was proposed that the trustees should meet when and as often as they thought fit, and the regulations confirmed in 1729 required them to do so.[8] Until the late 18th century there was no settled routine of meetings, a meeting was possibly called

1 WSA 2037/27; below, pp. 277–8.
2 WSA 2037/27.
3 e.g. below, pp. 148, 173, 194.
4 e.g. below, pp. 161, 201.
5 For the exception, below, p. 233.
6 Below, p. 350.
7 Below, p. 279.
8 TNA C 33/351, ff. 391v.–392 (below, p. 134); WSA 2037/8, orders proposed 1710.

as and when business seemed to require it, and the number of meetings in a year varied between five and none. In the mid 18th century there was often a meeting in June, and in 1781 the trustees decided to appoint the first Wednesday after 19 June as the day on which a general meeting should be held each year.[1] That decision remained in force only until 1791 and was disregarded as often as regarded. In 1791 the appointed day was changed to the first Wednesday in July, in 1810 to the first Wednesday in August, in 1847 back to the first Wednesday in July, in 1849 to the second Wednesday in July, and in 1852 to the second Thursday in July.[2] Meetings in summer sometimes coincided with sessions of the Wiltshire assizes. In 1827 the trustees postponed their meeting because several of them were engaged at the assizes, in 1829 they ordered that they would meet on the second Wednesday in August whenever the first should fall in the week of the assizes, and in 1852 they resolved that, if the commission day of the Wiltshire assizes should fall on the Thursday or a preceding day of the second week in July, they would meet on the third Thursday.[3]

Places

From 1726 the place at which the trustees met was usually named in the heading of the minutes, and in nearly all cases it was an inn no further from the almshouse than Marlborough. The first meeting of which there are minutes was held at the Bear in Charnham Street, part of Hungerford and then in Wiltshire,[4] and in the period 1726–50 the principal meeting places were the Blue Lion in Froxfield, the Green Dragon in Ramsbury (the house of the widow Essex Bell), and the Angel in Marlborough.[5] From 1750 the trustees nearly always met in Marlborough, until 1761 at the Angel, from 1765 to 1842 at the Castle, and from 1843 at the Ailesbury Arms. In 1762–3 they met twice at the Cross Keys in Froxfield and thrice at the Three Tuns in Marlborough.[6] Autumn and winter meetings were sometimes held at different places, and in the period 1795–1818 the trustees met six times in Marlborough town hall, each time in October. In view of their wealth and status it is very likely that the inn chosen was that thought to provide the greatest comfort and the best dinner. A room and the dinner were evidently booked by the steward, and in 1782 the trustees agreed that at future meetings at the Castle he should order dinner for the full number of trustees and that each trustee, including those who were absent, should pay 4*s*. for his meal.[7]

1 Below, p. 218.
2 Below, pp. 236, 268, 337, 340, 344.
3 Below, pp. 295–6, 298, 344.
4 Below, p. 140; for Charnham Street, *VCH Wiltshire*, iv. 350.
5 For Essex Bell, below, pp. 159, 175–6.
6 Below, pp. 192–6.
7 Below, p. 221.

Quorum

In 1698 the Lord Chancellor decreed that any five of the nine trustees whom he appointed would constitute a quorum,[1] and it was proposed in the regulations drafted in 1710 that the number needed would remain five.[2] In 1726, when there were again nine of them, the trustees ruled that any three were to be counted a quorum[3] but, because the decree was still in force, the rule was almost certainly invalid.[4] It apparently had no effect, the quorum remained five,[5] and between 1726 and 1783 seven general meetings attended by fewer than five trustees were abandoned for lack of a quorum.[6] In 1783 the trustees acknowledged the rule that five were needed for a quorum,[7] but later, as they did their 10-mile rule, they sometimes honoured it in the breach. At four general meetings business was conducted as usual although only four trustees were present. On one occasion the lack of a quorum was ignored.[8] On the others it was covered. In 1791 a fifth trustee signed the minutes, in 1795 a fifth and a sixth signed them, and those of 1855 were read and confirmed in 1856.[9]

Attendance

General meetings were usually attended by most of the current trustees. Most trustees attended most meetings, and some missed very few.[10] Henry Manvers Pierrepont (d. 1851), a trustee from 1839, attended all the general meetings 1840–50, and the Revd. Edward Pocock (d. 1839), a trustee for 41 years, missed only four. H. N. Goddard, a trustee from 1839, missed only four meetings between 1840 and 1866, and he missed that of 1854 only because he was on duty at Gosport as a major in the Royal Wiltshire militia.[11] Some, such as Thomas Bennet (d. 1754), a trustee for 40 years, and Henry Petty-Fitzmaurice (d. 1866), marquess of Lansdowne, a trustee for 14 years, attended fewer meetings than they missed. A few, William Sherwin (d. 1735), Sir Edward Seymour, bt. (d. 1740), and Edward, duke of Somerset, a trustee 1729–51, became inactive and were presumably absent from meetings.

From 1714 it was a rule that a trustee's right to nominate a widow to live in the almshouse depended on attendance at meetings. The rule was amended in 1783,[12] from when it was evidently enforced. In

1 TNA C 33/289, ff. 563v.–564 (below, p. 128).
2 WSA 2037/8, orders proposed 1710.
3 Below, p. 154.
4 Cf. Ward, *Somerset Hospital*, 27–8.
5 TNA C 33/351, ff. 391v.–392 (below, p. 134).
6 e.g. below, pp. 158, 184, 189, 197, 202.
7 Below, p. 225.
8 Below, p. 268.
9 Below, pp. 236–8, 246, 355–7.
10 For the trustees and the periods in which they served, below, pp. 392–401.
11 Below, p. 351.
12 Below, pp. 141, 222–3; cf. above, trustees (exercise of patronage).

1807, however, the rule was dispensed with in the cases of Charles, Lord Bruce, who was doing his duty in parliament, and the earl of Ailesbury, who attended view meetings and to the state of the almshouse.[1] That dispensation may have been for one year only, but the regulations published in 1834 gave to those who were absent from meetings because they were sick, or in attendance at parliament, unlimited exemption from the forfeiture of their turn to nominate.[2] Thereafter absent trustees sent their apologies and made their excuses, and it was frequently recorded that an absent trustee was ill or at parliament. 'Domestic affliction' (perhaps bereavement) was sometimes accepted as an excuse.[3] The trustees perhaps found themselves to be too lenient. At a meeting in 1845 those present excused the absence of the marquess of Ailesbury and his son Lord Ernest Bruce because they were at parliament, but they resolved that thenceforth attendance at parliament would not save an absentee from forfeiting his turn to nominate.[4] They nevertheless made an exception in 1848.[5] In 1854 Lord Bruce, still an M.P., proposed that the exemption taken away in 1845 should be given back. If that proposal were rejected he would propose instead that, since six of the trustees were M.P.s, their annual meeting should be held alternate years in London and Marlborough. A compromise was reached. From 1854 a trustee absent from a general meeting would be excused if he had sent a letter to the chairman giving his word that his attendance would be prevented by unavoidable public duty.[6]

General meetings were attended not only by the trustees but also by their officers.[7] The steward was expressly required to be present by the regulations proposed in 1710 and by later regulations,[8] and he was almost certainly present at every meeting. He took a clerk to assist him in the later 1760s and earlier 1770s, probably from 1840,[9] and possibly at other times. The chaplain of the almshouse attended meetings about 1700 and in the 1760s and 1770s.[10] In 1853 the trustees ordered that the officiating chaplain be requested to attend their meetings, an order which may imply that the chaplain already attended regularly and that the officiating chaplain did not.[11] From 1854 both attended, and the almshouse paid for their dinners.[12] The porter attended in the 1770s,[13]

1 Below, p. 263.
2 Below, p. 314.
3 Below, pp. 323, 355.
4 Below, p. 332.
5 Below, p. 338.
6 Below, p. 351.
7 The officers are discussed below, officers.
8 TNA C 33/351, ff. 391v.–392 (below, p. 134); WSA 2037/8, orders proposed 1710; below, p. 312.
9 WSA 2037/27; below, this section (minutes, signatures).
10 WSA 2037/26–7.
11 Below, p. 348.
12 WSA 2037/28.
13 Below, p. 214.

the bailiffs of Froxfield and Huish manors attended in the 1760s and 1770s, and the expenses of all of them were met from the almshouse's funds:[1] none is known to have attended otherwise.

Others attended general meetings occasionally and *ad hoc*. They included widows, tenants of the almshouse, tradesmen who had worked for the almshouse, and professional advisers. It is unlikely that widows attended frequently or in large numbers. From 1781 any widow whose pension had been suspended for unauthorized absence from the almshouse was called to a general meeting to explain why she should not be punished.[2] It is known that on a few occasions a widow attended in person, but on many others it is likely that the widow was absent and that the explanation was offered by letter or by another on her behalf.[3] Widows may also have attended to ask for leave of absence, to apply for places in the almshouse,[4] or to explain alleged misbehaviour.[5] Tenants may have attended even less frequently. On three occasions prospective tenants were called to attend, and in 1807 all those bidding to become tenants of a farm at Oare were apparently present at the meeting at which the tenant was chosen.[6] In 1761 a glazier was ordered to attend to explain his bill and in 1776, after repairs had been done at two farms, the tenants of the farms and the workmen who had submitted bills were ordered to attend the next meeting.[7] An executor of a steward attended in 1767, the attorney of the administrator of the will of the deceased steward in 1776, and in 1804 a valuer acting for the trustees.[8]

Chairmen

Which of the trustees attended the general meetings held in the period 1714–45 is known only from the signatures at the foot of the minutes. From 1746 the names of those present were listed at the head and the signatures remained at the foot. There was apparently a general rule that the order of signatures until 1745, and of the names of those present from 1746, should correspond to the order in which the trustees were appointed. In many cases the order was followed exactly and in many cases approximately although, for reasons which are obscure, the lay trustees who were appointed in 1713 were given precedence over the surviving clerical trustees who had been appointed in 1704.

1 WSA 2037/27.
2 Below, p. 221; below, almshouse life (absenteeism).
3 e.g. below, pp. 223, 228, 265, 292, 308, 324.
4 Below, pp. 230, 240.
5 Below, p. 334.
6 Below, pp. 147, 211, 231, 263–4.
7 Below, pp. 191–2, 210.
8 WSA 2037/27; below, pp. 211–12, 260.

In the 20th and 21st centuries the practice would have been for the first named trustee to have been the chairman who presided over the meeting. The practice was probably followed in the 18th century and was certainly followed in the 19th. The chairman of any meeting was thus in principle the longest serving trustee present at it.[1] From 1714 to his death in 1735 Francis Popham, although appointed only in 1713, was usually deemed the longest serving trustee. After him the longest serving trustees were, successively, Richard Jones (d. 1736), Thomas Bennet (d. 1754), the Revd. John Pocock (d. 1773), John Whitelock (d. 1787), Ambrose Goddard (d. 1815), William Northey (d. 1826), Charles, marquess of Ailesbury (d. 1856), and George, marquess of Ailesbury. At the great majority of meetings held while each was the longest serving trustee, and at which he was present, his was the first signature or the first name on the list of those present. Each was in effect chairman for life. Applied expressly to the trustee named first in the list the word chairman was used from 1802.[2] Sometimes the longest serving trustee was absent from a meeting and in that case the trustee present who had served longer than any other present might be expected to have been chairman in his place. That sometimes happened, happened without fail in the period 1856–66, but did not happen at about 28 general meetings from which the longest serving trustee was absent. At a few meetings the longest serving trustee was present and not chairman.[3] Perhaps he arrived late or, although present, was not in the best of health.

Classes and order of business

The items of business done at the meetings of the trustees, which have been classified in the edition printed below,[4] covered all aspects of the almshouse's affairs. The main classes are trusteeship, estate, almshouse, and, from 1828, the Mayo trust.[5] Trusteeship business included the choosing of new trustees, the absence of trustees from the meetings, the overall supervision of the almshouse's funds, the presentment of rectors of Huish, and the appointment of stewards and other officers.[6] Estate business, the underlying purpose of which was to maximize long-term profits from the estate, consisted of numerous items relating to the tenancy of farms and other premises, the condition of buildings, the improvement of agriculture, and the exploitation of woodland.[7]

1 Brief notes on the trustees are given below, pp. 392–401.
2 Below, p. 257.
3 e.g. below, pp. 257, 260.
4 Below, method of editing.
5 For the Mayo trust, below.
6 For the rectors and the officers, below, officers.
7 Cf. below, estate.

Almshouse business related to the maintenance, enlargement, and improvement of the buildings and to life in the almshouse, including the pensions and behaviour of the widows.[1]

The order in which the items of business were recorded in the minute books was probably that in which they came before the trustees and was presumably determined by the steward. From 1787 the examination of the steward's almshouse accounts was the first item of business and from 1828 his account of the funds of the Mayo trust was the second. Items of business were otherwise dealt with in no regular order.

Volume of business

In the 153 years 1714–1866 the trustees dealt with about 1,455 items of business at their general meetings. There were about 335 items of trusteeship business, about 660 of estate business, and about 365 of almshouse business. The volume of business gradually increased from an average of about 4 items a year 1720–49, to about 7 a year 1750–79, about 10 a year 1780–1839, and about 13 a year 1840–66. Almshouse business increased from about 1780, perhaps partly because the almshouse had been recently enlarged and perhaps partly because in 1781 the trustees resolved to take action against widows who were absent from it,[2] and trustee business tended to increase from 1834 as non-attendance of trustees began to be reported and excused.[3] In all periods the amount of estate business varied greatly from year to year.

Minutes, signatures

The regulations proposed in 1710 and other regulations all required the steward to take minutes at the meetings of the trustees,[4] and the minutes were entered in books for the most part neatly and legibly. Besides three initialled entries,[5] it is nowhere stated who wrote them. In the time of five stewards,[6] Thomas Kellway 1713–22, Charles Young 1745–66, Samuel Hawkes 1775–85, John Ward 1785–1829, and T. B. Merriman from 1840, most of the minutes were written by a single hand, and all were in a single hand 1714–20 and 1842–66. It appears that Kellway, Young, Hawkes, and Ward wrote most of the minutes themselves. Merriman evidently employed a clerk. In the time of the other stewards there were frequent changes of scribe. From the late

1 Cf. below, almshouse buildings; almshouse life.

2 For the enlargement, below, almshouse buildings (houses); for absenteeism, below, almshouse life.

3 Above, this section (attendance).

4 TNA C 33/351, ff. 391v.–392 (below, p. 134); WSA 2037/8, orders proposed 1710; below, p. 312.

5 Below, pp. 173, 281, 357.

6 For the stewards, below, officers.

18th century reports and other material were sometimes entered in the minute books with an exaggerated neatness and clarity attributable to the hand of a professional scribe.

The consistent neatness and legibility with which the minutes were written suggests that they were not entered in the books while the meetings were in progress. On the other hand, the signatures at the foot of the minutes appear to be genuinely those of the trustees present at the meetings. The most likely explanation of that paradox is that the meetings were held before dinner, the minutes were fair-copied while the trustees were at table, and the trustees signed the minutes before they left the meeting place. That explanation is supported by the writing, in 1799 and 1814, of entries below the signatures and before 'the meeting broke up' or 'the trustees separated'.[1] Sometimes from 1746 not every trustee who was listed as present at a meeting signed the minutes, and occasionally from 1829 the names of some of the trustees who had been present were pencilled in at the foot of the minutes but the trustees did not sign. Presumably in all such cases men had left the meeting place before the fair-copying of the minutes had been finished.

View meetings

The regulations proposed in 1710 and those confirmed in 1729 contained a rule that, among those held when and as often as they thought fit, the trustees should hold a meeting in Whitsun week each year. It was to be held at or near the almshouse in order to view the almshouse, the chapel, and the fittings and books in the chapel, and to choose a matron.[2] The meetings thus required were later called view meetings and were held in Whitsun week until 1803, when the trustees resolved that thenceforward they should be held on the third Wednesday in June.[3]

The proceedings of only 12 meetings held in Whitsun week are recorded in the minute books, none later than 1773. The meetings were apparently less formal than the general meetings. They possibly convened at the steward's house in the almshouse, were probably attended by the steward and only a few of the trustees, and could presumably proceed without a quorum. In 1758 and 1760, after their work at the almshouse was done, the meetings were adjourned to the Cross Keys at Froxfield;[4] the minutes for 1769 and 1771–3 record

1 Below, pp. 251, 275.
2 TNA C 33/351, ff. 391v.–392 (below, p. 134); WSA 2037/8, orders proposed 1710; for the chapel, below, almshouse buildings; for the matron, below, almshouse life.
3 Below, p. 258.
4 Below, pp. 185, 189.

that the trustees met at the Cross Keys,[1] but they probably did then what they did earlier. Evidence from 1748 suggests that, even when the minutes were entered in the books, the proceedings of the view meetings were only partially recorded.[2] In the 19th century view meetings may have been even less formal, and by 1834 it had become the practice for trustees living near the almshouse to view it and to report what they saw to the other trustees at the following general meeting.[3] By the early 19th century primary responsibility for the good order of the almshouse had apparently been assigned to, or assumed by, a single trustee, and that trustee attended the view meeting. In 1807 the trustee with primary responsibility was Lord Ailesbury,[4] from 1849 or earlier to 1863 Francis Leyborne Popham, and from 1865 T. H. S. Sotheron. From 1849 the view was taken by Leyborne Popham or Sotheron and by two other trustees nominated at the preceding general meeting.[5]

Although some items of trustee business and estate business were dealt with at view meetings, the main business was to inspect the almshouse. No matron was appointed after 1774. In the mid 18th century the trustees at the meeting gave orders for repairs to be made and authorized payment for them,[6] in the early 19th century it was apparently usual for them to draw up a list of the repairs which they thought necessary and submit it to the other trustees at the following general meeting,[7] and in the mid 19th century they apparently followed either procedure *ad hoc*. For example, in 1851 the viewing trustees gave orders and reported to the other trustees afterwards,[8] in 1864 they themselves commissioned a report,[9] and in 1857 and 1860 they referred proposed alterations to the almshouse to the general meeting.[10] The remit of the viewing trustees extended beyond inspection of the fabric to the behaviour and wellbeing of the widows. It seems that they went round the quadrangle from house to house to meet each widow and, from 1785, to check that they retained the bibles and prayer books which they had been given.[11] In 1803 the trustees at the general meeting resolved that every widow should be present at the view meeting, and in 1808 they resolved that only illness and not leave of absence could excuse a widow from being present.[12] The purpose of the resolutions may have been to ensure that each widow was in

1 Below, pp. 200, 203, 205–6.
2 TNA C 33/389, ff. 445 and v., 674–5; below, p. 177.
3 Below, p. 312.
4 Below, p. 263.
5 Below, pp. 339–40, 372, 381, 386.
6 e.g. below, pp. 162, 189.
7 e.g. below, pp. 255–6.
8 Below, p. 343.
9 Below, pp. 384–5.
10 Below, pp. 360–1, 373.
11 Below, pp. 229, 373; cf. below, almshouse life (religious worship).
12 Below, pp. 258, 266; for absenteeism, below, almshouse life.

her house on the day of the view rather than to bring all the widows together in a formal meeting. As they met the widows the viewing trustees might receive applications,[1] remonstrate with those who were breaking the rules of the almshouse,[2] or investigate complaints made by one against another.[3]

Special meetings

The idea of a special meeting was conceived after 1781, the year in which it was decided that general meetings should be held on the same day each year. Before then the trustees held 14 meetings at which they dealt with only one item of business, but none was described as special. In 1800 the steward was authorized to call a special meeting at his discretion,[4] in 1809 a meeting which took place was described as special,[5] and in 1821 the trustees expressly authorized the steward to convene a special meeting if he found two trustees who considered it expedient for him to do so.[6] Later meetings called special were held in December 1829 and January 1830 and in 1846 and 1853.[7] All the meetings were held in the usual places, except that of 1853 which was held in the steward's house. Those of 1829 and 1830 were attended by eight and five trustees respectively, numbers normal for general meetings in the 1820s and 1830s; the others were attended by an average of three. Each meeting was called for a particular item of business to be considered. In 1809 the trustees appointed a new surgeon, in 1829 and 1830 they dealt with the presentation of a rector of Huish and the appointment of a chaplain for the almshouse, and in 1846 and 1853 they discussed special items of estate business.

In 1822 a meeting of trustees at Beckhampton to discuss an exchange of lands was special but was not so called. On the other hand, in 1858 at what was called a special meeting the trustees dealt with the business of the Mayo trust and no almshouse business.[8]

Discord

The only evidence of discord among the trustees to be found in the minute books for 1714–1866 lies in the records of the special meetings held in 1829 and 1830. The steward called the first for 29 December 1829 to report that Charles Mayo had died and that the rectory of Huish and the chaplaincy of the almshouse were therefore vacant. The bishop's secretary had already been consulted and had opined that the deed by

1 Below, pp. 361, 380.
2 Below, p. 358.
3 Below, p. 373.
4 Below, p. 253.
5 Below, p. 267.
6 Below, p. 286.
7 Below, pp. 303–4, 334, 347.
8 Below, pp. 288, 367.

which a new rector was presented should be signed by every trustee. The eight trustees present at the meeting considered two candidates, William Bleeck and John Vilett. On a division four voted for each, whereupon the steward wrote to each of the three absent trustees to ask him to vote. Two voted for Bleeck and one for Vilett, and at the special meeting held on 26 January 1830 it was resolved that Bleeck should be presented as rector of Huish. The trustees present signed the presentation deed, and the steward was directed to transmit it to the absent trustees for them to sign. Bleeck was presented in 1830 and was appointed chaplain of the almshouse.[1]

Of the trustees present at the meeting in 1829 four, Ambrose Goddard, Thomas Vilett, Francis Warneford, and John Awdry, appear to have been natural supporters of Vilett, who lived at Swindon and was stipendiary curate of Lydiard Tregoze from 1815 and of Rodbourne Cheney from 1823. The Viletts were brothers and were related by marriage to Goddard and Awdry. Warneford's estates, like Goddard's, lay near Swindon. None of the four signed the minutes of the meeting and, when Vilett failed to win a majority, they evidently left it prematurely. The trustee who voted for Vilett after the meeting was the Revd. Edward Goddard, a distant relative also with an estate in north Wiltshire.[2] Of Vilett's five apparently natural supporters only one, Ambrose Goddard, attended the meeting in 1830 at which it was resolved to present Bleeck. He failed to sign the minutes and presumably left early.

ESTATE

The duchess of Somerset endowed Froxfield almshouse with Froxfield manor, the manor of Huish and Shaw, an estate at Chirton, and a farm at Milton Lilbourne and Fyfield.[3] The land of Huish adjoins that of a lost settlement called Shaw,[4] and for reasons which are obscure the word Shaw was added to the name of Huish manor. In the late 17th century the manor of Huish and Shaw included nothing at Shaw[5] and the double name was inappropriate. Froxfield manor consisted of land at Froxfield and nowhere else.[6] Huish and Shaw manor, however,

1 Below, pp. 303–5; for the chaplains, below, officers.
2 Brief notes on the trustees are given below, pp. 392–401; for John Vilett and the relationships, *Alum. Oxon. 1715–1886*, iv. 1473; Burke, *Landed Gentry* (1846), ii. 1479; (1906), 675; http://www.theclergydatabase.org.uk/persons (person ID 86818).
3 TNA PROB 11/474, ff. 176–93 (below, pp. 118, 121).
4 For Shaw, *VCH Wiltshire*, x. 8, 11; xi. 183.
5 Cf. ibid. x. 79; below, this section.
6 e.g. *Endowed Charities of Wiltshire* (southern division), 987–91; WSA 2037/119.

consisted not only of the land of Huish but also of land at Fyfield, Clench, Milcot, and Oare.[1] Each manor was held by the duchess in fee and the land of both was held of her by leases on lives or by copy of court roll. The estate at Chirton was held by the duchess at a low chief rent and consisted of a farm held of her at an improved rent and of premises held of her on lives; it was sometimes reputed a manor, perhaps because its land had at some time been held as several copyholds. The farm at Milton Lilbourne was held freely by the duchess and at an improved rent of her.[2] After inclosure in the 18th and 19th centuries the whole estate given by the duchess measured about 2,220 acres.[3]

Tenures

In the 17th century the usual method by which landowners derived income from their estates was to grant parts of them for a term specified in a lease or a copy of the court roll. The term was usually determinable on the death of the longest liver of three people named in the grant, its length was thus uncertain, and often it suited both parties for a grant to be renewed before the last life had ended. Grants by lease or copy might also be made in reversion. A sum of money was paid by the lessee on taking a lease, and a fine was paid by the grantee of a copyhold. Both payments were related to the value of the land being conveyed, to the expected length of the lives, and perhaps to other factors. They were negotiable and were the landowners' principal source of income from the land. Rents were usually nominal. In that method of deriving income the interests of the parties were finely balanced. Landowners in need of money might offer cut-price new leases or grants, while landowners with large estates or other sources of income might wait until lives had ended and offer leases or grants at higher prices.

The duchess and her advisers were wise enough to see that the best way to raise money for the maintenance of the almshouse and the widows who were to live in it would not be to make leases and grants which were determinable on death. Pensions paid to the widows had become quarterly by 1710,[4] a regular income was therefore necessary, and the estate was not large enough for the income generated as lives ended to be sufficiently regular and predictable. To reduce exposure to tenants and prospective tenants who, knowing that the trustees could not wait for money, might drive a hard bargain, the duchess directed

1 *VCH Wiltshire*, x. 79; cf. WSA 2037/119; for the name Milcot, below, this section (improvement of farms).

2 TNA PROB 11/474, ff. 176–93 (below, pp. 118–21); WSA 1300/290; 2037/26; for the chief rent, TNA C 38/260 (below, p. 127); WSA 2037/119; below, p. 293.

3 *Endowed Charities of Wiltshire* (southern division), 987–91.

4 WSA 2037/8, orders proposed 1710; for the pensions, below, almshouse life.

that no new lease for life should be granted and that no premium should be taken for granting a lease. Cottages, and houses which were not farmhouses, were evidently excepted. No land was to be leased for longer than 21 years from when the lease was executed. The trustees' only income from leaseholds was to arise from the yearly rents which, considering the value of the land, were to be as high as the tenants could afford to pay. Such rents were usually described as improved, sometimes as rack. The duchess also directed her trustees to grant no copyhold for more than three lives or in reversion, to lower the fines paid by the copyholders on entering their estates, and to raise the annual rents which they paid. No fine was to amount to more than a third of the value of the holding, and all rents were to amount to two thirds of what the improved rent for the holding would have been.[1]

In the late 17th century the duchess's directions were probably not novel and their effect on the income of the almshouse was not immediate, but they were forward looking and beneficial. So far as can be judged the trustees followed them. In addition to the farm with land at Milton Lilbourne and Fyfield and to that at Chirton, which had both been let at improved rents by 1692,[2] the principal farm at Huish was let at an improved rent in 1724,[3] and the two principal farms at Froxfield were let thus in 1758.[4] Rents from copyholds ceased to be nominal and in 1770 conventionary rents, nearly all from copyholds, totalled £156 a year.[5] The trustees diverged from the duchess's directions in 1773. They then resolved, except in respect of cottages, not to grant any copyhold anew nor to change or add any life named in grants which had already been made.[6] Their new policy, which was commonplace in later 18th-century Wiltshire, was to bring in hand each copyhold as the last life by which it was held ended and to lease it at an improved rent. Some lives lasted long, and lands at Froxfield, Clench, New Mill, and Oare were still held by copy in the 19th century.[7] The process could be accelerated. In 1800 four copyholds at Huish were surrendered in exchange for annuities,[8] and in 1812, in fairness or out of generosity, the trustees increased the annual payments to three of the former copyholders because the lands which they surrendered had since risen

1 TNA PROB 11/474, ff. 176–93 (below, pp. 118–19); for the exception of cottages, below, this section (cottages).
2 TNA C 38/260 (below, p. 127).
3 WSA 2037/179, lease, Pocock to Stagg, 1724.
4 Ibid. 2037/111, lease, Batson to Ivy, 1758.
5 Ibid. 2037/27 (below, p. 404); cf. 2037/119.
6 Below, p. 206.
7 WSA 2037/119; for the name New Mill, below, this section (improvement of farms).
8 Below, pp. 253–4; WSA 2037/119.

in value.[1] In 1834 they defined what they would grant by copy, or lease on lives, as cottages, gardens, and plots of land of 3 acres or less.[2]

Short-term leases gave several long-term advantages to the trustees. They did make their income more regular and more predictable,[3] even though it was received quarterly or half-yearly in arrears and no longer almost entirely in advance. Tenants for life, whether lessees or copyholders, may have been investors who sublet, but the tenants of lands held for 21 years or less at improved rents were usually farmers who occupied the land. Short-term leases to farmers, rather than long-term grants to investors, meant that the trustees could intervene more immediately and more frequently to promote the efficient working of their land, and they would never have to wait long to remove an unsatisfactory tenant. They were also given more opportunity to vary rents. Prosperous tenants could be asked to pay more, and temporary rent reductions could help good tenants in difficulty through no fault of their own. The trustees had an increasing power to determine the size, and the disposition of the land, of their farms, and it became worthwhile for them to invest in buildings. Lifeholders were obliged to maintain the buildings on their holdings,[4] but neither they nor their undertenants could be compelled to invest in new buildings. The incentive for a landowner to do so was weak when he was uncertain how long it would be before he could re-lease or re-grant the land, stronger when he knew that the land need not be out of his hands for long.

Improvement of farms

In the period 1692–1866 the almshouse trustees improved their rack-rent farms in several ways. They made some larger, some discrete from land in different ownership, and some more compact. They favoured the elimination of cultivation in common, did much to improve farmsteads, and in many minor ways promoted better husbandry.

At Froxfield the trustees owned about 640 acres.[5] Two leasehold farms mentioned in 1686, the Greater and the Lesser, were merged and in 1758 leased at an improved rent as Froxfield (later Manor) farm. About 1785 Froxfield farm measured 347 acres and five copyholds and a leasehold on lives comprised 260 acres. By 1812 the leasehold, called Tarrant's, and two copyholds had been brought in hand, merged, and leased at an improved rent as what was later called Brewery farm. Manor farm and Brewery farm were completely several from 1819, when their lands were among those at Froxfield inclosed by Act, and they were

1 Below, p. 271.

2 Below, p. 314.

3 cf. WSA 2037/27–8.

4 e.g. below, p. 153.

5 *Endowed Charities of Wiltshire* (southern division), 987–91.

merged in 1834. The lands of two other copyholds were leased as a single farm at an improved rent in 1838.[1] In 1845 Manor farm was of 472 acres, the other farm of 142 acres.[2] Most of the smaller farm was added to Manor farm in 1855.[3]

At Huish, where the trustees owned the whole parish except the glebe,[4] their principal farm was likewise enlarged. In 1742 a smaller farm and woodland were added to it,[5] in 1779 two former copyholds were added, and in 1801 the four copyholds surrendered in 1800 were added.[6] By those additions, and by a small exchange of land made in 1803 by the trustees and the rector of Huish, all the commonable land was accumulated in Huish farm and inclosed *de facto*.[7] In 1840 Huish farm was of 639 acres.[8] It was reduced in 1843 when 100 acres was transferred to the trustees' farm based at Oare.[9]

At Milton Lilbourne, Fyfield, Clench, and New Mill, all in Milton Lilbourne parish, the trustees owned about 590 acres.[10] The improvement of the farms at all four places was protracted.

A farm which consisted of a farmstead and land in Milton Lilbourne and a barn and land in Fyfield was already held at an improved rent in 1686.[11] The barn was blown down in the great storm of 1703 and, presumably because the land at Fyfield could no longer be worked economically from Milton Lilbourne, the farmstead and land at Milton Lilbourne was thenceforward leased as a separate farm.[12] From 1781, when the last of Milton Lilbourne's land was inclosed by Act, it was worked in severalty as a farm of 176 acres, and from 1820, when land at Fyfield was restored to it, it was of 198 acres.[13] From 1778 the tenants were members of a family called Warwick[14] and by 1853, when James Warwick gave notice to quit, the farm needed new improvements. Its land lay dispersed and had been worked efficiently only because the Warwicks held adjacent land of their own, and its farmhouse had become inadequate presumably because the Warwicks did not live in it. In 1853 land and buildings in Milton Lilbourne were

1 WSA 2037/27; 2037/111, lease, Batson to Ivy, 1758; 2037/119.
2 Ibid. tithe award.
3 Ibid. 2037/28.
4 Ibid. tithe award; *VCH Wiltshire*, x. 78–9, 81.
5 WSA 2037/179, lease, Whitelock to Brown, 1742; below, p. 170.
6 WSA 2037/27; 2037/179, lease, Goddard to Reeves, 1801; above, this section (tenures); below, pp. 231, 253.
7 *VCH Wiltshire*, x. 80–1; below, p. 258.
8 WSA tithe award.
9 Below, p. 329.
10 *Endowed Charities of Wiltshire* (southern division), 988–9, 991.
11 WSA 2037/108, lease, Kellway to Noyes, 1680; 2037/109, lease, Yate to Hungerford, 1709.
12 WSA 2037/26–8; 2037/109, lease, Yate to Hungerford, 1709.
13 *VCH Wiltshire*, xvi. 175; below, p. 284.
14 WSA 2037/27–8; 2037/111, lease, Whitelock to Warwick, 1778.

available for purchase and would, if added to it, improve the farm. The trustees had money in reserve but were advised by counsel that, to buy land, they might use only that part of it which had been received for compulsory sale of land and which was too small a sum to buy what was needed. They were released from their difficulty by their steward, T. B. Merriman, who himself bought a house and land in Milton Lilbourne and, by prior arrangement, gave both to the trustees by exchange. The land made the trustees' farm more workable, the house was made the farmhouse, and the farm was thus improved.[1]

Throughout the 18th and 19th centuries the land of Fyfield lay divided between Fyfield manor, which descended mainly in the Hungerford and Penruddocke families, and the estate of Froxfield almshouse. Most of the manor lay as a single farm, Fyfield farm.[2] The almshouse's estate was of about 290 acres,[3] which from 1693 to 1820 was held on lease by the lord of Fyfield manor or his tenant of Fyfield farm. In 1703, presumably soon after the barn was blown down, it was leased separately from the farm based at Milton Lilbourne. In 1713 Henry Penruddocke assigned it to his tenant of Fyfield farm, it was worked with that farm until 1820,[4] and between those dates the land of Fyfield thus lay inclosed *de facto*.[5] By allowing their land to be worked with Fyfield farm the trustees for long avoided the expense of erecting new buildings on it. On the other hand, the dispute over two small closes which began in 1781 might otherwise not have arisen,[6] and in the early 19th century, when J. H. Penruddocke was their tenant, the trustees admitted that there was nothing to be gained by an exchange of lands and *de iure* inclosure unless Penruddocke bore the whole expense.[7] In 1807 the trustees agreed to a future exchange based on shared expenses and the assignment of the whole of the southern part of Fyfield tithing to Penruddocke and of the northern part to them.[8] That exchange and *de iure* inclosure took place under an Act of 1818, the year in which Penruddocke's lease expired; the trustees declined to give up their land south of the Kennet and Avon canal in exchange

1 Ibid. 2037/114, deed, Kingstone to Merriman, 1853; below, pp. 347–9, 352–4.

2 *VCH Wiltshire*, xvi. 172–3, 177.

3 Below, p. 284.

4 WSA 332/181, deed, Hungerford to Warner, 1713; leases, Penruddocke to Cannings, 1733; Penruddocke to Cannings, 1756; Penruddocke to Stagg, 1776; Penruddocke to Stagg, 1798; 2037/108, lease, Warrington to Hungerford, 1693; 2037/109, leases, Yate to Hungerford, 1709; Yate to Warner, 1715; 2037/110, lease, Popham to Cannings, 1733; 2037/111, leases, Batson to Cannings, 1755; Whitelock to Penruddocke, 1776; 2037/112, lease, Goddard to Penruddocke, 1796; above, preceding paragraph.

5 *VCH Wiltshire*, xvi. 177.

6 For the dispute, below, this section (doubts, disputes, troublesome tenants).

7 Below, p. 262.

8 Below, pp. 263–5.

for Broomsgrove wood north of it.[1] Two points remained at issue. Until 1820 the trustees' land continued to be held by Penruddocke and worked by his tenant of Fyfield farm and, when the exchange was made, there was more timber standing on the land received from Penruddocke than on the land given to him. At a special meeting held in 1822 it was agreed how much rent Penruddocke should pay for 1818–20 and how much and in what way the trustees should pay for the excess timber.[2] The trustees' land at Fyfield, then compact, still lacked a farmstead. In 1820 the part of it south of the canal was restored to their farm at Milton Lilbourne, and in the early 1820s buildings on the other part, which became known as Hill Barn farm, were erected at Clench. From 1820 to 1845 Hill Barn farm was worked as a whole or in parts by men whose principal farmsteads stood elsewhere.[3] Between 1843 and 1845 a new farmstead, Broomsgrove Farm, was built on the Fyfield land, and in 1845, worked from it and for the first time, the trustees leased most of their land at Fyfield, Clench, and New Mill as a discrete and compact farm.[4]

Two small farms at Clench, referred to as the larger and the smaller, were held of the almshouse trustees by copy. Each comprised inclosed land and feeding rights on upland pasture. In 1805, as part of an exchange between the trustees and Thomas Brudenell Bruce, earl of Ailesbury, inclosed land was added to each to replace the feeding rights.[5] The larger farm, Batchelor's bargain, was first leased at an improved rent in 1747 and was of 48 acres in 1820. From 1747 to 1845 it was part of farms based elsewhere and from 1845 was part of Broomsgrove farm.[6] The smaller farm, 36 acres about 1832, was first leased at an improved rent in 1840.[7] It was apparently discrete but perhaps too small for significant improvement. The tenant emigrated in 1850, the farm was in poor condition in 1854, and in 1861, despite minor improvements, the trustees had to reduce the rent to keep the tenant.[8] In 1866 they thought it best, when it became vacant, to add it to their farm at Milton Lilbourne.[9]

A copyhold of 1 yardland, the land of which was some of a lost settlement called Milcot, was said to lie at a hamlet called Milcot Water

1 WSA 2037/112, lease, Goddard to Penruddocke, 1796; ibid. EA/119; below, pp. 280, 282, 286.
2 Below, pp. 286, 288–90.
3 Cf. *VCH Wiltshire*, xvi. 195; WSA 2037/27–8; ibid. A 1/345/324B; ibid. Milton Lilbourne, Pewsey, and Wilcot tithe awards; below, pp. 284, 290, 320, 328.
4 WSA 2037/28; below, pp. 329, 333.
5 *VCH Wiltshire*, xvi. 176–7; WSA 2037/119.
6 WSA 2037/27–8; 2037/119; below, pp. 176, 284.
7 *Endowed Charities of Wiltshire* (southern division), 991; WSA 2037/27.
8 *Endowed Charities of Wiltshire* (southern division), 995; WSA 2037/28; below, pp. 341, 352, 355, 376.
9 Below, p. 390.

or Millcroft Water. The name of the hamlet was further corrupted to Milkhouse Water. Another hamlet, called New Mill, grew up near Milkhouse Water in the late 18th century and early 19th,[1] and in that period the holding formerly said to lie at Milcot Water was said to lie at New Mill. It was of about 28 acres and was first leased at an improved rent in 1830. The lessee became the first tenant of Broomsgrove farm, of which the land at New Mill became part.[2]

Under an inclosure award made in 1803 by Act the trustees' land in Oare was concentrated to adjoin their land in Huish to the west.[3] It was held of the trustees as a single copyhold farm until 1808 when, 84 acres, it was leased at an improved rent.[4] Its buildings were poor and neglected and a tenant became insolvent and quitted.[5] To improve the farm the trustees built a new farmhouse in 1842–3, transferred 100 acres of Huish farm to it in 1844, and built a new farmyard on Huish Hill in 1845–6.[6]

The trustees' farm at Chirton, which included nearly all their land there,[7] could not be enlarged. It was improved by being made several in 1808, when the land there was inclosed by Act,[8] and in other ways.[9] The farm was of 269 acres after inclosure.[10] Premises called Pearson's or Hort's, consisting of two cottages and a small close, were held on lives until 1861, when they were brought in hand.[11]

Perhaps the trustees' most important investment in the long-term value of their farms was to keep the farmsteads in good repair and fit for existing purposes and to make them fit for new purposes. The duchess of Somerset directed that buildings were to be repaired by, and at the expense of, the tenants,[12] and in 1777 it was declared that the customary practice of the trustees was to impose such an obligation on their tenants.[13] Money was demanded from any tenant who, on quitting his farm, left buildings in disrepair, and allowances were made to new tenants entering on farms on which buildings needed repair.[14] The cost of building work, however, was sometimes shared between the trustees, who in the future might be able to charge higher rents for farms with

1 *VCH Wiltshire*, xvi. 168–9; below, pp. 144, 148, 191.
2 WSA 2037/27–8; 2037/119; cf. below, p. 333.
3 WSA 425/1.
4 Ibid. 2037/113, lease, Goddard to Fowler, 1807; 2037/119; cf. below, pp. 263–4 (Edmonds's).
5 WSA 2037/27; below, p. 326.
6 WSA 2037/27–8; below, p. 328.
7 WSA 2037/119.
8 Ibid. EA/77.
9 Below, this subsection (p. 42, nn. 1–2, 5; pp. 42–3).
10 *Endowed Charities of Wiltshire* (southern division), 989.
11 WSA 2037/27; 2037/119.
12 TNA PROB 11/474, ff. 176–93 (below, p. 119).
13 Below, p. 213.
14 e.g. below, pp. 153, 206–7, 213, 217, 384.

better buildings, and the tenants, for whom better buildings might make their farms more profitable for the period of their existing leases, and increasingly it was borne entirely by the trustees. From time to time extensive repairs were made to farm buildings;[1] barns were given new floors, new doors, and new roofs.[2] The trustees paid for the new farmhouses at Oare and on Broomsgrove farm and for others built at Froxfield in 1848–9 and Huish in 1864; one at Milton Lilbourne was being planned in 1866.[3] They also provided new buildings at Oare in 1830–1 following a fire, and the downland farmstead built in 1845–6 on their farm there was rebuilt in 1865–6 also after a fire.[4] New stables and new granaries were built,[5] and new buildings were erected for dairy farming,[6] cattle rearing, and pig farming.[7] In 1810, however, the trustees declined to share the cost of erecting a building to house a threshing machine at Froxfield,[8] and in 1812 they did no more than to allow timber for a horse house built for his threshing machine by their tenant at Milton Lilbourne.[9] In 1740 the trustees ordered their steward to insure against fire all the buildings on their rack-rent farms.[10] That policy, if taken out, evidently lapsed, but from 1783 the farmhouses at Froxfield, Huish, Chirton, and Milton Lilbourne were insured.[11] Because many farm buildings in Wiltshire, including those on the trustees' farm at Oare, had been set on fire maliciously in 1830, from 1831 the trustees insured the buildings on all their farms. A successful claim was made in 1864.[12]

The trustees favoured many schemes to improve husbandry. Sainfoin was grown on Froxfield farm and Huish farm, it was proposed to plough downland of Froxfield farm, and land on both farms was chalked.[13] Meadow land at Froxfield was improved and watered, and land at Fyfield and Clench was drained.[14] There were several schemes to improve the downland of the farm at Chirton: the trustees met part of the cost of a new pond in 1737 and of inclosing part of the sheep

1 e.g. below, pp. 151, 194, 196, 198–9 (Chirton); 186, 188, 190, 253, 255, 258, 261 (Froxfield); 206–7, 210, 213, 287 (Huish); 355 (Clench).
2 e.g. below, pp. 152, 163, 182 (Chirton); 172 (Huish); 179, 181 (Milton Lilbourne); 186, 188 (Froxfield).
3 WSA 2037/27–8; below, pp. 328, 333, 339–40, 383, 389.
4 WSA 2037/27–8; below, pp. 306, 383.
5 e.g. below, pp. 151, 181, 372 (Chirton); 182, 287 (Huish); 370, 372 (Broomsgrove); 390 (Froxfield).
6 Below, pp. 183, 219, 251, 258.
7 WSA 2037/27 (1837, 1838); 2037/28 (1859, 1860); below, p. 363.
8 Below, p. 267.
9 Below, p. 270.
10 Below, p. 170.
11 WSA 2037/27.
12 Below, pp. 306, 337, 383.
13 WSA 2037/27 (1837–8); 2037/119; below, pp. 156, 184–5, 333.
14 WSA 2037/27 (1834); 2037/28 (1859); below, pp. 255–6, 307, 335.

down in 1740, in 1785 they paid for a well to be dug, and in 1859 it was proposed to plough 36 acres.[1] In 1817 the trustees agreed to pay part of the cost of making Huish Hill easier to ascend, and in 1835 they did the same in respect of Oare Hill.[2]

Rents of farms

The trustees' purpose in converting tenures from lifehold to short-term and in improving farms was to give themselves an income which was high, regular, and predictable for the benefit of the almshouse and the widows living in it. They evidently succeeded in their purpose. In 1860 the rents from their seven farms totalled £2,049.[3]

As increasingly the almshouse's estate was leased at improved rents the annual income from it rose but, because the reduced income from fines and the sale of leases had to be set against it, the rise did not reflect an increase in the value of the estate. For a century after the almshouse was built there was no significant rise in improved rents. For example, the rent of the farm at Chirton was £100 in 1698 and £110 1788–98,[4] and that of Huish farm was increased in the mid 18th century only because the farm was enlarged and expensive repairs were made to its buildings.[5] In the late 18th century and early 19th the estate did become more valuable and improved rents were raised, partly because husbandry in common ceased and partly because, from the outbreak of war with France in 1793, prices for agricultural produce increased. The rent of the farm at Chirton, the land of which was inclosed in 1808, was increased in stages from 1798 to 1815, from when it was £280.[6] That of Huish farm, £361 from 1801 and £800 from 1813,[7] was likewise more than doubled. Froxfield farm was leased for 21 years at £210 from 1799 and, immediately after its land had been inclosed, for £410 from 1819.[8] Otherwise, as soon as the Napoleonic wars ended rents fell. Abatements from Michaelmas 1815 were given to three tenants and were to continue until the price of wheat in Wiltshire from Michaelmas to Michaelmas should average £24 a load.[9] The price of corn remained low in 1821,[10] the trustees agreed to a general reduction of rents from 1821–2 'on account of the depreciation

1 Below, pp. 168, 171, 229, 369.
2 Below, pp. 278, 315.
3 WSA 2037/28.
4 Ibid. 2037/27; 2037/119; TNA C 38/260 (below, p. 127).
5 WSA 2037/27; 2037/179, lease, Whitelock to Goodman, 1776; above, this section (improvement of farms); below, pp. 172, 182, 206–7, 213.
6 WSA 2037/113, lease, Goddard to Hayward, 1801; below, pp. 249–50, 254, 276.
7 WSA 2037/179, leases, Goddard to Reeves, 1801; Goddard to Robbins, 1813; below, p. 271.
8 WSA 2037/119; below, pp. 249–50, 284; cf. below, p. 271.
9 Below, p. 277.
10 Below, p. 286.

of agricultural produce',[1] abatements continued until 1828–9 or later,[2] and in the earlier 1830s most of the trustees' farms were re-leased at reduced rents. In 1837, after the price of corn had risen, the trustees ordered their steward to raise rents in appropriate cases,[3] but lower prices of agricultural produce were again translated to lower rents about 1850, and in 1851 and 1861 tenants succeeded in having their rents reduced by threatening to quit.[4] The duchess directed not only that every tenant should keep the buildings on his holding in good repair but also that he should pay all taxes levied on it.[5] The trustees, however, were not prevented from making allowances against rent as a way of sharing the cost of maintaining buildings or erecting new ones and, although the tenants paid the land tax, both a prospective tenant and the trustees no doubt considered the expected level of it when agreeing on the rent to be paid under a lease.[6]

Occasionally tenants of the trustees, perhaps like tenants everywhere, could not or would not pay their rent and fell into arrears. Three examples are given here. William Holloway held the trustees' land at Chirton and was in arrears in 1736, when the trustees ordered the steward to find out if the security for the payment of the arrears was adequate.[7] It was apparently not. Despite being distrained upon Holloway was £223 in arrears when he left the farm, and the arrears, later described as a desperate debt, were evidently never recovered.[8] Francis Pigott, who took a 21-year lease of Froxfield farm in 1799, in 1804 offered security for his arrears and in 1805 was given the chance to clear them by half-yearly payments of £50. In 1806, after a distress had been taken and the arrears reduced, he was given the chance to clear them by payments of £100 every 2 months. He accepted the offer with thanks,[9] but in 1808 he was in reduced circumstances, assigned his lease, and left the farm.[10] In one case a tenant seems to have overreached. In 1813, when corn prices were high, Huish farm was leased to William Robbins for 12 years at £800 and in 1816, when prices were lower, he was already in arrears. Although the trustees abated his rent it remained in arrears, from 1819 he was required to pay interest on what he owed, and, despite a revaluation of the farm and concessions offered by the trustees, he quitted the farm at Michaelmas 1822.[11] In 1805, when

1 Below, p. 287.
2 Below, p. 297.
3 WSA 2037/27; below, pp. 306, 309, 311, 315, 317.
4 Below, pp. 333, 341–5, 376.
5 TNA PROB 11/474, ff. 176–93 (below, p. 119).
6 e.g. below, pp. 154, 188, 284, 293, 306, 311.
7 Below, p. 166.
8 WSA 2037/27; below, pp. 174–5.
9 WSA 2037/119; below, pp. 250–1, 259, 261–2.
10 WSA 2037/119; below, p. 267.
11 Below, pp. 271, 277, 282, 285–6; cf. WSA 2037/27; 2037/179, lease, Northey to Taylor, 1822.

they were having difficulty with Pigott and perhaps for the first time, the trustees set deadlines for the payment of rent. The tenants were informed that rents due at Lady day (25 March) must be paid by the last Saturday in the following November and rents due at Michaelmas (29 September) by the last Saturday in the following May.[1] In 1815 the deadlines were made much less generous. Thenceforward Lady day rents were to be paid on the first Saturday in July, Michaelmas rents on the Saturday before Christmas.[2] From 1840 the deadlines were the last day of June and the last day of December.[3]

Woodland

The largest areas of woodland owned by the trustees stood on their manors. Almshouse coppice, 38 acres, and Ley coppice, 27 acres, stood at Froxfield and Coffer (later Gopher) wood, 22 acres, stood at Huish. There were smaller areas of woodland at Clench and Fyfield, and there were evidently small coppices or hedgerow trees at Milton Lilbourne, Oare, and Chirton.[4] Ley coppice had been reduced to 13 acres by 1819, and in that year the trustees authorized the tenant of Froxfield farm to grub the rest, which they judged to be of poor quality, and to plough the land;[5] the last 2 acres was not cleared until 1857 or later.[6]

The trustees' primary source of income from their woodland was the timber. Trees were cut for use directly in buildings to be erected or repaired, to raise money for the erection or repair of buildings, or to raise money for other expressed purposes or for general purposes. For example, timber was allowed in 1750 for repairs on a copyhold at Froxfield and in 1799 and 1812 for new farm buildings to be erected at Milton Lilbourne;[7] timber was sold in 1814–15 to pay for the almshouse's new gatehouse and for repairs at Huish,[8] in 1823–4 to meet some of the costs of the Fyfield inclosure award,[9] and in 1866, when £568 was raised, simply to add to the almshouse's general funds.[10] The trustees' secondary income from the woodland was from produce such as coppice wood, small trees, saplings, firewood, and bark. From 1700 or earlier they gave firewood to the widows,[11] and in 1734 the steward was apparently authorized to sell all the coppice wood of Coffer wood.[12] Later the right to take produce of the woodland was leased at

1 Below, p. 261.
2 Below, p. 276.
3 Below, p. 323.
4 WSA tithe awards; for Ley coppice, ibid. 2037/111, lease, Batson to Ivy, 1758.
5 Below, p. 284.
6 Below, p. 360.
7 Below, pp. 178, 251, 270.
8 Below, pp. 274, 276; for the gatehouse, below, almshouse buildings (houses).
9 Below, pp. 290–1.
10 Below, p. 389.
11 Below, almshouse life (firewood, coal).
12 Below, p. 166.

rack rent. Coffer wood was leased with Huish farm for a century or more from 1742,[1] and the woodland at Froxfield, no longer needed for faggots, was leased in 1796 and held on leases until about 1855.[2] Under his lease a tenant of woodland might not fell a timber tree or a tree likely to become a timber tree.[3]

The trustees' interest in the management of their woodland may have increased in the 1840s when, from time to time, the steward was directed to examine woodland, sell timber fit to be cut, plant new trees where necessary, and make new plantations if possible.[4] In 1851 arrangements were to be made to superintend the small coppices at Milton Lilbourne and Clench,[5] and in the 1850s and 1860s the trustees sold small oaks, saplings, bark, and faggots from Coffer wood and Almshouse coppice, which were then in hand.[6]

Cottages

In the 17th century cottages which had long stood on a manor are likely to have been held by copy of court roll, either on their own or with a very small holding of land. If a new cottage was built on the manor, including its waste, the builder or possessor was required to accept a grant of it from the lord of the manor, to make a payment on accepting the grant, and to pay rent thereafter. The grants were usually in the form of leases for 99 years on lives and, as with copyhold cottages and other lifeholds, the payments on acceptance were negotiable and the rents usually nominal. In the 18th century cottages stood on both the almshouse's manors and to exercise their manorial rights was apparently the trustees' only concern with them. Most were leasehold and most stood at Froxfield; of those on Huish manor some stood at Huish, some at New Mill, and two at Oare.[7] In the 1720s the trustees took stock of the cottages on both manors.[8] The result for Froxfield was that the steward was ordered to prosecute the builders, or eject the occupants, of cottages which lacked the 4 acres required by statute for the use of the occupants,[9] that the trustees were able to grant five cottages standing on the waste of the manor to the existing possessors, and that the trustees ordered the steward to bring an ejectment against the possessor of a cottage so that their claim to it might be tried.[10] The

1 WSA 2037/179, lease, Whitelock to Brown, 1742; ibid. tithe award.
2 Ibid. 2037/27–8; 2037/113, lease, Goddard to Merriwether, 1811; below, pp. 242, 247.
3 e.g. WSA 2037/113, lease, Goddard to Merriwether, 1811.
4 Below, pp. 324, 331, 339.
5 Below, p. 343.
6 WSA 2037/28.
7 Ibid. 2037/119.
8 Below, pp. 151, 154.
9 Below, p. 154; cf. 31 Elizabeth I c. 7: *Statutes of the Realm*, iv. 804–5.
10 Below, pp. 160, 162.

only apparent result for Huish was that in 1733 the trustees were in the process of ejecting the possessor of a cottage then standing on the waste who had refused to take a lease from them.[1] The 18th-century trustees did no more than to make new grants for lives by copy or lease, receive the payments on acceptance, and collect the rents. They did nothing to design, build, improve, or maintain cottages, and in 1773, when they decided to bring copyhold tenure on their estate to an end, they excepted cottages.[2]

No cottage was granted on lives after 1809,[3] and therefore lifehold tenure of cottages gradually ended in the 19th century. As lives ended cottages which had stood in the 18th century and may not have been built to last were demolished,[4] and in 1848 the trustees resolved expressly that old and poor cottages at Froxfield should be pulled down as they became untenanted.[5] At the same time the trustees began to see advantages in investing in cottages, and they built new cottages themselves for profit. Six new ones had been built at Huish by 1824, and another two were built there in 1835–6. The trustees sought a 4 per cent return on their investment,[6] and in 1838 the outgoing steward proudly reported that in the previous decade several new cottages had been built and were yielding about £20 a year.[7] New cottages were built at Froxfield and New Mill in the 1840s and at Froxfield and Chirton in the 1860s.[8] In 1866 the trustees owned 54 cottages. Rents totalled £143.[9]

The cottages built at Froxfield by the trustees were evidently intended to house the general population. It was noted in 1839 that accommodation there was much needed and in 1841 that the existing housing was in a bad state,[10] in 1844 four cottages were burned down,[11] and about 1860 five cottages were demolished to make way for a railway.[12] Nine new cottages built in the 1840s and nine built between about 1860 and 1866 were converted from old commercial buildings, incorporated their materials, or were built on their sites.[13] In 1862 the trustees resolved that in future every cottage newly built or formed by converting an existing building should as a rule have three bedrooms each with its own entrance, and in 1863 they expressed a wish to alleviate what, in respect of Froxfield, they called the evil of

1 Below, p. 165.
2 Below, p. 206.
3 Cf. *Endowed Charities of Wiltshire* (southern division), 989–91.
4 Below, pp. 268, 290, 297.
5 Below, p. 339.
6 WSA 2037/27; below, pp. 315–16.
7 Below, p. 319.
8 WSA 2037/27–8.
9 Ibid. 2037/28.
10 Below, pp. 321, 324.
11 WSA 2037/28.
12 Below, p. 373; cf. below, p. 383.
13 WSA 2037/28; below, pp. 322–5, 339–40, 375, 378, 384, 390.

overcrowding.[1] In aspiring to build additional and better cottages it is not clear whether they were motivated by morality, philanthropy, or a desire to increase income from rents. Most of the new cottages built at Huish were evidently occupied by farm workers and may have been built expressly to increase the value of Huish farm. Four of the new cottages which had been built there by 1824 were leased to the tenant of the farm, the two built in 1835–6 adjoined a downland farmyard which was part of the farm, and in 1860 the tenant held nine cottages with the farm.[2]

Other assets

Besides their agricultural land, woodland, and cottages the trustees owned malthouses, brewhouses, and three inns at Froxfield and a wharf and a public house at New Mill. Froxfield, on the main road from London to Bath and Bristol, was apparently a minor centre for malting and brewing, and for long the inns evidently flourished.[3] In the mid 19th century, after railways had been built, less traffic used the road and the inns declined.[4] The trustees also invested in allotment gardens and government securities.

The Cross Keys inn was standing in 1727 and, at much expense to the trustees, was upgraded between 1758 and 1762. In 1759 it was leased at an improved rent, in 1762 was leased with a house and a malthouse which by 1763 had also been repaired at much expense to the trustees,[5] and until the 1830s was apparently the heart of a successful business. New buildings erected before 1793 included a stable for 10 horses, a cellar for 60 hogsheads, an extension to a brewhouse, and a new parlour.[6] In 1793 the tenant, W. C. Noyes, sold his business, and assigned his lease, to William Newbury,[7] and about 1822 Newbury assigned his lease to John Brown, who was in partnership with one Hillary.[8] New buildings for Newbury, probably erected in the 1790s, included a new granary, a stable, a barrel house, a cellar, and a brewhouse. The cost was shared by him and the trustees, who expected a 6 per cent return on their outlay.[9] In 1801, when Newbury intended to rebuild the malthouse, the trustees offered him as much rough timber as was needed and £100 at 6 per cent, but in 1803, when Newbury claimed to have spent over £1,000 on the buildings at the Cross Keys, they

1 Below, pp. 378, 382.
2 WSA 2037/27–8; below, p. 315.
3 For Froxfield, *VCH Wiltshire*, xvi. 149–65.
4 Below, following paragraph.
5 Below, pp. 156, 185–8, 190, 192–3, 196–7.
6 WSA 2037/112, lease, Goddard to Noyes, 1791; below, pp. 187, 193, 229, 235.
7 *VCH Wiltshire*, xvi. 158; WSA 2037/112, lease, Goddard to Noyes, 1791.
8 *Early Trade Directories* (WRS xlvii), 62; WSA 2037/27.
9 WSA 2037/112, lease, Goddard to Newbury, 1796; below, pp. 244-5.

waived the £6 a year.[1] The business declined from the 1830s and Brown, who was subletting the premises and in financial difficulty, gave up the tenancy in 1836. The buildings were then in poor repair. The steward leased the premises in portions and recommended the demolition of the brewhouse, which had been vacant for many years.[2] The business continued on what was apparently a smaller scale. Part of the brewhouse had been demolished by 1842, in 1842–3 stables and a new and smaller brewhouse were built behind the inn,[3] and the old malthouse was demolished in 1848–9. The inn was repaired again in 1849,[4] but in 1865 the ratepayers of Froxfield petitioned the trustees to close it and the trustees did so at Michaelmas of that year.[5] The Blue Lion was described in 1718 as newly built.[6] It was first leased at an improved rent in 1808, was burned down in 1835, and had been rebuilt by 1837.[7] The Pelican was probably built in the mid 18th century and stood on copyhold land. Both inns stood at the east end of Froxfield village.[8] In 1862 the tenant for life, then aged about 88, offered to lease the Pelican to the trustees, who resolved to accept it, to repair it, to lease it as what they called a respectable small inn, and to close the Blue Lion.[9] By 1863 the Blue Lion had been closed and the Pelican leased at an improved rent.[10]

In 1810–11 the trustees accepted a proposal for John Liddiard to build a wharf on their land beside the Kennet and Avon canal.[11] The wharf was built and in 1818 the trustees leased it to Mary Liddiard at £5 a year.[12] Traffic on the canal, like that on the road through Froxfield, declined after railways were built,[13] and about 1854, when the buildings at it were in a bad state, the wharf was given to T. B. Merriman in the exchange made then.[14] Also at New Mill, a cottage on the land of Huish manor was open as the Greyhound public house in the late 18th century, when it was held on lives by W. C. Noyes, the tenant of the Cross Keys. In 1812 a new lease was made on lives,[15] one or more of which had evidently not ended by 1866.[16]

Between 1819 and 1835 the trustees leased 21 acres at Froxfield as 42 garden allotments.[17] In doing so they presumably intended to

1 Below, pp. 254, 258.
2 Below, pp. 316, 319, 321.
3 Below, pp. 325, 328.
4 Below, pp. 339–40.
5 Below, p. 387.
6 WSA 2037/109, lease, Pocock to Pethers, 1718.
7 Ibid. 2037/113, lease, Goddard to Trueman, 1808; 2037/119; below, p. 317.
8 *VCH Wiltshire*, xvi. 152; WSA 2037/119.
9 Below, p. 378.
10 WSA 2037/28; cf. below, pp. 384, 390.
11 Below, pp. 269–70.
12 Below, p. 280.
13 *VCH Wiltshire*, iv. 276–7.
14 Below, pp. 354, 356; cf. above, this section (improvement of farms).
15 WSA 2037/119; below, p. 229.
16 Cf. WSA 2037/28.
17 Ibid. 2037/27; ibid. tithe award; *Endowed Charities of Wiltshire* (southern division), 988; below, p. 282.

benefit the poor, but to have offered allotments at a cost to their estate would have been contrary to the duchess's direction to lease land at the highest rent possible.[1] Rents charged for allotments were about the same as those charged for equivalent agricultural land and totalled £19 in 1866.[2]

In 1755 the court of Chancery sanctioned a scheme under which money saved by the trustees to enlarge the almshouse was invested in the government securities traded as Old South Sea annuities. In 1767 the trustees held stock which had a face value of £2,600 and yielded £78 a year, thereafter they bought and sold stock as opportunity and need arose,[3] and in 1810 £235 9*s*. 5*d*. stock was acquired when the money received from the sale of land to the Kennet and Avon Canal company was invested.[4] In 1850 the trustees reduced their holding to £2,500,[5] and in 1853 that was paid off at par.[6] The £235 9*s*. 5*d*. from the sale of land was retained in cash for re-investment in land, and the residue, £2,264 10*s*. 7*d*. after a broker's commission had been paid, was used to buy consolidated annuities (consols) with a face value of £2,573 14*s*. 9*d*. and an annual yield of £77.[7] In 1855 £159 of the £235 was used to buy land and the rest to buy £83 consols. In the period 1829–32 the trustees also bought two Exchequer bills, each with a face value of £500 and a yield of £11 10*s*. a year. They were sold in 1843–4.[8]

Road, canal, railways

The main road from London to Bath and Bristol, beside which the almshouse was built, was turnpiked through Froxfield village in 1726.[9] In 1791 it was widened by taking in two strips of meadow belonging to the almshouse and by cutting down part of the bank between the almshouse and the road. The almshouse trustees sold the land, invested the proceeds, and reduced the rent paid by the tenant who held the meadow land by an amount equal to the interest from the investment. The turnpike trustees made good the damage caused by altering the bank.[10]

1 TNA PROB 11/474, ff. 176–93 (below, p. 119).
2 WSA 2037/28.
3 Ibid. 2037/27; TNA C 33/389, ff. 674–5; C 33/403, f. 564; C 33/447, ff. 471v.–472; cf. above, Attorney General *v* Grimston (1729–85).
4 WSA 2037/27; below, p. 267; cf. below, this section (road, canal, railways).
5 Below, p. 341.
6 *Endowed Charities of Wiltshire* (southern division), 995.
7 Below, p. 350.
8 *Endowed Charities of Wiltshire* (southern division), 985, 995; below, pp. 298, 319, 328.
9 For the turnpiking, *VCH Wiltshire*, iv. 257, 267.
10 Below, pp. 236, 239–40; cf. below, almshouse buildings (walls, gardens, paths).

The Kennet and Avon canal was opened across Froxfield parish in 1799[1] and was built across the trustees' land in Milton Lilbourne parish in 1806–7.[2] The trustees sold the land in Milton Lilbourne to the canal company in 1806. The proceeds were invested and, again, the interest was used to reduce the rent of the tenants whose land was taken.[3] The canal company was obliged to build a bridge over the canal where it crossed Fyfield's land but, because inclosure and exchange of lands was being considered, the bridge was not built and the company allowed £75 to the trustees on being released from its obligation.[4]

The Berks. & Hants railway was opened between Reading and Hungerford in 1847 and various schemes were made to extend it. In two of the schemes, one for a London, Bristol, and South Wales Direct railway and one for a Newbury–Bath railway, it was proposed to build a line across the almshouse's land at Froxfield. In 1846 the trustees resolved to oppose the South Wales line, and by implication the Newbury–Bath line, unless they were satisfactorily compensated for their land which would be taken and for the inconvenience which would be caused to the almshouse. Neither line was built. In 1858, however, the trustees assented to a proposal to extend the Berks. & Hants railway via Froxfield to Devizes: the marquess of Ailesbury was chairman of both the Berks. & Hants Extension Railway company and the almshouse trustees.[5] The trustees' property taken for the line was 2¾ acres and five cottages at Froxfield and 2½ acres at Milton Lilbourne. The company paid £472 10*s*. for the land and as compensation because the line severed some parts of the trustees' land from other parts, and £477 10*s*. for the five cottages to be replaced. The £472 10*s*. was set aside for future purchase of land, the cottages had been replaced by 1864, and in 1861 the trustees proposed to exchange their severed lands for lands on the right side of the track.[6]

Doubts, disputes, troublesome tenants

Perhaps like every other owner of an estate the almshouse trustees were occasionally confronted by doubts, disputes, and troublesome tenants. Most of the doubts and disputes arose over who owned a particular piece of land or a particular right, and the trustees faced claims made sometimes by other landowners and sometimes by their own tenants. Most of the tenants who caused trouble had failed to repair buildings or pay rent.

1 *VCH Wiltshire*, iv. 273–4.
2 K. R. Clew, *Kennet & Avon Canal* (1985), 69, 73.
3 *Endowed Charities of Wiltshire* (southern division), 991; below, p. 262.
4 Below, pp. 263–5, 288.
5 *VCH Wiltshire*, iv. 283, 285–6; below, pp. 334–5, 364.
6 Below, pp. 375–6, 381, 383–4.

In the earlier 18th century the trustees disputed with the tenant of the Rectory estate at Froxfield, which was owned by the dean and chapter of St. George's chapel, Windsor, and with the vicar of Froxfield. The first dispute was over the right to tithe wood from Almshouse coppice, the second over the ownership of a garden.[1] There were three cases of doubt about what land at Fyfield was part of Fyfield manor and what belonged to the trustees. The first led to the acquisition by the trustees of Pyke's Bear croft.[2] The second gave rise to a dispute over two small closes between John Cannings, who claimed them as part of his estate at New Mill held of the trustees by copy, and Charles Penruddocke (d. 1788), who claimed one as part of Fyfield manor and the other as land leased to him by the trustees: in 1792–3 the trustees proposed arbitration to Penruddocke's successor J. H. Penruddocke.[3] In the third the trustees thought that a tenant of Fyfield manor had encroached on their land.[4] The extent of the trustees' land at Chirton, which had been sold to the duchess of Somerset by Elizabeth Bing,[5] was likewise thrice questioned. In 1719 the trustees resolved to ask one Robert Bing about it,[6] a dispute over a plot of land had begun by 1749,[7] and a dispute over four cottages with the tenant who held the lifehold estate there until it fell in hand in 1861 ended in compromise in 1864.[8] In 1847 a similar dispute over cottages at New Mill had also ended in compromise.[9] In 1752, however, the trustees took a firmer line in a dispute over a driftway at Chirton. They simply ordered that the rival claims should be tried at the next Wiltshire assizes. The trial was held at Salisbury in 1753, the trustees' tenant was the plaintiff, and they met his costs when he was nonsuited.[10] The details of two disputes may perhaps be rehearsed. When Edmund Hungerford bought Fyfield manor in 1688 he also acquired an interest in a copyhold at Fyfield presumably held for a life or lives then in being. The copyhold was part of Huish manor and had been granted to one of the Ashe family, members of which sold Fyfield manor to Hungerford. It consisted of 6½ acres of arable, ½ acre of meadow, and the right to feed 80 sheep in common, and in the earlier 18th century the boundaries of its land were unknown. In 1715 the trustees began to make enquiries about it and in 1717 resolved to pursue a claim that it had sunk from Huish

1 Below, pp. 143–4, 146–7, 163–4; for the estate, *VCH Wiltshire*, xvi. 156.
2 Below, this paragraph.
3 WSA 332/286; below, pp. 241–3; for the Penruddockes, *VCH Wiltshire*, xvi. 173.
4 Below, p. 252.
5 *VCH Wiltshire*, x. 63.
6 Below, p. 149.
7 Below, this paragraph.
8 WSA 2037/119; below, pp. 382, 384.
9 Below, pp. 333, 337.
10 WSA 2037/119; below, pp. 180–1.

manor into Fyfield manor. In 1718, by when the life or lives had ended, they resolved to prefer a bill against Henry Hungerford if he refused to join them in marking out their land and valuing their right of common and, probably in Michaelmas term 1718, they exhibited a bill in Chancery for the discovery and recovery of the holding. In 1721, by when the land had still not been identified, Hungerford conceded. The trustees granted the holding to him in exchange for Pyke's Bear croft, 7 acres. Until lands were exchanged on *de iure* inclosure, however, the trustees leased that croft to successive lords of Fyfield manor.[1] In 1749 and 1752 the trustees appointed some of their number to investigate a complaint by the tenant of both their rack-rent and lifehold land at Chirton that it had been encroached on and that a wall which he had built on it had been demolished by a third party. The tenant, whose costs were met by the trustees, took action at law, withdrew from it, and by 1757 had accepted defeat and rebuilt the wall presumably on a new line.[2]

Matters of doubt or dispute between the trustees and their tenants were not minuted frequently. The custom of Huish manor was twice in doubt, in 1715–17 over whether, on the death of the last survivor of those named in a copyhold grant, his or her executors might hold the premises listed in the grant for 1 year after the death,[3] and in 1738 over whether a tenant had forfeited his copyhold because he had been convicted of felony.[4] A problem arose in 1779 when the incoming tenant of the trustees' farm at Milton Lilbourne complained that his buildings needed repair and that the farm was smaller than he had been led to believe.[5] Tenants who failed to maintain the buildings on their holdings frequently troubled the trustees who, when repairs had not been carried out, occasionally threatened to bring an ejectment against a tenant[6] or to prosecute an outgoing tenant or the executors of a deceased tenant.[7] A few tenants misappropriated trees. In 1724 the trustees were severe: they simply ordered the steward to either eject or prosecute two copyholders of Huish manor who had cut timber on their holdings and sold it.[8] In 1862 they considered themselves lenient: men working for the tenant had cut large limbs from trees growing on Broomsgrove farm, the tenant claimed that his orders had been exceeded, offered to pay for the trees or for the damage done, and

1 WSA 332/181, deed, Popham to Hungerford, 1721; 2037/27; below, pp. 143–5, 147; for the Ashes and the sale in 1688, *VCH Wiltshire*, xvi. 173.
2 Below, pp. 177, 179–82, 184.
3 Below, p. 146.
4 Below, p. 169.
5 Below, p. 217.
6 Below, pp. 144–7; cf. below, p. 148.
7 Below, pp. 151, 153, 155–6, 162–3.
8 Below, p. 152.

offered to give up land for a plantation, but the trustees did no more than to demand the sum at which the trees were valued.[1] The trouble caused to the trustees by tenants who did not pay their rent has already been referred to.[2]

ALMSHOUSE BUILDINGS

Houses

Soon after the death of the duchess of Somerset, which occurred in October 1692, Sir William Gregory took responsibility for the building of Froxfield almshouse. An inscription on a tablet set above its main gateway recorded that it was finished in 1694, but the court of Chancery gave June 1695, by when widows had been installed, as a legal completion date.[3] It is very likely that the tablet was inscribed and put up about the time that the building was finished and that 1694 is a more accurate date for its completion than 1695. Later the inscribed date may nevertheless have been changed to 1695.[4]

The almshouse was built, as the duchess directed, around a square courtyard and of brick. As it stood from 1694 to 1772 each of its four ranges was about 47 m. long. There was a house at each corner and seven houses in each range between them. In the south range, which had a principal front to the London road, there was a central gatehouse which incorporated the main gateway and a lodge for a porter. The house at the south-east corner was for the steward to use, and the other 30 houses were for widows. The house at the north-east corner and the house at the north-west corner was each separated from the north range by a narrow passage. In each of the widows' houses there was a ground-floor room, a room above it, a hearth in each room, and a passage, a staircase, and closets. No house had a cellar or a garret. The ground-floor rooms, each of which evidently incorporated a small kitchen or scullery, measured 14 ft. by 12–13 ft.[5] There was a cupola, presumably above the gatehouse, and, presumably in the cupola, by 1699 a clock had been fixed and a bell hung.[6]

As early as 1698 the trustees stated that the almshouse needed repairs which would cost £200,[7] and between 1699 and 1701 much

1 Below, pp. 377–8.
2 Above, this section (rents of farms).
3 Ward, *Somerset Hospital*, 29; TNA C 38/260 (below, p. 125); cf. above, foundation.
4 Cf. below, p. 274; for successive gatehouses and tablets, below, this sub-section.
5 Cf. Ward, *Somerset Hospital*, 28–9; TNA PROB 11/474, ff. 176–93 (below, p. 117); WSA 2037/86.
6 WSA 2037/26; below, p. 162.
7 TNA C 33/291, f. 116; C 38/260, report dated 11 February 1699.

work was done.[1] Between 1701 and 1772 the widows' houses were routinely maintained, and bills presented by tilers, masons, carpenters, blacksmiths, and glaziers were regularly paid.[2] For example, in 1758 each of the houses that needed it was to be whitewashed inside and brick floors were to be laid in houses which lacked them.[3] The cupola was repaired in 1731 and replaced by a new one in 1759. In 1732–3 a new lock and key was made for the main door of the almshouse, the tablet above the gateway was amended and the inscription made legible, and the clock was repaired and its face newly painted and figured.[4]

The duchess's direction that 20 new houses should be added to the almshouse was followed in the early 1770s. Building began in 1772, and again each house was to consist of a single ground-floor room and a room above it. The gatehouse, in the south range, and the steward's house, at the south-east corner, was each converted to a house for a widow, the seven houses between the steward's house and the house at the north-east corner were demolished, and the north and south ranges were extended eastwards. In the south range a new gatehouse was built immediately east of the old steward's house, and a new steward's house was built at the new south-east corner. Eight new houses for widows were built between them, and the new gatehouse thus became the centre of the extended range. To extend the north range 10 new houses were built, including that at the new north-east corner which was separated from the others by a narrow passage. As extended each range was about 105 m. long and the courtyard became a double square. Between the houses at the new corners seven houses were built as a new east range to replace the seven in the old one.[5] In June 1773 the widows living in the old seven were ordered to move to new houses,[6] their old houses were presumably demolished soon afterwards, and an inscription recorded that the extension of the almshouse was finished in 1773.[7] In 1774, evidently to further or complete a scheme by means of which the 20 new houses running anticlockwise from the new gatehouse were assigned to the 20 clergy widows, five clergy widows were asked to move to new houses.[8]

The new gatehouse was built with a cupola, a clock, and a bell, probably those which had been in place above the old gatehouse, and with a weathervane dated 1772. In 1783 the inscription to record the enlargement of the almshouse was added to the tablet bearing the

1 WSA 2037/26.
2 e.g. ibid.; below, pp. 154, 156–7, 161, 172, 199.
3 Below, p. 186.
4 Below, pp. 162, 165, 187.
5 TNA PROB 11/474, ff. 176–93 (below, p. 120); WSA 2037/119; for the plan, ibid. 2037/86.
6 Below, p. 206.
7 Ward, *Somerset Hospital*, 29; WSA 2037/27; for the inscription, below, this subsection.
8 Ward, *Somerset Hospital*, 31; WSA 2037/86; below, p. 207.

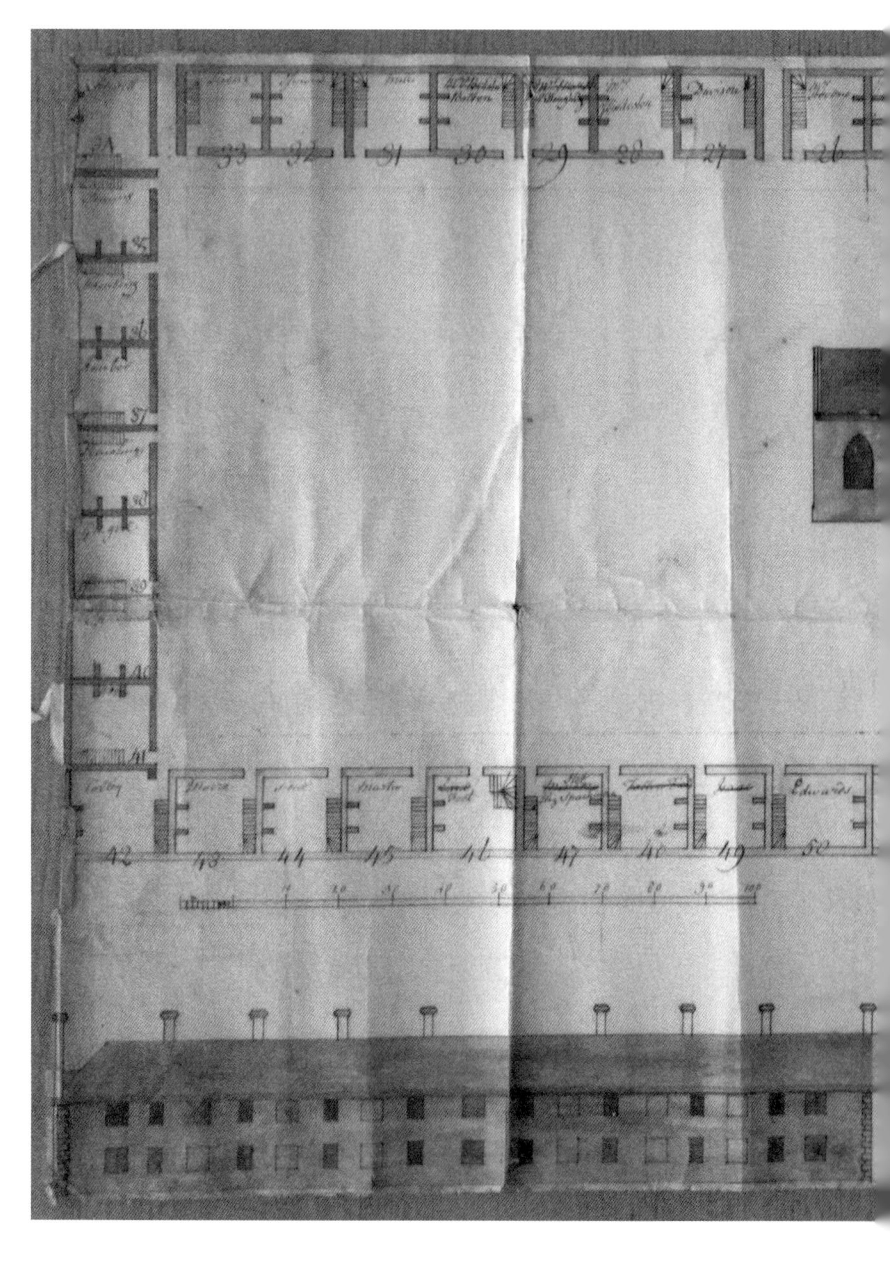

Ground-floor plan and south vi
(A new chapel was not built in the cen

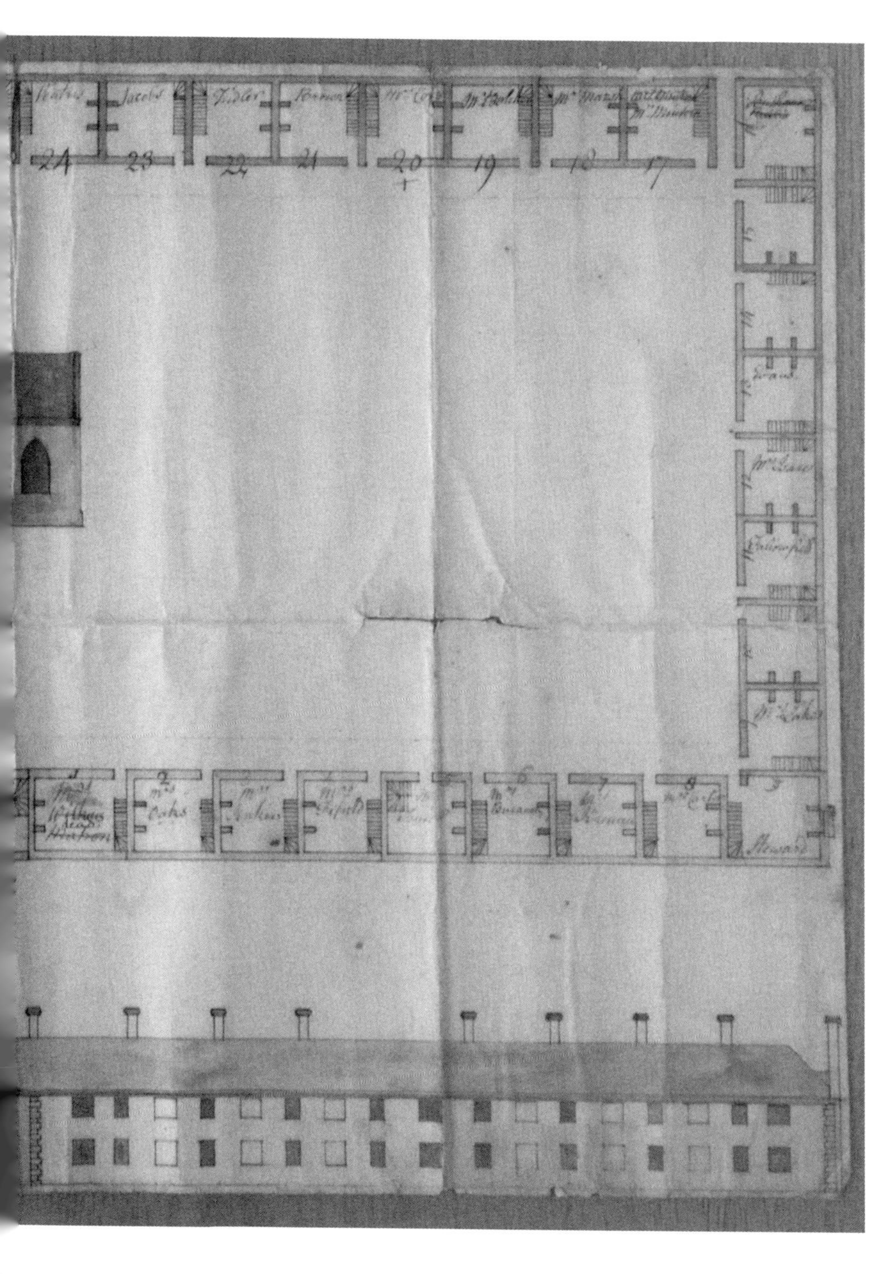

f Froxfield almshouse about 1774
f the enlarged quadrangle until 1814)

date 1694, and the tablet was put up on the new gatehouse.[1] In 1796 a new copper dial was fitted to the clock, and the two dials of the clock were painted.[2] In 1814, to dignify the approach to the new chapel from the London road, the trustees resolved to improve and ornament the gatehouse. Although they resolved that its brickwork should be stuccoed it was rebuilt in stone. The gateway was widened, new iron gates were hung, and the inscription on the tablet was engraved anew and, as the trustees supposed, corrected.[3] By 1822 it had evidently become possible for a person to pass through the gates when they were closed and locked, and impenetrable doors, presumably wooden, were then fitted over them.[4] For the convenience of the widows part of the porch was converted to a water closet in 1859.[5]

Routine maintenance of the almshouse continued after 1773, and the building was gradually improved. Roofs and drains were repaired and spouting (presumably gutters and downpipes) was replaced or fitted for the first time.[6] Work was done on the individual houses, especially on 24 of the 25 surviving old ones. The 25th was probably that at the old north-east corner which may have been much altered in 1772–3. The old houses were provided with new doors and windows in 1789, the 24 houses to the door of each of which, lacking one, a shed was to be fitted in 1790 were probably old ones, and in 1796 it was ordered that new windows should again be fitted in 24 old houses.[7] The doors and window frames, and the pediments over the doors, of all the houses were painted in 1825.[8] The words shed and pediment were perhaps used to describe small wooden canopies erected to provide shelter. Chimney pots, to help the smoke from fires to escape, were fitted to some houses in 1786,[9] and much boarding of floors, possibly to replace the bricks, was paid for in 1839–40.[10]

The almshouse had been insured against fire by 1748,[11] but it was apparently not until the 1790s that the trustees took into account the safety of the widows. In 1791 a committee considered how the main door could be kept locked at night but the widows leave the building in the event of fire. It failed to solve the problem and reported that the only solution lay with Lewis Evans, the vicar of Froxfield and the

1 Ward, *Somerset Hospital*, 29; *Gentleman's Magazine*, lxxi (1), facing p. 306; J. Buckler, watercolour in library of WANHS, Devizes, vol. iv. 16; WSA 2037/27.

2 WSA 2037/27; below, p. 247.

3 *VCH Wiltshire*, xvi. 163; WSA 2037/119; below, pp. 274, 276; for the chapel, below, this section.

4 Below, p. 288.

5 Below, p. 370.

6 e.g. below, pp. 232, 294, 329, 331, 336, 358, 360–1, 364, 370.

7 Below, pp. 234–6, 247; cf. WSA 2037/86.

8 Below, pp. 293–4.

9 Below, p. 232.

10 WSA 2037/27.

11 TNA C 33/389, ff. 674–5.

officiating chaplain, who was of a scientific mind and had undertaken to design a new lock.[1] Later the trustees turned their attention to minimizing the spread of fire in the almshouse, but not at any cost. A proposal of 1794 to build six party walls if the cost would not exceed £60[2] was evidently dropped, a resolution of 1802 to build four or six was rescinded because they would disfigure the almshouse, and in 1809 it was resolved to do no more than to build four or five in the roof space and only to do that if the cost was no more than £20.[3]

Bird's eye view of Froxfield almshouse, 1800

By her will the duchess gave money to pay for tables, bedsteads, and other durable furniture to be provided in each of the widows' houses,[4] and the new houses were evidently equipped as the old ones had been.[5] The question who was entitled to fixtures or fittings in the houses was raised in the early 19th century. In 1808 the trustees ruled that no incoming widow should pay for any improvement made by her predecessor; such improvement was to include wallpaper but exclude fittings deemed legally removable. If the incomer wished to accept and pay for any such legally removable fitting she was to be charged no more than two thirds of what her predecessor had paid for it; if she rejected it her predecessor or her predecessor's representatives might remove it if all damage caused by doing so was made good.[6]

1 Below, pp. 237, 240; for the locking of the door, below, almshouse life (regulations, rules); for Evans, *DNB*; below, officers (chaplain).
2 Below, p. 244.
3 Below, pp. 256–7, 266.
4 TNA PROB 11/474, ff. 176–93 (below, p. 117).
5 WSA 2037/27.
6 Below, p. 266.

Somerset Hospital
AT FROXFIELD.

Regulations respecting Fixtures, made at a Meeting of the Trustees, held the 3rd Day of August, 1825.

THE Widows appointed, subsequent to this day, are to be informed, that they will have to pay only for Grates and Shelves, (if they choose to take them) at a valuation of the articles as worth to take away.---If the new Widow does not take, the Executors may remove them, making good all damages.

With respect to all other Fixtures which it can be proved have been paid for by any Widow now in the Hospital, prior to this date, the Trustees will allow to the Executors for the same, or for such parts as the Steward shall think fit to retain, to be left as heir looms for the benefit of the succeeding Widows, two-thirds of the value, the same being valued as to take away.

All Fixtures (except Grates and Shelves) and other improvements, made by the present or any future Widows after this date, are to be left as heir looms for the benefit of their successors, without any remuneration. The valuer to be appointed by the Steward, and to be paid by the Executors and new Widow, in equal shares; and he must in all cases deduct from his valuation, what it would cost to make good the damages which would be occasioned, were the articles valued to be removed.

A new rule was made in 1825. In the case of articles which had been fixed in houses before then it was ruled that, other than grates and shelves, they were to be left for the benefit of the incomer, and the trustees, not she, would pay to the outgoer or her representatives two thirds of what the articles would be worth if taken away less the cost of making good. In the case of grates and shelves, if an incomer wished to accept them, she, not the trustees, must pay to the outgoer or her representatives what the value of them would have been if taken away less the cost of making good. All fixed improvements made after 1825 were to be left for, and taken by, incoming widows without payment.[1]

1 Below, p. 294.

The regulations promulgated in 1698, those proposed in 1710, and those confirmed in 1729 all required widows to pay for damage caused to the glass in their windows while they held their houses.[1]

Chapel

The duchess directed that a chapel should be built of brick in the middle of the quadrangle and that it should be furnished with plain seats, cushions, bibles, and all else that was necessary.[2] The chapel, like the almshouse, was built in the period 1692–4,[3] and thereafter the trustees maintained both the building and its furnishings.[4]

The plan to extend the almshouse included one proposal to build a new chapel in the centre of the enlarged quadrangle[5] and another to build one outside the quadrangle and among gardens immediately east of it.[6] Neither proposal was accepted, and the extension of 1772–3 left the chapel not at the centre of a square quadrangle but in the west part of a rectangular one and possibly too small for 20 more widows to worship in.[7] In 1775 the trustees thought about enlarging it and again about replacing it,[8] but it seems that the chapel remained in use as it was. It was repaired in 1788 and 1789,[9] and in 1798 the steward was authorized to commission a porch.[10] In 1813 one of the trustees, Edward Popham, rector of Chilton Foliat, represented that the chapel was in poor repair and of mean appearance. Another trustee, Thomas Brudenell Bruce, earl of Ailesbury, offered to pay for a new one to be built, and the offer was accepted.[11] The new chapel was begun in 1813 and finished in 1814.[12] It was built in the middle of the new quadrangle and with stone walls and an iron roof.[13] It was later said to have 18 pews and to seat 80.[14] The architect was Thomas Baldwin of Bath.[15] In 1818 it was reported by Thomas Cundy, an architect who was working for Charles, earl of Ailesbury, at Tottenham House, that dry rot was damaging the wainscot and floors, and the trustees ordered that remedial work should be done.[16] In 1858 one of the walls was thought

1 TNA C 33/351, ff. 391v.–392 (below, p. 132); C 38/267 (below, p. 136); WSA 2037/8, orders proposed 1710.
2 TNA PROB 11/474, ff. 176–93 (below, p. 117).
3 Ibid. C 33/289, ff. 250–2 (below, p. 122).
4 e.g. ibid. C 38/260, report dated 11 February 1699; below, p. 162.
5 WSA 2037/86.
6 Ibid. 2037/83.
7 Cf. *Gentleman's Magazine*, lxxi (1), facing p. 306.
8 Below, p. 209.
9 Below, pp. 233–5.
10 Below, p. 249.
11 Below, p. 273.
12 WSA 2037/119.
13 For the roof, below, p. 364.
14 p. 3 of a printed report by the trustees of the parochial charities of St. Margaret and St. John, Westminster, 1892, part of which survives in WSA 2037/1.
15 WSA 2037/87.
16 *VCH Wiltshire*, xvi. 29–30; WSA 2037/90; below, p. 281.

to be in danger of collapse and an offer made by George, marquess of Ailesbury, to pay for repairs was accepted.[1] In 1860 the trustees received a suggestion that a handrail fitted to the steps of the chapel would help invalid widows; in 1861 they ordered that one should be fitted, but only if Lord Ailesbury thought it desirable.[2]

The quadrangle and chapel of Froxfield almshouse, 1998

The seats fitted in the 1690s may have lasted in it until the old chapel was demolished about 1814. Other furnishings were less durable. The bible and the prayer book were occasionally repaired or replaced,[3] surplices were bought,[4] and in 1796 a pall, a cloth for the pulpit, and probably a cloth for the communion table were provided.[5] A cloth for the pulpit of the new chapel was ordered in 1814, and a new pall was bought in 1829–30.[6] The chapel linen was regularly washed and mended and the floor was swept.[7] In 1861 the trustees set aside £20 towards the cost of a stove which, like the handrail, was to be fitted only if Lord Ailesbury thought it desirable.[8]

Others

The almshouse's service buildings stood outside the quadrangle and were approached by way of the narrow passages through the north

1 Below, p. 364.
2 Below, pp. 373, 376.
3 WSA 2037/27; below, pp. 165, 174; for the widows' bibles and prayer books, below, almshouse life (religious worship).
4 WSA 2037/27; below, p. 174.
5 Below, p. 247.
6 WSA 2037/27; below, p. 274.
7 WSA 2037/27; below, p. 234.
8 Below, p. 376.

range.[1] Privies may have been set up north of the north range in the 1690s when the old houses were built, and new or additional privies may have been set up in 1772–3 when the new houses were built.[2] In the 1840s and 1850s the trustees accepted the need for replacements, additions, or improvements, and new privies were built in 1840–1 and between 1856 and 1858.[3] A wash-house and a brewhouse, built between 1781 and 1783 for the widows to use and possibly under one roof,[4] may have been the building called a wash-house and bakery which was rebuilt in 1857–8.[5] There is no evidence that the new building was used as anything but a wash-house.[6] Three proposals to store fuel under cover came to naught. The first, made when the almshouse was enlarged in 1772–3 was for 50 woodhouses;[7] the second, made in 1795, was for a communal coal house;[8] the third, made in 1844, was again for 50 woodhouses.[9] Only in 1856–7 was what was then called a fuel house provided for each widow.[10]

Walls, paths, gardens

To separate it from the outside world the almshouse was built with a low wall between its south range and the London road and with higher walls round its other three sides. The walls had probably been built by 1694.[11] The south wall was ornamental[12] and, after the almshouse was enlarged, it was lengthened eastwards. Its old part was replaced, and the new part built, in 1778; a broad terraced path was made outside it, and between 1781 and 1783 a flight of steps was built to link the road to the terrace and, through a gap in the wall, to the gatehouse.[13] In or soon after 1791, when the road was widened, the terrace was remade and the steps were rebuilt,[14] and in 1818, to enhance the approach to the new gatehouse and the new chapel, improvements were made following designs by Thomas Cundy.[15] The north wall enclosed gardens and the land on which the service buildings stood. In 1769 the east wall was raised and the ground on the outside lowered, evidently to

1 WSA 2037/83.
2 Ibid. 2037/27.
3 Ibid. 2037/27–8; 2037/92; below, pp. 323, 336, 358.
4 WSA 2037/27; below, p. 219.
5 WSA 2037/28; below, p. 361.
6 Cf. *Endowed Charities of Wiltshire* (southern division), 999.
7 WSA 2037/83.
8 Below, p. 246; cf. below, almshouse life (firewood, coal).
9 WSA 2037/91; below, p. 331.
10 WSA 2037/28; below, pp. 358, 360–1.
11 TNA C 38/260, report dated 11 February 1699; WSA 2037/26.
12 Cf. *Gentleman's Magazine*, lxxi (1), facing p. 306.
13 *VCH Wiltshire*, xvi. 163; Ward, *Somerset Hospital*, 29; WSA 2037/27; below, pp. 215, 219.
14 Below, pp. 239–40; cf. above, estate (road, canal, railways).
15 WSA 2037/89; below, p. 281.

stop an unauthorized back way into and out of the grounds of the almshouse.[1] A new east wall to enclose new gardens of the extended almshouse was paid for in 1780.[2]

The ground within the quadrangle may have been sown with grass in the 1690s, an unpaved path probably ran around the edge of it,[3] and in 1802, after the quadrangle had been doubled, a brick path was laid across it.[4] In 1838 it was ordered that trees planted against the houses should be removed, but shrubs might be grown in borders if they became no higher than 1 ft. above the path.[5] By the mid 19th century a pitched path had been made around the quadrangle and not far from its edge, and a gutter had been laid along the inner edge of the pitching. A plan to lay a path of pennant grit around the outer edge of the pitching was probably executed in 1858.[6] In 1863 the trustees ordered that gardens which had been made in the quadrangle should be given up and the ground turfed, and in 1864 the porter was directed to prevent the widows from making footpaths across the lawns and from playing croquet and other games on them.[7]

From about 1700 each widow had a plot in a walled kitchen garden. A gardener who was sent to Froxfield to 'set, cut, and divide' the garden, and who was paid in 1699, probably prepared 30 plots north of the north range.[8] About 1780 a new walled garden was laid out east of the extended almshouse, the trustees having failed in an attempt to acquire land for one north of the new part of the north range.[9] In 1801 the trustees ordered that the plot of any absent widow should be cultivated and that the cost of cultivation should be deducted from her pension.[10]

ALMSHOUSE LIFE

The poor widows

Women whose husbands died and who lacked an adequate private income could keep themselves from destitution in various ways. They might remarry, live with relatives, earn an income by their labour or intelligence, or perform a service in the household of someone who could afford to support them. For some women life in an almshouse, with a private house and a guaranteed income, may have seemed a better option than any other available to them.

1 Below, p. 201.
2 WSA 2037/27.
3 Cf. below, p. 320.
4 Below, p. 256.
5 Below, p. 320.
6 WSA 2037/93; below, p. 361; cf. WSA historic photograph collection, P40999.
7 Below, pp. 382, 385.
8 WSA 2037/26; cf. 2037/83.
9 Ward, *Somerset Hospital*, 29; WSA 2037/83; below, p. 215.
10 Below, p. 255.

The duchess of Somerset directed that widows admitted to Froxfield almshouse must be poor, honest, and leading a good life. Poor was defined as receiving a yearly income from property of less than £20[1] and from that definition, and from the inclusion of the relicts of clergymen, it seems that the widows in the mind's eye of the duchess were not those of the first or second poor. In the unlikely event that they gave it any thought the trustees could perhaps justify the exclusion of indigent widows on the grounds that, if women were indigent, they could not be leading a good life, and a proviso expressed in 1796, that a widow would only be admitted to the almshouse if she were 'well recommended in point of character',[2] probably applied in all cases. The lay widows who were admitted were probably the relicts of farmers, professional men, or tradesmen, and a few are known to have been.[3] With identical pensions and virtually identical houses[4] all the widows were set on the same plane as each other and, despite in the early 18th century the title Mrs. being reserved only for them,[5] some clergy widows may have felt that their social status was thus lowered. Some of the widows could afford to keep servants[6] and, although some seem to have become insolvent,[7] while they were receiving their pensions the widows were clearly not poor in the generally accepted sense. In 1892 a writer with an axe to grind reported rumours that earlier nearly all the widows had private means in addition to their pensions and that there were 20 pianos in the almshouse.[8]

From when the almshouse was built to the early 1770s there were four classes of widows living in it, manor widows, lay three-counties widows, clergy three-counties widows, and clergy London or Westminster widows. The early trustees made two mistakes. They nominated 5 manor widows instead of 10 or more, and 10 lay three-counties widows instead of 5 or fewer. That mistake had been corrected by about 1740, but thenceforward the trustees stuck to a ratio of 10 to 5 rather than using their discretion to nominate more manor widows and fewer three-counties widows. In 1714 there were 11 clergy three-counties widows whereas there should have been 10, and 4 London or Westminster widows whereas there should have been 5. From 1773, when the enlargement of the almshouse was completed, there were

1 TNA PROB 11/474, ff. 176–93 (below, pp. 117–18).
2 Below, p. 247.
3 WSA 2037/80 (below, pp. 419, 421–2, 427–8).
4 Above, almshouse buildings (houses); below, this section (pensions).
5 Below, pp. 138–9.
6 Below, p. 390.
7 e.g. below, pp. 230, 256–7, 326–7.
8 p. 4 of a printed report by the trustees of the parochial charities of St. Margaret and St. John, Westminster, 1892, part of which survives in WSA 2037/1.

seven classes of widows. Of the 15 counties-at-large widows, those from places outside the three counties, and of the 5 new London or Westminster widows, any 5 were to be clergy widows. The trustees, disregarding the flexibility offered to them and possibly to avoid confusion, nominated all 5 clergy widows from the counties-at-large, and thus from the 1770s 5 of the London or Westminster widows were clergy widows and 5 were lay widows. The new classes were thus lay counties-at-large widows, lay London or Westminster widows, and clergy counties-at-large widows.[1] The duchess of Somerset directed her trustees to place in each vacant house a widow of the same class as the one who had last occupied it,[2] and the corollary of that was that each house was to be used by widows of only one class. The mistakes made by the early trustees, and later the possibility that lay widows might occupy clergy houses,[3] meant that the direction was not always followed and that its corollary did not always apply. From 1774 the clergy widows in houses 1–20 were segregated from the lay widows in houses 21–50. Within each segregated area, however, each house was usually occupied by a widow of only one class and the houses assigned to each class were intermingled with those assigned to each other class.[4] Although Froxfield almshouse was built on Wiltshire soil, was endowed with lands only in Wiltshire, and from 1704 was governed by trustees who all lived in Wiltshire, a high proportion of the widows who lived in it came from outside the county. Of the 30 widows in 1714 half came from places in Wiltshire, the 5 manor widows, 7 lay three-counties widows, and 3 clergy three-counties widows. Besides the 4 from London or Westminster 8 of the others came from Berkshire and 3 from Somerset.[5]

In 1785, after the extension of the right to be admitted to the almshouse to widows living far from the trustees' homes, and perhaps because of it, the trustees defined what residential qualification a widow would need to be accepted as an applicant for a house. They resolved that widows would qualify if 40 days had elapsed between the time at which they came to live in the area covered by the class which they proposed to enter and the occurrence of the vacancy for which they proposed to apply. Alternatively, they would qualify if they were settled in that area,[6] and by settled the trustees clearly meant legally

1 Above, foundation, where the classes of widows are rehearsed; cf. Ward, *Somerset Hospital*, 31; for the mistakes, above, trustees (exercise of patronage); below, pp. 138–9.
2 TNA PROB 11/474, ff. 176–93 (below, pp. 117–18).
3 Above, trustees (exercise of patronage).
4 Ward, *Somerset Hospital*, 31; WSA 2037/86; above, almshouse buildings (houses).
5 Below, pp. 138–9.
6 Below, p. 228.

settled.[1] There is no evidence that the 40-day rule was ignored by the trustees. On the other hand, there is no evidence that any widow was asked to prove where she had lived for the 40 days prior to a house becoming vacant or what her legal place of settlement was. That a widow might easily qualify to apply for a house, whether or not the 40-day rule was strictly enforced, allowed houses to be occupied by widows who had spent their married lives, and perhaps much of their widowhood, outside any of the areas covered by the seven classes. One of the many examples of such widows is Ann Hay who was admitted as a clergy three-counties widow in August 1832 having probably lived at Rotterdam until the preceding January. Another is Margaret Richardson who was admitted as a clergy counties-at-large widow in August 1833; she had probably lived until 1832 at Wath, all the places of which name lie more than 150 miles from London.[2]

The admission papers for 1830–45 printed below[3] show that on average the marriage, or most recent marriage, of the 57 widows who were admitted to the almshouse in that period lasted 21 years. Four lasted more than 40 years, 10 less than 10 years. For example Mary Fowler, admitted in 1830, had married Thomas Fowler in 1780 and had been a widow since 1824; she died in 1835. Hannah Phillips married John Phillips in 1794, was widowed by his death in 1800, was admitted to the almshouse in 1830, and died in 1834 aged 65. The average age at death of the men whose relicts were admitted to the almshouse was 52. The oldest was the Revd. John Trusler who died in 1820 aged 85 and whose relict Mary Trusler was admitted in 1835 and had died by 1845.[4] The husbands who died young included Thomas Welch who married Elizabeth Fowler in 1821 when he was 29 and she was 45 and who died in 1828. Elizabeth entered the almshouse as his relict in 1836 aged 60 and died there in 1864. Not all the husbands whose death ended the shorter marriages died young. For example, Elizabeth Ann Belcher was admitted in 1842 as the relict of Robert Belcher who died in 1837 aged 71; she had married him in 1832, when he was a widower, and she had resigned her house by 1843. For widows admitted to the almshouse in the period the average length of time which passed between the death of their husbands and their admittance was 10 years. In four cases it was over 30 years and in nine cases less than 1 year. Elizabeth Maylor Periam was the relict of George Periam who, 9 years after their wedding, died in 1805 aged 42. She was nominated by John Awdry, and Thomas Merriman, the steward, wrote to her at

1 Cf. below, p. 314.
2 WSA 2037/80 (below, pp. 420–1).
3 Ibid. (below, pp. 418–32); except where stated, dates of death for the widows named in this paragraph have been taken from WSA 1635/7.
4 For Mary Trusler's date of death, ibid. 2037/80 (below, p. 431).

28 Carey Street offering to give her information presumably about the almshouse. She was admitted in 1838 and lived in the almshouse until 1852, when she died aged 75. The order to admit Delia Mary Cosens was given on 28 February 1834. She was the relict of the Revd. Reyner Cosens, who died aged 27 and was buried on 4 February. She left the almshouse in 1844 when she remarried.

On average about two of the houses in the almshouse became vacant each year in the period 1696–1710,[1] three to four in the period 1830–45.[2] Those figures, crudely interpreted, suggest that on average widows lived in the almshouse about 15 years. One of the long stayers was Charlotte Thomas, who was admitted in 1792 and lived there for 63 years. In 1846, needing care and attention, she left the almshouse and went to live at Devizes with her niece: in 1847 the trustees, dismissing a complaint that she was not well enough treated there, invited her to return. She evidently did return and was said to live in the almshouse when, in 1855, she died aged 100.[3] Another long stayer was Elizabeth Abbot, who lived in the almshouse over 40 years. She was an ally of Susannah Cherry in 1697, was matron 1726–32, and lived there until 1738, when she too died aged 100.[4] One of the short stayers was Mary Trimmer, the order to admit whom was given on 29 April 1845. She had been married to the Revd. Henry Trimmer of Norwich for 19 years and a widow for nearly 3 years. She had resigned her house by 23 May. The Hon. Barbara St. John, a daughter of Henry St. John (d. 1805), Baron St. John, married the Revd. Thomas Bedford in 1813. Bedford died in 1816 aged 28 and she was admitted to the almshouse as his relict in 1843. She had resigned her house by 1845.[5]

Although some widows resigned their houses and a few were expelled,[6] most of those who were admitted to the almshouse lived in it until their death; and although some entered the almshouse when they were young, the average age of the widows in it was high. That at death of the widows for whom age was given in Froxfield parish register was 80 in the period 1816–19 and 76 in the period 1856–8. In the period 1813–66 the register gives the age at death of about 85 widows: only 21 died aged under 70.[7] Besides being single and safe from destitution the widows in the almshouse were obviously healthy.

1 Cf. below, this section (occupancy).
2 WSA 2037/80 (below, pp. 418–32).
3 Ibid. 1635/7; 2037/27; below, pp. 336, 338.
4 TNA C 38/267 (below, pp. 130–1); WSA 1635/1; below, this section (matron).
5 WSA 2037/80 (below, pp. 428, 430–1); for the St. Johns, Burke, *Peerage* (1924), 1974.
6 For expulsions, below, this section (absenteeism).
7 WSA 1635/3; 1635/7.

Occupancy

All the 30 houses in the almshouse were occupied soon after the building was finished.[1] In 1714 nine of the widows who had lived in the almshouse in 1697 remained there, and there were nine vacancies.[2] If it can be assumed that some of the 21 houses which had become vacant since 1697 had done so more than once, those figures suggest that the trustees appointed in 1704 ceased to fill vacancies about 1709–10. They probably did so in the spring of 1710 when, perhaps disenchanted, they petitioned the court of Chancery to add to their number. In July 1713 new trustees were authorized to act with them,[3] and the nine vacancies were filled in October 1714.[4]

The 20 additional houses built in 1772–3 were also occupied soon after they were completed, and there were 43 or more widows living in the almshouse in 1778.[5] It seems that the trustees commissioned the new building only when their funds were already sufficient to pay the additional pensions,[6] and a statement made later which implied that additional houses were left empty while the trustees waited for their funds to grow may not have been correct.[7]

It is possible that by the later 18th century clergy widows, who may have spent their married life in a parsonage house, had become deterred from entering the almshouse by an expectation of a lowered social status.[8] Certainly from the 1770s houses for them sometimes remained vacant for longer than those for lay widows,[9] and in the 1830s it was still being said that it was with difficulty that clergy houses were filled.[10] In the period 1830–45, moreover, clergy widows entered the almshouse after an average of only 5 years of widowhood, and eight of the nine women who were admitted less than 1 year after the death of their husbands were clergy widows.[11] Those figures suggest that clergy houses were more readily available than lay ones for which, in effect, there may have been a long waiting list. Nevertheless, whether or not clergy houses were less in demand than lay ones, 48 houses were occupied in 1786, all 50 were occupied in 1793,[12] and, of 57 widows admitted to the 20 clergy houses and 30 lay houses 1830–45, 23 were

1 Ibid. 2037/26; TNA C 33/289, ff. 250–2 (below, p. 122).
2 Below, pp. 138–9.
3 For the trustees and the appointment of them 1704–13, above, Attorney General *v* Grimston (1699–1729).
4 Below, pp. 138–9.
5 WSA 2037/27.
6 Cf. TNA C 33/389, ff. 674–5; C 33/403, f. 564.
7 *Endowed Charities of Wiltshire* (southern division), 983.
8 Cf. above, this section (the poor widows).
9 Above, trustees (exercise of patronage).
10 *Endowed Charities of Wiltshire* (southern division), 984.
11 WSA 2037/80 (below, pp. 418–32).
12 Ibid. 2037/27; below, pp. 243–4.

clergy widows and 34 were lay widows.[1] Those facts suggest that the alleged difficulty in filling clergy vacancies was either exaggerated or usually overcome, and the almshouse was in general fully occupied until the 1860s or later.[2]

Pensions

The duchess of Somerset provided not only a house for each of 30 widows, latterly 50, but also a yearly sum of money. In the minute books the sum was sometimes called a dividend, sometimes a salary, and perhaps most often a stipend. Elsewhere it was called a pension and, to conform to modern usage, it has been so called throughout this introduction. It was to be met from what was left of the income from the almshouse's estate after certain other uses had been satisfied, and the pension of each of the 30 widows, latterly the 50, was to be equal to that of the others.[3]

The duchess assumed that the surplus income from the estate would at first be too small for adequate pensions to be paid and made special arrangements, but by December 1697 no pension had been paid.[4] In June 1698 the court of Chancery ordered that pensions should be paid forthwith and backdated to 1695, and it fixed the amount to be paid at about £2 8*s*. a year for 1695–8 and at a minimum of about the same for each of the 7 years 1698–1705.[5] In December 1698 the steward paid £9 12*s*. to each widow, perhaps a little more than was due from June 1695, and in each of the following 4 years, presumably because income from the estate exceeded expectations, he paid between £6 10*s*. and £7 10*s*.[6] Thereafter the trustees managed the estate so as to make the surplus income sufficient, and sufficiently regular and predictable, to pay pensions in full at a previously declared rate. The yearly pension was 7 gns. in the 1730s, 8 gns. from 1740. In 1748, when they knew that the trustees were saving money to enlarge the almshouse, the widows asked the court of Chancery to order them to increase their pensions. The court denied them[7] and only in 1771, when enough money had been saved,[8] was the pension increased. From Michaelmas 1771 it was 10 gns. Despite the increase in the number of recipients to 50, it was increased to £13 from 1778, more than half the increase of £2 10*s*. being met by subsuming the payment made to the widows in place

1 Ibid. 2037/80 (below, pp. 418–32).
2 Ibid. 2037/27–8.
3 TNA PROB 11/474, ff. 176–93 (below, pp. 118–20).
4 Ibid. (below, p. 120); above, foundation.
5 Above, Attorney General *v* Grimston (1697–8).
6 WSA 2037/26.
7 TNA C 33/389, ff. 674–5; cf. above, Attorney General *v* Grimston (1729–85).
8 Cf. above, almshouse buildings (houses).

of gowns.[1] The pension was increased to £14 from 1781 and to £15 from 1783, but when in 1791 the widows petitioned the trustees for a further increase their petition was dismissed as useless and improper.[2] From 1793 the trustees nevertheless increased the pension to 16 gns., 1 gn. being a true increase and 15*s.* being added to replace yearly gifts of faggots, and the widows thanked the trustees by letter.[3] Further increases were made as farm rents rose and afterwards. The widows were given 20 gns. a year from 1801, £24 from 1807, £28 from 1810, £32 from 1813, £36 from 1826, and £38 from 1832.[4] In 1838 the steward suggested to the trustees that to add to the widows' incomes was the most gratifying part of their duty: pensions were immediately increased to £40.[5] In 1851, however, after farm rents had fallen, they were reduced to £36 a year.[6] An application for an increase made in 1861 by 41 widows was rebuffed,[7] and pensions remained at £36 in 1866.[8]

The pension was paid quarterly, to each widow in person, and for many years at the steward's house in the almshouse. If a widow was absent on payday, and if she had leave of absence, she was paid later.[9] Until 1832 each widow was paid for a full quarter on the first payday after she was admitted, after 1832 only for the proportion of the quarter which had elapsed to the payday since the day of her admittance.[10] At the payday after a widow had resigned her house or died she or her representative was paid what was due from the previous payday. In case of death 1 gn. was added as a contribution to the cost of the funeral, and in appropriate cases the trustees deducted any financial penalty which the widow had incurred and the cost of repairing any window glass left broken when the widow left her house or died.[11]

Gowns

The duchess of Somerset directed that each widow should receive a gown each year about Christmas. The cost was to be met from the almshouse's estate as a first charge on either fines received on new grants of copyholds or, if they were insufficient, on the almshouse's other income. The gowns were to be of uniform cloth, colour, and

1 WSA 2037/27; below, pp. 204, 216; for the gowns, below, this section.
2 Below, pp. 219, 223, 237–8.
3 Below, pp. 242–4; for the faggots, below, this section (firewood, coal).
4 Below, pp. 255, 264, 268, 273, 295, 308.
5 Below, pp. 319–20.
6 Below, p. 343.
7 Below, p. 376.
8 WSA 2037/28.
9 Ibid. 2037/27; Ward, *Somerset Hospital*, 29.
10 Below, p. 308.
11 WSA 2037/26–8; below, p. 223; for the 1 gn., below, this section (burial); for the financial penalties and glass, below, this section (regulations, rules).

style. None was to cost more than £1 6*s*. 8*d*., and the most that might be spent on gowns in any year was therefore £40.[1] The gowns were received from the tailor and handed to the widows by the porter,[2] and they were to be worn by the widows in the almshouse's chapel.[3] In 1701, when the trustees paid £37 for 90 yards of cloth to make 30 gowns, and 28 gowns were made at a cost of 2*s*. each,[4] each gown cost the maximum amount permitted by the duchess. The last occasion on which gowns were given was probably Christmas 1770, and from 1771 the trustees gave each widow £1 6*s*. 8*d*. a year at Christmas instead.[5] The reasons for discontinuing the giving of gowns are obscure. The practice may have been thought anachronistic, and to keep the cost to £1 6*s*. 8*d*. a gown may have become difficult. From 1778 the £1 6*s*. 8*d*. was subsumed in the widows' pensions.[6]

Firewood, coal

The trustees of the almshouse, although not expressly directed to do so, took wood from their coppices at Froxfield and gave it to the widows as firewood.[7] They paid for the wood to be cut, faggoted, and taken to the almshouse: for example, 1,800 faggots were taken on one occasion in 1700 and 5,275 on one in 1771.[8] The faggots were probably stored in a common woodyard and, if so, to expect them to be shared equally among 30 widows was perhaps to invite disgruntlement. In 1716 the trustees found it necessary to order that no widow might meddle with the firewood of another even if she was absent, had resigned her house, or had died,[9] and in 1718 they ordered that no widow might sell her wood and re-iterated that, if a house became vacant, the wood given to the previous occupant should be left for the new one.[10] The winter of 1792–3 was probably the last in which faggots were given to the widows. In July 1793 the trustees estimated that the average yearly value of the wood to each widow was 15*s*., discontinued the practice of giving it, and added 15*s*. to pensions in place of it.[11]

Instead of giving an equal amount of fuel to each widow regardless of how much she might wish to use, in 1795 the trustees proposed to give a fixed sum, the 15*s*. of additional pension, and to lay in a stock of coal so that each widow might buy as much fuel as she wished at

1 TNA PROB 11/474, ff. 176–93 (below, p. 119).
2 Below, p. 167; for the porter, below, officers.
3 TNA C 33/351, ff. 391v.–392 (below, p. 135); C 38/267 (below, p. 132); WSA 2037/8, orders proposed 1710.
4 WSA 2037/26.
5 Ibid. 2037/27.
6 Below, p. 216.
7 TNA C 33/389, ff. 674–5; WSA 2037/119.
8 WSA 2037/26–7.
9 Below, p. 144.
10 Below, p. 148.
11 Below, p. 242.

a price lower than she would otherwise have had to pay. They gave money to the porter, directed him to buy coal, and ordered that a coal house should be built in the woodyard. Coal was bought and carried to the almshouse, but the scheme did not succeed.[1] In 1801 the porter's executors returned the money to the trustees, who resolved that they would spend nothing more on coal.[2] In making the proposal in 1795 the trustees perhaps anticipated the opening of the Kennet and Avon canal, but no coal could have been brought by canal to the wharf at Froxfield before 1810.[3]

Nursing

The trustees for long did nothing to arrange, or pay for, the medical care of the widows. The cost of caring for any who was sick or needed to be nursed was presumably met by the widow herself or by her family or friends. That changed in the 1780s. In 1782 the trustees paid an apothecary to attend on a widow whom they described as insane,[4] from 1785 they frequently paid for widows to be nursed in their houses, and from 1791 they appointed surgeons to treat the widows in return for a yearly salary.[5]

When the trustees began to pay for nursing they no doubt intended to confer an extra benefit on widows in need, but they acted in the absence of a directly expressed intention of the duchess of Somerset and despite a possible objection that the money spent on nursing for a minority of the widows could have been used to increase the pensions of them all.[6] In the 1780s and 1790s they may have paid the nurses directly.[7] From about 1800 it is more likely that the widows paid for their own nurses and that the trustees gave money to them to cover, or contribute to, the payment.[8] The cost to the trustees, £29 12*s*. 6*d*. in 1799 and £40 15*s*. 6*d*. in 1816, reached a peak about 1820.[9] By then, however, the amount given in individual cases had fallen. The trustees allowed 2*s*. 6*d*. a week for each nurse in the 1790s;[10] from 1818 the usual allowance was 1*s*. a week.[11] From the 1790s to about 1820 the trustees contributed to the cost of an increasing number of nurses or to nursing for longer periods, and the contribution made by individual widows probably rose too. The period in which the trustees were at their most liberal was that in which rents from the almshouse's estate

1 WSA 2037/27; below, p. 246.
2 WSA 2037/27; below, p. 255.
3 *VCH Wiltshire*, iv. 273–4; xvi. 151.
4 WSA 2037/27.
5 Below, officers (surgeon), where the duties and salary of the surgeon are discussed.
6 For the duchess's intentions, TNA PROB 11/474, ff. 176–93 (below, pp. 116–21).
7 Below, pp. 230–2, 237, 248.
8 e.g. below, pp. 262, 296–7.
9 WSA 2037/27.
10 Ibid.; below, pp. 248–9.
11 e.g. below, pp. 281, 296–7.

were at their most buoyant,[1] and from the 1820s the trustees contributed to the cost of fewer nurses or to nursing for shorter periods. The total cost fell from £26 in 1827, when they presumably contributed to the cost of 10 nurses throughout the year, to £18 in 1844 and £1 11*s.* in 1855.[2] There were vestiges of liberality. In 1824 the trustees conceded that a clerical pension not exceeding 10 gns. a year would not debar a widow from an allowance if she needed a nurse, and in 1825 they made a similar concession to lay widows.[3] Nevertheless by 1838, when the widows were receiving pensions equal to 15*s.* 6*d.* a week, the trustees may have thought them able to meet the whole cost of their own nursing. From 1858 they again paid nothing for nursing.[4]

A widow who felt a need for nursing might apply for a contribution to the cost of it or, if she was incapable, another might apply on her behalf. The application might be made at a general meeting of the trustees, at a view meeting, or, if a need was urgent, perhaps to a single trustee or the steward.[5] At their general meeting the trustees sometimes referred applications to a single trustee for consideration and decision.[6] What was wrong with widows who needed to be nursed was rarely recorded. In 1785 one was subject to fits and one was infirm and aged 86,[7] in 1802 one could do nothing for herself, in 1829 one was infirm and nearly 80, and in 1832 another was old and infirm.[8] They may have been typical.

To nurse widows in the almshouse caused a problem. Care may have been needed at any time but the gate to the almshouse was kept locked at night. In 1797 the trustees therefore expressed a preference for each nurse to be a widow living in the almshouse or the daughter of a widow living there who, perhaps, could be expected to sleep in her mother's house.[9] Many of the nurses may have fallen outside those categories. A rule made in 1844 by the trustees that, except in the case of severe illness or great need, no nurse might sleep in the almshouse[10] is more likely to have been designed to stop an existing practice than to prevent such a practice from developing. The comfort of the infirm was not neglected. In 1859 the trustees bought two large mahogany portable water closets to be used at the discretion of the surgeon and by bedridden widows.[11]

1 For rents, above, estate (rents of farms).
2 WSA 2037/27–8.
3 Below, pp. 292, 294.
4 WSA 2037/28.
5 For an application at a view meeting, below, p. 361.
6 Below, pp. 281, 291, 342.
7 Ward, *Somerset Hospital*, 27; below, pp. 228, 230.
8 Below, pp. 256, 298, 308.
9 Below, p. 248; for the gate, below, this section (regulations, rules); for resident daughters, cf. below, this section (children, inmates, men).
10 Below, p. 331.
11 WSA 2037/28; below, p. 370.

Sometimes widows were nursed away from the almshouse. In 1814 the trustees permitted a widow who needed much care to live with her son, to whom they remitted her pension, and they congratulated themselves on saving what they would have contributed towards her being nursed in her house.[1] They also saved money by permitting a widow to live in the lunatic asylum of Dr. E. L. Fox in Brislington House from 1814 to 1833 or later. To care for her in 1816 Dr. Fox was paid £61 10*s*.: £31 10*s*. was paid by the trustees instead of the widow's pension of £32 and the rest by a clerical fund in the diocese of Bath and Wells and by the Corporation of the Sons of the Clergy.[2] From 1845 to 1851 the trustees similarly paid for a widow to live in Fiddington House lunatic asylum.[3]

Burial

When there were 30 widows in the almshouse probably on average two died each year, when there were 50 probably three. For example, 48 houses became vacant by death in the period 1830–45.[4] In 1701 the trustees were already contributing to the cost of funerals, and they were still doing so in 1866.[5] By 1748 their contribution had become fixed at 1 gn.[6] Until about 1780 the money was given to the porter and almost certainly included the price of a coffin;[7] thereafter it was given to an executor or representative of each deceased widow.[8] Froxfield churchyard was evidently the usual place of burial.[9] In 1831 the trustees were asked to give land to enlarge the churchyard, admitted that the shortage of space there had been caused mainly by the interment of almshouse widows, but doubted that they might lawfully alienate the charity's land.[10] They gave the land in 1845.[11]

Regulations, rules

In return for their houses, pensions, gowns, fuel, nursing, and coffins the widows were required to obey what the trustees called variously orders, rules, and regulations. Dictionaries allow little difference in meaning between those various words, but throughout this introduction each of the three words is consistently used in a special context of its own.

1 Below, p. 274.

2 *Endowed Charities of Wiltshire* (southern division), 985; WSA 2037/27; below, pp. 275–6; for Dr. Fox, *Roll of the Royal College of Physicians of London*, ed. W. Munk, ii (London, 1878), 376–7.

3 WSA 2037/28.

4 Ibid. 2037/80 (below, pp. 418–32).

5 Ibid. 2037/26–8.

6 TNA C 33/389, ff. 674–5.

7 WSA 2037/26–7; for the porters and their duties, below, officers.

8 Ward, *Somerset Hospital*, 30; WSA 2037/27–8.

9 Cf. WSA 1635/1–3; 1635/7.

10 Below, pp. 307, 309.

11 WSA D 375/2/139, deed, Ailesbury to H.M. Commissioners; below, pp. 328, 330, 332.

Orders is applied to *ad hoc* commands not intended to be permanent or universal, rules to commands intended to be either, and regulations to any codex of rules. That is done however the steward used the words when entering the minutes and in an attempt to help the reader. This subsection deals mainly with the regulations and rules.

The first regulations to govern the behaviour of the widows were promulgated by the trustees in November 1698. They incorporated rules on attendance at chapel, the wearing of gowns, absence from the almshouse, children and inmates, reverence to superiors, respect to be shown by the widows to the chaplain, the trustees' officers, and one another, disorderly conduct, insobriety, swearing and cursing, and repair of window glass. If a widow broke a rule she was either to suffer a financial penalty or to be expelled from the almshouse. At the trustees' order the steward hung a copy of the regulations in the chapel. By 1699 the trustees had also ruled that the gate of the almshouse should be locked at 9 p.m.[1] Some of the widows disregarded the rules, denied the right of anyone to lock them in or out at night, and, claiming to hold their houses for life, denied the trustees the right to expel them. The most notable objector was Susannah Cherry, who by June 1699 had *inter alia* taken down the copy of the regulations and removed it from the chapel. The trustees asked the court of Chancery to confirm the rules and give them the power to punish those who broke them, but their request was not granted.[2] In 1702, however, the court recommended that the trustees should add two new rules to the regulations, one that the chaplain should do specified duties and one that the porter should lock the gate at night and unlock it in the morning. Although neither the regulations promulgated in 1698 nor the rules recommended in 1702 were confirmed by the court[3] the trustees evidently expected the widows to conform to them, and by 1704 a copy of them had been framed and again hung in the chapel.[4]

In 1710, at the trustees' request, new regulations were proposed by the master in Chancery to whom the cause Attorney General *v* Grimston stood referred. They contained 13 rules on the management of the trust, the duties of the steward, the chaplain, and the porter, the appointment and duty of a matron, and the behaviour of the widows. Of the eight which governed behaviour three concerned religious

1 TNA C 38/267 (below, p. 132); for the rules on religious worship, absenteeism, and children and inmates, below, this section; for the chaplain, below, officers; for window glass, above, almshouse buildings (houses).

2 TNA C 33/291, f. 540; C 38/267 (below, pp. 130–1); for the legal proceedings, above, Attorney General *v* Grimston (1699–1729); for Mrs. Cherry, below, this section (troublesome widows).

3 TNA C 33/297, f. 126 and v.; above, Attorney General *v* Grimston (1699–1729).

4 WSA 2037/26.

worship, absenteeism, and children and inmates, and others required the widows to be respectful and decent and not to be drunk or to swear or curse. For some lapses the penalties were more moderate than those stated in 1698. If a widow became unquiet, disorderly, or abusive her punishment would be not expulsion, as it would have been formerly, but the forfeit of no more than 6*d*. for each offence. For being drunk, swearing, or cursing a widow might be expelled not, as from 1698, for a first offence but only for a third. For the first she would forfeit 1*s*. and be admonished in the presence of the matron and two or three other widows, and for the second she would forfeit 2*s*. and be admonished by the chaplain in the chapel after the service on Sunday morning. Some penalties remained severe: if a widow were incontinent she would be expelled. Again appended to the regulations was an order to the steward to hang a copy of them in the chapel.[1] The court of Chancery did not confirm those proposed regulations. In the later 1720s the trustees claimed to think that it had done, and between 1710 and 1729 life in the almshouse was presumably governed as if it had.[2] Moreover, in 1716 and 1718 the trustees themselves made new rules, one on absenteeism, one forbidding the widows to force entry to the house of any widow who had died, and the two relating to firewood.[3]

In 1727 the trustees' right to expel a widow under a rule of 1710 was challenged, and in 1729 a master incorporated new regulations in a report and the court of Chancery confirmed them.[4] The regulations, which contained 15 rules, were similar to those proposed in 1710. In the rules on behaviour some penalties were increased. For lack of respect to their superiors the widows would forfeit their pension until they had satisfactorily submitted. For behaviour which was indecent towards the chaplain, the steward, or another widow, or which was unquiet, disorderly, or abusive, a widow would suffer the loss of a week's pension for a first offence, the loss of up to a month's pension for a second, and expulsion for a third. The times at which the porter was to lock and unlock the main gate were defined: in spring and summer it was to be locked at 9 p.m. and unlocked at 5 a.m., in autumn and winter at 7 p.m. and 7 a.m. There was new flexibility: on special occasions, and with the consent of the matron, the porter might open the gate when it would otherwise be locked. Like the earlier ones the new regulations were to be copied and a framed copy was to be hung in the chapel.[5]

1 Ibid. 2037/8, orders proposed 1710; TNA C 38/308; for the matron and her duty, below, this section; for the officers and their duties, below, officers.

2 TNA C 33/351, ff. 97, 175, 391v.–392 (below, pp. 133–7); below, p. 159; below, following paragraph.

3 Below, pp. 144–5, 147–8.

4 Above, Attorney General *v* Grimston (1699–1729).

5 TNA C 33/351, ff. 391v.–392 (below, pp. 134–6); what is probably the copy hung in 1729 survives unframed in WSA 2037/8.

New rules to define absenteeism and to punish absentees were made in 1748 and 1781,[1] in the later 18th century some of the old rules, in particular those relating to a matron and to some aspects of religious worship, were not being enforced, and in 1791 the trustees ordered that a written or printed copy of all the rules should be hung conspicuously in the almshouse.[2] In 1803 and 1808 the trustees made new rules, on absenteeism, attendance at view meetings, and the letting of houses or gardens,[3] and in 1834 they published revised regulations containing 22 rules.[4] To codify and confirm current practice the revision included new rules on the management of the trust and the new rules on absenteeism. There were also new rules on religious worship, and all reference to a matron was omitted.[5] Otherwise the regulations of 1834 differed little from those of 1729. The penalty for showing disrespect remained forfeiture of pension until due submission, the sliding scale of punishments for disorderly behaviour or the use of abusive language was unchanged, and the penalty for incontinence remained expulsion. For drunkenness, swearing, or cursing the penalty for the first offence was raised from admonishment and 1*s.* to admonishment and 5*s.*, and for the second from admonishment and 2*s.* to admonishment and 20*s.*; a widow who committed a third offence forfeited her pension for as long as the trustees thought fit and remained liable to expulsion. The times at which the porter must lock and unlock the main gate were not changed but, there being no matron, the new rule offered no flexibility. It was made a rule not that the revised regulations should be hung up but that a copy of them should be given to each widow on her admittance and that one should be kept by the porter.

The regulations of 1834 were still in force in 1866. In the 1840s the trustees made two new rules, one against auctions in the almshouse and one against servants or nurses sleeping there,[6] and in the 1850s they altered one. In July 1851, apparently as an experiment, they ordered that the main gate should be left unlocked until 10 p.m. each day for 2 months, in 1853, in the face of a petition from the widows, they ruled that it should be locked for the 30 minutes immediately before the start of each divine service in the chapel, and in 1859 the 10-o'clock closing of the gate in summer was, with some qualification, made a rule.[7]

1 Above, Attorney General *v* Grimston (1729–85); for absenteeism, below, this section.
2 Ward, *Somerset Hospital*, 21; below, p. 237.
3 Below, pp. 258, 266.
4 Below, pp. 311–14.
5 For the matron, religious worship, and absenteeism, below, this section.
6 Below, pp. 326–7, 331.
7 Below, pp. 343, 349, 370; cf. below, this section (religious worship).

In the period 1694–1866 the trustees were sometimes troubled by widows who lived in the almshouse. Most of the troubles arose from absenteeism or inmates and were small, there is little evidence of indecent, disrespectful, or abusive behaviour,[1] and so far as can be judged life in the almshouse was nearly always serene. The regulations set the standards and the widows generally seem to have lived up to them.

Matron

In 1702 the court of Chancery required the trustees to appoint a matron,[2] and in 1710 the master proposed that the widows, by a majority of themselves, should nominate one of their number who, if the trustees approved of her, was to be called the matron and empowered to oversee the others. The matron was to hold her office for only 1 year but could be nominated in successive years. While in office she was to carry a white wand, be respected by the other widows, and live constantly in the almshouse.[3] How soon after 1702 the trustees appointed a matron is obscure. Since they evidently expected the proposed regulations of 1710 to be followed, those appointed in 1713 may have empowered one soon after their appointment. The first unequivocal evidence of one is the appointment of Mary Welkstead in 1725. Elizabeth Abbot was appointed in both 1726 and 1727. Each of those matrons was a clergy widow.[4]

The duties proposed for the matron in 1710 were to report on the misdeeds of widows and on the validity of their excuses for absence from divine service or from the almshouse, to share in the sanctioning of inmates, and to be present at the first admonishment of any widow found guilty of drunkenness, swearing, or cursing.[5] In the regulations of 1729 the provision that she should be nominated by the other widows and the duty concerning inmates were dropped. The power to vary the hours at which the porter should keep the main gate locked was added, and she was to be paid £1 a year.[6]

Mrs. Abbot remained matron until, aged about 94, she was thought to be too old to remain in office. She was replaced in 1732 by Ann Story.[7] In 1735 Mrs. Story resigned because she considered herself ill treated by the other widows and was not replaced. In 1748 the court of Chancery ordered the trustees to appoint a new matron. The trustees

1 For Mrs. Cherry, Mrs. Gibbs, and Mrs. Powell, below, this section (troublesome widows).
2 TNA C 33/297, f. 126 and v.
3 WSA 2037/8, orders proposed 1710.
4 Below, pp. 138, 154, 156–7.
5 WSA 2037/8, orders proposed 1710.
6 TNA C 33/351, ff. 391v.–392 (below, pp. 134–6).
7 Below, pp. 164–5; for Mrs. Abbot, above, this section (the poor widows).

complained that the office was useless for the classic reason that, if a matron did her duty by reporting that others had misbehaved, those reported bore her ill will and deterred her from doing her duty, and they explained that it was for that reason that no widow had been willing to accept the office since 1735. They nevertheless obeyed the court and on 3 June 1748 appointed Martha Shepherd (d. 1762),[1] who remained matron until her death. In 1763 Sarah Wilkins was appointed to succeed Mrs. Shepherd,[2] and at the enlargement of the almshouse in 1772–3 house no. 1, the new one immediately east of the gatehouse, was assigned to her. The last payment of £1 was made to her in 1774, she probably died about then, and she was not replaced as matron.[3]

Religious worship

In her will the duchess of Somerset provided for clergymen to be paid to lead religious worship in the almshouse's chapel. She directed that at first prayers were to be read every day and that later, besides daily prayers, there was to be a Sunday service at which the clergymen would preach.[4]

The trustees appointed in 1698 expected that the chaplain would hold a daily service in the chapel and ruled that each widow should attend it in the gown which she had been given. Any widow absent without good cause was treated harshly: she was to forfeit 6*d.* for each service missed.[5] In the regulations proposed in 1710, when all the trustees were clergymen, a rule was more specific but in one place ambiguous. Divine service according to the Book of Common Prayer was to be performed in the chapel every day at 11 a.m., and on Sundays it was to include a sermon. Afternoon prayers were to be read at 3 p.m. either on every day or, perhaps more likely, only on Sundays. The almshouse's bell was to be rung to call the widows to the chapel, and every widow was required to attend and wear her gown. The penalty for missing a service was reduced to 2*d.* and the widows were given time to make their excuses.[6] The regulations confirmed in 1729 did not vary those rules, but they did make it clear that Sunday was the only day on which there was to be an afternoon service.[7]

1 TNA C 33/389, ff. 674–5; WSA 1635/2; below, p. 177; cf. above, Attorney General *v* Grimston (1729–85).

2 Below, p. 194.

3 WSA 2037/27; 2037/86.

4 TNA PROB 11/474, ff. 176–93 (below, p. 119); for how the chapel was served, below, officers (chaplain).

5 TNA C 38/267 (below, p. 132).

6 WSA 2037/8, orders proposed 1710; for the trustees in 1710, above, Attorney General *v* Grimston (1699–1729).

7 TNA C 33/351, ff. 391v.–392 (below, pp. 134–5).

The rules on religious worship confirmed in 1729 may not have been obeyed implicitly or for long. In 1786 the steward noted that the one by which the days and times of services were specified was not being fully complied with,[1] in 1809 the new chaplain was required to do no more than read prayers on Wednesdays and Fridays and hold a Sunday morning service at which he would preach,[2] and services on four weekdays and a second service on Sundays were thus dropped. The rule which required the widows to attend every service in the chapel also allowed them to make excuses to the matron and, between 1735 and 1748 and from 1774, was presumably unenforceable because no matron was in office.[3] There is, moreover, no evidence that any widow was punished for failing to worship. By the regulations published in 1834 divine service was to be performed every Wednesday and Friday and twice every Sunday, with a sermon at one or both of the Sunday services. Financial penalties, this time at the trustees' discretion, were again to be imposed on widows who missed a service without good cause.[4] Again there is no evidence that a widow was punished for having done so. In 1845 the trustees were told that the widows objected to persons who did not live in the almshouse obtruding themselves into the chapel, presumably to worship, and they ordered the steward to ask counsel whether they had the right to exclude such persons.[5] The trustees' wish to exclude them may have been father to the rule of 1853 that the almshouse's main gate should be locked before the start of services.[6]

To promote religious worship the trustees furnished the chapel with, *inter alia*, a bible and a prayer book.[7] They also provided the sacramental wine.[8] From the 1770s each widow was expected to have a bible and a prayer book for her personal use. The trustees were prepared to buy them and in 1771 spent £24 8*s*. in doing so.[9] In 1785 they qualified their liberality. At first they ordered the steward to buy books for any widow who had none in her house, but almost immediately afterwards they came to suppose that books given previously had been either lost by the widows or taken away by the representatives of deceased widows. They repeated the order to the steward, required all the widows to show their books yearly at the trustees' view meetings, and ordered that thenceforward the steward should replace the missing book of any widow at her own expense.[10] In 1798 they again resolved,

1 Ward, *Somerset Hospital*, 21. 2 Below, p. 266.
3 Cf. above, Attorney General *v* Grimston (1729–85); above, this section (matron).
4 Below, p. 312. 5 Below, p. 334.
6 Below, p. 349; cf. above, this section (regulations, rules).
7 Above, almshouse buildings (chapel).
8 e.g. TNA C 33/389, ff. 674–5; WSA 2037/27–8; below, p. 194.
9 WSA 2037/27. 10 Below, pp. 228–9.

when necessary, to give new books to widows and to replace old ones[1] and, for example, in 1820 they bought 10 new bibles and 10 new prayer books.[2] 1840 the trustees came to an agreement with the Society for Promoting Christian Knowledge: in return for a subscription of £1 a year the society undertook to supply the widows' bibles and prayer books.[3]

Absenteeism

A central provision of the duchess of Somerset's will was that, out of its endowment, a pension should be paid to each widow living in the almshouse.[4] The provision was unequivocal, so far as is known was never challenged on the grounds that it did not preclude the payment of a pension to a widow who had left the almshouse, but nevertheless caused the trustees much difficulty. It implied that they should stop the pension of any widow who left without resigning her house, whether or not she intended to return, and therefore that they should be certain that a widow was in fact absent and, in equity, inform themselves of the circumstances which had brought about the absence and take account of them. Although there is no evidence that widows sought admittance to the almshouse for the pension rather than the house, it became necessary to define for how long an absent widow might receive her pension and retain her house and how a widow who was absent beyond those periods should be dealt with.

The regulations promulgated in 1698 contained a simple and harsh rule. If a widow was absent for 7 consecutive days or more she would forfeit her pension for the whole period of her absence.[5] The regulations proposed in 1710 included a rule even more draconian. A widow absent for a week or more was to be punished by the forfeit of 5*s.* a week, probably then nearly double the pension. She would be spared, however, if the chaplain and the matron certified that her return had been prevented by sickness or other reasonable cause.[6] That rule, which allowed the trustees to waive punishment, by extension gave them the right to grant leave of absence and by 1715 they had begun to exercise it.[7] In 1716 they ruled that leave might not exceed 1 month, presumably 31 not necessarily consecutive days, in 1 year, but they again excepted widows absent for extraordinary reasons.[8] In 1729 the rule proposed in 1710 was confirmed. The penalty was reduced

1 Below, p. 249.
2 WSA 2037/27.
3 Below, p. 323.
4 TNA PROB 11/474, ff. 176–93 (below, pp. 118–20).
5 Ibid. C 38/267 (below, p. 132).
6 WSA 2037/8, orders proposed 1710.
7 Below, p. 143.
8 Below, p. 145.

from 5*s*. a week to all the pension which had become due during the absence, a penalty which had already been imposed on a widow in 1727, and the gloss applied to the rule in 1716 was not re-applied.[1] In 1729 and 1733 four widows who had overstayed their leave were treated leniently by the trustees. Another, old, infirm, and blind, was allowed to live with her son-in-law, to whom her pension was paid until her death.[2]

The rules of 1698, 1710, and 1729 had obvious flaws, especially if the disinclination of some widows to obey them is included. They did nothing, for example, to prevent a widow who attended chapel every Sunday, and was willing to risk the loss of 1*s*. a week for missing weekday services, from claiming her pension without setting foot in her house. No provision was made for checking how long a widow was absent from the almshouse, and no power to expel absentees was given to the trustees. In 1748 the trustees, lamenting that some houses had been vacant for 2 or 3 years because widows would neither return to them nor resign them, asked the court of Chancery to confirm a new rule. They proposed that they might expel a widow if, without being given leave by two of themselves and without reasonable cause, she was absent for more than 14 consecutive days or for more than 30 days in 1 year. The widows argued that the paucity of the pension forced them to spend time living with relatives as dependants and that two trustees would often be hard to find near Froxfield. They proposed 2 months instead of 14 days and 3 months instead of 30 days. The court of Chancery confirmed the rule proposed by the trustees.[3] One of the obvious flaws was removed by the new rule, but there was still no provision for checking how long a widow was absent and the trustees' right to withhold pension was ignored and presumably lapsed. Whereas expulsion could only be effected at the end of a process in which the circumstances of a widow's absence were examined a pension could be withheld immediately, and widows contemplating absenteeism may have been deterred less by the remote prospect of expulsion under the new rule than by the immediate prospect of losing their income under the old. There is evidence that it remained commonplace for widows to overstay their leave, that other widows deceived the steward on their behalf,[4] and in 1769, when they resolved to enforce it and to warn the widows that they would do so, the new rule was not having the effect desired by the trustees.[5] Perhaps relying on the rule of 1729 the

1 TNA C 33/351, ff. 391v.–392 (below, p. 135); below, p. 157.

2 Below, pp. 159, 165–6.

3 TNA C 33/389, ff. 285v.–286, 445 and v., 674–5; below, p. 176; cf. above, Attorney General *v* Grimston (1729–85).

4 Below, pp. 219–20.

5 Below, p. 201.

trustees did sometimes withhold pensions, in appropriate circumstances restored them, and, as an inducement to resign her house, in 1770 gave a year's pension to a widow who because of ill health had never lived in it and had otherwise not been paid.[1]

In 1781 the trustees made another new rule on absenteeism and in making it they acknowledged that many widows, especially the new counties-at-large ones, had relatives and friends living far from Froxfield whom they should be allowed to visit. The new rule was

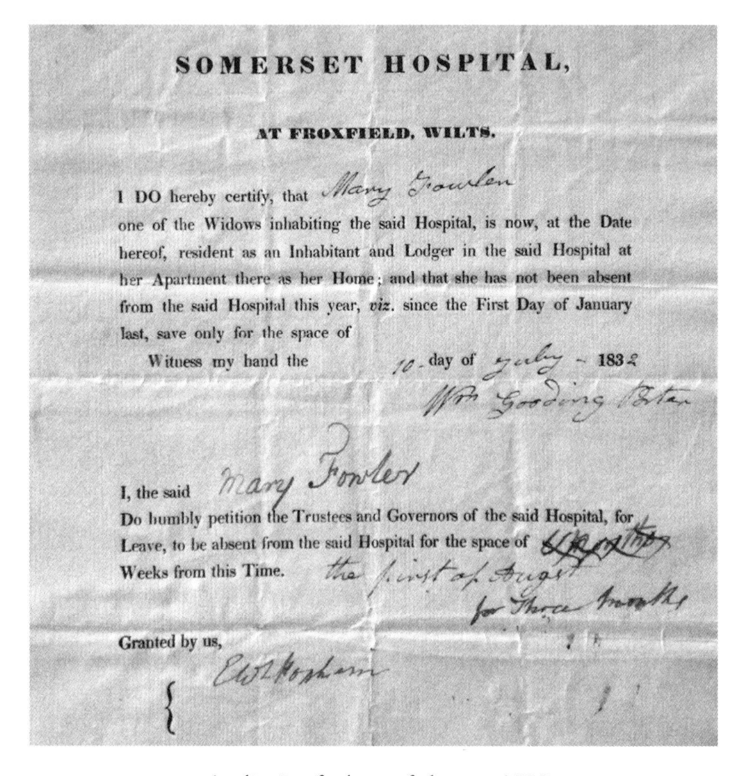
SOMERSET HOSPITAL,

AT FROXFIELD, WILTS.

I DO hereby certify, that Mary Fowler one of the Widows inhabiting the said Hospital, is now, at the Date hereof, resident as an Inhabitant and Lodger in the said Hospital at her Apartment there as her Home; and that she has not been absent from the said Hospital this year, *viz.* since the First Day of January last, save only for the space of

Witness my hand the 10 day of July 1832

Wm Gooding Porter

I, the said Mary Fowler

Do humbly petition the Trustees and Governors of the said Hospital, for Leave, to be absent from the said Hospital for the space of Weeks from this Time. the first of August for Three months

Granted by us,

E W L Popham

Application for leave of absence, 1832

less harsh than the old one and therefore perhaps more acceptable and more likely to be obeyed. It was also more meticulous and therefore more easily enforced. Each widow was permitted 13 weeks of absence every year, and for every absence she was required to apply for approval to two trustees. Printed application forms were held by the porter who, on request, passed one to the widow having certified on it that she was not already an absentee, specified which days she had already been absent in the year, and stated for how long she wished to be

1 Below, p. 202.

absent. The widow presumably took the completed form to any two trustees. To prevent him from being misled the porter was to register every Sunday the attendance record of every widow. To help widows who might wish to spend a winter with family or friends any part of the 13 weeks of one year might be run together with any part of the 13 weeks of the next. To penalize unauthorized absence the trustees claimed the right to impose the sanctions in the rules of both 1729 and 1748, thus enabling them to withhold pension and to expel. Every quarter the steward was to examine the porter's register, suspend the pension of any unauthorized absentee, and call the offending widow to the following general meeting of the trustees. If the widow there failed to show good cause why she should not be punished, or if she failed to attend, the trustees might expel her or punish her otherwise. The new rule, which took effect on 1 January 1782,[1] was confirmed by the court of Chancery in 1783. Before it was confirmed a master consulted the steward and the porter who both swore that it was beneficial.[2] It was incorporated in the regulations published in 1834, but so too were the rules of 1729 and 1748.[3] It is hard to understand why in 1834 the old rules were included. Both had been superseded and, by allowing the widows to have 7 days (1729) or 14 days (1748) of absence without having to ask, conflicted with the rule of 1781. They were couched in terms different from those of the rule of 1781 and the trustees may therefore have thought them useful and been reluctant to let them go.

The rule made in 1781 remained in force in 1866, and between those dates there were many occasions on which a widow's pension was suspended because she was absent without leave and many on which the trustees considered whether the arrears should be restored or forfeited or the widow expelled. Between 1781 and 1800 widows whose pensions had been suspended for absenteeism seem to have been treated leniently. A widow who lived away from the almshouse because she was ill was allowed to keep her pension in full,[4] and in other cases excuses were accepted and arrears paid.[5] The trustees seem to have been reluctant to withhold pension permanently or to expel, but they tried to bring absentees back, and to deter absenteeism, by the threat of doing so. Pensions were restored in return for promises to reside,[6] and on other occasions in return for an undertaking given by a widow to resign her house if she was again absent without leave.[7]

1 Below, pp. 219–21.
2 TNA C 38/713; cf. above, Attorney General *v* Grimston (1729–85).
3 Below, pp. 312–13.
4 Below, pp. 221–2.
5 Below, pp. 223, 228, 230, 235, 237, 242.
6 Below, pp. 230, 244.
7 Below, pp. 234, 248.

The trustees' policy is illustrated by the case of Elizabeth Davies, who was absent without leave several times between 1791 and 1803. In 1791 they decided first to withhold her arrears until she made a satisfactory excuse, secondly to withhold them indefinitely and to pay her nothing except when she was actually resident in the almshouse, and thirdly to expel her if she had not become resident by Christmas. In 1792 they offered her arrears to her if she submitted and in 1794 if she promised to reside, and in 1797, because her son was ill, they licensed an additional 3 months' absence if she would agree to forfeit her pension and resign her house if she failed to return at the end of it.[1] In 1803, when her pension was 2 quarters in arrear, the trustees agreed to pay her 1 quarter's arrears unconditionally but the second only if there was no objection to how she spent the first.[2] In 1798 the trustees were unaccountably generous to Margaretta Poole, a widow resident not in the almshouse but in Salisbury gaol. They conceded that she had been imprisoned through no fault of her own, felt sorry for her, sent her a year's pension, and in 1799 paid her arrears.[3]

Perhaps the trustees found themselves to have been too lenient. In 1800 they ruled that the pensions of all widows who had been absent for more than the 13 weeks without leave should be stopped and that in future arrears would not be paid to any unlicensed absentee no matter what the excuse. They did, incompatibly, give themselves the right to make exceptions,[4] but thereafter they do seem to have been less inclined to give back the money withheld from widows whose pensions had been suspended and more inclined to expel them. In 1801 they resolved to expel a widow who had been absent for 3 years and whose pension had been suspended, but they could not find a key to her house. In July 1802 they offered to distribute part of her arrears of pension among her creditors if she would relinquish her house within 3 months, the bribe was accepted, and by October 1802 the trustees had taken possession of the house and paid debts.[5] In 1803, to avoid further bribery, the question how to take possession of a deserted house was addressed directly. By then Mrs. Poole had been absent without leave for several years and had left her house locked with her goods inside. The trustees asked Richard Richards of Lincoln's Inn how they might lawfully take possession of the house and were advised by him that they might force the door if they had first held a meeting and signed a minute declaring that they had expelled the widow. He also advised them that they might do likewise in similar cases in the

1 Below, pp. 237–9, 241, 244, 248.
2 Below, p. 258.
3 Below, pp. 249, 251.
4 Below, pp. 253–4.
5 Below, pp. 255–7.

future. In October 1803 they ordered the porter to enter the house and resolved to admit a new widow to it.[1]

After 1800, as before, applications for absence were apparently treated by the trustees on their merits. Most may have been made routinely to two individual trustees in accordance with the rule of 1781 until, after 1814, E. W. Leyborne Popham was nominated by his fellow trustees to dispose of all such applications alone. In 1843 Leyborne Popham was replaced as the nominated trustee by Francis Leyborne Popham, who in 1856 was joined by the Revd. John Leyborne Popham as an additional nominee.[2] From 1856 probably either might dispose of any application. The applications for leave which did come before the body of trustees at their meetings were perhaps significant, difficult, or contentious and, after due consideration, some were accepted and some rejected. When the trustees accepted an application and gave a reason for doing so the reason was usually sickness, and in several cases they may have expected that the sickness of the widow whose pension they continued to pay would prevent her from ever returning to the almshouse.[3] The trustees gave no reason for rejecting applications[4] but a case in 1846, in which a widow's request for permanent leave was rejected and Francis Leyborne Popham was asked to grant extended leave if her health required it,[5] suggests that the unsuccessful applicants were not sick enough for extended leave.

The trustees at their meetings dealt not only with applications for leave of absence but also with reports that pensions of widows had been suspended for unlicensed absence. They might restore the arrears, withhold them, or expel the offending widows. Sometimes no reason was given for restoring arrears,[6] and when one was minuted it was usually that the widow had been sick, resigned her house,[7] or died. For example, in 1843 the trustees decided to withhold the pension of a widow who was absent without leave, and gave no reason: they changed their minds when they heard that her absence had been caused by an illness which had resulted in her death, and they paid the arrears to her representatives.[8] Sometimes the trustees restored arrears with a warning not to overstay in future, sometimes with a threat that if leave were again overstayed pension would then be forfeited, and on one occasion only after a widow had kept a promise to behave well for a

1 WSA 2037/119; below, pp. 258–9; for Richards, *Lincoln's Inn Admissions* (Lincoln's Inn, 1896), ii. 70.

2 Below, pp. 329, 358–9; for the Leyborne Pophams, below, pp. 396–7.

3 Below, pp. 262–3, 274, 288, 336.

4 e.g. below, pp. 288, 291.

5 Below, p. 336.

6 e.g. below, pp. 265–6, 268.

7 e.g. below, pp. 290, 295, 297.

8 Below, pp. 329, 331.

year.[1] When the trustees withheld arrears their reason for doing so, although not always minuted, seems to have been that the widow asking for them was a persistent offender. Sarah Bacon was thrice denied arrears, once because her absence without leave had been a second offence, once to mark the trustees' disapprobation of her conduct, and once because her absence had been unreasonable and repeated.[2] In 1822 the trustees threatened to expel a widow whose absence had been prolonged and whose pension had been suspended, and in 1827 they threatened another absent widow thus. One returned and if Mrs. Geary, who was threatened in 1827, was the Ann Geare who lived in the almshouse until 1842 both did.[3] In 1833 the trustees did expel a widow, as they had done in 1803. By August 1833 Ellenora Caddick had been absent without leave for nearly 2 years and she had left her house in what was called a disgraceful state of dilapidation. The steward wrote to tell her that the trustees thought that her house should be declared vacant and, he receiving no reply, the trustees declared it so.[4]

Although the trustees expelled widows and withheld pensions under the rule drawn up in 1781 and confirmed in 1783 and 1834, the rule was nevertheless often evaded, ignored, or flouted. In 1850 the steward informed the trustees that there was an increasing habit for widows to live away from the almshouse for most of the time, returning only to show themselves at chapel on Sundays. The trustees authorized him to retain part of the pension of a widow who had presumably indulged in the habit, and they ordered him to inform all the widows that the rule would be strictly enforced and that those attempting to evade its provisions would be severely punished.[5] By how much and for how long the widows' habit was curtailed is not clear. Fewer cases of absenteeism came before the trustees at their meetings in the 1850s and 1860s and, like earlier ones, were apparently treated on their merits.[6]

Children, inmates, men

Rules against widows keeping a child or other person in their houses were made in the regulations promulgated in 1698, those proposed in 1710, and those confirmed in 1729. No objection was raised if a child or inmate stayed for a week or less. A financial penalty was to be imposed if one stayed longer. The rule of 1729 defined ineligible inmates as children and maidwomen, and a clause was added to prevent each widow from having any man in her house after the main gate of

1 Below, pp. 274–6, 324.
2 Below, pp. 276, 281, 294–5.
3 WSA 1635/7; below, pp. 285, 288, 291, 294, 296.
4 Below, pp. 308, 310.
5 Below, p. 341.
6 e.g. below, pp. 373, 378, 385.

the almshouse had been locked. The penalty for entertaining a child or maidwoman for more than 1 week was 2*s*. 6*d*. a week; if a man stayed after hours the penalty was 2*s*. 6*d*. a night. Only by the written consent of two trustees could the rule be set aside.[1] The rule was reiterated in 1834 except that from then a writing of only one trustee was required to set it aside and no penalty for breaking it was specified.[2] It is likely that the rules of the late 17th century and early 18th reflected the trustees' intention to exclude children and other inmates from the almshouse rather than to license as many as the widows might wish to entertain. That seems especially so in the case of men. One of the trustees' concerns may have been that, if a widow died, a child who had been living with her might become a charge on them or the parish, and in 1719 they demanded indemnities from a widow whose bastard grandchild was probably living with her.[3]

Later in the 18th century widows did share their houses with children or servants, and the trustees, if written consent had not been given, evidently turned a blind eye to it. In 1732 they ordered the steward to require the widows to remove all children and inmates,[4] in 1796 they made the surgeon responsible for treating not only the widows but also their children, and in 1797 they apparently expected that daughters of widows would be living with their mothers.[5] In the 19th century the trustees may have become more determined to enforce the rule, and in the period 1817–41 they thrice suspended the pensions of widows who had broken it.[6] In 1843, apparently having noticed that in some way the rule had not been strictly enforced, they resolved that it should be,[7] in 1844 they nominated Francis Leyborne Popham to dispose of all applications for permission to entertain inmates, as he did those for absence, and ruled that no servant should spend a night in the almshouse except in emergency,[8] and in 1856, as for leave of absence, they nominated the Revd. John Leyborne Popham as an additional trustee to dispose of applications.[9] Widows nevertheless continued to break the rule and in the 1840s and 1850s the trustees continually tried to enforce it. The trustees ordered the expulsion of a widow's daughter and suspended pensions until unlicensed inmates had been ejected:[10] on the other hand, they restored pension when

1 TNA C 33/351, ff. 391v.–392 (below, p. 135); C 38/267 (below, p. 132); WSA 2037/8, orders proposed 1710.
2 Below, p. 313.
3 Below, p. 149.
4 Below, pp. 163–4.
5 Below, pp. 247–8; cf. above, this section (nursing); below, officers (surgeon).
6 Below, pp. 278, 318, 320, 324, 326.
7 Below, p. 329.
8 Below, p. 331.
9 Below, pp. 358–9.
10 Below, pp. 334, 336, 358, 361.

SOMERSET HOSPITAL, AT FROXFIELD, WILTS.

In consequence of the great irregularities which have arisen with regard to Inmates and Visitors, it is necessary for all Widows desirous of having permission for an Inmate, to renew their applications to Mr. Popham, before Monday the First of October, 1849.

EMBERLIN AND HAROLD, PRINTERS, MARLBOROUGH.

widows conformed and they licensed inmates when widows needed care or were ill.[1]

Other transgressions

Besides those involving absenteeism or the keeping of inmates few serious transgressions are referred to in the minute books for 1714–1866. In two cases important precedents were set and in a third two trustees are portrayed as acting with magisterial authority.

The house of a widow who was admitted to the almshouse in 1714 and who probably died soon afterwards was broken into. After an investigation by the steward, in 1718 the trustees resolved that in future any widow who forced entry to the house of a deceased widow would be severely punished. They thus made clear that the houses were to be treated as private property.[2] Between 1840 and 1842 the steward twice objected to a sale by auction being held in a widow's house, having understood from his predecessors that such sales were not permitted. One of the two sales was held by an officer of the sheriff in a case of debt and the other by the creditors of a deceased widow. The steward remonstrated against a third sale and, as a result, a complaint was made to a trustee either by or against him. At their meeting in 1842 the trustees simply prohibited sales by auction at the almshouse.[3]

In 1860 the two trustees who viewed the almshouse on 2 July heard that Mary Hemus, acting on information received from Elizabeth Marsh, had alleged that in 1856 Elizabeth Mary Powys had been incontinent with W. C. Gooding, who had been the porter since 1857, and with Stephen Snook, a baker and shopkeeper of Froxfield. The trustees, H. N. Goddard and Francis Leyborne Popham, who were

1 Below, pp. 358, 361, 364, 390–1.
2 Below, pp. 138, 146–8; cf. below, p. 143.
3 Below, pp. 326–7.

both J.P.s, conducted what was called a full hearing. They concluded that the allegation could not be proved and that for Mrs. Hemus to make it after more than 3 years was indiscreet, and they warned Mrs. Marsh to be more careful in what she said. After the hearing Mrs. Marsh and Mrs. Powys both complained about Mrs. Hemus and her servant. The trustees warned Mrs. Hemus that, if her servant was complained about again, her permission to keep one would be withdrawn.[1]

Troublesome widows

Just as they were by some of their tenants, the trustees were sometimes troubled by widows who lived in the almshouse. Besides dealing with widows who were persistently absent they were occasionally faced with widows who challenged their authority or whose personal behaviour impinged on others.

Susannah Cherry and Grace Gibbs, the two widows who challenged the trustees' authority, have already been mentioned.[2] Mrs. Cherry, the relict of Richard Cherry (d. 1695), vicar of Burbage,[3] was living in the almshouse in 1698 when she challenged the regulations promulgated in that year by the trustees. She was alleged to have entered the chapel, where they had been hung, taken them down, and carried them out of the chapel. With Elizabeth Abbot she took the key of the main gate of the almshouse from the porter's son and refused to return it or allow the gate to be locked. She abused the trustees and officers and despised their authority. When admonished by the trustees, who wished to expel her, she refused to submit, asserted that she held her house for life and was as secure in it as the trustees were in their own estates, and declaimed that she did not fear what the trustees could do to her.[4] Mrs. Cherry's lack of fear was justified. The court of Chancery refused to permit the trustees to withhold her pension or expel her,[5] and she remained both resident and abrasive. It was alleged that, when asked by the steward to live civilly and abide by the regulations, she reviled the trustees and that, when declaring that she would ignore the regulations, she called them 'fit for nothing but to wipe her breech or her shoes'. The trustees were discouraged by what they called Mrs. Cherry's disrespectful behaviour,[6] in 1704 described her as incorrigible and reported her as saying that 'if they forgave her she would do the same again', and in that year, perhaps in anger, disgust, or despair, resigned the trust.[7] Mrs. Cherry was not

1 Below, p. 373; for the trustees, below, pp. 395–6; for the porter, below, officers.
2 Above, Attorney General *v* Grimston (1699–1729).
3 WSA 1678/3.
4 Ibid. 2037/26; TNA C 38/267 (below, pp. 130–1).
5 Above, Attorney General *v* Grimston (1699–1729).
6 TNA C 38/267 (below, p. 131).
7 Ibid. C 33/301, ff. 259v.–260.

expelled and pension owed to her was presumably paid by the new trustees. She died in 1714 and was buried at Burbage.[1] Grace Gibbs, the trustees were informed in 1726, admitted lewd and scandalous people to her house at night and thus kept a disorderly house. If the information was correct the visitors evidently entered through a window from the London road. The trustees warned Mrs. Gibbs that she would be expelled from the almshouse if she indulged in such behaviour in future and barred the south window of her ground-floor room. By November 1727, however, they had received further evidence of Mrs. Gibbs's incontinency and disorderly life and, as they had done in respect of Mrs. Cherry, they first resolved to withhold her pension and secondly to expel her.[2] Mrs. Gibbs resisted, as Mrs. Cherry had done, but this time, in 1729, the court gave the trustees the right to take those actions. Mrs. Gibbs's counsel acknowledged to the court that her pension had been withheld because of her misbehaviour and the disrespect and bad language which she had offered to the trustees, but he insisted that she was sorry and in great distress and need and that she had submitted. Whether in mercy or because they had withheld them without legal right the court ordered the trustees to pay her arrears in full,[3] and they did so in 1730.[4] Mrs. Gibbs continued to live at the almshouse until, in 1740, she died.[5]

One of the widows whose personal behaviour was very troublesome was Elizabeth Powell, the relict of the Revd. Howell Powell, who was admitted to the almshouse between 12 October 1785 and 9 January 1786. The Powells' son was baptized at Froxfield in June 1786[6] and in July Mrs. Powell was ill.[7] In June 1791 the trustees were informed that Mrs. Powell was frequently drunk and was again ill. They nominated a committee to enquire into the facts and to employ an apothecary to visit her. If she was found to be ill medicines were to be given to her, if she was found to be deranged a nurse was to be employed to confine her and take care of her, but if she was found to be the author of her own misfortune she was to be punished. The punishment would be the forfeiture of pension or expulsion.[8] Mrs. Powell was attended on by James Blackman, a surgeon of Ramsbury, and was found guilty of drunkenness. 'Her intemperance appeared so habitual, and her conduct so violent and offensive, that the committee judged it necessary for the peace and safety of the hospital to remove her as soon as possible'. On being told of the committee's judgement,

1 WSA 1678/3.
2 Below, pp. 154–5, 156–7.
3 TNA C 33/351, ff. 97, 175, 391v.–392 (below, p. 137); above, Attorney General *v* Grimston (1699–1729).
4 Below, pp. 159–60.
5 WSA 1635/1.
6 Ibid. 1635/2; 2037/27.
7 Below, pp. 231–2.
8 Below, p. 237.

and on being offered an additional 6 months' pension, Mrs. Powell agreed to resign her house at Michaelmas 1791. By 17 September she had vacated the house and on 13 October her pension was paid up. The trouble for the trustees was that Mrs. Powell had nowhere to go. In June 1791 they evidently acknowledged that, if they stopped her pension and expelled her, she would become a pauper dependent on parochial relief, and they accepted that they would contribute to the cost of maintaining her at her place of settlement. They apparently shrank from leaving her to her fate, and between June and August 1791 they offered to compensate anyone who would take her. The steward wrote to Mr. Lloyd, a gentleman named by Mrs. Powell as her friend, and intimated that, if any of her relations would take the charge and care of her, and if she was kept far from Froxfield and gave no trouble to the inhabitants of the almshouse or the parish, an allowance towards her maintenance would be paid. Lloyd, 'after what he himself lately saw at Froxfield, declined taking any active part in her affairs'. He referred the steward to Mrs. Powell's brother-in-law Mr. Nash, an attorney at High Wycombe, to whom the steward sent a letter to the same effect as that sent to Lloyd. The answer, dated 24 August 1791, was equally unequivocal: 'Mrs. Powell's behaviour to me and her sister has been so very unbecoming that I am determined she never more shall enter my house'. Nash declared that 'under her present misfortunes, which she has thought proper to reduce herself to, I know of no benefit she can claim or expect but that of a pauper at her own parish'. When the trustees met on 17 September 1791, perhaps fearing that they might have to take her back, they resolved that until further notice no other widow should be placed in the house lately occupied by Mrs. Powell, who may have been living nearby. They ordered the steward to take the opinion of counsel on what was her legal place of settlement and, if Mrs. Powell would not 'voluntarily remove herself to some distant place', he was to help the parish officers of Froxfield to have her removed from the vicinity.[1] By October 1791 the trustees had paid counsel, paid for proceedings at law relating to the removal of Mrs. Powell, and paid one William Fowler for removing her.[2] Whither counsel advised the trustees to send Mrs. Powell is obscure. In 1792 they resolved that a new widow might be admitted to her house.[3]

Although Margaret Richardson's behaviour troubled the trustees she was perhaps as much sinned against as sinning. She was the relict of the Revd. John Richardson of Wath, who died in August 1832 aged 38, and was admitted to the almshouse in August 1833.[4] By 1840 her conduct in the almshouse had given rise to disapproval or suspicion

1 WSA 2037/27; below, pp. 237–9.
2 WSA 2037/27.
3 Below, p. 240.
4 WSA 2037/80 (below, pp. 420–1).

and Lord Ailesbury, then the longest serving trustee, had authorized an enquiry into it. In June 1842 Mrs. Richardson tried to hang herself. The steward reported her attempt to Lord Ailesbury, and a report on the state of her mind was commissioned. By 3 August Mrs. Richardson had written to the trustees to express regret for what she had done. Because she was contrite they resolved to forgive her, but she was warned that if she misbehaved again she would be expelled.[1] In 1845 Anne Waldron, another clergy widow, claimed that Mrs. Richardson had assaulted her. Mrs. Waldron may have included Mrs. Richardson in allegations that men had been admitted to the almshouse after the main gate had been locked, and the trustees implied that her conduct had frequently been disorderly. Mrs. Waldron's allegations were considered to be unfounded, and each widow forfeited a quarter's pension.[2] Mrs. Richardson was admonished in the chapel by the chaplain, who in 1846 informed the trustees that she had since behaved with propriety. He asked them to restore her arrears, but they refused his request.[3]

OFFICERS

In her will the duchess of Somerset authorized the trustees for the almshouse to appoint officers and directed them to appoint a chaplain.[4] To manage all sides of their affairs, trusteeship and their meetings, the estate, the almshouse buildings, and life in the almshouse, they appointed a steward. To deal with some estate matters they appointed bailiffs, a gamekeeper, and a woodward, and to deal with life in the almshouse they appointed the chaplain, a chapel clerk, a porter, and a surgeon.

Steward

The trustees' principal officer was at first called the receiver or the receiver and paymaster.[5] In 1698 he was already being called the steward,[6] and from 1722 his formal title was steward and receiver.[7] In the minute books edited below he was called steward more often than receiver, occasionally treasurer,[8] and sometimes clerk.[9] Throughout this introduction he is called the steward.

1 Below, p. 326.
2 Below, pp. 333–4; for Mrs. Waldron, WSA 2037/80 (below, p. 424).
3 Below, p. 336.
4 TNA PROB 11/474, ff. 176–93 (below, pp. 119–21).
5 Ibid. C 33/289, ff. 250–2 (below, p. 124), 563v.–564 (below, p. 129); C 33/301, ff. 73v.–74, 259v.–260; C 38/257.
6 Ibid. C 38/267 (below, p. 132).
7 e.g. below, pp. 150, 173.
8 e.g. below, pp. 207, 227.
9 e.g. below, pp. 248–9.

The stewards in the period 1695–1866 were William Bailey 1695–6, Alexander Thistlethwaite 1697 or 1698 to 1703, Joseph Wall 1703–12, Thomas Kellway 1713–22, Joseph Walker 1722–6, Thomas Franklin 1726–44, Charles Young 1745–66, Samuel Martin 1767–75, Samuel Hawkes 1775–85, John Ward 1785–1829, Thomas Merriman 1829–40, and T. B. Merriman from 1840.[1] Thistlethwaite was of Hungerford, Walker, Young, and Hawkes were of Marlborough, Martin was of West Kennett, and each was said to be a gentleman.[2] Presumably all the stewards were educated men with knowledge of, and experience in, legal affairs and estate management. Ward was an attorney in Marlborough, Thomas Merriman became his partner, and T. B. Merriman, his son, became his: they worked in premises in Silverless Street and presumably had a full-time office staff.[3]

As authorized by the duchess, the stewards were appointed by her trustees. Sir William Gregory appointed Bailey, to obey an order of the court of Chancery Sir Samuel Grimston appointed Thistlethwaite,[4] and the decree of 1698 confirmed the right of the new trustees and their successors to appoint future stewards. The trustees did remain subject to the direction of the court,[5] it was assumed that their choice of steward needed the court's approval,[6] and in two cases it was stated that the master to whom the cause Attorney General *v* Grimston stood referred made the appointment.[7] It is almost certain, however, that in all cases the master did no more than give formal approval to the trustees' choice, and in recording the appointment by the trustees of all stewards from Walker to Hawkes it was implied that the approval of a master, although necessary, would be a formality.[8] From 1786 the court no longer passed the steward's accounts[9] and the practice of it giving formal approval to the stewards appointed by the trustees ceased.

The court of Chancery sought security from stewards that they would present their accounts in the court once a year.[10] In 1698

1 This list is based on Ward, *Somerset Hospital*, 32, and the minute books edited below; additional information is from TNA C 33/289, ff. 250–2 (below, pp. 122–3; Bailey); C 33/291, f. 365 (Thistlethwaite); C 33/319, f. 629 and v. (Kellway); C 38/308 (Wall); ibid. PROB 11/530, ff. 208v.–209 (Wall); WSA 1050/14 (Ward); 1050/21 (Hawkes); 1079/2 (Young); 1176/2 (Martin); 2037/26 (Thistlethwaite).

2 *VCH Wiltshire*, xii. 97 (Martin); TNA C 38/257 (Thistlethwaite); below, pp. 150, 173, 199, 209.

3 *Early Trade Directories* (WRS xlvii), 4, 25, 52, 79, 124.

4 TNA C 38/260 (below, p. 125).

5 Ibid. C 33/289, ff. 563v.–564 (below, pp. 128–9).

6 Ibid. C 33/351, ff. 391v.–392 (below, p. 134); WSA 2037/8, orders proposed 1710.

7 TNA C 33/319, f. 629 and v.; C 38/283.

8 Below, pp. 150–1, 173, 199–200, 209; for Hawkes, cf. TNA C 33/447, ff. 471v.–472.

9 Above, Attorney General *v* Grimston (1729–85).

10 For the stewards' accounts, below, this sub-section.

Thistlethwaite and his sureties entered into a recognizance of £1,000 that he would do so,[1] Wall's recognizance was also of £1,000,[2] and the recognizance of each steward down to Hawkes was probably of the same amount. After the death or resignation of a steward the recognizance would be vacated when his accounts, or those of his executors or administrators, had been allowed by a master in Chancery. That having been done, and the recognizance of the incoming steward and his sureties having been accepted, the almshouse's muniments were delivered to the incomer.[3] In 1785 Ward bound himself to present accounts faithfully but, the court of Chancery having discontinued its scrutiny of the accounts, it seems that no security was sought from the Merrimans.[4] Moreover, as each of those succeeded the other there was no break in the presentation of the accounts or custody of the muniments.

While in office the steward's function, in general terms, was to give effect to the trustees' decisions. The decree of June 1698 made him accountable to the trustees and imposed on him the duties of paying the widows their pensions and of keeping the almshouse's muniments.[5] The regulations proposed in 1710 and those confirmed in 1729 required him to keep an account book, to attend the trustees' meetings and keep a minute book, to record penalties inflicted on the widows, and to publish the orders made by the trustees.[6] It is very likely that throughout the period 1695–1866 he gave the trustees advice on many matters. He wrote their letters and instructed their professional advisers,[7] and often he was authorized to make decisions and enter into agreements on their behalf.

In matters relating to trusteeship and meetings the steward did indeed act as a clerk and a treasurer, as both of which he was sometimes described. As a clerk he convened the meetings,[8] and at them he reported on actions already taken, received instructions as to future actions, and presumably guided the trustees through the business to be transacted. With or without assistance he entered the minutes[9] and prepared the deeds by which the almshouse and its estate were conveyed from time to time to existing and new trustees.[10] He gave notice of vacancies in the almshouse to the trustees who stood in turn

1 TNA C 33/291, f. 365.
2 Ibid. C 33/319, f. 629 and v.
3 e.g. ibid. C 33/301, ff. 521v.–522; below, pp. 151, 173, 200, 209.
4 Cf. below, pp. 227–8, 298, 322.
5 TNA C 33/289, ff. 563v.–564 (below, pp. 129–30).
6 Ibid. C 33/351, ff. 391v.–392 (below, pp. 134, 136); WSA 2037/8, orders proposed 1710.
7 e.g. below, pp. 175, 200, 219.
8 e.g. WSA 2037/27.
9 Above, meetings (minutes, signatures).
10 e.g. below, pp. 158, 198.

to nominate widows to fill them, and in the 19th century he sent out printed nomination forms.[1] As a treasurer he received the almshouse's income, made its disbursements, and presented accounts yearly.[2]

The steward acted in all matters relating to the estate. While there was copyhold tenure he held the manor courts.[3] About leaseholds he treated with tenants and potential tenants[4] and drew up the leases.[5] He received the rents,[6] represented the trustees in proceedings relating to statutory inclosure[7] and commutation of tithes,[8] arranged private inclosures and exchanges of land,[9] inspected and reported on buildings,[10] and performed multifarious other tasks. He was evidently empowered to settle minor matters without reference to the trustees,[11] and from 1843 he settled many estate matters in collaboration with G. W. Wroughton, one of the trustees.

In matters relating to the almshouse buildings and life in the almshouse the steward was as active as he was in estate matters. He made arrangements for the repair and improvement of the buildings,[12] including the chapel and its furnishings[13] and the service buildings,[14] and he paid those who did the work. He paid the widows' pensions once a quarter,[15] and for long did so in the house incorporated in the almshouse and reserved for his use.[16] He published the regulations and often imposed sanctions, usually the withholding of pension, on the widows who had not complied with them.[17] Thomas Merriman probably drew up the rules published in 1834.[18] The steward reported on an attempted suicide[19] and a dispute between widows,[20] consulted counsel about the expulsion of a widow and the use of the chapel,[21] and made rules for the sale of coal.[22] As in estate matters he usually acted on the instructions, or with the prior authority, of the trustees.

1 Above, trustees (exercise of patronage).
2 Below, this sub-section.
3 WSA 2037/27; below, pp. 143, 151, 161, 164.
4 e.g. below, pp. 213, 229, 250, 253–4, 283–4, 318–19.
5 e.g. below, pp. 154, 165, 170–1, 203, 211, 245.
6 e.g. WSA 2037/26–8; below, p. 210.
7 e.g. WSA 2037/27; below, pp. 213–14, 252, 275.
8 e.g. below, pp. 317, 327.
9 e.g. below, pp. 208, 215, 255, 258.
10 e.g. below, pp. 162–3, 340.
11 e.g. below, pp. 275, 317–18.
12 e.g. below, pp. 165, 203–4, 249, 294, 358, 360–1, 373.
13 e.g. below, pp. 165, 173–4, 209, 374.
14 e.g. below, pp. 246, 356, 358, 360–1.
15 WSA 2037/26–8.
16 Below, p. 380.
17 e.g. below, pp. 157, 165, 307, 318, 361.
18 Cf. below, p. 311.
19 Below, p. 326.
20 Below, pp. 333–4.
21 Below, pp. 258, 334.
22 Below, p. 246.

In minor matters and emergencies, however, he often acted on his own initiative, and his actions were endorsed by the trustees only *post factum*.

The decree of December 1697 required the steward to present accounts yearly, and it was evidently understood that the accounts were to be presented to the relevant master in Chancery.[1] Bailey was being prosecuted for his in 1698[2] and Thistlethwaite's to June 1698 were allowed by the master in July 1698.[3] By making the steward accountable to the trustees, however, the decree of June 1698 gave scope for the uncertainty or conflict which was to arise in 1704.[4] Thistlethwaite's accounts from June 1698 to Michaelmas 1703, when he ceased to act as steward, were demanded by the master, presented in 1704, objected to by the Solicitor General on behalf of the widows, and rejected by the master as imperfect. Thistlethwaite responded that the accounts had been allowed by the trustees and that therefore he had no case to answer before the master.[5] He spent a week in London, probably in 1706, to defend a prosecution over his accounts, in 1708 a commission was executed at the Bear in Charnham Street to examine them, and they were again passed by the trustees.[6] No further accounts were presented to a master until 1710 when, on referring a petition of the trustees to him, the Lord Chancellor ordered that the master should receive Wall's from Michaelmas 1703 to Lady day 1710. The master allowed those accounts and commented that the almshouse's revenue 'had not been frugally managed' in Thistlethwaite's time.[7] From then until 1785 the steward kept an account book and presented his accounts yearly both to the trustees and the relevant master.[8] The trustees twice took action because the accounts of a former steward were not presented promptly, against Walker's sureties in 1730[9] and against Martin's executrix and sureties in 1776.[10]

For his services to the almshouse the steward was paid a salary and was reimbursed for the expenses which he incurred. From 1698 to 1702, when the almshouse's estates were being surveyed, its buildings were being repaired, and the steward consequently had much to do, his salary was £40 a year.[11] By order of Chancery it was reduced to

1 TNA C 33/289, ff. 250–2 (below, p. 124).
2 Ibid. C 38/260 (below, p. 125).
3 Ibid. C 33/291, f. 365.
4 Ibid. C 33/289, ff. 563v.–564 (below, p. 130).
5 Ibid. C 38/283.
6 WSA 2037/26.
7 TNA C 33/317, f. 407 and v.; C 38/308.
8 Ibid. C 33/447, ff. 471v.–472; above, Attorney General *v* Grimston (1729–85); trustees (functions).
9 Below, p. 160.
10 Below, pp. 210–12; cf. above, Attorney General *v* Grimston (1729–85).
11 WSA 2037/26.

£20 a year from 1702.[1] By 1767 it had been increased to £30,[2] and in 1813, although the trustees then resolved to double it, it was increased to only £50.[3] In 1847 it was increased to £70 and in 1859 to £90.[4] Until about 1785 the greatest of the steward's regular expenses were those for travelling to London to be approved by a master and yearly to pass his accounts. He charged for attending the trustees' meetings and for holding the courts of Froxfield and Huish manors. In the later 18th century the costs of hiring a horse to take him to Froxfield to pay the widows' pensions were reimbursed and he charged fees *ad hoc* for extraordinary work.[5] In 1787 the trustees recognized that the steward had been subsidizing the almshouse out of his own pocket and resolved to reduce expenditure until he had been paid back.[6]

Besides his work for the almshouse the steward acted as the trustees' secretary and treasurer in respect of the Mayo trust.[7] From 1829 he reported annually on the trust's assets.[8] From 1852 he conducted the preliminary proceedings in the choice of exhibitioners, appointed and paid an examiner, and passed the examiner's report to the trustees and the trustees' thanks to the examiner. He paid the exhibitioners half-yearly,[9] and from 1859 was himself paid £20 a year for his work.[10] The steward also acted as the trustees' agent in respect of the Thistlethwaite trust.[11]

Manorial officers

The trustees appointed an officer to collect the conventionary rents of Froxfield manor and another to collect those of Huish manor.[12] The officer for Froxfield was called a bailiff in the 1760s and 1770s,[13] a hayward from the 1820s. None was appointed after 1832.[14] The officer for Huish manor was called a bailiff and was empowered to act on all the trustees' land except that at Froxfield. Besides collecting the conventionary rents he probably helped the steward at the manor court and in other dealings with the tenants, and a decision of the trustees made in 1799 that he might not give leave to tenants to grub fences or lop trees could suggest that decisions taken earlier in minor matters and on his own initiative had been accepted.[15] From 1724 his

1 TNA C 33/297, f. 126 and v.
2 WSA 2037/27.
3 Ibid.; below, p. 273.
4 Below, pp. 337, 369.
5 WSA 2037/26–7.
6 Below, p. 232.
7 For the Mayo trust, below.
8 Below, p. 299 sqq.
9 Below, p. 345 sqq.
10 Below, p. 369.
11 For the Thistlethwaite trust, below.
12 WSA 2037/26.
13 Ibid. 2037/27.
14 Ibid. 2037/130.
15 Below, p. 251.

salary was £4 a year.[1] Both bailiffs attended meetings of the trustees in the 1760s and 1770s.[2]

From the mid 18th century the office of bailiff of Huish manor was combined with that of gamekeeper and that of woodward at the same salary. The gamekeeper's duty was to preserve the game on the manor and the woodward's to look after the woodland and hedges and to preserve them.[3] There is no reference to a gamekeeper after 1809. Guy Warwick, the bailiff and woodward from 1815 to his death in 1850 and the lessee of the trustees' farm at Milton Lilbourne from 1832,[4] advised about the condition of woodland and buildings: that was presumably the service to the trust in recognition of which his salary was raised to £10 in 1827.[5] No successor to Warwick is known to have been appointed.

Chaplain

The provisions for a chaplain made in the duchess's will were potentially problematic, and the duchess evidently anticipated the problems. Although the widows were to be his parishioners and it would be his duty to cure their souls, none could compel the minister of Froxfield to accept the £10 to be offered by the trustees or visit the widows. The duchess therefore directed that, when the almshouse's income had risen sufficiently, the trustees themselves should choose a chaplain and pay him £30 a year from the estate. To save the £30 she gave the trustees her right to present a rector of Huish so that, when vacancies occurred, they could present rectors who would be the almshouse's chaplains without taking any reward from the almshouse's revenues. The rector's successors were to be similarly encumbered. Perhaps doubting that a rector of Huish could be compelled to serve a private chapel at Froxfield the duchess directed that, if any failed to do so, the trustees were to choose another chaplain and pay the £30 a year to him.[6]

John Snead (d. 1724), vicar of Froxfield, was the first chaplain of the almshouse and from 1698 or earlier was paid the £10 a year.[7] The rectory of Huish became vacant by death in 1702. In that year the trustees were embroiled in the court of Chancery, they failed to present a rector, and the bishop collated by lapse. The new rector, Francis Gibbs (d. 1751), evidently played no part in services at the almshouse's

1 Below, pp. 152, 168, 200.
2 WSA 2037/27.
3 Ibid.; below, pp. 188, 200, 205.
4 WSA 2037/27–8; for the date of death, ibid. 942/5.
5 Below, pp. 276, 293, 296, 307, 325.
6 TNA PROB 11/474, ff. 176–93 (below, pp. 119–21).
7 WSA 2037/26; for Snead, Phillipps, *Wiltshire Institutions*, ii. 40, 59; for his date of death, WSA 1635/1.

chapel.[1] Snead's successor as vicar of Froxfield, James Searle (d. 1765), also succeeded him as chaplain:[2] he was presumably paid either the £10 or, since he served in place of the rector of Huish, the £30. The trustees presented him as rector of Huish in 1751[3] from when, if the duchess's intentions were carried out, the payments would have ceased. Searle's successor as rector of Huish, Charles Curtis (d. 1775), was a pluralist[4] and was probably not appointed chaplain of the almshouse. Curtis's successor was Charles Mayo (d. 1829), who was also a pluralist, and Mayo's was William Bleeck. Both Mayo and Bleeck were appointed chaplain of the almshouse[5] but neither is known to have officiated at it.

From 1765 a chaplain who did officiate, and who came to be called formally the officiating chaplain, was appointed. He was probably chosen by the trustees, who from 1766 to 1809, a period in which there were five or more officiating chaplains, paid him the £30. There is no evidence that a rector of Huish made or approved a choice or augmented the salary. The chaplains included George Jenkins (1779–88), curate of Froxfield, and Lewis Evans (1788–99), vicar of Froxfield 1788–1827.[6] In 1809 the trustees resolved to increase the salary to £50 if, *inter alia*, the clergyman would provide himself with a suitable house not far from the almshouse.[7] They appointed Arthur Meyrick, who received the £50 and kept a boarding school at Ramsbury. Meyrick ceased to officiate in 1829, when T. G. P. Atwood, the new vicar of Froxfield, was appointed as the new officiating chaplain at the same salary. Atwood was still officiating in 1866.[8]

In 1857, perhaps feeling that it was anomalous to have both a chaplain and an officiating chaplain, the trustees thought about asking the bishop to allow a future rector of Huish to live at Froxfield. They resolved instead to try to acquire the advowson of Froxfield vicarage, which belonged to the dean and chapter of Windsor, in the hope that those they appointed as vicars would serve as resident chaplains. Despite two of them, the earl of Shelburne and Lord Ernest Bruce, each having a private conversation with the dean on the subject and

1 Phillipps, *Wiltshire Institutions*, ii. 46; above, Attorney General *v* Grimston (1699–1729); for Gibbs's date of death, WSA 1740/1.

2 Phillipps, *Wiltshire Institutions*, ii. 59; below, p. 166; for Searle's date of death, WSA 1635/2.

3 Below, p. 179.

4 Phillipps, *Wiltshire Institutions*, ii. 79, 82, 88; *VCH Wiltshire*, xvi. 148; for the date of death, WSA 616/3.

5 *VCH Wiltshire*, x. 18; below, pp. 208, 303–5.

6 *Endowed Charities of Wiltshire* (southern division), 984; *Wiltshire Returns to the Bishop's Visitation Queries 1783* (WRS xxvii), p. 107; *VCH Wiltshire*, xvi. 161; WSA 2037/27.

7 Below, p. 266.

8 *VCH Wiltshire*, xii. 46; xvi. 161; WSA 2037/27–8; below, p. 305.

despite the dean's sympathy with the object, they failed to persuade the dean and chapter to exchange or sell the advowson.[1]

The primary duty of the chaplains or officiating chaplains was to hold services and read prayers in the chapel.[2] They were given secondary duties by the regulations proposed in 1710 and those confirmed in 1729. In certain circumstances they were required to judge or admonish widows or to validate the excuses of widows suspected of breaking rules of the almshouse.[3] The chaplain evidently attended the trustees' meetings regularly and from 1854, if not earlier, the officiating chaplain also attended.[4]

Chapel clerk

From when the new chapel was opened in 1814 the steward appointed a chapel clerk. The trustees proposed a salary of £2 12*s*. a year: £2 10*s*. was paid.[5] The duty of the clerk was presumably to ensure that the chapel was clean enough and well enough equipped for the widows to worship in.

Porter

A porter was presumably appointed as soon as widows were admitted to the almshouse, and one succeeded another throughout the period 1714–1866. The known porters were Charles Milsom (d. 1733) from 1699 or earlier, Thomas Osmond (d. 1755), John Osmond from 1755 to his death in 1788, William Merriwether, John's son-in-law, 1788–92, Alexander Newman from 1792 to his death in 1798, Edward Newman 1798–1819, John Arman 1819–22, William Gooding 1822–57, and Gooding's son W. C. Gooding from 1857.[6] In 1792 the trustees ordered that Merriwether should be dismissed because, in defiance of two magistrates, one of whom was a trustee and to both of whom he had been impertinent, he had erected a scaffold and promoted a revel at Froxfield. He was given 3 months' notice and resigned.[7] In 1856 William Gooding became incapable and, until he replaced him as porter, his son was asked to do his duties.[8]

The porters did prescribed duties for which they were paid a salary, and they regularly did other work for which, until 1844,

1 Below, pp. 359–60, 367–9.
2 For the details, above, almshouse life (religious worship).
3 TNA C 33/351, ff. 391v.–392 (below, pp. 134–6); WSA 2037/8, orders proposed 1710.
4 Above, meetings (attendance).
5 WSA 2037/27–8; below, p. 274.
6 Most of the dates are taken from WSA 2037/27–8; see also below, pp. 130–1, 183, 234, 283, 361; for the dates of death, WSA 1635/1–3.
7 Below, pp. 241–2.
8 Below, p. 361.

they presented bills and were paid *ad hoc*.[1] A porter's lodge was incorporated in the almshouse's gatehouse but it seems to have lacked living accommodation,[2] and the porters down to 1819 probably subcontracted some or all of both their prescribed and *ad hoc* work. Some of those early porters were evidently prosperous. John Osmond was a builder,[3] Alexander Newman was described as a gentleman,[4] and Edward Newman held property for which he paid rent of £125 a year.[5] In 1702 the salary was £2 a year,[6] in 1755 and later £4.[7] In 1802 it was increased to £5 on condition that the porter attended chapel regularly, in 1806 it was increased to 7 gns., and in 1818 it was increased to £10.[8]

The prescribed duties were administrative and practical. In 1699 they were to lock and unlock the main gate of the almshouse and to look after the chapel.[9] Afterwards they may have become gradually more numerous. The porter admitted incoming widows,[10] distributed gowns,[11] and rang the bell to call the widows to the chapel.[12] In the 1770s he attended the trustees' general meetings,[13] and from 1781 he kept a register to show whether or not each widow was resident in the almshouse.[14] Much of the *ad hoc* work was carpentry, which was presumably done by the porters themselves, their employees, or their subcontractors.[15] In the 18th century the payment of 1 gn. to the porter each time a widow was buried almost certainly reflected or included a charge for making the coffin. The other work was done on the almshouse buildings.[16]

In 1819, to replace Edward Newman, the trustees evidently decided that, instead of employing a prosperous gentleman who would subcontract the porter's work, they would employ a handyman who would do the work himself. They gave the porter the use of the house left vacant by the widow who lived in the asylum at Brislington from 1814 to 1836. The house stood beside the main gate, and the porter may have lived in it.[17] In 1833 the trustees decided that the porter should

1 For the change in 1844, below, this sub-section.
2 Cf. above, almshouse buildings (houses).
3 WSA 2037/27; below, pp. 187–8.
4 WSA 1635/3.
5 Ibid. 2037/27.
6 Ibid. 2037/26.
7 Ibid. 2037/27; below, p. 183.
8 Below, pp. 256, 262, 281.
9 TNA C 38/267 (below, pp. 130–1).
10 Below, pp. 140–1, 143.
11 Below, p. 167.
12 *Endowed Charities of Wiltshire* (southern division), 986; WSA 2037/27; below, p. 234.
13 Above, meetings (attendance).
14 Below, pp. 220–1.
15 WSA 2037/27–8; below, pp. 154, 161, 187–8, 201, 415–16.
16 WSA 2037/27–8; for burial, cf. above, almshouse life.
17 *Endowed Charities of Wiltshire* (southern division), 985; WSA 2037/80 (below, p. 423); for the widow, above, almshouse life (nursing).

live in a house near, not in, the almshouse,[1] and by 1834 they had built one for him on the south side of the London road opposite the gatehouse.[2] Thereafter the porter's duties became many, varied, and tantamount to those of a caretaker.[3] In 1839 his salary was increased to £15.[4] In 1844 the trustees objected to the large amount charged for *ad hoc* work, increased his salary to £25, and required him to keep all neat and clean with his own tools and to toll the bell.[5] The salary was increased to £30 in 1863.[6]

Surgeon

From 1791 the trustees appointed medical practitioners to care for the widows at the trustees' expense. The medical practitioners were sometimes called apothecaries to indicate that they prepared, stored, and administered drugs, surgeons to indicate that they might apply themselves directly to a patient's body, or both.

In 1791 the trustees offered a salary to a surgeon who would attend once a week at the almshouse without being sent for, attend whenever sent for, and provide medicines and surgery for the widows. They appointed James Whitelock of Ramsbury for a year. Whitelock was paid £20 for the year and was evidently required to provide the necessary medicines at his own expense.[7] His contract was extended and he remained surgeon until 1798. He was absent in 1794, when one Condell substituted for him, and in 1796, when John Eyles of Ramsbury substituted for him. Eyles had proposed to him that he would attend at the almshouse on the widows and their children, supply them with medicines, and keep the medicines at Froxfield in readiness. In 1798 the trustees appointed Eyles in place of Whitelock, who had resigned.[8]

Eyles's salary was increased to £30 in 1802.[9] In 1809 it was increased to £40 on condition that he would keep sufficient medicines in the upper room of the gatehouse and attend at the almshouse twice a week routinely, more often if any widow was seriously ill, and as soon as possible when called for in an emergency. Soon afterwards Eyles resigned and the trustees appointed R. K. Marsh.[10] The salary was increased to £50 in 1814.[11] When Marsh resigned in 1824 his partner Alfred Kite, who had already been ministering to the widows, and William Bartlett of Great Bedwyn each offered himself as surgeon

1 Below, p. 310.
2 O.S. Map 1/2,500, Wiltshire, XXX. 14 (1885 edn.); WSA 2037/27.
3 e.g. below, p. 331.
4 Below, p. 321.
5 Below, p. 331.
6 Below, p. 382.
7 Below, pp. 236–8.
8 Below, pp. 241, 245, 247, 250.
9 Below, p. 256.
10 Below, pp. 266–7.
11 Below, p. 274.

and apothecary. In August 1824 the trustees chose Bartlett but allowed Kite to continue until the following Christmas.[1] In 1832 Bartlett was denied an increase in salary but in 1833, when he claimed that the widows required much attention and much medicine, his salary was increased to £60.[2] He resigned in 1843, when the trustees acted as they had in 1824. His partner James Lidderdale, who may already have been ministering to the widows, and R. H. Barker of Hungerford each offered himself as surgeon and apothecary. In August the trustees chose Barker but allowed Lidderdale to care for the sick widows until the following Christmas.[3]

PHILANTHROPY *IN EXCELSIS*?

Sarah, duchess of Somerset, was independently wealthy and of her own volition made many charitable gifts. She paid for Froxfield almshouse to be built and endowed it with an estate of land. Both the almshouse and the endowment were large, and the income from the land was for long sufficient to maintain the building and provide all those living in it with a pension large enough to sustain themselves. Only in the 20th century, after economic and social changes which the duchess could hardly have foreseen, did the income from the land become too small to serve those purposes. To give homes and pensions to hundreds of widows for hundreds of years seems very much like philanthropy *in excelsis*.

On the other hand, all the duchess's charitable gifts, besides two small ones to endow scholarships at Oxford and Cambridge, were to take effect after her death and therefore caused no loss to herself. What others may have lost, although potentially much, may not have been seen by the duchess, or felt by the possible recipients, as critical. The duchess was separated from her husband, who anyway had an income from his own estates, and at her death she had no living issue, sibling, or parent. When she made her will her niece was a member of a rich family and, as countess of Warrington, anyway predeceased her. The duchess's residuary legatees were two grandnephews and two grandnieces, none of whom was likely to become indigent and all of whom may nonetheless have benefited much under her will. Although her nearest relatives were not close, to make charitable gifts was not compulsory. That the duchess made them should probably be taken at face value as philanthropy of a high order.

In the case of Froxfield almshouse those who benefited from the duchess's philanthropy were described as poor widows. They were not,

1 Below, p. 292.
2 Below, pp. 308, 310.
3 Below, p. 329.

however, drawn from an impoverished underclass, were not the relicts of cottagers squatting on waste ground or of agricultural labourers, and were less likely to have been servants than to have had servants. The duchess's charity was intended not to lift widows out of destitution but to prevent widows who were comfortably off at the death of their husbands from sliding into it. The duchess grew up in the 1640s and, although he was so later and may then have prospered, her father may not have been rich in that period. The duchess may have intended that the widows who were to benefit from her charity should be drawn from a class not far below that in which she was brought up, whose potential difficulties as widows she was aware of, and with whom she empathized. If she intended to help only the widows with whom she empathized and not the poorest of widows her philanthropy might seem to be below the very highest. That she should endow a charity for housing the already destitute in a large almshouse, or for giving money, food, or other goods to them regularly whether or not they lived in an almshouse, may have been inconceivable to a wealthy duchess in the late 17th century. If conceivable, such a charity may have seemed unpalatable because poor rates were already levied on her estates, and unlikely to succeed because competent, experienced, and energetic trustees to manage it would have been hard to find. The duchess might nevertheless have given money to the very poor had she wished to.

Despite such objections, if philanthropy is practical benevolence, to found Froxfield almshouse, and to enable it to improve so many lives over so long a period, was philanthropy *in excelsis* however little the foundress herself lost and whoever the beneficiaries might have been.

THE MAYO TRUST

In 1775 the trustees of the almshouse presented Charles Mayo, then aged about 24, as rector of Huish and appointed him chaplain of the almshouse. From 1779 Mayo was also rector of Beechingstoke.[1] In 1817 he proposed to found a charity and endow it with land and shares, and he asked the almshouse trustees to be the trustees of the charity. They consented.[2] In 1828 Mayo proposed to give instead 3½ per cent annuities with a face value of £2,500, declared that he intended to help well educated Anglican clergymen who had ministered long and diligently without what he considered to be adequate reward in the form of preferment, and hoped that by doing so he would set an example which others, wealthier than he, would follow.[3] Mayo's

1 *VCH Wiltshire*, x. 18; WSA 2377/2; above, officers (chaplain).

2 Below, p. 278.

3 Below, pp. 297, 299–300.

declaration of trust was signed in February 1829. He gave the £2,500 to two of the almshouse trustees, who were to retain the money and the income from it as a growing fund which was not to be drawn on until 21 years after Mayo's death, and he provided for them to be replaced by other almshouse trustees when necessary. Mayo proposed that his help should be given in two ways. He directed the trustees to endow an exhibition of £70 a year for a scholar to study at an Oxford college, and he suggested that they should buy either one advowson or two. The exhibitioner was to be the son of a clergyman who had lived for 15 years or more in Wiltshire and was himself to have been born in Wiltshire or to have lived there for 15 years or more. The exhibition was to be enjoyed for no longer than 7 years. If an advowson was bought it was to be of a benefice from which a yearly income of £200 or more arose, and any clergyman presented to be an incumbent was to be an unbeneficed graduate who had ministered in Wiltshire for 15 years. Any church of which the advowson might be purchased was to stand south of Lancashire and Yorkshire. The purchase of an advowson was not to diminish the value of the exhibition.[1]

Charles Mayo died on 27 November 1829,[2] for 21 years from when the fund which he had given in trust was allowed to accumulate. In 1844–5 the nominal rate of interest was reduced from 3½ per cent to 3¼ per cent and in 1851 the fund stood at £5,864.[3] In 1850 the almshouse trustees appointed a committee, to consist of the three of their number who were then Mayo's trustees, to devise a procedure for choosing an exhibitioner as soon as possible after 27 November 1850.[4] The committee moved slowly[5] and advertized the exhibition only in March 1852. Applicants were to be under 19 years of age and examined. The exhibition was to be of £70 a year as Mayo directed, the exhibitioner was to be reported on half-yearly by a tutor at his college, and the exhibition was to be tenable for no more than 5 years and not 7 as Mayo directed. At their meeting in July 1852 the almshouse trustees chose the first exhibitioner. The examiner then was the Public Orator of the university of Oxford,[6] in 1856 the trustees resolved that thenceforward the name and address of each candidate and of the school at which he had been educated should be disclosed to them before the examination,[7] and in 1857 the examiner was a domestic chaplain of the bishop of London.[8]

Despite the payment of £70 a year to the exhibitioner, and a reduction of the rate of interest to 3 per cent, the capital of the trust

1 Below, pp. 299–303.
2 Below, p. 303.
3 Below, pp. 331, 334, 343.
4 Below, p. 342.
5 Below, p. 343.
6 Below, pp. 345–6.
7 Below, p. 359.
8 Below, p. 362.

continued to increase. In 1855, when it was £6,328, the almshouse trustees proposed to buy the advowson of a benefice. None suitable was found[1] and in 1857–8, after the dean and chapter of Windsor had declined their offer to buy the advowson of Froxfield with part of that capital, some trustees began to doubt the desirability of buying any other advowson. The matter was referred to a committee of the almshouse trustees, and a report was prepared by Sir John Awdry and read to the general meeting in July 1858.[2] In his report Sir John reflected on changes in attitudes and practices in the Church of England since what he called Mr. Mayo's time. By Mr. Mayo's time he probably meant not 1829 when Mayo stated his views but a time, long before then, when he formed them. Sir John contended that in Mayo's time a well off and beneficed clergyman might have found even a moderately poor parochial benefice attractive as an additional one for himself because non-residence and pluralism were then acceptable, and because services need not be frequent and a curate to perform them not expensive. He concluded that the well educated, hard working, and inadequately rewarded clergymen in Mayo's mind's eye were curates who served one church or more for non-resident or pluralist incumbents and received no more than a small stipend for doing so. By contrast Sir John thought that the many moderately poor benefices which had been formed since Mayo's time by the division of large parishes would not recommend themselves as additional benefices to men who already held a richer one because pluralism had become less acceptable and, because more services were required, the cost of a curate to provide them had become greater. He observed that the poorer benefices were then held singly as incumbents by men in the same class as those who were stipendiary curates in Mayo's time. In reporting his conclusions and observations Sir John implied that, in the 1850s, well educated clergyman who had been diligently ministering for 15 years or more would not be unbeneficed, and he argued that the best way to help clergymen of the class in Mayo's mind's eye was to pay for the education of their sons. He recommended not that an advowson should be bought but that a second exhibition should be offered and the trustees, while reserving their right to acquire the advowson of Froxfield if it became available, followed that recommendation.[3]

The second exhibition was of the same value, competed for in the same way, and held on the same conditions as the first.[4] A question arose about the eligibility of any candidate whose 19th birthday fell between the day of his recorded entry as a candidate and the day on

1 Below, pp. 356, 359.
2 Below, pp. 362, 365; for the offer, above, officers (chaplain).
3 Below, pp. 365–7.
4 Below, p. 368.

which the exhibitioner was chosen,[1] and in 1861 the trustees announced that they would pay particular attention to the qualifications of the parents of the candidates and, presumably because Mayo had not called for comparative assessments, that superior attainments alone would not ensure the success of any one candidate.[2] In 1863 they resolved that the 5 years should begin on the first day of the second term after the day on which the exhibitioner was chosen.[3] By 1866 the trust fund had continued to grow while the two exhibitions were being provided.[4]

THE THISTLETHWAITE TRUST

Gabriel Thistlethwaite (d. 1723), rector of Winterslow, gave by will £100 to augment Huish rectory. The money was given to the rector, Francis Gibbs, and was not invested. In 1766 Gibbs's sons Charles and George replaced it and invested it in Old South Sea annuities with a face value of £113 12*s.* 8*d.*, the income from which was given to the rector of Huish.[5] In 1791 that investment was transferred to the trustees for the almshouse, and thenceforward the income from it was received by the trustees and passed to the rector. In 1853 the stock was paid off at par and the proceeds were re-invested in consols with a face value of £128 19*s.*[6]

RECORDS

The text of this volume consists mostly of editions of documents or of parts of documents. The editions in the prelude have been prepared from documents in the Probate and Chancery classes among the public records in the National Archives at Kew, those in the main body of the text and in the appendix from documents among the muniments of Froxfield almshouse in the Wiltshire and Swindon History Centre at Chippenham.

The duchess of Somerset's will, under which the almshouse was built, endowed, filled, and managed, was proved, and copied into a register, at the Prerogative Court of Canterbury in 1704. That into which it was copied was among the many such registers placed in the care of the Public Record Office in 1970 and subsequently moved to Kew. The edition of extracts of the will printed in the prelude was

1 Below, pp. 371, 388.
2 Below, p. 377.
3 Below, p. 382.
4 Below, p. 391.
5 *Endowed Charities of Wiltshire* (northern division), 243–4; for the date of death, WSA 3353/2.
6 WSA 2037/27–8; below, pp. 236, 350.

made from the registered copy.[1] In 1697 the almshouse's affairs were exposed to the court of Chancery, and a cause Attorney General *v* Grimston was commenced. From 1698 the trustees were subject to the direction of the court in the management of the almshouse, and from then they and others occasionally petitioned the court for such direction.[2] The subject matter of a petition was usually referred to a master in Chancery for him to consider, the master reported back to the court and usually recommended a course of action, and, having considered the report, the court gave an order to convey its direction in response to the petition. The records of proceedings in Chancery survive in the National Archives in great abundance. To introduce the text printed below the only ones to have been examined are the books in which decrees and orders were entered and the volumes in which the masters' reports have been bound.[3] Editions of three decrees, of 1697, 1698, and 1729, and of two reports, of 1698 and 1700, are printed in the prelude.

In 1698 the court of Chancery ordered the steward to provide a chest with three locks and keys in which to keep the title deeds of the almhouse's estate.[4] The steward also kept the deeds by which the trustees accepted the trust placed in them and held the estate, all the writings generated by the business of the estate,[5] and account and minute books. When one steward succeeded another all the muniments were passed to the new one by the old one or his representative.[6] By 1780 the archive had evidently outgrown the chest and in that year the steward bought a bureau in which to keep it.[7] From 1785 the stewards, John Ward and his successors the Merrimans,[8] kept it at their offices in Marlborough. The descendent firm of solicitors, Messrs. Merriman, Porter & Long, deposited it in the Wiltshire Record Office at Trowbridge, part in 1971 and nearly all the rest in 1985, and in 2007 all the deposited records of the almshouse were moved to the new History Centre at Chippenham.[9] The administrative records among them include the three minute books edited as the main text printed below and the documents of which edited parts appear in the appendix.[10]

1 TNA PROB 11/474, ff. 176–93 (below, pp. 115–21).
2 Above, Attorney General *v* Grimston.
3 For the decrees and orders, TNA C 33; for the reports, C 38.
4 TNA C 33/289, ff. 563v.–564 (below, p. 129).
5 e.g. below, p. 173.
6 e.g. below, pp. 151, 173, 200, 209.
7 WSA 2037/27.
8 Above, officers (steward).
9 WSA depositors' files.
10 All but a few of the almshouse's muniments lie in the accession numbered 2037.

The edited minute books (2037/12–14) cover the periods 1714–75, 1776–1818, and 1818–66. The steward appointed in 1713, finding that the regulations proposed in 1710 required him to register the orders made by the trustees at their meetings, bought the first for 4*s.* from F. Buckeridge on 16 October 1714, and it is unlikely that a minute book was kept before then.[1] Each of the books consists of paper pages fastened between cardboard covers, and two were bound in leather. The first two measure 325 mm. × 210 mm.; their pages have not been numbered. The third measures 355 mm. × 241 mm.; its pages were numbered 1–257, probably after the book had been filled. The minutes which the books contain were written in black ink, except that between 1714 and 1718 some words were highlighted in red ink. In the third book brief marginal notes were made beside the first line of most entries to indicate the subject matter of the entry. The documents of which edited parts appear in the appendix are stewards' accounts and widows' admission papers. Thistlethwaite's accounts, for 1698–1703, were evidently written as a fair copy at a single sitting and probably not until 1708. They appear on 15 sheets of paper sewn together at the head.[2] Later accounts were written up in books. The oldest to survive contains those for 1766–7 and for each year until 1842–3.[3] The second oldest runs from 1843–4 to 1881–2.[4] The edited extracts are for the years 1702–3 (pages 10–11 of Thistlethwaite's accounts), 1770 (Martin's) when the accounts run from January to December, 1815–16 (Ward's) running August to August, and 1860–1 (T. B. Merriman's) running July to July. Those years were chosen to cover the period 1698–1866 roughly evenly, otherwise at random. The accounts for them are broadly typical. The edited admission papers are the first 58 in a series covering the period 1830–74 and run to 1845.[5] There is a set of papers for each widow admitted to the almshouse in that period. Each set contains a printed form, filled in partly by the steward and partly by the nominating trustee, by means of which the porter was ordered to admit the widow to a specified house which was vacant for a given reason. It also contains evidence, usually a copy of an entry made in a parish register, of both the widow's marriage and her husband's death. Occasionally other evidence was introduced.

METHOD OF EDITING

The six documents published here as the prelude are legal documents drafted in the late 17th century and earlier 18th by legal technicians,

1 WSA 2037/8, orders proposed 1710; below, p. 138; cf. above, Attorney General *v* Grimston (1699–1729).

2 WSA 2037/26.

3 Ibid. 2037/27.

4 Ibid. 2037/28.

5 Ibid. 2037/80.

and in each of them the draftsman used words in a way designed to avoid doubt and forestall a potential challenge by an opposing legal technician. For the 21st-century reader the use of words in that way at those times has, if not obscured the meaning of the documents, certainly increased the time needed to uncover it, and many of the words used in the originals have therefore been omitted in the edition here printed. Apart from a few intruded between square brackets, however, the words which remain are, and are in the same order as, those used in the originals. In the duchess of Somerset's will, for example, where her words were 'from that time forwards for ever afterwards the chaplain and his successors for ever shall have and receive out of the rents, issues, and profits of the manors and premises the yearly stipend or salary of £30 a year, to be paid to him by half-yearly payments' they are given as 'for ever afterwards the chaplain and his successors shall have out of the profits of the manors and premises the salary of £30 a year, to be paid to him half-yearly'. An exception is that the words 'the same', referring to what or who has been previously mentioned, have, if not omitted, usually been changed to 'that' or 'those'. In many places the technician drafting the original, presumably to close all loopholes and to cover all eventualities, used two or three words whereas, to a 21st-century layman, one would have been enough. In the edition the one word is used. For example, 'intents and purposes' is given as 'purposes' and 'right and interest' as 'right'. Likewise the draftsman often included both singular and plural and in the edition one has been omitted. For example, 'any child, children, or other person or persons' is given as 'any child or other person'.

In the text of the minute books as printed here the headings are the dates on which the meetings were held. The dates have been taken from the headings in the minute books themselves. In many cases an original heading also names the day of the week on, and the place at, which a meeting was held. In the edition the name of the place has been appended to the heading. The day of the week and other words, recording only that the meetings were those of the trustees of the almshouse, have been omitted. Otherwise the text of the minute books printed below is essentially a transcript. Some otiose words have been omitted, 'the same' has often been changed to 'that' or 'those', and in other small ways the text has been simplified. Although the wording of them has been little changed the entries in the minute books have been classified. Italicized subheadings have been intruded and each item of business at each meeting of the trustees has been placed under the one most appropriate. Items of business therefore appear in the edition in an order very often different from that in which they were recorded in the minute books and, presumably, came before the trustees. The document printed as an annexe to the minutes of the meeting held on 12 August 1829 has been edited by the method followed for the six documents in the prelude.

Among the materials published here as the appendix the list of trustees includes abbreviated titles of books used as authorities; the titles are given in full under the rubric Abbreviations and Notanda. The four examples of annual accounts drawn up by the steward are full transcripts. The information drawn from the admission papers of 1830–45 has been calendered and moderately abbreviated.

Throughout the following edition capitalization, spelling, and punctuation have been modernized. All dates are expressed according to the year of grace as it is now reckoned; quarter days are named as they appear in the original and their dates are given in Abbreviations and Notanda. Sums of money are shown in a standardized form. The spelling of some surnames has been modernized and, when it appears that only one person is in question, a standard form of a forename and of a surname have been adopted. Place names have been given their modern form and spelling: when in the original either is much different from the modern it is noted in italics within round brackets. In the index places in Wiltshire which were less than parishes are identified by the names of the parishes in which they lay; places elsewhere in England, except some major cities, are identified by the names of the counties in which they lay. Square brackets have been used to enclose editorial interpolations to amplify the original text, make its meaning clearer, report that it is deficient, or indicate that it contains a mistake made by the scribe. Marginal notes are also supplied between square brackets.

PRELUDE

EXTRACTS FROM THE WILL OF SARAH, DUCHESS OF SOMERSET, PROVED IN 1704

(TNA PROB 11/474, ff. 176–93)

IN THE NAME OF GOD, AMEN. I Sarah, duchess dowager of Somerset, late wife of the Rt. Noble John, duke of Somerset, deceased, and now the wife of the Rt. Hon. Henry, Lord Coleraine, being in good health of body and of perfect mind, praised be God, yet knowing the certainty of death and the uncertainty of the time thereof, having by my marriage agreement with my now husband, and by conveyances of my estate, reserved to myself a power to dispose of my estate real and personal although under coverture, do this 17 May 1686 make this my last will and testament.

First and principally I recommend my immortal soul into the hands of God, who gave it, assuredly trusting through the meritorious death and passion of Jesus Christ, my blessed saviour and redeemer, to receive full pardon and free remission of all my sins and a glorious resurrection amongst the just. My body I leave to the earth, from whence it came, to be interred in the abbey church at Westminster.

By one indenture tripartite bearing date 14 July 1682 made between me Sarah, duchess dowager of Somerset, of the first part, the Rt. Hon. Henry, Lord Coleraine, Baron of Coleraine in the kingdom of Ireland, of the second part, and the Rt. Hon. Sir Harbottle Grimston, bt., Master of the Rolls, since deceased, and Sir Samuel Grimston of Gorhambury, bt. (by the name of Samuel Grimston, esq., son and heir apparent of Sir Harbottle Grimston), of the third part, and by other conveyances, all the manors, messuages, lands, and hereditaments whereof I was then seised in fee simple are conveyed to Sir Harbottle Grimston and Samuel Grimston and their heirs upon trust that they, and the survivor of them and his heirs, should convey those manors and premises, and the profits thereof, to such persons and to such purposes as I, as well being married and though under coverture as being sole, should by any writing direct.

By one indenture quinquepartite bearing date 14 July 1682 made between me Sarah, duchess dowager of Somerset, of the first part, Henry, Lord Coleraine, of the second part, Sir Harbottle Grimston of the third part, Sir William Gregory, kt., then one of the barons of His Majesty's Court of Exchequer, of the fourth part, and Samuel

Grimston of the fifth part, several manors, messuages, lands, tenements, and hereditaments, lying as well in England as in Ireland, were granted to Sir Harbottle Grimston and Samuel Grimston [and] their executors and administrators for 99 years if I shall so long live. Terms of years, in the nature of mortgages of other manors, messuages, lands, tenements, and hereditaments, were thereby assigned to Sir Harbottle Grimston and Sir William Gregory [and] their executors and administrators. Pieces of plate, jewels, medals, and other things, mentioned in a schedule, all the ready money, debts and securities for money, plate, goods, cattle, chattels, household stuff, and all other the personal estate of me the duchess of Somerset were by that indenture granted to Sir Harbottle Grimston, Sir William Gregory, and Samuel Grimston, [and] their executors and administrators. [All] upon trust that Sir Harbottle Grimston, Sir William Gregory, and Samuel Grimston, and the survivors and survivor of them, [and] his [the survivor's] executors and administrators, should convey the manors, messuages, farms, lands, tenements, and hereditaments, the profits thereof, the advantage to be made of the manors and premises and the profits thereof, all the mortgages and securities for money and all the money thereupon due, all lands, tenements, and hereditaments to be purchased with, and all interest of, such money, and the jewels, plate, goods, chattels, money, and personal estate and the whole benefit to be had out of it, to such persons and to such purposes as I, as well being married and although under coverture as being sole, should by any writing direct.

Now I Sarah, duchess dowager of Somerset, taking advantage of the powers to me given in the indentures, and by virtue of those and all other powers in me vested, do by this my writing direct that my surviving trustees, Sir Samuel Grimston and Sir William Gregory, and their heirs, executors, and administrators, shall convey the manors, messuages, farms, lands, tenements, hereditaments, money, jewels, plate, household stuff, mortgages, debts, goods, and other estate real and personal, and the proceed thereof, to them conveyed, to the persons, for such purposes, and in such manner as I do in this my will, or in any codicil annexed to my will, give them to.

First I will that [for] my funeral expenses and the charge of erecting a tomb for me my executors shall lay out £800. I order that there shall not above £300 be expended in my funeral and that, if my funeral expenses shall not amount to £300, then what shall remain shall be added to the £500 and laid out on my tomb.

I give to the Rt. Hon. Henry, Lord Delamere, Sir Samuel Grimston, and Sir William Gregory £1,700 to be by them, the survivors and survivor of them, [and] his [the survivor's] executors and administrators, within 2 years after my decease laid out in the building and finishing of an almshouse for 30 poor widows to inhabit in. My will is that the almshouse shall be built in my manor of Froxfield near the village and church there on part of the 2 acres of land that I reserved to myself out of a lease I lately granted to Edward Savage of Wolfhall in the parish of Great Bedwyn. I devise the 2 acres to Henry, Lord Delamere, Sir Samuel Grimston, and Sir William Gregory, and their heirs, to be by them employed as the site of the almshouse and for none other purpose.

I will that the almshouse shall be built in the form of a quadrangle with a square court in the middle of it, that there shall be built a chapel in or near the middle of the court, and that the almshouse and chapel shall be built of brick. In the whole building there shall be 30 ground rooms and 30 chambers over them, with a chimney or hearth in every of the rooms and chambers but [with] neither cellars nor garrets, so every of the 30 poor widows shall have to herself one ground room and one chamber over it. I will that my executors shall lay out £200 for tables, bedsteads, and suchlike durable furniture for the rooms and chambers, for the making of plain seats in the chapel, and [for the] buying of things necessary and fit for the chapel, [such] as bibles for the minister and widows, and cushions and such other goods as are necessary for the furnishing of the chapel. Goods that shall be so bought for the chapel and for the widows' rooms shall there continue so long as they shall last.

Provided, and my will is, that, if I shall in my lifetime build the almshouse myself and fully finish it, then the gifts of £1,700 and £200 shall be void. If it shall happen that I shall in my lifetime begin the buildings and not live to finish them, then I will that my executors shall lay out on the building so much as shall suffice to finish it according to the design I have laid for it and no more.

My will is that, so soon as the almshouse shall be built and made fit to be inhabited, they Henry, Lord Delamere, Sir Samuel Grimston, and Sir William Gregory, the survivors and survivor of them, and his [the survivor's] heirs, shall make choice of, and place therein, 30 poor widows that are poor but honest and lead a good life. I will that 25 of the widows shall, before that time, be living in Wiltshire or in Somerset and Berkshire, that 10 of that 25 shall be ministers' widows if so many such poor widows shall be found living in the three counties, and that at least another 10 of that 25 shall be chosen out of my manors in Wiltshire if there shall be so many poor widows there. The other 5 of the 30 poor widows shall be ministers' widows living in or near the cities of London and Westminster. I will that the same rule, proportions, and qualifications shall be observed in all elections that shall be made of widows to fill up any vacancies that shall happen, so there shall be always in the almshouse 10 ministers' widows and 15 other widows that, before they were chosen into the almshouse, were inhabiting in

Wiltshire, Somerset, and Berkshire and 5 ministers' widows that were, before their election into the almshouse, residing in or about the cities of London and Westminster.

I declare my will to be that no widow that has lands or tenements of inheritance of the yearly value of £20 shall be elected into any room in the almshouse or receive any of the allowances given for the maintenance of the poor widows in the almshouse. I direct that each of the widows shall have an equal share of the maintenance made for them, but I will that they shall hold the rooms and maintenance during their widowhoods only and no longer. When any of the widows shall die or marry, Henry, Lord Delamere, Sir Samuel Grimston, and Sir William Gregory, the survivors and survivor of them, and his [the survivor's] heirs, shall choose other widows to inhabit in the almshouse during their widowhoods and to receive their shares of maintenance.

For the maintenance of the poor widows in the almshouse I give, and direct that Sir Samuel Grimston and his heirs shall settle in such manner as Henry, Lord Delamere, and Sir William Gregory, and the survivor of them and his heirs, shall think necessary [so] that they may be a perpetual maintenance for the widows, my messuage and farm of Milton and Fyfield which I purchased of Thomas Kellway, gentleman; which farm is now in lease for several years yet to come at the yearly rent of £150 or thereabouts. [I give] also my manors of Froxfield, [and] Huish and Shaw, and all my farms, lands, tenements, and hereditaments within those manors; which manors, when the present leases and estates therein shall determine, I hope will prove a considerable endowment for the almshouse. By the account I receive from my bailiffs and other officers the manors and farms of Froxfield, [and] Huish and Shaw, will, when the leases and estates now in being shall determine, be worth £640 a year or thereabouts.

For advancing the endowment of the almshouse in yearly value, and for raising more certain and constant maintenance for the poor widows, I will that, when the leases now in being of any of the farms in the manors of Froxfield, [and] Huish and Shaw, shall determine, the farms shall not be again leased for life. Nor shall any fine be taken for renewing [any], or making any new, lease of the farms, but, when the present leases shall determine, my will is that the farms shall be leased for no longer than 21 years and at the greatest improved yearly rents that can be gotten for them. The two leasehold farms in Froxfield, as I am informed by my officers, [will be] worth when it falls [*?rectius* they fall] in hand £120 a year; one of the leasehold farms in my manor of Huish will, when it falls in hand, be worth £100 a year and the other about £40 a year.

I will that Henry, Lord Delamere, Sir Samuel Grimston, and Sir William Gregory, the survivors and survivor of them, and his [the survivor's] heirs, shall take care that neither they, nor any other person who shall have power to grant any new leases, shall have power to grant any lease of the farms and lands which are now held by lease for lives, or years determinable on lives, other than for the best improved rent that can be gotten for them, without the payment of any fine and not for longer than 21 years in possession to commence from the making of such lease. Upon the granting of any estate of any [of] the copyhold messuages, lands, tenements, or hereditaments there shall not be any made for more than three lives, and [even] that in possession only and not in reversion. There shall not be taken any fine more than one third of the improved value of the copyhold tenement, and two thirds of the improved yearly value shall be reserved in rent and made payable half-yearly for it to be employed for the maintenance of the poor widows in the almshouse. Their maintenance shall be augmented as the rents of the manors and premises shall increase upon the determination of the leases and estates now in being and the granting of new leases and estates according to the direction aforesaid. In every lease to be made of the manors and premises the tenant shall be bound to pay all taxes and to keep the messuages and buildings in good repair.

My will is that the money that shall be raised by fines taken upon making new grants by copy shall be applied, in the first place, for buying a cloth gown for each of the poor widows yearly about Christmas, all the gowns to be made of the same sort of cloth and of the same colour and fashion [as each other]; none of the gowns shall exceed the price of 26*s.* 8*d.* In the next place [the money shall be applied] for the reparation of the almshouse, or rebuilding it if there shall be occasion. The residue, if any, shall be equally shared among the widows at such time as my trustees, or the survivors or survivor of them, and his [the survivor's] heirs, shall think fit. Until the fines shall amount to so much as shall pay for the gowns yearly, and make good the reparations, those things shall be done out of the profits of the premises before the making of any dividend to the widows.

Provided, and I will, that the minister or curate of Froxfield shall have out of the profits of the manors and premises, before any dividend shall be made among the poor widows, the salary of £10 a year for reading prayers daily with the widows and visiting such of them as shall happen to be sick, to be paid to him half-yearly until the income of the almshouse shall amount clearly to £300 a year. After the revenues shall amount to £300 a year or more I will that Henry, Lord Delamere, Sir Samuel Grimston, and Sir William Gregory, the survivors and survivor of them, his [the survivor's] heirs, and such others as they shall appoint to be governors of the almshouse, shall choose a chaplain for the almshouse to read prayers daily with the widows, preach to them once every Sunday, and visit them when they are sick. Thenceforth the payment of £10 a year to the minister or curate shall cease, and for ever afterwards the chaplain and his successors shall have out of the profits of the manors and premises the salary of £30 a year, to be paid to him half-yearly.

The residue of the profits [are] to be employed for, and shared equally among, the poor widows in manner and form aforesaid. But my will is that, when the rents of the manors and farms shall amount to more than £400 a year, all the overplus of rents and fines above £400 a year shall be applied for the adding to the almshouse [of] lodgings for 20 poor widows more, each widow to have one ground room and one chamber over it, who shall be placed therein so soon as they shall be built. And then the £400 a year, and all further increase of rents, shall be equally divided, after the salary of the chaplain shall be paid, among all the 50 widows.

I will that, of the 20 poor widows that shall be chosen to inhabit in the additional lodgings, 5 shall dwell in or about the cities of London and Westminster and the other 15 shall be chosen out of any part of England that is not above 150 miles from London, excepting Wiltshire, Somerset, and Berkshire, I having made provision for the widows of those three counties in the establishment of the first 30 widows in the almshouse. I will that 5 of the 20 shall be ministers' widows, and that the 20 shall be chosen in the same manner, and have the same qualifications, as the other 30 poor widows; save only in what relates to their place of habitation, in which particular this my last direction is to be observed. When the 20 widows shall be placed in the almshouse they shall have the gowns and equal shares of the revenues of the almshouse with the other widows without any distinction.

I will that all the rents of the manors, farms, lands, and tenements which I have given for the maintenance of the poor widows, and the money that shall be raised by fines for any copyhold estates in the manors, which I appoint shall not be taken but according to the rate and rule by me given, that shall become payable between my death and the finishing of the almshouse shall be kept in stock for the widows and not paid to them but as is hereinafter directed. I give £500 out of my personal estate to be added to the stock. The money that shall be raised by rents and fines, and the £500, shall be divided into 10 equal parts and one of the parts shall be equally distributed among the 30 widows in every year of the first 10 after the finishing of the almshouse as an increase of their maintenance; during which time they will need some addition to their revenue more than they will afterwards, it being probable that in 10 years the revenues of the almshouse will be increased by the falling [in] of estates in the manors given for the endowment.

My will is that Henry, Lord Delamere, Sir Samuel Grimston, and Sir William Gregory, the survivors and survivor of them, and his [the survivor's] heirs, shall be allowed all their necessary expenses in the execution of the trusts in them reposed. [They] shall also be allowed out of the profits of the premises all salaries and allowances as they shall pay or allow to stewards, bailiffs, receivers, and other officers to be employed about the premises.

I appoint Henry, Lord Delamere, Sir Samuel Grimston, and Sir William Gregory executors of this my last will and testament.

Codicil 10 February 1692

I will that my trustee Sir Samuel Grimston and his heirs shall convey, in such manner as Henry, earl of Warrington, and Sir William Gregory, and the survivor of them and his heirs, shall think necessary, the advowson of the church of Huish to such persons as Henry, earl of Warrington, and Sir William Gregory, and the survivor of them and his heirs, shall nominate. To the purpose that the person who shall be chaplain to the almshouse at Froxfield, if he be fit and capable, shall be presented to the church of Huish when the church shall become void next after my decease. Thenceforth all salaries provided in my will for the chaplain shall cease. My will is that the incumbent of the church and his successors shall be chaplain of the almshouse and shall by himself, or some sufficient curate to be approved by Henry, earl of Warrington, and Sir William Gregory, and the survivor of them and his heirs, discharge the duty of the chaplain as in my will is directed, without receiving any reward for that out of the revenues of the almshouse. I direct Henry, earl of Warrington, and Sir William Gregory, and their heirs, to make the best provision they can for the chaplain's due performance of his duty, but, if that cannot be secured by law, I will that the provision made in my will for the chaplain's maintenance shall stand.

I appoint the manor and farm of Chirton (*Cherrington* alias *Chirton*) for the better support of the poor widows in the almshouse. I direct that the manor and farm shall be settled on the almshouse as I have appointed the other maintenance of the widows to be settled. My will is that the profits of the lands that shall be made between the time of my death and the finishing of the almshouse shall be kept in stock for the widows and paid to them as the other fines and rents are to be paid.

To the end that the almshouse and chapel at Froxfield may be more firmly built and finished, I give £500 more to be laid out by my executors in the building and finishing besides the money that I have given in my will. I give £100 more to be laid out by my executors for the better furnishing of the chapel when it shall be built and for the better furnishing of the 30 poor widows' lodgings in the almshouse.

DECREE OF THE HIGH COURT OF CHANCERY, 21 DECEMBER 1697
(TNA C 33/289, ff. 250–2)

Between the king's Attorney General on behalf of Mary Farewell, Elizabeth Abbot, Jane Elks, Jane Stephens, Mary Randall, Olive Nevill, Frances Buckeridge, Anne Dewy, Isabel Hill, Hester Andrews, Alice Davidge, Dorothy Eastmond, Jane Whale, Agnes Avery, Sarah Mitchell, Grace Bryant, Elizabeth Shadwell, Alice Gibbons, Elizabeth Sims, Jane Walter, Amice Harding, Rachel Stuckey, Anne Gardiner, Elizabeth Roberts, Susannah Cherry, Mary Withers, Grace Franklin, Christian Coventry, and Joan Randall, the poor inhabitants of the hospital in Froxfield, plaintiffs, [and] Samuel Grimston, bt., Elizabeth Gregory, a widow, [and] William Gregory, esq., the heir of William Gregory, kt., deceased, defendants, this cause coming this day to be debated before the Rt. Hon. the Lord High Chancellor of England in the presence of counsel learned on both sides.

The substance of the plaintiffs' bill appeared to be that Sarah, late duchess of Somerset, … *the plaintiffs epitomized the clauses of the duchess's will in which the two deeds of 14 July 1682 are themselves epitomized, the clauses of the will in which the duchess directed how the almshouse was to be built, endowed, filled, and enlarged and how the endowment was to be managed and employed, and the clauses of the codicil relating to the endowment.* Soon after executing the writing the duchess died, Sir Harbottle Grimston being then dead. The earl of Warrington soon after dying, Sir Samuel Grimston refused the trust. Sir William Gregory took upon him[self] the execution thereof, caused the almshouse and chapel to be built, placed therein 30 poor widows who are qualified according to the duchess's will, did appoint a bailiff to receive the profits of the manors and premises appointed by the duchess for the maintenance of the widows, caused a draft of a settlement to be drawn for Sir Samuel to convey the manors and premises charged with the charity to persons, fitly qualified and living near the almshouses, as governors and trustees, and sent such draft to Sir Samuel to execute. Before it was executed Sir William died, leaving William Gregory his grandson and heir and, having made his will, Elizabeth Gregory his executrix, who has proved his will. Sir William Gregory being the surviving trustee to whom several terms of years in the nature of mortgages were transferred by a quinquepartite deed the same came to Elizabeth Gregory, his executrix. All other the personal estate of the duchess by that indenture came to Sir Samuel Grimston by survivorship, and he is the sole surviving executor of the duchess and trustee of the manor[s] and premises appointed for the maintenance of the widows and has the sole estate in law in them, but Sir Samuel refuses to execute a settlement of the charity according to the direction in the will and codicil or anyways to act in the trusts. The other defendants also refuse to act in the trust and Elizabeth Gregory, who has in her hands sums of money received by Sir William Gregory, her late husband [*rectius* father-in-law], belonging to the charity, refuses to pay them for the support of the widows who, for want thereof, are reduced to great necessity. That Sir Samuel Grimston may either take upon him[self] the execution of the trust or convey the manors and premises charged with the trust to some other persons to be appointed by this court, and that, until a settlement can be made, Sir Samuel may give authority to some persons to manage the trust and to receive the profits of the manors and premises, and the arrears thereof, and pay them to the widows for their support and maintenance and to be relieved in the premises, is the scope of the plaintiffs' bill.

Whereunto it was insisted by Sir Samuel Grimston's counsel that the defendant believes that Sarah, late duchess of Somerset, did execute such indenture[s] and make such will and codicil as in the bill is set forth, and that he is named one of the executors. The defendant did not think fit to undertake the trust and believes [that] Sir William Gregory took upon him[self] the execution thereof. [He] says that, in case the real and personal estate be vested in him by survivorship, he, being still unwilling to undertake the trust, does submit to the court to nominate fit persons for trustees. [He] is willing to transfer all his right in the real and personal estate as this court shall direct, being saved harmless, [being] discharged from all accounts and troubles, and being paid his costs.

The defendants Elizabeth Gregory and William Gregory also believe that the late duchess did execute such indentures and made such will and codicil for the founding [of] such hospital as in the bill is set forth, and that Sir William Gregory did act in the trust, cause an almshouse and chapel to be built, and placed therein 30 poor widows qualified according to the will. Elizabeth confesses that she finds by Sir William's accounts that he had received of the profits of the manors and farms given by the duchess for the maintenance of the almshouse, at [*i.e.* up to] the time the women were placed there, £404 0*s.* 3*d.* [She] says that from that time to the time of his [Sir William's] death one William Bailey received the profits, who ought to have paid them for the support of the widows. [She] says that Sir William died in May 1696, that she is his executrix and has proved his will, that the indentures, and will and codicil, are in her power, and that she is ready to produce them. [She] confesses that she has in money and bills that £404 0*s.* 3*d.*, and that she has of the duchess, [of] her personal estate unadministered by her testator, the further sum of £962 16*s.* 10*d.*; both which sums she is ready to account for, and pay over, to such persons as this court shall direct. [She] confesses that she has in her power several other deeds and writings relating to the charity which she is willing to deliver as this court shall direct. William Gregory says that he is lately come of age and has not intermeddled with the trust. Both the Gregorys are willing to do what in them lies for the settling of the charity according to the intentions of the duchess.

Whereupon, and upon long debate and hearing what was alleged by the counsel for all the parties, his lordship does think fit, and so orders, that Sir Samuel Grimston do attend Sir Richard Holford to declare whether he will accept of the trusts or not. Sir Samuel is forthwith to give authority to some person to be approved of by the master to receive the profits of the charity lands and the arrears unreceived by the former receiver, [all of] which is forthwith to be applied towards the relief of the poor widows according to the will of the duchess. Such person is first to give security, to be approved of by the master, to account yearly for the profits he shall from time to time receive. The authority to be given by Sir Samuel is not to be taken as any acceptance of the trust or to make him anyways liable for what shall be received under such authority, but is only to be given for the better carrying on of the charity until the matter in relation to the trustees shall be settled.

It is ordered that the Gregorys account before the master for the profits of the charity lands and of all other money belonging to the charity which has come to their hands or to the hands of Sir William Gregory or of any of their agents by their authority. The master is to state how much was received from the decease of the duchess to the finishing [of] the hospital but, in taking the account, is to make to the defendant[s] all just allowances.

The cost of this suit is to be taxed by the master and be paid out of the profits raised between the duchess's death and the finishing of the almshouse [and] remaining in Elizabeth Gregory's hands. It is ordered that the will of the duchess, as also the several deeds and writings relating to the charity lands, which are in the custody or power of the defendants, be produced before, and left with, the master. All deeds and writings relating to the premises which have been formerly brought before, and are now remaining with, any other master are to be transmitted to Sir Richard Holford, who is to look into the will and deeds and to state to this court the several questions which he shall find to arise. The master is to certify what number of persons are proper, and who are fitting, to be appointed trustees, who is the present steward, and who is fit to be the steward and receiver. The master is to prepare conveyances to be ready to be executed for the charity when the trustees shall be settled. After the master's report the plaintiffs are at liberty to apply to this court, whereupon such further directions shall be given as shall be just.

REPORT OF SIR RICHARD HOLFORD, 1 JUNE 1698
(TNA C 38/260)

Between the king's Attorney General on behalf of Mary Farewell and others, the poor inhabitants of the hospital in Froxfield, plaintiffs, [and] Samuel Grimston, bt., Elizabeth Gregory, a widow, and William Gregory, esq., the heir of William Gregory, kt., deceased, defendants.

In pursuance of an order of 21 December last I have, in presence of the plaintiffs' counsel and clerk in court, of Sir Samuel Grimston's agent and solicitor, and of the clerk in court and solicitor for Elizabeth Gregory and William Gregory, esq., considered of the matters to me referred.

Sir Samuel Grimston has declared that he does not accept the trust. According to the directions of the order I have approved an authority, which Sir Samuel has executed, empowering Alexander Thistlethwaite, gentleman, to receive the profits of the lands of the charity and the arrears unreceived by the former receiver. Mr. Thistlethwaite has given security before me to account yearly for the profits as shall be received by him, as by my former report dated 22 February last.

I have taken the account of Elizabeth Gregory, executrix of Sir William Gregory, who has annexed to her answer to the plaintiffs' bill a schedule of the rents of the manors and farms, given by Sarah, late duchess of Somerset, for the maintenance of the almshouse, from the time of the duchess's death; to which account the plaintiffs submit. I have annexed a true copy thereof to this my report. It appears that Sir William Gregory had in his hands at the time of his decease, in May 1696, £404 0*s.* 3*d.* received out of the profits of the estate from the decease of the duchess to the finishing of the hospital. I find by the defendant's answer that Sir William Gregory received £962 16*s.* 10*d.* out of the personal estate of the duchess, £500 whereof was by the will of the duchess to be kept as a stock for the 30 poor widows to be placed in the hospital, be added to what should be left of the profits of the estate from her death to the finishing [of] the hospital, and be divided into 10 equal parts. One of the 10 parts should be distributed between the 30 widows by equal shares in every of the first 10 years after the finishing [of] the hospital as an increase of their maintenance. I find that the hospital was finished in June 1695, and from that time Sir William Gregory empowered Mr. William Bailey to receive the profits of the estate, who has not yet accounted for them but is now prosecuted for his account.

As to the deeds belonging to the hospital and the several manors and lands given for the support thereof, [Elizabeth] Gregory has left with me the deeds mentioned in the second schedule to this my report annexed. She does insist that it may be very inconvenient to part with the original will and codicil of the duchess in regard [that] there are several other charities thereby given by the duchess which are not yet settled. The will and codicil being proved by witnesses in this court, for the preservation thereof she prays to have the custody of the original will and codicil until those charities are settled; she submitting in the meantime to produce them when required.

I have considered of fit persons to be trustees for the hospital and conceive that nine will be sufficient. Upon consideration and advice I name Alexander Popham of Littlecote, esq., Edward Seymour of Easton, esq., Francis Stonehouse of Great Bedwyn, esq., Francis Goddard of Standen, esq., Lovelace Bigg of Chilton Foliat, esq., Samuel Whitelock of Chilton Lodge, esq., Thomas Fettiplace of Fernham, esq., John Hippisley of Lambourn, esq., and John Blandy of Inglewood, esq., all of them near neighbours to the hospital. Five of them [shall] be a quorum. I have, according to the direction of the order, approved a conveyance to be executed by Sir Samuel Grimston and William Gregory, esq., to the trustees, have signed my allowance thereon, and do appoint Sir Samuel Grimston and William Gregory, esq., to execute it.

I have considered the several bills of costs produced before me. The plaintiffs' bill amounting to £155 4*s.* 2*d.* I have thought fit to tax at £139, to be paid to Mr. Turner, the plaintiffs' clerk in court, by Mrs. Gregory. Sir Samuel Grimston's bill amounting to £17 12*s.* 8*d.* I tax at £13 12*s.*, to be paid to Mr. William Lewis, solicitor to Sir Samuel, for the use of Sir Samuel. The bill for Mrs. Gregory and Mr. William Gregory amounting to £35 0*s.* 9*d.* I have taxed at £30 19*s.* 6*d.*, to be paid to Mr. John Rogers, their solicitor, for their use. Which three sums for costs of this suit, amounting to £183 11*s.* 6*d.*, being deducted out of the £404 0*s.* 3*d.* there will remain of that sum in the hands of Mrs. Gregory £220 8*s.* 9*d.*

Whereto the £500 being added will make £720 8*s.* 9*d.*, [which is] to be by her paid to Mr. Thistlethwaite for a stock according to the will. Being divided into 10 equal parts each part is £72 0*s.* 10½*d.*, [which is] to be distributed from the time of finishing the hospital for 10 years according to the will, of which 10 years 3 years will expire this instant June. So many of the widows as are living are to receive their 3 years' share, being to each £7 4*s.* 0¾*d.* For such as are dead their shares [are] to be brought to account by Mr. Thistlethwaite. The residue of the £720 8*s.* 9*d.* [after 3 years' payments], amounting to £504 6*s.* 3*d.*, I conceive ought to be placed on security at interest for the benefit of the widows, and the interest and one 10th of the principal [is] to be paid yearly to them for their better support according to the will.

After the £500 is taken out of the £962 16*s*. 10*d*. there will be £462 16*s*. 10*d*. remaining in Mrs. Gregory's hands.

I find that Warner South of Gray's Inn, esq., was employed by the duchess as her steward, was continued [as] steward by Mr. Justice [*i.e.* Sir William] Gregory during his life, and prays to be so continued, but those who prosecute for the charity insist that for the future there will be no occasion for any other steward than the receiver of the rents; wherein I do pray the determination of the court.

All which I submit to the judgement of this court.

[*Signed*] Richard Holford.

The first schedule to my report, being a schedule, annexed to Elizabeth Gregory's answer to the information of the Attorney General, containing an account of the rents of the manors and farms given by the duchess of Somerset for the maintenance of the almshouse at Froxfield from the time of her death.

[Income due from] the manor of Huish and Shaw £12 4*s*. 2*d*. a year, the manor of Froxfield £9 7*s*. 7*d*., Chirton farm £100, Milton farm £110; £231 11*s*. 9*d*.

Whereof received of Col. Hungerford in part of the rent for the farm of Milton, by a bill payable to the earl of Warrington, £55; out of the manors of Huish and Shaw, and Froxfield, William Bailey, the receiver, deducted for the bailiff's wages £1 and towards his own salary £5, and then paid to me out of those rents £15 11*s*. 9*d*.; £70 11*s*. 9*d*.

15 June 1695. An account made up with Mr. Bailey, receiver of the manors and [of the] farm of Chirton. The rents of the manor of Huish and Shaw £12 8*s*. 4*d*., arrears of rents out of it 6*s*. 8*d*., the rents of the manor of Froxfield £9 7*s*. 5*d*., 2 years' rent for the farm of Chirton £200, [total] £222 2*s*. 5*d*. Out of which rent Mr. Bailey deducts for bailiff's wages £1 and towards his own salary as receiver of the rents belonging to the almshouse £6, for attending commissioners about king's tax several times and for letters 3*s*. 2*d*., for expenses [of] two courts 8*s*., for 2 years' taxes and repairs out of the farm of Chirton £26 4*s*. 2*d*., for a quarter's tax for the coppice wood in Froxfield 9*s*., for 3½ years' chief rent out of Chirton farm £16 16*s*. 7*d*., for looking after the coppice wood and hanging a gate £1 18*s*., and for arrears of rent out of the manor of Huish 4*s*. [He] paid to me out of those rents £168 19*s*. 6*d*.

18 June 1695. Received of Col. Hungerford in part of the rent for the farm of Milton, by bill from Sir Francis Child, £100.

27 July 1695. Received then of Col. Hungerford in full for the rent for the farm of Milton, ending at Lady day last past, £65.

The second schedule to my report, being a schedule of the deeds, delivered by Mrs. Elizabeth Gregory, a widow, executrix of Sir William Gregory, kt., deceased, to me by virtue of an order of the court 2 March 1698, belonging to the manors and farms given by the Rt. Noble Sarah, late duchess dowager of Somerset, deceased, by her will for the endowment of an almshouse at Froxfield, which she appointed to be, and is since, built there.

There follows a list of 18 deeds relating to Chirton and 10 relating to Huish and Shaw and to Milton and Fyfield.

DECREE OF THE HIGH COURT OF CHANCERY, 3 JUNE 1698

(TNA C 33/289, ff. 563v.–564)

Between ... *the parties are named as they were in the preamble to the decree of 21 December 1697.*

Whereas this cause received a hearing before the Rt. Hon. the Lord High Chancellor 21 December last in the presence of counsel learned for all the parties, at which hearing his lordship did order ... *the orders made on that day, after the long debate, are epitomized.*

The master, having been attended by all the parties' counsel and agents, made his report bearing date 1 June instant and thereby certified that ... *the findings of Sir Richard Holford, as recorded in his report, but not the schedules attached to the report, are epitomized.*

This cause coming to be heard this day upon the master's report and before his lordship in the presence of counsel for all the parties, and upon reading the report, debate, and hearing what was insisted on by the counsel on both sides, his lordship does think fit and so order[s] that Sir Richard Holford's report do stand absolutely ratified and confirmed to be observed by all parties according to the true intent thereof.

[It is ordered] that £139 costs taxed for the plaintiffs be forthwith paid by Mrs. Gregory, out of the £404 0*s.* 3*d.* in her hands, to Mr. John Turner, the plaintiffs' clerk in court. Sir Samuel Grimston do forthwith execute the conveyance allowed by the master, on Mrs. Gregory's payment of the £13 12*s.* costs to Mr. William Lewis, his solicitor, for his use. William Gregory do execute the same conveyance, on payment of £30 19*s.* 6*d.* costs taxed for him and Mrs. Gregory to Mr. John Rogers, their solicitor, for their use. Thereupon Sir Samuel and Mr. Gregory are to be discharged of the trust, and indemnified, by this decree.

It is ordered that the conveyance to the nine trustees be confirmed and that they execute the trust. Any five of the trustees shall be a quorum to act in the trust, to make new elections of poor widows when there shall be vacancies [and] according to the direction of the will of the duchess and [to] powers in the conveyance, to make contracts and leases, to elect officers and appoint salaries, and to make proper orders for the better governing [of] the hospital, [all] as they or any five of them shall think fit subject to the directions of this court.

It is ordered that Mr. Alexander Thistlethwaite be confirmed receiver of the rents of the hospital and paymaster. Mrs. Gregory do forthwith pay to Mr. Thistlethwaite the £220 8*s.* 9*d.* remaining in her hands after the costs of this suit are paid, and do also pay to him the £500 for a stock for the poor widows. Upon such payment Mrs. Gregory is indemnified and discharged by this decree. That Mr. Thistlethwaite do out of the £220 8*s.* 9*d.* pay the several sums to the poor widows as are living, according to the directions of the master's report. [The shares of] such widows as are dead [are] to be applied to the increase of the charity. The £500 shall forthwith be placed out at interest on good security to be allowed by the master. The interest that shall be made thereof, together with the 10th parts of the £500 principal, shall be paid to Mr. Thistlethwaite and, [with] what shall be left of the £220 8*s.* 9*d.* in Mr. Thistlethwaite's hands, shall every Midsummer day during the 7 years to come of the 10 years be equally divided and distributed by Mr. Thistlethwaite to the widows according to the method as the master has divided them.

It is ordered that all the deeds mentioned in the schedule to the master's report shall be delivered by the master to Mr. Thistlethwaite, who is to provide a chest with three locks and keys, to be kept as the trustees shall appoint. As to the original will and codicil of the duchess, it is ordered that Mrs. Gregory do forthwith bring them into this court, there to remain for the benefit of all parties concerned to have resort thereto but not to be delivered out without the direction of this court. As to the original deeds of trust made of the charity, and [of] all other the duchess's charities, that now remain either in the hands of the defendants or in the custody of any of the masters of this court, [and] that concern the hospital of Froxfield with other lands, it is ordered that all such deeds be brought before, and left with, Sir Richard Holford to be by him sorted and scheduled. Copies of such schedules are to be delivered to such persons that desire them and, if there be occasion for any of those deeds to be made use of at any trial at law or otherwise, the parties that desire them are to be at liberty to apply to this court for them.

It is ordered that Mr. William Bailey, the former receiver, do attend the master and account upon oath for all that he has received of the profits of the charity land and how he has disposed thereof, in taking which account the master is to make him all just allowances. What the master shall certify to remain in his hands he is to pay to Mr.

Thistlethwaite, whose acquittance shall be a discharge to Mr. Bailey for it. Mr. Thistlethwaite is to be accountable to the trustees for all he shall receive and do about the premises.

It is ordered that Warner South, esq., the former steward of the courts of the manors belonging to the hospital, be continued steward of those courts.

What further costs shall be expended in this suit, or by any future suits, are to be paid out of the profits of the charity lands.

REPORT OF SIR RICHARD HOLFORD, 1 DECEMBER 1700
(TNA C 38/267)

Between ... *the parties are named as they were in the preamble to the decree of 21 December 1697.*

Pursuant to the order made in this cause 23 December last, whereby I am to state what orders have been made by the trustees for the governing [of] the hospital since the decree and how the widows have behaved themselves, the orders and the affidavits [were] to be produced before me, the trustees [were] to propose what orders are fit to be made, and I [was] to state the same. I have been attended by counsel on behalf of the trustees and by counsel on behalf of the poor widows. The trustees' agent has produced to me the orders made by the trustees for the better government of the almshouse and poor widows, a copy of which I have hereunto annexed. There have not been any other orders proposed to me save that their agent lately left with me a paper, seeming to be proposed by the trustees but not subscribed by anybody, a copy of which I have also annexed.

Mr. John Snead, clerk, made affidavit 10 June 1699 that he saw Mrs. Susannah Cherry, one of the widows, pull down the orders made by the trustees and carry them out of the chapel, speak despitefully of the trustees and the officers, and declare [that] she valued them not. He has heard Susannah Cherry both then and at other times abuse the trustees and officers and despise their authority. She and Elizabeth Abbot have acted contrary to the orders, and Susannah Cherry declared that she would do the same in spite of the trustees, or words to that effect.

Edward Plott made affidavit 15 June 1699 that he was present when the trustees took notice of Mrs. Cherry's misbehaviour and admonished her. Instead of submitting to their correction she declared, in the presence of the trustees, that she was put into the hospital for her life and that she did not fear what they could do to her, or [words] to that effect. She has declared the same several times since.

Charles Milsom made affidavit 2 June 1699 that he, being employed by the trustees as porter to the hospital to take care of the gates and look after the chapel, and being ordered by the trustees to lock the gates at 9 o'clock at night, entrusted his son (in his absence) to look to and lock the gates. [He] was informed by his son that Elizabeth Abbot, one of the widows, assisted by others, had taken away the keys from his son and that she and Susannah Cherry had refused to deliver him the keys, saying [that] they would not have the gates locked by him or any other person that the trustees should appoint. Susannah Cherry did then declare that she did not value what the trustees could do for that she had as much right to her place in the house for her life as they had to their estates.

Joseph Burton made affidavit 9 April 1700 that Susannah Cherry, when desired from Mr. Thistlethwaite to live civilly according to the orders, did speak very despitefully of the orders and very much slighted the trustees, especially Francis Stonehouse, esq., declaring that she valued the orders no more than any orders [that] this deponent should make, [that she] would take no more notice of them, and that they were fit for nothing but to wipe her breech or her shoes, or words to that effect.

Mr. Alexander Thistlethwaite made affidavit 24 June 1700 (since this order of reference) and sets forth the continued disrespectful behaviour of Susannah Cherry towards the trustees and their orders. [He says] that he has done nothing but by the order of the trustees and that the trustees have been discouraged by the ill-behaviour of Susannah Cherry and others, or to that effect. Elizabeth Abbot and Hester Andrews, upon their submission to the trustees, had been paid their allowances equal to the other widows'.

On the other side, Susannah Cherry made two affidavits, 20 December 1699 and 15 June 1700, that there was £14 due to her and that she had not received one penny thereof. Mr. Thistlethwaite had made stoppage of several sums and was angry with her for opposing him, and by reason of her poverty she was not able to make her defence. She had submitted to, and begged pardon of, several of the trustees, she never abused nor despised the orders, and [she] blames Mr. Thistlethwaite for his unkindness towards her.

Hester Andrews, another of the widows, made affidavit 29 April 1700 that there was at least £7 due to her, that Mr. Thistlethwaite refused to pay it, that she is in extreme poverty, that for above 3 months she has conformed to the orders, and that she believes [that] Mr. Thistlethwaite is not her friend and has occasioned the stop of her allowance.

John Farlow made an affidavit against Mr. John Snead, the chaplain to the hospital, whose affidavit is above mentioned, that Mr. Snead has been very unkind to the widows.

[All] which is the substance of what has been offered to me. All which I submit to the judgement of this court.
[*Signed*] Richard Holford.

Orders made by Alexander Popham, esq., Edward Seymour, esq., Francis Stonehouse, esq., Francis Goddard, esq., Lovelace Bigg, esq., Samuel Whitelock, esq., Thomas Fettiplace, John Hippisley, and John Blandy, esqs., trustees of a hospital in Froxfield, for the better governing of the hospital [and] to be observed by the inhabitants thereof.

That every one of the widows that are now inhabitants, or shall hereafter inhabit in the hospital, shall daily go into the chapel belonging to the hospital and there continue during divine service to be read by the chaplain, in the gowns given by the foundress, unless just cause can be given to the contrary; upon the penalty of forfeiting 6*d.* for every failure.

That every one of the inhabitants that shall be absent from the house 1 week or more at any one time shall forfeit her allowance for the time of such failure. The allowance [is] to be deducted by the steward of the hospital, for such uses as the trustees or any five of them shall direct, without the consent in writing first obtained under the hands of the trustees or any one or more of them.

That every one of the inhabitants that shall keep in the house any child or other person that does not belong to the hospital 1 week together or more shall forfeit their salaries for every time of such person inhabiting. To be deducted by the steward and for such uses as the trustees or any five of them shall direct.

That the inhabitants do behave themselves reverently to their superiors and respectively to one another, be not at any time unquiet in their behaviour [or] disguised by liquors, [and do not] swear or curse, under pain of being expelled the hospital.

That the inhabitants do each behave themselves soberly and respectfully to the chaplain of the hospital and [to] all the officers who are employed about the premises by the trustees, and not disturb any of them in the execution of their offices with their tongues or otherwise, upon pain of forfeiting 10*s.* for every such misdemeanour, to be deducted by the steward upon complaint [and] to be disposed of as the trustees or any five of them shall direct, or be[ing] expelled the hospital if the trustees or any five of them shall think fit.

That the inhabitants and every of them shall yearly allow out of their salaries sufficient to repair their glass windows belonging to their apartments as there shall be occasion.

We the trustees establish the orders and appoint the steward to hang up a copy of them in the chapel.

Witness our hands 3 November 1698.

24 June 1700. [Left by] Roger Meredith
We whose names are hereunder written, trustees of a hospital in Froxfield, hereby make the orders following this 27 October 1699.

We order the steward of the hospital to displace Susannah Cherry, one of the inhabitants, and to stop her salary due by virtue of the place, for the misdemeanours following: for keeping children in the house contrary to the orders, abusing the trustees and officers, and other misdemeanours contrary to the true meaning of the orders and the charity by declaring that she valued not what the trustees could do to her for that she had as good a title to her place as the trustees had to their estates, pulling down the orders, despising the trustees, and other misdemeanours. [The order is to be carried out] when we shall be empowered to displace.

Whereas the salaries of Elizabeth Abbot and Hester Andrews, two of the inhabitants of the hospital, were by direction of the trustees stopped for their abuses and misdemeanours contrary to the orders, we direct the steward to stop their salaries till further order.

We order that the above salaries, hereby ordered to be stopped, shall be applied towards discharging the disputes in law and otherwise, and [likewise] those salaries already stopped.

We agree that Edward Seymour, esq., one of the trustees of the hospital, do nominate one other widow in the place of Susannah Cherry upon her being expelled.

Edward Seymour, Francis Stonehouse, Lovelace Bigg, John Blandy, Thomas Fettiplace

24 June 1700. [Left by] Roger Meredith
The further order proposed, as mentioned in my report.

'Tis proposed for the good order and government of the hospital that the orders already made by the trustees be confirmed by the court, and that the trustees have a power to compel a submission to their authority by suspending or expelling the poor widows for disobedience to the orders or to any other orders that shall be made for the good government of the hospital and in pursuance of the decree.

DECREE OF THE HIGH COURT OF CHANCERY, 25 JULY 1729
(TNA C 33/351, ff. 391v.–392)

Between the Attorney General on behalf of the poor inhabitants of the hospital of Froxfield, plaintiffs, [and] Samuel Grimston, bt., and others, defendants.

Counsel on behalf of Francis Popham, Richard Jones, Samuel Whitelock, Thomas Bennet, Edward Ernle, Henry Hungerford, esqs., and George Popham, clerk, trustees of the hospital, this day attending [*rectius* attended] the Rt. Hon. the Lord High Chancellor touching their petition preferred unto his lordship 17 June last [and] praying directions upon Mr. Holford's report, dated 7 June last, containing several orders laid before him by the trustees for the better government of the hospital pursuant to an order of 19 February last. The master by his report certified that he conceived them to be necessary for the better management of the charity, which was directed and endowed by Sarah, late duchess dowager of Somerset, and established by the decree in this cause. The orders and rules being as follows.

1. That the steward for the hospital to be approved of by the Lord Chancellor provide paper books for keeping the accounts relating to the hospital, make due and fair entries of the particular branches of the revenues and of all his receipts, disbursements, and allowances (and when, how, and to whom paid and made), and produce it to the trustees when required.
2. That the trustees or any five of them meet when and as often as they think fit for the execution of the trust, and that the steward attend them and observe all orders by them made and diligently register them. More especially that the trustees or any five of them meet in the Whitsun week yearly at the hospital or as near thereto as conveniently they can. That they then view the hospital and [the] chapel, and the pulpit, seats, books, and what belongs to the chapel, and see that they be in good order. That they then elect one of the most grave and prudent widows of the hospital, to be nominated by the trustees and by them directed and empowered to oversee the rest and to take note of all miscarriages, neglects, and misdemeanours of the rest of the inhabitants. That she from time to time, assisted by the chaplain, inform the trustees or any two of them of what miscarriages, neglects, or misdemeanours shall be there committed (and when, how, and by whom). The widow to be nominated shall be called the matron during the year that she shall oversee the rest and, when out of her own apartment, shall constantly carry a white wand for distinction. [She] shall be chief and respected as such and constantly reside there for the time she is matron, unless permitted to be absent by two or more of the trustees. The matron shall be paid by the steward 20*s*. a year for her trouble in execution of the office, provided the trustees think she has done her duty.
3. That divine service according to the Book of Common Prayer be daily performed in the chapel by the chaplain of the hospital,

or by some other able minister to be by him procured; to begin every of the weekdays at 11 o'clock in the forenoon upon toll of the bell, and prayers and a sermon in the forenoon and prayers in the afternoon on every Sunday.

4. That every one of the widows shall constantly attend divine service in the chapel in their gowns provided for them by the trustees and shall there behave themselves devoutly and decently, under the penalty of *2d.* for every neglect unless hindered by sickness or other reasonable cause. [The cause is] to be allowed and testified by the chaplain and [the] matron to the trustees or some of them within 1 week after such neglect. None [is] to be liable to such penalty unless accused within a fortnight after such neglect.

5. That every one of the widows who shall be absent from the hospital 1 week or more at any one time, unless hindered by sickness or other reasonable cause to be testified by the chaplain and [the] matron and allowed by two or more of the trustees, shall forfeit for every such offence so much as her allowance shall come to for the time she shall be absent.

6. That none of the widows shall keep any child or maidwoman in the hospital for 1 week, or any man after the gate of the hospital is locked up, in any one year without the consent of two or more of the trustees in writing; on pain that she keeping such child, maidwoman, or man shall forfeit *2s. 6d.* for every week or night so offending.

7. That all the widows and inhabitants shall behave themselves respectively towards their superiors, and especially towards the trustees. In case any of the widows offend, she shall forfeit her pension until the offender shall have made due submission and acknowledgement to the satisfaction of the trustees.

8. That all the widows shall behave themselves decently towards the chaplain and [the] steward and towards each other, and that they be not unquiet, disorderly, or abusive in their language, conversation, or behaviour. In case any of the widows offend, and it be testified by [*rectius* to] any two of the trustees by the matron and [the] chaplain or either of them within 1 week, the person so offending shall forfeit 1 week's allowance for the first offence. For the second offence, testified as aforesaid, [she] shall be suspended so long as such trustees think fit, not exceeding 1 month, and shall forfeit her allowance during her suspension. For the third offence [she] shall be expelled out of the hospital by any five or more of the trustees.

9. That, if any of the widows shall be found guilty of living incontinently, or [of] any other great and heinous crime, the trustees or any five of them may expel such offender.

10. That, if any of the widows shall marry, she is thereupon within 10 days to depart from the hospital, or any five of the trustees, upon proof of the marriage, may expel her and suspend her pension from the time of her marriage.
11. That, if any of the widows shall be at any time disguised in drink or shall profanely swear or curse, she shall for the first offence forfeit 1*s*. For the second offence, having been admonished of the first in the presence of the matron and two or three of the other widows, she shall forfeit 2*s*. For the third offence, having been admonished of the second by the chaplain in the chapel presently after divine service, she shall forfeit her pension and be suspended. If she shall not within 1 month submit to, and prevail with, three of the trustees at least to take off her suspension and restore her, then any five of the trustees may expel her.
12. That all the pecuniary penalties shall be deducted by the steward out of the next shares payable to each widow offending, and that a due and fair entry thereof be made by the steward in a book by him for that purpose kept. The money shall be laid out in repairs of the hospital or as the trustees or any five of them shall direct.
13. That every one of the widows shall keep in repair the glass windows of their respective apartments from any damage done by themselves. If any of them neglect or refuse so to do, the steward shall deduct out of the quarterly stipend of such widow so much money as shall be sufficient to repair them and therewith repair those windows.
14. That the outward door of the hospital shall be locked by the porter between Lady day and Michaelmas every night at 9 o'clock and not opened till 5 o'clock the next morning, and between Michaelmas and Lady day every night at 7 o'clock and not opened till 7 the next morning, without leave of the matron upon some special occasion.
15. That the steward for the hospital do cause these orders and such other orders or reports as shall be made in confirmation by the High Court of Chancery to be fairly written in a full and plain character and forthwith hung up in a frame in a convenient place in the chapel, there to be read by the widows or who else shall desire to read them; and [be] new written as often as there shall be occasion.

Whereupon, and upon hearing the petition, and the report dated 7 June last [being] read, his lordship does order that the report do stand confirmed and that the rules therein contained be added to, and made part of, the decree of this cause, to the end [that] they may remain on record and obedience may be yielded thereto.

Mr. Mills, of counsel with Grace Gibbs, one of the poor widows, from whom the allowance of the charity has been withheld on account of her misbehaviour, disrespect, and ill-language given and shown to the trustees, now informing the court that she was sorry and in great distress and want, and Grace Gibbs having made her submission, it is ordered that the trustees pay to her the allowance due to her to this time.

MINUTE BOOKS OF FROXFIELD ALMSHOUSE

MINUTE BOOK 1714–75

(WSA 2037/12)

Preliminaries

16 October 1714

Received of Mr. Kellway 4*s*. for this book, by me, F. Buckeridge.

Undated notes

Thomas Osmond, porter.

Mr. Benet Goddard recommends Jane Kenton, lay widow at-large.

Lay Widows

Resident [at] Michaelmas 1714: 1, Mary Simonds, Marlborough (C); 2, Margery Gale, Fyfield (M); 3, Susan Horne, Shalbourne (C); 4, Elizabeth Kimber, Froxfield (M); 5, Grace Franklin, Clyffe Pypard (C); 6, Alice Keepings, Pewsey (C); 7, Mary Biffin, Wootton Rivers (M); 8, Mary Godfrey, Salisbury (C); 9, Jane Whale, Salisbury (C); 10, Elizabeth Sims, Fyfield (M); 11, Jane Stephens, Hungerford (C).

Admitted 19 October 1714: 12, Joan Pearce, Salisbury (C); 13, Joan Gigg, Froxfield (M); 14, Elizabeth Fisher, Chilton Foliat (C); 15, Frances Young, Hungerford (C).

Note. This lay widows list is directly contrary to the will, occasioned, I presume, by the several chasms, law suits, and elections of new trustees, and [by] the old trustees, in that interval, not keeping to the strict letter of the will. For as above C stands for county [and] M for manors there appears to be 10 lay widows of the county and but 5 of the manors. By the will there ought to be 10 of the manors of Wiltshire, if [they are] to be found, and 5 of the counties. Accordingly, from the trustees' minutes of 1 February 1715, when [it was] found out, they unanimously agreed to rectify it in their several and respective nominations for the future.

Clergy Widows

Resident [at] Michaelmas 1714: 1, Mrs. Mary Randall, Great Bedwyn; 2, Mrs. Sarah Hayes, Alton; 3, Mrs. Elizabeth Abbot, Hungerford; 4, Mrs. Mary Farewell, Hungerford; 5, Mrs. Elizabeth Housing, Stanford Dingley; 6, Mrs. Jane Elks, Chaddleworth; 7, Mrs. Anne Wootton, Tellisford; 8, Mrs. Mary Welkstead, Woodley; 9, Mrs. Clare Clifford, Middlesex; 10, Mrs. Sarah Jauncey, Middlesex.

Admitted 19 October 1714: 11, Mrs. Sarah Corey, Chew Magna; 12, Mrs. Susanna Wooford, Buttermere; 13, Mrs. Elizabeth Carter, London; 14, Mrs. Elizabeth Skicklethorp, London; 15, Mrs. Elizabeth Hathway, Berkshire.

Note. Mrs. Corey nominated by Mr. Whitelock: refused.

Rules

Extracted from the duchess of Somerset's will for the more ready assistance of the trustees in their election of widows for the hospital.

That the trustees make choice of, and place therein, 30 poor widows that are poor but honest and lead a good life.

That 25 of the widows shall before that time be living in Wiltshire or in Somerset and Berkshire.

That 10 of that 25 widows shall be ministers' widows if so many such poor widows shall be found living in the three counties.

That at least another 10 of that 25 shall be chosen out of my manors in Wiltshire if there shall be so many poor widows there.

That the other 5 of the 30 poor widows shall be ministers' widows living in or near the cities of London and Westminster.

That the same rules, proportions, and qualifications shall be observed in all elections that shall be made of widows to fill up any vacancies that shall happen, so there shall always be in the almshouse 10 ministers' widows and 15 other widows that, before they were chosen into the almshouse, were inhabiting in Wiltshire, Somerset, and Berkshire and 5 ministers' widows that were, before their election into the almshouse, residing in or about the cities of London and Westminster.

A List of the Trustees

Mr. Archdeacon Yate not active [*entry deleted*]; Mr. Edward Pocock presented Mrs. Elizabeth Hathway (clergy) [*entry deleted*]; Mr. Thomas Hawes presented Margery Walter (lay) [*entry deleted*]; Mr. Richard Gillingham presented Mrs. Susanna Wooford (clergy) [*entry deleted*]; Mr. William Sherwin not active; Sir Edward Seymour, bt., not active; Francis Popham, esq., presented Mrs. Susanna Wooford (clergy); Richard Jones, esq., presented Elizabeth Fisher (lay); Charles Tooker, esq., presented Mrs. Joan Gallimore (clergy); Samuel Whitelock, esq., presented Mrs. Corey (not accepted); Lovelace Bigg, esq., presented Frances Young (lay); Thomas Bennet, esq., presented Catherine Garlick (lay); Edward Ernle, esq., presented Joan Whithart; Mr. Hawes presented Margery Walter; Mr. Edward Pocock presented Mrs. Elizabeth Hathway; Mr. Gillingham presented Elizabeth Woodroffe; Francis Popham, esq., 8 September 1716 presented Mrs. Woodroffe; Samuel Whitelock, esq., 27 February 1717 presented Mrs. Elizabeth Davies; Richard Jones, esq., 24 March 1718 presented Mrs. Mary Slade;

Samuel Whitelock, esq., 9 April 1718 presented Elizabeth Anderson; Lovelace Bigg, esq., 7 March 1718 presented Elizabeth Weeks; Thomas Bennet, esq., 10 January 1718 presented Sarah Barnes; Edward Ernle, esq., 19 December 1719 [presented] Margaret Pipping; Mr. Edward Pocock [presented] Elizabeth Siney; Mr. Richard Gillingham [*entry deleted*]; Francis Popham, esq., 29 October 1719 presented Pethia Lomax; R. Jones, esq., presented Mrs. Neate, who did not accept [*entry deleted*]; S. Whitelock, esq. [*entry deleted*]; L. Bigg, esq. [*entry deleted*]; Thomas Bennet, esq., 29 September 1719 presented Frances Blake [*entry deleted*]; Edward Ernle, esq., 19 December 1719 presented Margaret Pipping [*entry deleted*]; Edward Pocock, clerk, presented Elizabeth Siney [*entry deleted*].

19 October 1714, a general meeting of eight of the trustees, who make a quorum, at the Bear, Charnham Street

Present

Francis Popham, Richard Jones, Samuel Whitelock, Lovelace Bigg, Thomas Bennet, Edward Ernle, esqs., Thomas Hawes, Richard Gillingham, clerks.

Trusteeship

It is ordered that Mr. Kellway, steward of the hospital, do write to Mr. Archdeacon [Yate] to recommend two clergymen's widows in the liberties of the cities of London and Westminster and [in] Middlesex, on the decease of Mrs. Alice Davidge and Mrs. Olive Nevill. Endorsed 'Twas done.

That in the letter Mr. Archdeacon be desired to recommend, besides that two, a clergyman's widow qualified as above in place of Mrs. Sarah Rusbach, lately deceased. *Endorsed* He could find not one.

That the porter have an order from Mr. Kellway under his hand to admit forthwith Joan Pearce of Salisbury, who had an order from Mr. Archdeacon Yate 22 December 1712 for her then admittance in place of Joan Arnold, deceased. *Endorsed* Admitted.

That the porter have an order as above to admit forthwith Joan Gigg of Froxfield, who had an order from Mr. Pocock 3 January 1713 for her then admittance in place of Mrs. Anne Carter, deceased. *Endorsed* Admitted.

That the porter have an order as above to admit forthwith Elizabeth Fisher of Chilton Foliat in place of Martha Clements, deceased. *Endorsed* Admitted.

That the porter have an order as above to admit forthwith Frances Young of Hungerford in place of Gertrude Kingston, deceased. *Endorsed* Admitted.

That the porter have an order as above to admit forthwith Mrs.

Sarah Corey, a clergyman's widow of Chew Magna, in place of Mrs. Susannah Cherry, deceased. *Endorsed* Refused.

That the porter have an order as above to admit forthwith Mrs. Susanna Wooford, a clergyman's widow of Buttermere, in place of Mrs. Elizabeth Towning, late of Middlesex, deceased, who by [a] mistake of the former trustees was put in for a Middlesex widow but [is] now found to be a supernumary. *Endorsed* Admitted.

That every trustee shall have liberty to nominate in his turn, as they are mentioned in the deed of trust, either a clergyman's or layman's widow on notice given him by the steward of his right to nomination; unless such trustee has absented himself from each general meeting of the trustees for one whole year [and] for that reason shall forfeit his turn of nomination for that time only. [In that case] the right of nomination shall pass to the next trustee in course. Upon any London or Middlesex vacancy Mr. Archdeacon Yate be desired to recommend to the rest of the trustees, and the trustee who has the next nomination shall have it saved to him till there happen another vacancy.

Signatures

Francis Popham, Richard Jones, S. Whitelock, Lovelace Bigg, Edward Ernle, Thomas Hawes.

1 February 1715

Trusteeship

It is ordered that Mr. Kellway do forthwith, out of the profits of the revenue of the hospital now in his hands, pay to Mr. Christopher Appleby, the trustees' solicitor, £22 for his bill. Mr. Appleby's receipt thereon shall be a discharge to Mr. Kellway for his so doing. *Endorsed* Accordingly paid.

Estate

That Mr. Kellway do enquire of Drewett what is become of John Bigg, the preceding tenant to Chirton, and to see Bigg's last acquittance, by reason [*i.e.* because] Mr. Wall did not receive the full rent by £11 1*s.* 10*d.* *Endorsed* Swore off by Bigg before a master [that] 'twas paid.

That Mr. Kellway do see Mr. Wall's last receipt for Edward Drewett of Chirton to know how the rent was paid from St. Thomas['s day] 1711 to Midsummer 1714. *Endorsed* Paid to the widows.

Agreed with William Tarrant for the late widow Quarrington's copyhold estate, valued by us at £12 a year, to take £20 for 2 years' profit due Lady day 1715 and 20*s.* for a heriot due on the death of the widow Quarrington, [she] being poor. [Tarrant is] to pay £28 fine for a lease of three lives and reserved rent [of] £8 a year, both lease and quit rent to be without any payments or deductions, [and] to have leave to Midsummer for nomination of his three lives. *Endorsed* Lease

Ordered and Agreed (on the Request of the said Thomas Warner for leave to plow up part of a Spewy ground, & plant the other part with a Witty bed & fence & preserve it) that he have leave so to doe, on Mr Tooker & Mr Earle's view, they find it advantagious for the Hospitall. (Twas viewd & approve[d])

Ordered that Charles Milsom Porter, doe keep in his safe custody from time to time the keys of all vacant chambers, immediately on the clearing of each chamber, and to deliver no key, till he have an Order of Admittance from Mr Keylwaie, under the Penalty of Expulsion from his place

Ordered and agreed, that whereas Henry Pyke (Tenn.t to the other part of Milton fforme) intends to plant ab.t Sixty lug of ffrith on the said Estate this Season, & preserve the same from Cattle. And whereas he hath but three years to come of his Lease, If any other Tenn.t should then advance the Rent of the fforme. That then the said Henry Pyke &c shall be allowed a just & reasonable price for his planting & preserving ye said ffrith.

Ordered and Agreed, That a Court be held for the Mannor of ffroxfeild the 22d instant at the fforme in ffroxfeild, that Mr Keylwaie demand the Herriotts presented last Court (in Mr Walls time) & also enquire by the oath of the Homage, what Lives are since fallen? what Herriotts due? what meadow or pasture plowed? what timber cut? or any other wast? by whome committed, and when; & all other things &c presentable at the same Court. (vide Courtbook)

Ordered and Agreed, That a Court be likewise held for the Mannors of Huish & Shawe on Tuesday the 1st day of March next at the fforme in Huish, that Mr Keylwaie request farmer Rich. Edmonds Tho: Weston, Rich.d Reeves & Jo.n Smith to attend, to prove what they know of a Coppyhold Estate intermixed with H. Hungerford's Esq.r in Hyfeild: & that Mr Keylwaie enquire by the oath of the Homage, what lives &c.? (as above) (ut supra)

Ordered That Mrs Clare Clifford have leave to goe to London for the space of two months from the date hereof, on Extraordinary Buisnesse.

Minutes of a meeting held 1 February 1715

sealed, fine received.

Ordered that Mr. Kellway be allowed 16*s.* for 2 years' quit rent, for which William Tarrant paid £20 as above for the 2 years' profit.

Agreed with farmer Thomas Warner for a rack-rent part of Milton farm in the late possession of H. Hungerford, esq., for £70 a year for 19 years to commence from Michaelmas next, without deduction for any taxes, assessments, or payments and according to his old lease.

Ordered on the request of Thomas Warner for leave to plough up part of a Spewy ground, and plant the other part with a withy bed and fence and preserve it, that he have leave so to do on Mr. Tooker's and Mr. Ernle's view and [if] they find it advantageous for the hospital. *Endorsed* 'Twas viewed and approved.

Ordered that whereas Henry Pyke, tenant to the other part of Milton farm, intends to plant about 60 lugs of frith on that estate this season and preserve it from cattle, and whereas he has but 3 years to come of his lease, if any other tenant should then advance the rent of the farm Pyke shall be allowed a reasonable price for his planting and preserving the frith.

Ordered that a court be held for the manor of Froxfield the 22nd instant at the farm in Froxfield, that Mr. Kellway demand the heriots presented [at the] last court, in Mr. Wall's time, and enquire by the oath of the homage what lives are since fallen, what heriots due, what meadow or pasture ploughed, what timber cut, or any other waste, by whom committed and when, and all other things presentable at the court. *Endorsed* See court book.

Ordered that a court be held for the manor of Huish and Shaw on Tuesday 1 March next at the farm in Huish, that Mr. Kellway request farmer Richard Edmonds, Thomas Weston, Richard Reeves, and John Smith to attend to prove what they know of a copyhold estate intermixed with H. Hungerford, esquire's, in Fyfield, and that Mr. Kellway enquire by the oath of the homage what lives etc., as above [*preceding entry*]. *Endorsed* As above.

Ordered that Mr. Kellway leave a note with Mr. John Liddiard of Froxfield acquainting him that 'tis the unanimous opinion of the trustees that he has no right to tithe wood out of the Almshouse coppice [and] that he must expect to be sued if he offers to take any this fellage.

Almshouse

Ordered that Charles Milsom, porter, do keep in his safe custody the keys of all vacant chambers immediately on the clearing of each chamber and deliver no key till he have an order of admittance from Mr. Kellway, under the penalty of expulsion from his places.

Ordered that Mrs. Clare Clifford have leave to go to London for 2 months from the date hereof on extraordinary business.

Signatures

Francis Popham, Lovelace Bigg, Richard Jones, Edward Ernle, Edward Pocock, Thomas Bennet, Richard Gillingham.

19 April 1716

Trusteeship

[Ordered] that Milton and Fyfield widows, for the future, be not deemed manor widows.

Estate

Ordered that Charles Milsom, porter, in consideration of 5*s*. etc. as by [the] lease, [of] the erecting [of] a good substantial house at his own charge on a waste piece of ground on the manor [of Froxfield] and [the] taking in [of] a piece of Edward Savage's ground (by his [*i.e.* Savage's] own voluntary and free consent, Milsom being his uncle) adjoining the lord's waste for a garden, and [of] paying 1*s*. a year quit rent, shall have a lease for three lives granted him.

That a bill be preferred against Henry Hungerford of Fyfield, esq., to discover the late Mrs. Ashe's copyhold estate belonging to the hospital, [which has] sunk into Mr. Hungerford's estate, the next term.

That the trustees and homage be allowed their expenses at the extraordinary court at Pewsey towards retrieving that copyhold estate.

That at the next court to be held for the manor of Huish and Shaw, before Midsummer day next, it be given in charge to present Catherine Pyke, widow, for her waste committed on her copyhold estate at Milkhouse (*Millcroft*) Water in that manor.

Ordered that Mr. Kellway do call on Mr. John Liddiard and demand £4 for the 2 last years' tithe wood [which] he took out of Froxfield coppice, forbid him taking any more, according to his promise made to Mr. Whitelock and Mr. Bigg, and show him Mr. Dodd's opinion on the same.

That Edward Drewett of Chirton be allowed £3 15*s*. for thatching his barn, according to the promise of the old trustees.

That Mr. Pocock, Mr. Ernle, and Mr. Tooker be desired to view Edward Drewett's building [to see] if it be according to his lease and to enquire after Hayward's trespass and quit rent. We submit Roger Hatter's case in renewing to those three trustees.

Almshouse

[Ordered] that Mr. Kellway do acquaint the widows [that] they do not presume to meddle with any widow's wood [whether the widow be] non-resident or [a house be] vacant, or [on] any pretence whatsoever, without the direction of three or more of the trustees. The trustees have resolved to punish the neglect of this order by deduction out of their allowance or [by] more severe methods.

The trustees have unanimously agreed that no widow have leave to be absent above 1 month in a year, which leave is to be granted under the hands of two trustees as formerly, that every widow absent [for a] longer time shall forfeit 5*s*. a week unless for extraordinary reasons to be allowed by the trustees at their next general meeting, and that Mr. Kellway send for the now absent widows and acquaint them all with this order.

Signatures

Francis Popham, Richard Jones, Lovelace Bigg, Edward Ernle, Richard Gillingham.

26 October 1717

Trusteeship

[Ordered] that upon the death of each widow Mr. Kellway do enter the time of her death in his book and immediately certify it to the trustee whose turn it is next to nominate: also whether lay or clergy, if lay whether of the manors or county, if clergy whether of London, Middlesex, or adjacent, or of the counties. The trustee shall be obliged within 6 months after such notice to fill up her vacancy with a widow of the same denomination and same county, having always respect to the other qualifications mentioned in the duchess's will. Till the full number of manor widows be nominated the trustee whose turn it is to name a lay widow be obliged to name a manor widow, provided there be any qualified according to the will and recommended within that time by any persons for the manors. The order of 19 October 1714 in relation to Mr. Archdeacon's recommending of London and Middlesex widows do stand. Mr. Kellway do acquaint each absent trustee with this order.

That Mr. Kellway do write to Mr. Appleby for the three decrees of Chancery relating to the conveying of the trust of Froxfield almshouse.

Estate

Ordered that the signing of Charles Milsom's lease be respited according to his petition till he has compounded with his creditors, and that then Mr. Kellway do carry the lease to five of the trustees separately for their signing.

That Mr. Kellway do prefer a bill against Henry Hungerford, esq., as soon as he can be better informed in relation to the surrender and copy mentioned in a paper in Mr. Kellway's custody and in other things relating to that affair.

That a court be held for the manor of Huish and Shaw [on] the last Tuesday in April next, and that it be given in charge to the jury to present Catherine Pyke, widow, for waste and dilapidations. If before that time she has not repaired her copyhold estate and given the trustees sufficient satisfaction for the damages then Mr. Kellway do enter to the estate.

That Mr. Popham, Mr. Jones, and Mr. Ernle be desired to view Drewett's building [to see] if [it remains] according to the covenants of his lease and to enquire after Hayward's trespass and quit rent. [We] submit Roger Hatter's case in renewing to those three trustees and [acknowledge] that they will be pleased to do it and make their report at the next general meeting.

That Mr. Kellway do give Mr. Liddiard a copy of the case of the wood in Froxfield coppice and Sir Samuel Dodd's opinion thereon, to be compared with the original by Mr. Liddiard in order to [allow] his showing of it to the dean and chapter of Windsor for their satisfaction, before the next meeting of the trustees. Till then the trustees' demands of Mr. Liddiard, and his demand of them, in relation to the wood shall be respited.

That the presentment made by the jury in relation to the executor's year against the lords at a court held 1 March 1715 for Huish and Shaw be not allowed, for there is no executor's year against the lord.

That Mr. Kellway have inspection to [*i.e.* should look at the record of] Mr. Wall's court of survey [to see] what the late John Smith's heriots are on the two copyhold estates in Froxfield, do demand it [*rectius* them] of the widow Smith, and report it at the next meeting of the trustees.

Almshouse

[Ordered] that Mr. Kellway do pay to Mrs. Farewell 30*s*. due [at] Michaelmas 1716 upon her signing a resignation of her chamber.

That Mr. Kellway do enquire into the misdemeanor in breaking open the chamber of Mrs. Joan Pearce and report it at the next meeting of the trustees.

That Mrs. Wootton be paid 20*s*. by Mr. Kellway in consideration of her losses in Mr. Wall's time and that it be entered in his voucher of 28 October last.

Signatures

Edward Pocock, Francis Popham, Lovelace Bigg, Richard Gillingham, Edward Ernle.

22 July 1718

Trusteeship

[Ordered] that Mr. Kellway do write to the master for copies of the three decrees of Chancery relating to the conveying of the trust of Froxfield almshouse.

That the trustees be desired to peruse Sir Richard Holford's order for the good government of the hospital at their next meeting.

Estate

Ordered that the lease of Milsom's house, said in the order of 19 April 1716 to be granted for three lives, be granted to him or the best bidder for 99 years absolute at 2*s*. a year quit rent, and [that] the money thereby arising be lodged in Mr. Kellway's hands for Milsom's creditors upon condition that each of them take 10*s*. for £1.

That Mr. Ernle be desired to wait on Mr. Hungerford and acquaint him that, whereas at a court held for Huish and Shaw 29 April last the homage presented ½ acre of meadow, 6 acres of arable in the common fields of Fyfield, and common for 80 sheep [to be] sunk into the estate of Henry Hungerford, esq., we desire him to appoint a person to meet such other as shall be nominated by the trustees to lay out those premises and agree on the yearly value of the commons, before Michaelmas next. On refusal Mr. Kellway [is] to prefer a bill against him next term.

Whereas Mr. Popham, Mr. Jones, and Mr. Ernle were desired to view Drewett's building [and] to enquire after Hayward's trespass and Hatter's case, Drewett built his mud wall and carthouse according to his lease. [It is ordered] that he have a lease for Pearson's *alias* Hort's house, [its] garden, and Pearson's close, about 100 lugs (be it more or less), in the late possession of John Hayward, under the yearly rent of 35*s*. free from all taxes, payments, and assessments, and set and keep it in good repair. [It is ordered] that Mary Hatter pay 4*s*. for 2 years' quit rent and £4 for 2 years' rack rent and have a lease granted her of the cottages and premises for 7 years, on her putting and keeping them in repair, free from all taxes and payments under the yearly rent of 40*s*.

[Ordered] that Mr. Kellway bring an ejectment or take possession of the copyhold estate of Catherine Pyke, widow, next term if she do not tenantably repair and submit herself to the judgement and award of the trustees at their next meeting for her waste and spoil on the estate.

That a short extract of the duchess's will so far as relates to the conveyance of Froxfield be sent to Mr. Liddiard for the conveying [of] it to Mr. Jones, [a] canon of Windsor.

That the order of 26 October last in relation to Smith's heriots do stand.

That Mr. Ernle and Mr. Kellway be desired to view the widow Banning's copyhold estate and report it at the next meeting.

That Farmer Pyke attend the trustees' next meeting in order to [allow] the setting [of] that estate to him or the best bidder, as shall be most advantageous to the hospital.

Almshouse

The trustees have ordered for the future severely to punish any widow that shall break open any door or casement on the death of each widow, but that immediately on such death the key of such deceased widow be conveyed by the porter to Mr. Kellway.

[Ordered] that no widow shall sell or alienate her wood on any pretence whatsoever, but that the wood belonging to each chamber shall remain to the next successor.

Next meeting

[Ordered] that the trustees meet again [on] the second Tuesday in September to consider Milsom's, Hayward's, and Pyke's affairs, and that they have notice to attend the meeting to prevent prosecution.

Signatures

Edward Pocock, Richard Gillingham, Lovelace Bigg, Francis Popham, Edward Ernle.

9 September 1718

Estate

Ordered that the signing of Pethers's lease for 99 years be respited till Charles Milsom has compounded with his creditors and that then Mr. Kellway do carry the lease to five of the trustees for their signing. *Endorsed* Compounded and lease signed.

Ordered that a court be held for Huish and Shaw at the usual place on Thursday 3 weeks after Michaelmas next to take the surrender of Catherine Pyke, widow, to her copyhold estate at Milkhouse (*Milcot*) Water and to pay her £70 for the surrender; and that the estate be granted to John Cannings by copy, according to the direction of the duchess's will, for £98 fine and £14 a year quit rent, [he] paying all taxes and payments [and] setting the premises in, and keeping them in, good repair during the three lives granted by the copy.

Ordered that Henry Pyke hold Milton estate for 1 year from Michaelmas 1718 under the same rent and covenants as by his now lease.

Signatures

Francis Popham, Richard Jones, Samuel Whitelock, Edward Pocock, Edward Ernle, Thomas Bennet, Lovelace Bigg.

12 August 1719

Trusteeship

[Ordered] that Mr. Bennet within 6 months present a county clergy widow in place of Mrs. Elizabeth Henson, who died 28 June last.

That Mr. Ernle within 6 months present a county clergy widow in place of Mrs. Anne Wootton, who died 15 July last.

Estate

Ordered that Roger Hitchcock's fine be granted for [*i.e.* set at] £30 for two lives, for which he has time to nominate till the next court held for Huish and Shaw. [He is to] pay £6 a year quit rent from Lady day 1719, £15 at Michaelmas [1719], and £15 at Lady day 1720.

Ordered that Mr. Jones and Mr. Ernle be desired to survey Milton estate, now Farmer Pyke's, within a month and [to] view the repairs; and then that they, with three more of the trustees, at any place they will appoint, have full power to let the estate to Farmer Pyke, or the best bidder, for what they think fit having relation to the duchess's will. *Endorsed* Out of repair.

That Mr. Ernle be desired to enquire of Mr. Robert Bing the name of such meadow and pasture ground as belong to Chirton farm, the number of acres of each ground, as of a meadow on the west side of Hort's house belonging to Froxfield almshouse.

Almshouse

Ordered that Mr. Kellway go to Mrs. Godfrey and assure her that 'tis the order of all the trustees that she be suspended her pay, or otherwise severely prosecuted, unless she give them and the parish satisfaction in relation to her daughter's bastard child; and that Mr. Kellway leave a copy of this order with her.

That Mrs. Garlick's place be vacant at Michaelmas 1719. *Endorsed* Turned out.

Signatures

Francis Popham, Richard Jones, Samuel Whitelock, Edward Pocock, Edward Ernle, Thomas Bennet, Lovelace Bigg.

21 June 1720

Estate

Agreed with Thomas Banning for a copy for his own life and his brother John's. [He is] to pay £20 a year quit rent free from all taxes and £60 fine at Michaelmas next.

[Ordered] that Mr. Kellway demand of Elizabeth Early something in lieu of a heriot for her taking a bed of Edward Plott's, who was a customary or copyhold tenant of the manor of Froxfield [and] who died since the last court possessed of the bed and other goods, which Elizabeth took too after the death of Edward.

The two following entries are crossed through

Edward Drewett of Chirton came before the trustees of Froxfield almshouse and surrendered two leases, one of Chirton farm and the other of Pearce's bargain in Chirton, [which he held] for a term of years unexpired. At the same time came Richard Walter *alias* Liney of Heddington, yeoman, and agreed with the trustees to take a grant of Chirton farm and Pearce's bargain from Lady day 1720 for 7 years, under the same covenants expressed in both the leases [and] with an advance of £7 a year above what is mentioned to be paid in both the leases.

Agreed between the trustees and Edmund Tarrant of Wilcot, husbandman, in consideration of the rent and covenants hereinafter expressed, to demise to him that messuage or tenement, arable lands, etc. now or late in the tenure or occupation of Henry Pyke, senior, his assignee or undertenant [and] lying in Milton. [He is] to hold from Michaelmas next for 7 years under the yearly rent of £85 payable quarterly without any deduction of taxes or payments, [and is] not to plough any meadow nor plough, sow, or plant with corn above two parts in three of the inclosed arable fields [in] the 2 last years of the term.

Almshouse

Ordered [that] Mrs. Weeks be paid from the time she came to the house.

9 May 1721

Certification

These are to certify [to] whom it may concern that John Bell, [an] infant, late of the parish of St. Botolph, Aldersgate, London, was buried in that parish [on] 1 March 1721, as appears by the register of that parish. In testimony whereof I have set my hand this 9 May 1721: Robert Savage, parish clerk. [*Other signatories*] Mary Brown; X, the mark of Sarah Richard.

3 July 1721

Confirmation

We whose hands are hereunder set take this certificate to be true, and take it as such. William Tarrant, churchwarden; Jesse Smith, overseer; Edward Savage, John Greenway.

26 October 1722

Trusteeship

We whose names are hereunder written, the trustees for managing the charity of the late duchess dowager of Somerset's foundation of Froxfield hospital, do by virtue of the power given us by the will of the duchess and since confirmed by decree of the High Court of Chancery, appoint Joseph Walker of Marlborough, gentleman, to be our steward and [the] receiver of the revenues of the hospital, Mr. Thomas Kellway, our late steward, having by reason of his great age and infirmities petitioned us to resign that employment. [*Signed*] Francis Popham, Edward Ernle, Lovelace Bigg, Edward Pocock, Richard Jones.

Ordered that Mr. Walker do this present Michaelmas term apply to Mr. Appleby, solicitor in Chancery, in whose hands the decrees and several other papers relating to this charity are lodged, to have them delivered to Mr. Walker for our perusal and custody. In case of the refusal of Mr. Appleby to deliver them, we empower our steward to apply to the proper master in Chancery or to move the court of Chancery, as he shall be by counsel advised, to obtain them or leave to take out copies of them.

We order Mr. Kellway, [our] late steward, to deliver to Mr. Walker all deeds, evidences, writings, and papers concerning the lands belonging to the charity so soon as Mr. Walker shall have given security in Chancery for the due execution of his stewardship pursuant to those decrees.

Signatures

Francis Popham, Richard Jones, Lovelace Bigg, Edward Ernle, Edward Pocock.

25 June 1723

Estate

It is ordered that Mr. Walker, the steward, do within 1 month demand of the widow Pyke, [the] executor of [Henry] Pyke, late tenant of Milton farm, belonging to the hospital, satisfaction for the waste done, or suffered, by him in the buildings belonging to the farm during his lease thereof. In case of her refusing to make such satisfaction we order our steward to prosecute her according to law.

Whereas we have been informed that some lands in the manor of Huish and Shaw are concealed from us to the injury of the charity, we order our steward to hold a court baron there within 1 month next and strictly give it in charge to the homage duly to enquire thereof and present what they shall find relating thereto and [relating] to anything else concerning the manor, especially the erecting [of] cottages. That the steward do otherways inform himself [of] what he can in relation thereto and report it at our next meeting.

Pursuant to an agreement by us or five of us made with Richard Walter *alias* Liney, tenant of Chirton farm, in consideration of his building a new stable there, the old one being ruinous and irreparable, and repairing the house and outhousing, [all] which appears by his bills to have cost £47 19*s*. 2*d*., we have thought fit to allow him towards his expense therein £25 and order our steward, by rateable proportions, to allow that out of the rent of the four quarters of this year as he shall pay it.

Signatures

Thomas Bennet, Lovelace Bigg, Edward Ernle, Francis Popham, Samuel Whitelock, Edward Pocock, Richard Jones.

8 April 1724

Estate

Ordered that John Gale of Wootton Rivers be bailiff of the manor of Huish and of the farms of Chirton, Milton, and Fyfield belonging to the hospital. We agree that he shall have for salary £4 a year to commence from Lady day last.

That the steward do search for Pyke's lease of Milton farm in order to lay [it] before Mr. Jones and Mr. Ernle [for them] to see his covenants for repair and in what condition he ought to have left the farmhouse and outhousing, [so] that we may settle the allowance to the new tenant, Tarrant, for those repairs done since he came on the farm.

That the steward do search for the accounts of Mr. Kellway, as far back as he can find them, and the oldest rent rolls of Huish and Froxfield manors, to satisfy us of the particulars of those rents as they then stood and how they have been improved since. If they are not to be found he shall make a rental of those quit rents as he shall find them appear by Mr. Joseph Wall's survey.

That, as it appears to us that Richard Edmonds and Roger Hitchcock, tenants by copy of court roll of the manor of Huish, have committed great waste by cutting timber off their estates there without assignment, we order our steward to enter on the estates or prosecute them, as he shall be by counsel advised; more especially as they sold such timber.

That the steward do make a lease from us to John Walter *alias* Liney of the house and garden late in the possession of Mary Hatter [and] lying at Chirton for three lives absolute. [The] consideration is for him to rebuild, £20 to be paid at [the] sealing, 3*s.* a year rent, heriot 5*s.*, and other covenants as usual.

That the steward do allow to Farmer Liney out of his next half year's rent £5 towards his making a barn door and barn floor at Chirton farm.

Signatures

Francis Popham, Samuel Whitelock, Richard Jones, Edward Ernle, Lovelace Bigg.

25 September 1724

Estate

Memorandum. Whereas there have lately been disputes between

Dr. Walter Ernle and John Walter *alias* Liney, tenant of Chirton (*Chirton* alias *Chirington*) farm belonging to the hospital, concerning seats in a pew in the parish church of Chirton, and they having been heard before us this day by themselves and [by] evidence, after thorough examination of the matters in dispute it was by us proposed to end the [dispute], and they so agree to do, in [the] manner following. Liney agreed to disclaim all right to the seat or pew or any part thereof, in consideration whereof Dr. Ernle agreed to give him in exchange two single seats elsewhere in the church that belong to him in right of another estate, called Nalder's, lying in the parish of Chirton. This we consent to ratify as far as in us lies as trustees of the hospital, to which the farm of Liney belongs and in right of which he lays claims to the seats in the pew claimed by Dr. Ernle.
Signatures
Francis Popham, Richard Jones, Edward Ernle, Samuel Whitelock.

6 April 1725

Trusteeship
We agree to add to us as trustees for the almshouse the Revd. Mr. George Popham, clerk, rector of Chilton Foliat, and Henry Hungerford of Fyfield, and we order Mr. Walker, our steward, forthwith to draw a deed of conveyance from us to them of the manors and lands settled for the endowment of the charity, in trust to us and them for the purposes of the will and [of the] decrees of the High Court of Chancery relating thereto.
Signatures
Francis Popham, Samuel Whitelock, Richard Jones, Edward Ernle, Thomas Bennet, Edward Pocock.

18 May 1725

Estate
Whereas William Dance and John Eatwell, two able workmen, have by our order viewed what repairs were wanting on the messuage, barns, stables, and outhouses of the farm of Huish, belonging to the charity, at the decease of Mrs. Catherine Thistlethwaite, the last life on the farm, and have this day brought before us an estimate thereof amounting to £31 19*s.* 6*d.*, it is ordered [that] the steward or bailiff do forthwith demand of Mrs. Edmonds of Salisbury, a widow, [the] executor or administrator of Catherine Thistlethwaite, £31 19*s.* 6*d.* On her refusal to pay it our steward [is] to proceed at law against her as he shall be by counsel advised. The steward or bailiff, or whom they send, [is] to deliver her a duplicate of the estimate.

Ordered [that] our steward do make enquiry of what cottages have been lately erected in Froxfield, either on the waste or otherwise, without laying 4 acres of land to each, and by whom. That he do prosecute the erectors or occupiers of them according to the statute in that case made or bring ejectments against them, as he shall be by counsel advised.

Almshouse

Ordered that Mrs. Welkstead be matron of the almshouse for this year and do carry her white wand, take notice of all irregularities, and represent them to the chaplain or steward [so] that they may be laid before us at our next meeting.

Ordered [that] our steward do defend the action brought against Charles Milsom and others by Edward Savage of Froxfield for making up the fence before the almshouse [and] next the highway, according to our former orders to him though not entered here before.

Signatures

Francis Popham, Richard Jones, Edward Ernle, Samuel Whitelock, Henry Hungerford.

6 September 1726, at the Blue Lion, Froxfield

Trusteeship

Whereas, when our number of trustees was greater, it was agreed by us that not less than five should be a quorum and should have power at any meeting to transact all affairs concerning the hospital, but, now our number being decreased, we order that any three of us shall be from henceforth accounted a quorum and have power to make such orders and agreements concerning the hospital as they shall think fit.

Estate

Whereas the lease, formerly granted by us to Richard Walter alias Liney, of Chirton farm will expire [on] 25 March next, we now agree to let the farm to Edward Carpenter for 8 years from that 25 March at the yearly rent of £98 clear from all taxes. If the land tax shall during that term advance to more than £15 a year we agree to allow Carpenter for such advance. If the land tax shall be less than £15 a year at any time during the term Edward Carpenter [is] to pay that [shortfall] to us as an advance of rent. We order our steward to draw a lease from us to Edward Carpenter accordingly.

Almshouse

We order our steward to pay Thomas Osmond his two bills for carpenter's work at the hospital amounting to £8 15*s*., and to William Gregory his bill for mason's work at the hospital amounting to £1 5*s*. 8*d*.

We order our steward to acquaint the widow Gibbs, now an

inhabitant of the hospital, that we have received information that she keeps a disorderly house by letting in lewd and scandalous people at unseasonable hours in the night and that, if she persists in that after our steward shall have so acquainted her, we hereby order that the widow Gibbs shall be utterly expelled [from] her house in the hospital. We order that the casement of the south window of her lower room shall be barred up.

Signatures

Francis Popham, Henry Hungerford, George Popham, Richard Jones, Samuel Whitelock.

Adjournment

We adjourn ourselves to this place to the 27th of this instant [September].

27 September 1726, the adjournment from the last meeting

Estate

At a meeting by us held 18 May 1725 our then steward was ordered to demand of Mrs. Edmonds, widow, executrix or administratrix of Mrs. Catherine Thistlethwaite, £31 19*s.* 6*d.* for repairs that were wanting on the messuage, barns, stables, and outhouses of the farm of Huish belonging to the hospital, and on her refusal to pay it our steward was to proceed at law against her. But, it not appearing to us that the [order] was put in execution, we now order our present steward to demand that sum of Mrs. Edmonds and, upon non-payment thereof, to proceed at law against her as by counsel shall be advised.

Whereas at the same meeting our then steward was ordered to make enquiry of what cottages had been erected in Froxfield without laying 4 acres of land to each and to prosecute the occupiers or erectors of them according to the statute in that case made, and it not appearing to us that anything was done in that affair, we now give the same order to our present steward.

We agree to grant to Jeffery Banks, blacksmith, by copy of court roll, a cottage with its appurtenances in Froxfield, value 30*s.* a year, lately fallen into our hands by the death of Ursula Cully, widow. [He is] to hold for his own life and the lives of Thomas Cripps and James Banks, both of Milton, brothers of Jeffery, at the yearly rent of 20*s.*; fine £8.

We order our steward to allow Farmer Tarrant £2 4s. 11½d., money which he paid to John Dear for pitching the stable and court at Milton farm as appears by bill and receipt.

We also order our steward to allow Farmer Tarrant 5s. 1d., which he paid to Henry Pearce for smith's work for the barn's doors at Milton farm as appears [by bill and receipt].

Ordered that it be referred to Edward Ernle and Henry Hungerford, esqs., for them to consider of the exchange of cow leazes belonging to Milton farm for lands of Mr. Clark's called Clay lands, three cow leazes for each acre, if we have such power.

Almshouse

Ordered that Mrs. Abbot for the year ensuing do carry a white wand, take notice of all irregularities, and represent them to the chaplain or steward [so] that it may be laid before us at our next meeting.

We order our steward to pay Jeffery Banks's bill dated 28 November 1724 for the smith's work at the almshouse, being 9*s.* 7*d.*

Signatures

Francis Popham, Edward Ernle, George Popham, Samuel Whitelock, Henry Hungerford.

6 November 1727, at the Green Dragon, Ramsbury

Estate

Whereas we formerly granted to Walter Stagg of Huish one farm there late in the possession of Mrs. Catherine Thistlethwaite for a term of years not yet expired, and upon the death of Walter Stagg the remainder of the term is vested in John Stagg, his son, now we hereby agree that, upon John Stagg's surrendering up the lease now in being, a new lease be by us granted to him for 13 years to commence from Lady day next at the yearly rent of £100, payable quarterly, and under the same covenants and agreements as are contained in the lease now in being. John Stagg shall be obliged by his new lease to sow a ground of arable land containing 14 acres, called Park End, part of the farm, with good sainfoin seed within 2 years from the commencement of the new lease. After that shall be so sown he is not to plough up any of the 14 acres during the term of 12 years. We further agree to put the messuage, barns, stables, and other housing on the farm in good tenantable repair within 2 years from the commencement of the new lease.

We agree to continue the order made at our last meeting, held at Froxfield 27 September 1726, concerning the prosecution of Mrs. Edmonds, and the order made at that meeting for the prosecution of persons that have built cottages in the manor of Froxfield, more particularly the persons that have built cottages in the chalk pit near the Cross Keys inn.

It is ordered that a copy of court roll be by us granted to Charles Stagg of a messuage or tenement and 1 yardland in the manor of Huish, lately fallen into our hands by the death of Ann Stagg, widow, mother of Charles, who held it for her widowhood. [He is] to hold for his own life and the life of Lawrence Stagg, his brother, at the yearly rent of £6, free from all taxes; fine £30.

Ordered that a lease be granted from us to Thomas Osmond of a cottage by him lately erected in the manor of Froxfield. [He is] to hold for 99 years if he, Barbara his wife, and Barbara their daughter, or either of them, shall so long live; yearly rent 1*s*., fine agreed to be remitted in consideration of building except only 5*s*., heriot 5*s*.

Ordered that our steward do prosecute all persons as have already, or hereafter shall, unlawfully cut and take any wood from any of the coppices belonging to the almshouse.

Almshouse

It is ordered that Mrs. Abbot, one of the hospital widows, shall be continued matron of the hospital for the ensuing year and that she [shall] carry her white wand as usual.

Whereas Frances Young, one of the widows inhabiting in the hospital, absented herself from her habitation for half a year ending at Michaelmas 1726 without our licence, for which crime we gave our steward a verbal order at our last meeting to stop her pay from thenceforth, and it now appearing to us that the memory and understanding of Frances Young was impaired by sickness and [that sickness] was the occasion of her forgetting the orders of the hospital, we order our steward to stop her pay during the half year she was absent only and to pay her equally with the rest of the widows of the hospital from Michaelmas 1726 until Michaelmas last, and so on until she shall be guilty of any like crime.

Ordered that our steward do forthwith pay to William Gregory his bill of £7 16*s*. 5*d*. for tiling and mason's work done at the hospital [and] beginning 3 October 1726.

That our steward do pay to Jeliosophet Kimber £2 10*s*. for lafts [?laths] used at the hospital, £1 8*s*. 8*d*. to Robert Hawkins for lime and tiles used there, £3 3*s*. to Thomas Osmond for carpenter's work there, and £3 4*s*. 8*d*. to Jeffery Banks, blacksmith, for work done at the hospital.

Whereas we formerly received information that Grace Gibbs, one of the widows of the hospital, lived incontinently and was guilty of other disorders there, for which crimes we gave our steward a verbal order to stop [*altered to* suspend] her pay till our next meeting, and we having now received further information of her incontinency and disorderly way of living, we order that she be forthwith expelled and turned out of her house in the hospital. If she quits her house within a fortnight from henceforth without giving us any further trouble, we order our steward to pay her equally with the rest of the widows inhabiting in the hospital until Michaelmas last, but, if she refuses to quit her house in a peaceable manner within that time, then we order that all monies which she claims from the duchess of Somerset's charity shall be wholly suspended and stopped.

Signatures

George Popham, Henry Hungerford, Richard Jones, Francis Popham, Edward Ernle.

18 March 1729, at the Green Dragon, Ramsbury

Adjournment

We adjourn this meeting to Friday seven-night next, to be held at this place.

Signatures

Francis Popham, Richard Jones, George Popham, Henry Hungerford, Edward Ernle.

28 March 1729

Adjournment

We further adjourn this meeting to Friday in the Easter week next, to be held at the sign of the Phoenix in Pewsey.

Signatures

Francis Popham, Edward Ernle, George Popham, Samuel Whitelock, Richard Jones.

[?**11 April 1729**]

No meeting for want of a quorum.

16 December 1729, at the Green Dragon, Ramsbury

Trusteeship

We elect Thomas Batson of Ramsbury, esq., William Jones of Ramsbury, esq., Edward Seymour of Easton, esq., Edward Grinfield of Rockley, in the parish of Ogbourne St. Andrew, esq., and John Pocock of Mildenhall, clerk, trustees of the hospital to be added to us, and we order our steward to draw a conveyance of the trust estate from us to them ready to be produced to us at our next meeting.

and see almshouse business

Estate

We agree to grant to Jason Early of Bagshot in the parish of Shalbourne a lease of a cottage and garden lying near to Froxfield church between the houses of Mr. John Liddiard on the west side and the house of the widow Smith on the south side. [He is] to hold during his own life and the lives of Michael Munday of Great Bedwyn and William Early, son of Alexander Early of Sunninghill in the forest of Windsor, at the yearly rent of 1s.; heriot, 1s.

Almshouse

We order our steward forthwith to prefer a petition to the Rt. Hon. the Lord High Chancellor setting forth the reasons of our withdrawing the yearly allowance of Grace Gibbs, one of the widows inhabiting in the hospital, and that our steward do make his report of the same at our next meeting.

It is ordered that our steward do forthwith pay the widows Mrs. Baskerville and Mrs. Dobbins, inhabitants of the hospital, all their arrears now due to them, [money] which was stopped by reason of their absence from the hospital, they having now produced to us proper certificates that they were forced to be absent longer than the time by us allowed them by reason of sickness.

Signatures

Richard Jones, Edward Ernle, Henry Hungerford, Samuel Whitelock, George Popham.

The following note is entered among undated notes on the first page of the minute book.

To appoint a meeting at the widow Bell's on Wednesday 6 May next at [the] request of Francis Popham, Richard Jones, Henry Hungerford, esqs., George Popham and [John Pocock], clerks.

6 May 1730, at the sign of the Green Dragon, Ramsbury

Trusteeship/Almshouse

Whereas by former order hereinbefore inserted and by us subscribed we did order Mr. Thomas Franklin, our present steward, to expel Grace Gibbs, one of the widows inhabiting in the hospital, and to suspend her allowance due as an inhabitant thereof, she being then charged with the crime of incontinency and being guilty of other disorders in the hospital, whereas we then apprehended that we had power to punish her for her crimes by virtue of rules and orders formerly proposed by Sir Richard Holford, kt., late one of the masters of the High Court of Chancery, for the better government of the hospital, [and so believed] until we were since informed that those orders were not then confirmed and made part of the decree of the High Court of Chancery formerly made in favour of the hospital, and [whereas], upon Grace Gibbs's petition to the Lord High Chancellor, his lordship has ordered us to pay to her all her arrears now due, therefore in obedience to his lordship's order we now order Mr. Franklin forthwith to pay to her £22 1s., which appears to us to be all [the] arrears due from us to her at Lady day last, it being the same sum paid to each widow during the suspension of Grace Gibbs. We order our steward to pay to Grace Gibbs such cost as shall be taxed by a master for her law charges, in endeavouring to recover of us her arrears, after it shall be so taxed.

Signatures

Francis Popham, Henry Hungerford, Edward Ernle, Richard Jones, John Pocock.

21 August 1730

Trusteeship

It is ordered that our present steward Mr. Franklin do in the next Michaelmas term proceed in the court of Chancery to compel the securities of Mr. Joseph Walker, our late steward, to pass his accounts in that court and to pay all arrears due from him to the hospital.

Estate

It is ordered that a lease be by us granted to John Munday of a messuage and four grounds, called the Great coppice, in Huish, with its appurtenances, now in the occupation of John Munday by virtue of a lease granted to him by Edward Ryder, esq., whose estate in the premises is now determined and fallen into our hands. [He is] to hold the premises for 14 years from the feast day of St. Michael the Archangel next at the yearly rent of £30 and the payment of all taxes, and under such other covenants and agreements as are contained in Mr. Ryder's lease to him.

It is ordered that it be a request to Henry Hungerford and Edward Ernle, esqs., that they view what repairs have been already made, and what others are wanting, at Huish farm.

Signatures

Francis Popham, Richard Jones, Henry Hungerford, Thomas Batson, Edward Grinfield, George Popham, John Pocock.

Adjournment

This meeting was adjourned to 7 September next.

14 October 1730

Estate

We order that leases be by us granted to John Andrews, Thomas Alexander, William Davies, Robert Newman, and John Day of their several cottages, with their appurtenances, erected on the waste ground of the manor of Froxfield, under the same rents, heriots, covenants, conditions, and agreements as are contained in our leases made of the several cottages in Froxfield, by virtue of an order hereinbefore by us made, and for such lives as they shall severally and respectively name at the next court to be held for that manor.

It is ordered that Jeffery Banks be at liberty to surrender his estate in a copyhold messuage and blacksmith's shop in the manor of Froxfield at the next court to be held in and for that manor, and at that court to take a new estate in the messuage and shop for his own life and the lives of Anne Banks his daughter and John Osmond, the son of Thomas Osmond of Froxfield, wheelwright, in consideration of 40*s*. to be then paid to us. We order our steward to take such surrender and to make such new grant at that court.

Signatures

Francis Popham, Richard Jones, Thomas Batson, Edward Seymour, Edward Ernle, Henry Hungerford, George Popham.

4 May 1731

Estate

It is ordered that, upon the surrender of a lease by Edward Carpenter formerly made by us to him of a messuage or tenement, garden, and close, together with other lands, [all] at Chirton, called Pearson's *alias* Hort's, a new lease of the same be by us granted to William Barnes of Chirton. [He is] to hold for 99 years determinable on the death of three such lives as he shall nominate, in consideration of £14, the new building of the messuage now very much decayed, the yearly rent of 1*s*., and 5*s*. for a heriot.

It is ordered that our steward do forthwith keep a court leet and court baron in and for the manor of Huish, particularly to enquire into all encroachments made on the commons and lands in that manor.

Almshouse

It is ordered that our steward do forthwith pay Thomas Osmond, carpenter, his bill of £3 9*s*. 8*d*. for work done in and about Froxfield hospital, and that he do forthwith cause the garden walls belonging to the almshouse to be put in repair.

Next meeting

The next meeting is to be held at the Blue Lion in Froxfield the Thursday in the Whitsun week [10 June].

Signatures

Francis Popham, Richard Jones, George Popham, John Pocock, William Jones, Thomas Batson.

10 June 1731

Estate

Ordered that a lease be by us granted to Robert Hailstone of Manningford of a messuage or tenement, [a] garden, [an] orchard, and about 5 acres of arable land thereto belonging, late a copyhold estate in the manor of Huish and upon the decease of Margery Chandler, widow of Thomas Chandler, fallen into our hands. [He is] to hold the messuage or tenement etc. for 99 years if he [and] Robert and Mary, his son and daughter, shall so long live, in consideration of a fine of £14, the yearly rent of 40*s*. clear from taxes, and 5*s*. for a heriot.

Ordered that Mr. Franklin do forthwith bring an ejectment against John White, the present possessor of a cottage in this [?Froxfield] manor, in order to try the title of it.

Almshouse

It is ordered that Samuel Dyson do forthwith glaze the windows of the houses in the hospital hereinafter mentioned, viz. Mrs. Bernard's, Mrs. Meden's, Mrs. Powell's, Mrs. Clement's, and Mrs. Early's, and that our steward do pay him for it, those windows being found out of repair by the widows when they first came to inhabit their houses. That Samuel Dyson do forthwith amend the leads of the cupola of the hospital and do paint the doors, doorcases, and window cases of the chapel and the timber work belonging to the cupola.

Signatures

Henry Hungerford, Richard Jones, Thomas Batson, William Jones, John Pocock.

9 July 1731

Estate

It is ordered that a lease be granted to farmer Thomas Tarrant of Milton farm, now in his possession. [He is] to hold from Michaelmas next for 11 years at and under the same rents, covenants, and agreements as are contained in the lease now in being of that farm and which will expire at Michaelmas next.

Ordered that our steward, Mr. Thomas Franklin, do pay to John Munday of Oare 40*s*. towards the repairing of the housing belonging to a farm late Mr. Ryder's at Huish, lately fallen into our hands and now granted by us to John Munday for 14 years from Michaelmas last.

Signatures

Richard Jones, Thomas Bennet, Henry Hungerford, William Jones, John Pocock.

29 May 1732, at the Green Dragon, Ramsbury

Estate

We order that our steward, Mr. Thomas Franklin, do within 10 days go to Chirton farm and there view what repairs are wanting on that farm which ought to be done by Edward Carpenter, the late tenant; and do immediately after such view require him to do them and, on his refusal, commence an action at law against him. We further order that our steward do, at the charges of the hospital, before the next harvest cause a sufficient floor to be made in the wheat barn on the farm, and to make a new pair of great doors to the barley barn next [to] the street there and a new well drock to the well belonging to the farm.

It is ordered that, upon the surrender of a lease by us formerly granted of a messuage or tenement, [a] garden, and [a] close, [all] called Pearson's *alias* Hort's, at Chirton to William Barnes of that place for the lives of William his son [and] Mary and Elizabeth his daughters, a new lease be by us granted to William the father. [He is] to hold for the lives of William his son and Elizabeth his daughter; Sarah, another of his daughters, to be added in the room of Mary, now deceased, in consideration of 40*s*.; under the same rents, covenants, and agreements as are contained in the lease to be surrendered.

It is ordered that our steward do within 1 month go to Froxfield and enquire, and inform himself, by the testimony of all the ancient inhabitants there what lands belong to the vicarage house of Froxfield [so] that they may be distinguished from the waste ground of the manor. That our steward do at the same time enquire, and inform himself, by the like testimony whether the garden at Froxfield which we lately granted by lease to William Sutton together with a cottage has been usually held with, and properly belonging to, the cottage, whether the garden do belong to any other person, and what lands and ways properly belong to the cottage and garden. That our steward do report the same at the next meeting.

We order our steward forthwith to receive of Anne Smith of Froxfield, widow, 20*s*. in lieu of a heriot due on the death of Robert Smith, her husband, who lately died possessed of a copyhold estate in the manor of Froxfield valued at £5 a year.

Almshouse

We order that our steward do within 1 month enquire what widows belonging to the almshouse are [in] any ways guilty of the breach of any of the orders lately by us made, and confirmed by the court of Chancery, for the better governing [of] the almshouse, and in particular the sixth order. That our steward do make his report to us at our next meeting.

Signatures

Richard Jones, Henry Hungerford, John Pocock, Thomas Batson, William Jones.

9 August 1732

Estate

Whereas we have received information from Mr. Franklin, our steward, that he cannot perform the orders of our last meeting by which he was obliged to enquire of several things in the manor of Froxfield, he not having sufficient authority to administer oaths to the persons necessary to be examined, therefore we order [that] Mr. Franklin do within 1 month keep a court baron within and for the manor of Froxfield, and that he do then and there enquire into the matters, and perform the orders of the last meeting, relating to Froxfield.

Signatures

Francis Popham, Thomas Bennet, Edward Ernle, John Pocock, Edward Grinfield, Thomas Batson.

22 September 1732, at the Blue Lion, Froxfield

Estate

It is ordered that our steward, Mr. Franklin, do preserve the depositions now taken between the present vicar of Froxfield and John Waite, occupier of a cottage and garden standing on the waste ground adjoining to the vicarage house.

Next meeting

Ordered that part of an order at a meeting dated 29 May last relating to William Sutton be referred to our next meeting, and we adjourn this meeting to Tuesday next at the Green Dragon in Ramsbury.

Signatures

Francis Popham, Thomas Batson, Edward Grinfield, George Popham, John Pocock.

26 September 1732, the adjournment from the last meeting

Almshouse

It is ordered that our steward, Mr. Franklin, do, as soon as can be, admonish the widows belonging to the hospital to remove their children and all inmates from it.

That our steward do forthwith order the widow Dismore and the widow Siney to reside constantly at their respective habitation in the almshouse and to constantly attend at prayers.

That our steward do at our next meeting report to us the particular behaviour of all the widows as to their compliance with the above mentioned orders.

Whereas we being informed that Mrs. Abbot, the present matron of the almshouse, by reason of her great age is become incapable to perform the office, we therefore choose Ann Story [as] matron of the almshouse for the year ensuing.

Ordered that our steward do cause a new lock and key to be made forthwith for the almshouse front door.

Signatures

Francis Popham, George Popham, Thomas Batson, Edward Grinfield, John Pocock.

3 August 1733, at the Green Dragon, Ramsbury

Trusteeship

Ordered that our steward do make up his accounts between this [day] and 12 October next, and that for the future he does annually make up his accounts.

Estate

Ordered that a lease be granted to John Cannings of Fyfield farm, now in the occupation of Thomas Warner by virtue of a lease which will expire at Michaelmas day 1734. [He is] to hold the farm from that Michaelmas day for 21 years at and under the same rents, covenants, conditions, and agreements as are expressed in Thomas Warner's lease. That our steward do forthwith draw a lease to John Cannings accordingly.

Ordered that our steward do forthwith proceed to get possession of a cottage standing on the waste ground of the manor of Huish [and] now in the possession of Thomas Alexander, he having refused to take of us a lease thereof [and] an ejectment being already brought for that purpose.

Almshouse

Ordered that our steward do, at the time he shall make his next quarter's payment to the widows of the almshouse, pay to Elizabeth Siney and Ann Dismore, two of the widows, 2 gns. each, being one quarter payable to them at St. Thomas's day last which was stopped by our steward by reason of their lodging out of the almshouse. Upon their humble submission and promise not to offend in the like nature for the future, payment is now ordered.

Ordered that our steward do forthwith cause the Bible of the chapel to be new bound, the common prayer book to be amended, and the clock belonging to the almshouse also to be amended; also to cause the several other necessary repairs about the roof and walls of the almshouse to be made, which were found to be wanting by such of us who viewed them in the Whitsun week last; also to cause the dial plate of the clock to be new painted and figured and the inscription over the door to be amended and made legible.

Ordered that our steward do pay to William Fench all the arrears which were due to his mother-in-law Frances Young, late one of the widows of the almshouse, now deceased, during the time she was maintained by Fench at his own house, she being so absent by reason of her blindness, old age, and other great infirmities and having permits granted her for that purpose.

Signatures

Francis Popham, Richard Jones, George Popham, William Jones, John Pocock, Henry Hungerford.

30 October 1734, at the Green Dragon, Ramsbury

Trusteeship

Ordered that Mr. Thomas Franklin, our steward, do forthwith pay to the Revd. Mr. James Searle, vicar of Froxfield and chaplain to the almshouse, £10 towards the rebuilding of the vicarage house of Froxfield, he having no place of residence belonging to the almshouse.

Estate

Ordered that our steward do forthwith cause the 2 acres of ground belonging to the farm late Mr. Ryder's at Huish, near the coppice called Huish Coffer at the upper part thereof, to be inclosed with a sufficient hedge at the expense of the charity. That our steward do let the ground for a term of years and for the best price he can get for it.

Ordered that our steward do forthwith enquire into the state of that coppice wood and that he sell and dispose thereof, either entire or by parcels to the best advantage.

Almshouse

Ordered that the apartment of Mrs. Cox, one of the widows of the almshouse, be forthwith put in repair, and that our steward do pay for such repairs out of the charity monies.

Signatures

Richard Jones, Thomas Batson, George Popham, William Jones, Francis Popham.

12 July 1736, at the Green Dragon, Ramsbury

Estate

It is ordered that Mr. Thomas Franklin, our steward, do enquire whether John Holloway of Orcheston (*Orson*), John Neate of Coate, and Edward Holloway of Netheravon are proper securities for the arrears of rent due from our tenant William Holloway and [for] all rent which shall grow due for our farm at Chirton on his lease now in being.

Ordered that we grant by copy of court [roll] to John Edmonds of

Oare in the parish of Huish, yeoman, a copyhold messuage and lands at Oare in the manor of Huish lately fallen into our hands on the death of Richard Edmonds. We order our steward at the next court to be held for that manor to admit John Edmonds tenant thereof. [He is] to hold from the feast day of St. Michael the Archangel next for his own life and the life of John Edmonds his son at and under the yearly rent of £16, a fine of £80, and a usual heriot for that estate. Our steward do receive of [the elder] John Edmonds all arrears of rent due from him at Michaelmas next, being £24.

Almshouse

Ordered that the porter of the hospital shall yearly receive the widows' gowns from the tailors that shall be employed to make them, and as often as he shall receive the gowns shall deliver one to each of the widows and take of them severally receipts for them. If at any time any gown shall be misemployed or lost by the porter he shall pay the value of such gown.

Signatures

Richard Jones, Thomas Batson, William Jones, Thomas Bennet, Edward Grinfield, Henry Hungerford.

2 June 1737

Trusteeship

We agree to elect Edward Popham of Littlecote, esq., Sir Michael Ernle of Brimslade, bt., John Morris, vicar of Aldbourne, trustees of the hospital to be added to us. We order our steward, Mr. Thomas Franklin, to draw a conveyance of the charity estates from us to them to the use of us and those new trustees.

Signatures

Thomas Bennet, Thomas Batson, John Pocock, William Jones, Henry Hungerford.

19 September 1737

Trusteeship

Ordered that, in pursuance of the duchess of Somerset's will, upon the death of a widow of the county-at-large, or other sooner determination of her estate in the almshouse, the next trustee whose turn [it] shall be to nominate shall put into the almshouse a widow residing in one of the duchess's manors given in charity in order to complete the number of the manor widows.

Ordered that our steward do for the future, on the death of every widow or other sooner determination of her estate in the almshouse, give notice thereof in writing to the next trustee whose turn it shall be to nominate; also of the denomination of the widow. In case there shall be any doubt or dispute about the qualification of the widow nominated it [is] to be referred to, and determined by, the trustees at their next general meeting.

Estate

Ordered that William Barnes of Chirton be allowed £11 out of the first year's rent of Chirton farm for digging and making a complete pond 20 yds. square on the most convenient part of the down belonging to the farm.

Ordered that William Barnes do plant 100 elms on the most convenient part of that farm in an husbandlike manner, that he be allowed 1*s.* for each tree out of the charity lands, and that he shall preserve them and, in case of failure of any trees, replant until such number shall grow.

Almshouse

Ordered that the widow Gordon be allowed her pay to Midsummer last, her order of admission being signed before quarter day though her admission was delayed by sickness till after that time.

Signatures

Thomas Bennet, Henry Hungerford, Thomas Batson, John Pocock, Edward Grinfield.

28 June 1738

Estate

It is ordered that John Bunce, servant to Henry Hungerford, esq., be appointed bailiff of the manor of Huish and of the manors of Chirton, Milton, and Fyfield, [all] belonging to the hospital. We agree that he shall have a salary of £4 a year from Midsummer day last.

That we grant by copy of court roll to Daniel Smith of Froxfield, yeoman, a messuage and lands in the manor [of Froxfield] lately fallen into our hands on the death of Anne Smith, widow. We order our steward, at the next court to be held for that manor, to admit Daniel Smith tenant thereof. [He is] to hold from the feast day of St. Michael the Archangel next upon his own life and the lives of George and John, sons of Stephen Smith of Kintbury, at and under the yearly rent of £4 free from taxes, fine of £28, and the usual heriot. That our steward do receive of Daniel Smith £4 10*s.*, which shall be due at Michaelmas next.

Signatures

Michael Ernle, E. Popham, William Jones, Thomas Batson, J. Morris.

11 August 1738, at the Green Dragon, Ramsbury

Estate

Ordered that our steward do at our next meeting produce a case stated with proper queries for Mr. Fazakerley's opinion on Roger Hitchcock's forfeiture of a copyhold estate in the manor of Huish by his being formerly convicted of felony. Our steward do in the meantime show such case to the inhabitants of Huish for their approbation and ask them if they will agree to Mr. Fazakerley's opinion.

Signatures

E. Popham, Michael Ernle, J. Morris, George Popham, Edward Grinfield, Thomas Batson.

9 October 1738, at the Angel, Marlborough

Estate

It is ordered that, [concerning] … [*MS. blank*] Smith, widow of Thomas Smith, late of Froxfield, upon her surrender of a bargain called the Horseshoe bargain at Froxfield Mr. Thomas Franklin, our steward, do then admit Joseph Drury of that place tenant thereof at the next court to be held for the manor of Froxfield. [He is] to hold it for his own life, and two such other lives as he shall nominate, at the quit rent of £10 13*s*. 4*d*. and in consideration of £160 to be laid out on rebuilding the messuage or tenement called the Horseshoe bargain. We order [that] our steward do mark out 10 trees towards the building of it.

Memorandum

That the above order was not pursued, Drury falling from his agreement.

Signatures

William Jones, Thomas Batson, Edward Grinfield, John Pocock, Michael Ernle.

26 January 1739, at the Angel, Marlborough

Trusteeship

It is ordered that Mr. Thomas Franklin, our steward, do forthwith prefer a petition to the Rt. Hon. the Lord Chancellor for his order in the disposal of the monies now in our hands, and which shall yearly increase by the income of the charity lands amounting to more than £400 a year, until they be laid out in building lodgings for 20 more poor widows to be added to the hospital according to the direction of the duchess's will.

Signatures

Michael Ernle, E. Popham, William Jones, Thomas Batson, John

Pocock, J. Morris, Edward Grinfield.

7 March 1740, at the Angel, Marlborough

Estate

It is ordered that our steward, Mr. Franklin, do draw a lease or leases of Huish farm, now in the possession of John Stagg, of a farm called Stubnail, now in the occupation of John Munday, and of a coppice called Huish Coffer pursuant to a contract signed by the new tenant, William Brown, with the proper and usual covenants to be inserted in the lease or leases.

Ordered that our steward do take out a policy of insurance from the Sun Fire Office, London, for the insuring from fire of the messuages, barns, stables, and other buildings on the farms following, to wit Chirton farm, Huish farm, and Milton farm.

Signatures

Michael Ernle, Thomas Batson, Henry Hungerford, Edward Grinfield, John Pocock.

29 September 1740, at the Angel, Marlborough

Estate

It is ordered that the copyhold estate at Froxfield late held by Alexander Platt for the life of Millicent Burton, widow, and on her death fallen into our hands, be granted to Alexander by copy of court roll, for three such lives as he shall nominate, at the next court to be held for the manor of Froxfield; at and under the yearly rent of £8 (free from taxes), the usual heriot, and a fine of £56; and £12 for the rent, and a heriot due on the death of the widow, since it fell into our hands. We order our steward to admit Alexander Platt tenant.

Ordered that the copyhold estate late Thomas Smith's called the Horseshoe bargain, in the manor of Froxfield and lately fallen into our hands by the death of his widow, be granted by copy of court roll to Samuel Smith, for three lives as he shall nominate, at the next court [to be held] for the manor; at and under the yearly rent of £10 13*s*. 4*d*. (free from taxes), the usual heriot, and a fine of £74 13*s*. 4*d*. We order our steward to admit Samuel Smith tenant.

Signatures

Thomas Batson, John Pocock, Edward Grinfield, E. Popham, William Jones.

18 November 1740, at the Green Dragon inn, Ramsbury

Estate

It is ordered that, whereas William Barnes has a lease from us of Chirton farm for 20 years at £94 yearly free from all taxes and repair, in which lease there is a proviso for making it void at the end of the first 4 years from the commencement of the term upon William Barnes's giving 6 months' notice, which he has given, and [it being] represented to us that he cannot hold the farm at that yearly rent we, being satisfied with the reasons by him given, agree to abate him out of that rent £10 yearly during the term he shall hold the farm. [We] also [agree] that he be allowed £5 towards his making an inclosure on the sheep down belonging to the farm. And we order our steward to draw a new lease to William Barnes of that farm accordingly.

Ordered that our steward do forthwith commence an action at law against John Munday, in such manner as he shall be advised, for the recovery of £15, being half a year's rent due from him to us at Michaelmas last for the farm aforesaid

Signatures

Michael Ernle, William Jones, George Popham, Thomas Batson, Edward Grinfield, Henry Hungerford.

12 March 1742, at the Green Dragon, Ramsbury

Estate

It is ordered that, on the surrender of a lease, dated 9 July 1731 and granted by us to Robert Hailstone, of a messuage and lands in the manor of Huish for 99 years determinable on the death of three lives therein named, a new lease be granted to William Matthews of Huish, to whom the lease has been transferred by Robert Hailstone by [an] indenture dated 16 October last. [He is] to hold the [premises] for 99 years determinable on the death of three such lives as he shall nominate, under a fine of £3 and under the same rents, heriots, covenants, and agreements as are expressed in the lease to Robert Hailstone.

Ordered that a further term of 11 years be granted to farmer Thomas Tarrant of Milton farm, belonging to the almshouse, to commence from Michaelmas next, at which time his present lease from us will expire. We order our steward to draw a lease accordingly from us to Thomas Tarrant, to commence from Michaelmas next for 11 years at and under the same rents, covenants, and agreements as are expressed in the lease now in being.

Signatures

Henry Hungerford, William Jones, Samuel Whitelock, Thomas Batson, Michael Ernle, Edward Grinfield, George Popham.

30 November 1742, at the Green Dragon, Ramsbury

Estate

Ordered that our steward do pay or allow £10 to William Brown, tenant of Huish and Stubnail farms, for the damages which he sustained by not entering till sometime in November 1740 on Stubnail, when he ought to have entered at the Michaelmas before, and towards the repairs of the bounds at Stubnail farm. That our steward do forthwith cause a good oaken barn floor to be laid in the west barn at Huish farm.

Almshouse

It is ordered that Mr. Thomas Franklin, our steward, do forthwith pay Anthony Pethers £2 14*s*. 10*d*., his blacksmith's bill for work done at the hospital.

Signatures

Samuel Whitelock, William Jones, Michael Ernle, Thomas Batson, John Pocock, Henry Hungerford.

12 September 1743, at the Angel, Marlborough

Estate

Ordered that, on the surrender or forfeiture of the estate which Mary Stagg, widow, now holds of us in the manor of Huish for her widowhood, a new estate be granted by copy of court roll to her son-in-law John Tarrant for his own life and such other life as he shall nominate; in consideration of the yearly rent of £12, to be paid for the future, and the usual heriot; in consideration that John Tarrant do give sufficient security that he will within 1 year from the time of his admittance rebuild all housing which has decayed and fallen down on the copyhold for want of repair and in the same manner as it stood thereon 20 years last past, and within the same time sufficiently repair all the housing now standing thereon; and in consideration that John Tarrant do surrender the copyhold estate for the benefit of his mother-in-law Mary Stagg in case she shall recover her senses so as to be capable of managing that copyhold, and in the meantime to maintain and provide for his mother[-in-law] in all [that is] necessary.

Ordered that, on the surrender of Jane Smith's widowhood in a copyhold estate at Froxfield, a new grant be granted by copy of court roll to Thomas Cripps, her son-in-law, for the lives of his wife and two daughters at the yearly rent of £8, free from taxes, and the usual heriot. We order our steward to proceed accordingly.

Ordered that, on the surrender of a cottage at Froxfield lately held by William Vincent by lease for his life, a new lease be granted to William Littman for his own life and two other lives as he shall nominate; under the yearly rent of 1*s*. and a fine of £6.

Almshouse

It is ordered that our steward do forthwith, at the expense of the charity, cause the following repairs to be performed: the tiling at the north-west corner of the almshouse, the widow Hamblin's house in the almshouse, the ivy to be taken off the chimneys in the almshouse, the widow Hamblin's windows to be amended, and the widow Holton's house in the almshouse to be amended. That our steward do, at the expense of the charity, provide proper mats for the chapel in the almshouse.

Signatures

Henry Hungerford, Michael Ernle, William Jones, John Pocock, Thomas Bennet.

5 January 1745, at the Angel inn, Marlborough

Trusteeship

We the trustees whose names are hereunto subscribed, by virtue of the powers given us by the will of the duchess and since confirmed by the decree of the High Court of Chancery, appoint Charles Young of Marlborough, gentleman, to be our steward and receiver of all manors, rents, revenues, and estates to the hospital belonging, the office being become vacant by the death of Mr. Thomas Franklin, the late steward. [*Signed*] Michael Ernle, John Pocock, Henry Hungerford, E. Popham, William Jones, Thomas Batson, Edward Grinfield.

Ordered that the executors or administrators of the late Mr. Thomas Franklin do deliver to Charles Young all deeds, evidences, court rolls, rentals, survey books, papers, and writings belonging to the charity in their custody or power so soon as Charles Young shall have given security for the due execution of his office pursuant to the decree of the court of Chancery in that behalf.

Next meeting

Ordered that the next meeting shall be on Wednesday 20 March 1745 at the Angel inn in Marlborough, and that the nominated steward do in the meantime acquaint the executors or administrators of the late Mr. Thomas Franklin that they are then to be prepared to make up their accounts.

Signatures

William Jones, Thomas Batson, Michael Ernle, Edward Grinfield, John Pocock, Henry Hungerford, E. Popham.

Endorsement

23 January 1745, sent Mrs. Franklin a copy of the last order by Mr. William Sutton. C[harles] Y[oung].

20 March 1745, at the Angel inn, Marlborough

Trusteeship

It is ordered that Mrs. Sarah Franklin, executrix of Mr. Thomas Franklin, the late steward and receiver, deceased, do forthwith deliver over to Mr. Charles Young, the steward and receiver elect, all deeds, evidences, court books, survey books, rentals, papers, and writings belonging to the charity.

Ordered that Mr. Charles Young do procure an office copy of the decree made on the hearing of a cause now depending in the court of Chancery wherein the Attorney General, on behalf of the poor widows inhabiting the hospital, was plaintiff and Sir Samuel Grimston, bt., and others [were] defendants.

Signatures

Michael Ernle, Henry Hungerford, Thomas Batson, William Jones, John Pocock.

23 July 1745, at the Angel inn, Marlborough

Almshouse

It is ordered that the steward elect do provide a new surplice of Holland, of 5*s.* an ell or thereabouts, and a new common prayer book for the service of the chapel belonging to the almshouse, and do pay for them.

Signatures

Michael Ernle, Henry Hungerford, William Jones, Thomas Batson, John Pocock.

3 October 1746, at the Angel inn, Marlborough

Present

Thomas Bennet, esq., William Jones, esq., Thomas Batson, esq., Henry Hungerford, esq., Sir Michael Ernle, bt., the Revd. Mr. John Pocock.

Trusteeship

At this meeting the trustees received the accounts of Mrs. Sarah Franklin, executrix of Mr. Thomas Franklin, the late receiver of the estates belonging to the charity, from Michaelmas 1742 to Michaelmas 1744, and took into consideration the affidavit of Mrs. Franklin written after the account. As to £18 3*s.* 6*d.*, in the affidavit alleged to be charged in Mrs. Franklin's own wrong, they find that Daniel Gibbons, in the affidavit named, did receive that sum for goods sold under the distress made on the goods of William Holloway, formerly the tenant of Chirton farm, part of the charity estate, for which sum

Daniel Gibbons at a former meeting of the trustees declared he was ready to account with Mrs. Franklin. They find that Mrs. Franklin has in the account charged herself with the £18 3*s*. 6*d*. and with the further sum of £222 16*s*. 6*d*., the outstanding arrear from Holloway, and no more, and that she has craved allowance in the account for the £222 16*s*. 6*d*. so that she stands charged with no more of the debt from Holloway than the £18 3*s*. 6*d*., which the trustees apprehend [that] she ought to be. As to the several sums of money amounting to £8 4*s*. 6*d*., in the affidavit mentioned to be paid by the late receiver and to be omitted in the account, Mrs. Franklin having produced vouchers for them the trustees think they ought to be allowed her; and that £8 4*s*. 6*d*. being deducted out of the sum of £324 17*s*. 11½*d*., the balance of the account as it now stands, the balance will then be reduced to £316 13*s*. 5½*d*. The trustees also find that Mrs. Franklin has at several times paid to Mr. Charles Young, the present receiver, several sums of money amounting to £290 which, being deducted out of the £316 13*s*. 5½*d*., there will then remain in the hands of Mrs. Franklin of the charity monies £26 13*s*. 5½*d*. and no more.

Whereas Mr. Thomas Franklin, in his account from Michaelmas 1741 to Michaelmas 1742, craved allowance for £335 as an outstanding arrear from William Holloway, and Mrs. Sarah Franklin, in her account from Michaelmas 1742 to Michaelmas 1744, has only charged herself with the before mentioned £18 3*s*. 6*d*. and £222 16*s*. 6*d*., together making £241, now we hereby acknowledge that £94, residue of the arrears of £335, was paid by Mr. Samuel Martin, late under-sheriff of Wiltshire, to Mr. Charles Young, the present receiver.

Estate

see trusteeship business

Signatures

Thomas Bennet, Michael Ernle, Henry Hungerford, William Jones, Thomas Batson, John Pocock.

14 May 1747, at the house of Essex Bell, widow, at Ramsbury

Present

William Jones, esq., Thomas Batson, esq., Henry Hungerford, esq., Sir Michael Ernle, bt., the Revd. Mr. John Pocock.

Trusteeship

Ordered that the steward do write to Sir Edward Seymour to know whether it be his pleasure to resign the trust.

Estate

Ordered that the steward do cause all the estates belonging to the hospital to be measured and mapped.

Almshouse

Whereas several of the widows do absent themselves from the hospital without leave of the trustees contrary to the rules established by the decree of the court of Chancery for the better rule and government thereof and do remain absent for a great time, and [whereas] it sometimes happens that they neither return nor make any proper resignation of their houses, whereby such houses stand long vacant and other deserving objects are deprived of the benefit of the charity in the meantime, now we direct that the steward do cause application to be made to the court of Chancery for the directions of the court therein and to remedy the mischief.

Signatures

Henry Hungerford, Michael Ernle, William Jones, Thomas Batson, John Pocock.

22 July 1747, at the house of Essex Bell, widow, at Ramsbury

Present

Henry Hungerford, esq., William Jones, esq., Thomas Batson, esq., Edward Popham, esq., Sir Michael Ernle, bt., the Revd. Mr. John Pocock.

Estate

Resolved that John Cannings may hold the estate at Milton called Batchelor's bargain, lately fallen into the hands of the trustees by the death of Charles Kellway, until Michaelmas 1748 under the yearly rent of £35.

Resolved that Thomas Banning have leave to change the life of John Banning, now in the copyhold estate which he holds in the manor of Huish and Shaw, for the life of his son Thomas, paying £4 4*s*. as a fine. The steward is ordered to make a grant of the estate by copy of court roll accordingly to Thomas Banning the elder under the usual rent and services.

Signatures

Henry Hungerford, William Jones, Thomas Batson, E. Popham, Michael Ernle, John Pocock.

1 December 1747, at the house of Essex Bell, widow, at Ramsbury

Present

William Jones, esq., the Revd. Mr. John Pocock, Henry Hungerford, esq., Thomas Batson, esq., Sir Michael Ernle, bt.

Estate

Resolved that a lease of Batchelor's bargain be granted to Mr. John Cannings from Michaelmas last for so many years as are to come in his lease of Fyfield farm, which he holds under Henry Hungerford, esq.; rent £31 15*s.* clear of taxes.

Resolved that a grant by copy of court roll be made to John Edmonds of the cottage and garden in the tithing of Oare in the parish of Wilcot and manor of Huish, lately fallen in by the death of Sarah Edmonds, widow, with the appurtenances, for the lives of him and his son John successively according to the custom of the manor; fine £2 10*s.*, rent 13*s.* 4*d.* a year clear of taxes, and all other works etc.

Resolved that Thomas Vernall have leave to add the life of Thomas Webb of Froxfield, labourer, in the cottage lately erected on the waste of the manor of Froxfield and granted to him by indenture of lease dated 18 March 1729; fine £2 10*s.*, rent and heriot as before.

Signatures

William Jones, Thomas Batson, John Pocock, Henry Hungerford, Michael Ernle.

3 June 1748, at the hospital

Present

Henry Hungerford, esq., John Pocock, clerk, Sir Michael Ernle, bt., Thomas Batson, esq., Edward Popham, esq.

Almshouse

Mrs. Martha Shepherd appointed matron for the year ensuing.

The hospital viewed, and orders given for the necessary repairs.

The chapel, pulpit, seats, books, and what belongs to the chapel viewed and found in good order.

Signatures

Henry Hungerford, John Pocock, Michael Ernle, Thomas Batson.

5 April 1749, at the Angel inn, Marlborough

Present

Henry Hungerford, esq., William Jones, esq., Thomas Batson, esq., the Revd. Mr. John Pocock, Sir Michael Ernle, bt.

Estate

Farmer William Barnes complained that one Frances Lavington, who claims a cottage adjoining to the lifehold estate of William Barnes which he holds under the charity, and which cottage, as he alleges, is partly built on the charity estate, has thrown down a wall which he built to part his ground from the cottage and has done him great damage in his garden and otherwise molested him in the possession of his lifehold estate. Mr. Henry Hungerford and Sir Michael Ernle are desired to take a view of the premises.

William Barnes requested to have a granary built on Chirton farm.

[It is] ordered that the steward do apply to Isaac Smith of Ogbourne to consider of the best method of building such granary and make an estimate of the charge of building a granary on nine stones.

Signatures

Henry Hungerford, William Jones, John Pocock, Michael Ernle, Thomas Batson.

27 February 1750, at the Angel inn, Marlborough

Present

Henry Hungerford, esq., William Jones, esq., Sir Michael Ernle, bt., the Revd. Mr. John Pocock, Thomas Batson, esq.

Estate

Ordered that an estate by copy of court roll be granted to Thomas Banning of that small dwelling house and 4 acres of land in Clench, in the manor of Huish and Shaw, with the appurtenances, for the lives of Thomas and Thomas his son; fine £10, rent 40*s*., and the usual heriot.

Ordered that an estate by copy of court roll be granted to Charles Liddle of that cottage and garden at Oare, in the manor of Huish and Shaw, for the lives of Charles and Mary Harris, the daughter of Joseph Harris, late of Oare, maltster; fine 20*s*., rent 10*s*., and the accustomed heriot. Fine now paid.

Ordered that the pates at Milton farm be repaired and a pump put in there.

Ordered that, in consideration that John Tull had rebuilt the cottage at Wick, in the manor of Huish and Shaw and now in the occupation of Alice Tull, his widow, a lease thereof be granted to Alice for 99 years if she, Daniel Kingston of Wick, labourer, and John, the son of William New of Burbage, gardener, or any of them, so long lives; rent 10*s*.

Ordered that a lease be granted to Joan Cully of the cottage in Wick, now in her possession, for 99 years if Joanna Crook, Mary Barley, and Richard Townsend, or any of them, so long lives; rent 10*s*., fine remitted in consideration of repairs and improvements formerly done by her.

Ordered that the steward do allow William Bunce, a copyhold tenant of the manor of Froxfield, six oaks to be taken out of the Almshouse coppice for the repairs of his copyhold.

Signatures

Henry Hungerford, Thomas Batson, William Jones, John Pocock, Michael Ernle.

15 May 1751, at the Angel inn, Marlborough

Present

Thomas Bennet, esq., William Jones, esq., Thomas Batson, esq., the Revd. Mr. John Pocock, Sir Michael Ernle, bt.

Trusteeship

We choose Ambrose Goddard, esq., Sir Robert Long, bt., John Whitelock, esq., the Revd. Mr. Thomas Talbot, and Thomas Bigg, esq., to be trustees in the room of Samuel Whitelock, esq., the Revd. Mr. George Popham, Henry Hungerford, esq., deceased, and of His Grace the duke of Somerset and Edward Grinfield, esq., who desire to resign. In regard that Edward Popham, esq., was not present at this meeting we refer it to him to name a new trustee in the room of the Revd. Mr. John Morris, who desires to resign.

Estate

Ordered that the receiver pay or allow to farmer Thomas Tarrant £4 17*s*. 6*d*. for carriage of materials for repairs of Milton farm.

Ordered that new doors be made of deal for the barn at Milton farm, and that the stable there be effectually repaired.

Upon a surrender of the estate of Charles Liddle in his copyhold cottage at Oare, let it be granted to John Jones for his life and the life of John his son; fine for exchanging two lives 40*s*.

Resolved that Huish farm, Huish Coffer, and Stubnail farm be let to John Tarrant for 8 years at £120 a year rent clear of taxes.

Ordered that the steward do the needful in relation to the matters in difference between the lord of the manor of Chirton and the trustees of this charity and in relation to Frances Lavington.

Ordered that a granary be built on Chirton farm.

Signatures

Thomas Bennet, William Jones, Thomas Batson, John Pocock, Michael Ernle.

17 September 1751, at the Angel inn, Marlborough

Present

Mr. Bennet, Mr. Jones, Mr. Batson, Mr. Pocock, Sir Michael Ernle, Sir Robert Long, Mr. Northey, Mr. Goddard, Mr. Bigg.

Trusteeship

A presentation of James Searle, clerk, chaplain of the hospital, to the rectory of Huish was executed.

1 May 1752, at the Angel inn, Marlborough

Present

William Jones, esq., Thomas Batson, esq., Sir Michael Ernle, bt., Ambrose Goddard, esq., Thomas Bigg, esq.

Estate

Ordered that a grant be made to Charles Head by copy of court roll of the copyhold bargain, part of the manor of Huish, late Mary Head's, for the lives of Charles and Elizabeth his daughter; fine £120, rent £20 clear of taxes, and the usual heriot.

Ordered that a grant be made to Henry Tuck by copy of court roll of the copyhold bargain, part of the manor of Huish, late Mary Tuck's, for the lives of Henry and William his son; fine £12, rent 40*s.* clear of taxes, and the usual heriot.

Signatures

William Jones, Thomas Batson, Michael Ernle, A. Goddard, Thomas Bigg.

4 July 1752, at the Angel inn, Marlborough

Present

Mr. Batson, Mr. Pocock, Sir Michael Ernle, Mr. Northey, Mr. Goddard, Mr. Bigg.

Estate

Resolved that the matter in difference in relation to the house of Frances Lavington shall, by the consent of the Revd. Mr. Caleb Colton, lord of the manor of Chirton, be referred to Sir Michael Ernle, William Northey, esq., and Ambrose Goddard, esq., and that they meet at Chirton on Monday 27 July thereon.

Ordered that the matter between William Barnes and Michael Burgess in relation to the driftway over Northborough be tried at the next assizes.

Signatures

Thomas Batson, John Pocock, Michael Ernle, W. Northey, Thomas Bigg.

29 May 1753, at the Angel inn, Marlborough

Present

Thomas Bennet, esq., Sir Michael Ernle, bt., Thomas Batson, esq., the Revd. Mr. John Pocock, Sir Robert Long, bt., William Northey, esq., Ambrose Goddard, esq., Thomas Bigg, esq., John Whitelock, esq., the Revd. Mr. Thomas Talbot.

Estate

Let a lease be granted to John Cannings the younger of Fyfield farm and Batchelor's bargain for 21 years from the expiration of the present lease of Fyfield farm, at the yearly rent of £102 clear of taxes.

Let a lease be granted to William Littman of the cottage at Froxfield late in the possession of William Vincent and now in the possession of William Littman; for 99 years if William Littman, James Vincent, aged about 17, the son of William Vincent, late of Froxfield, wheelwright, and William Vincent, aged about 14, [an]other son of William Vincent, deceased, or any of them, so long lives; fine £9, rent 1*s.*

Let a lease of Huish farm, Huish Coffer, and Stubnail farm be granted to John Tarrant for 9 years from Michaelmas last at the rent of £120 clear of taxes. Whereas Huish farm has been hitherto a Lady day's bargain and Stubnail farm has been a Michaelmas bargain and John Tarrant, pursuant to a former agreement, entered thereon accordingly, and whereas it appears to us that it will be beneficial to lay those farms together and make them both Michaelmas bargains, and John Tarrant has agreed to allow £24 for the half year's rent for Huish farm from Lady day 1752 to Michaelmas 1752, therefore let the receiver abate or allow to John Tarrant £24 10*s.*, the residue of the half year's rent.

Let the receiver pay William Barnes, the tenant of Chirton farm, £16 1*s.*, which he paid for the costs of a nonsuit in the cause wherein he was plaintiff against Michael Burgess touching the droveway claimed across Northborough.

Let the receiver pay to John Clements £20 5*s.* 6*d.* for measuring and mapping the manor of Froxfield, Fyfield farm, and Oare bargain.

Let a lease of Milton farm be granted to Thomas Tarrant for 7 years from Michaelmas next at £82 a year clear of taxes, and let a new barn's floor be laid.

Let the receiver pay Isaac Smith £80 for building the granary at Chirton farm.

Signatures

Robert Long, Michael Ernle, W. Northey, John Pocock, John Whitelock, Thomas Bigg, Thomas Batson, Thomas Talbot, A. Goddard.

11 May 1754, at the Angel inn, Marlborough

Present

Sir Robert Long, bt., William Northey, esq., Ambrose Goddard, esq., the Revd. Mr. John Pocock, the Revd. Mr. Thomas Talbot.

Estate

Leave is given to Mr. John Cannings to grub the hedgerow between the Elbow ground and Bottom mead on Fyfield farm, reserving to the trustees all trees growing in the hedgerow.

Let the receiver pay to William Barnes 33*s.*, which he paid for the costs of a non-prosecution in the action Barnes against Hayward and others relating to Frances Lavington's house.

Let oak timber be allowed for a new barn's floor at Chirton farm, the tenant finding workmanship and carriage of materials, and let the old floor be used in repairing the floor of the other barn.

Let a granary on nine stones be built at Huish farm, the tenant finding carriage of materials and straw for thatching it.

Let the rails belonging to Huish churchyard be new made.

Signatures

Robert Long, W. Northey, Thomas Talbot, John Pocock, A. Goddard.

10 October 1754, at the Angel inn, Marlborough

Present

Sir Robert Long, Sir Michael Ernle, the Revd. Mr. Pocock, Ambrose Goddard, esq., Thomas Batson, esq.

Estate

Let a lease be granted to Mr. Benjamin Merriman of the cottage at Wick, part of the manor of Huish, late in the possession of Alice Tull, widow; for 99 years from this day if he, aged about 32, Elizabeth his daughter, aged about 5, and John, the son of William New of Burbage, aged about 9, or any of them, so long lives; rent 10*s*.; consideration, surrender of the present lease and £4 10*s*. fine, now paid.

Signatures

Robert Long, Michael Ernle, John Pocock, A. Goddard, Thomas Batson.

26 October 1754, at the Angel inn, Marlborough

Present

Thomas Batson, esq., John Pocock, clerk, Edward Popham, esq., Sir Michael Ernle, bt., William Northey, esq., Thomas Bigg, esq., Thomas Talbot, clerk.

Trusteeship

Ordered that the following scheme be laid before the master to whom the cause relating to this charity stands transferred touching the application of the savings out of the charity estate until it shall be wanted for building houses for 20 widows more: that the savings be vested in government securities and that the dividends and produce be laid up for the benefit of the charity.

Almshouse

The orders made by the trustees who visited the hospital in Whitsun week last are hereby confirmed.

Signatures

Thomas Batson, John Pocock, E. Popham, Michael Ernle, W. Northey, Thomas Bigg.

22 May 1755, at the hospital

Present

Thomas Batson, esq., John Pocock, clerk, John Whitelock, esq.

Almshouse

The hospital [was] viewed and orders [were] given for the necessary repairs.

7 July 1755, at the Angel inn, Marlborough

Present

Thomas Batson, esq., Edward Popham, esq., Sir Michael Ernle, bt., Sir Robert Long, bt., Thomas Bigg, esq., John Whitelock, esq.

Trusteeship

We elect Thomas Goddard of Swindon, esq., Richard Goddard of Marlborough, esq., and William Liddiard of Ogbourne, esq., to be trustees of this charity in the room of Thomas Bennet, esq., William Jones, esq., and Ambrose Goddard, esq., late trustees, deceased.

Estate

Let a cowhouse be built at Milton farm for six cows, the tenant finding straw and thatching.

Let £5 be allowed Thomas Tarrant for laying a yellow deal floor on oaken sills in the parlour at Milton farm.

Let the receiver allow John Tarrant £32 11*s.* 3*d.*, which he has paid for repairs at Huish and Stubnail farms, as by bill now produced and allowed.

Let the receiver pay John Eyles, carpenter, £19 9*s.* 10*d.*, his bill for repairs at Huish and Stubnail farms.

Let a grant be made to Alexander Platt of the copyhold tenement at Froxfield late in the tenure of Elizabeth Smith, widow, deceased, for the lives of Alexander, aged about 50, Amy Drury, aged about 20, the daughter of Joseph Drury of Froxfield, innholder, and Robert Drury, aged about 12, son of that Joseph; fine £50, rent £10, and the accustomed heriots.

Almshouse

We appoint John Osmond to be porter of the hospital; £4 a year salary.

Signatures

Thomas Batson, E. Popham, Michael Ernle, Robert Long, Thomas Bigg.

1 October 1756, at the Angel inn, Marlborough

Present

None of the trustees attended.

7 October 1756, at the Angel inn, Marlborough

Present

Sir Robert Long, bt., Sir Michael Ernle, bt.

23 October 1756, at the Angel inn, Marlborough

Present

Thomas Batson, esq., Edward Popham, esq., Sir Michael Ernle, bt., Thomas Bigg, esq., John Whitelock, esq.

Trusteeship

We elect George Hungerford of Studley, esq., to be a trustee of this charity in the room of the Revd. Mr. Thomas Talbot, who has resigned.

Estate

Let Charles Head be permitted to add one life in his copyhold at Huish at the fine of £60, rent and heriot as before.

Signatures

Thomas Batson, E. Popham, Michael Ernle, John Whitelock, Thomas Bigg.

7 June 1757, at the Angel inn, Marlborough

Present

Thomas Batson, esq., the Revd. Mr. Pocock, Edward Popham, esq., Sir Michael Ernle, Sir Robert Long, Thomas Bigg, esq., Thomas Goddard, esq., Richard Goddard, esq., William Liddiard, esq., George Hungerford, esq.

Estate

Let the receiver pay to William Barnes 40*s.* which he paid for removing and new making 4 lugs of mud wall on Chirton farm, which had been presented by the homage as standing on the waste.

Let the copyhold bargain at Huish, late Roger Hitchcock's, be granted to John Rudman of Manningford for his life and the life of William his son; rent £7, fine £42.

Let the house and malthouse at Froxfield now in the occupation of Elizabeth Rotherham, widow, be granted to her by lease for 7 years from Michaelmas next at the rent of £7.

Sir Michael Ernle, Mr. Pocock, and Mr. Liddiard are desired to view Froxfield farm and consider of Mr. Ivy's proposal for breaking up the down.

Let 2 tons of timber be allowed to John Cannings for repairs.

Signatures

Thomas Batson, G. Hungerford, John Pocock, T. Goddard, W. Liddiard, E. Popham.

3 September 1757, at the Angel inn, Marlborough

Present

Thomas Batson, esq., Edward Popham, esq., Sir Michael Ernle, bt., Thomas Bigg, esq., John Whitelock, esq., John Pocock, clerk, Richard Goddard, esq., William Liddiard, esq.

Estate

Sir Michael Ernle, Mr. Pocock, Mr. Whitelock, and Mr. Liddiard are desired to treat with Elias Ivy about letting Froxfield farm.

Almshouse

The orders made by the trustees who visited the hospital 1 June 1757 are hereby confirmed.

Let the receiver admit Elizabeth Ashburner, widow, the relict of Robert Ashburner, late of Newbury, clerk, deceased, into the hospital as a clergy widow.

Signatures

Michael Ernle, E. Popham, Thomas Batson, John Pocock, W. Liddiard, Richard Goddard, John Whitelock, Thomas Bigg.

18 May 1758, at the hospital, and adjourned to the Cross Keys, Froxfield

Present

Thomas Batson, esq., the Revd. Mr. Pocock, Sir Michael Ernle, bt., Richard Goddard, esq., William Liddiard, esq.

Estate

Let the house now in the possession of the widow Lockeram *alias* Rotheram be put in repair.

Ordered that the receiver do pay the following bills for repairs done at the Cross Keys at Froxfield. To Anne Smith for bricks and lime, tiles and paving bricks, £27 17*s*.; William Gale, bricklayer, £12 12*s*. 2*d*.; John Rogers, carpenter, £17 14*s*. 11½*d*.; Edward Cotterell, money disbursed by him to pay the labourers, £8 6*s*. 6*d*.; Henry Cox for carriage of materials, £2 9*s*.; Anthony Pethers, blacksmith, 19*s*.; James New for thatching, £2 17*s*. 9*d*.; Elias Ivy for carriage, 14*s*.; Mr. Stephen Pearse for three loads of straw, £2 2*s*.; Edward Tarrant for three loads of straw, £2 5*s*.; Aaron Liddiard for poles, £5 5*s*. 7½*d*.;

John Osmond for lath[s] and nails, 8*s.* 1*d.*; Alexander Platt for carriage, £2 5*s.* [Total] £85 16*s.* 1*d.*

Let John Osmond's life be added in the cottage wherein he now lives, and the life of Anne his wife be put in and exchanged for the life of Barbara his mother; fine £3, rent and heriot as before.

Almshouse

Let all necessary repairs be done to the hospital, such of the widows' houses as want it be whitewashed, and such of the ground floors as have not already been done be covered with bricks.

Next meeting

Notice [is] to be given for a meeting to be held at the Angel inn at Marlborough on 9 June 1758.

Signatures

Thomas Batson, Michael Ernle, Richard Goddard, John Pocock, W. Liddiard.

9 June 1758, at the Angel inn, Marlborough

Present

Sir Robert Long, bt., Sir Michael Ernle, bt., Edward Popham, esq., Thomas Batson, esq., the Revd. Mr. Pocock, Thomas Goddard, esq., Richard Goddard, esq.

Estate

The agreement made by the trustees for the letting of Froxfield farm to Elias Ivy is hereby confirmed.

26 June 1759, at the Angel inn, Marlborough

Present

The Revd. Mr. Pocock, Sir Michael Ernle, Thomas Bigg, esq., John Whitelock, esq., Richard Goddard, esq., William Liddiard, esq.

Estate

Let the life of John Banning, aged 27, the son of Thomas Banning, be added in the copyhold bargain of Thomas at Huish in place of Thomas Banning, junior, deceased; fine £4, rent and heriot as before.

Ordered that the following repairs be done at Froxfield farm. The roof of the carthouse at the end of the oat barn to be repaired; the roof of the granary to be repaired; the wall on the west side of the house to be taken down and rebuilt; a new room with a chamber over it and a cellar under it to be added at the south end of the house; a pump to be put into the well and the well to be steened; a woodhouse to be built at the end of the stable.

In consideration that William Selby erected the cottage at Froxfield now in his possession, and of a fine of £14, let a lease be granted to him thereof for 99 years determinable on the deaths of Thomas his son [and] Mary and Elizabeth his daughters; rent 2*s*. 6*d*.

In consideration that William Jason will substantially repair the cottage in Froxfield now in his possession, let the rent thereof from 30 May 1757 to Michaelmas last be remitted to him. Let a lease be granted to him for 99 years if he, Sarah his wife, William his son, or any [of] them, so long lives; fine £20, rent 2*s*. 6*d*. [*Margin*. Received]

In consideration that Thomas Kimber will substantially repair the cottage at Froxfield now in the occupation of Nicholas Kimber, let the rent thereof from 30 May 1757 to Michaelmas last be remitted to him. Let a lease be granted to Thomas for 99 years if he, Mary his wife, Mary his daughter, or any of them, so long lives; fine £20, rent 2*s*. 6*d*. [*Margin*. Received]

Ordered that notice be given to Anne Pethers to quit possession of the cottage at Froxfield at Michaelmas next.

Let the life of John Osmond be added in the cottage at Froxfield in his possession; fine £9, rent and heriot as before.

Let the cottage now in the occupation of Anne Pethers be converted into a stable for Edward Cotterell. [*Entry marked with a cross*]

Let the receiver pay the following bills for repairs. To John Osmond, carpenter, £78 9*s*. 8*d*.; Anthony Pethers, blacksmith, £19 6*s*. 10*d*.; Robert Hawkins for bricks, tiles, and lime, £31 1*s*. 11*d*.; James New, thatcher, £16 6*s*. 3*d*.; Edward Newman for rope yarn, £1 19*s*. 4½*d*.; Joseph Gregory, bricklayer, £24; Elias Ivy for money disbursed by him in payment of labourers and for money due to him for carriage of materials, £82 9*s*. 9*d*.; John Osmond for repairs at Elizabeth Lockeram's, £2.

Ordered that a new stable be built at the Cross Keys at Froxfield to hold 10 horses, and the house be put into tenantable repair, Edward Cotterell agreeing to pay £21 a year clear of taxes from Michaelmas next and 40*s*. a year clear of taxes for the cottage now in [the] possession of Anne Pethers.

Almshouse

Ordered that John Osmond build the cupola at the hospital according to the plan now produced by him.

Signatures

Michael Ernle, W. Liddiard, John Pocock, Richard Goddard, John Whitelock, Thomas Bigg.

15 October 1759, at the Angel inn, Marlborough

Present

The Revd. Mr. Pocock, Edward Popham, esq., Thomas Bigg, esq., John Whitelock, esq., Richard Goddard, esq.

Trusteeship

£600 Old South Sea annuities desired by the trustees to be purchased.

Estate

Let the little parlour at the Cross Keys have a new yellow deal floor laid.

Let a yellow deal floor be laid in the parlour chamber at the Cross Keys.

Let the chimney at the west end of the house be repaired. [*Margin.* Gale offered to do it for £1 11*s.* 6*d.*]

Let the receiver allow Edward Cotterell the land tax for the Cross Keys from Michaelmas 1757 to Michaelmas 1759.

Ordered that the receiver pay the following bills for repairs. To Elias Ivy, a bill paid by him for brick and lime, £47 10*s.* 5*d.*; to Elias Ivy, a bill paid by him to John Scamell for carriage of timber, £1 7*s.*; to John Osmond, carpenter, his bill by measure for the two barns and other work at Froxfield farm, £40 10*s.* 5*d.*; to John Brasher, his bill for carriage, £4 11*s.* 10*d.*

Signatures

E. Popham, John Pocock, John Whitelock, Thomas Bigg, Richard Goddard.

25 April 1760, at the Angel inn, Marlborough

Present

The Revd. Mr. John Pocock, Sir Michael Ernle, Thomas Bigg, esq., Richard Goddard, esq., George Hungerford, esq.

Estate

Ordered that the receiver pay the following bills for repairs and materials. To Mr. Richard Bailey, timber merchant, £223 8*s.* 10¼*d.*; to Robert Hawkins for bricks and lime, £47 4*s.* 7*d.*; to Joseph Gregory, bricklayer, for repairs at the Cross Keys, £16 3*s.* 8*d.*; to John Rawlins for bricks and lime, £44.

Let a deputation be made to John Tarrant to be gamekeeper of the manor of Huish.

Let the receiver do the needful to recover possession of the cottage at Froxfield now in the occupation of Anne Pethers, widow, if she shall not quit the possession in 1 week from hence.

Next meeting

Thursday 29 May for a meeting at Froxfield.

Signatures

John Pocock, Michael Ernle, Thomas Bigg, G. Hungerford, Richard Goddard.

29 May 1760, at the hospital, and adjourned to the Cross Keys, Froxfield

Present

The Revd. Mr. John Pocock, Edward Popham, esq., Sir Michael Ernle, Sir Robert Long, Thomas Bigg, esq., George Hungerford, esq., Thomas Goddard, esq., Richard Goddard, esq.

Trusteeship

Ordered that the receiver do lay the duchess's will and the copy of the decree of the court of Chancery before us at our next meeting, and all other proceedings had relating to the hospital, in order [for us] to consider further of the application made to us by the widows for building 20 additional lodgings pursuant to the will of the foundress.

Estate

Let a new lease be granted for three lives to Joseph Eyles, fine £6, heriot 1*s*., rent as before, if he shall produce a certificate that the lives on the present lease are now in being.

Almshouse

Let repairs be done at the hospital as follows. A new door be made to the house belonging to the widow Mintern; the drains to be cleansed belonging to the hospital.

Next meeting

Ordered that the receiver do give notice of a meeting to be held at the Angel inn at Marlborough on Thursday 26 June next.

Signatures

John Pocock, E. Popham, Michael Ernle, Robert Long, Thomas Bigg, G. Hungerford, T. Goddard, Richard Goddard.

26 June 1760, at the Angel inn, Marlborough

Present

The Revd. Mr. John Pocock, Edward Popham, esq., Sir Michael Ernle, Thomas Bigg, esq., Richard Goddard, esq.

27 October 1760, at the Angel inn, Marlborough

Present

John Pocock, clerk, Thomas Goddard, esq., Richard Goddard, esq.

10 November 1760, at the Angel inn, Marlborough

Present

John Pocock, clerk, Edward Popham, esq., Sir Michael Ernle,

John Whitelock, esq., Thomas Goddard, esq., Richard Goddard, esq.
Trusteeship

We choose Francis Popham, esq., and George Stonehouse, esq., to be trustees in the room of Thomas Batson, esq., and William Liddiard, esq., deceased.

Ordered that the receiver do lay before the trustees at their next meeting a copy of his account from Michaelmas 1758 to Michaelmas 1759.
Estate

Ordered that the receiver do pay the following bills for repairs, they having been referred at the meeting on 26 June last to the consideration of Mr. Pocock, who makes no objection thereto. To John Osmond, carpenter, for repairs at Froxfield farm, by measure, £81 6*s.* 8*d.*; to him for the same, by day work, £66 16*s.* 2*d.*; Joseph Gregory, bricklayer, for repairs at Froxfield farm, £70 11*s.* 2*d.*; Anthony Pethers, blacksmith, for repairs at Froxfield farm, £32 3*s.* 5*d.*; John Osmond, carpenter, for materials used in repairs at the Cross Keys, £29 7*s.* 8*d.*; John Osmond for work at the Cross Keys, £18 10*s.* 2*d.*; Anthony Pethers, blacksmith, for work at the Cross Keys, £7 2*s.* 2*d.*; Elias Ivy for work with his team in carriage of materials for repairs, etc., £41 2*s.* 8*d.*; James New for thatching the stable at the Cross Keys, £4 8*s.* 6*d.*; John Hicks, stonemason, for chimney piece etc. to Froxfield farm, £5 11*s.* 2*d.*; James New for thatching at Froxfield farm, £1 13*s.* 11*d.*; Edward Newman for rope yarn used in thatching, 18*s.* 2½*d.*
Signatures

Michael Ernle, E. Popham, T. Goddard, John Whitelock, Richard Goddard, John Pocock.

30 May 1761, at the Angel inn, Marlborough

Present

John Pocock, clerk, John Whitelock, esq., Thomas Goddard, esq., Richard Goddard, esq., Francis Popham, esq.
Estate

Let a new lease of Chirton farm be granted to William Barnes for 12 years from Lady day last at the present rent of £84 a year clear of taxes. What repairs are now necessary, after he has done what he is obliged to, are to be done for him.

In consideration of a surrender to be made of a lease dated 18 March 1729 and of a lease dated 8 June 1731, let a new lease be granted to William Barnes of the premises comprised in the two indentures of lease; for 99 years if John Barnes, aged 21, William Barnes, aged 19, Harry Barnes, aged 18, the sons of William Barnes the younger and grandsons of William Barnes [the lessee], or any of them, so long lives; fine £18 10*s.*, rent 4*s.*, and 10*s.* for a heriot.

In consideration of a surrender to be made by William Matthews of an indenture of lease dated 12 March 1742 and of £3 for a fine, let the life of Thomas Roberts, aged about 18, the son of Samuel Roberts of Wilcot, maltster, be added in the room of Benjamin Matthews, deceased; rent £2, heriot 5*s.*

Let a lease be granted to John Andrews of Savernake park, yeoman, of the cottage at Froxfield late in the possession of John Waite, deceased; for 99 years if John Waite, junior, son of that John Waite, Miriam, the daughter of John Waite, senior, James Andrews Kimber, aged about 9, son of Edward Kimber of Froxfield, labourer, or any of them, so long lives; fine £4, rent 1*s.*, heriot 1*s.*

Almshouse

Ordered that the receiver do pay to Joseph Gregory his bill for repairs at the hospital, £6 15*s.* 6*d.*

Ordered that John Dyson do attend at the next meeting to explain his bill.

Signatures

John Pocock, John Whitelock, T. Goddard, Richard Goddard, F. Popham.

26 October 1761, at the Angel inn, Marlborough

Present

John Pocock, clerk, Edward Popham, esq., Sir Michael Ernle, John Whitelock, esq., Francis Popham, esq.

Estate

Ordered that the copyhold bargain called Milkhouse (*Milcot*) Water, in the manor of Huish, late in the possession of John Cannings, deceased, be granted to Thomas Cannings of Littleton, in the parish of Kimpton, for the lives of Thomas Cannings, aged about 14, and John Cannings, aged about 3, sons of Thomas Cannings, and the life of the longer liver of them, successively according to the custom of the manor; fine £56, rent £14, and the usual heriot when it shall happen.

Ordered that the copyhold estate in the manor of Huish now in the possession of Charles Stagg for his life be granted to him for the life of James Stagg, aged about 23, son of Charles, [and to James] for his life in reversion after the death of Charles; fine £12, rent and heriot as before.

Ordered that, upon a surrender to be made by Cornelius Bettridge of his present lease determinable on the death of William Bettridge, a new lease be granted to Cornelius of the cottage at Froxfield now in his possesion; for 99 years if William, aged about 30, William Freegood, aged about 13, the son of John Freegood of Little Bedwyn, William

Jackson, aged about … [*MS. blank*] years, the son of William Jackson of Hungerford, or any of them, shall so long live; fine £13, rent as before.

Ordered that the receiver do pay the following bills for repairs and materials etc. To Mr. Richard Bailey, timber merchant, £6 1*s*. 6¾*d*.; to Robert Hawkins for bricks etc., £4 6*s*.; to John Osmond, carpenter, for repairs of the old stable at the Cross Keys, £1 1*s*. 10*d*.; to John Smith, glazier, for work at Froxfield farm, £16 0*s*. 5½*d*., [and] for work at the Cross Keys, £8 19*s*. 5¾*d*.; to James New for flakes and laying them over the cellar and [the] new stable at the Cross Keys, £3 2*s*.; to Elias Ivy for removing the nuisance in the High Road near the hospital [caused] by rubbish formerly thrown there, £4 12*s*. 2*d*.

Almshouse

Let John Gregory of Chilton Foliat, bricklayer, be employed in doing what repairs shall be necessary at the hospital.

and see estate business

Signatures

E. Popham, F. Popham, Michael Ernle, John Pocock, John Whitelock.

2 August 1762, at the Three Tuns, Marlborough

Present

The Revd. Mr. Pocock, Edward Popham, esq., Thomas Goddard, esq., Richard Goddard, esq., Francis Popham, esq.

Estate

Ordered that a grant by copy of court roll be made to Joseph Drury of the tenement, part of the manor of Froxfield, late in the possession of Alexander Platt, deceased, for the lives of Joseph Drury, aged about 27, Robert Drury, aged about 20, and Amy Drury, aged about 30, the sons and daughter of Joseph; fine £56, rent and heriot as before.

Ordered that the receiver pay William Humphreys's bill for a stone drock for Farmer Ivy, and carriage, 14*s*.

Almshouse

Ordered that the receiver pay John Dyson, glazier, his bill for repairs at the hospital from 22 February 1759 to this day, £14 8*s*. 7½*d*.

Next meeting

Notice of meeting on Monday 30 August at the Cross Keys, Froxfield.

Signatures

John Pocock, E. Popham, T. Goddard, Richard Goddard, F. Popham.

30 August 1762, at the Cross Keys, Froxfield

Present

Sir Michael Ernle, Sir Robert Long, Thomas Goddard, esq., Richard Goddard, esq., Francis Popham, esq.

Estate

Ordered that a lease be granted to Edward Cotterell for 7 years from Michaelmas next of the messuage and malthouse in Froxfield late in the possession of the widow Lockeram, now deceased, at the rent of £10 10*s*. a year clear of all taxes. The trustees agree with Edward Cotterell, in consideration of that rent, to lay out the full sum (if necessary) of £80 in repairs of the messuage and malthouse. Edward Cotterell is to keep the messuage and malthouse in sufficient tenantable repair after the £80 is laid out in the repairs. If the messuage and malthouse shall be repaired for a lesser sum than £80, the trustees agree to abate 1*s*. in the pound for so much money as it shall be deficient [*i.e.* less than £80] out of the yearly rent.

Ordered that a lease be granted to Edward Cotterell for 7 years of the Cross Keys, now in his possession, and the cottage late in the possession of Anne Pethers, widow, at the rent of £23 a year clear of all taxes. The trustees are to allow Edward Cotterell £12, for which sum he is to build a cellar on the premises with brick [and] large enough to hold 3 score hogsheads. The trustees are to allow him the further sum of £10, for which he is to put the cottage into good and sufficient tenantable repair and to leave it and the Cross Keys at the end of the term.

Almshouse

Ordered that the receiver pay John Osmond his bill for the repairs of the cupola at the hospital, on condition that he do enter into articles to be drawn up by the receiver to keep the cupola in repair during his life, fire and tempest excepted, £29 4*s*. 6*d*.

Signatures

Robert Long, Michael Ernle, F. Popham, T. Goddard, Richard Goddard.

23 June 1763, at the Three Tuns, Marlborough

Present

The Revd. Mr. Pocock, Sir Michael Ernle, Thomas Goddard, esq., Richard Goddard, esq., George Stonehouse, esq.

Trusteeship

see next meeting

Estate

Ordered that a grant by copy of court roll be made to Charles Stagg of the copyhold estate late in the possession of Charles Stagg, his father, deceased, in the manor of Huish, for the lives of Charles, aged about 26, and Elizabeth Stagg his sister, aged about 24; fine £30, rent and heriot as before.

Ordered that a lease be granted to John Tarrant the younger of the bargain at Froxfield late in the possession of Edward Tarrant, deceased; for 99 years if John, William and Edward the twin sons of Edward, or any of them, so long lives, in trust for William and Edward; fine £40, rent and heriot as before.

Let the life of Sarah Pethers, aged about 14, the daughter of Anthony Pethers, be added in his copyhold bargain at Froxfield; fine £8, rent as before.

Let the heriot on the death of Thomas Banning be compounded at 2 gns.

Ordered that John Butcher, carpenter, be employed to do the repairs at Huish farm and Chirton farm according to the estimates made by him.

Let timber be allowed for repairs of the pound at Froxfield, to wit for 3 rails, 3 posts, and 3 uprights, to be had from John Osmond. Let the old posts be used for spurs or uprights.

Almshouse

We choose Sarah Wilkins to be matron of the hospital in the room of Martha Shepherd, deceased. [She is] to hold the office from old Midsummer next with the usual salary of 20*s*. yearly.

Ordered that, for the future, the bottles in which the sacrament wine is delivered be returned to the person who sells it and not charged or paid for. The porter is to take care that the bottles are returned accordingly.

Next meeting

Complaints having been made that lay widows have been admitted into the hospital in the room of clergy widows, [it is] ordered that the steward do give notice of a meeting of the trustees on Friday 29 July next at the Cross Keys at Froxfield to consider of that matter and [do] mention in the notice the occasion of that meeting.

Signatures

John Pocock, Michael Ernle, T. Goddard, Richard Goddard, George Stonehouse.

29 July 1763, at the Cross Keys, Froxfield

Present

The Revd. Mr. Pocock, Edward Popham, esq., Thomas Goddard, esq., Richard Goddard, esq., George Stonehouse, esq.

Trusteeship

see almshouse business

Somerset Hospital at Froxfield in Wilts &c – At the Meeting of the Trustees for managing the Charity of the Hospital aforesaid held 29th July 1763 at the Cross-Keys in Froxfield –

Present

The Revd. Mr. Pococke
Edward Popham Esqr.
Thomas Goddard Esqr.
Richard Goddard Esqr.
George Stonehouse Esqr.

Ordered the Receiver do pay Edward Cottrell the Sum of forty Pounds being part of the Sum layd out by him in the Repairs of the Messuage & Malthouse in Froxfield late in the possession of Elizth. Lockeram Decd.

Ordered the Receiver do give Notice of ~~another~~ Meeting to be held for the Hospital on Tuesday in the next Michaelmas Quarter Sessions of the peace at the Three Tuns in Marlbro

Ordered that the Receiver do in the mean time inspect Edward Cottrells Accounts delivered in & make a Report of the same to the Trustees at the next Meeting & that the Receiver do Attend thereat.

Ordered that the Receiver do not pay Sarah Cobby & Mary Gingell two of the Widows now inhabiting the Hospital & lately Nominated by Mr. Whitlocke & Mr. Hungerford any further quarterly Dividends unless the sd. Mr. Whitlocke & Mr. Hungerford do make it appear at the next Meeting that the said Widows are duly qualifyed to succeed the Widows in whose Room they were Nominated; and that the Receiver do write to the sd. Mr. Whitlocke & Mr. Hungerford in relation thereto –

John Pococke T. Goddard
E Popham Geo Stonehouse
Ri. Goddard

Minutes of a meeting held 29 July 1763

Estate

Ordered [that] the receiver do pay Edward Cotterell £40, being part of the sum laid out by him in the repairs of the messuage and malthouse in Froxfield late in the possession of Elizabeth Lockeram, deceased.

Ordered that the receiver do in the meantime inspect Edward Cotterell's accounts delivered in, make a report of them to the trustees at the next meeting, and attend thereat.

Almshouse

Ordered that the receiver do not pay Sarah Cobley and Mary Gingell, two of the widows now inhabiting the hospital and lately nominated by Mr. Whitelock and Mr. Hungerford, any further quarterly dividends unless Mr. Whitelock and Mr. Hungerford make it appear at the next meeting that those widows are duly qualified to succeed the widows in whose room they were nominated. That the receiver do write to Mr. Whitelock and Mr. Hungerford in relation thereto.

Next meeting

Ordered [that] the receiver do give notice of [a] meeting to be held for the hospital on Tuesday in the next Michaelmas quarter sessions of the peace, at the Three Tuns in Marlborough.

Signatures

John Pocock, E. Popham, T. Goddard, George Stonehouse, Richard Goddard.

4 October 1763, at the Three Tuns, Marlborough

Present

The Revd. Mr. Pocock, John Whitelock, esq., Thomas Goddard, esq., Richard Goddard, esq., George Stonehouse, esq.

Trusteeship

see almshouse business

Estate

Ordered that the receiver do pay Zabulon Carter his bill of £24 3*s*. for planks for a barn floor at Huish, for laths for repairs there, and for planks for a barn floor at Chirton.

Whereas at the meeting held on 30 August 1762 the trustees agreed to let the messuage and malthouse at Froxfield, late in the possession of Elizabeth Lockeram, to Edward Cotterell for 7 years from old Michaelmas then next at the yearly rent of £10 10*s*. clear of all deductions, and agreed to lay out £80 in the repairs thereof; whereas the repairs came to £97 11*s*. 5*d*.; whereas the trustees then agreed to let to him the inn at Froxfield called the Cross Keys, and the cottage adjoining late in the possession of Anne Pethers, for 7 years from old

Michaelmas then next at the yearly rent of £23 clear of all deductions, and agreed to allow him £12 for building a cellar and £10 for repairing the cottage; and whereas the building [of] the cellar and the repairs of the cottage came to £45 18*s*. 11*d*.; now, in consideration thereof, Edward Cotterell doth hereby agree with the trustees to accept a lease of the inn and cottage for 13 years from 10 October instant at the yearly rent of £23 clear of all deductions, to accept a lease of the messuage and malthouse for 13 years from 10 October instant at the yearly rent of £12 10*s*. clear of all deductions, and to execute the counterparts of the leases when required. [*Signed*] Edward Cotterell.

Ordered that the receiver do pay to Edward Cotterell the several bills hereinafter mentioned for the repairs above mentioned, which have been paid by him, viz. for the repairs at Lockeram's £97 11*s*., for making the new cellar £33 15*s*., for the repairs of the cottage £12 3*s*. [Total] £143 9*s*.

Ordered that the receiver do pay to Edward Cotterell £27 1*s*., being monies laid out by him in building the new stable at the Cross Keys in 1759.

Almshouse

Whereas Mr. Whitelock acknowledges that the widow Cobley was nominated by him in mistake and Mr. Hungerford has not made it appear that Mary Gingell is duly qualified, it is ordered that the receiver do give notice to Sarah Cobley and Mary Gingell to quit the hospital and that he do not pay them any further dividends.

Signatures

John Pocock, John Whitelock, T. Goddard, Richard Goddard, George Stonehouse.

30 July 1765, at the Castle inn, Marlborough

Present

The Revd. Mr. Pocock, Richard Goddard, esq., George Stonehouse, esq.

30 August 1765, at the Castle inn, Marlborough

Present

The Revd. Mr. Pocock, Edward Popham, esq., Thomas Goddard, esq.

12 September 1765, at the Castle inn, Marlborough

Present

The Revd. Mr. John Pocock, Edward Popham, esq., Thomas

Goddard, esq., John Whitelock, esq., Richard Goddard, esq., George Stonehouse, esq.

Trusteeship

We choose William Jones, esq., and the Revd. Mr. Richard Pocock to be trustees in the room of Thomas Bigg, esq., and George Hungerford, esq., deceased.

Ordered that the receiver do prepare a conveyance of the charity estate from the old trustees to Francis Popham, esq., George Stonehouse, esq., William Jones, esq., and the Revd. Mr. Richard Pocock in trust for them and the old trustees for the charity.

Ordered that the receiver do immediately lay out £1,600 in Old South Sea annuities in the names of Sir Robert Long, bt., and Edward Popham, esq., in trust for this charity, being part of the savings of the charity estate in the receiver's hands, and that the dividends thereof be laid up for the benefit of the charity.

Ordered that the receiver do apply to the court of Chancery for their directions for building 20 additional lodgings to the hospital for 20 widows more, pursuant to the will of the foundress, the trustees having laid out in Old South Sea annuities £2,600, being part of the savings of the charity estate now in hand.

Estate

Ordered that the receiver do pay the following bills. To William Barnes the elder for bills paid by him for repairs at Chirton farm: to John Draper for bricks and lime, £16 8*s*.; to Daniel Topp, sawyer, £3 6*s*. 9*d*.; to John Witchell, blacksmith, £3 12*s*. 4*d*.; to Zabulon Carter for laths, £2 10*s*. 8*d*.; to Edward Dear for bricks and lime, £14 4*s*. 10*d*.; to John Wells, thatcher, £1 10*s*. 6*d*.; to John Hayward, carpenter, £24 6*s*. 11*d*.; to William Swan, junior, ironmonger, £4 2*s*. 4*d*.; to John Spencer, glazier, £3 19*s*.; to his son William Barnes for board, £5 7*s*. 3*d*.; to John Butcher for several journeys made by him to view the repairs, £1 1*s*. 6*d*.

Signatures

John Pocock, E. Popham, John Whitelock, T. Goddard, Richard Goddard.

25 June 1766, at the Castle inn, Marlborough

Present

The Revd. Mr. John Pocock, Sir Michael Ernle, bt., Sir Robert Long, bt., Thomas Goddard, esq., George Stonehouse, esq., the Revd. Mr. Richard Pocock.

Trusteeship

Ordered that the orders made at the meeting held 12 September last be forthwith obeyed.

and see estate business

Estate

Ordered that the receiver do pay the following bills for repairs and materials. To John Tarrant the elder for bills paid by him for repairs at Huish farm: to John Butcher, carpenter, £4 18*s.* 8*d.*; to John Fiddler, thatcher, £7 14*s.* 2*d.*; to William Francis, ironmonger, £3 12*s.* 6*d.*; to Thomas Windsor, blacksmith, £3 7*s.* 4*d.*; to William Jordan, bricklayer, £16 13*s.*; to John Eyles, carpenter, £18 16*s.* 7*d.* To John Tarrant the younger for bills paid by him for repairs at Huish church: to William Jordan, bricklayer, £5 7*s.* 8*d.*; to John Eyles, carpenter, £2 10*s.*; to Edward Dear, brickmaker, for materials, £9 2*s.* To Mary Collins, widow, for glazier's work done at Huish church, 12*s.* 6*d.* To William Barnes the elder for bills paid by him for repairs at Chirton farm: to John Hitchins, bricklayer, £18 7*s.* 3*d.*; to John Hayward, carpenter, 15*s.* 11*d.* To William Barnes the elder his bill for carriage of materials used in repairs at Chirton farm, £29 9*s.* Bills for repairs at the hospital: to John Dyson, glazier, £17 1*s.* 8*d.*; to John Gregory, mason, £24 12*s.* 9*d.*; to John Osmond, carpenter, £9 17*s.* 2*d.*; to Elias Ivy for carriage of materials, £1 8*s.*; to Anthony Pethers, blacksmith, £5 15*s.* 5*d.*

In consideration of a surrender to be made by John Osmond of the copyhold bargain late in the possession of William Bunce, let a grant by copy of court roll be made to John for the lives of him, Martha Osmond his daughter, aged about 16 months, and Ann, the daughter of George Tucker of Corsham, maltster, aged about 2 years; yearly rent 40*s.* over and besides the former rent.

Almshouse

see estate business

Signatures

Robert Long, John Pocock, Michael Ernle, Richard Pocock, T. Goddard, George Stonehouse.

14 July 1767, at the Castle inn, Marlborough

Present

Edward Popham, esq., Sir Michael Ernle, William Northey, esq., Thomas Goddard, esq., Richard Goddard, esq., George Stonehouse, esq., the Revd. Mr. Richard Pocock.

Trusteeship

We, by virtue of the powers given us by the will of the late duchess dowager of Somerset and since confirmed by the High Court of Chancery, appoint Samuel Martin of Kennett, gentleman, to be our steward and receiver of all manors, rents, revenues, and estates to the hospital belonging, the office being become vacant by the death of Mr. Charles Young, the late steward.

Ordered that the executors of the late Mr. Charles Young do deliver to Samuel Martin all deeds, evidences, court rolls, rentals, survey books, papers, and writings belonging to the charity in their custody or power as soon as Samuel Martin shall have given security for the due execution of his office pursuant to the decree of the court of Chancery in that behalf.

Almshouse

That the apartment in the hospital lately occupied by Widow Gilbert be put in proper repair.

Signatures

E. Popham, Michael Ernle, W. Northey, T. Goddard, Richard Goddard, George Stonehouse, Richard Pocock.

3 August 1768, at the Castle inn, Marlborough

Present

Edward Popham, esq., the Revd. Mr. John Pocock, John Whitelock, esq., Thomas Goddard, esq., Richard Goddard, esq., George Stonehouse, esq., Francis Popham, esq., the Revd. Mr. Richard Pocock.

Estate

We appoint John Tarrant of Huish, yeoman, to be our bailiff for the manor of Huish and Shaw and of the manors of Chirton, Milton, and Fyfield, [all] belonging to the hospital, and we agree that he shall have a salary of £4 a year from this day.

Signatures

E. Popham, F. Popham, George Stonehouse, Richard Pocock, John Pocock, John Whitelock, T. Goddard, Richard Goddard.

18 May 1769, at the Cross Keys inn, Froxfield

Present

Revd. Mr. John Pocock, Edward Popham, esq., Sir Michael Ernle, bt., Thomas Goddard, esq., Richard Goddard, esq., Francis Popham, esq., George Stonehouse, esq., the Revd. Mr. Richard Pocock.

Trusteeship

Ordered that the receiver do forthwith purchase £1,000 in Old South Sea annuities in the names of Edward Popham and Thomas Goddard, esqs., in trust for the charity, being part of the savings of the charity estate in the receiver's hands, and that the dividends thereof be laid up for the benefit of the charity.

Ordered that the receiver do forthwith lay the will of the foundress and all necessary papers, orders, etc., with a full state of the powers of the trustees, before some eminent counsel for his opinion on them, in order to ground their application to the court for directions relating to the disposition of the savings in hand and to erecting more tenements at the hospital.

Ordered that all former orders and decrees of the court and trustees relating to the residence of the widows be put in execution, the receiver first giving notice thereof to the widows at the hospital.

Almshouse

Ordered [that] the following bills be paid. For repairs at the hospital: to Anthony Pethers a blacksmith's bill, £7 7*s.* 6*d.*; to John Gregory a mason's bill, £11 19*s.*; to John Dyson a glazier's bill, £16 11*s.* 3*d.*; to John Osmond a carpenter's bill, £25 14*s.* 6*d.* To Edward Popham, esq., for bricks had at his kiln, £4 0*s.* 3*d.* To Thomas Palmer for bricks and lime, 17*s.* To Elias Ivy a bill for carriage of bricks, lime, sand, etc., £2 5*s.* To John Drury a bill for carriage of bricks, lime, sand, etc., £3 19*s.* 6*d.*

Ordered that the garden wall of the hospital towards the east side near the woodyard be raised and the ground on the outside lowered, and the widows [be] severally informed that, if any of them shall be instrumental towards injuring or destroying the wall, for the future the offender will be punished for it.

and see trusteeship business

Next meeting

The next meeting [is] to be at the Castle inn at Marlborough 9 June next in the morning.

Signatures

E. Popham, John Pocock, Michael Ernle, T. Goddard, F. Popham, George Stonehouse, Richard Pocock, Richard Goddard.

9 June 1769, at the Castle inn, Marlborough

Present

The Revd. Mr. John Pocock, Edward Popham, esq., Sir Michael Ernle, bt., William Northey, esq., John Whitelock, esq., Thomas Goddard, esq., Richard Goddard, esq.

Trusteeship

The trustees then executed deeds of lease and release of the lands belonging to the hospital to Francis Popham, esq., George Stonehouse, esq., and Mr. Richard Pocock, who were elected some time ago in the room of Thomas Batson, William Liddiard, and Thomas Bigg, esqs., all deceased, to the use of them and the old trustees.

Estate

We confirm an agreement made by our steward for the sale of a cottage at Froxfield, late Webb's, to John Dobson under the yearly rent of 20*s.*; for 99 years, to be determinable with the lives of three persons to be named by John, and a fine of 5 gns. [We] order a lease to be prepared accordingly.

Signatures

John Pocock, E. Popham, Michael Ernle, John Whitelock, T. Goddard, Richard Goddard.

7 November 1770, at the Cross Keys inn, Froxfield

Present

John Whitelock, esq., Richard Goddard, esq., George Stonehouse, esq., Mr. Richard Pocock.

29 December 1770, at the Castle inn, Marlborough

Present

Mr. John Pocock, Richard Goddard, esq., Francis Popham, esq., George Stonehouse, esq., Mr. Richard Pocock.

Trusteeship

We choose Ambrose Goddard of Swindon, esq., John Walker of Compton Bassett, esq., and Lovelace Bigg of Chilton Foliat, esq., to be trustees in place of Thomas Bigg, esq., Sir Robert Long, bt., and Thomas Goddard, esq., all deceased.

Memorandum. William Jones, esq., who was formerly elected in the room of Thomas Bigg, esq., died before any conveyance of the charity lands was made to him or his acting under the trust.

Estate

We confirm the grant and agreement made by our steward with John Banning for adding his son Thomas's life in his copyhold tenement in the manor of Huish, under the fine of £5.

Almshouse

Ordered that the steward do forthwith insure the hospital from fire in the Sun Fire Office at £1,000 in the whole.

Ordered that our steward do pay Mrs. Ann Latournell 1 year's annuity of 8 gns. for all arrears due to her on her signing her resignation of her apartment in the hospital and a release of all future claims thereto, she having never resided therein and declaring her ill health never will permit her to reside.

Ordered that our steward do pay Mrs. Priscilla Smith all the arrears of her annuity, we being satisfied by [a] certificate under the hands of two surgeons who attended her in a disorder that prevented her residence in the hospital during the time the arrears were incurred.

Next meeting

We agree to meet again on Thursday in next Whitsun week at Froxfield.

Signatures

John Pocock, Richard Goddard, F. Popham, George Stonehouse, Richard Pocock, John Whitelock.

24 May 1771, at the Cross Keys inn, Froxfield

Present

John Whitelock, esq., Richard Goddard, esq., George Stonehouse, esq., Mr. Richard Pocock, Ambrose Goddard, esq.

Trusteeship

Ordered that the receiver do purchase £1,000 Old South Sea annuities, part of the money now in his hands belonging to the charity, in the names of Edward Popham, esq., and Ambrose Goddard, esq., for the benefit of the charity.

Estate

Ordered that the receiver do prepare leases for 21 years from Michaelmas last of the Cross Keys inn, with the appurtenances, of the cottage late Anne Pethers's, and of the tenement and malthouse late Lockeram's, all in Froxfield, to Thomas Noyes under the rents and covenants contained in leases intended to be granted of those premises to Edward Cotterell, deceased; save only that Thomas Noyes is to put into good repair the walls and all bricklayer's work of the old stable adjoining to and part of late Pethers's tenement, the trustees agreeing to put a new roof on it and to find tiles, laths, and nails sufficient to cover it; also except all allowances made or intended to be made to Edward Cotterell towards repairs.

Almshouse

Ordered that the small repairs, mentioned in a paper this day delivered to the receiver and signed by us, be done to the hospital, which we have this day viewed.

Next meeting

The next meeting [is] to be at the Castle inn in Marlborough on the second Monday in July next.

Signatures

John Whitelock, Richard Goddard, George Stonehouse, Richard Pocock, Ambrose Goddard.

8 July 1771, at the Castle inn, Marlborough

Present

John Pocock, clerk, John Whitelock, esq., George Stonehouse, esq., Richard Pocock, clerk, Ambrose Goddard, esq.

Almshouse

Ordered [that] the receiver do collect together as many building materials of oak and deal timber, bricks, and lime this present summer as he reasonably can, and on the best terms, paying for them as soon as they shall be delivered at Froxfield, towards the building [of] more tenements pursuant to the will of the foundress.

[Ordered] that he prepares a plan of the present buildings of the hospital, as well as of those intended to be added, against the next meeting.

Next meeting

The next meeting [is] to be at the Castle inn at Marlborough 21 September next.

Signatures

John Pocock, John Whitelock, George Stonehouse, Richard Pocock, Ambrose Goddard

21 September 1771, at the Castle inn, Marlborough

Present

Richard Goddard, esq., Francis Popham, esq., George Stonehouse, esq., Revd. Mr. Richard Pocock, Ambrose Goddard, esq., John Walker, esq., Lovelace Bigg, esq.

Trusteeship

We elect Charles Penruddocke of Compton Chamberlayne, esq., and Edward Ernle of Brimslade, Doctor in Divinity, as trustees of the charity in the room of William Northey, esq., and Sir Michael Ernle, deceased.

Almshouse

Ordered [that] the receiver do contract on the best terms he can with some person or persons for removing the earth on the east end of the present hospital sufficient for the laying out [of the] ground on a level with the present buildings and square for the erection of 20 new tenements, with the addition of seven more tenements in the room of the present seven in the east end, so as to make the whole number of tenements to form one entire square on one level. And to exchange with the dean and chapter of Windsor, and Mr. Gilmore their present lessee of the parsonage of Froxfield, their acre of land adjoining to the present hospital for an acre of the hospital's lands, with an intent to inclose it for the purposes aforesaid.

Ordered that the receiver pays 10 gns. a year to each of the widows inhabiting the hospital, the first quarterly payment to be made on the next quarter's day.

Signatures

Richard Goddard, F. Popham, George Stonehouse, Richard Pocock, Ambrose Goddard, John Walker, Lovelace Bigg.

12 June 1772, at the Cross Keys inn, Froxfield

Present

John Whitelock, esq., the Revd. Mr. Richard Pocock, Lovelace Bigg, esq.

Almshouse

The repairs of the hospital [were] surveyed and orders given for amending the defects.

11 July 1772, at the Castle inn, Marlborough

Present

John Whitelock, esq., George Stonehouse, esq., Revd. Mr. Richard Pocock, John Walker, esq., Lovelace Bigg, esq., Charles Penruddocke, esq., Sir Edward Ernle, bt.

Estate

We hereby nominate John Moody of Milton to be our gamekeeper for the manor of Huish and Shaw to preserve the game there; also woodward of all the lands and tenements belonging to the hospital, except what lies in the manor of Froxfield, to look after the timber, woodlands, and hedges to preserve them; both during our pleasure only, under the yearly salary of £4.

Let the farm at Huish to Mr. Henry Goodman of Easton and his son James, late in the possession of John Tarrant, for 12 years from Lady day last old style, [the] tenant paying land tax and all other taxes and doing all repairs; under the yearly rent of £120, the tenants entering into a lease under such covenants as our steward shall advise to be reasonable and proper.

Let the farm at Chirton to William Barnes, the present occupier, for 12 years from the end of the present lease granted to his father; under the yearly rent of £100, the tenant paying the land tax and all other taxes and outgoings and keeping the whole in tenantable repair, he entering into a lease for that term under the like covenants as are contained in the present lease.

Let our steward agree with the widow of John Tarrant, late of Huish farm, deceased, for the best price he can reasonably get for the exchange of one or both the lives of Mr. Gilmore and his son in their late copyhold estate in the manor of Huish for such lives as the widow shall nominate.

Signatures

John Whitelock, George Stonehouse, Richard Pocock, John Walker, Lovelace Bigg, Charles Penruddocke, Edward Ernle.

4 June 1773, at the Cross Keys, Froxfield

Present

Francis Popham, Richard Pocock, George Stonehouse, Lovelace Bigg, Sir Edward Ernle.

Almshouse

Ordered that the repairs mentioned in a paper this day delivered to the receiver and signed by us be done to the hospital, which we have this day viewed.

Ordered that the widows inhabiting the east end of the hospital do remove from their habitations there to the additional buildings lately built, according to an appointment made by us this day and delivered to our receiver. We order 1 gn. to be paid by our receiver to each of those widows on condition [that] they remove to their several apartments, appointed by us, within 1 month.

We order that no allowance be made to the widows who shall neglect to remove within the time.

Adjournment

Adjourned to Wednesday 30 June instant at the Castle inn in Marlborough.

Signatures

F. Popham, George Stonehouse, Richard Pocock, Lovelace Bigg, Edward Ernle.

30 June 1773, at the Castle inn, Marlborough

Present

John Whitelock, esq., George Stonehouse, esq., the Revd. Mr. Richard Pocock, Lovelace Bigg, esq., Ambrose Goddard, esq., Sir Edward Ernle, John Walker, esq.

Trusteeship

We this day examined and stated a year's account with our receiver from Michaelmas 1770 to Michaelmas 1771, and then adjourned to 18 September next to the Castle inn in Marlborough.

We this day came to a resolution not to renew or instate any life in any copyhold estate within any manor belonging to the hospital (except cottages), in order by degrees to increase the annual payment to the widows inhabiting the hospital.

Estate

Ordered that our steward do erect a room of about 12 feet square adjoining the kitchen at the farm at Huish lately held by John Tarrant, deceased, and a new brick wall to the garden in the room of the present mud wall, and that he does survey the defects of repairs in the buildings, gates, and bounds belonging to the farm and cause such parts thereof belonging to the trustees to be repaired. [He is ordered] to enforce the repairs as shall belong to the going-out tenant to be done, or otherwise to compound with the representatives of the late tenant for a sum of money in lieu thereof.

Also [the steward is ordered] to survey all other buildings in the manor of Huish and to report to us the condition of them.

and see trusteeship business

Signatures

John Whitelock, George Stonehouse, Richard Pocock, Ambrose Goddard, John Walker, Lovelace Bigg, Edward Ernle.

12 October 1774, at the Castle inn, Marlborough

Present

George Stonehouse, esq., Revd. Mr. Richard Pocock, Ambrose Goddard, esq., John Walker, esq., Lovelace Bigg, esq., Charles Penruddocke, esq.

Almshouse

Ordered that every widow admitted to a tenement in the almshouse who shall be absent from her tenement on the day on which their quarterly payments shall be made to them on 5 April every year, without having licence for such absence under the hands of two trustees, shall forfeit the whole year's allowance of wood. [The forfeited wood is] to be divided equally between all others of the widows who shall then be resident in the almshouse.

Ordered that our treasurer do pay to Mrs. Mintern, Mrs. Fallowfield, Mrs. Isaac, Mrs. Marsh, and Mrs. Belcher 1 gn. each on their removing into the new built tenements allotted for clergy widows, such tenements to be chosen by ballot in case they cannot agree themselves.

Next meeting

The next meeting [is] to be at the Castle inn in Marlborough on Thursday 29 December next.

Signatures

George Stonehouse, Ambrose Goddard, Lovelace Bigg, Richard Pocock, John Walker, Charles Penruddocke.

5 January 1775, at the Castle inn, Marlborough

Present

George Stonehouse, esq., Revd. Mr. Richard Pocock, Ambrose Goddard, esq., Lovelace Bigg, esq., Charles Penruddocke, esq., Sir Edward Ernle, bt.

Estate

Agreed to let the farm at Fyfield, now in possession of the representatives of the late John Cannings at £70 a year, and the lands called Pyke's Bear croft, now in possession of Charles Penruddocke, esq., at the yearly rent of £5, to Mr. Penruddocke for 21 years from the determination of the present lease made to John Cannings; at the yearly rent of £100 clear of land tax and all other taxes and payments, and under the like covenants on the lessee's part [as] are contained in the present lease.

Signatures

George Stonehouse, Richard Pocock, Lovelace Bigg, Edward Ernle, Ambrose Goddard.

29 April 1775, at the Castle inn, Marlborough

Present

John Whitelock, esq., George Stonehouse, esq., Richard Pocock, clerk, Ambrose Goddard, esq., John Walker, esq., Lovelace Bigg, esq., Charles Penruddocke, esq., Sir Edward Ernle, bt.

Trusteeship

Executed a presentation of the rectory of Huish to Mr. Charles Mayo, clerk, M.A., and elected him chaplain of the hospital.

Estate

Agreed to exchange the close of arable land called Hurley ground, of about ¾ acre in the parish of Milton, with Mr. Michael Ewen for land of his of equal value in the same parish, and we leave it to the commissioners acting under an Act of Parliament for inclosing the common field lands in Milton to fix the value of such lands so to pass in exchange. We order deeds of exchange to be prepared accordingly by our steward.

Let the farm called Batchelor's at Clench to the present tenant, Mr. Henry Pyke, for 21 years from the expiration of the present lease [and] under the yearly rent of £45; in all other respects the covenants and agreements on the lessee's part to be the same as are contained in his present lease.

Let Mr. Elias Ivy add two lives in the tenement at Froxfield lately burnt to the ground, without any fine on condition of his rebuilding it substantially at his own expense.

Let Mr. Joseph Smith add one life in his tenement, burnt to the ground at the same time, without fine on condition [that] he rebuilds also at his own expense. We order him some timber, if it can conveniently be had, at the discretion of our steward.

Signatures

John Whitelock, George Stonehouse, Richard Pocock, Ambrose Goddard, John Walker, Lovelace Bigg, Charles Penruddocke, Edward Ernle.

14 June 1775, at the Castle inn, Marlborough

Present

George Stonehouse, esq., Charles Penruddocke, esq., Ambrose Goddard, esq., Lovelace Bigg, esq., the Revd. Richard Pocock, Sir Edward Ernle, bt.

Trusteeship

The receiver's account of money disbursed on the new buildings at Froxfield amounting to £2,823 6*s.* 10*d.* was this day examined and approved, and in token thereof we signed it.

Ordered that the receiver do prepare estimates for repairing and enlarging the present chapel and for building a new chapel, and a plan for the same, against the next meeting.

Almshouse

see trusteeship business

Adjournment

Adjourned to 16 September next at the Castle inn.

Signatures

George Stonehouse, Richard Pocock, Ambrose Goddard, Lovelace Bigg, Charles Penruddocke, Edward Ernle.

7 October 1775, at the Castle inn, Marlborough

Present

John Whitelock, esq., George Stonehouse, esq., Revd. Richard Pocock, Ambrose Goddard, esq., John Walker, esq., Lovelace Bigg, esq., Charles Penroddocke, esq., Sir Edward Ernle.

Trusteeship

We the trustees, by virtue of the powers given us by the will of the late duchess dowager of Somerset and since confirmed by the High Court of Chancery, appoint Samuel Hawkes of Marlborough, gentleman, to be our steward and receiver of all manors, rents, revenues, and estates to the hospital belonging, the office being become vacant by the death of Mr. Samuel Martin, the late steward.

Ordered that the executors of the late Mr. Samuel Martin do deliver to Samuel Hawkes all deeds, evidences, court rolls, rentals, survey books, papers, and writings belonging to the charity in their custody or power as soon as Samuel Hawkes shall have given security for the due execution of the office pursuant to the decree of the court of Chancery in that behalf.

Signatures

John Whitelock, George Stonehouse, Richard Pocock, Ambrose Goddard, John Walker, L. Bigg, Charles Penruddocke, E. Ernle.

MINUTE BOOK 1776–1818
(WSA 2037/13)

12 June 1776, at the Castle inn, Marlborough

Present

John Whitelock, esq., George Stonehouse, esq., Revd. Richard Pocock, clerk, Ambrose Goddard, esq., Lovelace Bigg, esq., Sir Edward Ernle, bt., Charles Penruddocke, esq.

Trusteeship

The executrix of the late Mr. Martin, the late steward and receiver of the revenues of this charity, having hitherto neglected and refused to deliver the deeds, rentals, survey books, and other papers and writings remaining in his hands touching the charity as [she was] ordered [to] at our last meeting, or to make out and deliver a state of his accounts or to prove his will or administer to his effects, it is therefore ordered that notice be given to his executrix forthwith to deliver up the deeds, rentals, and other writings to our present steward Mr. Hawkes, and at our next meeting to deliver in a state of the accounts of Mr. Martin with the balance thereon due. Notice of this order and of the day of the next meeting is also ordered to be given to Sir Edward Baynton, bt., and John Talbot, esq., the sureties in the court of Chancery for our late steward on his being appointed receiver of the revenues.

It is also ordered that our present steward do prepare a state of the case relative to the present affairs of the charity, to be laid before some eminent counsel in that court for his opinion and directions as to the properest manner of proceeding.

and see adjournment

Estate

The several workmen who have delivered in bills for repairs done at Huish farm and Chirton farm are ordered to attend, at the next meeting, with Farmer Goodman and Farmer Barnes, the tenants.

Ordered that for the future the tenants settle their accounts half-yearly when a year's rent is due and pay their rents accordingly to the steward.

Adjournment

The meeting is adjourned to the Castle inn, Marlborough, to Saturday 27 July next, when the trustees propose to fill up the vacancies in the trust, of which the steward is to give notice to the trustees in his circular letter.

Signatures

John Whitelock, George Stonehouse, Richard Pocock, L. Bigg, Ambrose Goddard, Charles Penruddocke, E. Ernle.

27 July 1776, at the Castle inn, Marlborough

Present

John Whitelock, esq., Richard Pocock, clerk, John Walker, esq., Lovelace Bigg, esq., Charles Penruddocke, esq., Sir Edward Ernle, bt.

Trusteeship

At this meeting the opinion of counsel on a state of the case since the death of the late receiver, in pursuance of our order made at the last meeting, was produced, recommending the filing [of] a bill in Chancery and, if necessary to substantiate proceedings, making the administrator of the late receiver and his sureties parties. But, the trustees being informed that since the last meeting administration with the will annexed of the late receiver has been granted to William Philpot of Beckhampton, yeoman, [it is] ordered that notice be given to such administrator forthwith to deliver to our present steward all deeds, writings, court books, and other papers relating to the charity and, at our next meeting, to deliver in a full state of that receiver's accounts touching the rents of the estates belonging to the charity since the last account [was] settled. The further consideration of the matter is deferred till the next meeting.

Estate

Resolved that our steward do prepare a lease of Huish farm to Mr. James Goodman, to be executed at our next meeting, pursuant to the contract made with him at a meeting held 11 July 1772. In case of his refusal to execute it, [it is] ordered that a bill in Chancery be filed against him to enforce the performance of his contract according to the terms thereof.

Next meeting

The next meeting is appointed to be held at the Castle inn, Marlborough, on Saturday 21 September next, of which James Goodman has notice in writing now given him with a copy of this order.

Signatures

John Whitelock, Richard Pocock, John Walker, L. Bigg, Charles Penruddocke, E. Ernle.

21 September 1776, at the Castle inn, Marlborough

Present

John Whitelock, esq., Francis Popham, esq., George Stonehouse, esq., Revd. Richard Pocock, Ambrose Goddard, esq., John Walker, esq., Lovelace Bigg, esq., Charles Penruddocke, esq., Sir Edward Ernle.

Trusteeship

At this meeting Mr. Locke, attorney for Mr. Philpot, the administrator of the goods etc. of the late receiver Mr. Martin, produced his accounts since the last account, to Michaelmas 1772. Viz. an account to Michaelmas 1773, which was settled by the trustees 5 January 1775, when the balance in his hands was £2,954 19*s.* 8*d.*; an account to Michaelmas 1774, the balance thereon being £1,609 12*s.* 5*d.*, and an account to Michaelmas 1775, the balance being £422 6*s.*, both which accounts the trustees have examined and approve. All those accounts are to be settled and allowed by the master in the High Court of Chancery and are left for such purpose, together with the vouchers, in the hands of our present steward.

Adjournment

Adjourn to the Castle inn, Marlborough, to Monday 23 December next.

Signatures

John Whitelock, F. Popham, George Stonehouse, John Walker, L. Bigg, Charles Penruddocke, E. Ernle.

1 April 1777, at the Castle inn, Marlborough

Present

John Whitelock, esq., Richard Pocock, clerk, Ambrose Goddard, esq., John Heneage, esq., Lovelace Bigg, esq., Sir Edward Ernle, bt.

Trusteeship

Resolved that such of the trustees who live in the neighbourhood will, on the Tuesday in the Whitsun week, view the repairs and state of the building at the almshouse.

Estate

Numerous applications having been made to rent the farm at Huish now in the occupation of James Goodman, who is to quit at Michaelmas next, [it is] ordered that the farm be let to such who will give the highest improved rent for it, that the steward do by letter acquaint the farmers who have applied to him of this resolution and of the present yearly rent and other circumstances relating to the farm, and [that he] desire their answers in writing to be sent to him on or before the … [*MS. blank*]

Almshouse

see trusteeship business

Next meeting

The next meeting is appointed to be held on Wednesday 11 June next at the Castle inn, Marlborough.

Signatures

John Whitelock, Richard Pocock, Ambrose Goddard, J. Heneage, L. Bigg, E. Ernle.

11 June 1777, at the Castle inn, Marlborough

Present

John Whitelock, esq., Revd. Richard Pocock, Ambrose Goddard, esq., John Heneage, esq., Lovelace Bigg, esq., Charles Penruddocke, esq.

Trusteeship

see almshouse business; next meeting

Estate

We approve the agreement made by our steward with John Reeves of Clench for letting Huish and Stubnail farms to him from 10 October next for 12 years at the yearly rent of £150, the tenant paying all taxes and other deductions and keeping and leaving the premises in good repair.

Whereas many repairs have been done in and about the farm at Huish since letting it to Mr. James Goodman, the present tenant, and he has delivered in bills for such repairs amounting to £200 and upwards, some of which bills have been paid by him and others remain unpaid, [and whereas] there remains 2 years' rent in arrear from him at Lady day last, and at Michaelmas next he is to quit the farm at his own desire signified at a former meeting, we order the steward to call on him to pay the rent in arrear or otherwise to take proper measures for recovering it. Likewise [we order the steward] to cause the present state of the buildings, gates, stiles, and fences belonging to the farm to be surveyed, and an estimate taken of the deficiencies in reparations, which according to the minute of the agreement made with James Goodman by our late steward Mr. Martin, the customary practice of letting the farms belonging to the charity, and the express directions of the will of the foundress, are to be performed by, and at the expense of, the tenants or occupiers of the farms. Thereupon, and upon James Goodman putting those premises into good repair or allowing a proper sum of money for such purpose, our steward is authorized to pay, or otherwise allow to him, those bills so delivered amounting to £200 and upwards, together with such money as he has already paid on account. [Our steward is] to settle all other accounts with him or, in default thereof, to pursue such methods as may be advised by counsel touching those outstanding bills, enforcing the repairs now wanting, and bringing all matters in dispute relative thereto to a legal decision.

Ordered that notice be given to Mr. Tarrant, the tenant of the farm at Milton, to produce his lease (if any) of the farm or to quit the farm at old Michaelmas 1778; likewise to put the farm, and the several buildings thereon, in good repair.

Ordered that our steward do attend on all proper occasions in case any proceedings be had relative to the Act for inclosing the common fields at Milton, take care of the trustees' interests, and do what may be necessary for carrying the Act into execution.

Ordered that the receiver do pay the arrears of John Moody's salary as bailiff.

Almshouse

Ordered that the repairs at the almshouse be forthwith done according to an account taken 20 May last at a meeting of three of the trustees at Froxfield.

That, instead [of] 1*s.* 6*d.*, 5*s.* be from this time allowed to John Osmond, the porter, for his trouble and expenses in attending the meetings.

Ordered that ... [*MS. blank*] Feltham, widow of the Revd. ... [*MS. blank*] Feltham of Chettle, be admitted as a clergy widow at-large into the hospital, there being at present many vacancies and no applications.

Next meeting

At the next meeting the trustees intend to choose new trustees in the place of such as are dead, of which the steward is to acquaint the absent members, and the next meeting is appointed at the Castle inn 20 September next.

Signatures

John Whitelock, Ambrose Goddard, Richard Pocock, J. Heneage, L. Bigg, Charles Penruddocke.

20 September 1777, at the Castle inn, Marlborough

Present

The Revd. Richard Pocock, Ambrose Goddard, esq., John Heneage, esq., Lovelace Bigg, esq., Sir Edward Ernle, bt.

Trusteeship

At this meeting the receiver produced his account of receipts to Michaelmas 1776 and of disbursements, the charge with which he debits himself amounting to £2,250 14*s.* 2*d.* and his discharge to £1,386 6*s.* 10*d.*, the balance in his hands being £864 7*s.* 4*d.*; which accounts were approved and signed at this meeting.

Estate

At this meeting the trustees executed a lease of Huish and Stubnail farm to John Reeves from old Michaelmas next, for 12 years at the yearly rent of £150.

Signatures

Richard Pocock, Ambrose Goddard, J. Heneage, E. Ernle, L. Bigg.

17 June 1778, at the Castle inn, Marlborough

Present

John Whitelock, esq., Revd. Richard Pocock, Ambrose Goddard, esq., Lovelace Bigg, esq., Charles Penruddocke, esq., Sir Edward Ernle, bt.

Trusteeship

Ordered that the trustees will at the next meeting elect new trustees in place of such as are dead, in case a sufficient number of trustees to make a quorum shall attend; of which the steward is to give notice to all the trustees previous to the meeting.

Estate

The trustees, taking into consideration the condition of Milton farm and the present rent thereof, are of opinion that Farmer Tarrant, the tenant, has been very deficient in performing the covenants contained in his lease in the article of repairs and otherwise, and that it [*i.e.* the farm] is much underlet. Farmer Tarrant having expressed a desire to renew his lease, the trustees order and empower the steward to enter into a contract with him for a lease for 8 years from 10 October next at the yearly rent of £120; under the usual covenants for paying taxes, keeping and leaving the premises in repair, and leaving the fields in a due course of cultivation, Thomas Tarrant procuring sureties for the payment of the rent and performance of the covenants.

In case Farmer Tarrant should not make a new contract for Milton farm, the steward is to agree with any other person for it on the terms above specified.

Almshouse

Ordered that the wall in front of the almshouse at Froxfield be built by … [*MS. blank*] Gale according to a plan sometime since delivered to the trustees.

That the steward do apply to Mr. Gilmore, the lessee under the college at Windsor, in order to procure an exchange of an acre of glebe land lying north of the hospital [and] belonging to Mr. Gilmore for land of equal value belonging to the trustees. If that can be effected it is ordered that the gardens for the new erected buildings be laid out on the north of the almshouse.

Adjournment

The meeting is adjourned to the Castle inn, Marlborough, to Saturday 19 September next.

Signatures

Richard Pocock, Ambrose Goddard, L. Bigg, Charles Penruddocke, E. Ernle.

19 September 1778, at the Castle inn, Marlborough

Present

John Whitelock, esq., Revd. Richard Pocock, Ambrose Goddard, esq., John Heneage, esq., Lovelace Bigg, esq., Charles Penruddocke, esq., Sir Edward Ernle, bt.

Trusteeship

We choose Sir James Tylney Long, bt., Sir William Jones, bt., William Northey, esq., and Francis Stonehouse, esq., to be trustees for this charity in place of Edward Popham, esq., Richard Goddard, esq., John Pocock, clerk, and George Stonehouse, esq., deceased, and order the steward to prepare a conveyance of the estate belonging to the charity from the present trustees to Sir James Tylney Long, Sir William Jones, William Northey, and Francis Stonehouse, esqs., in trust for them and the present trustees.

Estate

The copyhold estate at Huish lately held by the widow of John Tarrant being fallen in hand by the death of Joseph Gilmore, the last life, upon the complaint and application of the widow Tarrant the trustees order £10 to be paid her as a compensation for four [?acres of] sainfoin planted thereon, on condition that her tenant yields up the quiet possession of that copyhold bargain at Michaelmas next.

Almshouse

The trustees order the dividend of the profits of the charity estate payable to the poor widows, inhabitants of the hospital, to be raised from 10 gns. a year each to £11 13*s*. 4*d*. each, and that £1 6*s*. 8*d*. usually paid at Christmas in lieu of a gown be added to the £11 13*s*. 4*d*. to make the annual pay to each widow £13; to be paid by four quarterly payments of £3 5*s*. to commence from old St. Thomas's day next.

Signatures

John Whitelock, Richard Pocock, Ambrose Goddard, J. Heneage, Lovelace Bigg, Charles Penruddocke, E. Ernle.

16 June 1779, at the Castle inn, Marlborough

Present

John Whitelock, esq., Richard Pocock, clerk, Ambrose Goddard, esq., John Walker Heneage, esq., Lovelace Bigg, esq., Charles Penruddocke, esq., Sir Edward Ernle, bt., William Northey, esq.

Estate

In case Thomas Noyes, the tenant of the Cross Keys inn and the other premises at Froxfield lately occupied by Edward Cotterell, shall forthwith put them into good repair and enter into a covenant with sufficient sureties for keeping and leaving them in repair, for the regular payment of the rent, and for not assigning any part of the premises to any person without licence in writing first obtained, upon these terms the steward may treat with Thomas for a lease. Otherwise let the same be offered to Farmer Blake or any other person willing to become tenant.

Upon the representation of James Warwick, the tenant of Milton farm, of the want of repairs and of a diminution in the number of acres belonging to the farm as it was at first estimated and valued by him, [it is] ordered that our steward do give notice to Thomas Tarrant, the late tenant, to do the necessary repairs and perform the other covenants contained in his lease according to the tenor thereof. In case of any let or refusal [the steward is] to prepare and lay a case before Mr. Mansfield for his opinion as to the bringing [of] an action or other means of compelling him to the due performance of his covenants, and [he is] to make a proper allowance to James Warwick for the deficiency of land, if any. Instead of a third, the trustees consent that a fourth only of the arable in the inclosures be left as summer fallow, and that James be allowed to sell such of the last year's crop of hay as cannot properly be spent by him on the premises to the next coming-on tenant at a price to be fixed by two referees to be by them chosen. If they cannot agree [they are] to refer the price between them to a third person to be chosen by the referees.

The steward is to make a contract for letting the farm at Froxfield, late in the occupation of Elias Ivy, on the plan, as near as may be, proposed and recommended by Mr. Black, who has surveyed the farm.

Almshouse

Whereas there are several vacancies in the hospital at Froxfield for widows of clergymen and no applications made for them, [it is] ordered that the steward do make known such particulars as may be requisite by an advertisement to be published in the papers.

Signatures

John Whitelock, Richard Pocock, Ambrose Goddard, J. Walker Heneage, L. Bigg, Charles Penruddocke, E. Ernle, William Northey.

18 September 1779, at the Castle inn, Marlborough

Present

John Whitelock, esq., Richard Pocock, clerk, Ambrose Goddard, esq., John Heneage, esq., Lovelace Bigg, esq., Charles Penruddocke, esq., Sir Edward Ernle, bt., Sir William Jones, bt., William Northey, esq.

Estate

At this meeting the trustees executed a lease of Milton farm to

James Warwick.

The trustees approve of the agreement made by the steward with John Andrews for a lease of the farm at Froxfield from Michaelmas next, and order a lease to be prepared accordingly.

Almshouse

The steward is ordered to admit such widows of clergymen, as appear to be proper objects and are duly qualified, who have [made] or may make application in consequence of the advertisement lately published for filling up the vacancies.

Signatures

Richard Pocock, Ambrose Goddard, J. Walker Heneage, E. Ernle, Charles Penruddocke, William Northey.

21 June 1780, at the Castle inn, Marlborough

Present

John Whitelock, esq., Revd. Richard Pocock, John Walker Heneage, esq., Sir William Jones, bt., William Northey, esq.

Trusteeship

Examined and allowed the accounts of Mr. Samuel Hawkes, the receiver, a balance of £670 18*s.* 7*d.* remaining in his hands.

Estate

Whereas at a meeting 29 April 1775 it was ordered that Mr. Elias Ivy should add two lives in his tenement at Froxfield, then lately burnt down, without fine on condition of his rebuilding it substantially, and it having been rebuilt accordingly, upon the proposal of his executor Jason Ivy to surrender his present lease and take a new lease for 99 years determinable with three lives and to pay a fine of £6, the trustees approve thereof.

Signatures

John Whitelock, Richard Pocock, William Jones, J. Walker Heneage, William Northey.

27 June 1781, at the Castle inn, Marlborough

Present

Richard Pocock, clerk, John Walker Heneage, esq., Ambrose Goddard, esq., Lovelace Bigg, esq., Charles Penruddocke, esq., Sir James Tylney Long, bt.

Trusteeship

For the future let the general annual meeting of the trustees be on the Wednesday next after 20 June, unless the 20th falls on a Wednesday.

Estate

Ordered that the receiver do employ Mr. Webb or Mr. Richardson, land surveyors, to go over and take a survey of the farm at Fyfield in order to estimate and ascertain the expediency and advantage of laying the lands in the tithing of Fyfield in severalty and of discharging them from tithe by a compensation in land or otherwise, and [to] report to the trustees at their next meeting [so] that, if it be thought proper, an application may be made to Parliament for carrying it into execution.

Estimates having been delivered at this meeting of repairs wanting at the farm at Froxfield amounting to £70, of the expense of building a dairy house there amounting to £30, and of the expense of building a brewhouse and wash-house at the hospital for the use of the poor widows amounting to £96, the trustees approve thereof and leave the carrying [of] that into execution to the order and discretion of their steward; as also preparing a flight of steps, either of brick with a kerb of wood or with brick and stone, in the front of the hospital towards the turnpike road.

Almshouse

Ordered that the yearly dividends to the widows be raised from £13 to £14 from the next quarter day.

Several of the poor widows at the hospital, having been absent at the last quarterly day of payment, and others of them, though then present yet having seldom or never resided at their apartments in the hospital, and [*?rectius* have] thereby forfeited their right to the yearly allowance of coppice wood, viz. Mrs. Bradford, Mrs. Carter, Mrs. Bally, Mrs. Higgins, Mrs. Willoughby, Mrs. Whitelock, Mrs. Thomas, Mrs. M. Kimber, Mrs. Lucas, and Mrs. Flint. [It is] ordered that the portions of wood so forfeited by those widows be distributed by the porter among the other poor widows inhabiting the hospital.

and see estate business

Signatures

J. Walker Heneage, Richard Pocock, Charles Penruddocke, James Tylney Long, L. Bigg.

15 September 1781, at the Castle inn, Marlborough

Present

John Whitelock, esq., Richard Pocock, clerk, Ambrose Goddard, esq., John Walker Heneage, esq., Lovelace Bigg, esq., Charles Penruddocke, esq., Sir James Tylney Long, bt., Sir William Jones, bt., William Northey, esq.

Almshouse

Whereas by certain regulations confirmed in Chancery 25 July 1729 it is ordered, among other things, 'that every one of the widows who shall be absent from the hospital 1 week or more at any time, unless hindered by sickness or other reasonable cause to be testified by the chaplain and [the] matron and allowed by two or more of the trustees, shall forfeit for every such offence so much as her allowance shall come to for the time she shall be absent'; whereas by another rule of the trustees of 3 June 1748, confirmed in Chancery 5 August 1748, 'it is ordered that, for the better government of the hospital and of the poor persons therein, if any of the poor widows shall at any time absent herself from the hospital for 14 days at any one time, or at several times for 30 days, in any 1 year without the licence of two or more of the trustees in writing first obtained, unless really hindered by sickness or some reasonable cause allowed by the trustees at a general meeting to be held for the affairs of the hospital, or by the major part of them so assembled, every widow so absenting herself shall for such offence be expelled from the hospital and from her house therein, and that shall be deemed vacant'; and whereas it appears to us by the report of our steward, and by the report of the porter, that, of the widows admitted and receiving the charity, divers of them never reside there at all for any continuance and many others are absent for months together either without leave or after the time has been long expired for which leave was granted, and that during their absence it is a frequent practice of the friends of such widows, especially near the time of each quarterly payment in order to deceive our steward, to wait on the neighbouring trustees for the purpose of procuring permission for them to go away for a month when, in truth, they have already been absent for a long time preceding. By these evasions, contrary to the plain design of the institution, the buildings left unoccupied run to decay and more proper objects of the charity are excluded.

To remedy those abuses and to enforce those regulations having regard to the difference of times and circumstances, the extension of the charity to more distant counties, and the increased number of widows, and desirous for these and other reasons to allow them all proper indulgence in the article of absence, it is ordered that the steward do prepare printed forms to be left with the porter which each widow shall procure before she makes application to any two or more of the trustees for leave to absent herself from the hospital. The porter shall certify under his hand that the widow is then abiding at the hospital as a lodger at her apartment there as her home, but specifying therein the days or weeks (if any) that such widow may have been absent in that year, and he shall then fill up her petition for as many additional weeks as she shall choose provided the number together do not exceed 13 weeks in 1 year. [So] that the porter may ascertain the residence of each widow more exactly he shall keep a book with all their names and 52 columns for the weeks in the year, and every Sunday shall mark down what widows have been present and what absent in the preceding week; but with this restriction, that no widow shall be deemed present at any time unless she lodges in her own apartment in the hospital. To make some provision for such widows as may wish occasionally to spend a winter with their friends or relations, and to save them travelling expenses, it is further permitted to those who petition for leave of absence near the end of the year to procure at the same time a second petition to two or more of the trustees praying that their time of absence for the next year may be allowed in the first months of it. All widows are to leave directions with the porter where letters will reach them when absent.

It is further ordered that printed copies of the above regulations, or the purport of them, be distributed to each widow at the time of the next quarterly payment and sent to such as are absent; with this further notice, that strict obedience to them is expected from 1 January next under the penalties set forth in the orders of 1729 and 1748.

The steward each quarter shall examine the porter's book and suspend the quarterly dividend of such non-residents as shall offend against the regulations till the next general meeting of the trustees, which meeting each widow so offending shall have notice to attend, if she can be heard of, to show cause why she should not be expelled from the hospital or otherwise punished according to the discretion of the trustees.

Signatures

J. Walker Heneage, L. Bigg, Ambrose Goddard, Richard Pocock, James Tylney Long, Charles Penruddocke, William Northey.

26 June 1782, at the Castle inn, Marlborough

Present

John Whitelock, esq., Richard Pocock, clerk, Ambrose Goddard, esq., John Walker Heneage, esq., Lovelace Bigg, esq., Sir James Tylney Long, bt.

Trusteeship

Examined and allowed the accounts of Mr. Samuel Hawkes, the receiver, a balance of £605 18*s.* 11½*d.* remaining in his hands.

It is agreed by the trustees now present that, at every future meeting at the Castle, the steward shall order a dinner for the full number of trustees and that each of them shall pay 4*s.* for his ordinary although absent. The steward is to acquaint the absent trustees of this regulation.

Almshouse

It appearing to the trustees that Mrs. Frances Lucas, one of the widows formerly communicated to and many years resident at the hospital as one of the poor widows on that endowment but now residing with her son at Hungerford, is incapable from her great age and infirmities of being conveyed to or of residing at her apartment in the hospital, [it is] ordered that the steward do pay the quarterly dividend accruing or to grow due from 1 January last to the order or appointment of Frances Lucas, or her receipt for it, as it shall become payable during such inability or until some further order be made at a future meeting of the trustees; notwithstanding the rules established at the last meeting, her case appearing to the trustees to be particular and not to fall within the general regulations concerning residence then intended to be enforced.

Signatures

John Whitelock, Richard Pocock, Ambrose Goddard, J. Walker Heneage, L. Bigg, James Tylney Long.

25 June 1783, at the Castle inn, Marlborough

Present

John Whitelock, esq., Richard Pocock, clerk, Ambrose Goddard, esq., John Walker Heneage, esq., Lovelace Bigg, esq., Charles Penruddocke, esq., William Northey, esq.

Trusteeship

Ordered that the steward take the proper measures for applying to the court of Chancery for confirming the order made 15 September 1781. It is recommended to Mr. Bigg and Mr. Pocock to revise the several orders now in force for the better managing [of] the hospital and report them at the next meeting.

Ordered that the nomination to future vacancies in the hospital for manor widows shall not be taken, as formerly, by the trustees in turn in succession but, on account of the numerous applications, it is ordered that the widows in the several manors having claims shall from time to time deliver in a short state in writing of the nature of their pretensions for the trustees at their next and future meetings, to be by them considered of and determined upon.

It appearing to the trustees that there still remain three vacancies in the hospital for widows of clergymen, and that no applications have been made by such persons as are duly qualified notwithstanding repeated advertisements, it is ordered that such apartments, and others in the like situation for the future, shall be filled by lay widows of the proper counties when such vacancies happen as shall not, upon due notice given in the public papers or one of them, be claimed or solicited for within 1 year after the vacancy happens.

Resolved that every trustee who shall have been absent at two of the general annual meetings successively shall from thenceforth forfeit his turn of nomination to vacancies in the hospital, until he shall attend in person at some subsequent meeting and pay the forfeits he may have incurred by a resolution of the trustees at their last general meeting in June 1782.

Almshouse

Upon the application of Mrs. Lloyd and Mrs. Lake, two of the widows inhabiting the hospital whose quarterly dividend has been retained by the steward for not conforming to the late order made concerning residence, and it appearing that their absence beyond the limited time was occasioned by sickness, [it is] ordered that the dividends in arrear be paid to them the next quarter. Mrs. Willoughby, another of the widows whose dividend for several quarters has been withheld by the steward for not residing, having for some time inhabited her apartment in the hospital and promised at this meeting to observe the rules made by the trustees for the future, it is ordered that her arrears be also paid.

Ordered that the dividends of the rents payable to the poor widows inhabiting the hospital be raised from £14 to £15 each. Where a poor widow happens to die in the middle of a quarter the steward shall pay the proportional share of such widow's last quarterly dividend, up to the day of her death, to her representatives.

Next meeting

Agreed that the trustees will meet at the Castle inn on Saturday 13 September next.

Signatures

Richard Pocock, J. Walker Heneage, L. Bigg, Charles Penruddocke, Ambrose Goddard, E. Ernle, William Northey.

13 September 1783, at the Castle inn, Marlborough

Present

John Whitelock, esq., Richard Pocock, clerk, Ambrose Goddard, esq., John Walker Heneage, esq., Lovelace Bigg, esq., Charles Penruddocke, esq., Sir Edward Ernle, bt., Sir William Jones, bt., William Northey, esq.

Trusteeship

We choose John Awdry of Notton, esq., and James Sutton of New Park, esq., to be trustees in place of Francis Popham and Francis Stonehouse, esqs., and order the steward to prepare a conveyance of the charity estate from the present trustees to the new trustees now chosen, in trust for them and the old trustees.

Almshouse

Ordered that the steward do issue his warrant to the porter for the admission of Mary Preston as a clergy widow of the county of Somerset, and Mary Millington as a manor widow, into the vacant apartments in the hospital.

The steward is ordered to pay the dividends of rents that have accrued to Eleanor Tarrant since her admission, although she has not yet been able to take up her residence at the hospital.

Next meeting

We agree to meet at the Castle inn at Marlborough on Wednesday 8 October next in order to take into consideration, and come to some resolutions concerning, an application to Chancery respecting the rules and orders for managing the charity.

Signatures

Richard Pocock, J. Walker Heneage, L. Bigg, Charles Penruddocke, William Northey.

8 October 1783, at the Castle inn, Marlborough

Present

Richard Pocock, clerk, Sir Edward Ernle, bt., Lovelace Bigg, esq., Sir William Jones, bt., William Northey, esq.

Trusteeship

At this meeting for taking into consideration the state of the charity, the rules made for the management thereof, and other matters relative thereto, it appears to the trustees

That, in consequence of a resolution of the trustees made at a meeting [on] 30 June 1773 not to renew or instate any life in any copyhold estate within the manors belonging to the hospital (except cottages), in order by degrees to increase the annual payment to the widows inhabiting the hospital, none of the copyhold bargains have been renewed since that time.

That the purposes to which the fines to be taken on such renewals are appropriated by the duchess's will have been, and may be, fully answered and made up to the poor widows by the dividends on £2,600 stock in Old South Sea annuities now remaining, which are annually applied for the benefit of the hospital and its inhabitants and accounted for by the receiver.

That the cloth gowns formerly delivered to the poor widows yearly about Christmas have been discontinued for many years, and the cost price or worth in money, being £1 6*s*. 8*d*. for each gown, has been added to and made part of the annual dividend payable quarterly to each widow.

That as fast as the revenues of the lands belonging to the hospital would admit of it the trustees have raised the shares payable to the poor widows, from £10 10*s*. a year and £1 6*s*. 8*d*. for the gown as they stood in 1778 to £15 a year, the £1 6*s*. 8*d*. for the gown included, being the annual dividend now paid to each of the poor widows.

That, since the extension of the charity to a greater number of widows, the trustees have endeavoured to fill the new apartments according to the directions of the duchess's will, but some of those appropriated to the widows of clergymen are vacant and often are so for a long time, no clergy widows properly qualified being to be found within the districts appointed by the will. In which case the trustees are of opinion [that] it would be for the advantage of the charity to fill such vacant apartments with clergy widows from other districts and, after a certain time and notice given in the public papers, if no clergy widows properly qualified can be found, to have a power of nominating lay widows to such vacant tenements.

That ever since 1729 the number of trustees has been increased from nine to 12, which last number is barely sufficient to secure the attendance of five so often as is necessary.

That, since the number of widows has been increased and the charity extended, it has been found necessary to make some new regulations for enforcing the rules concerning residence at the hospital and to enlarge the time of absence, with leave of the trustees, from 1 month to 3 months in every year, as is set forth more particularly in an order of the trustees made 15 September 1781. The regulations made by that order having been found upon trial to answer the purpose, it is resolved and ordered that the steward do take the proper measures for getting the order of 15 September 1781 confirmed in the High Court of Chancery.

At this meeting also the trustees came to the following resolutions.

That in their judgement it will be for the benefit of the charity and the improvement of the trust estate to adhere to the order made [on] 30 June 1773 and, as the lives fail whereon the copyhold bargains are now held, to suffer them to come into possession to be then leased out at improved rents.

That the method of paying the widows now in use, by quarterly payments as above mentioned, is most beneficial, and that the present annual dividend of £15 is the utmost the revenues of the charity estate and stock in the Funds will allow after deducting the necessary expenses.

That, upon the death of every clergy widow or other vacancy in the clergy widows' apartments, if there be no immediate application or no clergy widow can be found properly qualified within 1 month, the steward do make known such vacancy by advertisement in the public papers according to the districts: that is to say, in some London evening paper for vacancies from the cities of London and Westminster and in the *Salisbury Journal* for the several counties. In case no application be made by clergy widows residing in the proper districts for 12 months, or of clergy widows wherever they may reside for 24 months, from the publication of such advertisement, then it shall be lawful for the trustees to fill such vacant apartments, according to the tenor of this resolution, either at the end of 12 months with a clergy widow duly qualified in other respects though from a different district or at the end of 24 months with a lay widow duly qualified and resident in the district wherein the vacancy may happen.

That our steward do pursue all proper measures by petition or otherwise for bringing the orders and resolutions, and other matters above stated or such parts thereof as may be advised, before the Lord Chancellor for his lordship's directions therein.

Whereas the £2,600 Old South Sea annuities originally subscribed and still remaining in the names of Sir Robert Long, bt., and Edward Popham, esq., in trust for the charity is now vested in Mrs. Popham, the relict of Francis Popham, esq., deceased, the eldest son and representative of Edward Popham [*margin*: Dorothy, executrix; Francis, executor of Edward], who survived Sir Robert Long, in trust, [it is] ordered that our steward do prepare a state of the case to be presented to Mrs. Popham and that she be requested to do all necessary acts for transferring the [annuities] to two or more of the trustees in trust for the benefit of this charity.

Signatures

Richard Pocock, J. Walker Heneage, Ambrose Goddard, L. Bigg, Charles Penruddocke, William Jones.

4 July 1784, at the Castle inn, Marlborough

Present

Richard Pocock, clerk, Lovelace Bigg, esq., Sir Edward Ernle, bt., Sir William Jones, bt., William Northey, esq.

Trusteeship

The parish church at Huish being very much out of repair and in danger of falling down, at this meeting several estimates of the expense of repairing, and of taking down and rebuilding, it were delivered in. It appears that neither the tenant under this trust of the farm at Huish, nor the other parishioners who are chiefly copyholders in the manor of Huish, can or might at this time be required to put the church into such repair as is necessary. It has also been represented to the trustees that the Revd. Mr. James Rogers, who with his family usually attends divine service in that parish, has proposed to lay out £20 towards ceiling the church, that John Reeves, the tenant of the farm, who is obliged by his lease to contribute £5 towards the repairs of the church, is willing to advance £5 more, and [that] the Revd. Mr. Mayo, at his own expense as rector, is to repair or rebuild the chancel. The trustees therefore, in order that everything necessary may be done in a proper manner, appoint and desire Sir Edward Ernle, bt., one of the trustees of this charity, Mr. Rogers, and Mr. Mayo to review estimates and enter into contracts with proper workmen for the doing thereof as is intended in a decent, frugal, and effectual manner. [It is resolved] that their thanks be given to Mr. Rogers for his very civil offer. [*Margin.* The costs to the trust, amounting to £162 16*s.* 1¾*d.*, are entered in the account book at the end of J. Ward's second account]

Estate

At this meeting the trustees executed a lease to James Warwick of Milton farm and, in consideration of his engaging to enter into an agreement for leaving one third, instead of one fourth, part of the arable land belonging to his farm fallow or in grass in the last year of his lease for the next tenant, and [leaving] 6 acres more of arable land to be winter fallowed for turnips by the next tenant, at such price for this last 6 acres as they can agree upon, [it is] ordered that the treasurer pay James Warwick £10.

and see trusteeship business

Signatures

Richard Pocock, L. Bigg, Edward Ernle, William Jones, William Northey.

22 June 1785, at the Castle inn, Marlborough

Present

John Whitelock, esq., the Revd. Richard Pocock, clerk, Ambrose Goddard, esq., John Walker Heneage, esq., Lovelace Bigg, esq., Charles Penruddocke, esq., the Revd. Sir Edward Ernle, bt., Sir James Tylney Long, bt., Sir William Jones, bt., William Northey, esq.

Trusteeship

We the trustees whose names are hereunto subscribed, by virtue of the powers given us by the will of the late duchess dowager of Somerset and since confirmed by the High Court of Chancery, appoint John Ward of Marlborough to be our steward of all manors and receiver of all rents, revenues, and estates to the hospital belonging and to hold courts and do all other things to the offices of steward and receiver belonging, the offices being become vacant by the death of Samuel Hawkes, gentleman.

At this meeting examined and allowed the accounts of the late receiver and his representatives, the balance whereof is £156 0*s.* 5*d.*

An application having been made to Mrs. Dorothy Popham, in consequence of an order of the trustees made 8 October 1783, to transfer £2,600 Old South Sea annuities belonging to the charity to two or more of the trustees in trust for the charity, and she having signified her consent thereto on being properly discharged and indemnified, [it is] ordered that the new steward do prepare a proper deed between the trustees and Mrs. Popham whereby she may be authorized and requested to transfer the stock, and the dividends due thereon, to Sir James Tylney Long, bt., Ambrose Goddard, esq., and Lovelace Bigg, esq., and [he may] indemnify and discharge her from the trust and from the consequences of such transfer, and whereby Sir James Tylney Long, Ambrose Goddard, and Lovelace Bigg may declare the trust of the stock and dividends to be for the benefit of the charity.

Almshouse

The steward is to purchase new bibles and prayer books to be ready for such of the widows as have none in their rooms.

The allowance to Mary Alexander for nursing Mrs. Murray to be continued during her illness.

Mrs. Lampard, an absentee, having appeared and made her excuses: allowed them and ordered her dividend and arrears to be paid.

Signatures

John Whitelock, Ambrose Goddard, E. Ernle, J. Walker Heneage, William Northey, Charles Penruddocke, L. Bigg.

17 September 1785, at the Castle inn, Marlborough

Present

Richard Pocock, clerk, Charles Penruddocke, esq., John Walker Heneage, esq., Lovelace Bigg, esq., James Sutton, esq., Sir William Jones, bt., William Northey, esq.

Trusteeship

Whereas it is expedient [that] some uniform rule should be adopted in interpreting who are the proper objects of this charity, it is resolved that the trustees will in future confine their nominations to such widows as shall be settled in some parish in the district from whence they are to be selected or whose last place of residence shall have usually been in such district for 40 days previous to the vacancy.

It is also resolved that, instead of sending orders to the steward for admission of widows into the hospital, which is attended with inconvenience and expense to the widows, orders shall in future be directed and sent to the porter for the admission of lay widows to vacant houses unless, on examination of the decrees and orders of the court of Chancery, it shall appear that the court shall have given other directions.

The steward produced a bond, with sufficient sureties, faithfully to account for all sums of money coming to his hands as receiver, which was deposited in the hands of Mr. Bigg for the benefit of the trust.

At this meeting the trustees present executed a deed authorizing and requesting Mrs. Dorothy Popham to transfer £2,600 Old South Sea annuities to Ambrose Goddard, esq., Lovelace Bigg, esq., and Sir James Tylney Long, bt., in trust for the charity and indemnifying and discharging her from the trust.

Estate

Agreed with farmer John Barnes for a fresh lease of Chirton farm for 12 years from Lady [day] next at £110 a year, clear of land tax, and repairs; with similar covenants as in the [existing] lease except in such particulars as our steward and he shall think proper to vary for the benefit of the farm, and in consideration that the tenant shall enter into reasonable covenants to be required by the steward.

Ordered that he [John Barnes] be allowed the money he has expended in digging a well on the down, and that he be allowed brick and lime at the kiln for a wall against the south-east side of the stable.

Agreed with William Crook Noyes to accept a surrender of his lease of a house at New Mill and [to] grant him a fresh lease without fine, for 99 years if he and his daughters Elizabeth and Alice, or any of them, shall so long live, in consideration of the quit rent being raised to £1 a year.

The steward is also to agree with William Crook Noyes for a lease of his bargain at Froxfield for 21 years from Michaelmas next at £40 a year clear, or as much more as he can agree for, and to enlarge the brewhouse according to the estimate given in by John Osmond.

Almshouse

Ordered that Ann Hancock and Sarah Calvert be admitted in place of Ann Willoughby and Celia Whitelock, to hold from the time of their nomination in June last.

Whereas many of the bibles and prayer books allowed for the use of the widows in the hospital have either been lost or mislaid by them or carried away by their representatives, who ought to have left them for the benefit of succeeding widows, whereby the trust is put to unnecessary expense, it is ordered that the steward do deliver new bibles and prayer books to such of the widows as have none, and that the widows shall produce their bibles and prayer books to the trustees annually at the view meetings of the trustees. The representatives of deceased widows, and widows marrying or resigning their houses, shall deliver up to the steward at the succeeding payday next after the death, marriage, or resignation the books belonging to their respective houses for the benefit of the succeeding widows. In default of such delivery, or if it shall appear that any of the widows shall have destroyed or damaged her books, the steward shall stop and retain so much of the stipend made or payable to the widows or their representatives making such default as shall be sufficient to replace [them], and the steward shall therewith replace such books as shall be wanting.

The steward is ordered to pay Eleanor Tarrant her arrears, her absence being occasioned by illness.

The steward is to allow any sum a week, not exceeding *2s. 6d.*, for nursing Mrs. Oaks, a clergy widow aged 86, she being very infirm.

and see trusteeship business

Signatures

Richard Pocock, William Jones, L. Bigg, J. Walker Heneage, Charles Penruddocke, James Sutton.

11 January 1786, at the Bear inn, Devizes

Present

Ambrose Goddard, esq., John Walker Heneage, esq., Lovelace Bigg, esq., Sir James Tylney Long, bt., John Awdry, esq.

Almshouse

Anne Smith, widow, an absentee without leave for more than a year, having made proper submission and promised never to absent herself from the Somerset Hospital without leave, nor to ask leave but at a general meeting of the trustees, it is ordered that she be permitted to continue in the hospital. It is further ordered that six quarterly payments due to her on 5 January instant, but which she has forfeited by her contempt of the rules respecting residence, shall be applied by the steward in compounding with and satisfying the creditors of her, and for her benefit in such manner as has been agreed upon by her.

Mrs. Esther Humphreys, a clergy widow, having signified to the steward her intention of resigning her tenement and stipend, [it is] ordered that immediately on her resignation Mrs. Hannah Rider, a clergy widow mentioned by Sir James Tylney Long, be appointed to succeed her if she shall appear properly qualified. [*Margin.* Not qualified]

Signatures

L. Bigg, Ambrose Goddard, J. Awdry, J. Walker Heneage, James Tylney Long.

27 July 1786, at the Castle inn, Marlborough

Present

Richard Pocock, clerk, Ambrose Goddard, esq., Lovelace Bigg, esq., Charles Penruddocke, esq., John Walker Heneage, esq., Sir Edward Ernle, bt., Sir James Tylney Long, bt., Sir William Jones, bt., John Awdry, esq.

Trusteeship

Whereas the order made on 25 June 1783 for admission of manor widows by the trustees at their general meetings may prevent tenements becoming vacant from being occupied for a considerable time, and [whereas] it is judged more convenient that the future nominations of manor widows, as also of clergy widows, shall be taken in turn by the trustees, it is ordered that the nomination to future vacancies in the hospital for manor widows and clergy widows shall be taken by the trustees in turn, distinct and separate from their turns to the nomination of other lay widows. In order that the trustee whose turn it shall be to nominate a manor or clergy widow may know what widows have applied for manor and clergy vacancies, [it is] ordered that the steward keep a list of all manor and clergy widows, candidates for places in the hospital, in the order [in which] they apply, to which end the trustees will send the names of such widows as apply to them to the steward. When a vacancy for a manor or clergy widow shall happen the steward shall send to the trustee having the nomination of a fresh widow a copy of the list of such of the candidates as are qualified to succeed to it, provided that ... [*MS. blank*] Munday of Broad Town, widow, shall have the first manor vacancy.

Examined and allowed the first account of Mr. John Ward, the receiver, for 1785, on which there is a balance of £291 8*s.* 8*d.* due to him.

Examined the bills for rebuilding Huish church. [It is] ordered that the receiver discharge what remains due thereon after deducting the charge of 1 gn. for a plan and 7*s.* 6*d.* for measuring charged by John Eyles.

Estate

Allowed of a proposal made by Henry Tombs to the steward for taking a lease of a poor cottage in bad repair near the Cross Keys in Froxfield which lately fell in hand on the death of Stephen Wentworth; for the lives of himself [and] John and Henry his sons in consideration of the yearly rent of 20*s.* and a fine of 5 gns. [*margin*: received and accounted for in account no. 2]. A lease was accordingly executed at this meeting.

Also [executed]: a lease to John Barnes of Chirton farm and another to William Crook Noyes of a cottage at New Mill, pursuant to orders made 17 September last.

At this meeting John Reeves attended and desired to take a fresh lease of Huish farm, with the bargains held therewith, for 12 years to commence at the expiration of the present lease in order that he may with safety plant sainfoin on the farm. [It is] ordered that the steward have power to agree with him at the yearly rent of £200 and under similar covenants and conditions to those in his present lease, except as to such alterations as will be proper in consequence of bargains fallen in hand since the making of that lease.

Almshouse

Ordered that the receiver pay Mrs. Elizabeth Barnes 1 gn. for attending and nursing Mrs. Elizabeth Powell.

Ordered that two squares of the roof of the north-west corner of the hospital be repaired by new lathing and fresh laying the tiles.

It is permitted that pots may be put on the tops of the chimneys of such of the poor widows' houses as are smokey, at the discretion of the steward, the expense being in the whole not more than 6*s.* a tenement.

and see trusteeship business

Signatures

Richard Pocock, J. Walker Heneage, Charles Penruddocke, Edward Ernle, Ambrose Goddard, James Tylney Long, William Jones, L. Bigg, J. Awdry.

27 June 1787, at the Castle inn, Marlborough

Present

Ambrose Goddard, Lovelace Bigg, Charles Penruddocke, John Walker Heneage, esqs., Sir James Tylney Long, Sir Edward Ernle, Sir William Jones, bts., James Sutton, John Awdry, William Northey, esqs.

Trusteeship

Examined and allowed the second account of Mr. John Ward, the receiver, for 1786, on which there is a balance of £113 11*s.* 0¾*d.* due to him.

It appearing to the trustees that the net receipt of the hospital has for some years been insufficient to pay the widows' salaries and the other outgoings, that the receiver has from time to time advanced large sums of money for those purposes out of his own pocket, [and] that the balance that will be due to him after paying the ensuing Midsummer quarterages will be £160 or thereabouts, it is resolved that the trustees will suspend their future nominations till 6 months after any vacancy which may happen until such time that the receiver shall be reimbursed all monies by him so advanced. In order to effect that purpose at an early period the receiver is required to enforce the payment of all arrears from tenants which may be due from time to time in the most effectual manner.

Estate

Approved of the proposal of John Osmond mentioned in a separate state of proposals for stating [*i.e.* granting an estate in] certain houses in Froxfield, and the steward is to agree with Joseph Drury and Charles Cook on the terms mentioned in that state of proposals if they are willing to give the fines therein mentioned.

Ordered that Farmer Barnes shall be allowed materials for rebuilding the brewhouse provided he will do carriage, find straw, and pay for workmanship.

Signatures

J. Walker Heneage, James Tylney Long, William Jones, Charles Penruddocke, J. Awdry, William Northey, L. Bigg, E. Ernle, Ambrose Goddard, James Sutton.

25 June 1788, at the Castle inn, Marlborough

Present

Ambrose Goddard, esq., John Walker Heneage, esq., Lovelace Bigg, esq., Sir William Jones, bt., William Northey, esq., James Sutton, esq.

Trusteeship

Examined and allowed the third account of Mr. John Ward, the receiver, for 1787, on which there is a balance of £42 12*s.* 9¼*d.* due from him.

and see next meeting

Estate

Ordered that Farmer Barnes shall be allowed the expenses of building a brewhouse, he performing carriage of materials and finding straw and thatching.

Almshouse

Ordered that the hospital shall be forthwith repaired according to the particular taken upon view of the hospital on 13 May last, and that the chapel windows shall be repaired with new glass and the porter's lodge, gate, and posts painted and repaired.

Let Jane Stiles be admitted into the hospital in place of Mary Millington, a manor widow, deceased.

Let Elizabeth Brown be admitted to the tenement vacant by the death of Catherine Parry, a widow at-large. Emma Springett is to be admitted to the tenement vacant by the death of Mary Oaks, a Wiltshire widow.

Next meeting

At the next meeting the trustees intend to choose new trustees in place of such as are deceased, of which notice is to be given to such of the trustees as are absent. The next meeting is appointed at the Castle inn on Saturday 13 September next.

Signatures

Ambrose Goddard, J. Walker Heneage, L. Bigg, William Jones, William Northey, James Sutton.

19 September 1789, at the Castle inn, Marlborough

Present

Ambrose Goddard, esq., John Walker Heneage, esq., Lovelace

Bigg, esq., Sir James Tylney Long, bt., William Northey, esq., John Awdry, esq.

Trusteeship

We choose the Rt. Hon. Thomas Bruce, earl of Ailesbury, James Montagu the younger of Alderton, esq., the Revd. Edward Popham of Chilton, clerk, Doctor in Divinity, and the Revd. Thomas Goddard Vilett of Swindon, clerk, Doctor of Laws, to be trustees in place of Sir Edward Ernle, the Revd. Richard Pocock, clerk, John Whitelock, esq., and Charles Penruddocke, esq., deceased, and order the steward to prepare a conveyance of the charity estate from the present trustees to the new trustees in trust for them and the old trustees.

Examined and allowed the fourth account of Mr. John Ward, the receiver, for 1788, the balance whereof, being £188 14*s.* 10¼*d.*, is to be carried to the next account as due from him.

Estate

The leases to John Reeves of Huish farm, and two cottage leases, were executed pursuant to former agreements.

Agreed with William Merriwether to accept of a surrender of a lease of three tenements in Froxfield late Osmond's, [held] for the life of Barbara Tucker [and] dated 13 October 1759, and to grant him a fresh lease for three lives, to be nominated by him in 1 month, for a fine of £80.

Ordered that the steward give notice to Farmer Andrews that the trustees insist upon his immediately paying up his arrears, and that they insist on his paying at least all the rent that was due at Michaelmas 1788 before Christmas next.

The steward is to sell such elm and ash timber as can be spared from the Huish and Milton estates, not exceeding the value of £150, on such terms as he can agree for.

Almshouse

The steward is at liberty to pay Mrs. Mary Haddon her arrears if she will sign an undertaking to resign in case of any future absence without leave.

We appoint William Merriwether to be porter and woodman for Froxfield in the room of his father-in-law, deceased, and allow him as a salary for that business, and for ringing the chapel bell, £5. Mrs. Brown is to be continued as washer and mender of the chapel linen and sweeper of the chapel.

We allow John Osmond 40*s.* for ringing the bell etc. for the last year.

The minutes of repairs taken at Whitsuntide by the steward as necessary to be done to the hospital was examined, and it is ordered that such repairs be done and that new doors and windows to the old tenements and chapel, as included in the estimates given in by the

workmen, be immediately set about.
Signatures

Ambrose Goddard, J. Walker Heneage, L. Bigg, James Tylney Long, J. Awdry, William Northey.

28 July 1790, at the Castle inn, Marlborough

Present

John Walker Heneage, esq., Sir James Tylney Long, John Awdry, esq., Ambrose Goddard, esq., William Northey, esq., Lovelace Bigg Wither, esq., the earl of Ailesbury, James Montagu, esq., the Revd. Edward Popham, D.D., the Revd. Thomas Goddard Vilett, LL.D.
Trusteeship

Examined and allowed the fifth account of Mr. John Ward, the receiver, for 1789, the balance whereof, being £215 7*s*. 5¼*d*., is to be carried to the next account as due from him.

The deed of trust appointing new trustees was executed by all the trustees present at this meeting.

It is resolved that in future no trustee shall rent or occupy any part of the charity estate.
Estate

The trustees approve of the contract made by the receiver with James Warwick for the sale of 116 timber trees for £205, one moiety to be paid on 10 October next and the remainder on 10 October 1791.

The receiver is to allow James Warwick 2 gns. out of his rent towards the church rate extraordinary on the recasting of Milton bells.

Agreed with Joseph Drury to grant him a reversionary copy of the Pelican inn with the stables, garden, and ½ acre of land, likewise a house, barn, and stable in Froxfield in the occupation of him, with two paddocks of land near or adjoining, and a cottage in the occupation of William Pope, for the life of his son Joseph, aged 16; fine £70, quit rent in reversion £4.

Agreed to grant a fresh lease to William Crook Noyes of the Cross Keys, and other property rented by him, for 21 years from Michaelmas 1791 at £35 10*s*. a year, and to allow him materials for building a parlour etc. on the terms proposed by him and entered in the contract book or survey.
Almshouse

Ordered that the treasurer pay widow Anne Smith her arrears if she shall return to the hospital before the next payday, her absence having been occasioned by necessity.

Ordered that sheds be put to the doors of 24 of the tenements which have none according to William Merriwether's estimate, and that windows shall be made in the tenements no. 1 and no. 50 in the kitchen to look into the court.

Signatures

William Northey, Ailesbury, J. Montagu, E. Popham, T. G. Vilett, Ambrose Goddard, J. Walker Heneage, L. Bigg Wither, J. Awdry, James Tylney Long.

22 June 1791, at the Castle inn, Marlborough

Present

Dr. Popham, Ambrose Goddard, esq., Dr. Vilett, William Northey, esq.

Trusteeship

Examined and allowed the sixth account of Mr. John Ward, the receiver, for 1790, the balance whereof, being £327 14*s.* 5¾*d.*, due from him is to be carried to the next account.

The trustees approve of the transfer of £113 9*s.* 2*d.* Old South Sea annuities to Sir James Tylney Long, Ambrose Goddard, esq., and Lovelace Bigg, esq., in trust for augmenting the rectory of Huish pursuant to the will of Gabriel Thistlethwaite [*interlineated*: of Winterslow], clerk, dated 24 April 1718 [and] proved at Salisbury, to a deed of trust executed by Messrs. Charles Gibbs and George Gibbs dated 13 February 1766, and to a memorandum endorsed on the deed of trust respecting the Old South Sea annuities belonging to this charity dated 17 September 1785.

Resolved that in future the general annual meeting shall be on the first Wednesday in July instead of the first Wednesday after 20 June, and that the treasurer shall of his own authority give a month's notice thereof to all the trustees.

and see almshouse business

Estate

Ordered that the steward allow Farmer Andrews materials for a barn floor and for rebuilding the end of a stable, and that he allow Farmer Drury some timber for doors at the Pelican, at the steward's discretion.

Ordered that the committee [named below], or any two of them, be empowered to treat and agree with the trustees of the turnpike road from Newbury to Marlborough for improving it by allowing them to take in certain parts of the land belonging to the charity estate in Froxfield adjoining the narrow parts of the road, upon the trustees of the road making a reasonable compensation and erecting proper walls, fences, and other conveniences where the alterations shall render them necessary.

Almshouse

Ordered that the treasurer signify to Mr. Blackman and Mr.

Whitelock of Ramsbury, Messrs. Garlick, Pinckney, and Maurice of Marlborough, and Mr. Smith of Hungerford, surgeons, that they are at liberty to deliver propoals, sealed up, to the treasurer, stating upon what terms they can attend once a week without being sent to, and so often upon being sent to as shall be necessary, at the Somerset hospital and provide the widows there with medicines and surgery for 1 year, which proposals shall be taken into consideration at the next meeting.

It having been represented to the trustees that Widow Powell has been frequently guilty of drunkenness and that she is now very ill, it is ordered that Lovelace Bigg Wither, esq., the earl of Ailesbury, and Dr. Popham, or any two of them, be a committee to enquire into the facts and to employ an apothecary to visit her, report her case, and supply her with medicines if they think fit. The committee is to take such measures for the punishment of the widow by suspending her stipend, or any part of it, or by expelling her from the hospital and making some weekly allowance out of her stipend towards her maintenance at the place of her settlement, or not, till further order as the committee shall judge expedient. If it shall appear to the committee that the widow is deranged they are to employ a nurse to confine and take care of her.

Ordered, on the petition of Widow Clowes, that the treasurer pay her her arrears, notwithstanding her absence for the reasons stated in her petition.

Ordered that the steward suspend the stipend of Elizabeth Davies during her absence without leave unless she produces a satisfactory excuse for her having been absent.

Ordered that the several repairs of which memorandums were made at the view meeting be done, and that the iron window frames shall be painted where necessary.

The case of Mrs. Jouring, who petitions for an allowance towards her surgeon's bill, to be further considered at the next meeting.

Ordered that the workmen's bills for repairs to the hospital shall be left with the carpenter, who is to examine whether the works charged for have been done properly and whether the charges are reasonable, previously to the bills being discharged.

Ordered that the rules for the government of the widows, or an abstract of them, be written or printed and hung up in a conspicuous part of the hospital, and that the widows be required to comply with the rules except in such cases as they have usually been dispensed with.

Ordered that the before named committee be desired to consider of some effectual means whereby the door of the hospital may be kept locked in the night, and at the same time securing to the inhabitants the means of retreat in case of fire.

The petition of the widows for an advance of salary is rejected by the trustees, who will advance the yearly stipend when they are satisfied the revenues will admit of it without any application from the widows, which is considered as useless and improper.

Signatures

Ambrose Goddard, William Northey, E. Popham, T. G. Vilett, Ailesbury.

17 September 1791, at the Castle inn, Marlborough

Present

Ambrose Goddard, John Walker Heneage, Lovelace Bigg Wither, esqs., Sir James Tylney Long, bt., John Awdry, esq., the earl of Ailesbury, Dr. Popham, Dr. Vilett.

Trusteeship

The report of the committee appointed at the last meeting respecting widow Elizabeth Powell and as to the improvement of the road through Froxfield was read. The trustees approve of and confirm what has been done by the committee. [*Margin.* See report entered on the two next pages]

Estate

see following report

Almshouse

Ordered that the steward take the opinion of counsel as to the place of Widow Powell's legal settlement and assist the parish officers of Froxfield in getting her removed to her parish, at the expense of the trust, if she will not voluntarily remove herself to some distant place. The steward has a discretionary power to allow any further sum not exceeding half a year's stipend for her expenses in removing out of the country.

Resolved that no other widow shall be placed in the tenement lately occupied by Widow Powell until further order.

Ordered that the treasurer pay Mr. Blackman two bills amounting to £3 8*s.* 3*d.* for attendance on Widows Powell and Noyes.

Ordered that Mr. James Whitelock be employed for 1 year from the 29th instant to attend the hospital once a week, or oftener if necessary, and provide the widows with medicines and surgery at the stipend of £20, according to his proposal.

The trustees have examined a state of the income and average expenditure of the trust and are of opinion that no addition to the widows' stipend can at present be made.

Ordered that the arrears due to widow Elizabeth Davies be suspended until further order, that no part of her stipend hereafter to grow due be paid her but for such time as she shall actually reside in the hospital, and that, if she shall continue non-resident until Christmas, she shall from thenceforth be expelled.

and see following report

Signatures

Ambrose Goddard, L. B. Wither, James Tylney Long, J. Awdry, Ailesbury, E. Popham, T. G. Vilett.

The report of the committee of trustees appointed at the last meeting

The committee enquired into the charges preferred against Widow Powell for drunkenness and found them true. Her intemperance appeared so habitual, and her conduct so violent and offensive, that the committee judged it necessary for the peace and safety of the hospital to remove her as soon as possible. But, the intention of the committee being communicated to her, she entered into a voluntary agreement to resign her tenement and stipend at Michaelmas next upon being paid her stipend down to that time and half a year forward to Lady day next, which the committee consented to, and she afterwards gave up the key of her tenement to the porter. The steward has since sent to Mr. Lloyd, a gentleman named by the widow Powell as her friend, the particulars of that agreement and intimated that, if any of her relations would take the charge and care of her, some allowance might possibly be obtained, on application to the trustees, towards her maintenance provided she was kept at a distance from, and gave no disturbance to, the inhabitants of the hospital or parish of Froxfield. Mr. Lloyd replied [that] he was not surprised, after what he himself lately saw at Froxfield, at the account lately given of Widow Powell. He declined taking any active part in her affairs and referred the steward to her brother-in-law Mr. Nash, attorney, at High Wycombe, to whom the steward wrote a letter nearly to the same effect as that he had written to Mr. Lloyd. [He] received the following answer from Mr. Nash dated 24 August 1791. 'I have been favoured with yours of 31 July respecting Mrs. Powell leaving Froxfield hospital, which is very unpleasant for me and Mrs. Nash to be acquainted with, although I must confess it was a thing I at some time expected from her conduct. Mrs. Powell's behaviour to me and her sister has been so very unbecoming that I am determined she never more shall enter my house. Nor will any of her relations admit her again to their houses. Therefore, under her present misfortunes, which she has thought proper to reduce herself to, I know of no benefit she can claim or expect but that of a pauper at her own parish. I am totally unacquainted where that may be, but should think either Ham or the parish of Chalfont St. Peter.'

The committee have agreed with the trustees of the two districts of turnpike road between Marlborough and Newbury that the road shall be made straighter and wider by cutting off a strip of meadow opposite the Cross Keys inn and a strip of meadow opposite Alexander Newman's house belonging to the trust estate, [by] lengthening the bridge over the river, and by cutting down part of the bank in front of the hospital and rebuilding the steps. The trustees of those districts have engaged to pay the full value of the land to be taken from the meadows and to make proper drains and fences and a handsome footpath under the hospital wall, as by an agreement entered into by the trustees will more fully appear. The committee are of opinion that the road and village will be greatly improved by such alterations without any detriment to the trust estate, conceiving that the interest of the purchase money should be allowed to the tenant of the meadows during the remainder of his lease as a compensation for the land to be added to the road.

The committee have not been able to fix on any eligible method for keeping the hospital door locked and yet securing a retreat for the widows in case of fire, but Mr. Evans, the chaplain, has undertaken to make a model of a lock which may probably answer the purpose.

(Signed) L. Bigg Wither, E. Popham, Ailesbury

4 July 1792, at the Castle inn, Marlborough

Present

Sir James Tylney Long, bt., Ambrose Goddard, esq., John Walker Heneage, esq., Lovelace Bigg Wither, esq., John Awdry, esq., James Montagu, esq., Revd. Dr. Vilett, Revd. Dr. Popham.

Trusteeship

Examined and allowed the seventh account of Mr. John Ward, the receiver, for 1791, the balance whereof, being £178 18*s.* 6¼*d.* due from him, is to be carried to the next account.

The order made at the last meeting that no widow shall be placed in late Powell's tenement is rescinded, and the trustee whose turn it is to present a widow to that vacancy is at liberty to do it.

Frances Berry of Broad Town Mill, widow [*margin*: admitted], Barbara Tucker of Froxfield, widow [*margin*: admitted], Elizabeth White of Ham, widow, and ... [*MS. blank*] Martin of Froxfield, widow, [*interlineated*: and Sarah Haskins, a manor, three-counties, or at-large widow, added September 1794] have applied to the trustees assembled at this meeting for nominations and are all of them considered as objects of this charity and qualified either for manor tenements or as Wiltshire lay widows, and Widow Martin as a widow for a county-at-large. Ordered that, upon vacancies happening for any tenements for which the above widows are qualified, the steward do communicate to the trustee whose turn it shall be to present to the vacant tenement the names of the above widows, in the order in which they stand, with the recommendation of the trustees present at this meeting of the above widows. In case the trustee whose turn it is shall nominate one of the above persons he shall not thereby lose his turn to the next nomination.

Estate

Ordered that the steward transmit a copy of Cannings's case, now read, to Mr. Penruddocke's steward with a request that the merits of it may be discussed in the most friendly and amicable manner either at the next meeting or at any other time more agreeable to Mr. Penruddocke.

Almshouse

The receiver is allowed to pay Widow Davies her arrears on her making a proper submission for having exceeded her leave of absence.

Ordered that Mr. Whitelock's contract shall be continued for another year if he chooses to undertake the care of the widows on the same terms [as] he did at the last meeting.

Ordered that the repairs minuted by the steward on the day of the view meeting be executed forthwith.

John Richmond Webb, esq., and Dr. Vilett represented to the trustees at this meeting that the porter of the hospital, after a revel at Froxfield had been prohibited by them as magistrates, has erected a scaffold and encouraged the holding [of] a revel at that place to the great dissatisfaction and inconvenience of the inhabitants, and that, upon those magistrates remonstrating with him on the impropriety of his conduct, he behaved with great impertinence. Ordered that the porter be discharged at Michaelmas next and that another shall be appointed in his place at the next meeting, which is to be held at the Castle inn at Marlborough on Wednesday 3 October next.

and see trusteeship business

Signatures

J. Walker Heneage, Ambrose Goddard, L. B. Wither, James Tylney Long, J. Montagu, T. G. Vilett, E. Popham, J. Awdry.

3 October 1792, at the Castle inn, Marlborough

Present

Sir James Tylney Long, bt., Ambrose Goddard, esq., the Revd. Dr. Vilett.

Estate

The case of John Cannings, with four depositions on oath in its support, having been received by the trustees, they direct the steward to write to Mr. Penruddocke to inform him that they will be glad to join with him in an amicable reference of the matters in question to two indifferent persons, one to be named by him and the other by the steward, who is directed to convene a meeting of the trustees at discretion to give further directions in case Mr. Penruddocke should give no answer within a reasonable time or if his answer should be

unfavourable to an amicable adjustment of the matters in difference.
Signatures
Ambrose Goddard, James Tylney Long, T. G. Vilett.

3 July 1793, at the Castle inn, Marlborough

Present
Ambrose Goddard, Lovelace Bigg Wither, John Awdry, James Sutton, esqs., the Revd. Dr. Popham, the Revd. Dr. Vilett, William Northey, esq.
Trusteeship
Examined and allowed the eighth account of Mr. John Ward, the receiver, for 1792, the balance whereof, being £435 16*s.* 5¾*d.* due from him, is to be carried to the next account.
Estate
Ordered that the steward procure an accurate survey and valuation, by Mr. Richardson or some other person, of the farms rented by John Hungerford Penruddocke, esq., and Henry Pyke, those farms coming next in turn for fresh leases. The trustees are willing to have all questions respecting the ascertaining [of] the property of the trust from the freehold and other property of John Hungerford Penruddocke referred to one or more arbitrators, at the discretion of the steward, as the first step towards a treaty for a fresh lease of the farm, which the trustees are disposed to grant to Mr. Penruddocke upon proper terms to be hereafter agreed upon.
Ordered that the steward have power to agree with Henry Berry for a fresh lease of a cottage at New Mill, now in lease to Richard Townsend, on the terms mentioned in the proposal.
Mr. Merriwether having resigned his employments at Froxfield, [it is] ordered that the steward employ some person to take the management of the woods into his hands for 1 year and sell the wood coming in course, that their value may be ascertained previous to their being let at rack rent, and that no more wood be distributed to the widows, that part of the charity being liable to abuse.
Almshouse
Ordered that the steward pay Anne Smith's arrears of stipend.
Ordered that, in lieu of the allowance of wood to the widows, which is computed to be of the average yearly value of 15*s.* to each widow, an addition of £1 16*s.* a year be made to their stipends to raise them to 16 gns. a year, the first quarter to commence and be paid on the 5th instant.
The steward has power to employ such person or persons, as he thinks fit, to do the business of the porter and carpenter till a fit person is appointed by the trustees.

and see estate business

Signatures

Ambrose Goddard, L. B. Wither, William Northey, J. Awdry, James Sutton, E. Popham, T. G. Vilett.

9 November 1793, at the Castle inn, Marlborough

Present

Ambrose Goddard, Lovelace Bigg Wither, John Walker Heneage, James Montagu, esqs., the Revd. Dr. Popham.

Estate

The trustees resolved to consent to the intended application for a canal from Newbury to Bath.

The steward is ordered to discharge Thomas Palmer's bill for bricks etc. amounting to £24 2*s*. 4*d*.

Almshouse

The trustees took into consideration Mr. Whitelock's request for an advance of stipend but are of opinion [that] the income of the trust estate will not admit of it and that the trustees having, at the time a surgeon was appointed, determined to engage with a fit person on the most reasonable terms that were offered they are not at liberty to alter them.

Ordered that the letter addressed by the widows to the trustees of this charity be entered in the minute book.

Signatures

Ambrose Goddard, J. Walker Heneage, J. Montagu, L. B. Wither, E. Popham.

Copy of the letter to which the last order refers

Gentlemen

We beg leave to return you our thanks for the acceptable addition you have been pleased to make to our stipends. We are gratefully sensible of the attention you have always paid to the discharge of your trust and to the promotion of our interest and comfort, and your humanity and kindness to us will ever be remembered and acknowledged with respect and gratitude by, gentlemen, your most obliged humble servants.

(Signed by) Sarah Sharpe, Mary Whitaker, Rebecca Lloyd, Betty Fyfield, Anne Smith, Martha Jones, Ann Prosser, Mary Haddon, Charlotte Thomas, Elizabeth Brown, Mary Evans, Jenny Isaac, Sarah Vincent, Hannah Rider, Susannah James, Susannah Higgate, Elizabeth Milne, Mary Davison, Mary Brown, Elizabeth Davies, Elizabeth Jouring, Martha Holmes, Flouinell Alexander, Ann Munday, Sarah Merriman, Sarah Spackman, Frances Berry, Martha Goodman, Ann Smart, Ann Williams,

Sarah Askey, Jane Stiles, Ann Sherer, Ann Clowes, Jane Kidman, Mary Sanwell, Sarah Clark, Mary Palmer, Ann Noyes, Mary Kimber, Ann Hopkins, Eleanor Pullen, Mary Foot, Phyllis Sanders, Mary Hill, Anna Maria Campbell, Mary Crook, Margaret Murray, Ann Powell, Mary Lampard.

13 September 1794, at the Castle inn, Marlborough

Present

Ambrose Goddard, John Walker Heneage, Lovelace Bigg Wither, John Awdry, William Northey, James Sutton, esqs., the earl of Ailesbury, Dr. Popham, Dr. Vilett.

Trusteeship

Examined and allowed the ninth account of Mr. John Ward, the receiver, for 1793, the balance whereof, being £380 10*s.* 8¾*d.* due from him, is to be carried to the next account.

Estate

An application from William Newbury for a granary, stable, and barrel house, and an estimate given amounting to £100: the trustees allow them on condition [that] he will engage to perform carriage of materials *gratis*, pay interest at 6 per cent for the money to be laid out, and keep and leave the buildings in repair.

Ordered that the coppice be kept in hand another year and that the steward be at liberty to sell such timber therein as is not in an improving state.

The trustees have taken Mr. Richardson's recommendation into consideration and are of opinion that the expenses of the reference between Mrs. Penruddocke and the trust should be paid as he advises but that they cannot give up any other part of the timber belonging to the trust consistent with their duty.

Almshouse

Ordered, on consideration of the cases of the three absentee widows whose stipends have been stopped, that, on their promise to be resident in future, Sarah Askey's arrear be paid to her and Charlotte Thomas's and Elizabeth Davies's arrears [be paid] to Alexander Newman for their debts due to him, with their consent.

The repairs ordered at the view meeting are approved.

Resolved that, for the better preservation of the almshouse from fire, six party walls be built in it, if that can be done for an expense not exceeding £60. [*Margin.* Between 7–8, 13–14, 21–22, 28–29, 36–37, 43–44]

Ordered that Mrs. Sarah Haskins, who is qualified as a manor, three-county, and county-at-large widow, be recommended in the same manner, and next to, Mrs. Tucker and Mrs. White. [*Margin.*

Nominated]

Mr. Condell is to be continued as surgeon and apothecary on the same terms as Mr. Whitelock was engaged, until his [?Mr. Whitelock's] return.

Nurses to Widow Kimber and Widow Clowes were allowed.

Signatures

Ambrose Goddard, William Northey, J. Awdry, J. Walker Heneage, J. Sutton, Ailesbury, L. B. Wither, T. G. Vilett, E. Popham.

1 July 1795, at the Castle inn, Marlborough

Present

Ambrose Goddard, Lovelace Bigg Wither, John Walker Heneage, esqs., the earl of Ailesbury, the Revds. Dr. Popham, Dr. Vilett.

Trusteeship

Examined and allowed the tenth account of Mr. John Ward, the receiver, for 1794, the balance whereof, being £326 16*s.* 1*d.* due from him, is to be carried to the next account.

Estate

Resolved that the trustees will meet again at the town hall, Marlborough, on Wednesday 7 October next at 11 o'clock in the morning to take into consideration a treaty for the renewal of Mrs. Penruddocke's and Mr. Henry Pyke's leases and other matters.

Ordered that a lease be granted to Alexander Newman of the estate which fell in hand on his wife's death, for ... [*MS. blank*] years at £40 a year from Michaelmas 1796 on the terms agreed upon and minuted in the survey book.

Allowed Farmer Reeves one half of his bills amounting to £15 16*s.* 8*d.* for rebuilding a workshop etc. at Huish.

Ordered that Mr. Hammond's bill amounting to £63 12*s.* 11*d.* for a new cellar built for William Newbury at Froxfield, for which he is to pay interest, be discharged.

Agreed with William Newbury to build him a brewhouse at the estimate given in by John Hammond, amounting to £154, on condition that he take a lease of the whole premises for 38 years from Michaelmas next and pay an additional rent of £6 per cent for the money expended in the cellar and brewhouse, he being allowed to assign his lease at pleasure on sufficient security being given for payment of the rent and performance of the covenants.

Ordered that the receiver prepare a lease accordingly and a contract with Mr. Hammond for erecting the building at that estimate.

Almshouse

The repairs ordered at the view meeting are approved. It is also ordered that a new sink be made at the brewhouse, that the window frames, where necessary, shall be renewed and painted as well as the old ones which want paint, that there shall be steps to the north garden, [and] that the pavement, where necessary, shall be repaired.

Resolved that, in order to supply the poor widows with fuel on easier terms than they buy it [on] in winter, a coal house shall be immediately erected in the woodyard under the receiver's directions. A stock of coal [shall be] laid in before the winter to be sold to the widows at stated days, under the care of Mr. Alexander Newman, at a price to be fixed at the next meeting and under such regulations as the receiver shall find it necessary to adopt.

Adjournment

The meeting is adjourned to Wednesday 7 October next at 11 o'clock in the morning at the town hall, Marlborough, of which the receiver is to give notice.

Signatures

L. B. Wither, E. Popham, Ailesbury, T. G. Vilett, J. Walker Heneage, Ambrose Goddard.

7 October 1795, at the town hall, Marlborough

Present

Ambrose Goddard, esq., John Awdry, esq., James Montagu, esq., the Revd. Dr. Vilett.

Estate

Ordered that a fresh lease be granted to John Hungerford Penruddocke, esq., of the farm at Fyfield rented by the late Charles Penruddocke, esq., from the expiration of the present lease; for 21 years at £200 a year clear of all deductions, if he chooses to accept it.

That a fresh lease be granted to Henry Pyke, gentleman, of his bargain at Clench from the expiration of his lease; for 21 years at £60 a year clear of all deductions, if he chooses to accept it.

Signatures

Ambrose Goddard, T. G. Vilett, J. Awdry, J. Montagu, James Sutton, J. Walker Heneage.

6 July 1796, at the Castle inn, Marlborough

Present

The earl of Ailesbury, John Awdry, esq., James Sutton, esq., the Revd. Dr. Popham, Ambrose Goddard, esq., Lovelace Bigg Wither, esq., John Walker Heneage, esq.

Trusteeship

Examined and allowed the eleventh account of Mr. John Ward, the receiver, for 1795, the balance whereof, being £46 12*s.* 4½*d.* due from him, is to be carried to the next account.

The receiver is directed to advertize the present vacancies for three-county clergy widows in [the] manner directed by the rules of the trustees confirmed in Chancery.

and see almshouse business

Estate

Ordered that a lease be granted of the coppices at Froxfield to William Merriwether for 14 years from Michaelmas next at £25 a year, on such terms and conditions as the receiver shall agree upon with him.

Leases to Mr. Penruddocke at £200, to Mr. Henry Pyke at £60, to Mr. Newbury at £54, and to Alexander Newman at £40 a year were executed by the trustees present.

Almshouse

Ordered that the clock face and cupola at Froxfield and the staircase be repaired, that new windows shall be put into 24 old tenements beginning at no. 27, to be executed by degrees, eight in a year, and that a new cloth for the pulpit and communion table, and a pall, be provided.

Mr. Whitelock is allowed to appoint Mr. J. Eyles of Ramsbury to be his substitute as surgeon and apothecary to the hospital during his absence, at 26 gns. a year to commence from Michaelmas next, on condition that he pays full and due attendance at the hospital on the widows and their children and supplies them with sufficient medicines, which he is expected to keep in readiness at Froxfield, according to the proposals contained in his letter to Mr. Whitelock dated 24 May last.

The trustees, taking the case of Charlotte Thomas into consideration, agree to allow her one half of the stipend which has been stopped in consequence of her absence up to this time, upon her giving up her tenement and fixtures in good order.

The trustees agree that, if Mrs. West of Middlesex, an Irish minister's widow, be well recommended in point of character, she shall be admitted to a vacancy in the hospital if the trustee who has the nomination thinks fit to appoint her to it.

and see trusteeship business

Signatures

Ambrose Goddard, J. Walker Heneage, L. B. Wither, J. Awdry, James Sutton, Ailesbury, E. Popham.

5 July 1797, at the Castle inn, Marlborough

Present

The earl of Ailesbury, John Walker Heneage, esq., Lovelace Bigg

Wither, esq., William Northey, esq., Ambrose Goddard, esq., the Revd. Thomas Goddard Vilett, LL.D.

Trusteeship

Examined and allowed the twelfth account of Mr. John Ward, the receiver, for 1796, the balance whereof, being £57 3*s.* 10½*d.* due to him, is to be carried to the next account.

Estate

The trustees allow Farmer Reeves oak plank for a barn floor.

The clerk is to send a carpenter to see what timber is absolutely necessary for repairs to Newman's (late Smith's) farm, and the clerk is at liberty to allow what he thinks fit.

Almshouse

Widow Elizabeth Davies's excuses for absence to this time are taken in consideration, as well as her application for further time on account of the illness of her son. The trustees agree to allow her another quarter's absence on condition of her agreeing to forfeit her situation and stipend in case she shall not return at that time and be resident in the hospital.

Nurses are allowed to Widows Sherer and Tucker from Whitsuntide last at 2*s.* 6*d.* a week each, to be engaged by the steward. Widows, or daughters of widows, of the hospital [are] to be preferred.

Ordered that the front doors and windows of the tenements as most want it be painted now or next spring.

Signatures

T. G. Vilett, L. B. Wither, William Northey, J. Walker Heneage, Ailesbury.

4 July 1798, at the Castle inn, Marlborough

Present

Ambrose Goddard, esq., John Walker Heneage, esq., Lovelace Bigg Wither, esq., William Northey, esq., James Sutton, esq., the Revd. Dr. Popham, the Revd. Dr. Vilett.

Trusteeship

The steward's account was examined and allowed, upon which a balance of £152 2*s.* 10*d.* is due to him.

The trustees present choose the Rt. Hon. Lord Bruce, John Richmond Webb of Milton, esq., and the Revd. Edward Goddard of Clyffe Pypard, clerk, to be trustees in place of Sir William Jones, bt., Sir James Tylney Long, bt., and James Montagu, esq., deceased, and ordered the steward to prepare a conveyance of the charity estate from the present trustees to the new ones, in trust for them and the old trustees to the uses of the present deed of trust.

Estate

It is agreed that Alexander Newman be allowed £60 to purchase timber for repairs as mentioned at the last meeting.

It is referred to the clerk to treat with Farmer Andrews for a fresh lease of his farm, if he chooses to agree on the terms upon which the clerk has the private instructions of the trustees now present within 6 weeks. If not, Mr. Ward is directed to advertize the farm to be let.

Agreed that a lease shall be granted to Edward Coxhead of a piece of waste for a cottage on such terms as may be agreed on with the clerk.

Almshouse

Allowed Widow Noyes 2*s*. 6*d*. a week for a nurse.

The repairs ordered at the view meeting are approved of and, Widow Rider's proposal for subscribing 1 gn. and locks and hinges towards a porch to the chapel being approved [*margin*: not advisable], [it is] ordered that the clerk be at liberty to order a porch to be made if the estimate does not appear very high.

Ordered that the widows' bibles and prayer books be replaced or renewed where necessary.

The steward is allowed to remit to Widow Poole 1 year's stipend to Midsummer 1798, during which period it appears to the trustees [that] she has been confined in Salisbury gaol from unavoidable misfortunes not imputable to her own misconduct, and [she] being an object of great charity. But the trustees cannot give authority for the payment to her of any further stipend until she is able to return to her tenement.

Adjournment

The trustees adjourn this meeting to Wednesday 3 October next at 11 o'clock at the town hall in Marlborough.

Signatures

Ambrose Goddard, L. B. Wither, William Northey, T. G. Vilett, James Sutton, E. Popham.

3 October 1798, at the town hall, Marlborough, pursuant to adjournment

Present

Ambrose Goddard, esq., John Awdry, esq., Revd. Dr. Popham, Revd. Dr. Vilett, Revd. Edward Goddard.

Trusteeship

The deed of trust to new trustees was executed by the trustees present.

Estate

Ordered that the clerk advertize Froxfield farm to be let in such manner as he thinks best.

Ordered that Mr. Gale of Stert be desired to look over Chirton farm and report his opinion therein, and that, if the present tenant will not give as much as he thinks it worth, the clerk have power to call a meeting of the trustees to take the matter into further consideration.

The trustees hereby signify their assent to an application to Parliament for an Act to inclose the common fields etc. in the township of Oare.

Signatures

Ambrose Goddard, E. Popham, T. G. Vilett, E. Goddard, J. Awdry.

1 December 1798, at the Castle and Ball inn, Marlborough, held pursuant to notice

Present

Ambrose Goddard, esq., the Revd. Dr. Vilett, the Lord Bruce, the Revd. Edward Goddard, John Richmond Webb, esq.

Estate

The trustees approve of the agreement entered into by the clerk with Francis Pigott for Froxfield farm at £210 a year, and order a lease to be made to him for 21 years from Michaelmas next.

The trustees approve of a trial being made by the clerk to bring about an inclosure of Chirton fields.

Ordered that the clerk take the opinion of the trustees individually as to the propriety and expediency of redeeming the land tax, that he be guided by the majority of opinions in proceeding to the measure, and that he have power to convene another meeting of the trustees if he thinks it necessary.

It is agreed that Farmer Barnes may hold Chirton farm for 1 year from Lady day next at £133 a year, but that his having a lease for a term at that rent be reserved for the consideration of the next general meeting.

The trustees signified their assent to the Oare Inclosure Bill.

Almshouse

Ordered that Widow Davison's and Widow White's excuses for absence be allowed and their salaries paid.

The trustees appoint Mr. Eyles surgeon in the room of Mr. Whitelock, [who has] resigned.

The clerk is to allow Widow Jouring a nurse at such pay, and for such time, as shall appear necessary.

Signatures

T. G. Vilett, J. R. Webb, E. Goddard, Bruce.

3 July 1799, at the Castle inn, Marlborough

Present

William Northey, esq., the Revd. Dr. Popham, the Revd. Dr.

Vilett, John Richmond Webb, esq., the Revd. Edward Goddard.

Trusteeship

The steward's account was examined and allowed, upon which a balance of £237 10*s.* 7*d.* is due to him.

Estate

The trustees agreed to grant a fresh lease of Ireson's cottage to William Newbury for the life of William Ireson and the lives of William Newbury and W. B. Newbury his son for a fine of 16 gns. A lease being prepared, they have executed it; also a lease to Francis Pigott of Froxfield farm as agreed at the last meeting.

Ordered that the bailiffs shall not have liberty to give leave to grub fences or lop trees to any of the tenants of the charity estate.

It is agreed that Thomas Barnes shall hold Chirton farm for 1 year from Lady day next at £137 clear.

The trustees present are of opinion that it is not expedient to redeem the land tax.

Ordered that the clerk pay the proportion of expense of Oare inclosure out of the charity income and take interest from the lifeholder.

Almshouse

The steward is to pay Widow Poole's arrears.

Signatures

T. G. Vilett, E. Popham, William Northey, J. R. Webb, E. Goddard.

Estate

Before the meeting broke up it was agreed with James Warwick that he shall have a fresh lease, for 7, 14, or 21 years from Michaelmas next at the option of either landlord or tenant, at £130 a year clear. Timber for a barn of 3 bays, to be left on the premises, not to exceed 48 tons, [and] to be cut under the inspection of Mr. Webb, shall be allowed. The trustees will allow 20 gns. for staddle stones, iron nails, and other materials. Which barn James shall build in a substantial manner at his own expense and keep and leave in repair, and he shall be allowed timber for a milkhouse to be also cut under Mr. Webb's inspection. [*Signed as above*]

Almshouse

Before the meeting broke up it was resolved that, as Mr. Evans has withdrawn himself from the duty of the chapel without having applied to the trustees for leave, they are of opinion [that] he ought not to be reinstated. [*Signed as above*]

2 July 1800, at the Castle inn, Marlborough

Present

Ambrose Goddard, esq., John Walker Heneage, esq., Lovelace Bigg

Wither, esq., John Awdry, esq., the Revd. Dr. Popham, the Revd. Dr. Vilett, the Lord Bruce, John Richmond Webb, esq., the Revd. Edward Goddard.

Trusteeship

The steward's account is examined and allowed, on which a balance of £12 4*s.* 7*d.* is due to him.

Resolved that the manors of Wootton Rivers and Thornhill, as well as the manors of Froxfield, Huish and Shaw, and Broad Town, are within the meaning of the late duchess of Somerset's will as her manors from which 10 poor widows were to be nominated.

Resolved that the following widows, viz. Amy Rawlins of Wootton Rivers [*margin*: nominated], Mary Godley of Broad Town, Lucy Cain of Newbury [*margin*: married], Dina Bedford of Clyffe Pypard [*endorsed*: incapable of taking the situation], if duly qualified as manor widows, be successively recommended to the trustees as manor vacancies happen. In case the trustee whose turn it shall be to nominate shall nominate one of the above widows he shall not thereby lose his turn but shall nominate to the next clergy or manor vacancy. [*Margin*. Other applications: Mary Wilmot, Froxfield; Jane May, Froxfield; Jane Mortimer, Ogbourne, for Wootton. But the trustees, October 1803, objected to these sort of appointments as preventing the progress of the turns]

Estate

Resolved that Mr. Ward, for Froxfield and Huish, confer with Mr. Bradford, for Broad Town, on the expediency of applying to Parliament for an Act to lay in severalty the common fields in those manors, and that they give the necessary notices and report their opinions at the adjournment of this meeting.

Resolved that this meeting approves of the application to Parliament for the inclosure of Chirton fields.

Resolved that Farmer Reeves's and William Newbury's applications for fresh leases be taken into consideration at the adjourned meeting, and that Farmer Barnes be continued another year at the same rent.

Ordered that a lease be granted to Thomas Dobson of Bettridge's cottage at Froxfield for two additional lives for a fine of £14.

The clerk is directed to send to Mr. Penruddocke a copy of Mr. Webb's statement of his tenant's encroachments on the almshouse property, with a request that he will have the matters complained of enquired into and redressed.

Almshouse

Ordered that the clerk pay Mr. Harold's bill for bibles and prayer books amounting to £21 6*s.* [*Margin*. Done]

Ordered that an estimate be made of the expense of party walls to divide the almshouse into six or eight parts as a security against fire.

[*Margin*. See September 1794]
and see trusteeship business
Adjournment
The meeting is adjourned to Wednesday 8 October next at the same place at 11 o'clock in the forenoon.
Signatures
J. Walker Heneage, Ambrose Goddard, L. B. Wither, J. Awdry, E. Popham, Bruce, J. R. Webb, T. G. Vilett, E. Goddard.

8 October 1800, at the town hall, Marlborough

Present
Ambrose Goddard, esq., John Walker Heneage, esq., Dr. Vilett, Lord Bruce, John Richmond Webb, esq., John Awdry, esq.
Trusteeship
Ordered that Mr. Ward be invested with a discretionary power to call a special meeting of the trustees.
Estate
Ordered that Mr. Gale be employed to value Farmer Reeves's farm [*margin*: Huish farm], that Mr. Ward be authorized to make agreements with the lifeholders in Huish to surrender their bargains on annuities to be settled by him, [and] that Farmer Reeves be then treated with for a lease of the whole, subject to the approbation of Dr. Vilett and Mr. Webb. Mrs. Tarrant having offered to surrender in consideration of an annuity of £40, that is agreed to.

The steward is at liberty to allow a new carthouse with a brick arch in the yard, and such repairs as he shall think necessary, at Froxfield farm, the tenant finding straw, thatching, and carriage.

It appearing that it will be for the benefit of the trust to lay Froxfield common fields in severalty, and that application to Parliament in conjunction with the trustees of the manor of Broad Town for an Act for that purpose would be desirable, with powers if practicable for exchanging any part of the lands belonging to the trustees with their consent to be signified at a meeting to be called for the purpose, but, it being suggested that a general inclosure Act may take place which may save considerable expenses, [it is] resolved that the application shall be deferred till further order. Mr. Ward is empowered to call a meeting of the trustees at his discretion to take the business into further consideration.

Ordered that a lease be granted to Mr. Newbury of his farm at Froxfield for 8 years from Michaelmas 1800 at his present rent, but to be void in case of an inclosure.
Almshouse
Ordered that the stipends of Mary Haddon, Hannah Rider,

Elizabeth White, Eleanor Pullen, Margaretta Poole, and Elizabeth Bailey, and all other widows who have been absent more than 13 weeks without leave, shall be stopped, and that no widow shall in future be paid on any pretence who shall have been absent without leave or beyond the time allowed; reserving power to Dr. Vilett and Mr. Webb, or any two trustees, at any meeting to take the special circumstances of the case of any widow into consideration and make [an] order at their discretion.

The consideration of adopting party walls in the almshouse to prevent a fire from extending is referred to the next meeting.

Signatures

J. R. Webb, Thomas Goddard Vilett, Bruce, J. Awdry, J. Walker Heneage.

1 July 1801, at the Castle inn, Marlborough

Present

Lovelace Bigg Wither, esq., John Awdry, esq., the Revd. Dr. Popham, John Richmond Webb, esq., the Revd. Edward Goddard.

Trusteeship

Examined and allowed the receiver's account, the balance whereof is £249 12*s.* 10*d.* due to the trustees.

Estate

The terms made by Mr. Ward with Farmer Reeves and the lifeholders of Huish are approved of and agreed to at this meeting.

Ordered that Mr. William Newbury be allowed rough timber at Huish or Milton sufficient, with such old materials as can be brought into use, to rebuild his malthouse on a plan and contract to be approved of by the clerk. When the work is done, approved of, and certified to the next meeting the trustees will advance him £100 toward the expense on his covenanting to pay an additional rent of £6 a year.

It is agreed that a lease of Chirton farm be granted to William Hayward and Harry Hayward, both of Chirton, nephews and legatees of the late Farmer Barnes, for 14 years from Lady day last at £137 a year for the 2 first years, and £180 afterwards, clear of all deductions. They shall be allowed one half of the cost of timber for defending frith hedges to be planted and raised against South mead and Cowland, they covenanting to raise them to complete quick hedges.

Leases to William Newbury, Farmer Reeves, and Thomas Dobson were executed by the trustees; also a lease to Harry Barnes for three lives, fine £36.

Mr. Ward may allow Farmer Reeves and Mr. Pyke to grub certain hedges if, on viewing them, he thinks proper to consent thereto. [He may consent] also to the taking down [of] Tarrant's barn, it being in a very decayed state and of no use to keep up.

The trustees cannot agree to Farmer Pigott's application for an allowance for improvements of meadows, which the length of his lease will give time for him to reap the benefit of, but will allow the expense of painting his parlour.

It is referred to Mr. Ward to consider of and arrange an exchange with the rector of Huish of his land and common rights in the fields below [the] hill for a paddock adjoining the glebe land and such other land as shall be considered an equivalent by the commissioners named in the Oare Inclosure Act.

Almshouse

Ordered that the repairs directed at the view meeting shall be done.

Allowed the clerk to charge 4 gns. paid to Widow Corlett in his next account.

Ordered that application be made to the person who has the key of Widow Haddon's tenement for that key, with a promise of indemnity, and that another widow be appointed in her stead, she having been absent upwards of three years.

Ordered that the gardens of absentees be cultivated at their expense and the cost stopped out of their stipends.

The trustees, taking into consideration the income and outgoings of the trust estate, resolve that the stipend to the widows be advanced to 20 gns. a year, the first payment to commence on the 5th instant.

Resolved that no further expense respecting coals shall be incurred by the trustees.

Signatures

L. B. Wither, Ambrose Goddard, E. Popham, J. R. Webb, J. Awdry, E. Goddard.

7 July 1802, at the Castle inn, Marlborough

Present

Ambrose Goddard, esq., John Walker Heneage, esq., Lovelace Bigg Wither, esq., the lord Bruce, the Revd. Dr. Popham, the Revd. Dr. Vilett, the Revd. Edward Goddard.

Trusteeship

Resolved that Mrs. Corlett's name be added to those widows who are to be recommended to the trustees for a manor vacancy.

Examined and allowed the receiver's account, the balance whereof, being £229 4*s*. 1*d*., is due to the receiver.

Estate

Ordered that the steward allow Farmer Pigott all or such part of the bills he has paid for repairs as he shall think fit, as well as those incurred but not paid; likewise that the steward allow such further necessary repairs as he shall think fit on condition that the farmer complete the intended improvements in the Marsh meadow to the steward's satisfaction.

The trustees consent to Mr. Gilmore's erecting a skilling on their ground at the end of his stable on condition of his paying the yearly acknowledgement of 6*d*.

The steward is authorized to state [*i.e.* grant an estate in] the cottage called Cripps's on such terms as he can agree upon with Edward Newman, but to except the paddock adjoining.

Agreed to state the shop in Froxfield to Edward Newman for his life by a reversionary copy for a fine of £32.

The trustees executed the lease to William Hayward ordered at the last meeting.

Almshouse

Resolved that the clerk write to Mrs. Combe in answer to her letter of 24 July 1801 to the following effect: that provided Mrs. Haddon relinquishes her tenement before October the trustees authorize Mr. Ward to distribute part of the arrear which would have been payable to her up to Midsummer 1801, in case she had resided, among her creditors, but that in case it shall not be then surrendered he is authorized to take proper steps to remove her.

Resolved that, if the answer to Mr. Ward's letter be not satisfactory, he shall state a case and take the opinion of counsel as to the measures most advisable to be taken.

The trustees allow the apothecary £30 a year from 1 June last.

The porter [is] to be allowed £5, instead of £4, a year for his salary on condition of his attending the chapel service regularly.

The trustees allow Mrs. Price the quarter's stipend due Lady day under special circumstances stated to the trustees but not to be considered as a precedent.

The trustees allow Widows Smart and Askey nurses at 1*s*. 6*d*., and Widow Sharpe who is unable to do anything for herself [at] 2*s*. 6*d*., a week from Lady day last.

Ordered that a brick-paved path be made across the quadrangle at Froxfield.

The trustees confirm the orders for repairs made at the view meeting.

Resolved that four or six party walls, under the directions of Dr. Popham, shall be erected in the hospital as a safeguard in case of fire. [*Margin*. Afterwards deferred]

and see trusteeship business

Adjournment

The trustees adjourned the meeting to the same place on Wednesday 6 October next at 11 o'clock in the forenoon and directed the clerk to give notice to the absent trustees that at that meeting fresh trustees will be elected in the room of those deceased.

Signatures

L. B. Wither, Ambrose Goddard, J. Walker Heneage, E. Popham, T. G. Vilett, Bruce, E. Goddard.

6 October 1802, at the Castle inn, Marlborough

Present

John Walker Heneage, esq., chairman, Ambrose Goddard, esq., William Northey, esq., the Revd. Dr. Popham, the Revd. Dr. Vilett, John Richmond Webb, esq., the Revd. Edward Goddard.

Trusteeship

The trustees present unanimously elect Thomas Michell, esq., of Standen House, and Francis Warneford, esq., of Sevenhampton, to be trustees in place of John Awdry, esq., and James Sutton, esq., deceased, and ordered the steward to prepare a conveyance of the trust estate from the present trustees to the new ones in trust for themselves and the old trustees to the uses of the present deed of trust.

Almshouse

Ordered that the building [of] the party walls ordered at the last meeting be relinquished, it appearing difficult to carry them into execution without disfiguring the building.

The trustees accede to Mrs. Combe's proposal on behalf of Mrs. Haddon and on receipt of possession of her tenement. The clerk is ordered to pay her debts in Wiltshire and Berkshire, contracted before she left Froxfield, out of the arrears of her stipend.

Signatures

J. Walker Heneage, E. Popham, William Northey, Ambrose Goddard, T. G. Vilett, J. R. Webb, E. Goddard.

6 July 1803, at the Castle inn, Marlborough

Present

Lovelace Bigg Wither, esq., William Northey, esq., Dr. Vilett, John Richmond Webb, esq., Revd. Edward Goddard, Col. Warneford, Thomas Michell, esq., Revd. Dr. Popham.

Trusteeship

The clerk's account was examined and allowed. The balance of £516 12*s.* 5*d.* due to him is to be carried to the next account.

The steward is to enquire into the characters of Mary Wilmot and Jane May of Froxfield, who apply to be added to the manor list of recommendation, and certify them to the next meeting.

Estate

Allowed £9 to Mr. Newman on account of a milkhouse erected by him, and £5 towards a cowhouse.

Allowed Farmer Pigott £117 4*s*. 11*d*., money expended in repairs and such further repairs as in a list signed by him.

Allowed Farmer Drury one half of the bills for timber for repairs at the Pelican.

Allowed Messrs. Hayward timber for a barn floor to be purchased at Devizes.

The clerk is to look at the improvement proposed to the fence of the lower watermeadow opposite the college and to make such allowance towards it as he thinks reasonable.

The trustees agree to the purchase made by Mr. Ward of ½ acre in Huish of John Reeves in trust for the trustees at 15 gns., and [approve] of an exchange made with Farmer Pontin of another ½ acre in the same field for a cottage in Oare and a fee-farm rent of 6*s*.

It appearing that some important exchanges may be effected in Clench and Fyfield the steward is authorized to employ some person qualified to scheme such exchanges, to be brought forward for consideration at the next meeting.

The improvements in building by Mr. Newbury having been considered the trustees give up the interest of £100, which he was to have paid, instead of allowing any further sum towards the expense he has been at, which he states at upwards of £1,000.

The exchanges with the rector of Huish are approved of.

Almshouse

Resolved that the clerk take opinion of counsel [about] what method can be taken to expel Widow Poole and obtain possession of her tenement.

At the recommendation of the visiting trustees

Resolved that the view meeting in future be the third Wednesday in June.

That the trustees not give leave of absence but for some reasonable cause, to be specified on the printed paper.

That it be made a condition that the widows be present at the view meeting.

That no widow be permitted to let her house, nor her garden, except to the porter for the purpose of its being kept in order.

Ordered that the steward pay Mrs. Davies one quarter's arrear of stipend. It is left to his discretion to allow the other quarter if it shall appear that she has applied the one quarter properly.

The repairs ordered at the view meeting are confirmed.

and see trusteeship business

Adjournment

Adjourned to Wednesday 5 October next at 11 o'clock in the forenoon.
Signatures
L. B. Wither, William Northey, E. Popham, T. G. Vilett, Thomas Michell, E. Goddard.

5 October 1803, held by adjournment

Present
Ambrose Goddard, esq., the Revd. Edward Popham, D.D., the Revd. Thomas Goddard Vilett, LL.D., the Revd. Edward Goddard, Thomas Michell, esq.
Almshouse
It appearing to the trustees that widow Margaretta Poole has absented herself from her tenement and from the hospital at Froxfield for more than a twelvemonth, without leave and without even having applied for leave of absence, contrary to the regulations confirmed in Chancery for the government of the hospital and of the poor persons therein, leaving her tenement shut up and receiving damage, and preventing a more fit object of the charity from inhabiting it, it is declared that she is expelled and amoved from her tenement, from the hospital, and from all stipend on account of such her absence. It is ordered that the door of the tenement of Margaretta Poole shall be opened by the porter and that a proper object of the charity be nominated, by the trustee whose turn it is to nominate a widow, to the vacant tenement in the room of Margaretta Poole.
Signatures
Ambrose Goddard, E. Popham, T. G. Vilett, E. Goddard, Thomas Michell.

4 July 1804, at the Castle inn, Marlborough

Present
Lovelace Bigg Wither, esq., William Northey, esq., Revd. Dr. Popham, John Richmond Webb, esq., Revd. Edward Goddard.
Trusteeship
The clerk's account was examined and allowed. The balance of £453 2*s.* 11*d.* due to him is to be carried to the next account.
Estate
It is referred to the clerk to take the security offered by Farmer Pigott for his arrear of rent.
The report of the receiver respecting the exchange at Clench being taken into consideration, [it is] resolved that it be referred to Mr. John Butcher to value the estates at Clench and afterwards to

confer with Mr. Gale as to any grounds whereon there may be any material difference of opinion, and that a further report be made at the adjournment of this meeting.

The trustees approve of William Newman's proposal for adding two lives in a cottage at Froxfield for a fine of £12, and allowed William Hayward a load of bricks.

Almshouse

Ordered that the repairs noted at the view meeting be executed.

The clerk is ordered to pay Dr. Blackman's fees for attending Widow Surridge.

Adjournment

The meeting was then adjourned to Wednesday 3 October next at the town hall, Marlborough, at 11 o'clock in the forenoon.

Signatures

L. B. Wither, E. Popham, William Northey, J. R. Webb, E. Goddard.

3 October 1804

Estate

The trustees took into consideration the proposed exchange between Lord Ailesbury and the trust and examined Mr. Butcher thereon. [They] are satisfied that it is proper to be carried into execution provided that the trust are put to no expense and that the buildings on Cully's farm be put into good and substantial repair, upon which condition the trustees will execute with Lord Ailesbury the proper deeds for confirming the exchange as far as they legally may.

The trustees do not think it worthwhile to eject the occupier of Tyler's lot.

Signatures

Ambrose Goddard, J. R. Webb, T. G. Vilett, Thomas Michell, E. Goddard.

3 July 1805, at the Castle inn, Marlborough

Present

Lovelace Bigg Wither, esq., chairman, Ambrose Goddard, esq., William Northey, esq., Revd. Dr. Vilett, Revd. Edward Goddard.

Trusteeship

The clerk's account was examined and allowed. The balance of £193 6*s*. 10*d*. due to him is to be carried to the next account.

Estate

The deeds of exchange between the earl of Ailesbury and the trustees were approved and executed. [*Margin*. At Clench]

Allowed Farmer Pigott £80 on account of bills for repairs on his promise that he shall never ask for any further allowance and that he pay £50 half yearly in addition to that allowance on account of his arrears, besides the growing rent from Michaelmas last: the first £50 to be paid immediately and the remaining payments to be made on the third Saturday in December and [the] third Saturday in June yearly till the arrear is discharged.

The trustees, taking into consideration the return of arrears of rent and the inconvenience the trust suffers from the payment of interest of balances of money deficient on the trust account, direct the clerk to give notice to the tenants that they are in future expected to pay the half year's rent due Lady day on or before the last [*changed from* third] Saturday in November [*changed from* December], and the half year's rent due Michaelmas on or before the last [*changed from* third] Saturday in May [*changed from* June] yearly.

The payment made by Farmer Pigott for property tax on Salam are allowed.

A lease may be granted to William Merriwether of the east end of Horseshoe mead for 12 years from Michaelmas next at £4 a year, with liberty to erect and afterwards remove a neat ash shed. [*Margin.* Small mead]

The clerk is to inform Mr. Penruddocke that the trustees are willing to enter into a treaty for a general exchange in Fyfield, if desired by him, on the same terms as have been adopted with Lord Ailesbury, Mr. Penruddocke being at liberty to name a valuer to meet the person to be appointed on behalf of the trustees by the clerk.

Almshouse

Ordered that the repairs noted at the view meeting be executed.

Signatures

Ambrose Goddard, L. B. Wither, William Northey, T. G. Vilett, E. Goddard.

2 July 1806, at the Castle inn, Marlborough

Present

Ambrose Goddard, esq., Lovelace Bigg Wither, esq., William Northey, esq., Revd. Dr. Popham, Revd. Edward Goddard, Thomas Michell, esq.

Trusteeship

The clerk's account was examined and allowed. A balance of £73 19*s.* 2*d.* due from him is to be carried to the next account.

The clerk is to give notice that at the next meeting new trustees will be elected in place of such as are deceased.

Estate

The trustees, taking into consideration the case of Farmer Pigott, and it appearing that since the clerk took a distress he has reduced his arrear considerably, consent that the goods distrained may be given up upon his promise of paying £100 every 2 months, the first payment to be on 2 September next, till his rent and arrear is discharged. On any default in payment of his instalments the clerk is to take a fresh distress. [*Margin.* I thankfully accept these conditions, F. Pigott]

Mr. William Merriwether having applied for a lease for three lives of a small parcel of meadow, which he under-rents of Mr. Pigott, opposite the Cross Keys, at 10*s.* 6*d.* a year, for the purpose of building tenements in which he engages to lay out £150 and to pay 6*d.* a year during Mr. Pigott's lease and 10*s.* 6*d.* a year afterwards, the trustees agree to those terms.

The clerk is desired to inform Mr. Penruddocke, in answer to his letter proposing that one half of the expense of the proposed exchange may be paid by the trust, that the trustees, having in Lord Ailesbury's case thought it right that his lordship should pay all the expenses relating to the exchange with him, do not think themselves at liberty to depart from that rule in the present case, especially as no advantage to the trust would be obtained during Mr. Penruddocke's lease, but that they will be ready at any time to renew the treaty for a general exchange with him when it shall appear more desirable to both parties than it seems to be at present.

The trustees agree to execute individually a conveyance of land taken for the Kennet and Avon canal in the parish of Milton at the price fixed by Mr. Davies on the part of the trustees. [They] direct the clerk to lay out the purchase money in Old South Sea annuities in the names of the trustees in whose names there is now trust money in that fund, and to pay the existing tenants out of the dividends such allowance for loss of land during their leases as he shall think reasonable.

The lease to Thomas Dobson, granted 6 years ago but withheld for want of his paying the fine, may be delivered to him on payment of such additional sum as the clerk shall think fit.

Almshouse

The orders made at the view meeting are confirmed.

Mrs. Williams's petition for payment of a quarter's salary to 6 January last is allowed although she did not take possession till several days after under special circumstances now stated.

Mrs. Cockayne and Mrs. Askey may be allowed 2*s.* a week for nurses from the present quarter.

The trustees agree to allow the porter an addition of £2 7*s.* to his present salary.

The trustees consent that the widow Martha Tash Sherman

have leave of absence for a twelvemonth to be under the care of her friends. Her stipend during that time may be allowed, but not longer unless it shall be ordered at the next general meeting under any special circumstances which may be then represented in her behalf.

Signatures

Ambrose Goddard, L. B. Wither, William Northey, E. Popham, E. Goddard, Thomas Michell.

1 July 1807, at the Castle inn, Marlborough

Present

Ambrose Goddard, esq., William Northey, esq., Revd. Dr. Popham, Revd. Dr. Vilett, Revd. Edward Goddard, Lovelace Bigg Wither, esq.

Trusteeship

The clerk's account was examined and allowed. The balance of £365 2*s.* 3*d.* due from him is to be carried to the next account.

Resolved that the order respecting the absence of trustees at two general meetings made in 1783, being a forfeiture of their nominations, shall be dispensed with as to Lord Bruce, who is attending [to his] duty in Parliament, and the earl of Ailesbury, who attends the view meetings and to the state of the hospital.

The trustees present unanimously elect Robert Wilsonn, esq., of Purton and John Pearse, esq., of Chilton to be trustees in place of J. W. Heneage, esq., and John Richmond Webb, esq., deceased, and ordered the steward to prepare a conveyance of the trust estate from the present trustees on the trusts of the present deed of trust.

Estate

The application of Farmer Reeves for an allowance on account of rebuildings being considered the trustees allow him £20 on that account, but cannot allow anything on account of rebuildings, except rough timber, in future.

The cottage called Tyler's being given up [it is] agreed to grant a lease at the same quit rent to William Newbury for three lives for a fine of 12 gns., out of which the clerk is to discharge the quit rent now in arrear.

Ordered that the steward take Mr. Davies's opinion on the plan and expediency of an exchange with Mr. Penruddocke at the equal expense of both parties and, if his opinion is favourable to it, the clerk is to prepare an agreement between the trustees and Mr. Penruddocke referring such exchange to Mr. Davies.

Ordered that the estate late Edmonds's shall be advertized to let at Michaelmas twelvemonth, proposals to be sent sealed to the clerk against the adjournment.

Almshouse

Resolved that the stipend of the widows be increased to £24 a year, the first quarterly payment to be made on the 5th instant.

Adjournment

The meeting is adjourned to Wednesday 7 October next at 11 o'clock in the forenoon at the Castle inn, Marlborough.

Signatures

Ambrose Goddard, T. G. Vilett, E. Goddard, L. B. Wither, E. Popham, William Northey.

7 October 1807, at the Castle inn, Marlborough

Present

The Revd. Thomas Goddard Vilett, LL.D., the Rt. Hon. Lord Bruce, Thomas Michell, esq., Robert Wilsonn, esq.

Trusteeship

The deed of trust directed to be prepared was executed by the parties present.

Estate

Robert Fowler being the highest bidder present at this meeting for late Edmonds's bargain at Oare, at £155 a year, the trustees direct the clerk to enter into an agreement with him for a lease on such terms and conditions and for such term of years, and take such security, as he shall think fit.

The opinion of Mr. Davies being highly favourable to a division and exchange of property in Fyfield the following preliminary stipulations were committed to writing, signed by John Hungerford Penruddocke, esq., and the trustees present, and directed to be handed to the other trustees. The business [is] to be further considered after the arbitrators have met, a regular agreement [is] to be then prepared and entered into, and the clerk has discretionary power to call a special meeting of the trustees if he thinks it necessary.

Copy of the stipulations

Memorandum of an agreement made 7 October 1807 between John Hungerford Penruddocke, esq., of the one part, and Ambrose Goddard, esq., and the other undersigned trustees of the estates late of Sarah, duchess dowager of Somerset, for the maintenance of 50 poor widows at Froxfield of the other part. The parties agree that the tithing of Fyfield shall be surveyed by Thomas Davies, esq., and John Charlton, esq., or by such surveyor as they shall appoint, and that the lands and commons belonging to John Hungerford Penruddocke and [to] the trustees shall be valued by Thomas Davies and John Charlton. An exchange shall be made between J. H. Penruddocke and the trustees whereby all the lands belonging to the trustees shall be laid together, or as nearly so as conveniently may be, at the north end of the tithing and the lands of J. H. Penruddocke at the south end. The expenses of the survey, valuation, and exchange, with the deeds for confirming the exchange, [are] to be at the joint expense of J. H. Penruddocke and the trustees. Provided that Thomas Davies and John Charlton, before they proceed on the business, shall nominate an indifferent person to be called in as an umpire in case of their disagreement but not otherwise. It is agreed that the removal of the barn now standing at Staplehouse, the question whether a bridge over the canal shall be dispensed with, and the disposal of the compensation to be allowed by the canal company in case it is dispensed with shall be referred to the arbitrators. It is also agreed that the tithes of the lands to be taken by, or remain to, the trustees shall also be taken in exchange by the trustees if the arbitrators recommend it. Before anything on these heads is finally decided it is desired that a report of the opinion of the arbitrators shall be made to the trustees and to J. H. Penruddocke.

Signed J. H. Penruddocke, Ambrose Goddard, T. G. Vilett, Bruce, Thomas Michell, Robert Wilsonn.

6 July 1808, at the Castle inn, Marlborough

Present

Ambrose Goddard, esq., L. B. Wither, William Northey, Thomas Michell, esqs., Revd. Dr. Vilett, Revd. E. Goddard, Robert Wilsonn, esq.

Trusteeship

The clerk's account was examined and allowed.

Estate

The clerk is at liberty to agree with Mr. Newbury and Mr. Merriwether for the lands in their occupations at 20*s*. an acre for renewing leases, 8, 12, or 16 years.

The trustees approve of the clerk's agreement with Joseph Drury for exchange of a life in Pepall's cottage and agreed to execute a lease thereof.

The trustees agree to receive a surrender of Widow Trueman's lease, of which 9 years are to come, at Michaelmas next and to grant a fresh lease from that time for 30 years at £7 a year, with covenant that she keep, and leave, in good repair all buildings thereon.

Almshouse

A letter from Mrs. Davies being read and her case considered [it is] resolved that, under the circumstances of her case, her absence is excused, the clerk is at liberty to pay the present quarter's stipend to her in London, and she is allowed 6 weeks further leave of absence from this time.

Ordered that each widow do appear [at] the view meeting, notwithstanding leave of absence, unless prevented by illness, in which case she is to send a certificate from some medical man of her inability to return to Froxfield.

Resolved that no payment shall be required from any new appointed widow for papering or any other improvement done by a deceased widow, except for such articles as can be legally deemed removable fixtures and for such not more than two thirds of what such deceased widow paid for it as nearly as can be estimated. In case only of the new appointed widow refusing to take or pay for such fixtures at such reduced value the representatives of the deceased shall be allowed to take them away, making good all damage done in removing thereof.

Signatures

Ambrose Goddard, Robert Wilsonn, L. B. Wither, William Northey, T. G. Vilett, Thomas Michell, E. Goddard.

5 July 1809, at the Castle inn, Marlborough

Present

Ambrose Goddard, esq., Lovelace Bigg Wither, esq., Thomas Michell, esq., Revd. Dr. Popham, Revd. Edward Goddard, John Pearse, esq.

Trusteeship

The trustees present examined the clerk's account with the vouchers and allowed it. The balance of £741 0*s*. 4½*d*. due from the accountant is to be carried to the next account.

Estate

The clerk may allow Messrs. Hayward any number of bricks, not exceeding 4,000, as a foundation for a mud wall.

Almshouse

Ordered that four or five party walls within the roof of the hospital be made as a security in case of fire, provided it can be done at an expense not exceeding £20.

Resolved that the salary of the chaplain be increased to £50 a year, on condition of his engaging to provide himself with a suitable residence within a moderate distance of the hospital and to perform morning service, with a sermon, on Sundays and prayers [on] Wednesdays and Fridays.

Resolved that the stipend of the apothecary be advanced to £40 a year from this time, on condition that he provides a sufficient quantity of medicines to be deposited at the hospital in the room over the lodge in readiness to be administered as occasion may require, and that he attends at the hospital at least twice a week, oftener in case of any serious illness of a widow, and at all times as soon as possible on being sent for on any illness or emergency.

Signatures

Ambrose Goddard, L. B. Wither, E. Popham, William Northey, E. Goddard, John Pearse.

4 October 1809, at the town hall, Marlborough, for the special purpose of appointing a surgeon in the place of Mr. Eyles, who is removed to Margate

Present

Revd. E. Goddard, Thomas Michell, esq.

Almshouse

Those trustees hereby appoint Mr. Robert Kerslake Marsh to be surgeon and apothecary to the hospital from 1 December next in place of Mr. Eyles.

Signatures

E. Goddard, Thomas Michell.

4 July 1810, at the Castle inn, Marlborough

Present

Lovelace Bigg Wither, esq., Dr. Popham, Francis Warneford, esq., William Northey, esq.

Trusteeship

The trustees present examined the clerk's account with the vouchers and allowed it. The balance of £1,251 3*s.* 11*d.* appearing due from the accountant is to be carried to the next account.

Ordered that the steward prepare a conveyance of the land sold to the canal company and of the land sold by the company to the trustees, and that the balance of the money received for land be laid out in South Sea stocks in the names of the trustees in whose names the other stock is invested.

Estate

The trustees appoint James Warwick to be bailiff and woodman for the manor of Huish and Shaw with the farms in Milton and Pewsey.

The trustees took into consideration the application of Mr. Henry Sellwood of Froxfield farm for an allowance on account of building a threshing machine house or to allow him to take away the house, and woodwork laid down for the use of the machine, at the end of the lease. The trustees prefer allowing of such removal, which they hereby agree to, and to allow Henry Sellwood 10 gns. on account of the expense he has incurred in painting.

Almshouse

The trustees took into consideration the causes of Mrs. West's and Mrs. Davies's absence beyond the time of their leaves and, being satisfied thereon, allow the receiver to pay their arrears.

and see adjournment

Adjournment

Resolved that this meeting be adjourned to the town hall in Marlborough on Wednesday 3 October next at 11 o'clock to consider if the present state of the trust estate will admit of an advance of £4 a year to the widows' stipends, and of the expediency of fixing on a day in August for the general annual meeting instead of the present time of meeting.

Signatures

L. B. Wither, William Northey, E. Popham, Francis Warneford.

3 October 1810, at the town hall, Marlborough, pursuant to adjournment

Present

Ambrose Goddard, esq., the Revd. Dr. Vilett, the Revd. Edward Goddard.

Trusteeship

The trustees, in confirmation of the opinion of the trustees at the last meeting, order that the general annual meeting of the trustees shall be held on the first Wednesday in August.

Almshouse

The trustees, taking into consideration the state of the income, [the] balance in hand, and [the] probable advance of rents in a few years, agree, in confirmation of the opinion of the trustees at the last meeting, that an advance of £4 a year may be made to the widows' stipends to commence from Midsummer last, the first quarter to be paid at Michaelmas 1810, and order that accordingly.

Signatures

Ambrose Goddard, T. G. Vilett, E. Goddard.

Estate

The trustees approve of the conditions made by Mr. Ward with Farmer Warwick for letting the Froxfield coppices to him at £12 an acre for each cut clear of all deductions, the cuts being 12 years' growth; Warwick agreeing to leave a very large number of stores at an allowance to be made by the steward for the value of such stores, which are not afterwards to be cut.

Also they agree to the steward's entering into stipulations with Gen. Popham for the removal of the cottages at Oakhill if possible.

Signatures

James Warwick, T. G. Vilett, E. Goddard.

7 August 1811, at the Castle inn, Marlborough

Present

Revd. Dr. Popham, Lord Bruce, Revd. Edward Goddard, Robert Wilsonn, esq., John Pearse, esq.

Trusteeship

The trustees present examined and allowed the receiver's account, the balance whereof, being £281 12*s.* 2*d.*, is to be carried to the next account as due from him.

Estate

The trustees approve of the steps taken by the steward in building two tenements at Huish in order that the cottagers lately resident in the parsonage house might be received into them, Mr. Mayo having agreed to rebuild the parsonage house. They authorize the receiver to erect two other tenements there if he shall deem it expedient.

The trustees agree to allow Robert Fowler rough timber and half the workmanship for a carthouse if he will find sawing, straw, and thatching and pay the other half of the workmanship.

The trustees will allow Mr. Sellwood elm plank for a barn floor on condition that he will have it constructed on the plan of one, built by the late Jasper York of Swindon, to be turned up when not using, and that he be at the expense of carriage and sawing and subject to the steward's directions therein.

Memorandum, made about January 1810

Clench, New Mill, ¾ acre

John Liddiard wants to make a wharf for Milton on a lease. Pyke will give [the land] up to him. The lease to be for 21 years from Michaelmas next at £5 a year [to the trustees] from [the] end of Pyke's lease. Account of expenses of the wharf to be kept and, if trustees disapprove of granting lease or choose to determine it, they may do it on 12 months' notice or [on] paying what he expends in making the wharf between now and the Froxfield trustees meeting, the account being previously inspected and approved by Mr. Thomas and J. Ward.

Liddiard afterwards entered into a sort of agreement with Chandler of New Mill, who was at part of the expense of the building, but they afterwards disagreed and it was a question at the meetings in July and October 1810 whether the lease should be granted to Liddiard or Chandler. It was at last recommended to Mr. Pyke to keep it in his own power and allow both parties an equal and impartial trading at it, paying the allowed wharfage, etc. Mr. Pyke, at the meeting 11 August, objected to this arrangement and said [that] his engagement was with Liddiard only and he considered him entitled to hold for [the] remainder of his own term. See resolution.

The trustees consent to Mr. Pyke's making an under-lease to John Liddiard for the remainder of Mr. Pyke's term at £5 a year. On the expiration of that term, if the trustees shall not choose to continue the lease to John Liddiard for a further term of 14 years, he must rely on the trustees for making him such allowance as they shall think proper on account of the money he has expended.
Signatures
E. Popham, Bruce, E. Goddard, John Pearse, Robert Wilsonn.

5 August 1812, at the Castle inn, Marlborough

Present
Lord Bruce, Dr. Popham, Dr. Vilett, Mr. Pearse, Revd. Edward Goddard, Mr. Northey.
Trusteeship
The trustees examined and allowed the receiver's account, the balance whereof, being £317 2*s.* 11*d.* due from the receiver, is to be carried to his next account.
Estate
The trustees executed a lease of a cottage at New Mill, late William Crook Noyes's, to his assignee Thomas Somerset.

They have allowed Farmer Warwick timber for a horse house for a threshing machine.

They agree to grant a lease to William Merriwether of the coppices at Froxfield on the terms settled by Mr. Ward.

Ordered that the account settled with Edward Newman to Michaelmas 1811, on which a balance of £164 4*s.* 6*d.* is due, be allowed, that he pay the odd £4 4*s.* 6*d.*, and that his proposal of giving his note, with his brother-in-law John Hawkins as his surety, for £160 payable with interest, one half at Christmas and the remainder at Midsummer next, be accepted; and that he be allowed to hold the estate late Cripps's, for the same term as he holds his rack-rent bargain, at £41 10*s.* a year [*margin*: ending at Michaelmas 1817], but that he be required to pay no more rent to Edward Tarrant till he produces the lease by which he claims to hold Tarrant's estate for his life.

Ordered that a lease be granted to William Newbury on the terms specified in the minutes of 6 July 1808.

Ordered that the steward be authorized to sell such pollards on Fyfield farm as are proper to be sold and to allow such of them as may be used for the horse house above mentioned.

Ordered that the clerk be empowered to treat and contract with

Mr. Pulse for the tithes belonging to him [and] issuing out of the trust estate.

Also that he be empowered to make Rudman, Stagg, and White some annual allowance towards the loss they have eventually sustained by having surrendered their lifeholds on terms very inadequate to the advanced value of land.

Mr. Sellwood is at liberty to produce a person well recommended as a tenant for Froxfield farm at the adjournment of this meeting.

Ordered that Huish farm be let by tender and that the proposals be submitted to the trustees at their adjournment.

Adjournment

Adjourned to the second morning of the Michaelmas sessions at the town hall, Marlborough.

Signatures

William Northey, E. Popham, D.D., T. G. Vilett, Bruce, E. Goddard, John Pearse.

7 October 1812, at the town hall, Marlborough

Present

Ambrose Goddard, esq., Revd. Edward Goddard, Robert Wilsonn, esq.

Estate

The trustees entered into agreement with Mr. William Robbins for a lease of Huish farm from Michaelmas 1813 for 12 years at £800 on conditions specified in the agreement.

They postponed licensing Mr. Sellwood to assign the lease of Froxfield farm till it be considered by the trustees at large whether the trust ought not in reason to participate in the advantages.

The trustees executed the leases to Messrs. Newbury and Merriwether ordered at the last meeting.

4 August 1813, at the Castle inn, Marlborough

Present

Ambrose Goddard, esq., William Northey, esq., the Revd. Dr. Popham, the Revd. Dr. Vilett, Lord Bruce, the Revd. Edward Goddard, Robert Wilsonn, esq.

Trusteeship

The trustees examined and allowed the receiver's account, the balance whereof, being £307 10*s.* 2*d.* due from the receiver, is to be carried to the next account.

The trustees present unanimously elect Thomas Goddard, esq., and John Awdry, esq., to be trustees in place of Lovelace Bigg Wither,

The Trustees examined and allowed the Receivers account the balance whereof being £ 307 . 10 . 2 — due from the Receiver is to be carried to the next acc.

Stipend

The State of the Income & expenditure of the Trust was laid before the Trustees, Whereby it appears That £4. a year may be added to the Widows Stipend from this time. which was ordered accordingly making the Stipend amount to £ 32 a year to each Widow —

Froxfield Chapel

At this Meeting the Rev.d Dr Popham represented to the Trustees that the that the Chapel belonging to the Hospital was found on his last visitation of it to be in very bad repair and very mean in its appearance, whereupon Lord Bruce signified to the meeting that his Father the Earl of Ailesbury one of the Trustees, was desirous, if it should be approved of by his Brethren, to erect a new Chapel for the Widows, at his own entire expence. The Trustees most thankfully accept his Lordships munificent Offer and express their desire that a record of the Gift in suitable Terms may be placed, by the Trustees, on the New Chapel, and request Lord Bruce to present their best acknowledgments to his Lordship

Minutes of a meeting held 4 August 1813

esq., and Thomas Michell, esq., and ordered the steward to prepare a conveyance of the trust estate to vest it in the new trustees jointly with the present trustees.

At this meeting the trustees, taking into consideration the increased income of the trust estate to £2,147 a year, that they have been able within the memory of the senior trustee to advance the stipend of the widows from 8 gns. to £32 a year, but that no advance within that period has been made to the salary of the receiver, agreed to double it, which was ordered accordingly.

Estate

The trustees agreed that the copy to Thomas Cannings of a small estate at New Mill, which has been withheld by the steward, may be delivered to him under the particular circumstances of the case.

It is agreed that the overplus value of timber at Fyfield shall be sold, and the money paid to Mr. Penruddocke, if it shall appear that he can legally dispose of it.

Almshouse

The state of the income and expenditure of the trust was laid before the trustees. It appears that £4 a year may be added to the widows' stipend from this time, which was ordered accordingly, making the stipend £32 a year to each widow.

At this meeting the Revd. Dr. Popham represented to the trustees that the chapel belonging to the hospital was found on his last visitation of it to be in very bad repair and very mean in its appearance, whereupon Lord Bruce signified that his father, the earl of Ailesbury, one of the trustees, was desirous, if it should be approved of by his brethren, to erect a new chapel for the widows at his own entire expense. The trustees most thankfully accept his lordship's munificent offer, express their desire that a record of the gift may be placed by the trustees on the new chapel, and request Lord Bruce to present their best acknowledgements to his lordship.

Signatures

Ambrose Goddard, William Northey, E. Popham, Bruce, T. G. Vilett, E. Goddard, Robert Wilsonn.

3 August 1814, at the Castle inn, Marlborough

Present

The Revd. Dr. Vilett, Robert Wilsonn, esq., John Pearse, esq., John Awdry, esq., Revd. Dr. Popham, William Northey, esq., the earl of Ailesbury (late Lord Bruce), Francis Warneford, esq., John Awdry, esq. [*?rectius* the Revd. E. Goddard]

Trusteeship

The trustees examined and allowed the receiver's account, the balance whereof, being £85 6*s.* 10*d.* due from him, is to be carried to the next account.

The minutes of the last meeting being read, and it appearing that since the last meeting Thomas Goddard, esq., and the Rt. Hon. Thomas Bruce, earl of Ailesbury, have died, the trustees present unanimously elect Edward William Leyborne Popham, esq., and Thomas Grimston Estcourt, esq., to be trustees in place of Thomas Goddard and the earl of Ailesbury. In consequence of the death of Thomas Goddard before the deed, directed at the last meeting to be prepared, was prepared [it is] ordered that the steward prepare a conveyance of the trust estate to vest it in John Awdry, the trustee elected at the last meeting, Edward William Leyborne Popham, and Thomas Grimston Estcourt jointly with the present trustees.

Estate

The trustees allow the steward to subscribe £10 if the farmers in Froxfield will enter into an adequate subscription to give a dinner to the poor on the re-establishment of peace.

The trustees approve of the sale of timber at Huish and Milton for defraying the expense of seasoned timber for the general repair and building at Huish farm.

Almshouse

An application being read from Mr. Marsh for an increase of his salary as apothecary the trustees, taking into consideration the labour of his office, ordered that £10 be added to his salary.

The steward is directed to appoint a person to act as chapel clerk at a salary of 52*s.* a year.

The steward is permitted to pay Elizabeth Ann Graves the arrear of her stipend stopped for absence.

It appearing that Widow Corlett has occasion for more care and attention than is likely to be paid to her in the hospital, and that it will be a considerable saving to the trust to have her under the care of her son, the steward is allowed, under the special circumstances, to remit her stipend to Mr. Thomas Corlett on receiving half-yearly certificates from the minister of the parish where she resides of her being alive.

The arrears of Widow Vincent's stipend are ordered to be paid to her representative.

The trustees allowed Widow White's daughter to be paid the arrears of the annuity of £6 up to Michaelmas next after her decease, which happened in January last.

Resolved that the gateway of the hospital be enlarged and iron gates and pales used instead of the present ones, and that the brickwork of the lodge be stuccoed and the inscription newly engraved. The Revd. Dr. Popham is requested to correct it and to order a new pulpit cloth.

Signatures

T. G. Vilett, E. Goddard, John Pearse, J. Awdry, E. Popham, D.D., Francis Warneford, Ailesbury, Robert Wilsonn, William Northey.

Estate

Before the trustees separated they resolved that the steward shall give the necessary notices of application to Parliament for an Act to inclose the common fields of Froxfield and Fyfield, and that he obtain the opinion of Mr. Parsons as to the value of Chirton farm, against the adjournment of this meeting.

Adjournment

Resolved that this meeting be adjourned to Tuesday 18 October next at the same place at 12 o'clock.

Signature

William Northey, chairman.

18 October 1814, at the Castle inn, Marlborough, by adjournment

Present

Robert Wilsonn, esq., Thomas Grimston Estcourt, esq., Revd. Edward Goddard, Lt. Gen. Popham.

Trusteeship

Mr. Goddard having signified his desire to assign the Old South Sea annuities standing in his name to fresh trustees it was resolved that they be assigned to Messrs. Northey, Pearse, and Estcourt. A deed declaring the trusts thereof, being ready prepared, was, with the conveyance of the trust estate to new trustees, executed by the trustees now present.

Estate

The trustees resolve on an application to Parliament for the inclosure of the common fields at Froxfield, that Mr. Benjamin Haynes shall be named in the Act as the commissioner and Mr. John Hayward of Rowde as surveyor, and that, in case of the death, refusal, or incapacity of either party, another shall be chosen by the trustees at a meeting to be called by the clerk for that purpose. [The clerk] has a discretionary power to insert such provisions in the Bill as shall appear expedient and to call a special meeting of the trustees should any circumstance occur rendering such meeting necessary.

Almshouse

The trustees approve of the removal of Mrs. Mary Morgan to the care of Dr. Fox of Brislington, and of the payment to Mrs. Evans of her arrears in consideration of her resignation.

The case of Mrs. Graves was considered by the trustees, who directed the arrear of her stipend to be postponed till the next meeting [so] that it may be known how she conducts herself in the meantime.

The arrears of Mrs. Bacon's stipend are permitted to be paid but on condition that, if she again exceeds her leave of absence, her stipend is to be forfeited.

The trustees present approve of the alterations making in the lodge at Froxfield as sanctioned by Dr. Popham and as far as they can form a judgement.

Signatures

E. Goddard, Robert Wilsonn, E. W. L. Popham, Thomas Grimston Estcourt.

2 August 1815, at the Castle inn, Marlborough

Present

The Revd. Dr. Vilett, the Revd. Edward Goddard, Francis Warneford, Thomas Grimston Estcourt, John Awdry, Edward William Leyborne Popham, esqs.

Trusteeship

The receiver's account was examined and allowed.

Estate

The trustees agree to exchange Mary Cook's life, and to add a third life, in Charles Cook's house at Froxfield for a fine of £32.

The trustees agree to sell such timber as can, in the opinion of Guy Warwick, be conveniently and properly appropriated towards defraying the expenses of the lodge at Froxfield.

The trustees agree to let Chirton farm to Messrs. Hayward if they will give £280 a year for 3 years, but if not [it is] ordered that the farm be let by tender.

The clerk is to give notice to the tenants that in future the Lady day rents are to be paid on the first Saturday in July and the Michaelmas rents on Saturday before Christmas day.

Almshouse

Let Widow Graves's pay, that was stopped at the last meeting, be paid to her.

The trustees allow Mrs. Currie being paid to the time of her leaving Froxfield.

The clerk is directed to apply for payment of the clergy subscriptions due to Mrs. Morgan towards defraying [the] expense of continuing her at Brislington.

and see estate business

Signatures

Thomas Goddard Vilett, E. Goddard, Francis Warneford, E. W. L. Popham, Thomas Grimston Estcourt, John Awdry.

7 August 1816, at the Castle inn, Marlborough

Present

Mr. Northey, the earl of Ailesbury, Dr. Vilett, Mr. Pearse, Mr. Estcourt, Revd. Edward Goddard, Gen. Popham.

Trusteeship

The receiver's account was examined and allowed.

Resolved that at the next meeting two gentlemen shall be elected trustees in place of Mr. Goddard and Dr. Popham, deceased; of which the clerk is to give notice in his circular letter giving notice of the meeting.

Estate

Applications from Mr. William Robbins, Robert Fowler, and Messrs. William and Edward Hayward for abatements of rent from Michaelmas 1815 were taken into consideration. It was agreed to allow £160 a year to Mr. Robbins out of his rent, £35 a year to Fowler, and £28 a year to Messrs Hayward, but to be returned to the present rents when wheat shall average in Wiltshire from Michaelmas to Michaelmas £24 a load.

The trustees also allowed Mr. Robbins £78 10*s.* out of his arrear on account of his improvements, on condition that the remainder of his arrear be discharged before the end of October next.

The clerk reported the arrangements made with Edward Newman and William B. Newbury of Froxfield and [the trustees] approve of them, except that instead of 7 years for Edward Newman's holding the cottages the term be limited to Michaelmas 1820, when the farm lease will expire.

Almshouse

Ordered that widows Honor Morgan and Sarah Bacon be paid their arrears stopped on account of absence, that having been satisfactorily accounted for.

Signatures

William Northey, Ailesbury, T. G. Vilett, E. W. L. Popham, E. Goddard, Thomas Grimston Estcourt.

6 August 1817, at the Castle inn, Marlborough

Present

William Northey, esq., Revd. Edward Goddard, Francis Warneford, esq., Robert Wilsonn, esq., John Pearse, esq., E. W. L. Popham, esq., T. G. Estcourt, esq.

Trusteeship

The trustees examined and allowed the receiver's account, in which there is a balance of £198 8*s.* 9*d.* due to him.

The minutes of the last meeting being read, it appearing that it was then resolved that at the next meeting two gentlemen should be elected trustees in place of Mr. Goddard and Dr. Popham, deceased, of which due notice has been given to the trustees by the clerk in his circular letter, and another vacancy having since occurred by the death of Dr. Vilett, the trustees present unanimously elect Ambrose Goddard, esq., J. H. Penruddocke, esq., and Henry Read, esq., to be trustees in place of Ambrose Goddard, senior, esq., Dr. Popham, and Dr. Vilett, and [resolve] that the new trustees shall come into the nomination lists after the present nine trustees shall have successively nominated widows.

A letter from Mr. Mant being read and the case of Edward Tarrant taken into consideration, the trustees authorize the clerk to make a donation of £10 to be placed in the hands of Mr. Mant for the charitable relief of Edward Tarrant, but to inform Mr. Mant that the trustees cannot hold themselves justified in making any payment, or sending any further relief, to Edward Tarrant.

Estate

Resolved that notice be given of an intended application to Parliament for an Act to inclose the common lands in Froxfield and Fyfield and that Mr. Gale, if he will accept the appointment, be named as sole commissioner.

The trustees agree to allow £20 to Mr. Robbins in consideration that he will lay out £30 more in making the hill at Huish more easy of ascent, being a permanent benefit to the trust.

Almshouse

The clerk is directed to give notice to Mrs. Price that, if her son continues to reside in the hospital at Froxfield, her stipend will be suspended. The clerk is directed to suspend payment of her stipend during his residence.

Mayo trust

A paper was read addressed to the trustees by the Revd. Charles Mayo proposing to vest an estate consisting of a messuage and 30 acres of land at Beechingstoke and four Kennet and Avon Canal shares in the trustees for certain charitable purposes under their patronage, and desiring their acceptance of the trust and patronage.

It is resolved by the trustees present that they will accept of the intended trust and will be extremely ready to render every assistance in their power to carry into effect the benevolent intentions of the respectable and charitable donor, whom, during his long connection with them, they have invariably had occasion to hold in the highest esteem and regard.

Signatures

E. W. L. Popham, E. Goddard, John Pearse, Francis Warneford,

William Northey, Thomas Grimston Estcourt.

5 August 1818, at the Castle inn, Marlborough

Present

The earl of Ailesbury, John Awdry, E. W. L. Popham, J. H. Penruddocke, esqs.

Trusteeship

The receiver's account was examined and allowed but, there not being a quorum, the trustees present determined to adjourn to the town hall in Marlborough on Wednesday 21 October next at 12 o'clock at noon and directed the clerk to apprise the trustees that, at that meeting, all circumstances respecting the exchange with Mr. Penruddocke, the re-letting [of] the new farm, Mr. Thomas Pyke's bargain at Clench, an exchange of a small parcel of land with the earl of Ailesbury, the wharf at Clench, and several other matters will be taken into consideration.

Estate

see trusteeship business

Signatures

Ailesbury, John Awdry, E. W. L. Popham, J. H. Penruddocke.

The following minutes are copied into a fresh book and signed by the trustees.

21 October 1818, at the town hall, Marlborough, and adjourned to the house of Mr. John Ward

Present

The earl of Ailesbury, chairman, Francis Warneford, esq., Revd. Edward Goddard, Gen. Popham, John Pearse, esq., Gen. Read.

Trusteeship

The trustees in whose names the South Sea stock belonging to the trust estate is vested are desired to sell it, at such time as the steward shall find necessary, towards paying for timber on the lands taken in exchange and the expenses of the inclosure. The money [is] to be replaced by sale of timber and by appropriating a part of the improved income.

The case of Widow Tarrant as represented by the Revd. Mr. Marshall was considered. The clerk is to inform that gentleman that, as the trustees present in turn, Mrs. Tarrant is at liberty to apply to any trustee but they cannot make a general order for her admission into the hospital.

The same answer may be given to Widow Batt.

Estate

The circumstances of the proposed exchange with Mr. Penruddocke being taken into consideration the trustees agree that, if Mr. Penruddocke will take land of the value of £40 a year for Broomsgrove coppice and the tithes thereof, the trustees will agree to those terms.

Resolved that when Mr. Penruddocke shall have fixed on a tenant for his estate at Fyfield, provided that takes place [with]in 6 months from this time, Gen. Popham, Gen. Read, and Mr. Edward Goddard, or any two of them, at a meeting to be appointed by the steward for that purpose, will be ready to treat with such person, if approved of, for a lease of the farm, excepting the coppice, at the commissioner's valuation, to take place at Michaelmas 1819. But the trustees will expect a guarantee from Mr. Penruddocke for performance of covenants and that one half of the advance on the rent shall be paid for the current year.

Resolved that Batchelor's bargain, except the coppices called Battle coppice and Rook grove and except the wharf and gardens, be let at a valuation to be made by Mr. Gale, and that Mr. Pyke have the preference of renting it.

Resolved that a lease of the wharf for 14 years from Michaelmas last be granted to Mary Liddiard at £5 a year clear on her entering into covenants for keeping and leaving it in complete repair.

Resolved that, as soon as the commissioner shall have laid out the farms at Froxfield, the Manor farm shall be advertized to be let by tender, the three before named trustees or any two of them at a meeting having power to accept or reject any such tender without regard to the amount. It is agreed that the land adjoining Lord Ailesbury's water mead shall be exchanged to his lordship for his land in Froxfield field at their respective values.

It is referred to the steward, with the assistance of Mr. Gale, to negotiate with Thomas Cannings for a surrender of his copyhold on an annuity for the life of the copyholder and the widowhood of his present wife.

Charles Cook having petitioned for permission to exchange a life and add a life on his copyhold house and shop, which he holds for the lives of himself and Mary Cook, with [the] intention of selling his interest, it is resolved that, if the steward shall approve of the person to whom he proposes to sell, they will accept a surrender of his interest and grant a copy to such person for the life of Charles Cook and two fresh lives to be named by the purchaser at a fine of £55.

On new letting the farms at Froxfield the steward is to require proper stipulations for preserving and raising the quick fences intended to be planted on the sides of the Bath road.

and see trusteeship business

Almshouse

The state of the chapel was taken into consideration and a report by Mr. Cundy, an architect who has surveyed it, was read, by which it appears that the dry rot is damaging the wainscots and floors and that something must be immediately done to prevent the rot extending further. The trustees approve of the remedy recommended by Mr. Cundy with the addition, if necessary, of raising the floors of the pews for more effectually killing the rot and drying the woodwork.

Resolved that an estimate shall be applied for to Mr. Cundy of the expense of applying the proposed remedies, that in the meantime Mr. Reason be directed to cut away the decayed wood and make openings for letting in the air, and that the ordering of further remedies be referred to the earl of Ailesbury and the three other before mentioned trustees or any two of them.

The trustees agree to have the steps reset with parapet walls and an iron wicket according to a plan afforded by Mr. Cundy, and a drain [is] to be made under the road.

The proposed plan of laying a footpath of Hannam stone round the area, of 15 inches wide which it is estimated may be done at about 20*d.* a foot [as] the whole expense, was taken into consideration and approved. But the execution [is] to be deferred till the funds of the trust will be sufficient to justify the expense.

Leave is granted to Mary Habgood to be absent for the winter months.

A letter from Widow Bacon being taken into consideration it is resolved that, in order to enforce better obedience to the rules of the hospital, the trustees consider it necessary to refuse the allowance of the stipend which was stopped during her absence, [it] being the second offence.

Martha Holmes's petition for 1*s.* a week to a nurse is referred to Gen. Popham.

It is agreed to advance the porter's salary to £10.

and see trusteeship business

These minutes are entered in a fresh book and signed by the trustees. [*Signed*] J.W.

MINUTE BOOK 1818–66
(WSA 2037/14)

21 October 1818

The minutes of the meeting entered here were copied from those in the previous book, where they were not signed

Signatures

Ailesbury, E. Goddard, E. W. L. Popham, Francis Warneford, H. Read, John Awdry.

4 August 1819, at Marlborough

Present

Mr. Northey, earl of Ailesbury, Revd. E. Goddard, Col. Warneford, Mr. Goddard, Gen. Read, Mr. Awdry, Mr. Estcourt, Mr. Penruddocke, Gen. Popham.

Trusteeship

The steward's account was examined and allowed.

Estate

Mr. Robbins is required to pay interest on his arrear in future, to discharge it in the course of the present year, and pay his rent regularly. The loss of £18 which the trust have sustained by his being in arrear must be set against his request of £10 [*rectius* £20] allowance for lowering Huish Hill.

The trustees agree to an exchange with Mr. Gilmore by giving land in the common field to him in exchange for his three pieces of inclosed glebe in Froxfield.

The trustees are not willing to extend the term to Miss Liddiard in a lease of the wharf beyond 14 years as mentioned at the last meeting.

The trustees decline granting a lease to Mr. Hayward unless at an advanced rent but will allow rough timber for floor [boarding] and weatherboarding.

The copy to Josiah Wooldridge for the lives of his two sons and of Mary, instead of Charles, Cook of Cook's cottage and shop at Froxfield is approved.

The exchange with Mr. Penruddocke being considered the trustees are of opinion that it is not expedient to give land for timber so as to make the canal [their] boundary but that, if Mr. Penruddocke can procure land in Froxfield or any parish adjoining Froxfield or Milton, the trustees will be willing to exchange the lands coming to them on the south side of the canal in Fyfield for an equivalent in value.

It is referred to the commissioner and [the] steward to make such arrangements and divisions of farms at Froxfield as shall be found expedient and to let some parcels of land to the poor for gardens.

Ordered that a lease be granted to Edward Newman of the houses, stable, and paddock which he now rents at £22 a year, except the little paddock; for 21 years at £26 a year clear and under covenants for his keeping and leaving the premises in repair. Provided that the commissioner, on his dividing and new arranging the farms, shall not find any part of the houses, grounds, or appurtenances desirable to be taken into the hands of the trustees.

Almshouse

On consideration of Widow Tarrant's case and of circumstances that have come to the steward's knowledge since the last meeting [it is] resolved that she shall be placed in the hospital on the first manor vacancy. In the meantime £10 a year shall be allowed towards her support by half-yearly payments, the first to be paid immediately and the next on 5 January next.

The trustees appointed John Arman to be porter to the hospital in the room of Edward Newman.

The trustees approve of the repairs done at Froxfield chapel and direct that the remaining bills for it be forthwith discharged.

Signatures

Thomas Grimston Estcourt, Ailesbury, E. Goddard, John Awdry, William Northey, H. Read, Francis Warneford, A. Goddard, E. W. L. Popham.

9 August 1820, at the Castle inn, Marlborough

Present

William Northey, esq., the earl of Ailesbury, the Revd. Edward Goddard, Francis Warneford, esq., Thomas G. Estcourt, esq., Ambrose Goddard, esq., John Pearse, esq., Gen. Popham.

Trusteeship

The steward's account was examined and allowed.

The clerk produced a statement of the probable income and expenditure of the trust calculated as commencing from Michaelmas next. [It is] resolved that the further consideration of the statement shall be deferred till the next meeting.

Estate

A lease to Edward Newman ordered at the last meeting was produced and executed.

The trustees approve of the intended allotments and exchanges at Fyfield and Froxfield and signed their consent to the several exchanges agreed upon pursuant to the directions of the Act for inclosing the common lands in Froxfield and Fyfield.

The clerk reported that, to forward the inclosure at Froxfield and prevent the mismanagement of lands by a longer continuance of the uncertainty of occupation than necessary, he had agreed with Mr. William Sellwood, with the advice of the commissioner and by authority of the Act, to determine his lease at Michaelmas 1819, being 1 year before the end of the term, upon an allowance of £200 on account of the rent being so much less than the letting value, a further allowance of £150 to be paid by the coming-on tenant on account of the advantage of taking the farm in a b[etter] state than under the conditions of the lease it might have been if held another year, and an allowance of £20 on account of building materials left on the farm.

The clerk reported that he had entered into treaty with the following persons for fresh letting such parts of the estate as have been newly arranged under the Inclosure Act and of such farms the leases whereof are expired or expiring.

In Froxfield from Michaelmas 1819

Mr. John Halcomb. Manor farm containing ... [*MS. blank*] at £410 [and] 13 acres of Ley coppice at £7 16*s*.; the whole of Ley coppice, being of very inferior quality, to be converted into arable at his expense. Term asked for.

Mr. William Newbury, since deceased. Several old inclosures and new allotments containing together 189a. 2r. 9p. at £230. The clerk is allowed to let this farm to the person who may take the brewery, if approved of as a tenant.

Mr. Joseph Drury. Almshouse coppice, 34 [acres], part of the farm lands, 28 [acres], part of Horse mead, ¼ [acre], [all] at £52.

William Bird. 3 acres in East field at £4 10*s*.

Daniel Read. 2a. 2r. 9p. near Cross Keys at £3 16*s*.

Cottagers. 13 gardens at £4 10*s*.

In Milton from Michaelmas 1820

James Warwick. Milton farm, 175a. 3r. 24p., valued at £200 17*s*. 9*d*.

In Fyfield from Michaelmas 1820

James Warwick. 21a. 2r. 37p., part of Fyfield farm, at £42.

Mr. Thomas Pyke. Barn and 268a. 0r. 7p., remainder of Fyfield farm, at £350, £8 being taken off for land tax out of £400 a year for the whole as valued subject to land tax.

At Clench from Michaelmas 1818

Thomas Pyke. House, barns, homestead, and part of lands at Clench, 48a. 1r. 9p., at £66.

Mary Liddiard. The wharf at £5.

Coppices taken in hand. Rook grove, 6a. 0r. 27p., [and] Battle coppice, 1a. 1r. 32p.

Daniel Banning. Late Widow Banning's copyhold tenement, 5a. 3r. 14p., in hand, £17.

The trustees approve of the foregoing arrangements and treaties and direct leases to be prepared to the following persons for the terms and at the rents set against their respective names: to Mr. John Halcomb for 12 years at £417 16*s*., to the person who may be accepted tenant in the place of the late Mr. Newbury for 12 years at £230, to Mr.

Joseph Drury for 12 years at £52, to Mr. James Warwick for 12 years at £242, to Mr. Thomas Pyke for 12 years at £416.

The clerk produced Mr. Evans's application to rent the cottage in front of the vicarage house, which the trustees agree to, but not to grant a lease for a term of years.

Mr. Pyke's application for allowance towards improving his buildings and yard at Clench is referred to the clerk.

A petition of William Robbins for a further abatement of rent was taken into consideration. The trustees, after so great an abatement as was made in 1815, do not feel justified in making a further abatement, but they have no objection to take the matter into further consideration after Mr. Gale, at Mr. Robbins's expense, shall have inspected the farm and reported his opinion in its state and value. They reserve to themselves the liberty to adhere to the present rent if they shall think fit notwithstanding [that] such valuation may be less.

Almshouse

The trustees considered the applications and letters in favour of two persons applying to be employed as carpenter and prefer John Arman, the porter, to do the carpenter's work at the hospital.

The clerk is allowed to pay Mrs. Biggs £2 retained on account of 2 weeks absence beyond her leave, on her promising not to absent herself again without leave. [*Margin.* Mrs. Biggs was paid January 1821 at quarter day]

Widows Haywood, Mary Habgood, Maria West, and Tarrant, having represented special circumstances as reasons for their petitioning for 3 months' leave of absence this year and 3 months' in the spring of 1821, with which the trustees are satisfied, [it is] ordered that leave be given to them accordingly.

The petition of Widow Tarrant for an allowance for apprenticing her son was read but cannot be complied with.

Signatures

William Northey, Thomas Grimston Estcourt, E. W. L. Popham, Ailesbury, Francis Warneford, Ambrose Goddard, E. Goddard, John Pearse.

1 August 1821, at the Castle inn, Marlborough

Present

William Northey, esq., the marquess of Ailesbury, the Revd. Edward Goddard, John Awdry, esq., Thomas Grimston Estcourt, esq., Edward William Leyborne Popham, esq., Ambrose Goddard, esq., John Hungerford Penruddocke, esq., Francis Warneford, esq.

Trusteeship

The clerk's account was examined and allowed.

The trustees elect Sir John Dugdale Astley and Maj. Thomas Vilett of … [*MS. blank*] to be trustees in place of Robert Wilsonn, esq., and Henry Read, esq., deceased, and direct that a deed of trust be prepared for vesting the trust estates in them and the remaining trustees against the next meeting.

The clerk is at liberty to convene a special meeting of the trustees in the Michaelmas sessions week, or at any time afterwards, if it shall appear to two of the trustees to be expedient.

Estate

The case of Mr. William Robbins and Mr. Gale's valuation being taken into consideration, together with the state of his arrear, the trustees are willing, during the present low price of corn and on condition that the arrear due Lady day last be paid, half within 9 weeks and the other half within 16 weeks, and the future rent [be] paid half-yearly at Christmas and Midsummer according to the late regulation, agree to throw back £70 out of the year's arrear due at Michaelmas 1820 and the like allowance out of his present year's rent. On this determination being communicated to Mr. Robbins's brother-in-law he expressed his fears that Robbins will not be able to go on with the farm and requested permission for him to resign at Michaelmas twelvemonth. He was informed that the trustees could not answer to that at present but, if they adjourned the meeting, it might be considered if Mr. Robbins should then bring forward his application.

It is agreed to grant a lease to Robert Fowler for 8 years.

It is required that Mr. Penruddocke or his undertenant pay rent for Fyfield farm, exclusive of the coppice, for 2 years ending Michaelmas 1820 at the following rate, viz. for 1819 £242 and for 1820 £292; and [that] Mr. Penruddocke in addition engages to pay the net produce of 2 years' cut of Broomsgrove coppice in lieu of £50 a year charged less for the farm held by Stagg without the coppice, which was intended to have been included in the exchange but, it being afterwards given up, Mr. Penruddocke took the coppice back again.

Signatures

John Awdry, Thomas Grimston Estcourt, E. Goddard, J. H. Penruddocke, William Northey, Ailesbury, Francis Warneford, E. W. L. Popham, A. Goddard.

7 August 1822, at the Castle inn, Marlborough

Present

William Northey, esq., Revd. Edward Goddard, Francis Warneford, esq., Thomas Grimston Estcourt, esq., Edward William Leyborne Popham, esq., John Pearse, esq., Ambrose Goddard, esq., John Awdry, esq.

Trusteeship

The receiver's account is examined and allowed.

and see estate business

Estate

The terms proposed for a lease of Huish farm to Mr. William Taylor for 12 years from Michaelmas next at £550 a year are approved of. [It is] ordered that a lease be accordingly prepared.

The application from Mr. William Robbins for the allowances mentioned at the last meeting, and a continuation of them for the current year, was taken into consideration. His request to be allowed till Lady day 1823 for payment of his rent and arrears was also considered. [It is] resolved that if Mr. Robbins will give proper security for payment of the rent and arrears by four instalments, on 20 October, 20 November, 1 February, and 25 March, the allowances shall be made.

The trustees, taking into consideration the applications from many of the tenants for a temporary allowance on account of the depreciation of agricultural produce, have agreed to allow out of the year's rent becoming due at Michaelmas next the percentages stated in a paper produced by the clerk and signed by the chairman.

Messrs. Northey, Estcourt, and Pearse are desired to sell the South Sea annuities at such times as they think fit and to pay thereout [of] the rate for the Froxfield and Fyfield inclosure and exchange: for Froxfield £699 18*s.* 5*d.*, for Fyfield £388 3*s.* 4*d.*, for Mr. Merriwether's share, if he secures yearly interest on the whole sum charged in respect of his estate, £24 19*s.* 1*d.*, for Widow Drury's share, in consideration of the short time the estate may probably be enjoyed, she being 84 years of age, £10 10*s.*

It is left to the clerk to allow some part of the expense it will be necessary for James Warwick to incur in replacing old buildings and walls on his farm at Milton, and to allow Mr. Halcomb timber for repairs at Froxfield to be taken from the trust estate at Fyfield at his expense.

A new stable is allowed to be erected at Huish farm at the expense of the trust, the old one being incapable of repair. The great barn, when it cannot longer be kept up, must necessarily be rebuilt at the expense of the trust.

It appearing that £1,230 and some interest is to be paid for timber on the estate taken in exchange from Mr. Penruddocke, and he having expressed a desire that out of such money the rate in respect of his estate at Fyfield and some expenses of improvements may be paid, the trustees refer it to Mr. Estcourt, Mr. Pearse, Col. Warneford, Mr. Goddard, and Gen. Popham, or any three of them, to take the whole of that business into consideration on Mr. Penruddocke's indemnifying the trustees. They are desired to meet for that purpose at Beckhampton on 5 September next.

The circumstances respecting the rent due from Mr. Penruddocke for Fyfield farm and cuttings of coppice to be then considered, it is understood that part of the South Sea stock may be applied in payment of the money for timber at Fyfield as soon as it is settled by the above deputation in what manner the money is to be appropriated. The deputation is authorized, either at such meeting or at any adjournment, to make an order for a sale of timber. The £75 allowed by the canal company to the trustees in consideration of their not requiring a bridge at Fyfield [is] to be applied towards payment of the expenses of the Fyfield inclosure.

Almshouse

The clerk is to inform Mrs. Haywood that her pay during her absence without leave cannot be allowed and that, if she does not forthwith return to the hospital, another widow will be appointed in her place.

The applications by Mrs. Bacon and Mrs. West for the sums forfeited by their absences without leave cannot be complied with.

The clerk is allowed to pay Mrs. Phillips £4 in part of her pay but cannot allow the remainder.

Mrs. Day being severely afflicted with palsey and incapable of being removed to the hospital, the clerk is allowed to pay her out till she is sufficiently recovered to return to her apartment.

Mrs. Tarrant's application for leave to be absent for 6 months or more every year cannot be complied with, nor her pay during her absence without leave be allowed.

The trustees are of opinion that a pair of doors would be desirable to shut at nights over the iron gates in the entrance to the hospital, and refer it to Gen. Popham and the marquess of Ailesbury to fix on the plan of executing the work so as to prevent the admission of persons after the gates are locked.

Signatures

William Northey, E. Goddard, Thomas Grimston Estcourt, John Awdry, E. W. L. Popham, A. Goddard, Francis Warneford, John Pearse.

5 September 1822, a meeting of the deputation of the trustees held at Beckhampton inn

Present

Francis Warneford, Edward William Leyborne Popham, Ambrose Goddard, Thomas Grimston Estcourt, esqs., and John Hungerford Penruddocke, esq., and Sir John Dugdale Astley.

Estate

The case and opinions of Mr. Preston and Mr. Sidebottom

respecting timber on the exchanged lands at Fyfield and the application of the money were read and considered. It was agreed that the timber on the exchanged lands, as far as it will go, shall be set one part against the other and that the balance in value, with interest upon it, may be applied in payment, upon Mr. Penruddocke's bond of indemnity to the trustees and to the commissioner, first of the sum charged upon him and to be by him charged on the allotted and exchanged lands for the expenses of the inclosure and exchange and in the costs of such charge; also in payment of such buildings and other permanent improvements on the lands allotted and exchanged to Mr. Penruddocke as are or shall be approved of, and ordered, by the commissioner; and the residue to be paid to the Accountant General under the regulations of the General Inclosure Act as soon as the necessary papers, charges, bonds, etc. can be prepared and settled and the award made.

The trustees considered the case, with all its circumstances, respecting the advance to be paid by Mr. Penruddocke for 2 years from Michaelmas 1818 and agree that they will accept of Mr. Penruddocke a rent of £396 [*interlineated evidently as a correction*: £296] a year for those years.

The consideration about a fall of timber is deferred till another meeting.

Adjournment

This meeting is adjourned to Wednesday 16 October next at the town hall in Marlborough.

Note. There being no business requiring the attention of the trustees, they did not attend at the adjournment.

6 August 1823, at the Castle inn, Marlborough

Present

Francis Warneford, esq., chairman, John Pearse, esq., Revd. Edward Goddard, John Awdry, esq., John Hungerford Penruddocke, esq.

Trusteeship

The minutes of the deputation of trustees at their meeting at Beckhampton on 5 September last were read as above entered and were approved of by this meeting.

The trustees examined the accounts of the receiver, upon which a balance of £547 5*s.* 11*d.* is due to the trust, and allowed them.

and see estate business

Estate

Ordered that the allowances to the tenants out of their year's rents becoming due at Michaelmas next be the same as were made out of the preceding year's.

The receiver reported his having sold the South Sea stock, the produce of which appears on his account, that he has paid the inclosure expenses and sundry other charges appearing on his accounts, and that other works are in the course of execution, particularly a new stable at Huish farm and three cottages at Huish in the place of three that were in a state of decay from age and incapable of repair. He has applied under the directions of the commissioner, on Mr. Penruddocke's bond of indemnity, £895 11*s.* 5*d.* and £196 11*s.* 3*d.*, in part of £1,328 8*s.*, the money required to be paid for timber on the exchanged property at Fyfield. The remaining £236 5*s.* 4*d.* is to be paid into the bank as soon as an order on the petition of Mr. Penruddocke can be obtained for that purpose. [*Margin.* To be paid for timber £1,328 8*s.*, paid Mr. Penruddocke's rate £895 11*s.* 5*d.*, his improvements £196 11*s.* 3*d.*, to pay to the bank £236 5*s.* 4*d.*; [total] £1,328 8*s.*] There being a considerable balance in hand the clerk has purchased £700 Old South Sea annuities in the names of Messrs. Northey, Estcourt, and Pearse towards replacing the stock that has been sold out.

Also that the award of the commissioner of the Froxfield and Fyfield inclosure has been completed and executed, and Mr. Merriwether has executed a security for payment of interest of the rate on his copyhold estate.

The trustees approve of and ratify the foregoing proceedings.

Ordered that the receiver take measures for a sale of timber in the ensuing season and apply the produce towards replacing the stock that has been sold and in paying for such new buildings as may be erected under the authority of the trustees.

At this meeting Mr. Thomas Pyke applied for an allowance of £75 on account of the inconvenience he has sustained by being without barn and stable room at the new farm and [of] some expenses incurred by him. He also requested to have an addition made to his barn at the new farm.

Ordered that the clerk allow Mr. Pyke £25 paid by him for materials, £25 for workmanship, and £12 10*s.* on account of the inconveniences he sustained by bad entry etc. The trustees allow of the addition to his barn.

Almshouse

Ordered that the doors and windows of the tenements, the cupola, and other outside woodwork of the hospital be painted where necessary, on contract as noted at the view meeting.

Mrs. Grace Gale's stipend having been stopped at the last payday in consequence of her absence on the day of the view meeting, and she having stated that she had leave of absence and was prevented returning by illness, the clerk, on her producing a certificate to that effect, is allowed to pay her stipend.

The meeting approves of the orders for repairs given at the last view meeting.

Mrs. Haywood's application through Mr. Marsh for leave of absence was considered and cannot be allowed.

Mrs. Bradshaw's application for a nurse is referred to Gen. Popham.

Mrs. West's application for payment of her arrears cannot be complied with.

Signatures

Francis Warneford, E. Goddard, John Awdry, J. H. Penruddocke, John Pearse.

4 August 1824, at the Castle inn, Marlborough

Present

William Northey, esq., chairman, Revd. Edward Goddard, Gen. Popham, Mr. Awdry, Sir J. D. Astley, Mr. Goddard, Maj. Vilett, Mr. Penruddocke.

Trusteeship

The trustees examined the account of the receiver, upon which a balance of £686 8*s*. 7*d*. is due to the trust; to be carried to the next account.

Ordered that £735 9*s*. 5*d*. Old South Sea annuities be purchased in the names of Messrs. Northey, Pearse, and Estcourt in addition to the stock already in their names, and that additional investments be made as money shall be raised by sale of timber and from surplus of rents until £2,835 9*s*. 5*d*. Old South Sea annuities, exclusive of £113 9*s*. 2*d*. belonging to the rectory of Huish [and] being the amount of the stock that has been sold by order of the trustees, shall be reinvested.

The steward reported that he obtained an order of the court of Chancery for payings and that he has paid £235 5*s*. 4*d*. into the bank in the name of the Accountant General, being the balance of timber on the Fyfield exchange as explained in the minutes of the last meeting.

and see estate business

Estate

Ordered that the allowances to the tenants out of their year's rents becoming due at Michaelmas next be the same as last year, but from Michaelmas next the allowance [is] to be reduced from 15 to 10 per cent.

The steward produced an account of timber sold pursuant to the orders of the trustees and of the money received and remaining due, and, it appearing that two lots of oak remain unsold and that there are many other trees damaged and proper for being cut, it is referred to the steward to make further sales as he shall deem advisable for raising further sums to replace the trust stock.

Mr. William Hayward complaining that the rent of his farm is too high [it is] ordered that it be valued by Mr. Hayward of Rowde, surveyor. The tenant was informed that he must be considered as engaged to abide by his opinion.

Ordered that a surrender of a lease be accepted [from], and a new lease be granted to, Mr. John Brown of a tenement in Froxfield, near the Cross Keys, which he holds for the lives of Charles Cook and Mary Surrell; for the lives of Mary and two others to be named by Mr. Brown, for a fine of £32. [*Note*. Not followed]

and see trusteeship business

Almshouse

Mrs. West's application for her arrear, under the special circumstances stated by her, is allowed.

Mrs. Bacon's petition for allowance of £12 in arrear to her was read but not allowed, but it is referred to the trustees at the next meeting to consider whether the arrear or any part of it can be allowed.

Mrs. Atwood's case was mentioned but the trustees consider it necessary to enforce the rules of the charity concerning residence and do not allow of the excuse offered for her exceeding her leave of absence.

The clerk is directed to warn Mrs. Cole and Mrs. West that, if they do not immediately discontinue their practice of going to lodge in the public house called the Pelican, which the trustees consider as very uncreditable, their next quarter's stipend will be detained. It is ordered accordingly.

Mr. Marsh resigned the office of surgeon and apothecary and Mr. Kite, his partner, and Mr. Bartlett of Great Bedwyn offered themselves as candidates. The majority of the trustees present elected Mr. Bartlett but, to show that such election has not proceeded from any disapprobation of Mr. Kite's conduct, they direct that he shall continue in the care of the sick widows till Christmas next when the present half-year expires.

Mrs. West's case being stated by Mr. Kite, the apothecary, [it is] ordered that an allowance of 2*s*. 6*d*. a week be made for a nurse to sleep in her apartment at such times as she shall be resident therein.

Ordered that such clergy widows as have no other income than the trust stipend, and clergy allowances not exceeding 10 gns. a year, shall not be debarred by such latter allowance from being allowed a nurse when it shall be reported by the surgeon of the hospital that a nurse is necessary.

Signatures

William Northey, E. W. L. Popham, J. H. Penruddocke, Thomas Vilett, A. Goddard, E. Goddard, John Awdry, J. Dugdale Astley.

3 August 1825, at the Castle inn, Marlborough

Present

The marquess of Ailesbury, chairman, Sir John Dugdale Astley, bt., Lt. Gen. Popham, Thomas Grimston Bucknall Estcourt, esq., Lt. Col. Warneford, Maj. Vilett, John Awdry, esq., Revd. Edward Goddard, Ambrose Goddard, esq., John Pearse, esq.

Trusteeship

The trustees examined the account of the receiver, upon which a balance of £121 18*s.* 2*d.* due to the trust is to be carried to the next account.

It appears by the receiver's accounts that, in addition to £700 Old South Sea annuities purchased prior to the meeting in August 1823, £735 9*s.* 5*d.* in that fund has been purchased pursuant to an order made at the last meeting, a further £700 was purchased on 22 July last, and there only remains to be purchased £700 Old South Sea annuities in order to replace the stock that has been sold for the purposes mentioned in the preceding minutes.

Estate

The trustees examined the accounts of the sales of timber and coppice wood and directed that, as soon as the lots upon which balances become due at Michaelmas next are paid for, the accounts be entered in the general account book of this charity.

Ordered that the allowances to rack-rent tenants, which for the current year ending at Michaelmas 1825 were reduced from 15 to 10 per cent by order of the trustees at the last meeting, shall be continued to Michaelmas 1826 and then discontinued altogether.

An agreement [is] to be made with William Hayward for his being continued tenant at a clear yearly rent of £216 12*s.* 6*d.* from Michaelmas last from year to year as long as both parties please, under proper stipulations as to occupation and going off, being the amount of Mr. John Hayward's valuation deducting £11 land tax and £3 16*s.* net quit rent payable to the duke of Marlborough.

It is referred to the clerk to make terms with David Wilson for the possession [of his holding] and [for] remunerating the expense he has been at in building on Huish Hill if he can do so on reasonable terms, or to grant, if he will take [it], a lease for a long term of years at 1*s.* quit rent.

The clerk is allowed to pay £8 to Mr. Guy Warwick for attention to considerable works in Huish and Fyfield, but this allowance shall not be considered as a precedent.

Almshouse

Ordered that the doors, window frames, and pediments over the doors of the hospital be painted by James Pickett at the estimate given in by him amounting to £5 13*s.* 3*d.*

Ordered that the ground against the west side of the hospital be lowered. The clerk is authorized to have iron or copper spouts put to the west side of the almshouse as an experiment of their use for keeping the apartments more free from damp.

Ordered that lay widows not having more income, exclusive of the trust stipend, than 10 gns. may be allowed the same privileges by the trustees as were given to clergy widows with such limited income at the last meeting respecting nurses.

Ordered that allowances for fixtures to executors of deceased widows, and to retiring widows, shall be subject to the following regulations. As to grates and shelves: the incoming widow [is] to have the option of taking or refusing to take them at a valuation of the articles as worth to take away, the outgoing widow making good the walls etc. As to other fixtures which the deceased or retiring widow shall have paid for prior to this date the trustees will allow to the executors of such widows, for the benefit of the incoming widow, two thirds of the value as to take away of such improvements, deducting the costs of making good the walls or floors, but such allowance is only to refer to improvements as have hitherto been made, and paid for, by the deceased or retiring widow and not to any future improvements, which shall be left for the benefit of succeeding widows without remuneration.

The cases of several widows whose stipends have been stopped having been considered [it is] ordered that the clerk pay to Elizabeth Phillips her arrear of stipend of £4, to Elizabeth Haywood her arrear of stipend of £8, to Sarah Bacon £6, part of her arrear, the other part being withheld to mark the disapprobation of her conduct in having in an unusual degree infringed the rules of the hospital. The arrears of stipend to Letitia Cole amounting to £17 shall not be allowed. The clerk, however, is to pay her the regular stipend in future during her good behaviour, but on any future misconduct she is to be expelled. To Grace Atwood £4 [is to be paid] in part of her arrear of £8.

Signatures

Ailesbury, J. Dugdale Astley, J. G. Bucknall Estcourt, E. Goddard, E. W. L. Popham, John Pearse, Thomas Vilett, Francis Warneford, John Awdry, Ambrose Goddard.

2 August 1826, at the Castle inn, Marlborough

Present

The Revd. Edward Goddard, the marquess of Ailesbury, Thomas G. Bucknall Estcourt, esq., John Awdry, esq., John Hungerford Penruddocke, esq., E. W. L. Popham, esq., Francis Warneford, esq.

Trusteeship

The trustees examined the account of the receiver, upon which there appears a balance in his hands of £228 3*s.* 5*d.* which is to be carried to his next account.

The receiver reported that £700 Old South Sea annuities has been purchased out of the trust fund, whereby it appears that the whole of the stock that was sold for payment of the expenses of the inclosures and exchanges at Froxfield and Fyfield, and consequent new erections, has been replaced in the names of the three trustees in whom the stock was originally invested.

Estate

The allowances to the tenants whose rents were fixed upon the inclosure, of £10 per cent out of their rents, are to be continued for the year ensuing.

and see trusteeship business

Almshouse

The trustees, on a statement of the income and probable expenditure of the trust, order that £4 a year be added to the widows' stipends, making in the whole £36 a year, the first quarter to be paid at Michaelmas next.

Mrs. Atwood having resigned her situation at Froxfield the stipend which was detained on account of her absence without leave is allowed to be paid.

The application of Widow Cole for payment of her stipend is rejected on account of her misconduct. A like application from Widow Bacon is rejected on account of her unreasonable and repeated absences without leave.

Signatures

J. Awdry, E. W. L. Popham, Ailesbury, J. H. Penruddocke, T. G. Bucknall Estcourt, Francis Warneford, E. Goddard.

3 August 1827, at the Castle inn, Marlborough, held on Friday 3 August, the usual day of meeting having been found inconvenient on account of the engagement of several of the trustees at the assizes

Present

The marquess of Ailesbury, chairman, Revd. Edward Goddard, Francis Warneford, esq., Lt. Gen. Popham, Sir John Dugdale Astley, bt., Thomas G. Bucknall Estcourt, esq., Ambrose Goddard, esq., John Pearse, esq., Thomas Vilett, esq., John Awdry, esq.

Trusteeship

The trustees examined the account of the receiver to Michaelmas last, upon which there appears a balance in his hands of £445 17*s.* 5*d.* which is to be carried to his next account.

On account of the special circumstance of the assizes happening to be on the usual day of the annual meeting of the trustees, the postponement of the meeting by the clerk to this day is approved of by the trustees present at this meeting.

Estate

The allowances to tenants to be continued as last year for the year ensuing.

The trustees decline fresh stating [*i.e.* granting an estate in] the tenements at Froxfield held by Mr. John Hawkins and the tenement at Huish held by Miss Liddiard.

The clerk is commissioned to purchase the cottage at Huish belonging to Thomas Alexander, to build two tenements on late Stagg's garden, and to place Alexander in one of them for his life [*note*: and Elizabeth his wife, see agreement], he being 75 years of age, rent free and with [a] condition that Mary Stagg may be accommodated with a lodging in it.

The trustees allow the salary of Guy Warwick, in consideration of his services to the trust, to be raised to £10 a year.

Ordered that the brewhouse at Huish farm be taken down and a new one built to be 18 ft. by 16 ft., the tenant doing carriage of all materials. [*Margin*. Memorandum: on taking down the brewhouse it was found that a quantity of wood had been walled into the old chimney and, in a charred state, might have occasioned the destruction of the house had the building remained longer so as for the wood, when in a burning state, to have communicated with anything combustible]

Almshouse

The clerk is to allow nurses at 1*s.* a week to the widows Wells, Barnes, and Tarrant.

Ordered that, in case Widow Geary shall not be heard of and give satisfactory reasons for her extraordinary absence by the next quarterly payday, the clerk shall take possession of the tenement and send a nomination paper to the trustee who shall then be in turn.

Signatures

Ailesbury, chairman, John Pearse, Thomas Vilett, Ambrose Goddard, John Awdry, E. W. L. Popham, T. G. Bucknall Estcourt, Francis Warneford.

6 August 1828, at the Castle inn, Marlborough

Present

Lt. Col. Warneford, chairman, Revd. Edward Goddard, John Pearse, esq., John Awdry, esq., T. G. B. Estcourt, esq., J. H. Penruddocke, esq.

Trusteeship

The trustees examined the account of the receiver of the rents to Michaelmas last, upon which there appears to be a balance in his hands of £596 3*s.* 4*d.* which is to be carried to the next account.

Estate

It is the opinion of the trustees that no alterations be made at present in the rack rents, except making the same allowances per cent as last year.

The clerk is authorized to remove the tenement lately rented by the Revd. Mr. Evans, to have two tenements erected in a more convenient situation, and to let the site of the removed cottage to the Revd. Mr. Atwood, the vicar of Froxfield.

Almshouse

The application of Elizabeth Wells of no. 42 for a nurse, and of Elizabeth Batt for a nurse, were considered. The clerk is authorized to allow 1*s.* a week for each from this time.

Under the special circumstances of Grace Gale's illness and removal from the hospital to Broad Town the clerk is authorized to pay the arrears of her stipend to her at Broad Town, and to continue the payment of her stipend there if the Revd. E. Goddard and the surgeon who attends her shall certify her incapability of returning to Froxfield.

Mayo trust

At this meeting there was laid before the trustees a communication from the Revd. Charles Mayo, chaplain of Froxfield college, in which, after representing the unfortunate situation of those well educated and deserving clergymen of the established church who after having for a great time discharged the sacred duties of their profession are without any prospect of preferment, he generously proposes to place into the hands of the trustees of this charity £2,500 3½ per cents to be applied by them, under the stipulations in the intended deed of trust [and] when it shall have accumulated to a sufficient sum, in the purchase of the advowson of two livings to be presented to clergymen of the above description, and to the establishment of an exhibition in the university of Oxford to which shall be appointed the sons of clergymen of the above description. It is resolved that the trustees are duly impressed with the importance of the design, and generosity of the intentions, of Mr. Mayo and that they readily undertake the trust with which he proposes to invest them. [They] beg to express their admiration of Mr. Mayo's generous and charitable intentions.

Signatures

Francis Warneford, J. G. Bucknall Estcourt, J. H. Penruddocke, John Pearse, J. Awdry, E. Goddard.

12 August 1829, at the Castle inn, Marlborough

Present

The marquess of Ailesbury, chairman, the Revd. E. Goddard, Lt. Col. Warneford, John Pearse, esq., Gen. Popham, Ambrose Goddard, esq., Sir J. D. Astley, bt., Lt. Col. Vilett.

Trusteeship

We the trustees whose names are hereunto subscribed, by virtue of the powers given to us by the will of the late Sarah, duchess dowager of Somerset, and since confirmed by the High Court of Chancery, appoint Thomas Merriman of Marlborough, gentleman, to be our steward of all manors and receiver of all rents, revenues, and estates to the hospital belonging and to hold courts and do all other things to the offices of steward and receiver belonging, the offices having become vacant by the death of John Ward, gentleman.

At this meeting examined and allowed the accounts of the late receiver and his representatives, the balance whereof, being £907 13*s*. 7*d*. due from them, they are to pay over to the new receiver.

Ordered that the receiver lay out £500, part of the balance, in the purchase of Exchequer bills and hold them for the benefit of the funds of the charity.

Ordered that whenever the first Wednesday in August shall happen, as in the present year, to be in the week for holding the assizes in Wiltshire the annual meeting of the trustees shall be held on the second Wednesday of that month.

Estate

Ordered that the tenement at Huish lately occupied by William Cook and let with the farm at Huish be rebuilt, and such other improvements made in the other buildings on that farm as the steward shall think necessary, not exceeding in the whole £40.

An application was made by Mr. John Brown, the lessee of the brewery, malthouse, etc. at Froxfield, for a renewal of his lease, which will expire in 1833, on account of the time which would be requisite for the removal of brewery implements into a new situation in case of his quitting his present buildings. [It is] ordered that Mr. Brown's application be taken into consideration at the next meeting of the trustees, and in the meantime the steward is to make enquiry into the nature and value of the property.

The trustees executed a lease of Huish farm to Mr. George Young for 6 years from Michaelmas 1828 at the yearly rent of £550.

Almshouse

On the representation of Widow Batt as to her infirmities, and being in her 80th year, [it is] ordered that the allowance to her nurse be increased from 1*s*. to 1*s*. 6*d*. a week.

An application was made to the trustees at this meeting from Widow Cole to be paid the arrears of her stipend which were stopped a few years ago by order of the trustees. [It is] resolved that such request be not complied with.

Mayo trust

The receiver reported that £2,500 stock in the 3½ per cent reduced bank annuities has been transferred by the Revd. Charles Mayo to John Pearse, esq., and Thomas Grimston Bucknall Estcourt, esq., upon the trusts mentioned in the minutes of the last meeting.

He also laid before the trustees at this meeting an indenture dated 23 February 1829 prepared under the advice and approval of Richard Preston, esq., barrister-at-law, and made between the Revd. Charles Mayo of the one part and John Pearse and Thomas Grimston Bucknall Estcourt, esqs., of the other part, declaring the trusts of the £2,500 and otherwise for carrying into effect the generous and charitable intentions of Mr. Mayo as expressed in the minutes made at the last meeting. The trustees approve of the stipulations and regulations contained in the indenture.

Signatures

Ailesbury, E. W. L. Popham, Francis Warneford, John Pearse, Ambrose Goddard, Thomas Vilett.

The Revd. Charles Mayo's declaration of trust

Indenture made 23 February 1829 between the Revd. Charles Mayo, rector of Huish and chaplain of the Somerset hospital at Froxfield, of the one part and John Pearse of Chilton Foliat, esq., and Thomas Grimston Bucknall Estcourt of New Park, esq., of the other part. Charles Mayo was on or about 29 April 1775 presented to the rectory and parish church of Huish and elected chaplain of the hospital, and John Pearse and Thomas Grimston Bucknall Estcourt are two of the trustees of the hospital.

Charles Mayo is desirous to testify his attachment to the church establishment, by whose patronage he has been liberally maintained above half a century, and his respect for the trustees, by whom he has been patronized. [He is] convinced that the Church of England owes its stability and importance to the higher orders in it and that many men of worth and talents receive the reward of their merits by elevation to preferments. [He is] also of opinion that there is nothing in which the wellbeing of the kingdom is more interested than in having a body of respectable parochial clergy, whose exemplary character and discourses may check the progress of infidelity and of fanaticism and Calvinistic doctrines, and [in having] such body constituted of men of regular education and approved moral character, conversant in the doctrines and principles of our religion, impressed with a sense of the importance of their office, diligent in the discharge of its duties, and at the same time moderately independent in their circumstances. Though entertaining these sentiments, and feeling a high interest in the welfare and respectability of the church, [he is] also of opinion, and he observed it with regret, that there is no inconsiderable number of clergymen of merit who, after receiving an expensive education, have spent their whole lives in a diligent discharge of their duty without receiving the reward of their services. Being willing, as far as it depends on his limited means, to encourage others by his example to apply their larger means to the same purpose, [he] has determined to appropriate a fund to the purposes hereinafter expressed.

Charles Mayo has transferred £2,500 [in] £3 10*s*. per cent a year reduced annuities into the names of John Pearse and Thomas Grimston Bucknall Estcourt, and he has in contemplation to purchase and transfer other like annuities, or 3 per cent consolidated or other 3 per cent bank annuities, into the names of the persons who shall be the trustees of the £2,500 at such time as he may do so, subject to the trusts hereinafter expressed.

Charles Mayo does direct, and John Pearse and Thomas Grimston Bucknall Estcourt do consent, that John Pearse and Thomas Grimston Bucknall Estcourt, their executors and administrators, and the trustees substituted in their stead, shall stand possessed of the £2,500 [in] £3 10*s*. per cent annuities, of all other annuities to be purchased in his or their names by Charles Mayo, and of all accumulations thereof, on the trust hereinafter declared.

During the life of Charles Mayo, and 21 years from his death, the trustees shall receive the dividends of the annuities and lay out the dividends, and income arising, in the purchase of other annuities in increase of the fund, and [they shall have] authority to sell any of the £3 10*s*. per cent annuities and invest the produce in the purchase of other annuities. At the end of 21 years from the death of Charles Mayo the trustees of the annuities shall transfer them into the names of two or more persons as the trustees of the hospital, or the major part of them duly assembled and not being less than five members present, shall nominate. Such new trustees [are] to sign a memorandum acknowledging the amount of stock transferred to them. To the intent that the expense of such proceedings may be moderate, the expense of all such transfers, and of the letters of attorney authorizing them and the receipt of the dividends, [are] to be paid out of the dividends which shall become due in the year, ending on 31 December, in which such transfers shall be made and letters of attorney executed.

The trustees of the annuities [are] to be selected from the trustees of the hospital. A new trustee [is] to be, within 1 year after a vacancy, appointed in the place of each trustee who by death, resignation, or removal shall cease to be a trustee of the hospital.

After the expiration of the 21 years the trustees of the £3 10*s*., or £3, per cent annuities shall stand possessed of them as one aggregate fund, and of the future income thereof, upon the trusts hereinafter declared.

£70 a year, part of the income, shall be applied as an exhibition endowment or scholarship to be granted by the trustees of the hospital to the sons of clergymen, living or deceased, who shall have resided at least 15 years in Wiltshire, been exemplary in the discharge of their clerical duties, and [been] of approved character for morals and doctrine. The testimonials of these particulars [are] to be signed by three beneficed clergymen of Wiltshire, each of whom [is] to be resident within 15 miles of the place in which the clergyman whose son is to be benefited shall be resident or, if dead, was lastly resident. Such certificate [is] to be signed by the archdeacon of the district of which such clergyman shall be, or at his death was, resident. The sons [are] to be natives of Wiltshire or to have been resident, except while at school or attending college, at least 15 years in that county, [and are] to be scholars of exemplary character and conduct and of promising abilities and diligence in their studies. The trustees of the hospital [are] to have the right of confining the exhibition to any particular college in Oxford, or to extend it to any of the colleges, but the exhibition shall not be enjoyed by any person for more than 7 years and shall [otherwise] determine on the acceptance of a fellowship or of any benefice of £50 a year or upwards. The £70 a year shall be given to one person only and not be given in parts to several persons.

The trustees shall have authority, by rules which they may change, to regulate the election of scholars so qualified for the exhibition and to deprive any scholar, after his election, of the benefit of such exhibition for immorality or any other cause which to the trustees shall, in their uncontrollable discretion, seem meet. No deprivation or rule to be made at any meeting of the trustees shall be valid unless confirmed, with or without alterations, by a majority of the trustees present at a special or general meeting to be appointed at such preceding meeting and to be held for such purpose at their usual place of meeting within 13 months, but not sooner than 2 months, after such preceding meeting. Notice in writing of such special or general meeting, and of the purpose of it with reference to those objects, [is] to be given to each trustee, or left at his last place of abode or usual residence, 21 days before the day of such special or general meeting.

The trustees may, by their resolution at any one meeting to be confirmed at a general or special meeting, and at their option and only if they should think fit, purchase one advowson or, at different times, two several advowsons producing a net annual income not less than £200 each. [They should] cause the advowson or advowsons to be vested in them upon [the] trust that they convey the advowson or advowsons as part of the estate of the hospital on the appointment of new trustees.

[They] shall present to the church, or to each of the churches, of which the advowson shall be purchased a clergyman of the choice of all the trustees or the major part in number of them, which clergyman shall have graduated in the university of Oxford or of Cambridge and shall have resided at least 15 years, prior to his presentation, in Wiltshire. During that time [he] shall have been in holy orders and exemplary in his discharge of his clerical duties. [He] shall be a person of approved character for morals and doctrine and shall, at the time of such presentation, be of 40 years or upwards, without any clerical benefice with cure of souls, without any reasonable prospect of any such benefice, and not in his own right or in right of his wife or both rights conjointly have an income of £150 a year from real or personal property or any permanent security. The testimonials of each candidate [are] to be in these particulars certified by three beneficed clergymen of the county resident within 15 miles from the residence of the candidate, and [are] to be attested by the archdeacon of the district in which the candidate shall be resident.

The expense of purchasing such advowson or advowsons, of obtaining a title thereto, of investigating the title, of conveying them to the trustees, and of [engrossing] the necessary deeds of trust relating to the £3 10*s*., or £3, per cent annuities and [the] advowsons [are] to be paid out of the income of the annuities.

The advowson or advowsons to be purchased [are] to be of a church or churches situated south of the counties of York and Lancaster. No purchase shall be made of any advowson to reduce the £70 for exhibitions, and for that purpose the trustees shall be bound, prior to such purchase, to appropriate by purchase, transfer, or otherwise £2,333 6*s*. 8*d*. [of] £3 per cent annuities to answer the £70 a year for the exhibition.

In case there should be any surplus of income remaining after the discharge of the existing trusts the surplus, and so much of the £70 as may not become payable by reason that there shall be a vacancy or suspension in the right to receive [it], shall be applied for charitable purposes as the trustees of the hospital shall by the resolution of any meeting, to be confirmed with or without alterations at a general or special meeting convened under a special notice, direct. Apprenticing, or assisting the daughters of clergymen in straitened circumstances, is recommended, though not prescribed, to the trustees.

In all cases of alterations of the resolution of a first meeting such alterations, to be valid, shall be adopted by each of the two next meetings by the trustees then present or the major part of them.

The trustees hereby appointed, the trustees to be appointed, and the trustees of the hospital shall be charged only for such money and property as [they] shall actually receive by virtue of the trusts, notwithstanding their signing any receipt for the sake of conformity or any letter of attorney for facilitating the execution of the trusts. Any one of them shall not be answerable for the acts or defaults of the others, but each only for his own. They shall not be answerable for any banker, broker, or other person in whose hands any part of the trust monies or property shall be deposited or who shall be authorized to make transfers or receive dividends. They shall not be accountable for the rise or fall in the value of funded property or the deficiency in title or value of any advowson to be purchased; nor for any other misfortune, loss, or damage which may happen in the execution of the trusts, except [if] it should happen through their own wilful default. In that case each person shall alone be answerable for such loss as shall arise from his own default.

It shall be lawful for the trustees named, future trustees, and the trustees of the hospital, out of the money which shall come to their hands by virtue of the trusts, to reimburse to themselves, and to allow their co-trustees, all expenses, and fees to counsel for advice, which they may incur in the execution of the trusts. [The trustees may] allow the accounts of any trustee who shall depart this life or be discharged from the trusts and receive, and give discharges for, the money which shall appear to be the balance of those accounts; without any responsibility in the person paying the money to see the application thereof or be answerable for the misapplication of it, so [long] as such account shall be allowed by the trustees of the hospital.

Signed, sealed, and delivered by Charles Mayo in the presence of Leonard Perry, servant to Mr. Mayo, Thomas B. Merriman, solicitor, Marlborough, [and] James Bradford, solicitor, Swindon; by John Pearse in the presence of Thomas Merriman; by Thomas Grimston Bucknall Estcourt in the presence of James Bradford.

29 December 1829, at the Castle inn, Marlborough, in pursuance of special notice given in consequence of the death of the Revd. Charles Mayo, the chaplain to the hospital and the rector of Huish.

Present

Francis Warneford, esq., in the chair, John Pearse, esq., John Awdry, esq., Gen. Popham, T. G. B. Estcourt, esq., Ambrose Goddard, esq., Sir J. D. Astley, bt., Col. Vilett.

Trusteeship

The steward reported that the Revd. Charles Mayo had departed this life on 27 November last, whereby the rectory of Huish and the chaplaincy to the hospital had become vacant.

He also reported that he had, through his agent, consulted the secretary of the bishop as to the mode of presenting to that rectory, who expressed his opinion that it was necessary that the presentation should be signed by each of the trustees.

The trustees took into consideration the qualifications of the candidates who made application to succeed Mr. Mayo in the rectory of Huish and, on a division, there appeared to be four who voted for the Revd. John Vilett and four who voted for the Revd. William Bleeck. The numbers therefore being even it was resolved that in consquence thereof, and also of the opinion expressed by the bishop's secretary, the steward should write to the three absent trustees, the marquess of Ailesbury, the Revd. E. Goddard, and John Hungerford Penruddocke, esq., and request that they will severally signify to him by letter for which of the two gentlemen each of them will vote. It was resolved that whichever of the gentlemen shall have a majority of votes, including those of the three absent trustees, shall be presented to the rectory of Huish.

Resolved that the trustees will defer until their next meeting the appointing of a chaplain to the hospital.

Adjournment

Ordered that this meeting be adjourned to this same place to Tuesday 26 January 1830 at 12 o'clock at noon.

Signatures

John Pearse, E. W. L. Popham, J. G. Bucknall Estcourt, J. Dugdale Astley. [The names of Col. Warneford, Mr. Awdry, Mr. A. Goddard, and Col. Vilett were pencilled in by the clerk, but they did not sign]

26 January 1830, at the Castle inn, Marlborough, in pursuance of the last adjournment

Present

John Pearse, esq., M.P., in the chair, Gen. Popham, T. G. B. Estcourt, esq., A. Goddard, esq., Sir J. D. Astley, bt.

Trusteeship

The steward produced letters addressed to him, in consequence of the resolutions at the last meeting of trustees, by the marquess of Ailesbury and J. H. Penruddocke, esq., who severally signified that they voted in favour of the appointment of the Revd. William Bleeck to the rectory of Huish, and a letter from the Revd. Edward Goddard signifying his vote to be in favour of the appointment of the Revd. John Vilett.

It appearing that there is a majority of one vote in favour of Mr. Bleeck, six of the trustees having voted for him and five of them for Mr. Vilett, [it is] resolved that the Revd. William Bleeck be presented to the rectory of Huish.

A presentation of Mr. Bleeck to that rectory was accordingly executed by such of the trustees as are present at this meeting, and the steward is to transmit it to the absent trustees for their signature.

Almshouse

Resolved that the Revd. William Bleeck be elected, and he is hereby appointed, the chaplain of the hospital.

The trustees being fully sensible of the exemplary manner in which the Revd. Arthur Meyrick has discharged the duties of the office of chaplain for upwards of 20 years, during which he has officiated as the representative of the late Mr. Mayo, take this opportunity of recording their approbation of his conduct.

Signatures

John Pearse, E. W. L. Popham, J. G. Bucknall Estcourt, J. Dugdale Astley. [The name of Mr. A. Goddard was pencilled in by the steward, but he did not sign]

4 August 1830, at the Castle inn, Marlborough

Present

The Revd. E. Goddard, Col. Warneford, John Pearse, esq., T. G. B. Estcourt, esq., John Awdry, esq., Gen. Popham, Ambrose Goddard, esq., J. H. Penruddocke, esq.

Trusteeship

The trustees examined the account of the receiver of the rents to Michaelmas last, upon which there appears to be a balance in his hands of £549 12*s.* which is to be carried to the next account.

It also appears that the receiver has purchased, and still holds, an Exchequer bill for £500 agreeably to the order of the trustees made on 12 August 1829.

Ordered that £20 be allowed towards the expense of building a charity school room at Chirton, at which place there is at present no establishment for the education of the poor, and the trustees of the Heytesbury charity having made a similar contribution.

Estate

Ordered that an addition of a sitting room and [a] bedroom be made to the farmhouse at Chirton for the accommodation of the family [of], and rendering it more fit for, the tenant at an expense not exceeding £50.

The late rector of Huish having rented a piece of waste land containing about 20 perches at £1 1*s.* a year, and the present rector being desirous of adding it to his rectory garden, [it is] ordered that it be let to him for a long term, provided he shall continue the rector, at the same rent of £1 1*s.* a year.

and see trusteeship business

Almshouse

Ordered that Mrs. Parker be paid the quarter's stipend to Midsummer last, she having received her nomination to a tenement previous to the quarter day but having from accidental circumstances been delayed in producing one of her necessary certificates.

Mayo trust

It appears from a separate account produced by the receiver that the amount of stock in the 3½ per cent reduced annuities standing in the names of John Pearse and T. G. B. Estcourt, esqs., trustees of the fund established by the late Revd. C. Mayo, had accumulated to £2,835 4*s*. 2*d*.

Signatures

J. Awdry, John Pearse, J. H. Penruddocke, E. Goddard, T. G. Bucknall Estcourt, Francis Warneford, E. W. L. Popham.

3 August 1831, at the Castle inn, Marlborough

Present

The marquess of Ailesbury, the Revd. Edward Goddard, Lt. Col. Warneford, Lt. Gen. Popham, Sir J. D. Astley, bt., Lt. Col. Thomas Vilett.

Trusteeship

The trustees examined the account of the receiver of the rents to Michaelmas 1830, upon which there appears to be a balance of £668 11*s*. 5*d*. which is to be carried to the next account.

Ordered that £15 be allowed towards the building of a poorhouse at Chirton, which appears to be much wanted by the parish.

Estate

The steward reported that in November last a barn, carthouse, and other outbuildings, part of the farm buildings in the occupation of Robert Fowler at Oare, were wilfully set fire to and burnt down and that he had ordered the rebuilding of them. He also reported that, there being a considerable quantity of oak and elm timber at and near Oare fit for cutting, he had sold as much in value as would pay for the erection of the new building.

The steward also reported that, in consequence of the numerous farm buildings in Wiltshire which have of late been maliciously set fire to, he had effected an insurance from fire in the Sun Fire Office for £7,500.

Mr. Thomas Pyke having given notice at Lady day last that he would quit at Michaelmas next the farms which he rents at Fyfield and Clench the steward employed Mr. Iveson to value them, and he produced such valuation amounting to £335 a year from which, however, is to be deducted £10 a year for land tax. Mr. Iveson was of opinion that an abatement of £30 might reasonably be made on account of there being no farmhouse on either of the estates and in consideration of the present state of agricultural concerns, making the net rent £295 a year; on which terms the steward has agreed to let the farms to Mr. Thomas Pyke, junior, the son of the present tenant, from Michaelmas next.

The several matters aforesaid are approved of and confirmed by this meeting.

Mr. Iveson having recommended an outlay for a few years by landlords and tenant of £10 a year each in draining on Fyfield and Clench farms, the steward is authorized to expend that sum annually in that improvement provided the tenant shall do the same.

The steward reported that, pursuant to the minute made at the meeting of the trustees on 12 August 1829, he had directed Mr. Guy Warwick to look over the brewery, dwelling house, malthouse, and Cross Keys public house at Froxfield now held on lease by Mr. John Brown at the rent of £54 a year, which lease will expire at Michaelmas 1833, and he produced Mr. Warwick's estimate of the [value] at £90 a year. [It is] ordered that the steward be authorized to let the premises to Mr. Brown on [a] lease not exceeding 7 years from Michaelmas 1833 at £90 a year, the tenant paying all taxes and doing all repairs.

An application was made by the Revd. Mr. Atwood, the vicar of Froxfield, for a small piece of ground for enlarging the churchyard at Froxfield. The trustees will take this matter into consideration at their next meeting, but at present they doubt the propriety of their permanently giving up any of the trust land.

and see trusteeship business

Almshouse

An application was made on behalf of Mrs. Cole for her arrears of dividends, which have been stopped by the steward. The trustees are of opinion that the conduct of Mrs. Cole has been such as would render it improper in the steward to pay these arrears to Mrs. Cole.

Mayo trust

It appears from a separate account produced by the receiver that the amount of stock in the 3½ per cent reduced annuities standing in the names of John Pearse and T. G. B. Estcourt, trustees of the fund established by the late Revd. C. Mayo, had accumulated to £2,945 8*s.* 2*d.*

Signatures

Ailesbury, E. W. L. Popham, E. Goddard, Thomas Vilett, J. Dugdale Astley, Francis Warneford.

1 August 1832, at the Castle inn, Marlborough

Present

The Revd. Edward Goddard, Lt. Col. Warneford, Lt. Gen. Popham, John Awdry, esq., Lt. Col. Vilett, T. G. B. Estcourt, esq., Sir J. D. Astley, bt.

Trusteeship

The trustees examined the account of the receiver of the rents to Michaelmas 1831, upon which there appears to be a balance of £437 5*s.* 10*d.* which is to be carried to the next account.

Estate

Ordered that the steward be authorized to expend not exceeding £30 in the alteration of a road at Huish, by which the farm there would be materially convenienced and about ½ acre of land be saved.

Almshouse

On an investigation by the trustees of the state of revenue and expenditure of the trust estate they are of opinion that an increase of £2 a year may be made to the widows' stipends. They order that such increase be made and that the first payment thereof be made at Michaelmas next.

Ordered that on all future appointments of widows the stipend of the widow shall commence from her taking possession of her tenement and not from the preceding quarter day as heretofore.

An application from Mr. Bartlett, the surgeon and apothecary to the hospital, for an increase of salary was taken into consideration, but the trustees are of opinion that they ought not at present to comply with Mr. Bartlett's request.

Ordered that a nurse be allowed to Margaret Lowder on account of her age and infirmities, but her application to be allowed to live away from the hospital cannot be complied with.

An application from Mrs. E. A. Graves for payment to her of £18 arrears, which had been stopped, is to be further considered at a future meeting.

An application from Mrs. Mary Fowler for a quarter's stipend in consequence of her appointment having been made a few days after 5 April 1830 cannot be complied with.

The steward having withheld the last quarter's stipend from Mrs. Bradshaw in consequence of her absence without leave [it is] ordered that a moiety of the sum stopped be paid to her, she having produced a certificate of ill health and having promised not again to transgress the rules of the hospital.

Mrs. Ellenora Caddick's application to be paid for the last quarter, which has been stopped in consequence of her absence without leave, is ordered not to be granted. [*Margin.* The quarter stopped was due 6 April 1832. She was paid the one due July 1832]

Under the circumstances stated respecting Mrs. Hay, widow of the Revd. Richard John Hay, who died at Rotterdam having been appointed by the bishop of London to an English chapel there, [it is] ordered that she may be admitted, if appointed, to one of the clergy tenements now vacant. [*Margin.* Mrs. Hay was a Wiltshire woman.

See letter with her nomination]

Mayo trust

It appears by a separate account produced by the receiver that the amount of stock in the 3½ per cent reduced annuities standing in the names of John Pearse and T. G. B. Estcourt, esqs., trustees of the fund established by the late Revd. C. Mayo, had accumulated to £3,062 3*s.* 6*d.*

Signatures

Francis Warneford, E. W. L. Popham, John Awdry, E. Goddard, Thomas Vilett, T. G. Bucknall Estcourt.

7 August 1833, at the Castle inn, Marlborough

Present

The marquess of Ailesbury, Lt. Col. Warneford, the Revd. E. Goddard, John Pearse, esq., John Awdry, esq., Lt. Gen. Popham, T. G. B. Estcourt, esq., Ambrose Goddard, esq., Sir J. D. Astley, bt., Lt. Col. Vilett.

Trusteeship

The trustees examined the account of the receiver of the rents to Michaelmas 1832, upon which there appears to be a balance of £502 18*s.* 6*d.* which is to be carried to the next account.

Ordered that the name of Col. Thomas Vilett be added to those of John Pearse, esq., and T. G. B. Estcourt, esq., in the investment of the South Sea annuities belonging to the trust and of the Mayo trust fund.

Estate

The steward produced a valuation at £344 11*s.* 3*d.* a year by Messrs. J. Iveson and W. R. Brown of the farm at Froxfield now in lease to Messrs. William and Thomas Halcomb, the executors of the late Mr. John Halcomb, at £417 16*s.*, which lease expires at Michaelmas next [and] from which an allowance has for several years past been made of 10 per cent.

Ordered that the steward be authorized to let the farm to Messrs. Halcomb at the valuation of £344 11*s.* 3*d.* on a lease for 12 years determinable, at the expiration of the first 4 or 8 years, on 12 months' notice to be given by either party.

The application made to a former meeting of the trustees for the grant of a small piece of land for enlarging the churchyard at Froxfield was again considered. In as much as the crowded state of the present churchyard has been occasioned in a great measure by the interment of inhabitants of the hospital the trustees think it reasonable that some accommodation of the kind applied for should be afforded. Gen. Popham and Mr. Pearse are requested to inspect the situation and to report their opinion to the next meeting of the trustees.

Almshouse

It appearing that Mrs. Ellenora Caddick has absented herself without leave from her tenement, no. 15, for nearly 2 years and that she has left it in a very disgraceful state of dilapidation, and the steward having read a copy of a letter written by him to Mrs. Caddick on 20 June last informing her that it was the opinion of the trustees who attended the last view meeting that the tenement ought to be considered as vacant and that another clergy widow should be appointed thereto, to which letter no answer has been returned by Mrs. Caddick, [it is] resolved unanimously that this tenement be considered as vacant and that another widow be appointed by the trustee in rotation in the stead of Mrs. Caddick, and that Mrs. Caddick be informed thereof.

It is the opinion of the trustees that it would be beneficial that a commodious house for the residence of the porter should be provided near to the hospital. Gen. Popham and Mr. Pearse are authorized to give such directions for building a house, or otherwise for that purpose, as they shall think proper.

The minute made at the last meeting of the trustees on the application of Mrs. Graves was further considered. The steward is authorized to pay Mrs. Graves £10 in part of the arrears petitioned for by her and no more.

An application was renewed at this meeting by Mr. Bartlett, the surgeon and apothecary, for an increase of salary on account of the great attention required from him and the large quantity of medicines used. On consideration of the circumstances the trustees resolve that Mr. Bartlett's salary be advanced from £50 to £60 a year.

Mayo trust

It appears by a separate account produced by the receiver that the amount of stock in the 3½ per cent reduced annuities standing in the names of John Pearse and T. G. B. Estcourt, esqs., trustees of the fund established by the late Revd. C. Mayo, had accumulated to £3,177 13*s*. 10*d*.

and see trusteeship business

Signatures

Ailesbury, Francis Warneford, J. Dugdale Astley, J. Awdry, Thomas Vilett. [The names of Revd. E. Goddard, Mr. Pearse, Gen. Popham, Mr. Estcourt, Mr. Ambrose Goddard were pencilled in by the clerk, but they did not sign]

6 August 1834, at the Castle inn, Marlborough

Present

Lt. Col. Warneford, the Revd. E. Goddard, Lt. Gen. Popham,

Ambrose Goddard, esq., J. H. Penruddocke, esq., Sir J. D. Astley, Lt. Col. Vilett.

Trusteeship

The trustees examined the account of the receiver of the rents to Michaelmas 1833, upon which there appears to be a balance of £546 18*s.* 3*d.* which is to be carried to the next account.

The steward produced a copy of proposed rules and regulations of the more important kind for the management of the hospital, which are approved of and confirmed. It is ordered that they be printed and that a copy be sent to each trustee and to each of the widows and the porter.

Estate

The steward produced a valuation at £499 19*s.* a year by Messrs. Iveson and Brown of the farm at Huish now in lease to Mr. George Young at £550 a year, which lease expires at Michaelmas next. It appearing that such valuation was made on the supposition that the land tax was to be paid by the trustees [it is] ordered that the steward be authorized to let the farm to Mr. Young according to that valuation deducting the amount of land tax, such land tax being continued to be paid by the tenant.

The steward also produced a valuation of the farm at Froxfield lately in lease to Mr. John Brown, such valuation being £190 18*s.*; at which rent the steward has let the farm to Messrs. Halcomb, which is confirmed.

Almshouse

see trusteeship business

Mayo trust

It appears by a separate account produced by the receiver that the amount of stock in the 3½ per cent reduced annuities standing in the names of John Pearse and T. G. B. Estcourt, esqs., trustees of the fund established by the late Revd. Charles Mayo, had accumulated to £3,290 10*s.* 7*d.*

Signatures

Francis Warneford, Ambrose Goddard, Thomas Vilett, E. W. L. Popham, J. Dugdale Astley. [The initials of the Revd. E. Goddard and J. H. Penruddocke were pencilled in by the clerk, but they did not sign]

The following are the most important of the subsisting rules, orders, and regulations for the government of the hospital, revised, approved of, and confirmed at a general meeting of the trustees held at Marlborough 8 [*rectius* 6] August 1834.

1. The steward shall keep regular books of accounts.

2. The steward shall attend meetings and enter minutes of the proceedings. The trustees shall meet yearly on the first Wednesday in August unless the Wiltshire assizes should happen to be held in that week, in which case the meeting shall be on the Wednesday following. [*Notes.* 4 August 1847, altered to first Wednesday in July; 4 July 1849, altered to second Wednesday in July; 16 July 1852, altered to second Thursday in July, unless assizes]
N.B. The trustees resident in the neighbourhood usually view the state of the hospital and all the apartments belonging to it about a month before the general annual meeting and report thereupon to such meeting.
3. Divine service shall be performed in the chapel every Wednesday and Friday, and twice a day every Sunday with a sermon.
4. The widows shall constantly attend divine service and, while present, behave with propriety. In case of the absence of any widow without satisfactory explanation her quarter's allowance shall be suspended until the pleasure of the trustees is known, and such fine may be imposed as the trustees in their discretion shall think fit.
5. Any widow desirous of leave of absence may be furnished by the porter for her signature with a printed form, which shall be presented to the trustees, wherein shall be specified the length of absence she requires, which shall not exceed altogether 13 weeks in any year. The porter shall then certify under his hand that the widow applying is, at the time of application, abiding at her apartment in the hospital as her home, and how many days or weeks, if any, such widow may have been absent during the year in which such application is made. In order that the porter may ascertain the residence of each widow more exactly he shall keep a book with the names of each widow and 52 columns for each week in the year and shall every Sunday note down which widows have been present in, and which absent from, the hospital during the preceding week. No widow shall at any time be deemed present unless she shall lodge in her own apartment in the hospital. To make provision for widows who may wish occasionally to spend a winter with their friends or relations, and to save travelling expenses, those who petition for leave of absence at the end of one year may at the same time present a second petition for leave of absence during the following year, and the length of absence allowed during 2 years may be allowed in the end of 1 year and the beginning of the next at the same time. All widows shall leave directions with the porter where letters will reach them when absent.
6. Every widow who shall be absent from the hospital for a week or more at any one time, unless hindered by some reasonable cause, shall forfeit her allowance during her absence. If absent for 14 days at any one time, or for any 30 days in any one year, without the licence in writing of some trustee, unless hindered by sickness or other reasonable cause, [she] shall be liable to be expelled and her house deemed vacant.

7. The steward shall each quarter examine the porter's book and suspend till the next general meeting of the trustees the quarterly dividend of such widows as by non-residence shall offend against the above regulations. Of which meeting every widow so offending shall have notice requiring her to attend thereat, provided she can be found, [so] that she may show cause, if she can, why she should not be expelled or otherwise punished according to the discretion of the trustees.
8. No widow shall keep any child or maidservant in the hospital for a whole week without the consent in writing of some trustee, nor any man after the gate is locked.
9. All the widows shall behave respectfully towards each other and all persons belonging to the hospital, and especially towards the trustees, chaplain, and steward, under forfeiture of stipend until due submission or amendment.
10. If any widow shall be guilty of disorderly behaviour or abusive language, and it shall within 3 weeks be sufficiently testified to two trustees, the offender shall forfeit a week's allowance for the first offence, her allowance for any time not exceeding a month for the second offence, and for the third offence may by five or more of the trustees be expelled.
11. Any widow found guilty of living incontinently, or of any other heinous offence, may by five or more trustees be expelled.
12. If any widow shall contract marriage she shall, within 10 days thereafter, depart or be expelled. Her allowance shall from the date of the marriage be suspended.
13. Any widow found guilty of drunkenness, cursing, or swearing shall for the first offence forfeit 5*s*., for the second shall, after admonition by any of the trustees or by the chaplain or steward, forfeit 20*s*., and for the third shall, having been admonished of the second by the chaplain in the chapel, forfeit her allowance during the discretion of the trustees and be liable to expulsion.
14. Every widow shall keep in repair the glass windows of her apartments from any damage done by herself or inmates.
15. The outward door of the hospital shall be locked by the porter at 9 o'clock every night from Lady day till Michaelmas and not opened till 5 o'clock the next morning, and be locked at 7 o'clock every night and not opened till 7 o'clock the next morning from Michaelmas till Lady day.
16. Two lists shall be kept of the vacancies which take place in the hospital. One shall contain the vacancies among the clergy and manor widows and the other the vacancies among the lay widows not being manor widows. Each trustee shall in turn nominate a widow in each list as places shall become vacant.
17. The steward shall on every vacancy give notice thereof in writing to the trustee whose turn it shall be to nominate, and of the district from which another widow is to be nominated. Such trustee shall be obliged

to fill up such vacancy within 6 months after the date of the notice. In case there shall be any doubt or dispute about the qualification of the widow to be nominated it shall be referred to, and determined by, the trustees at their next general meeting.

18. Every trustee who shall absent himself from two general annual meetings successively, due notice thereof having been given to him by the steward, unless prevented by sickness or by attendance in Parliament, shall forfeit his turn to nominate until he shall attend a meeting in person. The right of nomination shall pass to the trustee next in rotation. [*Note*. 6 August 1845 attendance in Parliament expunged]
19. On any vacancy in clergy widows' apartments, if no clergy widow properly qualified shall be nominated within 3 months from the time of the vacancy happening, the steward shall make known such vacancy by advertisement in some London newspaper, in case of a vacancy for London and Westminster, and in some one or more Wiltshire newspaper for the several counties. If no application shall be made by a clergy widow from the proper district within 12 months or by a clergy widow from a different district, but in other respects duly qualified, within 24 months from the date of such advertisement, then the trustees may supply such vacant apartment at the end of such 24 months with a lay widow resident within the district for which the vacancy happened.
20. In order to adopt a uniform rule for determining who are proper objects in cases of vacancies, the trustees will confine their nominations of widows to be chosen from a particular district to such whose parochial settlement shall be within such district at the time of the vacancy occuring, or whose last place of residence shall have usually been within such district for 40 days previous to such vacancy.
21. No lease, or copy of court roll, for lives shall be granted of any part of the trust estates, except of cottages and gardens and of small plots of land, not exceeding in any one case 3 acres, adjoining or near thereto.
22. A copy of these rules and orders shall be delivered to each widow at the time of her admission to the hospital, and a copy shall also be preserved by the porter.

5 August 1835, at the Castle inn, Marlborough

Present

Lt. Col. Warneford, the Revd. E. Goddard, Lt. Gen. Popham, John Pearse, esq., Sir J. D. Astley, bt.

Trusteeship

The trustees examined the account of the receiver of the rents to Michaelmas 1834, upon which there appears to be a balance of £413 9*s*. 3*d*. which is to be carried to the next account.

Estate

Several hundred pounds having been lately raised by voluntary subscription and expended in the improvement of Oare Hill, by which several estates belonging to the trustees are materially benefited by having the communication with Marlborough market opened to them, the steward is authorized to subscribe 20 gns. on behalf of the trustees as a contribution towards such improvement.

On the application of Mr. George Young [it is] ordered that two cottages be built near his down barn at an expense not exceeding £100, provided the steward shall find that they may be let at not less than £4 4*s.* a year.

Ordered that Mr. W. R. Brown be employed to value the farm at Chirton in the occupation of Mr. W. Hayward and the farm at Milton in the occupation of Mr. Guy Warwick. The steward is authorized to let those farms at Mr. Brown's valuation.

An application was made by Charles Naish, the purchaser of a cottage at Froxfield now in lease to the representatives of Charles Cook, for leave to put in two additional lives. The trustees do not consent to comply with such application.

Mayo trust

It appears by a separate account produced by the receiver that the amount of stock in the 3½ per cent reduced annuities standing in the names of John Pearse and T. G. B. Estcourt, esqs., trustees of the fund established by the late Revd. Charles Mayo, had accumulated to £3,407 10*s.* 7*d.*

Signatures

Francis Warneford, John Pearse, John Awdry, E. W. L. Popham, J. Dugdale Astley, E. Goddard.

3 August 1836, at the Castle inn, Marlborough

Present

The marquess of Ailesbury, the Revd. Edward Goddard, Lt. Gen. Popham, John Awdry, esq., Ambrose Goddard, esq., Sir J. D. Astley, bt., Lt. Col. Vilett.

Trusteeship

The trustees examined the account of the receiver of the rents to Michaelmas 1835, upon which there appears to be a balance of £203 10*s.* 5*d.* which is to be carried to his next account.

The trustees now present elect Earl Bruce, the Revd. John Ashfordby Trenchard, D.D., and William Codrington, esq., to be trustees in place of William Northey, esq., Francis Warneford, esq., and John Pearse, esq., deceased, and direct that a deed of trust be prepared for vesting the trust estates in them and the remaining trustees against the next meeting of the trustees.

In addition to the name of Col. Vilett, ordered at the meeting of trustees held 7 August 1833, it is now ordered that the name of Sir J. D. Astley be added [to] that of Mr. Estcourt (Mr. Pearse having lately died) in the investment of the South Sea annuities belonging to the trust and of the 3½ per cent annuities being the Mayo trust fund.

Mr. Estcourt having been prevented by his parliamentary duties from attending this day [it is] resolved that the cause of his non-attendance be allowed as satisfactory.

Estate

The steward reported that two new cottages had been built on Huish Hill in pursuance of the order made at the last meeting of the trustees but that, it having been thought very desirable to cover the cottages with slate instead of thatch in a situation adjoining to the farmyard and where it would be difficult to obtain a supply of water in case of fire, the expense had been increased to £120, and that he had let the cottages at a corresponding increase of rent, viz. at £5 per annum. The trustees approve of the expenditure of £120 for the reasons stated by the steward.

The steward read a letter from Mr. John Brown, the renter of the brewery buildings, dwelling house, malthouse, and Cross Keys public house at Froxfield under an order made 3 August 1831, proposing to give up his tenancy from Lady day last. It appearing that the premises are underlet by Mr. Brown at considerably higher rents than he pays to the trustees [it is] ordered that the offer of Mr. Brown be accepted.

Mayo trust

It appears by a separate account produced by the receiver that the amount of stock in the 3½ per cent reduced annuities standing in the names of John Pearse and T. G. B. Estcourt, esqs., trustees of the fund established by the late Revd. Charles Mayo, had accumulated to £3,527 15*s.* 10*d.*

and see trusteeship business

Signatures

Ailesbury, chairman, E. W. L. Popham, E. Goddard, John Awdry, Thomas Vilett. [The names of Sir J. D. Astley and Mr. A. Goddard were pencilled in by the clerk, but they did not sign] [*Margin.* Mr. Penruddocke was ill and unable to travel]

16 August 1837, at the Castle inn, Marlborough

Present

Revd. Edward Goddard, chairman, John Awdry, esq., T. G. B. Estcourt, esq., Sir J. D. Astley, bt., J. H. Penruddocke, esq., Lt. Col. T. Vilett, the Revd. Dr. Trenchard, William Codrington, esq.

Trusteeship

The trustees examined the account of the receiver of the rents to Michaelmas 1836, upon which there appears to be a balance of £106 7*s.* 11*d.* which is to be carried to his next account.

The trustees now present executed a conveyance of the trust estates to Earl Bruce, the Revd. John Ashfordby Trenchard, D.D., and William Codrington, esq., the three new trustees chosen at the meeting held 3 August 1836, vesting the estates in such new trustees jointly with themselves.

A declaration of the trusts of £2,600 South Sea stock belonging to the charity, of £235 9*s.* 5*d.* of the same stock, the produce of the exchange of lands with the Kennet and Avon Canal Company, and of £113 9*s.* 2*d.* of the same stock held in trust for the rector of Huish was executed by Thomas G. Bucknall Estcourt, esq., Sir John Dugdale Astley, bt., and Thomas Vilett, esq., the trustees into whose names those stocks have been transferred, in pursuance of the minutes of 7 August 1833 and 3 August 1836.

Estate

Resolved that the steward be authorized and directed to take the necessary steps for obtaining a commutation of the tithes of the estates belonging to the trustees of the Somerset hospital, under the Act of Parliament for that purpose, as soon as he shall think it desirable to proceed in the respective parishes.

In furtherance of the foregoing resolution the trustees now present signed a power of attorney, under the powers of that Act of Parliament, authorizing Messrs. Thomas Merriman, Thomas Baverstock Merriman, and William Clark Merriman, or either of them, to act for them in the execution of the Act.

The trustees having in consequence of the low price of corn found it necessary in the course of the last five or six years to reduce the rents of several of their farms, and the prices of corn having now become considerably higher, the steward is authorized and directed to consult some competent land valuer and to require an advance in the present rents in respect of such farms for which he shall be advised an increased rent ought now to be paid.

An application was made to this meeting by James Langfield of Ramsbury, who had built by contract a new house and offices at Froxfield in place of the Blue Lion public house which was some time ago burnt down, stating that in consequence of Mr. Merriman having interfered on behalf of the trustees he had finished the work in a more substantial manner than was at first intended, that the property would be increased in value nearly £300, and that he had incurred a loss of nearly £60 which, being a man with a large family, he was totally unable to bear. Therefore he prayed some contribution towards his loss. The trustees, being satisfied that the statement made by James

Langfield is in a great measure correct and that the value of the trust property has been increased, order that he be paid £15 towards his loss in the hope that Mr. Ball, the person with whom he contracted, will make him a similar allowance.

Almshouse

The steward stated the circumstances under which he had thought it right to withhold from Widow Scriven the payment of her quarter's stipend to Lady day last, namely that she persisted in suffering one of her daughters, whose conduct was very objectionable, to remain in her tenement notwithstanding repeated admonitions given to her by the steward to the contrary. [It is] resolved that the trustees approve of this step taken by the steward and that, in case Mrs. Scriven shall commit any further infraction of the rules of the hospital, the steward report her case specially to the trustees and suspend her stipend.

Mayo trust

It appears by a separate account produced by the receiver that the amount of stock in the 3½ per cent reduced annuities standing in the names of T. G. B. Estcourt and Thomas Vilett, esqs., and Sir J. D. Astley, bt., had accumulated to £3,648 7*s.* 11*d.*

Signatures

E. Goddard, chairman, Thomas Vilett, J. H. Penruddocke, T. G. Bucknall Estcourt, J. Dugdale Astley, J. A. Trenchard, William Codrington. [The name of Mr. Awdry was pencilled in by the clerk, but he did not sign]

1 August 1838, at the Castle inn, Marlborough

Present

Revd. Edward Goddard, chairman, John Awdry, esq., Gen. Popham, T. G. B. Estcourt, esq., Sir J. D. Astley, bt., Ambrose Goddard, esq., Lt. Col. T. Vilett.

Trusteeship

The trustees examined the account of the receiver of the rents to Michaelmas 1837, upon which there appears to be a balance of £16 5*s.* 10*d.* which is to be carried to his next account.

The following letter addressed by the receiver was produced and read, and ordered to be entered upon the minutes of the meeting.

To the Trustees of the Somerset Hospital at Froxfield
My Lords and Gentlemen
In compliance with the order made at your meeting on 16 August 1837 the several principal farms belonging to the trust have been revalued, and I am happy to say that I have concluded agreements with the present

tenants at an advance of rents in the whole of £160 to commence chiefly from Michaelmas next.

Besides this additional income your rental will be further increased about £45 in the current year by the falling in of a copyhold bargain at Froxfield on the death of a Mrs. Merriwether.

As it is probable you may think fit, in consequence of this increase of income, to consider whether some early addition may not be made to the stipend of the widows, I beg leave to submit to your consideration the following circumstances as connected with the general state of the affairs of the trust.

In August 1829, when I had the honour of being appointed your receiver, the balance in the hands of my predecessor which was paid over to me amounted to £907 13*s.* 7*d.* The balance in hand on my present account is only £16 5*s.* 10*d.* During this period I have, however, invested £1,000 in Exchequer bills, which I now hold on behalf of the trustees, and the stipends of the widows have for the last 6 years been increased £2 a year, amounting to £600. There have also been expended during the same period, besides the customary annual expenses of the estate, upwards of £700 in building a house for the porter and several new cottages, which cottages produce an income of about £20 a year.

It is to be observed too that the very low prices of corn during these years occasioned a considerable diminution of rents.

Mr. John Brown, the tenant of the brewery, dwelling house, malthouse, and the Cross Keys public house at Froxfield at £90 a year, having fallen into pecuniary difficulties, I have been obliged to take to his bargain and to let it to several different tenants. The premises were left by Mr. Brown much out of repair and consequently a considerable expenditure will be necessary to reinstate them, but to remunerate for this I have obtained an increase of rent of about £20 a year exclusive of the brewery, which may either be pulled down and the materials sold for defraying the expense of the before mentioned dilapidations or be used in erecting a brewery, on a much smaller scale at the back of the dwelling house, if the tenant will give an adequate rent for such brewery, which I think it not improbable he may agree to do.

Exclusive of the above, the necessary expenses attending the commutation of tithes, and the valuation of the farms, I am not aware of any material outlay now required from the trust funds, and I beg leave to express my hope that the foregoing statement will not only satisfactorily account for the reduced balance in my hands but will also enable the trustees to decide whether they may safely exercise the most gratifying part of their duty by adding somewhat to the present stipends of the widows.

I have the honour to be, my lords and gentlemen, your most obedient servant.

Thomas Merriman

Marlborough, 1 August 1838

Estate

A letter was read from Mr. William Kingstone complaining of his not having been accepted as tenant of Hill Barn farm in the parish of Milton. The trustees do not see any necessity for their interference in this business.

A letter was read from Mr. Stephen Snook requesting a lease for 21 years from the death of Mrs. … [*MS. blank*] Hawkins, upon whose life he holds a tenement and shop at Froxfield, on the ground of his proposing to lay out a considerable sum in putting the premises in complete repair. [It is] resolved that a lease or agreement shall be granted to Mr. Snook for 21 years from Michaelmas next at a rent of £20 a year clear of all taxes and repairs, provided he shall expend at least £75 in substantial repairs to the satisfaction of the steward and shall covenant to keep the premises in good repair.

and see trusteeship business

Almshouse

On an investigation by the trustees of the state of revenue and expenditure of the trust estate they are of opinion that an increase of £2 a year may be made to the widows' stipends. They accordingly order that such increase be made and that the first payment thereof be made at Christmas next.

Widow Scriven (no. 40) applied to the trustees to rescind the order made at their last meeting for withholding from her a quarter of a year's stipend. [It is] resolved that the trustees see no reason for rescinding their order.

Ordered that all trees, not shrubs, planted against any tenement in the quadrangle be removed and that no flower border be permitted to remain higher than 1 ft. above the adjoining footpath.

Mayo trust

It appears by a separate account produced by the receiver that the amount of stock in the 3½ per cent reduced annuities standing in the names of T. G. B. Estcourt and Thomas Vilett, esqs., and Sir J. D. Astley, bt., had accumulated to £3,776 8*s.* 1*d.*

Signatures

E. Goddard, T. G. Bucknall Estcourt, E. W. L. Popham, Ambrose Goddard, J. Dugdale Astley, Thomas Vilett.

7 August 1839, at the Castle inn, Marlborough

Present

The marquess of Ailesbury, John Awdry, esq., Gen. Popham, Ambrose Goddard, esq., Sir J. D. Astley, bt., Col. Vilett, William Codrington, esq.

Trusteeship

The trustees examined the account of the receiver of the rents to Michaelmas 1838, upon which there appears to be a balance of £427 14*s*. 8*d*. which is to be carried to his next account.

The non-attendance at this meeting of Earl Bruce, who has been absent at two meetings of the trustees, was excused on the ground that Parliament is still sitting.

The trustees now present elect the Rt. Hon. Henry Pierrepont and Horatio Nelson Goddard, esq., to be trustees in place of the Revd. Dr. Trenchard, D.D., and the Revd. Edward Goddard, deceased, and direct that a deed of trust be prepared for vesting the trust estates in them and the remaining trustees against the next meeting of the trustees.

Estate

The old brewhouse at Froxfield formerly occupied by Mr. John Brown having been many years vacant, and it being represented to the trustees that cottage accommodation for the population in the parish of Froxfield is much wanted, [it is] ordered that the steward obtain a plan and estimate of the expense of converting the materials of the brewhouse into six or eight cottages, and resolved that the marquess of Ailesbury, Gen. Popham, and Sir John Astley be authorized to inspect any such plans and estimates and to give such orders on the subject as they shall think proper.

Almshouse

Ordered that the salary of the porter be advanced £5 a year from Michaelmas next, making his salary from that time £15 a year.

Mayo trust

It appears by a separate account produced by the receiver that the amount of stock in the 3½ per cent reduced annuities standing in the names of T. G. B. Estcourt and Thomas Vilett, esqs., and Sir J. D. Astley, bt., had accumulated to £3,908 19*s*. 11*d*.

Signatures

Ailesbury, E. W. L. Popham, J. Dugdale Astley, Thomas Vilett, William Codrington, Ambrose Goddard, John Awdry.

5 August 1840, at the Castle inn, Marlborough

Present

The marquess of Ailesbury, John Awdry, esq., Gen. Popham, Ambrose Goddard, esq., Sir J. D. Astley, bt., Col. Vilett, the Earl Bruce, the Rt. Hon. Henry Pierrepont.

Trusteeship

The trustees examined the account of the receiver of the rents to Michaelmas 1839, upon which there appears to be a balance of £19 10*s*. 8*d*. which he is to pay over to his successor in office.

The following letter from Mr. Merriman was read.

To the Trustees of the Somerset Hospital at Froxfield
My Lords and Gentlemen
Having already taken the liberty of addressing a letter to each individual trustee signifying my intention to tender my resignation of the office of steward at your annual meeting to be held on this day, I now beg to resign into your hands that important and honourable office the duties of which you have for many years most kindly entrusted to my management.
In doing this permit me, my lords and gentlemen, to offer to you my most cordial and respectful thanks for the confidence and liberality with which I have been invariably honoured, and to assure you that, so long as it may please God to continue to me the enjoyment of health and strength, I shall not merely with willingness but with the greatest pleasure lend to my successor any assistance which my long acquaintance with the affairs of the trust may enable me to afford.
I have the honour to be, my lords and gentlemen, your much obliged and most obedient servant.
Thomas Merriman
Marlborough, 5 August 1840

Moved by Gen. Popham, seconded by Mr. Awdry, and resolved unanimously that the trustees have learnt with sincere regret the intention of Mr. Merriman to resign the office of steward to the Somerset hospital at Froxfield, of which he has executed the duties during a period of 11 years with the most zealous attention, and beg to express to him how fully sensible they are of his valuable services and to offer to him their best and warmest acknowledgements.

Moved by the marquess of Ailesbury, seconded by Sir J. D. Astley, and resolved unanimously that Thomas Baverstock Merriman of Marlborough, gentleman, be, and he is hereby by virtue of the powers given by the will of the late Sarah, duchess dowager of Somerset, and since confirmed by the High Court of Chancery, appointed, steward of all manors and receiver of all rents, revenues, and estates to the hospital belonging, and [he is] to hold all courts and do all other things to the office of steward and receiver belonging.

T. G. B. Estcourt, esq., being detained in London by his duties in Parliament his absence at this meeting is on that account excused, as is the absence of J. H. Penruddocke, esq., on account of ill health.

Estate

The state of the buildings at Froxfield, both at the old brewhouse and at Mr. Francis's house and workshops, was considered. It is referred to the marquess of Ailesbury, Gen. Popham, Sir J. D. Astley, and Mr. Pierrepont, or any two of them, to give such directions either for pulling down part and selling the materials, for repairing, or [for] converting into cottages any portion as they may think fit. The steward is directed to obtain plans and such other information as may be necessary for enabling the trustees to judge of the measures most advisable to be adopted, and he is to convene a meeting of the before mentioned trustees when he is prepared with the information.

Ordered that in future the tenants of the charity estates be required to pay their rents as follows, viz. the half-year's rents due at Michaelmas in the last week of December and the half-year's rents due at Lady day in the last week of June.

Almshouse

Ordered that a sufficient number of new privies be built at the hospital under the direction of the before mentioned trustees.

The steward is directed to subscribe, in the name of the trustees, 1 gn. a year to the district Society for Promoting Christian Knowledge for the convenience of being supplied with bibles and prayer books from that society.

Mayo trust

It appears by a separate account produced by the receiver that the amount of stock in the new 3½ per cent reduced annuities standing in the names of T. G. B. Estcourt, esq., Thomas Vilett, esq., and Sir J. D. Astley, bt., had accumulated to £4,048 6*s.* 8*d.*

Signatures

Ailesbury, chairman, J. Dugdale Astley, Henry Pierrepont, Thomas Vilett, Ambrose Goddard.

4 August 1841, at the Castle inn, Marlborough

Present

T. G. B. Estcourt, esq., in the chair, J. Awdry, esq., Ambrose Goddard, esq., Sir J. D. Astley, bt., Col. Vilett, the Rt. Hon. H. Pierrepont, H. N. Goddard, esq., William Codrington, esq.

Trusteeship

The trustees examined the account of the receiver of the rents to Michaelmas 1840, upon which there appears to be a balance of £190 7*s.* which he is to carry to his next account.

The Revd. Mr. Bleeck, the chaplain, having applied for some aid towards building a room for a Sunday school at Huish, [it is] resolved that £50 be appropriated to the fund for building such school and that Sir John Astley and Mr. Pierrepont be requested to examine the premises and confer with Mr. Bleeck as to the appropriation of the money.

The marquess of Ailesbury and Lord Bruce being prevented from attending this meeting by domestic affliction, and Gen. Popham and Mr. Penruddocke by ill health, their absence is excused.

Estate

The steward stated that, in the opinion of the surveyors whom he had consulted, it would be more desirable to pull down the present brewery at Froxfield and to build cottages from the ground than to convert any portion of the brewery buildings into cottages. [It is] ordered, in consequence of the general bad state of the habitations at Froxfield, that eight new cottages be built there on a site to be selected by Sir J. D. Astley and Mr. Pierrepont and under their supervision, and that if necessary one of the Exchequer bills should be sold to defray the expense.

The steward is empowered to agree with Mr. Drury, the owner of a cottage held for his life under the trustees, for a surrender of his interest in case it should be thought desirable to use the site for part of the new cottages.

Sir John Astley and Mr. Pierrepont are requested to report to the next meeting what they consider expedient to be done with regard to the house and buildings at Froxfield occupied by Mr. J. C. Francis.

The steward is directed to have the timber at Huish examined, [to] produce a general report thereon at the next meeting, and to order any portion thereof, that may appear to be desirable in the meantime, to be cut.

and see trusteeship business

Almshouse

The steward is directed to pay to Mrs. Braim, an inmate of the hospital, £30, the amount of stipend withheld by him from her in consequence of her absence without leave, and he is directed to admonish her to be very cautious not again to exceed her leave of absence.

Mrs. Graves, one of the widows, having received into her apartment a daughter and three grandchildren who have been resident there a fortnight without leave, the steward is directed to order the immediate removal of them under pain of suspension of salary.

Mayo trust

It appears by a separate account produced by the receiver that the amount of stock in the new 3½ per cents standing in the names of T. G. B. Estcourt, esq., Thomas Vilett, esq., and Sir J. D. Astley, bt., had accumulated to £4,193 15*s*.

Signatures

T. G. Bucknall Estcourt, Henry Manvers Pierrepont, Thomas Vilett, J. Dugdale Astley, John Awdry, William Codrington, H. N. Goddard, Ambrose Goddard.

3 August 1842, at the Castle inn, Marlborough

Present

The marquess of Ailesbury, in the chair, John Awdry, esq., Rt.

Hon. Henry Pierrepont, A. Goddard, esq., T. G. B. Estcourt, esq., Col. Vilett, Earl Bruce.

Trusteeship

The trustees examined the account of the receiver of the rents to Michaelmas 1841, upon which there appears to be a balance of £189 18*s*. which he is to carry to his next account.

The trustees now present unanimously elect the Lord Ernest Augustus Charles Brudenell Bruce, M.P., George Wroughton Wroughton, esq., and Francis Leyborne Popham, esq., to be trustees in place of John Hungerford Penruddocke, esq., Sir John Dugdale Astley, bt., and William Codrington, esq., and direct that a deed of trust be prepared for vesting the trust estates in them and the remaining trustees against the next meeting of the trustees.

Gen. Popham and H. N. Goddard, esq., being prevented from attending this meeting by ill health their absence is excused.

Estate

The steward reported that he had, in pursuance of the minute of the last meeting, agreed with Mr. Drury to give up to him the stables and yard and one small cottage, part of late Hawkins's lifehold and adjoining Mr. Drury's homestead, and to fence off the yard, in exchange for Mr. Drury's lifehold cottages and garden adjoining the old brewhouse.

Mr. Pierrepont recommended that a small brewhouse, with stabling adjoining, should be erected at the back of the Cross Keys public house at Froxfield in lieu of that part of the old brewhouse which has been left standing and [which] would require a considerable outlay to make it efficient, and [in lieu] of the present stabling, which is very bad. [Also] that the lifehold cottage now obtained from Mr. Drury, and a small cottage near the Cross Keys, should be repaired and that six new cottages should be built on a site which he had marked out. He had given directions accordingly.

Mr. Pierrepont also reported that he considered it expedient to allow the materials and £25 towards the repairs and alterations at the house occupied by Mr. John Francis, which had been pointed out to him on the spot, and that Francis was willing to complete such repairs and alterations on those terms, which are approved of accordingly.

The steward presented the report of Mr. Guy Warwick as to the timber at Huish, in consequence of whose recommendation no timber had been cut.

An application from Messrs. W. and T. Halcomb, the tenants of the Manor farm and late Brown's farm at Froxfield, praying for a reduction of rent in consequence of the diminished value of the farms by the discontinuance of coach horses on the road was read, and the steward reported that Mr. Wickham had given notice of his intention to quit the malthouse at Froxfield in consequence of there being no land to occupy with it and of the amount of the rent. [It is] resolved that the trustees see no reason for reducing Messrs. Halcomb's rent and, in case of their declining to hold on the present terms, the steward is directed to make such arrangements for dividing their holdings as may seem desirable.

The steward is directed to do such repairs as are absolutely necessary to the house and buildings at Oare occupied by John Edmonds which are of a very inferior description and were left in bad condition by the late tenant, who quitted insolvent.

The several tenements in the hospital, and the porter's house, having been assessed to the poor's rate the steward is directed to take an opinion of counsel as to the rateability of the property and, in case it shall appear to be chargeable, he is to pay the rates from time to time. He is to take the necessary steps for reducing the present rating of £3 per house if possible.

A letter from the Revd. T. G. P. Atwood applying for permission to rent 10 acres of land was read. [It is] resolved that such request be acceded to provided he can make the necessary arrangements with Messrs. Halcomb, the tenants of the farm.

A letter from several occupiers in Froxfield complaining of annoyance by the watering of one of the farm meads was read. The steward is directed to investigate the matter before the next meeting of the trustees.

Almshouse

Mrs. Graves's daughter and grandchildren having quitted her apartment in April last the steward is directed to pay her the three quarters stipend which he had withheld in pursuance of the order of the trustees at their last meeting.

The steward reported that, in consequence of Mrs. Richardson having attempted to hang herself in June last, he had considered himself called upon to make enquiry into the circumstances and that he had reported the matter to the marquess of Ailesbury, under whose direction the former enquiry into the conduct of Mrs. Richardson had been made in 1840. By desire of his lordship and Mr. Pierrepont he had had a report from the Medical Officer of the establishment and from Mr. Gardner, another medical gentleman, as to her state of mind. A letter from Mrs. Richardson expressing regret for what had occurred was read. [It is] resolved that in consequence of her expression of contrition her late conduct be forgiven, but the steward is directed to write to Mrs. Richardson and inform her that on any future complaint steps will be taken for removing her from Froxfield.

The steward reported that, having for the last 20 years understood from the two former stewards that auctions in the apartments in the hospital were not permitted, he had on two occasions objected to such sales being held, by the sheriff's officer under an execution and by the creditors of a deceased widow, and that he had remonstrated against a subsequent sale which had occasioned a complaint to be made to one of the trustees. [It is] ordered that in future no sales by auction be allowed in the houses or on any part of the hospital premises.

and see estate business

Mayo trust

It appears by a separate account produced by the receiver that the amount of stock in the new 3½ per cents standing in the names of Thomas Grimston Bucknall Estcourt, esq., and Thomas Vilett, esq., trustees of the fund established by the late Revd. Charles Mayo, had accumulated to £4,341 10*s*. 9*d*.

Signatures

Ailesbury, Thomas Vilett, Ambrose Goddard, T. G. Bucknall Estcourt, John Awdry.

2 August 1843, at the Ailesbury Arms inn, Marlborough

Present

T. G. B. Estcourt, esq., M.P., in the chair, Thomas Vilett, esq., the Rt. Hon. Henry Pierrepont, H. N. Goddard, esq., the Lord Ernest Bruce, Col. Wroughton, F. L. Popham, esq.

Trusteeship

The trustees examined the account of the receiver of the rents to Michaelmas 1842, upon which there appears to be a balance of £200 0*s*. 11*d*. due to him which he is to be allowed in his next account.

The trustees now present executed a conveyance of the trust estates to the Lord Ernest Augustus Charles Brudenell Bruce, M.P., George Wroughton Wroughton, esq., and Francis Leyborne Popham, esq., the three trustees chosen at the meeting held on 3 August 1842, vesting the estates in such new trustees jointly with the old trustees.

The trustees now present signed a new power of attorney authorizing Messrs. Thomas Baverstock Merriman and William Clark Merriman, or either of them, to act for the trustees in the execution of the Tithe Commutation Act.

Upon full consideration of all the circumstances with regard to the applications of Mrs. Havart and Mrs. Marenday to be admitted to the clergy tenements now vacant the trustees are of opinion that, as neither of those widows is duly qualified according to the resolution of 17 September 1785 and the rules for governance of the hospital, the regulations should be strictly adhered to and that the 12 months specified by rule 19 should be allowed to expire before any widow, other than one duly qualified, is nominated.

Mr. Awdry being prevented from attending this meeting by ill health his absence is excused.

Estate

The steward reported that, having in pursuance of the order of the trustees at their last meeting commenced repairing the old farmhouse at Oare, the building was found to be so very defective as not to warrant any outlay upon it, that he had therefore consulted such of the trustees as could be conveniently assembled at the time of the Wiltshire quarter sessions held at Marlborough in October last, and [that] by their authority a new house had been built on a small scale under the immediate direction of Col. Wroughton. [It is] resolved that [his actions] be approved of and confirmed and that such further repairs as are necessary should be done there.

The steward reported that he had had six new cottages and a new brewhouse and stabling erected at the Cross Keys at Froxfield, that he had a considerable amount of necessary repairs done to various other cottages, and that some further repairs to cottages were still wanting.

The steward is directed, in pursuance of the minute of 4 August 1841, to sell a £500 Exchequer bill to defray these expenses and the cost of the new house at Oare.

Two letters from the Revd. Francis Dyson on the subject of his wish to add a life in property at Chirton held by him for two lives, or that the trustees would purchase his present interest, were read. [It is] resolved that the trustees feel that they cannot depart from their resolution to decline renewing lifeholds.

A renewed application having been made by Messrs. Halcomb for abatement in their rent the trustees do not consider that any abatement should be made.

The steward stated the circumstances under which an arrear of £40 appeared in the account to be due in respect of Hill Barn farm, occupied by Messrs. Goodman and Burfitt. The steward is directed to endeavour to obtain a reference of the matters in difference between Mr. Burfitt and Mr. Goodman, and Col. Wroughton is requested and empowered, with the assistance of the steward, to endeavour to effect some arrangement or compromise of the matter.

An application from the parish of Froxfield for the grant by the trustees of a piece of ground for the enlargement of the churchyard, and a contribution towards the cost of consecration, was read. The minutes of 3 August 1831 and 7 August 1833 on this subject were likewise read. [It is] resolved that the trustees are willing to grant a piece of ground and request Col. Wroughton and Mr. Popham to select a site, but the trustees do not feel that they are called upon to contribute towards the consecration thereof.

The steward is directed to make the necessary arrangements, under the direction of Col. Wroughton, for adding about 100 acres to the farm at Oare occupied by Mr. John Edmonds by taking that portion from the farm occupied by Mr. George Young.

Ordered that the steward, under the direction of Col. Wroughton, make an entirely new arrangement and letting of all the lands belonging to the almshouse in the parish of Milton and, if thought desirable, to build a new farmhouse on a spot to be selected by Col. Wroughton and to make such alterations in the buildings as Col. Wroughton may think proper. If necessary he is to sell the other Exchequer bill to pay for it.

The steward is directed immediately to investigate the circumstances as to some cottages and land at Milton, supposed to belong to the trustees and now encroached on or held by some person not entitled, and to take such measures as shall be necessary.

and see trusteeship business

Almshouse

Mrs. Bree having left the hospital without leave and having been absent from the view meeting the steward is directed to withhold her stipend until she conforms to the rules.

The trustees request Francis Leyborne Popham, esq., to be good enough to dispose of applications for leaves of absence to the widows in the same manner as was done by the late Gen. Popham.

Representation having been made of some irregularities prevailing in the college [it is] ordered that all the rules as to internal arrangement, particularly rule 8, be strictly enforced.

Col. Wroughton and Mr. Popham are requested to employ some surveyor to inspect and report on the general state of the almshouse and premises and several improvements now suggested, and to order them in case they think it desirable.

Mr. Bartlett resigned the office of surgeon and apothecary, and Mr. Lidderdale, his partner, and Mr. Barker of Hungerford offered themselves as candidates. The trustees present unanimously elected Mr. Barker but, to show that such election has not proceeded from any disapprobation of Mr. Lidderdale's conduct, they direct that he shall continue the care of the sick widows till Christmas next, when the present half year expires.

and see trusteeship business

Mayo trust

It appears by a separate account produced by the receiver that the amount of stock in the new 3½ per cents standing in the names of Thomas Grimston Bucknall Estcourt, esq., and Thomas Vilett, esq., trustees of the fund established by the late Revd. Charles Mayo, had accumulated to £4,487 11*s.* 7*d.*

Signatures

T. G. Bucknall Estcourt, Henry Pierrepont, Thomas Vilett, G. W. Wroughton, H. N. Goddard.

7 August 1844, at the Ailesbury Arms inn, Marlborough

Present

The marquess of Ailesbury, Ambrose Goddard, esq., Col. Vilett, Rt. Hon. Henry Pierrepont, H. N. Goddard, esq., Lord Ernest Bruce, M.P., Col. Wroughton, F. L. Popham, esq.

Trusteeship

The trustees examined the account of the receiver of the rents to Michaelmas 1843, upon which there appears to be a balance of £412 7*s*. 11½*d*. which he is to carry to his next account.

The steward read a letter from Mr. H. G. Awdry stating the intention of his father John Awdry, esq., to resign his trusteeship. The trustees, doubting the sufficiency of such letter as a resignation, think it better to decline acting on it.

T. G. Bucknall Estcourt, esq., and John Awdry, esq., being prevented from attending this meeting by ill health their absence is excused. Earl Bruce having been absent from two successive meetings his patronage is suspended under rule 18.

Estate

The trustees approve of the settlement made with Messrs. Goodman and Burfitt by allowing £10, part of the arrear, towards drainage etc. done by them.

Col. Wroughton and Mr. Popham having approved of a piece of ground, part of Horseshoe mead, staked out for the proposed addition to the churchyard at Froxfield, the steward is directed to prepare the necessary grant thereof to the parish, at the cost of the parish.

The steward reported that, Messrs. Halcomb having served him with notice of their intention to quit at Michaelmas next the farms at Froxfield rented by them, Mr. Thomas Halcomb had applied to become tenant of the Manor farm at a reduced rent but, as Mr. Halcomb did not intend to reside there, he had, in compliance with the expressed wishes of the trustees at their last meeting and by desire of such trustees as he could refer to at the time, declined to treat with Mr. Halcomb. He also stated that he had, under the direction of Col. Wroughton, given notice to Mr. W. Wickham to quit the malthouse in order to effect a general re-letting of the property at Froxfield.

The steward also reported that, having been unable to let the Froxfield farms solely in consequence of the state of cultivation and bad entry, he had after much negotiation arranged for an arbitration which is now in progress. [It is] resolved that the trustees approve of what has been done by the steward and direct him to make such arrangement, under the direction of Col. Wroughton, for letting the property at Froxfield as shall appear to be most advantageous.

The steward is directed, under the superintendance of Col. Wroughton, to take the necessary steps for selling such timber on the hospital estate as may be fit to cut and to plant where necessary.

A letter was read from Mr. Goodman applying for a return of the back rent which has been charged to him under the report and recommendation of Mr. Iveson of 5 January 1844. [It is] resolved that the further consideration of that be deferred until Mr. Goodman has quitted.

Almshouse

The steward stated that, finding that the absence of Mrs. Bree from the hospital as referred to by the minute of 2 August 1843 had been occasioned by severe indisposition which terminated in her death shortly after the meeting, he had paid the full amount of her stipend to her representatives, which is approved of and confirmed.

Mr. Money, the surveyor employed in pursuance of the minutes of the last meeting to report on the state of the hospital, having recommended considerable repair to the roof and some drains to be made, the steward stated that such works had been done accordingly.

The trustees considered the proposed plans for ranges of wood-houses in the two back courts and refer it to Col. Wroughton and Mr. F. Popham to give such orders for them as they may think proper.

Mr. Popham is requested to dispose of all applications for permissions for inmates in the hospital as well as applications for leaves of absence.

Resolved that no servant or nurse be allowed to sleep in the hospital except in case of severe illness or urgent necessity.

The trustees, observing on the large amount annually charged by the porter for mowing and [for] cleaning up the chapel and quadrangle, gardens, and courts about the hospital, desire that no similar bills be allowed in future but that the porter's salary be increased to £25 a year to cover such expenses. He is expected to keep the whole clean and neat for that sum, such increase to include tolling [the] bell and all tools.

Mayo trust

It appears by a separate account produced by the receiver that the amount of stock in the new 3½ per cents standing in the names of Thomas Grimston Bucknall Estcourt, esq., and Thomas Vilett, esq., trustees of the fund established by the late Revd. Charles Mayo, had accumulated to £4,635 12*s*.

Signatures

Ailesbury, G. W. Wroughton, Ernest Bruce, F. Leyborne Popham, H. N. Goddard, Thomas Vilett, Ambrose Goddard.

6 August 1845, at the Ailesbury Arms inn, Marlborough

Present

T. G. B. Estcourt, esq., M.P., in the chair, Earl Bruce, Ambrose Goddard, esq., Col. Vilett, Rt. Hon. H. Pierrepont, H. N. Goddard, esq., Col. Wroughton, F. L. Popham, esq.

Trusteeship

The trustees examined the account of the receiver of the rents to Michaelmas 1844, upon which there appears to be a balance of £676 15*s*. 3*d*. which he is to carry to his next account.

Some doubt having arisen as to the extent of the district comprised in the classes of widows for London and Westminster [it is] resolved that the trustees will in future confine their nominations to widows deriving their qualification from some place within 10 miles of Temple Bar.

The trustees now present unanimously elect Thomas Henry Sutton Sotheron, esq., M.P., and George Heneage Walker Heneage, esq., M.P., to be trustees in place of Gen. Edward William Leyborne Popham and John Awdry, esq., deceased, and direct that a deed of trust be prepared for vesting the trust estates in them and the remaining trustees against the next meeting of the trustees.

The marquess of Ailesbury and Lord Ernest Bruce being prevented from attending this meeting by attendance in Parliament their absence is excused.

Resolved that from henceforth the exemption from attending meetings of the trustees by attendance in Parliament be expunged from rule 18.

Estate

The steward reported that the conveyance of 27 poles, part of Horseshoe mead selected by Col. Wroughton and Mr. Popham for the addition to Froxfield churchyard, executed by the trustees since the last meeting had been perfected. The ground would be consecrated as soon as an appointment could be obtained from the bishop.

The result of the reference with Messrs. Halcomb on their quitting Froxfield farm was stated by the steward to have been an award of £313 17*s*. 6*d*. against Messrs. Halcomb for miscultivation of lands and dilapidations of buildings besides other matters in kind, and of costs amounting, exclusive of their own solicitor, to about £217.

The steward reported that, in consequence of the late season of the year at which, from the resistance made by Messrs. Halcomb, the umpire's decision could be obtained, he had been unable to make an advantageous division of the farms. He had therefore, under the advice of Col. Wroughton, let the whole to Mr. John Redman at £620 a year, which is approved of and confirmed.

Col. Wroughton and Mr. Popham are requested to direct such alterations and removals of barns and buildings at Froxfield, Huish, and Milton as they may think desirable, to discontinue, if they think fit, the large malthouse at Froxfield, which will require a considerable sum to be laid out on it, and to convert it into cottages or such other buildings as may seem advantageous.

The trustees approve of the letting of the farm at Fyfield and Clench, on which a new house has been built at Broomsgrove, to Mr. William Kingstone.

The steward reported that in consequence of the objections made to the entry on the farm he had, in conjunction with Mr. Kingstone, entered into a reference with Messrs. Goodman and Burfitt. An award of £46 had been made against Mr. Burfitt, and a quantity of straw, which had been removed, had been ordered to be brought back both by him and by Mr. Goodman.

Mr. Goodman's application for a return of the £30 paid by him as back rent, the consideration of which was postponed from the last meeting, was again considered. [It is] ordered that £25 be repaid to Mr. Goodman and the remainder be held as a partial outset against the expenses incidental to the reference.

Mr. W. Hayward having applied for a reduction of his rent the steward is directed to ascertain whether any improvements can be made on the farm with a view to increase the annual value and whether the rent now paid is a fair one.

Mr. Redman having applied for assistance towards chalking about 14 acres on Froxfield farm [it is] resolved that no allowance be made in the first instance, but the trustees will be disposed to make any fair allowance for chalking done by him to the land in question in case of Mr. Redman's death or quitting the farm within 5 years.

Mr. John Banning having claimed that the cottages at New Mill erected by him are built on his own freehold and, although the trustees consider the site to belong to the hospital estate, it appearing that he had built them under the supposition that the land was his own the steward is directed to make, with the concurrence Col. Wroughton, such terms with Banning as may appear equitable, regard being had to any liability he may have been under to repair the old cottages which had gone to decay.

Almshouse

The steward reported that in consequence of complaint by Mrs. Waldron, an inmate of the hospital, of violent conduct towards her by Mrs. Richardson, another inmate, he had reduced Mrs. Waldron's statement into writing and submitted it to Col. Wroughton and Mr. Popham. He also reported that, the whole body of widows having complained of serious imputations thrown at the respectability of the establishment by statements made by Mrs. Waldron and her daughter, who was resident with her under leave, that men were admitted into the quadrangle after the closing of the gate and at late hours, which appeared to be without foundation, he had in consequence retained both from Mrs. Richardson and Mrs. Waldron their last quarter's stipend and had directed both to attend the trustees this day. Mr. Popham explained all the circumstances of the cases as they had come to his knowledge from the enquiry he had made. [It is] resolved that the last quarter's allowance retained from each of them by the steward be forfeited, that Mrs. Richardson be admonished by the Revd. W. Bleeck, the chaplain, in the chapel upon her disorderly conduct, which has been frequently brought under the notice of the trustees, and that Mrs. Waldron's daughter be no longer permitted to remain in the hospital.

In consequence of persons having obtruded themselves into the chapel, to the annoyance of the widows, the steward is directed to take an opinion of counsel as to the powers of the trustees to exclude other persons than inmates of the hospital from the chapel and to take such measures as may appear proper to exercise the rights of exclusion.

Mayo trust

It appears by a separate account produced by the receiver that the amount of stock in the new 3½ per cents, now 3¼, standing in the names of Thomas Grimston Bucknall Estcourt, esq., and Thomas Vilett, esq., trustees of the fund established by the late Revd. Charles Mayo, had accumulated to £4,794 13*s.* 7*d.*

Signatures

T. G. Bucknall Estcourt, Bruce, G. W. Wroughton, F. Leyborne Popham, G. H. Walker Heneage, Thomas Vilett, H. N. Goddard, T. H. S. Sotheron, Ambrose Goddard.

9 April 1846, a special meeting held at the Ailesbury Arms inn, Marlborough

Present

The Rt. Hon. Earl Bruce, Horatio Nelson Goddard, esq., Col. Wroughton.

Estate

The steward stated that, in consequence of the proposed London, Bristol, and South Wales Direct railway Bill having passed the Standing Orders of the House of Commons, he had thought it his duty to bring under the notice of the trustees the line as laid out through the hospital estate at Froxfield and the probability of annoyance being felt by the inmates of the hospital from the proposed line being close to the garden wall and across the garden allotments appropriated to the poor. He had therefore called the present meeting by direction of Col. Wroughton and Mr. Popham.

The trustees inspected the plan and section of this part of the line.

Resolved [that] it is the opinion of the trustees now present that a petition should be presented to the House of Commons against the London, Bristol, and South Wales Direct railway unless such terms can be arranged as to the course of the railway, for the land to be taken, and for the inconvenience to the almshouse as Col. Wroughton shall think proper to accept. Col. Wroughton is requested to take such steps in the matter as he may think desirable.

The trustees also request and authorize Col. Wroughton to arrange such terms as he may think proper for the land to be taken, and damages to be occasioned, by the proposed London, Newbury, and Bath Direct railway.

Almshouse

see estate business

Signature

H. Goddard

5 August 1846, at the Ailesbury Arms inn, Marlborough

Present

The marquess of Ailesbury, T. G. B. Estcourt, esq., A. Goddard, esq., Rt. Hon. Henry Pierrepont, H. N. Goddard, esq., Lord Ernest Bruce, Col. Wroughton, F. L. Popham, esq., T. H. S. Sotheron, esq., G. H. W. Heneage, esq.

Trusteeship

The trustees examined the account of the receiver of the rents to Michaelmas 1845, upon which there appears to be a balance of £92 7*s*. 6½*d*. which is to be carried to his next account.

A conveyance for vesting the trust estates in T. H. S. Sotheron, esq., and G. H. W. Heneage, esq., trustees elected 6 August 1846, jointly with the old trustees was executed at this meeting.

Estate

Col. Wroughton and Mr. Popham are requested to give such orders as they may think proper for spouting to the farmhouse and the almshouses by doing either the whole at once, or part at a time, as they may think proper.

The steward is authorized to convert about 3 acres of meadow on Froxfield farm into water mead, on the tenant paying 5 per cent interest on the cost.

The steward is authorized to make such terms with Richard Coombs for his renting the malthouse and property as Col. Wroughton may sanction.

Mr. Redman's application to be allowed the value of tithe straw, taken by him on his entry but which he would be unable to sell on his quitting, is acceded to.

Col. Wroughton reported that he could purchase the house late Banning's at New Mill for £90, which is approved of.

Almshouse

It appearing that Widow Thomas has occasion for more care and attention than is likely to be paid to her in the hospital, is unfit to be trusted alone, and it will be a considerable saving to the trust to have her under the care of her niece, the steward is allowed, under the special circumstances, to remit her stipend to Mr. Witty on receiving half-yearly certificates from the minister of the parish where he resides of her being alive, during her inability or until some further order from the trustees.

An application was made by Mrs. Ann Hay for leave for permanent absence from the hospital, which the trustees do not think should be granted. But the trustees request Mr. Popham to dispose of any applications for extension of leave from time to time if her health should require it.

The steward is directed to inform Mrs. Kirby and Mrs. Wride that the trustees will require a due adherence to the rules respecting inmates and will suspend the stipend of any widow acting in contravention of them.

Col. Wroughton and Mr. Popham are requested to make such arrangements respecting the privies and conveniences in the quadrangle as they may think proper.

The Revd. the chaplain reported that he had admonished Mrs. Richardson in the chapel, represented that she had subsequently conducted herself with propriety, and applied for a restoration of her stipend, which the trustees do not think should be granted.

and see estate business

Mayo trust

It appears by a separate account produced by the receiver that the amount of stock in the new 3½ per cents, now 3¼, standing in the names of T. G. B. Estcourt, esq., and Thomas Vilett, esq., trustees of the fund established by the late Revd. Charles Mayo, had accumulated to £4,949 13*s*. 5*d*.

Signatures

Ailesbury, Ernest Bruce, Ambrose Goddard, F. Leyborne Popham, H. N. Goddard.

4 August 1847, at the Ailesbury Arms inn, Marlborough

Present

The marquess of Ailesbury, in the chair, A. Goddard, esq., Earl Bruce, the Rt. Hon. H. M. Pierrepont, H. N. Goddard, esq., Lord Ernest Bruce, Col. Wroughton, F. L. Popham, esq.

Trusteeship

The trustees examined the account of the receiver of the rents to Michaelmas 1846, upon which there appears to be a balance of £567 11*s.* 8½*d.* due to the receiver which is to be charged in his next account.

Mr. Estcourt being the sole surviving trustee under the minutes of 7 August 1833 and 3 August 1836 of the £2,600 South Sea stock belonging to the charity, £235 9*s.* 5*d.* of the same stock, the produce of the exchange of lands with the Kennet and Avon Canal Company, and of the £113 9*s.* 2*d.* of the same stock held in trust for the rector of Huish it is ordered that the stock be transferred into the names of Horatio Nelson Goddard, esq., and Francis Leyborne Popham, esq., together with Mr. Estcourt, and that the usual declaration of trust be prepared for their signature.

An application from the Revd. G. P. Cleather for assistance towards repewing, and increasing the accommodation in, the parish church at Chirton was read. [It is] resolved that the trustees will give £20 towards that object, and regret that the present state of their finances does not warrant a larger contribution.

Ordered that in future the annual meetings shall be held on the first Wednesday in July instead of the first Wednesday in August.

Resolved that the steward's salary be increased to £70 a year.

Estate

The arrangement made by the steward for obtaining possession of the cottages at Clench, claimed by Mr. T. Banning as his freehold, on payment of £85 as a remuneration for his outlay thereon was approved.

Ordered that a new policy of insurance against fire be effected in respect of the whole of the hospital property. The steward is directed to obtain proper estimates of the sums to be insured in respect of each building.

The steward is directed to make such arrangements, under direction of Col. Wroughton and Mr. Popham, for the accommodation of Mr. Joseph Drury by alteration of his barns as may appear desirable.

The steward is also directed to build, under the direction of those gentlemen, three or four cottages at Froxfield on a site to be selected by them.

An application from George Benger for reduction of his rent for the Cross Keys at Froxfield is referred to Col. Wroughton, with the assistance of the steward.

and see trusteeship business

Almshouse

The steward reported that in consequence of complaints made by Miss Thomas of the treatment experienced by her mother, whose residence with Mrs. Witty at Devizes was sanctioned at the last meeting, he had represented the matter to the trustees at the view meeting and had by their desire requested Mr. Barker to visit Mrs. Thomas and report on her case.

The trustees, being of opinion that the discomforts complained of have been greatly exaggerated, do not feel called upon to interfere, but direct the steward to inform Miss Thomas that it is perfectly competent to her mother to return to Froxfield if she pleases. Mr. Popham is requested to give such order, in case of her returning, as he may think proper or desirable for the security of the establishment.

Mayo trust

It appears by a separate account produced by the receiver that the amount of stock in the new 3½ per cents, now 3¼, standing in the names of T. G. B. Estcourt, esq., and Thomas Vilett, esq., trustees of the fund established by the late Revd. Charles Mayo, had accumulated to £5,127 18*s.* 5*d.*

T. G. Bucknall Estcourt, esq., being now the sole surviving trustee of the Revd. C. Mayo's trust fund the trustees now present nominate Horatio Nelson Goddard, esq., and Francis Leyborne Popham, esq., to be trustees together with Mr. Estcourt. The steward is directed to get the stock properly transferred into their names.

Signatures

Ailesbury, H. N. Goddard, Henry Pierrepont, Ambrose Goddard, F. Leyborne Popham, G. W. Wroughton, Ernest Bruce.

5 July 1848, at the Ailesbury Arms inn, Marlborough

Present

Ambrose Goddard, esq., in the chair, Earl Bruce, Rt. Hon. Henry M. Pierrepont, H. N. Goddard, esq., Lord Ernest Bruce, Col. Wroughton, F. L. Popham, esq., G. H. W. Heneage, esq.

Trusteeship

The trustees examined the account of the receiver of the rents to Michaelmas 1847, upon which there appears to be a balance of £25 11*s.* 11½*d.* due to the receiver which is to be charged in his next account.

Mr. Estcourt having been absent from two successive meetings his patronage is suspended under rule 18.

Mr. Sotheron being absent in consequence of compulsory attendance on an election committee in Parliament his absence is excused.

Estate

Col. Wroughton reported that he had acceded to a suggestion by Mr. James Warwick, junior, for setting out and straightening the boundary between the farmhouse garden at Milton and the adjoining property belonging to Mr. Warwick, which is approved.

The steward is directed to ascertain whether some plantations cannot be made on various parts of the estate and to have such made as may be approved of by Col. Wroughton.

Ordered that a new farmhouse be built at Froxfield in the meadow between the house now occupied by Mr. Richard Coombs and the almshouse, that a portion of the malthouse be converted into three cottages, [that] the old farm[house] be pulled down and such materials as can be made available be used in the new building, and that Col. Wroughton and Mr. Popham be requested to settle the plans and arrange for the detail of the work.

Ordered that such of the old cottages at Froxfield as appear unfit to stand be pulled down as they become untenanted.

Almshouse

An application from Mrs. Cole for payment of her stipend forfeited many years since is refused.

Mayo trust

It appears by a separate account produced by the receiver that the amount of stock in the new 3½ per cents, now 3¼, standing in the names of T. G. B. Estcourt, esq., H. N. Goddard, esq., and F. L. Popham, esq., trustees of the fund established by the late Revd. Charles Mayo, had accumulated to £5,304 9*s.* 8*d.*

Signatures

Ambrose Goddard, Bruce, G. H. Walker Heneage, Henry Pierrepont, F. Leyborne Popham, G. W. Wroughton, H. N. Goddard, Ernest Bruce.

4 July 1849, at the Ailesbury Arms inn, Marlborough

Present

The marquess of Ailesbury, in the chair, T. G. B. Estcourt, esq., A. Goddard, esq., Earl Bruce, Rt. Hon. Henry M. Pierrepont, H. N. Goddard, esq., Lord Ernest Bruce, F. L. Popham, esq., T. H. S. Sotheron, esq., G. H. W. Heneage, esq.

Trusteeship

The trustees examined the account of the receiver of the rents to Michaelmas 1848, upon which there appears to be a balance of £386 15*s.* 4½*d.* due to the receiver which is to be charged in his next account.

Resolved that the view of the hospital be taken in each year by

Mr. Popham and two trustees to be appointed at the annual meeting, and that Mr. Sotheron and Mr. Heneage be the trustees to view in the ensuing year. Each trustee [is] to be at liberty to appoint a substitute in case of his being unable to attend.

Resolved that in future the annual meeting be held on the second Wednesday in July instead of the first Wednesday as at present.

Estate

The steward reported that the new farmhouse at Froxfield was complete and that three cottages, and various outbuildings for the convenience of the house occupied by Mr. Richard Coombs, had been erected with the old materials on the site of the old malthouse.

A porch being considered desirable at the farmhouse at Froxfield the steward is authorized to contribute £5 in case the tenant should think fit to erect one.

The steward also reported that the back part of the Cross Keys public house at Froxfield was in danger of falling in, and that the house occupied by Mr. S. Snook, which fell into hand a few years since, was so damp and unhealthy as to be scarcely habitable. The steward is authorized, under the direction of Col. Wroughton and Mr. Popham, to repair the Cross Keys, which it is estimated may be done for about £50, and to make such alterations in the house lately occupied by T. Giles at Froxfield as may make it suitable for S. Snook, at an estimated expense of £90. He is authorized to pull down such part of S. Snook's house and buildings as may appear unfit to stand.

A letter from Mr. Drury of Froxfield applying for a new barn having been read the steward is directed to procure a report as to the desirability of incurring any expense by building at this time on Mr. Drury's holding.

Almshouse

see trusteeship business

Mayo trust

It appears by a separate account produced by the receiver that the amount of stock in the new 3½ per cents, now 3¼, standing in the names of T. G. B. Estcourt, esq., H. N. Goddard, esq., and F. L. Popham, esq., trustees of the fund established by the late Revd. Charles Mayo, had accumulated to £5,491 4*s*. 7*d*.

Signatures

Ailesbury, chairman, Henry Pierrepont, Ambrose Goddard, H. N. Goddard, Ernest Bruce, Bruce, G. H. Walker Heneage.

10 July 1850, at the Ailesbury Arms inn, Marlborough

Present

The marquess of Ailesbury, in the chair, T. G. B. Estcourt, esq.,

Earl Bruce, Rt. Hon. Henry M. Pierrepont, H. N. Goddard, esq., Col. Wroughton, F. L. Popham, esq.

Trusteeship

The trustees examined the account of the receiver of the rents to Michaelmas 1849, upon which there appears to be a balance of £762 16*s*. 5*d*. due to the receiver which is to be charged in his next account.

Ordered that £335 9*s*. 5*d*. of the £2,835 9*s*. 5*d*. Old South Sea annuities be sold and the produce applied towards the balance due to the steward, which has arisen in consequence of the expenditure on new buildings and improvements.

Messrs. Sotheron and Heneage having been unable to attend a view meeting with Mr. Popham this year they are requested to view the hospital next year.

Estate

An application from the farm tenants of the trust property for assistance in consequence of the reduced price of agricultural produce was read. [It is] ordered that the steward request Mr. John Iveson to ascertain and report whether any reduction of rent or other allowance should be made for the year from Michaelmas 1849 to Michaelmas 1850 and to lay his report before Col. Wroughton, Mr. H. N. Goddard, and Mr. Popham on the first day of the Michaelmas quarter sessions, who are authorized to act therein and make such reduction as they may think fit.

Application having been made by Mr. Robert Pyke to quit the small farm at Clench in consequence of his being about to emigrate Col. Wroughton is requested, with the assistance of the steward, to make such arrangement as he may think proper for a re-letting.

The steward is directed to do such repairs only in the course of the year as may appear necessary, under the sanction of Col. Wroughton and Mr. Popham.

and see trusteeship business

Almshouse

The steward reported that, in consequence of the increasing habit of widows absenting themselves from their apartments for the principal part of their time and returning to show themselves at chapel on Sundays only, he had, under the direction of Mr. Popham, retained £8, part of the stipend for the Michaelmas quarter 1849, from Mrs. Elizabeth Kirby for absenting herself without leave, which is approved. A letter from Mrs. Kirby applying for payment of the sum retained was read, but the trustees consider that the case is not one in which the sum retained should be paid.

The steward is directed to inform all the widows that strict adherence to the rules for residence will be required and any attempts at evasion will be severely dealt with.

The application for nurses for Mrs. Skillman, Mrs. Barnes, and Mrs. Drake are referred to Mr. Popham, with the assistance of the surgeon, to deal with as he may think fit.

Mayo trust

It appears by a separate account produced by the receiver that the amount of stock late new 3½ per cents, now reduced 3¼, standing in the names of T. G. B. Estcourt, esq., H. N. Goddard, esq., and F. L. Popham, esq., trustees of the fund established by the late Revd. Charles Mayo, had accumulated to £5,669 9*s.* 1*d.*

Resolved that Messrs. Estcourt, H. N. Goddard, and F. L. Popham, with such other of the Froxfield trustees as may think proper to attend any of their meetings, be appointed a committee to prepare rules for carrying into effect the objects of the Revd. Charles Mayo's charity; with power to take legal advice, and to adopt such measures as they may find necessary, with a view to the election of an exhibitioner at the earliest practicable period after the expiration of the 21 years for which the fund was directed to accumulate.

Signatures

Bruce, Henry Pierrepont, G. W. Wroughton, F. Leyborne Popham, H. N. Goddard.

8 July 1851, at the Ailesbury Arms inn, Marlborough

Present

The marquess of Ailesbury, in the chair, Lord Ernest Bruce, M.P., Col. Wroughton, F. L. Popham, esq., T. H. S. Sotheron, esq., M.P., G. H. W. Heneage, esq., M.P., A. Goddard, esq.

Trusteeship

The trustees examined the account of the receiver of the rents to Michaelmas 1850, upon which there appears a balance of £363 9*s.* 5½*d.* due to the receiver which is to be charged in his next account.

Resolved that Col. Wroughton and Mr. H. N. Goddard be requested to view the hospital next year in conjunction with Mr. Popham.

In consequence of the day for the annual meeting having been changed this year [it is] resolved that trustees not attending this meeting do not fall within the terms of the rule forfeiting patronage for non-attendance this year.

Estate

The steward having received notice from Mr. John Redman of his intention to quit Froxfield farm at Michaelmas next, and having received subsequent offers from him for a continuance at a greatly reduced rent, he is directed to endeavour to make terms for re-letting to Mr. Redman if he can do so, under the advice of Mr. Iveson, so that the rent be not less than £480 for the ensuing year only and, in case of not agreeing, to take the proper steps for letting to a new tenant.

The steward is directed to refer to Mr. Iveson for his opinion as to the rents to be taken from the farm tenants for the current year, keeping in view the opinion of the trustees that the recommendation for reduction for the last year should not be exceeded except in any special case.

Ordered that the steward do such repairs in the ensuing year as may be directed by Col. Wroughton or Mr. Popham.

The steward is directed to re-arrange and equalize the cottage rents in all cases in which alteration may be necessary.

The steward is directed, under the sanction of Mr. Popham, to make the piece of ground at Froxfield, the site of the house lately occupied by S. Snook with the gardens, available to some useful purpose.

The steward is directed to make such arrangement, under the direction of Col. Wroughton, as may be thought desirable with regard to superintendence and management of the small coppices at Milton and Clench.

and see almshouse business

Almshouse

In consequence of the necessity for making such great reduction in the rents of the farms [it is] ordered that the stipend payable to the widows be reduced to £9 a quarter until further order.

The porter is directed to allow the gates of the hospital to remain open till 10 o'clock at night till 1 September in the present year, with power to Mr. Popham to order the gates to be closed at 9 if he think fit.

Mr. Heneage made a report of the late view of the hospital, when several orders were given.

Mayo trust

It appears by a separate account produced by the receiver that the amount of stock late new 3½ per cents, now reduced 3¼, standing in the names of T. G. B. Estcourt, esq., H. N. Goddard, esq., and F. L. Popham, esq., trustees of the fund established by the late Revd. Charles Mayo, had accumulated to £5,864 6*s*.

Mr. Popham stated that the committee consisting of Mr. Estcourt, Mr. H. N. Goddard, and himself, to whom the subject of forming rules for the late Mr. Mayo's charity was referred, were not prepared with their report.

Resolved that Mr. H. N. Goddard and Mr. Popham, with Mr. Sotheron (in place of, and with the sanction of, his father Mr. Estcourt), be appointed a committee for this purpose. They are requested to have the matter put in such a state as to enable the trustees to proceed to the election of an exhibitioner at their next annual meeting.

Signatures

Ambrose Goddard, F. Leyborne Popham, G. H. Walker Heneage, T. H. S. Sotheron, G. W. Wroughton, Ernest Bruce.

16 July 1852, at the Ailesbury Arms inn, Marlborough

Present

Col. Wroughton, in the chair, T. G. B. Estcourt, esq., A. Goddard, esq., Earl Bruce, H. N. Goddard, esq., Lord Ernest Bruce, F. L. Popham, esq., T. H. S. Sotheron, esq., G. H. W. Heneage, esq.

Trusteeship

The trustees examined the account of the receiver of the rents to Michaelmas 1851, upon which there appears to be a balance of £514 6*s.* 5½*d.* due to the receiver which is to be charged in his next account.

Resolved that the day for the annual meeting be in future on the second Thursday in July, instead of the second Wednesday as at present, subject to postponement to the following Thursday in case the first mentioned day, or any preceding day in that week, should be the commission day of the Wiltshire assizes.

The trustees now present unanimously elect Sir John Wither Awdry, kt., and the Rt. Hon. Henry Petty-Fitzmaurice, commonly called earl of Shelburne, to be trustees in place of Col. Thomas Vilett and the Rt. Hon. Henry Manvers Pierrepont, deceased, and direct that a deed of trust be prepared for vesting the trust estates in them and the remaining trustees against the next meeting of the trustees.

Resolved that Sir John Awdry and Lord Shelburne be requested to view the hospital next year in conjunction with Mr. Popham.

The absence of the marquess of Ailesbury is excused in consequence of the alteration of the day of meeting.

Estate

The steward reported that in pursuance of the minutes of the last meeting he had agreed with Mr. John Redman, the tenant of the farm at Froxfield, for 1 year only, from Michaelmas 1851 to Michaelmas 1852 at £500, and that, being unable previous to Lady day last to arrange with Mr. Redman terms for a further continuance of his tenancy, Mr. Redman had given notice of his intention to quit at Michaelmas next. The steward further reported that he had, with the sanction of Mr. Popham and under the advice of Mr. Iveson, agreed for his occupancy of the farm from Michaelmas 1852 to Michaelmas 1853 at £500 a year, the tenant to lay out not less than £10 in permanent repairs, which is approved.

The steward is directed to endeavour to make terms with Mr. Redman, under the direction of Mr. Popham, for a permanent letting to him at £500 a year, unless better terms may be obtained by the steward, with the concurrence of some competent valuer.

Col. Wroughton reported that, finding some of the buildings at Huish and Clench in such a state from general decay that slight expenditure on them would be thrown away, he had directed a thorough repair, and that he had ordered the cutting of about £300-worth of timber towards the expenses.

Mr. Popham is requested to give such order as he may think fit with regard to the erection of woodhouses to cottages at Froxfield.

Mr. Iveson's report on the rents was read and the steward is directed to act on it.

A proposal from Dr. Somerset to effect a small exchange of lands at Milton is referred to Col. Wroughton to ascertain the practicability of it.

Col. Wroughton is requested to make such arrangements, and to give such directions, for repairs to the farmhouse and buildings at Milton as he may think proper.

Mayo trust

It appears by a separate account produced by the receiver that the amount of stock late new 3½ per cents, now reduced 3¼, standing in the names of T. G. B. Estcourt, esq., H. N. Goddard, esq., and F. L. Popham, esq., trustees of the fund established by the late Revd. Charles Mayo, had accumulated to £6,037 11*s*. 9*d*.

The report of the committee appointed for managing the Revd. Charles Mayo's charity was read, approved of, and confirmed, with the exception that the trustees think the exhibition should not be confined to Brasenose college.

Resolved that the exhibiton should be tenable for 5 years only and be open to all the colleges in the university, and that certificates of progress be required half-yearly in compliance with the recommendation of the report.

The trustees proceeded to the election of a scholar or exhibitioner on the foundation of the late Revd. Charles Mayo. There appeared as candidates John Harries Llewellyn and Arthur John Cadwallader Llewellyn, sons of the Revd. David Llewellyn of Easton, Henry Cleather, son of the Revd. George Parker Cleather of Chirton, and Hugh Allan, the son of the Revd. Hugh Allan of Cricklade. It was resolved that Hugh Allan should be appointed to the exhibition. The period of 5 years, for which it is tenable, [is] to commence from this day.

He [the receiver] had paid, by desire of Mr. Popham, £20 to the Revd. R. Michell, the Public Orator of the university of Oxford, for his fee for the examination of the candidates for the exhibition, which he had charged in the account.

Signatures

G. W. Wroughton, T. G. Bucknall Estcourt, Ernest Bruce, J. W. Awdry, F. Leyborne Popham, Bruce, G. H. Walker Heneage, T. H. S. Sotheron, H. N. Goddard.

Copy of the report of the committee appointed for managing the Revd. Charles Mayo's charity

In compliance with the resolutions of the trustees of the Somerset hospital at their annual meetings in July 1850 and [July 18]51 we beg to lay before the general body of the trustees the following report of what appears requisite towards the fulfilment of the wishes of the donor of the scholarship. As we were in July 1851 requested to have the matter put in such a state as to enable the trustees to proceed to the election of an exhibitioner at their next annual meeting we hope that no serious objections will be raised to what we have done up to the present time. The strong expressions in the trust deed that the persons elected should be 'scholars of exemplary character and conduct and of promising abilities and diligence in their studies' induced us to require that an examination should take place at Marlborough in order to ascertain correctly the relative proficiency of the candidates and to prevent, as far as in our power, the possibility of the scholar elected being subsequently rejected at any examination for his academic degrees from a want of classical attainment. We also were, and are, unanimously of opinion that the ages of the candidates should not exceed 19, to be ascertained by the production of their baptismal certificates, although we recommend that this rule should on the present occasion be relaxed so as to admit as candidates all who were of the required age at the period when the powers of the trust ought strictly to have been first brought into operation. We took care that proper notices should be given in March last and we requested the examiner to report the result of his opinion of the proficiency of the candidates according to his own best judgement. We also now recommend that a half-yearly certificate of the continuous diligence of the elected scholar be required of one of the tutors of his college for 5 years, which we consider is the longest period each exhibition should be held by any one scholar, and that, if a preference be given to any college at Oxford, the college of Brasenose be selected in this first instance, of which Mr. Mayo was himself a member.

The accompanying papers and certificates, and report of Mr. Michell, the Public Orator of Oxford, who kindly consented to act as examiner, will more fully develop the regulations hereby recommended for this and all future elections under this trust.

(Signed) T. G. Bucknall Estcourt, T. H. S. Sotheron, H. N. Goddard, F. Leyborne Popham.

9 May 1853, a special meeting held at the steward's house in Marlborough

Present

Earl Bruce, in the chair, H. N. Goddard, esq., Col. Wroughton, T. H. S. Sotheron, esq.

Trusteeship

see estate business

Estate

The steward reported that he had convened the present meeting, at the desire of such of the trustees as he had been enabled personally to consult, in consequence of the tenant of Milton farm having given notice of his intention to quit at Michaelmas next and of the difficulty which he apprehended in re-letting on anything like terms adequate to the value, by reason of the lands lying so much dispersed [and] there being neither a sufficient farmhouse nor buildings necessary for carrying on the farm.

He further stated that he had agreed to purchase at valuation some cottages and lands belonging to the tenant and lying intermixed with the hospital property with a view to the trustees taking to them, if they should be pleased so to do, and effecting thereby an improvement in their estate.

He further reported that a house and lands belonging to the devisees in trust for sale of Mr. James Warwick, senior, deceased, the uncle of the present tenant and himself the occupier of the farm for many years, were advertized for sale by auction on Wednesday 11th instant. The greater part of the lands now for sale were highly desirable to be added to the hospital property for the purpose of connecting some of the detached portions and of saving the building of a new farmhouse.

The opinions of counsel taken by the steward as to the power to lay out the South Sea annuities belonging to the trust in the purchase of lands was read. The reports of Mr. Westbury as to the eligibilities of the properties now in the market and of their value were also read.

The trustees present consider that the opinion of counsel now read precludes them from laying out the proceeds of the South Sea annuities, other than the £235 9*s*. 5*d*. South Sea annuities arising from sale of land to the Kennet and Avon Canal Company, in this purchase desirable as they consider it to be if they had the means.

Mr. Merriman having expressed a willingness to purchase the whole of the estate of Mr. James Warwick (late Mr. James Warwick, junior) in Milton, including no. 212, the piece referred to in Mr. Westbury's report as eligible for a site for a house, and to take lands of the hospital in exchange for it, [it is] resolved that this offer be accepted, that the canal money be applied so far as it will extend in purchasing a portion of such land, and that the remainder of the value be made up by giving him lands in exchange.

Resolved that Mr. Merriman be authorized to purchase no. 168 (lot 2 in the particular of sale of the estate of the late Mr. James Warwick, senior) if it can be obtained at a reasonable price and that, if purchased by him, it should be considered as comprised in the foregoing arrangement.

Col. Wroughton was requested and authorized to superintend and give such directions for effecting the arrangements as he may think proper.

The steward is directed to make the best terms he can for letting the hospital estate at Milton either permanently or until further instructions can be given by the general body of trustees.

Signatures

T. H. S. Sotheron, H. N. Goddard, G. W. Wroughton.

14 July 1853, at the Ailesbury Arms inn, Marlborough

Present

Col. Wroughton, in the chair, H. N. Goddard, esq., F. L. Popham, esq., G. H. W. Heneage, esq., M.P., Sir J. W. Awdry, kt., T. H. Sutton Sotheron, esq., M.P.

Trusteeship

The trustees examined the account of the receiver of the rents to Michaelmas 1852, upon which there appears to be a balance of £345 4*s.* 11½*d.* due to the receiver which is to be charged in his next account.

The minutes of the special meeting of trustees convened by the steward on 9 May last on the subject of Milton farm and various properties there were read, approved of, and confirmed by this meeting.

Ordered that the officiating chaplain be in future requested to attend the annual meeting. The steward is to pay for his dinner.

Resolved that Earl Bruce and Mr. Sotheron be requested to view the hospital next year in conjunction with Mr. Popham.

The marquess of Ailesbury and Mr. Estcourt being prevented from attending this meeting by ill health their absence is excused.

Estate

The steward reported that in compliance with the order at the last meeting he had let Froxfield farm to Mr. John Redman at £510 a year, which was certified by Mr. John Iveson to be a fair rent.

The steward reported that he had been unable to obtain the piece of land no. 212 on the plan on what he considered reasonable terms, and he produced an offer from Mr. James Warwick to sell it at £450, which the trustees decline.

He also reported that he had purchased the piece of meadow no. 168 (lot 2 on the sale particular of the late Mr. James Warwick) at £225. He was in negotiation with the recent purchaser of a house and garden, late Stagg's, which was capable of being converted into a farmhouse, for attaching it to the hospital property [at Milton] by exchange or any other means.

Mr. Westbury's report of the ... [*MS. blank*] instant as to [Milton] farm and [the] exceedingly inconvenient situation of the lands was read.

The steward is directed to make such arrangements as may be found practicable, with the sanction of Col. Wroughton, for carrying out the projected exchanges or any of them, and for applying the £235 9*s.* 5*d.* South Sea annuities arising from sale to the Kennet and Avon Canal Company in making such purchases as can be effected thereby for the improvement of the hospital estate [at Milton].

The trustees approve of Mr. Giles Westbury or Mr. William Ferris to value the respective properties to be dealt with and to adjust any claims by the off-going tenant of [Milton] farm.

The steward is directed to make the best terms he can under the circumstances for re-letting the farm.

and see trusteeship business

Almshouse

A petition from the inmates of the hospital, numerously signed [and] requesting that the order given by the trustees who visited at Froxfield on the 14th last that the gates should be always closed half an hour before the time of divine service be rescinded, was read. The trustees think it not desirable to comply with that request and confirm the order given.

Mayo trust

It appears by a separate account produced by the receiver that the amount of stock late new 3½ per cents, now reduced 3¼, standing in the names of T. G. B. Estcourt, esq., H. N. Goddard, esq., and F. L. Popham, esq., trustees of the fund established by the late Revd. Charles Mayo, had accumulated to £6,128 6*s.* 1*d.* The dividend received in April last on this sum, amounting to £96 13*s.* 7*d.*, remains in his hands applicable to the payment of the year's stipend due on the 16th instant to Mr. Hugh Allan, the exhibitioner who was elected on the Revd. Charles Mayo's trust fund at the last annual meeting and of whose progress and conduct satisfactory certificates were produced.

Ordered that the balance of the next half-year's dividend, after payment of the expenses incurred in respect of the trust and election of an exhibitioner, be invested in addition to the principal now held on that trust.

Adjournment

Ordered that the meeting be adjourned to Wednesday 19 October next at 12 o'clock at the offices of Messrs. Merriman in Marlborough.

Signatures

G. W. Wroughton, H. N. Goddard, G. H. Walker Heneage, F. Leyborne Popham, J. W. Awdry, T. H. S. Sotheron.

19 October 1853

Estate

The business of the Milton exchanges and arrangement of the farm, for which it was supposed an adjournment might be desirable, not appearing to render such meeting necessary no trustee attended.

13 July 1854, at the Ailesbury Arms inn, Marlborough

Present

Col. Wroughton, in the chair, A. Goddard, esq., Earl Bruce, Lord Ernest Bruce, M.P., F. L. Popham, esq., T. H. S. Sotheron, esq., M.P., G. H. Walker Heneage, esq., M.P., Sir J. W. Awdry, kt.

Trusteeship

The trustees examined the account of the receiver of the rents to Michaelmas 1853, upon which there appears to be a balance of £114 17*s*. 6½*d*. in his hands which, however, includes £235 9*s*. 5*d*., part of the South Sea annuities lately held by the trustees and not re-invested when paid off, as after explained.

The steward stated that he had, under the direction of Col. Wroughton, sold by auction timber on the Huish and Milton estates to the extent of about £650 net, but the greater part of the money not being yet receivable in cash he had deferred including it in his account until the sale account should be completed.

The steward reported that, in the uncertainty which existed as to the proper course to be pursued in reference to the £2,500 South Sea annuities held as part of the trust property, i.e. whether to declare the option of taking the new £2 10*s*. per cent stock or to be paid off at par, he had not taken any measures for accepting the new stock and the whole had been paid off. £2,264 10*s*. 7*d*. (part of the £2,500, less broker's commission, received) had purchased £2,573 14*s*. 9*d*. 3 per cent consols, being a profit of £309 4*s*. 2*d*. for the hospital on that part of the stock. The £113 9*s*. 2*d*. held for the rector of Huish had purchased £128 19*s*. He further reported that he had retained in cash the £235 9*s*. 5*d*. arising from sale of land to the Kennet and Avon company in 1809, which should be re-invested in land, with a view of purchasing, if so determined, some lands at Clench lying intermixed with the hospital estate which he found were shortly to come into the market.

An application from the Revd. J. H. Gale, vicar of Milton, for assistance towards the erection of a parish school there was read. [It is] resolved that £25 be contributed and Col. Wroughton is empowered to order a contribution of a further sum not exceeding £15 if he should think it desirable.

Proposed by Mr. Popham, seconded by Mr. Sotheron, and resolved that, there being no parish day school in Froxfield, £3 3*s*. a year be subscribed annually towards the school at Little Bedwyn, so long as there shall not be an efficient day school at the former place and provided the children of the poor at Froxfield are received at Little Bedwyn on the same terms as the poor of that parish.

The following notice, having been sent by Lord Ernest Bruce to the steward with directions to transmit a copy to each trustee previous to the meeting, was read.

When a trustee, being a member of either [of the] Houses of Parliament, states in writing upon his honour that he is unavoidably detained by a committee or a morning sitting of the House, his attendance be excused. In the event of the above resolution being rejected Lord Ernest Bruce will take the liberty of moving the following resolution: considering that six trustees out of the present number are Members of Parliament the annual meeting will be henceforth held alternate years in London and Marlborough.

The first resolution was accordingly moved by Lord Ernest Bruce and seconded by Mr. Heneage.

Mr. Sotheron moved as an amendment that when a trustee shall address a letter to the chairman of the annual meeting giving his word that he will be prevented attending by unavoidable public duty he be excused.

Whereupon Lord Ernest Bruce withdrew his proposed resolution, and Mr. Sotheron's amendment was carried unanimously.

The attendance of the marquess of Ailesbury is excused on account of ill health, and of H. N. Goddard, esq., as actually doing duty at Gosport as major in the Royal Wiltshire militia, where his attendance is necessary.

Lord Shelburne having been absent from two successive meetings his patronage is suspended under rule 18.

Resolved that Lord Ernest Bruce and Mr. Sotheron be requested to view the hospital next year in conjunction with Mr. Popham. Their attention is particularly requested to the state of the drainage and other conveniences connected therewith, with power to employ any professional person to advise them and report thereon.

and see estate business

Estate

Claims having been made by Mr. James Warwick, the late tenant of Milton farm, to the right to break up a piece of newly made pasture of about 9 acres called Long croft and to some portions of the buildings, the steward reported that he had, under the advice of Mr. Westbury, compromised them by an allowance of £40, the buildings to remain and the land to continue as meadow.

The steward reported that he had, under the advice of Mr. Westbury, let Milton farm to Mr. Francis Church at £240 a year including the several newly purchased pieces and had let Mr. Church occupy a small piece of about 5 acres called Mead acre for 1 year rent free in lieu of any allowance on entry. The steward is directed to proceed to the completion of the necessary farm buildings, under the supervision of Col. Wroughton, at an estimated cost of about £300.

He also reported that, in consequence of the death of Mr. Thomas Holmes, the tenant of the small farm at Clench, and the bad state of the land, he had, by direction of Col. Wroughton, given notice to the executors to quit. He was in prospect of letting again at the full rent to a tenant who would not require much outlay for the house, which is of a very inferior kind. The steward is directed to make the best arrangement he can with regard to this farm, under the direction of Col. Wroughton.

The steward is directed to invest the £235 9*s*. 5*d*., or any portion thereof, in the purchase of part of the property of the late Mr. Thomas Higgins at Clench or of any other property which he may, under the advice of Col. Wroughton, consider advantageous to the hospital. Or, in the event of Col. Wroughton himself buying the part of Higgins's land desirable for the trust estate, the trustees will be ready to exchange for it a competent portion of the hospital estate at Huish or Oare. In case no eligible investment shall present itself the £235 9*s*. 5*d*. are to be again purchased into the funds with the stock now held in trust in the names of H. N. Goddard, esq., and F. L. Popham, esq.

The reports of Messrs. Westbury and Ferris as to the exchanges with Dr. Somerset and Mr. T. B. Merriman were read and approved and, papers having been already signed by 9 out of the 11 trustees for effectuating these exchanges by means of the Inclosure Commissioners, it is ordered that they be proceeded with and completed.

Messrs. Westbury and Ferris's report on Milton purchases, and exchanges with T. B. Merriman

Whereas it has been referred to us to apportion to Mr. T. B. Merriman an equivalent for certain houses and lands at Milton purchased by him and added to the farm there belonging to the trustees of the Froxfield almshouses we, having minutely inspected the property and likewise the property of the almshouse, are of opinion [that] the property so purchased is very essential to the almshouse farm. We do not see how it could have been let at its value without such purchases having been made, there being no farmhouse on it (the former tenant having lived in a house belonging to another person) and the lands being so intermixed with lands purchased [that] there appeared to be no situation to build a farmhouse convenient to the buildings already standing thereon [*i.e.* on the farm]. The house etc., late Stagg's (no. 209), having been purchased renders the present buildings available to a greater extent than they could be by any other means, and the orchard and garden (no. 208) attached thereto throw open the yard, buildings, and land to a meadow of the almshouse which was almost dissevered before and thereby makes it [*i.e.* the farm] more valuable. Before deciding on what lands should be allotted to Mr. Merriman we consulted the tenant of the almshouse farm [about] which lands it would be most desirable to give up from the farm. The cottages also which were purchased, and proposed to be given up to the almshouse, are situate much more advantageously to the farm than those proposed to be given up in exchange.

The property as described in the schedule no. 1 hereto annexed is that purchased by Mr. Merriman, and in the second schedule are described those [premises] that we award for the property so purchased. In making such award we have taken into our consideration the rent charges, land tax, and timber.

Dated 12 June 1854

(Signed) Giles Westbury, W. Ferris.

Schedule no. 1, lands purchased by Mr. T. B. Merriman and taken by, and let with, the hospital estate

A dwelling house consisting of two parlours, kitchen, scullery, and bedrooms, with stable, gig house, etc., and small garden (no. 209 on tithe map), 19p., intended for [the] farmhouse for the Milton estate; Ivy's meadow and orchard adjoining the above (208), 3r. 30p.; cottage and garden (204), 18p.; two cottages and gardens adjoining (205), 32p.; Moore's ground (272), 1a. 3r. 24p., arable, sandy loam; West Lady mead (275), 1a. 2r. 20p., arable, sandy loam; West Sands (171), 3a. 3r. 13p., arable, sandy loam; Broad Shore mead with land added (167), 2a. 0r. 26p., mead, sandy loam; Little Salisbury mead (168), 3a. 0r. 18p., mead, sandy loam. [Total] 14a.

Schedule no. 2, lands to be taken by Mr. Merriman from the trustees in exchange

Two cottages and gardens (no. 90a on tithe map), 35p., at New Mill; two cottages and gardens (90b, 91), 1r. 38p., at New Mill; yard and sheds (93), 3r. 22p., at New Mill, occupied by Miss Liddiard; arable land (89), 4a., at New Mill, occupied by Mr. J. Clack, sandy loam; arable land (98), 2r. 15p., at New Mill, occupied by Mr. Clack, sandy loam; pasture land (99, 100), 1a. 1r. 34p., at New Mill, occupied by Mr. Clack, peaty and wet; arable land (101), 3a. 1r. 16p., detached piece of Broomsgrove farm, part of the spoil bank of the canal; withy bed (102), 3r. 30p., wood, detached piece of Broomsgrove farm, part of the spoil bank of the canal; Mead acre (231), 4a. 3r. 21p., arable, pasture, and wood, not let with farm, sandy loam; new inclosure (384), 21a. 2r. 37p., arable, taken from farm, light sand. [Total] 38a. 2r. 8p.
(Signed) Giles Westbury, W. Ferris.

By another particular of same date accompanying the above report the values are given as under

The lands etc. taken by the hospital estate: annual value £61 15*s.* 2*d.*, value in fee £1,402 5*s.*, add timber £29 15*s.*, [total value] £1,432.
The lands taken by Mr. Merriman: annual value £50 11*s.*, value in fee £1,339 10*s.*, add timber £90 6*s.*, [total value] £1,429 16*s.*

Mr. Westbury's certificate on exchange with Dr. Somerset

I have seen and I know pieces of land called East Lady mead, containing 1a. 2r. 10p., belonging to the trustees of the Somerset hospital at Froxfield, [and] the piece called Lady mead, containing 2r. 21p., and the two pieces of Notts close, containing together 1r. 35p., [all] belonging to Dr. Somerset, which three last mentioned pieces are proposed to be given to the trustees in exchange for their piece called East Lady mead. I certify that the exchange is a fair and just one between the parties.
Dated 5 July 1854
(Signed) Giles Westbury

Almshouse
see trusteeship business
Mayo trust

It appears by a separate account produced by the receiver that the amount of 3¼ per cent stock standing in the names of H. N. Goddard, esq., and F. L. Popham, esq., trustees of the fund established by the late Revd. Charles Mayo, had, after payment of the expenses directed at the last meeting and three half-year's payments to Mr. Hugh Allan, the exhibitioner, accumulated to £6,228 6*s.* 1*d.*, leaving £35 1*s.* 7*d.* cash in hand to answer the half year (£35) becoming due on the 16th instant.

Signatures

G. W. Wroughton, Ambrose Goddard, T. H. S. Sotheron, F. Leyborne Popham, G. H. Walker Heneage. [The names of Lord Bruce, Lord E. Bruce, and Sir John Awdry were pencilled in by the clerk, but they did not sign]

12 July 1855, at the Ailesbury Arms inn, Marlborough

Present

Col. Wroughton, in the chair, H. N. Goddard, esq., F. L. Popham, esq., G. H. Walker Heneage, esq., M.P.

Trusteeship

The trustees examined the account of the receiver of the rents to Michaelmas 1854, upon which there appears to be a balance of £542 15*s*. 4*d*. in his hands, of which £76 3*s*. 3*d*. belongs to the fund arising from sale of land, leaving £466 12*s*. 1*d*. as the balance of the year's account.

The attendance of the marquess of Ailesbury is excused on account of continued ill health, of Mr. Sotheron by the state of his health from severe domestic affliction, and Sir John Awdry by unavoidable public duty.

Resolved that Earl Bruce and Col. Wroughton be requested to view the hospital next year in conjunction with Mr. Popham.

and see endorsements

Estate

The steward reported that he had, under the direction of Col. Wroughton and in compliance with the minutes at the last meeting, purchased by auction of the trustees of the late Mr. Thomas Higgins a field lying intermixed with the hospital lands at Clench with part of the £235 9*s*. 5*d*. arising from sale of lands to the Kennet and Avon Canal Company. After payment of purchase money and expenses there remained a balance of £76 3*s*. 3*d*. which he is directed to invest with the other trust monies in the 3 per cent consols.

That he had put the buildings on the small farm at Clench into repair and had added the newly purchased field to the farm, which was let to James Brewer at £78 10*s*. a year.

He also reported that he had taken steps for more conveniently arranging the field garden allotments at Froxfield, for effecting an improvement by removing the present unsightly and dilapidated barn near the front of the hospital and used as a workshop by William Gooding, and for the greater privacy of the hospital garden, which he is directed to carry out if he finds he can advantageously do so.

The steward is directed to erect woodhouses and oven[s] for the six new cottages at the west end of Froxfield village.

Mr. Merriman stated that in consequence of a refusal by Mr. Guy Warwick, occupier of the adjoining land, to permit the use of the ancient right of way from Milton street to Mead acre, one of the pieces taken by him [Merriman] in exchange, the matter had been referred to Mr. Alexander Meek of Devizes, who had not yet made his award.

Mr. Merriman is at liberty to use the names of the trustees in any proceedings against Mary Liddiard, the late tenant of New Mill wharf, for neglect of repairs to the wharf and buildings, which are found to be in a very bad state.

Almshouse

Complaint having been made of noises at night from dogs in and about the hospital the porter is directed to be vigilant in preventing strange dogs from being in the quadrangle and to prevent, so far as he can, nuisances arising from any dogs kept by the widows.

The steward is directed to obtain a plan for woodhouses for the accommodation of the inmates of the hospital.

The subject of increasing the stipend to the widows was discussed, but further consideration and decision was postponed in consequence of the small attendance of the trustees.

and see estate business

Mayo trust

It appears by a separate account produced by the receiver that the amount of new 3 per cent stock standing in the names of H. N. Goddard, esq., and F. L. Popham, esq., trustees of the fund established by the late Revd. Charles Mayo, had, after five half-yearly payments to Mr. Hugh Allan, the exhibitioner, accumulated to £6,328 6*s.* 1*d.*, leaving £77 9*s.* 5*d.* cash in hand, out of which another half-yearly payment of £35 will be due to Mr. Allan on the 16th instant.

Mr. Heneage gave notice that he would at the next meeting of the trustees move that in all future elections for the Mayo exhibition notice shall be given to each trustee, previous to the examination of the candidates, of the name and residence of each candidate and of the school where each of them has been educated.

That in all future advertisements respecting a vacancy for the Mayo exhibition an extract shall be given, and public attention called to that part, of the will [*margin*: it should have been trust deed] of the late Mr. Mayo which relates to the qualification of the parent of the candidate.

The steward is directed to look out for, with a view to purchasing, an advowson to be held under the trusts of Mr. Mayo's charity and to open negotiations in case he should meet with any appearing to be desirable, £200 a year being fixed by Mr. Mayo as the minimum. The trustees think the annual income should not exceed £400.

Signatures

G. W. Wroughton, G. H. Walker Heneage, H. N. Goddard, F. Leyborne Popham.

Endorsements

After the meeting had broken up a letter was received from Lord Ernest Bruce and addressed to the steward, of which the following is a copy.

By day mail
Immediate, Thomas B. Merriman, esq., Marlborough
Ernest Bruce
My Dear Sir
I am very sorry to be prevented attending the meeting of the trustees tomorrow by important business in Parliament, both at the morning sitting and in the early part of the evening, from which I cannot be spared. Having been so recently also at the view meeting I hope my attendance will be excused. I delayed writing to you till the last thing as I had hopes that I could attend.
Believe me, yours very faithfully,
Ernest Bruce, St. George's Place, Wednesday night.

These minutes were confirmed at the next meeting. Thomas B. M.

17 July 1856, at the Ailesbury Arms inn, Marlborough

Present

H. N. Goddard, esq., in the chair, Lord Ernest Bruce, M.P., Col. Wroughton, F. L. Popham, esq., T. H. S. Sotheron Estcourt, esq., M.P., G. H. Walker Heneage, esq., M.P., Sir J. W. Awdry, kt.

Trusteeship

The trustees examined the account of the receiver of the rents to Michaelmas 1855, upon which there appears to be a balance of £375 4*s.* 3*d.* in his hands which is to be carried to his next account.

A quorum of trustees not having been present on 12 July 1855 the minutes of that meeting were read and confirmed.

The steward stated that he had inadvertently sent a nomination paper to the earl of Shelburne (now Lord Wycombe) on the death of Mrs. Elizabeth Price, notwithstanding that his lordship's patronage was suspended for non-attendance at meetings, and that his lordship had nominated Mrs. Anne Marshall to supply the vacancy.

The trustees now present unanimously elect the Rt. Hon. Sidney Herbert, M.P., the Revd. John Leyborne Popham, and Ambrose Lethbridge Goddard, esq., M.P., to be trustees in place of Ambrose

Goddard, esq., Thomas Grimston Bucknall Estcourt, esq., and the marquess of Ailesbury, deceased, and direct that a deed of trust be prepared for vesting the trust estates in them and the remaining trustees against the next meeting of the trustees.

Resolved that Mr. Nelson Goddard and the Revd. J. L. Popham be requested to view the hospital next year in conjunction with Mr. F. L. Popham.

The marquess of Ailesbury (late Earl Bruce) and Lord Wycombe (late Lord Shelburne) having been absent from two successive meetings their patronage is suspended under rule 18.

Estate

The steward reported that he had, under the direction of Col. Wroughton, made a further sale of timber at Milton, the net proceeds of which, £226 11*s.* 6*d.*, will not be payable until September next and will therefore be credited in his next account.

Ordered that the steward complete the removal of the barn, and the erection of a new workshop for William Gooding, as approved by the trustees at the view meeting.

Almshouse

The steward reported that, finding at the last payday some of the widows had notwithstanding the remonstrance of the trustees at the view meeting on 20 June continued to have inmates in their houses without permission, he had retained that quarter's stipend from Anne Marshall and Emily Copinger. It appearing that they have now conformed to the rules the steward is authorized to pay the sums so retained. [*Margin.* Mrs. Marshall was paid at next payday in due course, Mrs. Copinger 22 July on urgent application – not to be taken as a precedent]

In compliance with the minutes of the meetings of 13 July 1854 [and] 12 July 1855, and of the directions of the trustees who viewed the hospital on 20 June last, the steward produced plans and estimates for completing the spouting round the hospital, for fuel houses, and [for] other improvements.

Ordered that the spouting round the hospital be completed, which it is estimated may be done for about £60.

The steward is directed to make new privies on the west side of the hospital in accordance with the plan produced and subject to such variation as shall be approved of by Mr. Popham, and to proceed with those suggested on the east side if found desirable.

Plans for fuel houses were produced, of which the trustees approve generally and refer it to Col. Wroughton and Mr. Popham to vary and carry out in any way they may think fit.

Resolved that the Revd. J. L. Popham be requested to dispose of applications for permissions for inmates in the hospital, and for leaves of absence, in the same manner as Mr. F. L. Popham, who will also continue to act, has hitherto done.

Mayo trust

It appears by a separate account produced by the receiver that the amount of new 3 per cent stock standing in the names of H. N. Goddard, esq., and F. L. Popham, esq., trustees of the fund established by the late Revd. Charles Mayo, had, after seven half-yearly payments to Mr. Hugh Allan, the exhibitioner, accumulated to £6,428 6*s.* 1*d.*, leaving £99 4*s.* 9*d.* cash in hand, out of which another half-yearly payment of £35 was payable to Mr. Allan on the 16th instant.

In compliance with the minutes of the last meeting the steward produced particulars of various advowsons offered to him for purchase by the Mayo trust, but as none of them appeared to him very eligible he had not entered into any negotiation.

Resolved that it is desirable to apply part of the 3 per cent annuities of the Revd. Charles Mayo's trust fund in the purchase of an advowson, that the steward communicate with Mr. Nelson Goddard and Col. Wroughton in case he hears of an advowson for sale which seems to him desirable according to the terms of Mr. Mayo's trust, and if they agree in his view that he summon a special meeting of the trustees.

Mr. Heneage, in compliance with the notice given by him at the meeting on 12 July 1855, moved, and it was resolved, that in all future elections for the Mayo exhibition notice shall be given to each trustee, previous to the examination of the candidates, of the name and residence of each candidate and of the school where each of them has been educated.

Signatures

H. N. Goddard, Ernest Bruce, T. Sotheron Estcourt, F. Leyborne Popham, J. W. Awdry, G. W. Wroughton, G. H. Walker Heneage.

9 July 1857, at the Ailesbury Arms inn, Marlborough

Present

H. N. Goddard, esq., in the chair, the marquess of Ailesbury, Col. Wroughton, F. Leyborne Popham, esq., T. H. S. Sotheron Estcourt, esq., M.P., G. H. Walker Heneage, esq., Sir J. W. Awdry, the earl of Shelburne, the Rt. Hon. Sidney Herbert, M.P., the Revd. J. Leyborne Popham, Ambrose L. Goddard, esq., M.P.

Trusteeship

The trustees examined the account of the receiver of the rents to Michaelmas 1856, upon which there appears to be a balance of £381 5*s.* 6*d.* in his hands which is to be carried to his next account.

The following resolution, having been sent by Mr. Heneage to the steward and a copy having been transmitted by him to each trustee, was now read. That it is most desirable that the chaplain to the college should reside at Froxfield and that, in the event of a future vacancy, application should be made to the bishop of the diocese asking permission of non-residence from Huish for such chaplain upon the condition of his residing at Froxfield and performing his duty in person at the college. If such permission should be obtained the trustees would endeavour to make such arrangements as might lead to his permanent residence either in the college or as near it as possible.

Mr. Heneage withdrew this resolution and it was resolved that it is desirable [that], and the steward is directed to ascertain whether, the trustees can by exchange or otherwise acquire the advowson of the vicarage of Froxfield with a view to it being connected with the chaplaincy of the hospital. The marquess of Ailesbury, Mr. H. N. Goddard, Mr. Sotheron Estcourt, and Mr. Heneage are appointed a committee to consider the whole subject of the chaplaincy and performance of the duties. They are requested to endeavour to devise a scheme whereby the purchase of advowsons for the Mayo trust, or an appropriation of part of that fund, may be made conducive to the appointment of a resident chaplain in close connection with the hospital.

The trustees executed the conveyance of the trust estates to the new trustees appointed at the last meeting.

Resolved that Mr. Sidney Herbert and Mr. A. L. Goddard be requested to view the hospital next year in conjunction with Mr. F. L. Popham.

A letter was received from Lord Ernest Bruce stating that he was prevented from being present at this meeting by the necessity of his personal attendance on Her Majesty in his official capacity. His absence is therefore excused.

Estate

Mr. George Young, the tenant of Huish farm, being desirous of relinquishing his tenancy in favour of his son William, and Mr. William Hayward, the tenant of Chirton farm, being likewise desirous of relinquishing his tenancy in favour of his son ... [*MS. blank*], at Michaelmas next, the trustees approve of and sanction such arrangements and changes of tenancy.

Mr. Redman's application for permission to grub the remaining 2 acres or thereabouts of Ley copse, permission for grubbing the whole of which was given to the former tenant Mr. John Halcomb in 1820 but not completed, is granted.

and see almshouse business

Almshouse

The steward reported that the several works and conveniences at the west end of the hospital, and the fuel houses, ordered at the last meeting had been completed and those at the last site were in progress, but there was a deficiency of six fuel houses. He produced a plan for rebuilding the wash-house and bakery, which is in a bad state of repair, and making the six fuel houses in one block of building with the wash-house upon a scheme suggested to, and approved by, the trustees who viewed the hospital on 5 June. He also stated that the heavy iron, and some other, spouting fixed many years ago to the south side of the quadrangle now wanted to be repaired throughout, at the estimated cost of about £10 in the whole.

The propriety of commencing the foregoing and other works, strongly recommended by the trustees who viewed the hospital, was discussed. The following were sanctioned and ordered, at estimated cost: the new privies, wash-house, and fuel houses, £150; spouting, £10; drainage of the yards and quadrangle, £100; pennant stone pavement and gutters at the hospital, £195 [*note*: see minute 21 October 1818]; Milton farm buildings to complete, £162.

The pavement [is] to be postponed to the commencement of next year.

The trustees sanctioned the expenditure, involving as it does part of the current income of next year, under the peculiar circumstances of the case and the expediency of commencing certain works before the next meeting.

The steward reported that in consequence of Mrs. Elizabeth Welch having kept her two sisters in her house after refusal of permission for more than one inmate he had withheld her quarter's stipend at Lady day. As she has now conformed to the rules the steward is authorized to pay her the sum retained.

Mrs. Ellen Lalande, who has permission for her granddaughter as an inmate, having applied at the view meeting for a nurse [it is] ordered that a nurse be not allowed under the circumstances.

The steward reported that William Gooding, the porter, having shortly after the last annual meeting become incapable of performing any of the duties, he had, with the approbation of Mr. Popham, placed William Gooding the younger, the son of the porter, in the office temporarily and that it has been executed to his entire satisfaction. [It is] resolved that William Gooding the son be appointed porter, in the expectation that he permits his father and family to remain in the house. [*Note*. William Gooding died 4 September 1859; William Gooding the son was sent to a lunatic asylum and his brother Richard appointed in his stead 14 July 1870; Aaron Brown appointed 13 July 1871]

and see trusteeship business

Mayo trust

It appears by a separate account produced by the receiver that the amount of new 3 per cent stock standing in the names of H. N. Goddard, esq., and F. L. Popham, esq., trustees of the fund established by the late Revd. Charles Mayo, had, after nine half-year's payments to Mr. Hugh Allan, the exhibitioner, and the investment of the surplus dividends, accumulated to £6,528 6*s.* 1*d.*, leaving £80 7*s.* 7*d.* cash in hand, out of which the last half-yearly payment of £35 will become payable to Mr. Allan on the 16th instant.

The resolution passed at the last meeting on the motion of Mr. Heneage with reference to the Mayo exhibitions was read for the purpose of being confirmed at this meeting in compliance with the directions in Mr. Mayo's trust deed. It was resolved that in all future elections for the Mayo exhibition notice shall be given to each trustee, previous to the examination of the candidates, of the name and residence of each candidate and of the school where each of them has been educated.

The resolution at the last meeting with reference to the purchase of an advowson for the Mayo trust was also read for confirmation. It was resolved that it is desirable to apply part of the 3 per cent annuities of the Revd. Charles Mayo's trust fund in the purchase of an advowson, that the steward communicate with Mr. Nelson Goddard and Col. Wroughton in case he hears of an advowson for sale which seems to him desirable according to the terms of Mr. Mayo's trust, and if they agree in his view that he summon a special meeting of the trustees.

The period of 5 years for which the Mayo exhibition was conferred on Mr. Hugh Allan expiring on the 16th instant the steward reported that he had, in accordance with the course pursued in 1852, given notice that the trustees would at this meeting proceed to elect another exhibitioner. In compliance with the directions received from Messrs. H. N. Goddard, F. L. Popham, and T. H. S. Sotheron Estcourt, the committee by whom the arrangements for the election in 1852 were made, the candidates, of whom a list had been sent to each trustee in compliance with the order at the last meeting, had been examined by the Revd. Edward Parry, domestic chaplain to the Lord Bishop of London, who was one of the examiners for this year at Marlborough college. One of the candidates, Francis William Atwood, having withdrawn during the examination Mr. Parry's report with respect to the other five candidates, and the required testimonials, were laid before the meeting. The five remaining candidates appear to be Arthur Henry Harington, William Henry St. Amand Wilton, James Lawrence Littlewood, Joel Francis Mullins, and Philip Ashby Phelps.

The trustees proceeded to the election of a scholar or exhibitioner on the foundation of the late Revd. Charles Mayo. It was resolved that Arthur Henry Harington, son of the Revd. John Harington of Little Hinton, should be appointed to the exhibition, to commence from 1 October next and to be tenable for 5 years provided the good conduct and progress of the exhibitioner be duly and regularly certified in accordance with the directions of the founder and the regulations laid down in 1852.

and see trusteeship business

Signatures

H. N. Goddard, chairman, T. Sotheron Estcourt, A. L. Goddard, F. Leyborne Popham, G. H. Walker Heneage, J. L. Popham, G. W. Wroughton, J. W. Awdry, Ailesbury, Shelburne, Sidney Herbert.

8 July 1858, at the Ailesbury Arms inn, Marlborough

Present

The marquess of Ailesbury, in the chair, H. N. Goddard, esq., Lord Ernest Bruce, M.P., Col. Wroughton, F. Leyborne Popham, esq., G. H. Walker Heneage, esq., Sir J. W. Awdry, the earl of Shelburne, the Rt. Hon. Sidney Herbert, M.P., the Revd. J. Leyborne Popham.

Trusteeship

The trustees examined the account of the receiver of the rents to Michaelmas 1857, upon which there appears to be a balance of £36 15*s.* 10*d.* in his hands which is to be carried to his next account.

Resolved that the marquess of Ailesbury and Mr. Sidney Herbert be requested to view the hospital next year in conjunction with Mr. Popham.

A letter was read from the Rt. Hon. T. H. S. Sotheron Estcourt stating [that] he was prevented by unavoidable public business from being present at this meeting and his absence is excused. Mr. A. L. Goddard's reason for absence is considered insufficient.

and see Mayo trust business

Estate

Ordered that a wall or other sufficient fence be erected from the brook to the house occupied by John Francis of Froxfield and that the house, outbuildings, and fence walls on Stephen Snook's house there be repaired where necessary, but the erection of a new shed as applied for is postponed for the present and the steward is to make the best arrangement he can with the tenants for contribution by them towards the cost according to the circumstances in each case.

An application having been made by Mr. John Redman for pigsties and for additional shed room at Froxfield farm for the convenience of feeding and fattening cattle, the steward is directed to erect pigsties suitable to the farm on a site to be determined by Mr. Popham and under his superintendence as to plan and construction. They do not consider it necessary for the trust estate to incur at this time the cost of erecting stalls for cattle.

The steward is authorized to give notice to the executors of the late John Edmonds in order to determine the present tenancy of the small farm at Oare, and to effect a re-letting either to a member of the family or to a stranger, under the direction of Col. Wroughton.

The tenant of Chirton farm having applied for some repairs to the outbuildings the steward is directed to do what may appear necessary, under the direction of Col. Wroughton and keeping in view that the state of the buildings there is such as to render a heavy expenditure at no distant time necessary, [and] to have the work so done as to be available for future alterations at the buildings on that farm.

A scheme having been put forth for making a railway from Hungerford to Devizes the steward is empowered to assent on behalf of the trustees in case application should be made for an Act of Parliament.

Almshouse

In consequence of an appearance of one of the walls of the chapel giving way, and the trustees at the view meeting having ordered a report to be made on the state of the walls and roof, which is of iron, the report of Mr. James May was produced. The steward stated that, the chapel having been built at the expense of Thomas, late earl of Ailesbury (see minutes of 4 August 1813), he had thought it right to communicate with the marquess of Ailesbury in order that his lordship's builder might, if thought desirable, inspect the building. Reports from each of these persons were read and the marquess of Ailesbury expressed his wish to take the repair on himself as the chapel had been built by his grandfather, a proposal which was thankfully accepted, and the trustees desire to offer to his lordship their best acknowledgements for his liberality.

A report on the state of the roof at the west end of the hospital was also produced. [It is] ordered that Mr. Money be employed to survey the roof and the steward is directed to have such portion as may appear most wanting, or most desirable, first done for an expenditure of £75, which is considered sufficient for the present year.

Mr. Barker, the surgeon of the hospital, having reported that, in consequence of the extreme state of Mrs. Catherine Carpenter, it is proper that a nurse in addition to her granddaughter should sleep in the house permission is granted.

The trustees sanction the occupation of the steward's house in the hospital by Mrs. ... [*MS. blank*] Smith provided she conforms to all the rules of the establishment and quit at any time on being required. She will be expected to give sufficient guarantee of ability to maintain herself so as not to require parochial assistance.

Mayo trust

It appears by a separate account produced by the receiver that the amount of new 3 per cent stock standing in the names of H. N.

Goddard, esq., and F. L. Popham, esq., trustees of the fund established by the late Revd. Charles Mayo, had, after all the payments had been made to Mr. Hugh Allan, the exhibitioner, and the investment of the surplus dividends, accumulated to £6,628 6*s.* 1*d.*, leaving £133 18*s.* cash in hand.

A letter from the chapter clerk of the dean and canons of Windsor, who declined to part with the advowson of the vicarage of Froxfield with a view to connect that benefice with the chaplaincy of the hospital, was read. The steward stated that from various causes it had not been found practicable to arrange a meeting of the committee to whom the subject of the arrangement of the chaplaincy had been referred, and in consequence of the serious doubts entertained by some of the trustees, and lately communicated to him, as to the desirability of purchasing an advowson he had taken no further steps for that purpose.

A report from the committee to whom the subject of the chaplaincy and Mayo trust was referred was read. [It is] resolved that it be adopted and copied with the minutes of this meeting.

Resolved that Sir John W. Awdry, by whose able assistance the report was prepared, be added to the committee, who are continued for the purposes mentioned in the minute of the last meeting.

The resolution passed at the last and preceding meetings relative to the purchase of an advowson for the Mayo trust was read. [It is] resolved unanimously that such resolution, being at variance with the report, be rescinded except so far as regards the acquisition of the advowson of Froxfield if it can be arranged.

Resolved unanimously that it is desirable to appropriate part of the income of the Mayo charity to another exhibition, in addition to that already founded, to the same amount and on the same terms.

The steward reported that in consequence of Mr. Arthur Henry Harington, the exhibitioner on the Mayo foundation elected at the last meeting, not having matriculated till 3 February and not gone into residence at his college (Wadham) till 25 May last no payment had been made in respect of the exhibition, which by the minute of [the] last meeting was to date from 1 October 1857. [It is] ordered that payment to Mr. Harington date from 3 February last and that the 5 years' term of his exhibition date from that period, subject to the regulations under which he was appointed.

Report of the committee on the Mayo trust

Mr. Mayo's main object was to improve the condition of laborious and estimable but ill-paid Wiltshire clergymen. His secondary object was to do it in connection with the Froxfield trust.

Now, whatever is paid in aid of the education and support of the sons and daughters of the clergy is a virtual addition to the endowments of the church, whereas what is laid out in the purchase of advowsons is no such addition but a mere transfer of patronage to the trustees.

The effect of this was not the same in Mr. Mayo's time. Though the purchase of advowsons was no addition to the endowment of the church the transfer of patronage of livings above the poorest to trustees, who he hoped would bestow it according to his wishes, was an improvement of the prospects of that class of the clergy whom it was his object to benefit. These were well educated and laborious men free from all fanaticism and extravagance and without interest to procure them preferment.

This seems to be a fair statement of his general object, by which trustees probably will feel they ought to be guided even if they think themselves bound rather to follow their own convictions than Mr. Mayo's views of the application of these principles to the divisions of his own day. These views, as appears from the instrument of foundation, were those of a moderate man greatly attached, both from theory and from gratitude, to the connection between church and state as important to the influence of the church through the position of her ministry but free from the torpor and apathy commonly imputed to those who relied most on that connection, and greatly dreading Calvinistic doctrine and practices imputed to that section of the clergy with whom that doctrine was most prevalent.

The character, however, and circumstances of those whom he intended to benefit may be regarded abstractedly from any party differences. Now, the poor and laborious clergy of his day were for the most part stipendiary curates often serving two or three churches. The facilities for non-residence and pluralities, and the greater laxity as to the duty required, then gave to a very small benefice a pecuniary value over and above what was necessary to obtain the services of a curate. At the present day the small benefices are by subdivision of larger ones much more numerous and, not being worth the acceptance of men of more interest, are for the most part held singly by men of the same class who formerly were curates, who are consequently more numerous and not much more wealthy than the curates of Mr. Mayo's time while much more is expected of them.

In order, therefore, to carry out Mr. Mayo's object by the purchase of advowsons they ought to be of a greater value than the minimum named by him or the social effect intended by him will not result, and even then many men of the class whom he intended to benefit will not be eligible.

Whilst, therefore, the trustees have a free discretion, after providing one exhibition, to invest in advowsons within the limits directed, it may be considered that unless there be special reason for doing so the spirit of his injunctions will be better carried out by the application of his funds to the other objects named by him.

We are of opinion that some surplus ought every year to be laid by in order gradually to extend more and more widely the educational benefits of the trust, but the present accumulations are sufficient to call for the consideration of an immediate extension beyond the single exhibition supplied by the trust.

Present amount of stock: new 3 per cents £6,628 6*s*. 1*d*., cash in hand £133 18*s*. Income, within a trifle of £200 a year.

Next meeting

Resolved that a meeting of the trustees be held at the town hall in Marlborough on Tuesday 19 October next at 12 o'clock for the purpose of further considering, and confirming or annulling, the several resolutions passed this day with reference to the Mayo trust.

Signatures

H. N. Goddard, chairman, G. W. Wroughton, G. H. Walker Heneage, J. L. Popham, F. Leyborne Popham, J. W. Awdry.

19 October 1858, a special meeting of the trustees, as trustees of the Mayo trust, held at the town hall, Marlborough, at 12 o'clock, in pursuance of a resolution passed at the meeting held on 8 July last for the purpose of further considering, and confirming or annulling, the several resolutions passed with reference to the Mayo trust.

Present

H. N. Goddard, esq., chairman, the Rt. Hon. the Lord Ernest Bruce, M.P., F. Leyborne Popham, esq., the Rt. Hon. T. H. S. Sotheron Estcourt, M.P., G. H. Walker Heneage, esq., Sir J. W. Awdry, Ambrose L. Goddard, esq., M.P.

Trusteeship

It is directed that the notices for the next annual meeting contain a notification that the salary of the steward will be brought under consideration.

and see Mayo trust business

Mayo trust

A notice of the time, place, and object of this meeting had been given to each trustee, or left at his dwelling house, more than 21 days before the day of meeting.

The minutes of the meeting of the trustees held on 8 July last so far as relates to the Mayo trust, and the report of the committee, were read.

The minutes of 16 July 1852 and the report of the committee on the regulations to be observed in the election of a Mayo exhibitioner thereto appended were also read.

A letter from Lord Shelburne reporting a personal communication with the Very Revd. the dean of Windsor with a view to ascertain how far there was any probability of the advowson of Froxfield being obtained for either the Froxfield or Mayo trusts, and being thereby made available for the chaplaincy of the hospital, was read. Lord Ernest Bruce also stated the purport of an interview he had had with the dean for the same object.

Resolved that the best thanks of the trustees be given to Lord Shelburne and Lord Ernest Bruce for the trouble and interest they have taken. Their lordships are requested to offer the thanks of the trustees to the Very Revd. the dean of Windsor for the very obliging manner in which he has received the application, and for the assistance which he has been ready personally to afford in a matter which appears surrounded by too many difficulties to enable any further progress to be made, at all events for the present.

Resolved that in case of a vacancy happening in the vicarage of Froxfield it will be desirable for the trustees to communicate with the dean in order that the convenience and advantage of the hospital may if possible be consulted in the new appointment.

The minutes of the meeting of the trustees held on 8 July last in reference to the postponement of purchasing an advowson and establishing another exhibition on the Mayo trust were confirmed without alteration.

Mr. Merriman, as steward and receiver of [the] charities, is to take the necessary steps for the trustees electing another exhibitioner on [the] Mayo trust at their next annual meeting, the election to be conducted in the same manner and with previous examination of candidates as on the former occasions. The examiner is, however, to be requested not to state the relative qualifications of the candidates but their competency according to the terms of Mr. Mayo's deed, with an extract from which he is to be furnished. The notices and advertisements for the election are also to contain a similar extract.

Resolved that Mr. Heneage be added to the committee to whom Mr. Merriman is to refer in case of need during the proceedings for the election.

Signatures

H. N. Goddard, G. H. Walker Heneage, J. W. Awdry, A. L. Goddard, F. Leyborne Popham. [The names of Lord E. Bruce and T. H. S. Sotheron Estcourt were pencilled in by the clerk, but they did not sign]

Endorsement

Copy of a note by Lord Shelburne ordered to be entered in the minute book 14 July 1859

In conversation with me the dean was kind enough to observe that in any case of vacancy in the living of Froxfield his own disposition personally would be to consult the wishes of the trustees in appointing another incumbent, that he could not of course pledge his successors, but that he believed that we should probably find them equally ready to do the same thing. S[helburne]

14 July 1859, at the Ailesbury Arms inn, Marlborough

Present

The marquess of Ailesbury, in the chair, H. N. Goddard, esq., Col. Wroughton, G. H. Walker Heneage, esq., the earl of Shelburne, the Revd. J. Leyborne Popham.

Trusteeship

The trustees examined the account of the receiver of the rents to Michaelmas 1858, upon which there appears to be a balance of £242 1*s*. 10*d*. in his hands which is to be carried to his next account.

Resolved that the steward's salary be increased £20 a year and that he be allowed to charge in future £20 a year to the Mayo trust fund as receiver and manager of that trust and for conducting elections as they occur.

Resolved that Mr. H. N. Goddard and Mr. Sotheron Estcourt be requested to view the hospital next year in conjunction with Mr. Popham.

Letters were read from Mr. Sotheron Estcourt, Mr. Sidney Herbert, and Sir John Awdry stating that they were prevented by unavoidable public business from being present at this meeting and their absence is excused.

Mr. A. L. Goddard having been absent from two successive annual meetings his patronage is suspended.

Estate

The steward reported that he had agreed with Mr. Henry Edmonds, son of the late Mr. John Edmonds, for the tenancy of the small farm at Oare on the same terms as the present holding.

A cottage on Huish Hill, which had been sometime claimed as belonging to the overseers of that parish, having been brought by the steward into [the] possession of the trustees is in such a state as to be past repair. [It is] ordered that it be pulled down and a sufficient cottage or double cottage [be] built in lieu thereof in the village of Huish, under the direction of Col. Wroughton.

The steward stated that he had not erected a new stable at Chirton for the reasons mentioned in his report, which was put on the table. Col. Wroughton is requested to look at the farm and to make such arrangements as he may think proper as well for breaking up 36 acres of down at the south end of the farm as to the buildings in general. Various suggestions were made for alteration in the plans proposed for the buildings, particularly by converting the barn, now running in a line with the dwelling house, into stabling or by some other arrangement of the buildings. Col. Wroughton is requested to give such orders therein as he may think most advantageous to the hospital estate.

Col. Wroughton is requested to give directions for building such stabling, and making such alteration in the yard, as may be necessary at Broomsgrove farm at a cost not exceeding £300.

Mr. William Hayward, the late tenant of Chirton farm, having offered to exchange a piece of meadow adjoining a small mead of the trustees at Chirton (each piece being so small as to be scarcely worth occupying by itself) for a small piece adjoining his house and garden, and the exchange being an advantageous one to the trustees not only in the land itself but for the timber on Hayward's piece, which he proposes to give up to the trustees with a view to it being cut and applied so far as suitable for the new buildings to be erected for his son on the trust property, the trustees now present signed the necessary application to the Inclosure Commissioners for their order for the exchange.

Almshouse

The steward reported that the trustees at the view meeting directed the repair of a further portion of the hospital roof in accordance with Mr. Money's report, at a cost of about £87.

Mrs. Smith, to whom permission to occupy the steward's house was given at the last meeting, not having availed herself of the offer, and the house having remained altogether unoccupied, the steward reported that he had, with the concurrence of some of the trustees whom he had consulted, allowed Mrs ... [*MS. blank*] White, a daughter of the late Mr. Welford, solicitor, of Marlborough, to use it during pleasure, which is approved.

The minute of 8 July 1851 as to leaving the hospital gates open till 10 at night in the summer was read. [It is] ordered that the gates be left open till 10 o'clock from 1 June to 1 September, with power to Mr. F. L. Popham to order them to be closed if he thinks fit.

The Revd. J. L. Popham is requested to ascertain how far a portion of the building at the entrance porch can be converted into a water closet for the use of the widows at night, to be open only during such time as the gates are closed. He is requested to give necessary orders for the work.

Ordered that two portable water closets be purchased and placed under the control of the medical attendant for the use of widows who may be bedridden.

Mayo trust

It appears by a separate account produced by the receiver that the amount of new 3 per cent stock standing in the names of H. N. Goddard, esq., and F. L. Popham, esq., trustees of the fund established by the late Revd. Charles Mayo, had, after two half-year's payments to Mr. Arthur Henry Harington, the exhibitioner, and the investment of the surplus dividends, accumulated to £6,728 6*s.* 1*d.*, leaving £97 15*s.* 2*d.* cash in hand.

The minutes of the last annual meeting, 8 July 1858, on the subject of the chaplaincy and the appropriation of the Mayo trust fund were read; also the minute of the special meeting of 19 October last. Whereupon the trustees resolved to proceed to the election of a second exhibitioner on the Mayo trust.

The steward having, under the direction of such members of the committee as he could communicate with, conducted the preliminary proceedings in accordance with the course pursued in 1852 and 1857 four of the candidates who sent in testimonials and papers had been examined by the Revd. Edwin Palmer of Balliol college, Oxford, M.A., one of the examiners this year at Marlborough college.

The candidates appeared to have been George Alexander Allan, son of Revd. Hugh Allan, Cricklade St. Mary, Alexander Hooper Etty, son of Revd. Simeon James Etty, Wanborough, Joel Francis Mullins, son of the Revd. George Mullins, Chalfield, Corsham, Philip Ashby Phelps, son of Revd. John Phelps, Little Langford, Edward Popham, son of Revd. William Popham, Christchurch, Bradford, John Edward Tompson, son of the late Revd. Edward Henry Tompson, Lyneham, of whom Mr. Tompson withdrew on account of his age exceeding 19 years and Mr. J. F. Mullins was prevented by severe illness from attending the examiner. Having been a candidate in 1857 Mr. Mullins was then examined with the others, and a statement of the circumstances of his case by the Revd. Herbert Plater was read. Testimonials of the several candidates were referred to and put on the table.

Notice was taken that of two of the other candidates P. A. Phelps attained the age of 19 on 2 May last and Edward Popham on 2 November 1858, and that there was a deficiency of a few months in the period of residence of the Revd. William Popham, the father of Mr. Edward Popham, as required by Mr. Mayo's trust deed.

The report of the committee in 1852 specifying the ages of the candidates and conditions of qualification was referred to.

It was resolved that Mr. P. A. Phelps be admitted a candidate, Lord Shelburne assenting only on account of the peculiarity of the circumstances but without prejudice to the general question as to whether the candidate's age is to be reckoned in future as starting from the day of election or from the day of his recorded entry as a candidate.

Resolved that Mr. Edward Popham is not eligible.

J. F. Mullins not having been able to attend the examination is considered not eligible. [*Margin*. Mr. Mullins died on 12 July 1859]

The trustees proceeded to the election of a scholar or exhibitioner on the foundation of the late Revd. Charles Mayo. It was resolved that Mr. Philip Ashby Phelps, son of the Revd. John Phelps of Little Langford, should be appointed to the exhibition, to commence from 1 October next and to be tenable for 5 years provided the good conduct and progress of the exhibitioner be duly and regularly certified in accordance with the directions of the founder and the regulations laid down in 1852.

and see trusteeship business

Signatures

Ailesbury, chairman, G. H. Walker Heneage, H. N. Goddard, G. W. Wroughton, J. L. Popham, Shelburne.

12 July 1860, at the Ailesbury Arms inn, Marlborough

Present

H. N. Goddard, esq., in the chair, the marquess of Ailesbury, Col. Wroughton, F. Leyborne Popham, esq., G. H. Walker Heneage, esq., Sir J. W. Awdry, the Revd. J. Leyborne Popham, Ambrose L. Goddard, esq., M.P.

Trusteeship

The trustees examined the account of the receiver of the rents to Michaelmas 1859, upon which there appears to be a balance of £62 1*s.* 7*d.* due to the receiver which he is to charge in his next account.

Resolved that Lord Ernest Bruce and Mr. Sotheron Estcourt be requested to view the hospital next year in conjunction with Mr. Popham.

And [resolved] that the trustees to be appointed in future be taken in rotation according to [*changed to* their order of] seniority.

Letters were read from the Rt. Hon. T. H. S. Sotheron Estcourt and the Rt. Hon. Sidney Herbert stating that they were prevented by unavoidable public business from being present at this meeting and their absence is excused, as is also the absence of Lord Ernest Bruce who is prevented by sickness from attending.

Estate

The steward reported that he had, under the direction of Col. Wroughton, erected a new stable at Broomsgrove farm and that some fencing to complete the yard and some alteration in the buildings would be requisite. He had, likewise under Col. Wroughton's directions, had a new stable erected at Chirton, but the further alterations in the buildings on that farm and the removal of the cottage at Huish had been postponed in order that the cost might be distributed over more than 1 year's accounts. [It is] ordered that the same be completed under the direction of Col. Wroughton.

The steward reported that he had placed the plans and particulars of the trust property required for the Berks. & Hants railway in the hands of Mr. Giles Westbury of Andover with instructions to treat with the company for it, viz. about 2½ acres at Milton and about 2¾ acres with five cottages at Froxfield. [It is] resolved that the appointment of Mr. Giles Westbury be confirmed. He is authorized to act for the trustees in regard to the sale of the lands and compensation under the direction of Messrs. H. N. Goddard, F. L. Popham, and Revd. J. L. Popham, who are appointed a committee for the purpose of this negotiation with power to any two of them to act, and to give such order as they may think fit, with regard to the immediate erection of cottages at Froxfield in lieu of those intended to be removed.

Almshouse

The trustees, Messrs. H. N. Goddard and Francis L. Popham, who viewed the hospital on the 2nd instant, reported that after having visited the inmates they proceeded to investigate charges preferred by Mrs. Mary Hemus (apartment no. 9), upon information stated to have been furnished to her by Mrs. Elizabeth Marsh (no. 7), against Mrs. Elizabeth Mary Powys (no. 6) under rule 11 for incontinence in 1856 with William Clark Gooding, appointed porter in July 1857, and Mr. Stephen Snook, baker and shopkeeper in Froxfield. After a full hearing the trustees came to the decision 'that there is no proof of the charges alleged against Mrs. Powys either with reference to William C. Gooding or Mr. S. Snook, and that they think the preferring [of] such charges after a lapse of upwards of 3 years, to say the least, very indiscreet on the part of Mrs. Hemus, and Mrs. Marsh was admonished to be more careful in future in making any statements respecting persons connected with the establishment'.

The viewing trustees further reported that Mrs. Powys and Mrs. Marsh, at the termination of the hearing, made various complaints against Mrs. Hemus and her servant, whereupon Mrs. Hemus was informed that if any future cause of complaint against her servant arose the permission to have one in her apartment would be withdrawn.

An application was made by Mrs. Elizabeth Cooke, a clergy widow, whose stipend for two quarters had been withheld under rules 6 and 7 by the steward at the payday on the 6th instant in consequence of her absence for 9 weeks beyond the time for which she had leave. The steward is directed to pay Mrs. Cooke the amount of stipend retained, except £5 which the trustees declare to be forfeited.

The steward is directed to have a survey made of the roof of the hospital and to give such order as is necessary for repair of it.

A suggestion having been made to the trustees at the view meeting that a handrail at the chapel steps would be a convenience to invalid widows they declined to give any instructions thereon, but directed the application to be mentioned at the annual meeting.

The steward is directed to have handrails placed at the steps in such manner as shall appear most conducive to the object in view and without detriment to the appearance of the building.

Mayo trust

It appears by a separate account produced by the receiver that the amount of new 3 per cent stock standing in the names of H. N. Goddard, esq., and F. L. Popham, esq., trustees of the fund established by the late Revd. Charles Mayo, had, after four half-year's payments to Mr. Arthur Henry Harington and one half-year's payment to Mr. Philip Ashby Phelps, the exhibitioners, and the investment of the surplus dividends, accumulated to £6,828 6*s.* 1*d.*, leaving £80 11*s.* 6*d.* cash in hand.

Signatures

H. N. Goddard, chairman, G. W. Wroughton, F. Leyborne Popham, J. W. Awdry, A. L. Goddard, J. L. Popham, Ailesbury. [The name of Mr. Heneage was pencilled in by the clerk, but he did not sign]

11 July 1861, at the Ailesbury Arms inn, Marlborough

Present

The marquess of Ailesbury, in the chair, H. N. Goddard, esq., Lord Ernest Bruce, M.P., Col. Wroughton, F. Leyborne Popham, esq., the Rt. Hon. T. H. S. Sotheron Estcourt, M.P., G. H. Walker Heneage, esq., Sir J. W. Awdry, the earl of Shelburne, the Revd. J. Leyborne Popham, Ambrose L. Goddard, esq., M.P.

Trusteeship

The trustees examined the account of the receiver of the rents to Michaelmas 1860, upon which there appears to be a balance of £213 9*s.* 4*d.* in his hands which is to be carried to his next account.

Resolved that in compliance with the minute of the last annual meeting the marquess of Ailesbury and Mr. H. N. Goddard be the trustees to view the hospital next year in conjunction with Mr. F. L. Popham.

Lord Herbert being prevented by ill health from attending this meeting his absence is excused. [*Note.* Lord Herbert died 2 August 1861, universally beloved and lamented. Thomas B.M.]

and see estate business

Estate

An application by Mr. Redman for some addition to his house at Froxfield, in which there is an insufficiency of bedrooms, was considered and a plan was produced, the execution of which is estimated to cost £134 towards which Mr. Redman offers to contribute one half. The trustees sanction the proposed alteration, if Mr. Redman will take the work on himself, at an allowance of £60.

The steward reported that he had, in compliance with the resolution at the last annual meeting and under the direction of the trustees to whom this matter was referred, arranged with the Berks. & Hants Extension Railway Company at £950 in the whole as the compensation to be paid for the land and cottages, and damage to the hospital estates, at Froxfield and Milton. £472 10*s*. was for purchase money for the land and severance and £477 10*s*. for the rebuilding of five cottages at Froxfield, which he had undertaken in order to avoid having the money paid into the court of Chancery and the consequent delay and expenses of orders for laying it out in erecting such cottages which would be necessary. He had, under the direction of the before mentioned trustees, converted a portion of the Blue Lion stables into three cottages and had employed Mr. Money of Donnington to prepare plans for a good double cottage to be erected at the corner of the field allotments. The trustees approve what has been done and direct the steward to proceed to the erection of the cottages under the direction of Messrs. H. N. Goddard, F. L. Popham, and Revd. J. L. Popham.

The steward stated that, in consequence of a representation made to him by the secretary of the Berks. & Hants Railway Company that the trustees were of opinion that a rent charge should be taken under the powers of the Lands Clauses Consolidation Acts instead of the £472 10*s*. for the sale money of the lands required for the railway, he had, under the direction of the gentlemen to whom the sale was referred, written a circular to all the trustees for the purpose of collecting their opinions on the proposed substitution. [He stated] that, the opinions being pretty equally divided, the marquess of Ailesbury and Mr. Sotheron Estcourt, the chairman and vice-chairman of the railway company, had directed the final arrangement of this question to stand over for this meeting.

Resolved that it is desirable to invest the £472 10*s*., when received from the Berks. & Hants Railway Company, with the view of re-investing it in the purchase of land for the improvement of the property of the charity.

The steward stated two proposals for exchanges of lands cut off by the railway, one at Froxfield of 3r. 29p. of arable severed from the farm for 1a. 2r. of water meadow and rushes belonging to the settled estate of Mr. Popham, and the other with Mr. Cusse of 4a. 2r. 1p. at Milkhouse Water for 6a. 2r. 35p. severed from his land, for which, however, a further quantity of land would be required from the hospital estate to make up the value.

The steward is directed to carry out the exchange with Mr. Popham and to endeavour, with the sanction of Col. Wroughton, to make terms with Mr. Cusse. Col. Wroughton is authorized to select any piece of land belonging to the hospital which he may think can be advantageously used for the purpose.

An application from Mr. W. G. Brown for permission to dig clay for bricks in one of the fields on Broomsgrove farm in the occupation of Mr. J. J. Kingstone is referred to the steward, who is authorized, under the sanction of Col. Wroughton and with the consent of the tenant, to make such terms as may be considered fair.

Ordered that a fence wall to the yard of Mr. Kingstone's farm be built as proposed by the plan now produced.

A plan was laid before the meeting for alterations in the house and yard at Chirton, of which the trustees approve generally, and the whole are referred to Col. Wroughton to give such order as he may think fit for the execution of the work.

James Brewer having given notice of his intention to quit the small farm at Clench, and being about to do so unless a reduction should be made in his rent, the steward is authorized to make terms for Brewer's continuing the farm if he can do so, under the sanction of Col. Wroughton, at a reduction to a rent not lower than £60.

The steward is authorized to expend £15 on the house at Froxfield occupied by John Humphreys and lately fallen into hand if he shall find that he can thereby put it into a proper state.

Almshouse

An application signed by 41 of the widows for an increase of the stipend and setting forth the inconvenience sustained by them by the reduction made in 1851 was read. Of those who signed, it appears that 18 only were in the hospital before the reduction. The trustees will be ready to make an increase in the stipend whenever the state of the hospital funds will warrant it.

The minutes of the last meeting as to a handrail at the chapel steps was read and that order is renewed, the work to be executed under the direction of the marquess of Ailesbury if his lordship should think it desirable. The trustees authorize the contribution of £20 for the expense of a stove in the chapel, to be erected also under the direction of the marquess of Ailesbury if he shall think proper.

Mayo trust

It appears by a separate account produced by the receiver that the amount of new 3 per cent stock standing in the names of H. N. Goddard, esq., and F. L. Popham, esq., trustees of the fund established by the late Revd. Charles Mayo, had, after six half-year's payments to Mr. Arthur Henry Harington and three half-year's payments to Mr. Philip Ashby Phelps, the exhibitioners, and the investment of the surplus dividends, accumulated to £6,828 6*s.* 1*d.*, leaving £125 11*s.* 2*d.* cash in hand.

Messrs. H. N. Goddard, F. L. Popham, and Sotheron Estcourt

are appointed a committee for directing the course of proceeding, the advertisement, and all details preliminary to an election of a scholar on the Mayo exhibition at the next annual meeting of the trustees. In all future advertisements an extract is to be given [of], and public attention to be called to, that part of the trust deed of the late Mr. Mayo which relates to the qualification of the parents of the candidate, and attention [is to be] called to the fact that, under the terms of the trust, superior attainments alone will not necessarily ensure the success of any particular candidate.

Signatures

Ailesbury, H. N. Goddard, J. W. Awdry, G. W. Wroughton, Shelburne, G. H. Walker Heneage, A. L. Goddard. [The names of Lord E. Bruce, Mr. F. L. Popham, Mr. Sotheron Estcourt, Revd. J. L. Popham were pencilled in by the clerk, but they did not sign]

10 July 1862, at the Ailesbury Arms inn, Marlborough

Present

The marquess of Ailesbury, in the chair, H. N. Goddard, esq., Col. Wroughton, F. Leyborne Popham, esq., G. H. Walker Heneage, esq., Sir J. W. Awdry, the earl of Shelburne, the Revd. J. Leyborne Popham.

Trusteeship

The trustees examined the account of the receiver of the rents to Michaelmas 1861, upon which there appears to be a balance of £161 9*s.* 10*d.* in his hands which is to be carried to his next account.

Lord Ernest Bruce and Col. Wroughton are, in accordance with the minute of 12 July 1860, the trustees to view the hospital next year in conjunction with Mr. F. L. Popham. Col. Wroughton being unable to attend, the Revd. J. L. Popham will view as his substitute.

The Rt. Hon. T. H. S. Sotheron Estcourt being prevented from being present at this meeting by severe illness his absence is excused.

Estate

The steward submitted to the meeting an account of the sum received from the Berks. & Hants Railway Company for the destruction of cottages at Froxfield taken for that work, upon which there is a balance unexpended of £308 17*s.* 3*d.*, subject to an unsettled claim by the builder, applicable to the construction of cottages in lieu of those destroyed.

The steward reported that in consequence of many trees on Broomsgrove farm, in the occupation of Mr. J. J. Kingstone, having been much injured in the last winter by cutting off large limbs he had, under the direction of Col. Wroughton, had a valuation made of the damage, which is estimated at £37 16*s.* 6*d.* Mr. Kingstone admitted having given the order, which, however, had been exceeded by the workmen employed, and stated his willingness to take the trees at a valuation or to pay a fair sum for the damage done and, if necessary, to give up land for a plantation. [It is] resolved that Mr. Kingstone be required to pay the £37 16*s*. 6*d*., the amount of such valuation, and in case of his refusal immediately to comply with these terms, which the trustees consider very lenient under the circumstances, the steward is to give Mr. J. J. Kingstone notice to quit his farm.

The steward stated that, in consequence of the advanced state of the last season at which the plans for new cottages were sent by Mr. Sotheron Estcourt and the subsequent extraordinary demand for bricks, he had not built the two further cottages in lieu of those taken by the Berks. & Hants Extension railway. The foundations having been dug out he had suspended operations in consequence of Mr. Drury, the holder of the Pelican public house at Froxfield for his life, having offered it to the trustees at an annual rent for the remainder of his interest, whereby an opportunity would be afforded of discontinuing one of the public houses at that end of the village and converting it into cottages. It appearing that by reason of Mr. Drury's advanced age (about 88) the prospect of long further continuance of his holding cannot be considered great, the steward is authorized, under the direction of Mr. F. L. Popham, to arrange terms with Mr. Drury for obtaining the Pelican, to convert the Blue Lion house and buildings into three cottages out of the money received from the railway company, and to repair the Pelican and make it sufficient for a respectable small inn.

Some conversation having then ensued with regard to the accommodation to be given to tenants in cottages belonging to the trust it was resolved that it should be adopted as a general principle, unless in cases where special directions are given to the contrary, that in any new cottages built, or old buildings converted into cottages, there shall be three bedrooms and separate entrances to them.

It was further resolved on account of peculiar circumstances in connection with the conversion of the Blue Lion building that Mr. Popham, who has kindly undertaken to control the further proceedings in this matter, should have a discretionary power to dispense with the above resolution as regards separate entrances if he should find it expedient to do so.

Almshouse

The application of Mrs. Elizabeth Gough, no. 25, for payment of her quarter's stipend to Midsummer, withheld by the steward in consequence of her absence beyond her leave, the same thing having occurred in the preceding quarter, is acceded to. The quarter may be paid with the Michaelmas quarter.

10th July 1862.

Cottages — General Order about Bed Rooms: & separate Entrances. —

Some Conversation having then ensued with regard to the accommodation to be given to Tenants in Cottages belonging to the Trust, it was resolved that it should be adopted as a general principle (unless in Cases where special directions are given to the Contrary) that in any new Cottages built, or old buildings converted into Cottages there shall be 3 bedrooms and separate entrances to the same —

Conversion of Blue Lion Exception to the above Order —

It was further resolved on account of peculiar Circumstances in Connexion with the Conversion of the Blue Lion building, that Mr. Popham who has kindly undertaken to controul the further proceedings in this matter should have a discretionary power to dispense with the above resolution as regards separate entrances if he should find it expedient to do so. —

No. 19. Vacant may be filled by another clergy Widow

The House No. 19. (Clergy 3 Counties) having become Vacant on 16th Oct 1860 — and the Vacancy having in Compliance with Rule 19 been advertized in Jany. 1861 — Col. Wroughton the Trustee to whom the nomination belongs is at liberty under Rule 19 to put in a Clergy Widow from some other District

Minutes of a meeting held 10 July 1862

The house no. 19 (clergy, three-counties) having become vacant on 16 October 1860, and the vacancy having in compliance with rule 19 been advertized in January 1861, Col. Wroughton, the trustee to whom the nomination belongs, is at liberty under rule 19 to put in a clergy widow from some other district.

An application made by Mrs. Jacob to the trustees who viewed the hospital for permission to exchange her house, no. 14, for no. 19, which had been and is still vacant, is not permitted.

The trustees who viewed the hospital on the 10th *ultimo* reported that in their opinion the steward's house might be beneficially appropriated to one of the clergy widows in one of the smaller houses. The steward is directed to have the house, hitherto used by him for paying the widows, repaired and fitted up for the reception of a clergy widow, and the present occupier of the house no. 15 is to have the option of moving into the steward's house, to be henceforth designated as no. … [*MS. blank*] if she should accept the offer.

Mayo trust

It appears by a separate account produced by the receiver that the amount of new 3 per cent stock standing in the names of H. N. Goddard, esq., and F. L. Popham, esq., trustees of the fund established by the late Revd. Charles Mayo, had, after eight half-year's payments to Mr. Arthur Henry Harington and five half-year's payments to Mr. Philip Ashby Phelps, the exhibitioners, and the investment of the surplus dividends, accumulated to £6,828 6*s.* 1*d.*, leaving £158 2*s.* 7*d.* cash in hand.

In accordance with the minute of the last meeting, 11 July 1861, the trustees proceeded to the election of a scholar or exhibitioner on the foundation of the Revd. Charles Mayo, deceased.

The candidates who sent in applications and testimonials are Charles Herbert Mayo, aged 17, son of the Revd. William Mayo of Salisbury, William Henry Atkinson Emra, aged 18, son of the Revd. John Emra of Redlynch near Salisbury, George Alexander Allan, aged 18, son of the Revd. Hugh Allan of Cricklade, George Nutt, aged 16, son of the Revd. George Nutt of Shaw near Melksham, John Henry Wilkinson, aged 17, son of the Revd. M. Wilkinson, D.D., of West (*Bishop's*) Lavington near Devizes, Charles Clark, aged 17, son of the Revd. Thomas A. Clark of Chippenham.

The report by the Revd. Edwin Meyrick, vicar of Chiseldon, on his examination of the several candidates was read.

Resolved that Mr. John Henry Wilkinson, son of the Revd. Matthew Wilkinson, D.D., is appointed to the exhibition on the foundation of the Revd. Charles Mayo, deceased, to commence from 3 February next and to be tenable for 5 years provided the good conduct and progress of the exhibitioner be duly and regularly certified in accordance with the directions of the founder and the regulations laid down in 1852. The exhibitioner is expected to matriculate in or before Easter term next.

The steward is directed to write to Mr. Meyrick and express the special thanks of the trustees for his report on the candidates and his

very judicious observations in regard to their respective merits.
Signatures
H. N. Goddard, J. L. Popham, J. W. Awdry, G. W. Wroughton, G. H. Walker Heneage. [The names of Lord Ailesbury, Mr. F. L. Popham, and Lord Shelburne were pencilled in by the clerk, but they did not sign]

9 July 1863, at the Ailesbury Arms inn, Marlborough

Present
The marquess of Ailesbury, H. N. Goddard, esq., Lord Ernest Bruce, M.P., Col. Wroughton, F. Leyborne Popham, esq., G. H. Walker Heneage, esq., Sir J. W. Awdry, the Revd. J. Leyborne Popham, Ambrose L. Goddard, esq., M.P.
Trusteeship
The trustees examined the account of the receiver of the rents to Michaelmas 1862, upon which there appears to be a balance of £79 15*s.* 9*d.* in his hands which is to be carried to his next account.

Mr. Francis L. Popham and Mr. Heneage are in accordance with the minute of 12 July 1860 the trustees to view the hospital next year.

The Rt. Hon. T. H. S. Sotheron Estcourt and the marquess of Lansdowne being prevented by continued illness and absence abroad on account of health from being present at this meeting their absence is excused.

At this meeting the trustees present executed a conveyance of 2a. 2r. 32p. in Froxfield and 2a. 2r. 6p. in Milton to the Berks. & Hants Railway Company, and signed a petition to the court of Chancery for investment of the purchase money in 3 per cent consols in the names of Lord Ernest Bruce, Revd. J. L. Popham, and A. L. Goddard, esq., three of the trustees of the hospital estates.
Estate
The steward submitted to the meeting an account of the sum received from the Berks. & Hants Railway Company for the destruction of cottages at Froxfield taken for that work, upon which account there is a balance unexpended of £93 4*s.* 7*d.*, subject to an unsettled claim by the builder.

The steward reported that he had, under the directions of Col. Wroughton, given instructions for some repairs necessary to the farmhouse at Milton, which is approved.

In consequence of the state of the farmhouse at Huish, which is of most inconvenient arrangement and construction and is now from natural decay past repair, the subject having been frequently incidentally before the trustees but from time to time postponed, the steward produced a plan prepared under direction of Col. Wroughton for altering so much of the present house as is fit to stand and for constructing a dwelling house suitable to the farm. [It is] ordered that it be carried into effect under the order in all respects of Col. Wroughton.

A reference to Mr. William Ferris relating to the cultivation and occupation of Milton farm by Mr. John Church, as agreed to by the steward, is approved of and confirmed.

A cottage at Froxfield having become vacant by the death of Joseph Stagg, and the steward having kept it unlet with a view to throw it and the adjoining cottage into one, he is directed to carry out that suggestion and to make such arrangements as may be practicable for effecting some further alleviation of the evil of overcrowding so prevalent in Froxfield.

The lifehold at Chirton consisting of a small house, a cottage, and [a] piece of land having fallen in hand by the death of Harry Barnes the steward is directed to take the best measures he can, under the advice of counsel, for enforcing the right of the trustees to the cottages fronting the street and claimed by him of the representatives of the late leaseholder, and to put the property into a proper state for habitation so far as circumstances will permit.

and see trusteeship business

Almshouse

Ordered that the gardens of late years made in the quadrangle be discontinued and the ground be covered with turf.

Resolved that the porter's salary be increased from £25 to £30.

Mayo trust

It appears by a separate account produced by the receiver that the amount of new 3 per cent stock standing in the names of H. N. Goddard, esq., and F. L. Popham, esq., trustees of the fund established by the late Revd. Charles Mayo, had, after nine half-year's payments to Mr. Arthur Henry Harington and seven half-year's payments to Mr. Philip Ashby Phelps, the exhibitioners, and the investment of the surplus dividends, accumulated to £6,828 6*s.* 1*d.*, leaving £225 16*s.* 1*d.* cash in hand.

Messrs. H. N. Goddard, Revd. J. L. Popham [*note*: another name was intended to be added but in the hurry was omitted] are appointed a committee for directing the course of proceeding, and details preliminary, to the election at the next annual meeting of a scholar on the Mayo exhibition in place of Mr. Philip Ashby Phelps, whose tenure of the present exhibition will expire on 1 October 1864.

Resolved that in all future elections on the Mayo charity the term of 5 years shall begin to run from the first day of the second term after the day of election or as soon after as the interest of the former exhibitioner shall expire.

Signatures

H. N. Goddard, chairman, Ernest Bruce, F. Leyborne Popham, G. H. Walker Heneage, J. L. Popham, G. W. Wroughton, A. L. Goddard.

14 July 1864, at the Ailesbury Arms inn, Marlborough

Present

The marquess of Ailesbury, H. N. Goddard, esq., Lord Ernest Bruce, M.P., Col. Wroughton, F. Leyborne Popham, esq., G. H. Walker Heneage, esq., Sir J. W. Awdry, the marquess of Lansdown, the Revd. J. Leyborne Popham, Ambrose L. Goddard, esq., M.P.

Trusteeship

The trustees examined the account of the receiver of the rents to Michaelmas 1863, upon which there appears to be a balance of £262 15*s.* 8*d.* in his hands which is to be carried to his next account.

Ordered that for the current year the subscription to the Little Bedwyn schools be augmented to 5 gns. The Revd. J. L. Popham is requested to obtain particulars showing the extent to which the schools are used by the poor of Froxfield.

Mr. Heneage having been prevented from attending the view meeting this year he, with Sir John Wither Awdry and the marquess of Lansdowne, are in accordance with the minute of 12 July 1860 the trustees to view the hospital next year. [*Note.* Lord Lansdowne arranged, after the meeting, with Sir J. Awdry and Mr. Heneage to meet on Whit Tuesday. J.P. to remind the three trustees of this a few days beforehand]

A letter was received from the Rt. Hon. T. H. S. Sotheron Estcourt asking to be excused from attending this meeting on account of ill health and his absence is excused.

Estate

The steward submitted to the meeting an account of the sum received from the Berks. & Hants Railway Company for the destruction of cottages at Froxfield taken for that work, upon which there is a balance unexpended of £57 4*s.* 1*d.*

The steward reported that in the night of Sunday 15 May a barn and stable on Huish Hill on the farm occupied by T. E. Bennet, together with two straw ricks, had been burnt. He had taken steps for prosecuting Frederick Webb, committed for the offence, with every prospect of a conviction. Also he had given order for rebuilding and hoped that the cost would not much, if at all, exceed the amount received from the Sun Fire Office. [*Note.* Work completed]

The steward reported the commencement of the building [of] a new farmhouse at Huish at a cost of £585 under plans approved by Col. Wroughton, and an alteration by covering the brewhouse with slate, and making two bedrooms over, at an additional cost of about

£30 under Col. Wroughton's direction. [*Note*. Not quite completed]

He also reported the commencement, under Col. Wroughton's sanction, of some necessary repairs to the farmhouse at Milton at a cost of about £30 to the trustees after deducting certain portions arranged to be paid by the tenant, and the representatives of the late tenant, by Messrs. Ferris and W. Baverstock. [*Note*. Contract completed]

He also reported a settlement, after much discussion and on terms approved by Mr. Money, for the alteration by Messrs. May and Gooding and converting [of] certain buildings at the Blue Lion at Froxfield into cottages in lieu of those destroyed by the Berks. & Hants Extension railway.

An application by Mr. Harry Hayward for materials for the construction of a cowhouse in his farmyard, he doing all labour, is granted to the extent of £10, the steward to be careful that the building is properly executed.

The opinion of counsel, taken in pursuance of the order at the last meeting of the trustees relative to the right to four cottages in front of the piece of ground comprised in the lease which has lately determined, showing that there was some doubt as to the result in case of litigation the steward reported that he had entered into negotiation with Mr. C. Chandler, the holder of the lease, who proposed to give up all claim to the cottages as freehold on having a new lease granted to him for 21 years certain at a small annual rent as a remuneration for his outlay on the property. He had suggested a lease for the life of Mr. Thomas Chandler, the late holder of the property, which Mr. Chandler considered insufficient.

The trustees will grant a lease of the four cottages, with pieces of garden land (about 6p. each) at present let with them, for 14 years at a rent of 20*s*., the tenant keeping them in repair. The cost of the lease and counterpart [is] to be paid by the tenant.

The steward is directed to make such arrangements with regard to the cottages opposite the farm, and to the house near the church by dividing it and making two cottages, as shall be directed by Col. Wroughton.

Ordered that the sporting rights at Froxfield, given up by F. L. Popham, esq., be let to the Revd. J. L. Popham.

Resolved that Mr. Merriman be requested to provide before the next meeting of the trustees an Ordnance map showing in red or blue the property of the trust as accurately as may be consistent with the smallness of the scale, the object being more to show generally the situation of the various lots than to define boundaries.

and see trusteeship business

Almshouse

The report on the roof of the hospital ordered at the view meeting not having been transmitted in time for this meeting [it is] ordered that it, when obtained, be referred to Mr. F. L. Popham, who is requested to give such order thereupon as he may think necessary.

The porter is directed to be vigilant in preventing the grass plots in the quadrangle from being used as footpaths or for playing at croquet or other games.

Mrs. Applegate, no. 41, not being in a state of mind fit for her to return to Froxfield the steward is authorized to pay her stipend quarterly to her son on production of a report from the medical officer of the establishment that she is properly treated.

Mayo trust

It appears by a separate account produced by the receiver that the amount of new 3 per cent stock standing in the names of H. N. Goddard, esq., and F. L. Popham, esq., trustees of the fund established by the late Revd. Charles Mayo, had, after nine half-year's payments to Mr. Philip Ashby Phelps and one half-year's payment to Mr. John H. Wilkinson, the exhibitioners, and the investment of £180 15*s.* in the purchase of £200 further stock out of the surplus dividends, accumulated to £7,028 6*s.* 1*d.*, leaving £120 11*s.* 5*d.* cash in hand.

In accordance with the minutes of the last meeting, 9 July 1863, the trustees proceeded to the election of a scholar or exhibitioner on the foundation of the Revd. Charles Mayo, deceased, in place of Mr. P. A. Phelps.

The candidates who had sent in applications and testimonials are Charles Herbert Mayo, aged 19, son of the Revd. William Mayo of Salisbury, candidate at last election, decided to be now disqualified by age exceeding 19 years; George Nutt, aged 18, son of the Revd. George Nutt, Shaw, Melksham, candidate at last election; James Alexander Wilson Atwood, aged 16, son of the Revd. Thomas George Patrick Atwood of Froxfield; Frederick Cooper, aged 18, son of the Revd. Robert Cooper, late of Stratford sub Castle, deceased, decided to be not qualified for want of sufficient residence of his father as a clergyman in Wiltshire and insufficient certificate; Charles Henry Dowding, aged 17, son of the Revd. Benjamin Charles Dowding of Southbroom, Devizes.

The report by the Revd. James Fraser on his examination of the candidates was read.

Resolved that Mr. George Nutt, son of the Revd. George Nutt, is appointed to the exhibition on the foundation of the Revd. Charles Mayo, deceased, to commence from the first day of Hilary term next (14 January 1865) and to be tenable for 5 years provided the good conduct and progress of the exhibitioner be duly and regularly certified in accordance with the directions of the founder and the regulations laid down in 1852.

The exhibitioner is expected to matriculate on or before Hilary term next.

The steward is directed to write to the Revd. James Fraser and express the thanks of the trustees for his report on the candidates and his very judicious observations in regard to their respective merits.

Resolved that Sir John Awdry and Mr. Nelson Goddard be appointed a standing committee with power to decide on all matters relative to the Mayo trust, and that they be requested to report to the trustees at their next meeting whether they can suggest any alteration in the rules relating to that trust.

Signatures

Ailesbury, chairman, G. H. Walker Heneage, Lansdowne, J. W. Awdry, A. L. Goddard, J. L. Popham, Ernest Bruce, F. Leyborne Popham, G. W. Wroughton, H. N. Goddard.

1 August 1865, at the Ailesbury Arms inn, Marlborough

Present

The marquess of Ailesbury, H. N. Goddard, esq., Lord Ernest Bruce, M.P., Col. Wroughton, the Rt. Hon. T. H. S. Sotheron Estcourt, G. H. Walker Heneage, esq., Sir J. W. Awdry, the Revd. J. Leyborne Popham, Ambrose L. Goddard, M.P.

Trusteeship

The trustees examined the account of the receiver of the rents to Michaelmas 1864, upon which there appears to be a balance of £240 5*s.* 10*d.* in his hands which is to be carried to his next account.

A minute of the trustees on 19 October 1858 was read relative to an occurrence of vacancy in the vicarage of Froxfield. The steward was directed, in case of a vacancy, immediately to communicate with the marquess of Ailesbury or the marquess of Lansdowne and send a copy of such minute.

In consequence of the day for the annual meeting having been changed this year [it is] resolved that trustees not attending this meeting do not fall within the terms of the rule forfeiting patronage for non-attendance.

The Revd. J. L. Popham and Mr. A. L. Goddard are, in accordance with the minute of 12 July 1860, the trustees to view the hospital next year in conjunction with the Rt. Hon. T. H. S. Sotheron Estcourt.

Estate

Resolved that the widow of the late Harry Hayward be allowed to continue in the occupation of the farm at Chirton provided security for payment of the rent and proper cultivation of the farm be given to the satisfaction of Col. Wroughton. In case of such security not being given [let] a notice to quit be given before next Lady day.

Col. Wroughton is requested to inspect the property at Milton, obtain a particular of what is requisite, and give such directions as he may think proper.

The steward reported that possession of the whole property at Chirton had only just now been obtained. Therefore no repairs had been done. Col. Wroughton was requested with the steward to make such arrangement of the property as he should think fit.

The steward reported that he had demanded from Mr. Thomas Chandler £35 5*s.* for rents received by him and that, after much negotiation, Mr. Chandler had offered £30 in discharge of his liabilities. [It is] resolved that the steward accept the £30.

The lease to Mr. Thomas Chandler for 14 years of cottages and gardens at Chirton pursuant to the resolution of the last meeting was executed by the trustees present. The steward was directed to exchange it for a counterpart executed by Mr. Chandler.

A memorial from ratepayers at Froxfield praying for the discontinuance of the Cross Keys public house at Froxfield was read. The steward reported that the present tenant, William Wise, was under notice to quit at Michaelmas next.

Resolved that William Wise be required to quit and the house discontinued as an inn, that the premises be converted into a blacksmith's shop and cottages, and that the present blacksmith's shop occupied by ... [*MS. blank*] Humphreys be converted into a shop, [all] at an expense not exceeding £150 and the whole [to] be done and let under the superintendence of the Revd. John Popham.

The steward is directed to write a letter to the memorialists informing them of the determination of the trustees.

Resolved that notice be given to the present tenant of the Pelican inn to quit at Michaelmas 1866. The steward is to report to the next meeting as to the probable increase of rent which may be obtained for those premises in consequence of the shutting up of the Cross Keys.

Almshouse

Resolved that the request of the widows for a bench to be placed near the road be granted and that the sort of bench and situation be left to the Revd. John Popham.

Resolved that the steward represent to Mrs. Marshall, one of the widows in the hospital, that her putting a permanent partition in her room downstairs is improper and contrary to rule and, although the trustees will not now require it to be removed, they disapprove of it.

An estimate for some repairs at the porter's house was laid before the meeting and, with the omission of new iron paling, it was allowed. It was ordered that materials be allowed the porter for repairing the present paling.

Mayo trust

It appears by a separate account produced by the receiver that the amount of new 3 per cent stock standing in the names of H. N. Goddard, esq., and F. L. Popham, esq., trustees of the fund established by the late Revd. Charles Mayo, had, after the whole 10 half-year's payments to Mr. Philip Ashby Phelps, three half-year's payments to Mr. John H. Wilkinson, one half-year's payment to Mr. George Nutt, the exhibitioners, and the investment of £89 12*s*. 6*d*. in the purchase of £100 further stock out of the surplus dividends, accumulated to £7,128 6*s*. 1*d*., leaving £61 18*s*. 9*d*. cash in hand.

It is directed that the clerk return the papers of every candidate for the Mayo exhibition whose father, whether living or deceased, shall not have resided 15 years in Wiltshire, who shall himself not be a native of the county or have been resident, except whilst at school or attending at college, 15 years in the county, or whose age will, at the date of the election, exceed 19 years. Provided that, if the candidate or his parent shall dispute the fact of failure in any of the above conditions of eligibility, the clerk shall refer to Sir John Awdry and Maj. Goddard who may direct whether he shall be admitted to examination subject to the opinion of the trustees on the objection.

Signatures

Ailesbury, chairman, A. L. Goddard, H. N. Goddard, Ernest Bruce, G. H. Walker Heneage, G. W. Wroughton, J. L. Popham, J. W. Awdry.

26 July 1866, at the Ailesbury Arms inn, Marlborough

Present

The marquess of Ailesbury, H. N. Goddard, esq., Lord Ernest Bruce, M.P., Col. Wroughton, F. Leyborne Popham, esq., the Rt. Hon. T. H. S. Sotheron Estcourt, Sir J. W. Awdry, the Revd. J. Leyborne Popham, Ambrose L. Goddard, esq., M.P.

Trusteeship

The trustees examined the account of the receiver of the rents to Michaelmas 1865, upon which there appears to be a balance of £32 in his hands which is to be carried to his next account.

The steward drew the attention of the trustees to the fact that the recent death of the marquess of Lansdowne had created a second vacancy in the number of trustees but that no notice for an election could under the circumstances of the case have been given. [It is] resolved that the steward, with his notice of the meeting for next year, do give notice that an election to fill vacancies will take place.

Lord Ernest Bruce and Col. Wroughton are, in accordance with the minute of 12 July 1860, the trustees to view the hospital next year in conjunction with T. H. S. Sotheron Estcourt, esq.

and see estate business

Estate

Col. Wroughton reported that he had found it necessary to have two cottages at Chirton rebuilt, but had not done anything to the repairs of the house lately occupied by William Trueman as he awaited the decision of the trustees relative to the suggested exchange for the purposes of the churchyard.

Col. Wroughton reported that he had carefully examined the property at Milton, was quite of opinion that it would be useless to attempt to make the present house fit for the tenant, and that a dairy and other buildings were requisite. Therefore he had only ordered such repairs as were absolutely necessary to the farm buildings and suggested that a new house should be built on a better site. Col. Wroughton laid before the meeting plans for a new house. [It is] resolved that the house as recommended by Col. Wroughton be built under his superintendence on the site to be fixed by him.

The steward reported that he had, under the direction of Col. Wroughton, sold timber at Broomsgrove, Clench, Milton, and Chirton, the net proceeds of which, £568 10*s*., will not be all payable until November next and will therefore be credited in his next account.

The steward is directed to have the timber at Huish examined and, under the direction of Col. Wroughton, order any portion thereof, that may appear to be desirable, to be cut, and to cut such further quantity on Broomsgrove, Clench, and Milton as Col. Wroughton shall approve.

Letter from the Revd. G. E. Cleather, vicar of Chirton, to Col. Wroughton dated 2 April 1866 with reference to a proposed addition to the churchyard at Chirton to be effected by an exchange of lands between the trustees and the authorities of that parish: the property required by the parish is the house and garden immediately adjoining the churchyard formerly held under lease by Mr. Thomas Chandler and they propose to give in exchange a garden with a cottage on it situated close to the two new cottages recently erected, the quantity of land in each case being about equal.

Resolved that the trustees are desirable to accede to the proposal if the parishioners can make it appear to the [Inclosure] Commissioners that the property proposed to be given by them in exchange is a fair equivalent to the trustees'. The steward is directed to instruct a surveyor to view the property and if necessary arrange with Col. Wroughton some course which will be fair between all parties.

The Revd. J. Leyborne Popham reported that in pursuance of the directions of the last meeting he had inspected the property at Froxfield occupied by John Humphreys and the late Cross Keys after

William Wise had quitted it. [He] found that it would not answer to make the latter into a blacksmith's shop and that it would be unadvisable to make any material alteration at Humphreys's holding. Therefore he had directed the Cross Keys to be made into a dwelling house for Charles Withers and a hovel adjoining into a shop, whereby an unsightly and ill adapted wooden house which he occupied was removed. Charles Withers now paid a rent of £14 for his house and shop, with the meadow, and was to pay £2 extra for future years. Two cottages were in progress from part of the old brewery and would be ready for habitation by Michaelmas next, and there is still sufficient building for conversion into another cottage or for a schoolroom as the trustees may decide. [It is] resolved that the deviation from the directions of the last meeting is approved. The steward is directed to get the cottages completed forthwith.

Application having been made on the part of the parishioners of Froxfield for aid towards establishing a school in that parish by converting certain rooms at the back of the late Cross Keys for that purpose [it is] resolved that the trustees are willing to do so, and to [give] aid towards keeping up such school, provided the parishioners are ready to do their part, and that Mr. John Popham and Maj. Goddard be a committee for making arrangements for this object having regard on the part of the trustees to the amount which will be contributed by the parishioners themselves.

The steward laid before the meeting the applications for renting the Pelican inn at Froxfield and was directed to offer it to Edward Howard Beard at an increase of rent to £50 and, if he should decline, to advise with Mr. Popham in selecting another tenant.

The steward laid before the meeting a plan for a stable and outbuildings to the farmhouse at Froxfield occupied by Mr. Redman and stated that Mr. Redman was willing to pay one half the expense. Mr. J. L. Popham and Mr. A. L. Goddard having informed the meeting that they thought it very desirable the steward was directed to have it done under competent supervision.

Col. Wroughton informed the trustees that he thought that in case James Brewer, the tenant of a small property at Clench, should quit the holding it might be desirable to add his land to the holding of Mr. Church of Milton. The steward was directed to bear this in mind.

Almshouse

A letter was read from Mrs. Taylor of no. 16 in the hospital [requesting] to be allowed to keep her servant in her house during the night as, hers being a corner house, she had a third room for the servant, her health was such as might require instant attention, and her daughter, who lived with her, was quite incapable from ill health to give her the necessary assistance. Mr. Barker, the surgeon, having verbally confirmed Mrs. Taylor's statement and having given a written certificate to that effect [it is] resolved that Mrs. Taylor's request be granted during such time as Mr. Barker may consider it necessary.

An estimate for iron paling to the porter's house at Froxfield was laid before the meeting. [It is] resolved that £8 be allowed to Mr. Gooding for doing the work according to the estimate and to the satisfaction of the steward.

Mayo trust

It appears by a separate account produced by the receiver that the amount of new 3 per cent stock standing in the names of H. N. Goddard, esq., and F. L. Popham, esq., trustees of the fund established by the late Revd. Charles Mayo, had, after five half-year's payments to Mr. J. H. Wilkinson and two half-year's payments to Mr. George Nutt, the exhibitioners, accumulated to £7,128 6*s.* 1*d.*, leaving £145 1*s.* 6*d.* cash in hand.

The subject of the next election for the Mayo scholarship was considered and it appeared that none would occur until 1868.

Signatures

Ailesbury, H. N. Goddard, T. Sotheron Estcourt, G. W. Wroughton, Ernest Bruce, J. L. Popham, J. W. Awdry.

APPENDIX

TRUSTEES APPOINTED 1686–1856

The dates at which those listed below were trustees of Froxfield almshouse have been taken from deeds in WSA 2037/2 and from the minute books edited above.

Ashfordby Trenchard (formerly Ashfordby), John (1771–1838), of Stanton Fitzwarren, a trustee from 1836 to his death. He inherited Stanton Fitzwarren manor in 1778, and he took the additional surname Trenchard in 1801 when he inherited lands in Somerset. He was a Doctor of Divinity and was rector of Stanton Fitzwarren from 1822 to his death. Burke, *Commoners*, iv; *Alum. Oxon. 1715–1886*; WSA 1999/9.

Astley, Sir John Dugdale (1778–1842), bt., of Everleigh, a trustee from 1821 to his death. He inherited the Everleigh estate in 1818, was an M.P. 1820–34, and was created a baronet in 1821. Burke, *Peerage* (1924); *VCH Wilts.* x–xi, xvi.

Awdry, John (d. 1802), of Notton, a trustee from 1783 to his death. He lived in the manor house at Notton and was the owner of an extensive estate in the neighbourhood of Notton. He was a J.P., D.L., and high sheriff of Wiltshire. Burke, *Landed Gentry* (1952); *VCH Wilts.* vii; WSA 109.

Awdry, John (1766–1844), of Notton, a trustee from 1813 to his death. He lived in the manor house at Notton, succeeded his father John (d. 1802) as owner of an extensive estate, and was a J.P. and D.L. Burke, *Landed Gentry* (1952); *VCH Wilts.* vii; WSA 109.

Awdry, Sir John Wither (1795–1878), of Notton, a trustee from 1852. He lived in the manor house at Notton and succeeded his father John (d. 1844) as owner of an extensive estate. He was Chief Justice of the Supreme Court of Judicature at Bombay, a J.P. and D.L. for Wiltshire, and from 1847 to 1861 chairman of Devizes quarter sessions. Burke, *Landed Gentry* (1952); *VCH Wilts.* v, vii; WSA 109.

Batson (formerly Davies), Thomas (d. 1759), of Ramsbury, a trustee from 1729 to his death. He took the surname Batson in 1701, succeeded his father as lord of Hilldrop manor in Ramsbury, and lived in the house in Ramsbury now called Parliament Piece. *VCH Wilts.* xii.

Bennet, Thomas (d. 1754), of Salthrop, a trustee from 1713 to his death. In 1703 he inherited Costow manor in Wroughton parish and a lease of Salthrop manor under the London Charterhouse. In 1709 he bought a manor in Broad Hinton and in 1739 he gave Costow manor in exchange for Salthrop. *VCH Wilts.* xi–xii; WSA 551/5.

Bigg, Lovelace (1661–1725), of Chilton Foliat, a trustee 1698–1704 and from 1713 to his death. He bought the Chilton House estate in Chilton Foliat in 1689. Burke, *Commoners*, ii; *VCH Wilts.* xvi.

Bigg (latterly Bigg Wither), Lovelace, of Chilton Foliat, a trustee from 1770 to 1810 x 1813. He inherited the Chilton House estate in 1772, sold it in 1792, and was a Wiltshire J.P. He took the additional surname Wither in 1789. *VCH Wilts.* xvi; WSA A 1/100 (1797).

Bigg, Thomas (d. 1761), of Chilton Foliat, a trustee from 1751 to his death. He inherited the Chilton House estate in 1740. *VCH Wilts.* xvi; WSA 735/5.

Blandy, John, of Inglewood, a trustee 1698–1704. He owned the Inglewood estate at Kintbury. *VCH Berks.* iv.

Booth, Henry (1652–94), earl of Warrington, a trustee from with effect 1692 to his death. He succeeded his father as Baron Delamere in 1684, was an extreme Whig, took an active part in the revolution of 1688, and was created earl of Warrington in 1690. *Complete Peerage*; *Hist. Parl., Commons*, 1660–90.

Brudenell Bruce, Charles (1773–1856), marquess of Ailesbury, of Savernake, a trustee from 1798 to his death. As Lord Bruce he was M.P. for Marlborough 1796–1814. He succeeded his father as earl of Ailesbury and owner of the Savernake estate in 1814, and was created marquess of Ailesbury in 1821. *Complete Peerage*; *Hist. Parl., Commons*, 1790–1820; *VCH Wilts.* xvi.

Brudenell Bruce, Ernest (1811–86), marquess of Ailesbury, of Tottenham Park, a trustee from 1842. As Lord Ernest Bruce he was M.P. for Marlborough 1833–68. He succeeded his brother as marquess of Ailesbury and owner of the Savernake estate in 1878. *Complete Peerage*; *VCH Wilts.* v, xvi.

Brudenell Bruce, George (1804–78), marquess of Ailesbury, of Savernake, a trustee from 1836. As Earl Bruce he was M.P. for Marlborough 1826–30. He succeeded his father as marquess of Ailesbury and owner of the Savernake estate in 1856, and was Lord Lieutenant of Wiltshire from 1863. *Complete Peerage*; *VCH Wilts.* xvi.

Brudenell Bruce (formerly Brudenell), Thomas (1729–1814), earl of Ailesbury, a trustee from 1789 to his death. In 1747 he succeeded to the barony of Bruce and estates in Wiltshire and elsewhere. In 1767 he took the additional surname Bruce and in 1776 was created earl of Ailesbury. He owned the Savernake estate and was Lord Lieutenant of Wiltshire from 1780. *Complete Peerage*; Burke, *Peerage* (1924); *VCH Wilts.* xvi.

Codrington, William (1790–1842), of Wroughton, a trustee from 1836 to his death. He was the lessee of Wroughton manor under the dean and chapter of Winchester and owned other land. Burke, *Landed Gentry* (1855); *VCH Wilts.* ix, xi.

Ernle, Edward (d. 1734), of Brimslade, a trustee from 1713 to his death. He lived at Brimslade House in Savernake. *VCH Wilts.* xvi.

Ernle, Sir Edward (born *c.* 1713, d. 1787), bt., of Brimslade, a trustee from

1771 to his death. He was a Doctor of Divinity, rector of Draycot Cerne 1747–60, and rector of Avington from 1760 to his death. He succeeded to the baronetcy on the death of his brother in 1771 and lived at Brimslade House. G.E.C. *Baronetage*; *VCH Wilts.* xiv, xvi; http://www.theclergydatabase.org.uk/persons (person ID 26862).

Ernle, Sir Michael (born *c.* 1704, d. 1771), bt., a trustee from 1737 to his death. He succeeded to the baronetcy in 1734, and in that year he succeeded his father as the occupant of Brimslade House. G.E.C. *Baronetage*; *VCH Wilts.* xvi.

Estcourt (latterly Bucknall Estcourt), Thomas Grimston (1775–1853), of New Park, Devizes, a trustee from 1814 to his death. He acquired the New Park estate on the death of his father-in-law James Sutton in 1801 and the Estcourt estate based at Shipton Moyne on the death of his father in 1818. He took the additional surname Bucknall in 1823. He was chairman of Devizes quarter sessions from 1802 or 1806 to 1836, M.P. for Devizes 1805–26, recorder of Devizes 1828–33, and M.P. for Oxford university 1826–47. *DNB*; *Hist. Parl., Commons*, 1790–1820; *VCH Wilts.* v, vii.

Fettiplace, Thomas (d. 1710), of Fernham, a trustee 1698–1704. He inherited the manor of Fernham in Shrivenham parish and held manors in Melksham and Preshute parishes in the right of his wife. *VCH Berks.* iv; *VCH Wilts.* vii, xii.

Geddes, Michael (born *c.* 1647, d. 1713), of Compton Bassett, a trustee from 1704 to his death. He was a Scot educated at the universities of Edinburgh and Oxford, a chaplain in Lisbon 1678–88, chancellor of Salisbury cathedral from 1691 to his death, rector of Compton Bassett 1693–1710, and rector of East Hendred from 1710 to his death. He was a Doctor of Laws and an anti-popish author. *DNB*; A. L. Humphreys, *East Hendred* (London, 1923); Le Neve, *Fasti, 1541–1857, Salisbury*; Phillipps, *Wiltshire Institutions*.

Gillingham, Richard (born *c.* 1654, d. 1719), a trustee from 1704 to his death. He was rector of Ham from 1688 to his death. *Alum. Oxon. 1500–1714*; Phillipps, *Wiltshire Institutions*; WSA, bishop's transcripts, Ham, bundle 2.

Goddard, Ambrose (1695–1755), of Swindon, a trustee from 1751 to his death. He inherited Swindon manor from a kinsman in 1742 and held it until his death. Burke, *Landed Gentry* (1906); *VCH Wilts.* ix.

Goddard, Ambrose (born *c.* 1727, d. 1815), of Swindon, a trustee from 1770 to his death. He was an agent for the Post Office in Lisbon until 1772, M.P. for Wiltshire 1772–1806. He inherited the manor of Swindon from his brother in 1770 and bought Wanborough manor in 1811. *Hist. Parl., Commons*, 1754–90, 1790–1820; *VCH Wilts.* ix.

Goddard, Ambrose (1779–1854), of Swindon, a trustee from 1817 to his death. He inherited Swindon manor from his father in 1815. He was a J.P. and D.L. of Wiltshire and was high sheriff 1819–20. He was M.P. for Cricklade 1837–41. Burke, *Landed Gentry* (1906); *VCH Wilts.* v, ix.

Goddard, Ambrose Lethbridge (1819–98), of the Lawn, Swindon, a trustee from 1856. He inherited Swindon manor from his father in 1854. He was a J.P. and D.L. for Wiltshire and a county councillor. He was M.P. for Cricklade 1837–68 and 1874–80. *WAM* xxx; *VCH Wilts.* v, ix.

Goddard, Edward (born *c.* 1761, d. 1839), of Clyffe Pypard, a trustee from 1798 to his death. He was lord of Clyffe Pypard manor and, having presented himself, vicar of Clyffe Pypard, both from 1791 to his death. He was a Doctor of Divinity and a J.P. Burke, *Landed Gentry* (1906); *Alum. Oxon. 1715–1886*; *VCH Wilts.* ix.

Goddard, Francis (d. 1724), of South Standen, a trustee 1698–1704. In 1684 he inherited the manors of Standen Hussey, Clyffe Pypard, and Little Bedwyn. He sold Little Bedwyn 1695–1700 and Standen Hussey in 1719. He was a J.P. and D.L. Burke, *Landed Gentry* (1906); *VCH Berks.* iv; *VCH Wilts.* ix, xvi.

Goddard, Horatio Nelson (1809–1900), of Clyffe Pypard, a trustee from 1839. He inherited Clyffe Pypard manor from his father in 1839. He was a J.P. and D.L. and was high sheriff of Wiltshire in 1860. He was a major in the Royal Wiltshire militia and took a leading part in the public business of the county. *WAM* xxxi; *VCH Wilts.* v, ix.

Goddard, Richard (d. 1771 x 1778), of Marlborough, a trustee from 1755 to his death.

Goddard, Thomas (1722–70), of Swindon, a trustee from 1755 to his death. He inherited Swindon manor from his father in 1755. He was M.P. for Wiltshire 1767–70. *Hist. Parl., Commons*, 1754–90; *VCH Wilts.* ix.

Goddard, Thomas (1777–1814), of Swindon, a trustee from 1813 to his death. He was the eldest son of Ambrose Goddard (d. 1815) and was M.P. for Cricklade 1806–12. *Hist. Parl., Commons*, 1790–1820.

Gregory, Sir William (1625–96), a trustee from with effect 1692 to his death. He was a Herefordshire lawyer and landowner, an M.P. 1678–9, and Speaker of the House of Commons in 1679. He was knighted in 1679. From 1679 to 1686 he was a Baron of the Exchequer and from 1689 to his death a judge of the King's Bench. *DNB*

Gregory, William. He was the grandson of Sir William Gregory and, as his heir, was a trustee 1696–8. He came of age in or shortly before 1697.

Grimston, Sir Samuel (1644–1700), bt., a trustee from with effect 1692 to 1698. He was the son of the lawyer and politician Sir Harbottle Grimston, whom he succeeded in 1685 as owner of the Gorhambury estate in Hertfordshire. He was an M.P. from 1668. *DNB*; *Hist. Parl., Commons*, 1660–90.

Grinfield, Edward (d. 1759), of Rockley, a trustee 1729–51. He inherited Rockley manor from his father and owned land in Great Somerford. *VCH Wilts.* xii, xiv.

Hawes, Thomas (d. 1717), a trustee from 1704 to his death. He was vicar of Ramsbury from 1685 to his death and, as prebendary of Netherbury in Terra, was a canon of Salisbury cathedral from 1695. *Alum. Oxon. 1500–1714*; Le Neve, *Fasti, 1541–1857, Salisbury*.

Herbert, Sidney (1810–61), Baron Herbert, of Wilton House, a trustee from 1856 to his death. He was an M.P. from 1832 to his death, held office in several governments, and managed the Wilton estate because his half-brother, the earl of Pembroke and of Montgomery, lived abroad. He owned Lea and Cleverton manor and was created Baron Herbert of Lea in 1861. *DNB*; *VCH Wilts.* xiv.

Hersent, John (d. 1705 or 1706), a trustee from 1704. He was ordained deacon in 1667, and was rector of Llanddewi Velfrey from 1686, rector of Bladon with Woodstock 1686–1702, and rector of Pewsey from 1702 to his death. *Alum. Oxon. 1500–1714*; WSA 490/479.

Hippisley, John (d. 1722), of Lambourn, a trustee 1698–1704. He was the lord of Grandisons manor in Lambourn. *VCH Berks.* iv.

Hungerford, George (d. 1764), of Studley, a trustee from 1756 to his death. In 1754 he inherited the manors of Studley, Rodbourne, and Westcourt in the parishes of Calne, Malmesbury, and Yatesbury respectively. *VCH Wilts.* xiv, xvii.

Hungerford, Henry (d. 1750), of Fyfield, a trustee from 1725 to his death. He inherited Fyfield manor in 1713 and held it until his death. *VCH Wilts.* xvi.

Jones, Richard (born before 1679, d. 1736), of Ramsbury, a trustee from 1713 to his death. He inherited Ramsbury manor in 1686 and bought property nearby. He was M.P. for Marlborough 1712–13 and for Salisbury 1713–15. *Hist. Parl., Commons*, 1690–1715; *VCH Wilts.* xii.

Jones, William (d. 1753), of Ramsbury, a trustee from 1729 to his death. In 1736 he inherited the Ramsbury Manor estate from his brother Richard. *VCH Wilts.* xii.

Jones, William (born *c.* 1743, d. 1766), a trustee from 1765 to his death. In 1753 he inherited the Ramsbury Manor estate from his father. *VCH Wilts.* xii.

Jones (formerly Langham), Sir William (d. 1791), bt., of Ramsbury Manor, a trustee from 1778 to his death. His wife inherited the Ramsbury Manor estate from her brother William in 1766. He assumed the surname Jones and was created a baronet in 1774. *VCH Wilts.* xii.

Leyborne Popham (formerly Leyborne), Edward William (1764–1843), of Littlecote, a trustee from 1814 to his death. In 1804 he inherited the Littlecote estate, which he enlarged, and in 1805 he assumed the additional surname Popham. He was a general in the army, a J.P., and in 1830 high sheriff of Wiltshire. Burke, *Landed Gentry* (1952); *VCH Wilts.* xii, xvi; *Army List*.

Leyborne Popham, Francis (1809–1880), of Littlecote, a trustee from 1842. He inherited the Littlecote estate from his father in 1843. He was a J.P. and D.L. Burke, *Landed Gentry* (1952); *VCH Wilts.* xii.

Leyborne Popham, John (1811–72), of Chilton Foliat, a trustee from 1856.

A younger son of Edward William Leyborne Popham, he was rector of Chilton Foliat from 1835 and, as prebendary of Yetminster Prima, a canon of Salisbury cathedral from 1849. Le Neve, *Fasti, 1541–1857, Salisbury*; *Alum. Oxon. 1715–1886*; Burke, *Landed Gentry* (1952).

Liddiard, William (d. 1760), of Ogbourne St. Andrew, a trustee from 1755 to his death. His father owned Ogbourne Maizey manor 1743–63, and he bought another estate in Ogbourne St. Andrew in 1740. *VCH Wilts.* xii.

Long, Sir Robert (1705–67), bt., of Draycot Cerne, a trustee from 1751 to his death. He succeeded to the baronetcy and the Draycot Cerne estate in 1729, and he was M.P. for Wootton Bassett 1734–41 and for Wiltshire 1741–67. G.E.C. *Baronetage*, iii; *Hist. Parl., Commons*, 1715–54; *VCH Wilts.* xiv.

Michell, Thomas (d. 1809), of South Standen, a trustee from 1802 to his death. He came from a landed family of Chitterne All Saints and he held South Standen manor in the right of his wife. Hoare, *Modern Wilts.* Heytesbury; *VCH Berks.* iv.

Montagu, James (d. 1797), of Alderton, a trustee from 1789 to his death. In 1790 he inherited estates at Lackham and Alderton. Aubrey, *Topog. Colln.* ed. Jackson; Burke, *Commoners,* ii.

Morris, John (d. 1774), a trustee 1737–51. He was vicar of Aldbourne from 1731 to his death and vicar of Box from 1740 to his death. Phillipps, *Wiltshire Institutions.*

Northey, William (born *c.* 1721, d. 1770), of Compton Bassett, a trustee from 1751 to his death. He inherited Compton Bassett manor in 1738 and sold part of it in 1758 and the rest in 1768. He was an M.P. from 1747 to his death. *Hist. Parl., Commons*, 1715–54; *VCH Wilts.* xvii.

Northey, William (born *c.* 1753, d. 1826), of Lockeridge, a trustee from 1778 to his death. He was the son of William Northey (d. 1770) and in 1778 lived at Lockeridge, where there was a gentleman's residence. He was of Box Hall and of Woodcote and was M.P. for Newport 1796–1826. *Hist. Parl., Commons*, 1790–1820; *VCH Wilts.* xi.

Pearse, John (born *c.* 1759, d. 1836), of Chilton Foliat, a trustee from 1807 to his death. He was a London clothier who in the period 1790–1828 served as director, deputy governor, and governor of the Bank of England. He was also the manager and director of the Sun Fire Office and manager of the Sun Life Office. In 1796 he bought Chilton Lodge in Chilton Foliat and later estates nearby. He was M.P. for Devizes 1818–32. *DNB*; *Hist. Parl., Commons*, 1790–1820; *VCH Wilts.* xvi.

Penruddocke, Charles (1743–88), of Compton Chamberlayne, a trustee from 1771 to his death. In 1769 he inherited the Compton Chamberlayne estate and Fyfield manor. He was M.P. for Wiltshire from 1770 to his death. *Hist. Parl., Commons*, 1754–90; *VCH Wilts.* xvi.

Penruddocke, John Hungerford (1770–1841), of Compton Chamberlayne, a trustee from 1817 to his death. In 1788 he inherited the Compton

Chamberlayne estate and Fyfield manor from his father. He was a J.P., D.L., sheriff of Wiltshire in 1817, and M.P. for Wilton 1821–32. Burke, *Landed Gentry* (1937); *VCH Wilts.* xvi; *Hist. Parl., Commons*, 1820–32; Hoare, *Modern Wilts.* South Damerham.

Petty-Fitzmaurice, Henry (1816–66), marquess of Lansdowne, a trustee from 1852 to his death. From 1836 he was styled earl of Shelburne. He was M.P. for Calne 1837–56, entered the House of Lords as Lord Wycombe in 1856, and held office in Whig governments. From 1859 to 1863 he was chairman of the GWR, and in 1863 he succeeded his father as marquess of Lansdowne and as owner of the Bowood estate. *DNB*; *VCH Wilts.* xvii.

Pierrepont, Henry Manvers (1780–1851), of Conholt Park, a trustee from 1839 to his death. He inherited the Conholt estate in 1826. He was an envoy to the court of Denmark and a privy counsellor. Burke, *Peerage* (1924), s.v. Manvers; *VCH Wilts.* xvi.

Pocock, Edward (born *c.* 1648, d. 1726), a trustee from 1704 to his death. He was the son of Edward Pocock, professor of Hebrew and Arabic at Oxford university, and was himself an oriental scholar. He was a canon of Salisbury cathedral as prebendary of Winterbourne Earls 1675–7, Durnford 1677–93, and Netherbury in Ecclesia 1693–1726. He was rector of Mildenhall from 1692 to his death. *DNB*; Le Neve, *Fasti, 1541–1857, Salisbury*; *VCH Wilts.* xii.

Pocock, John (born *c.* 1685, d. 1773), of Mildenhall, a trustee from 1729 to his death. He succeeded his father as rector of Mildenhall in 1727 and was rector until 1763, and he was also vicar of Compton 1731–67. As prebendary of Gillingham Minor he was a canon of Salisbury cathedral from 1746 to his death. *Alum. Oxon. 1500–1714*; Le Neve, *Fasti, 1541–1857, Salisbury*; *VCH Wilts.* xii.

Pocock, Richard (d. 1787), of Mildenhall, a trustee from 1765 to his death. He was presented as rector of Mildenhall by his kinsman John Pocock in 1763 and was rector until his death. *VCH Wilts.* xii; Phillipps, *Wiltshire Institutions*; WSA 1532/5.

Popham, Alexander (born *c.* 1670, d. 1705), of Littlecote, a trustee 1698–1704. He inherited Littlecote manor in 1674 and was M.P. for Chippenham 1690–8 and for Bath from 1698 to his death. *Hist. Parl., Commons*, 1690–1715; *VCH Wilts.* xii.

Popham, Edward (1712–72), of Littlecote, a trustee from 1737 to his death. He inherited the Littlecote estate from his father Francis in 1735 and was an M.P. from 1738 to his death. *Hist. Parl., Commons*, 1715–54; *VCH Wilts.* xii, xvi.

Popham, Edward (1738–1815), of Chilton Foliat, a trustee from 1789 to his death. He was a younger son of Edward Popham (d. 1772), a Bachelor and Doctor of Divinity, and rector of Chilton Foliat from 1778 to his death. He was vicar of Lacock from 1779 to his death. Burke, *Landed Gentry* (1952); *Alum. Oxon. 1715–1886*; *VCH Wilts.* xvi; WSA 735/9.

Popham, Francis (born *c.* 1682, d. 1735), of Littlecote, a trustee from 1713 to his death. He inherited the Littlecote estate in 1705. He was M.P. for Wootton Bassett 1706–10 and for Chippenham 1711–13. *Hist. Parl., Commons*, 1690–1715; *VCH Wilts.* xii, xvi.

Popham, Francis (born *c.* 1734, d. 1780), of Littlecote, a trustee from 1760 to his death. He inherited the Littlecote estate from his father Edward in 1772. *Alum. Oxon. 1715–1886*; *VCH Wilts.* xii, xvi.

Popham, George (born *c.* 1687, d. 1744), a trustee from 1725 to his death. He was rector of Chilton Foliat from 1714 to his death. *Alum. Oxon. 1500–1714*; WSA 735/5.

Read, Henry (d. 1821), of Crowood, a trustee from 1817 to his death. He inherited the Crowood estate in Ramsbury parish in 1786 and was a lieutenant general in the army. *VCH Wilts.* xii; *Army List*.

Richmond Webb, John (d. 1805), of Milton Lilbourne, a trustee from 1798 to his death. He owned an estate in Milton Lilbourne from 1754 and land in Berkshire. He was a Wiltshire J.P. *VCH Berks.* iv; *VCH Wilts.* xvi; WSA A 1/100 (1797).

Seymour, Sir Edward (1663–1740), bt., of Easton (latterly of Maiden Bradley), a trustee 1698–1704. He was re-appointed in 1713 but was not active as a trustee thereafter. He was an M.P. at intervals from 1690 to 1715 and succeeded to the baronetcy in 1708. He lived in the manor house at Easton probably from *c.* 1693 to *c.* 1708. Burke, *Peerage* (1924), s.v. Somerset; *Hist. Parl., Commons*, 1690–1715; *VCH Wilts.* xvi.

Seymour, Edward (1695–1757), duke of Somerset, of Easton (latterly of Maiden Bradley), a trustee from 1729 to his resignation in 1751. He lived in the manor house at Easton probably until 1740, when he succeeded his father as baronet. In 1750 he succeeded in his claim to the dukedom of Somerset. He attended a meeting of the trustees in 1730, none thereafter. In 1747 the other trustees invited him to resign the trust. Burke, *Peerage* (1924); *Complete Peerage*.

Sherwin, William (born *c.* 1669, d. 1735), a trustee from 1704 but never active as one. He was vicar of Headington from 1693, rector of Collingbourne Ducis from 1700 to his death. As prebendary of Seaford he was a canon of Chichester cathedral from 1703 and a residentiary canon there from 1718 to his death. Le Neve, *Fasti, 1541–1857, Chichester*; *Alum. Oxon. 1500–1714*; *VCH Wilts.* xi.

Sotheron (formerly Estcourt, latterly Sotheron Estcourt), Thomas Henry Sutton (1801–76), of Bowden Park, a trustee from 1845. He took the surname Sotheron in place of Estcourt in 1839 and added Estcourt after Sotheron in 1855. He succeeded his father T. G. Bucknall Estcourt as owner of the New Park and Estcourt estates in 1853 and owned an estate in Yorkshire. He was an M.P. 1829–32 and 1835–65, took office in a Tory government in 1858, and was Home Secretary in 1859. He set up the Wiltshire Friendly Society. *DNB*; *WAM* xvi; *VCH Wilts.* vii, x.

Stonehouse, Francis (1653–1738), of Great Bedwyn, a trustee 1698–1704. He owned West Bedwyn manor, lived at Stock House in Great Bedwyn and latterly at Hungerford Park in Hungerford, and in 1719 bought South Standen manor in Hungerford parish. He was frequently returned as M.P. for Great Bedwyn in the period 1679–1702. *Hist. Parl., Commons*, 1660–90, 1690–1715; *VCH Berks.* iv; *VCH Wilts.* xvi.

Stonehouse, Francis (d. 1779), of South Standen, a trustee from 1778 to his death. He inherited South Standen manor from his brother George in 1777. *VCH Berks.* iv.

Stonehouse, George (d. 1777), of South Standen, a trustee from 1760 to his death. He inherited South Standen manor in 1758. *VCH Berks.* iv.

Sutton, James (born *c.* 1733, d. 1801), of New Park, a trustee from 1783 to his death. He was M.P. for Devizes 1765–80 and inherited the New Park estate in 1775. *Hist. Parl., Commons*, 1754–90; *VCH Wilts.* vii, x, xii.

Talbot, Thomas, of Collingbourne Ducis, a trustee 1751–6. He was rector of Collingbourne Ducis from 1743. In 1756 he resigned as rector and as a trustee and moved to Margam. Phillipps, *Wiltshire Institutions*; WSA 2037/119.

Tooker, Charles (d. 1716), of East Kennett, a trustee from 1713 to his death. He inherited East Kennett manor in 1700. *VCH Wilts.* xii.

Tylney Long (formerly Long), Sir James (1736–94), bt., of Draycot Cerne, a trustee from 1778 to his death. He had assumed the additional surname Tylney by 1778. He was a Wiltshire M.P. from 1762 to his death. In 1767 he inherited the Draycot Cerne estate on the death of his father Sir Robert Long, in 1784 he succeeded to the estates of his uncle, and in 1785 he bought the Seagry House estate. *Hist. Parl., Commons*, 1754–90; Burke, *Ext. and Dorm. Baronetcies*; *VCH Wilts.* xiv.

Vilett, Thomas (1789–1846), of Swindon, a trustee from 1821 to his death. He was a lieutenant colonel of the Royal Wiltshire militia and a J.P. and D.L. Burke, *Landed Gentry* (1840).

Vilett, Thomas Goddard (1750–1817), of Swindon, a trustee from 1789 to his death. He was a Doctor of Laws and from 1791 to his death was rector of Draycot Foliat. *Alum. Oxon. 1715–1886*; *VCH Wilts.* ix; WSA 1357/24.

Walker (latterly Walker Heneage), John (1730–1806), of Compton Bassett, a trustee from 1770 to his death. He inherited half of Compton Bassett manor in 1758, bought the rest in 1768, and owned lands elsewhere in Wiltshire and in Somerset. He took the additional surname Heneage in 1777. He was M.P. for Cricklade 1785–94. *Hist. Parl., Commons*, 1754–90; *VCH Wilts.* ix–x, xvii.

Walker Heneage (formerly Wyld), George Walker (1799–1875), of Compton Bassett, a trustee from 1845. In 1806 he succeeded John Walker Heneage as owner of the Compton Bassett estate and other lands and in 1818 he took the surname Walker Heneage in place of Wyld. He was a J.P., a D.L., high sheriff of Wiltshire in 1829, and M.P. for Devizes 1838–57.

Burke, *Landed Gentry* (1937); *VCH Wilts.* v, viii–x, xvii.

Warneford, Francis (1761–1835), of Warneford Place, Sevenhampton, a trustee from 1802 to his death. He inherited the Sevenhampton estate in 1784 and was a D.L. of Wiltshire and a lieutenant colonel of the Wiltshire militia. *Alum. Oxon. 1715–1886*; Burke, *Landed Gentry* (1952); F. E. Warneford, *Warnefords* (1991), 286–7, 308.

Whitelock, John (d. 1787), of Chilton Lodge, a trustee from 1751 to his death. He inherited the Chilton Lodge estate from his father Samuel in 1743 and sold it in 1767. From 1773 or earlier until his death he lived at Marridge Hill House in Ramsbury parish. *VCH Wilts.* xii, xvi; WSA 500/7.

Whitelock, Samuel (d. 1743), of Chilton Lodge, a trustee 1698–1704 and from 1713 to his death. He inherited the Chilton Lodge estate in 1690 and held it until his death. *VCH Wilts.* xvi; *VCH Berks.* iv.

Wilsonn, Robert (d. 1819), of Purton, a trustee from 1807 to his death. He married into the Goddard family and held an estate in Purton in his wife's right. Burke, *Landed Gentry* (1906); *VCH Wilts.* xviii.

Wroughton (formerly Montagu), George Wroughton (1788–1871), of East Stowell, a trustee from 1842. He was a lieutenant colonel in the army. He took the surname Wroughton in 1825, when he inherited part of Wilcot manor, held the whole manor from 1839, and lived at Stowell Lodge. Burke, *Commoners*, ii; *VCH Wilts.* x; *Army List.*

Yate, Cornelius (born *c.* 1650, d. 1720), a trustee from 1704 to 1714 or later. He was vicar of Marlborough 1677–1707, as prebendary of Bishopstone a canon of Salisbury 1691–6, archdeacon of Wiltshire from 1696 to his death, and vicar of Islington St. Mary from 1707 to his death. *Alum. Oxon. 1500–1714*; Le Neve, *Fasti, 1541–1857, Salisbury*; Phillipps, *Wiltshire Institutions.*

ACCOUNTS

Account of Alexander Thistlethwaite, steward and receiver, for 1702–3 (from WSA 2037/26)

Receipts

Received of Mr. Hungerford for rent due for Milton and Fyfield farm at Lady day 1702, £55

Received of Mr. Hayward for rent for Chirton farm due at the same time, £55

Disbursements

Due as before to this accountant, £67 4*s.* 11*d.*

26 May 1702. Paid 27 of the widows of the hospital £3 apiece as by their receipt appears, Sarah Hayes, Jane Elks, Alice Davidge, Sarah Mitchell, Mary Farewell, Olive Nevill, Grace Bryant, Elizabeth Abbot, Hester Andrews, Susanna Haysome, Mary Randall, Jane Whale, Elizabeth

Shadwell, Anne Shergold, Jane Walter, Alice Gibbons, Joan Arnold, Grace Franklin, Jane Stephens, Anne Dewy, Anne Bailey, Elizabeth Sims, Agnes Avery, Dorothy Eastmond, Alice Small, Elizabeth Roberts, Anne Wootton, £81

28 July 1702. Paid the widow Harding's daughter what was due to the widow before her death, by the trustees' direction, £5 5*s.*

2 September 1702. Paid Mr. Snead, the chaplain, half a year's salary due Lady day 1702, £5

4 May 1702. Paid one Tuck of Hungerford for timber for repairing Chirton farm as by bill and receipt appears, £8

26 May 1702. Paid Mr. Hamblin of Hungerford for broad cloth for 15 gowns, 3 yards to each, £18 10*s.*

24 May 1702. Paid Mr. Toe of Hungerford for the like as by bill and receipt appears, being both for the year 1701, £18 10*s.*

3 June 1702. Paid Harper, a tailor, for making 15 of the gowns as by bill and receipt appears, £1 10*s.*

13 May 1702. Paid Blundy, a tailor, for making 13 of the gowns, £1 6*s.*

This accountant's salary due Lady day 1702, £20. Note: the salary now went off to £20 a year, the estates being surveyed and buildings repaired etc.

14 April 1702. Paid one King for hair for the use of the hospital as by his receipt appears, 6*s.* 2*d.*

2 June 1702. Paid Mr. Tuck for Mrs. Buckeridge, one of the widows, she dying and this accountant having engaged for the same as by receipt appears, 18*s.*

17 June 1702. Paid Wilkins the woodman for cutting the widows' wood, faggoting, and other business as by bill and receipt appears, £5 15*s.* 4*d.*

21 May 1702. Paid Farmer Tarrant for carrying the widows' wood as by receipt appears, £2 13*s.* 8*d.*

10 March 1702. Paid Horne of Hungerford for clock lines as by his receipt appears, 4*s.*

Paid Milsom for digging sand for the hospital, 5*s.*

Paid Milsom, the porter of the hospital, or to his order, 2 years' salary due Midsummer 1702 as by receipt appears, £4

Paid for making the widow Wootton's former gown, 2*s.*

Paid Tuck for more timber as by the bill aforesaid and receipt appears, £4

Paid in the whole this half year, £245 4*s.* 1*d.*

Received in the whole this half year, £110

So rest due to this accountant, £135 4*s.* 1*d.*

Receipts

Received of Mr. Hungerford half a year's rent for Milton and Fyfield farm due at Michaelmas 1702, £55

Received of Mr. Hayward half a year's rent for Chirton farm due at the same time, £55

Received of Noyes, the former tenant of Chirton, being arrears of rent, by the trustees' order, £20

Disbursements

Due as before to this accountant, £135 4*s*. 1*d*.

10 December 1702. Paid 26 widows of the hospital £3 10*s*. apiece as by their receipt appears, Alice Davidge, Mary Farewell, Elizabeth Roberts, Olive Nevill, Grace Bryant, Elizabeth Abbot, Hester Andrews, Mary Randall, Jane Whale, Dorothy Eastmond, Elizabeth Shadwell, Jane Walter, Alice Gibbons, Jane Stephens, Anne Dewy, Anne Bailey, Joan Arnold, Sarah Hayes, Alice Small, Jane Elks, Elizabeth Sims, Anne Wootton, Anne Shergold, Susanna Haysome, Grace Franklin, Agnes Avery, £91

13 October 1702. Paid Mrs. Mitchell, one other of the widows, as by her receipt appears, £3 10*s*.

30 November 1702. Paid Mr. Butler for nails for the hospital as by his bill and receipt appears, 16*s*. 6*d*.

23 November 1702. Paid Kimber the carpenter for work done at the hospital as by his bill and receipt appears, 16*s*. 11*d*.

18 January 1703. Paid Burton, a mason, for work done at the hospital as by his bill and receipt appears, £1

23 December 1702. Paid Tubb for cleansing the hospital clock as by receipt appears, 3*s*.

4 March 1703. Paid Burton for more work done at the hospital as by receipt appears, £1 1*s*. 6*d*.

19 January 1703. Paid Mr. Snead, the chaplain, his half year's salary due at Michaelmas 1702 as by receipt appears, £5

25 September 1702. Paid Mr. Liddiard for straw and work done for the hospital as by receipt appears, £2 3*s*.

23 April 1703. Paid Wilkins the woodman for cutting wood and making faggots for the hospital as by receipt appears, £4 18*s*.

7 June 1703. Paid Platt for 1 year's looking after the woods belonging to the hospital and carrying the widows' faggots as by receipt appears, £3 15*s*.

Paid Mrs. Buckeridge before her death, 15*s*.

Paid a labourer to place up bricks etc. at the hospital, 6*s*.

Paid another labourer for the same purpose, 4*s*. 6*d*.

Half a year's salary due to this accountant Michaelmas 1702, £10

Paid this half year in the whole, £260 13*s*. 6*d*.

Received this half year in the whole, £130

Rest due to this accountant, £130 13*s*. 6*d*.

The account of Samuel Martin, receiver of the rents and profits of the charity estate, for the balance of his last account, for the arrears allowed him therein, and for 1 year's rents and profits arising out of the estates and ending at old Michaelmas 1770 (from WSA 2037/27)

Charge

To the balance of the last account stated to Michaelmas 1769, £1,594 16*s.*

Arrears allowed therein of farm rents: from William Holloway, a desperate debt of long standing before the late receiver's time, £222 16*s.* 6*d.*, [and] from William Munday, the like, £15

Fyfield farm in possession of executors of John Cannings, deceased, at £70 a year, for 1 year's rent due at Michaelmas 1770, £70

Batchelor's bargain in possession of the same at £32 a year clear of all taxes, to year's rent due Michaelmas 1770, £32

Huish and Stubnail farms and the coppice called Huish Coffer in possession of John Tarrant at £120 a year clear of all taxes, to 1 year's rent due at Michaelmas 1770, £120

Milton farm in possession of Thomas Tarrant at £82 a year clear of all taxes, to 1 year's rent due Michaelmas 1770, £82

Pyke's Bear croft in possession of Charles Penruddocke, esq., at £5 a year clear of all taxes, to 1 year's rent due at Michaelmas 1770, £5

Chirton farm in the possession of William Barnes at £84 a year clear of all taxes, to 1 year's rent due at Michaelmas 1770, £84

Two cottages, two gardens, and a close of meadow at Chirton in possession of William Barnes by lease for 99 years determinable on lives at 4*s.*, to 1 year's rent due at Michaelmas 1770, 4*s.*

Two farms at Froxfield called the greater and the lesser in the possession of Elias Ivy at £120 a year clear of all taxes, to 1 year's rent due at Michaelmas 1770, £120

A messuage at Froxfield called the Cross Keys inn and a cottage, late in the possession of Anne Pethers but now of William Noyes, who married the widow Cotterell, at £23 a year clear of all taxes, to 1 year's rent due at Michaelmas 1770, £23

A messuage and malthouse late in the possession of Elizabeth Lockeram but now of William Noyes at £12 10*s.* a year clear of all taxes, to 1 year's rent due Michaelmas 1770, £12 10*s.*

To 1 year's conventionary rents arising out of the manor of Huish and Shaw due at Michaelmas 1770, £103 17*s.* 4*d.*

The like for the manor of Froxfield due at Michaelmas 1770, £52 12*s.* 10*d.*

To 1 year's dividend on £1,000 Old South Sea annuities due 10 October 1770, £30

To 1 year's dividend due on £1,600 due 10 October 1770, £48

To a heriot received of John Banning, 10*s.* 6*d.*

To cash received of John Banning for adding his son's life, £5

Total charge on receiver, £2,621 7*s.* 2*d.*

Disbursements

10 January

1. Paid 23 widows their quarterly dividend due at old Christmas 1769, Mary Mintern, Jane Kidman, Mary Oaks, Mary Fallowfield, Jenny

Isaac, Mary Todd, Mary Buchanan, Mary Belcher, Martha Davenport, Margaret Marsh, Elizabeth Mills, Sarah Spackman, Elizabeth Vincent, Jane Simms, Jane Webb, Barbara Osmond, Mary Moore, Margaret Rawlins, Elizabeth Martin, Sarah Hopkins, Mary Stone, Mary Gingell, Elizabeth Scriven, £48 6*s.*

2. Paid Mary Gingell four quarters to Michaelmas last, she being absent when the other widows were paid, £8 8*s.*

5 February

3. Paid the chaplain half a year to Christmas last, £15

4. Paid a bill for bricks used at the hospital, £2 0*s.* 6*d.*

5. Paid John Gregory a mason's bill, £6 16*s.* 5*d.*

6. Paid Elizabeth Newman for making 15 gowns at Christmas 1769, £1 17*s.* 6*d.*

7. Paid Daniel Ezzard the like, £1 17*s.* 6*d.*

9 April

8. Paid 27 widows their quarter's dividend due at Lady day last, Margaret Marsh, Mary Mintern, Sarah Wilkins, Jane Kidman, Mary Fallowfield, Mary Oaks, Jenny Isaac, Mary Todd, Mary Buchanan, Mary Belcher, Martha Davenport, Barbara Jenkins, Frances Lucas, Elizabeth Mills, Sarah Spackman, Elizabeth Vincent, Jane Simms, Jane Webb, Barbara Osmond, Mary Moore, Margaret Rawlins, Elizabeth Martin, Sarah Hopkins, Mary Stone, Elizabeth Hamblin, Mary Gingell, Elizabeth Scriven, £56 14*s.*

9. Paid Elizabeth Hamblin one quarter's dividend due 5 January last, she being absent when the other widows were paid, £2 2*s.*

10. Paid Sarah Wilkins the like dividend of 5 January last, being absent at that time, £2 2*s.*

11. Paid Frances Lucas five quarters' dividend due at the same time, she being absent at the several days of payment, £10 10*s.*

12. Paid Barbara Jenkins half a year's dividend due at the same time, she being also absent, £4 4*s.*

13. Paid 1 year's insurance to Lady day 1771, £2 10*s.*

9 July

14. Paid 27 widows their quarter's dividend to old Midsummer day, Mary Fallowfield, Priscilla Smith, Mary Mintern, Mary Oaks, Jane Kidman, Sarah Wilkins, Jenny Isaac, Mary Todd, Mary Buchanan, Mary Belcher, Elizabeth Fyfield, Martha Davenport, Margaret Marsh, Barbara Jenkins, Elizabeth Mills, Sarah Spackman, Elizabeth Vincent, Jane Simms, Jane Webb, Barbara Osmond, Mary Moore, Margaret Rawlins, Elizabeth Martin, Sarah Hopkins, Mary Stone, Frances Lucas, Mary Gingell, £56 14*s.*

15. Paid Betty Fyfield two quarters' dividends due at Lady day last, she being absent at that time, £4 4*s.*

16. Paid Priscilla Smith, another absentee, to the same time, £6 6*s.*

17. Paid the matron 1 year's salary to Midsummer 1770, £1
18. Paid Elizabeth Scriven's executor one quarter to 5 July 1770 and for her burial, £3 3*s*.

6 August
19. Paid Mr. Lucas's bill for cloth for the widows' gowns to Christmas 1769, £36

3 September
20. Paid John Gregory mason's bill, £7 8*s*. 9*d*.

15 September
21. Paid William Humphreys a freemason's bill, £4 4*s*. 6*d*.

16 October
22. Paid 27 widows their quarter's dividend due the 10th instant, Margaret Marsh, Mary Mintern, Sarah Wilkins, Barbara Jenkins, Jane Kidman, Mary Fallowfield, Mary Oaks, Priscilla Smith, Jenny Isaac, Mary Buchanan, Betty Fyfield, Mary Belcher, Mary Todd, Martha Davenport, Elizabeth Hamblin, Elizabeth Mills, Sarah Spackman, Elizabeth Vincent, Jane Simms, Jane Webb, Barbara Osmond, Mary Moore, Margaret Rawlins, Elizabeth Martin, Mary Stone, Sarah Hopkins, Sarah Cobley, £56 14*s*.
23. Paid Elizabeth Hamblin one quarter's dividend to Midsummer last, being absent at that time, £2 2*s*.
24. Paid Mary Stone for washing the chapel linen to Michaelmas last, 10*s*.

5 November
25. Paid James Field's bill for lime, £1 8*s*.

7 November
26. Paid John Tarrant a year's salary as bailiff of Huish due at old Michaelmas last, £4

25 September [*?rectius* November]
27. Paid the chaplain half a year's salary due at Midsummer last, £15

3 December
28. Paid the porter a year's salary due at Michaelmas last, £4
29. Paid John Osmond for faggoting and mending bounds, £13 1*s*. 9*d*.
30. Paid him his bill for repairs, £15 7*s*. 1*d*.
31. Paid the blacksmith's bill for repairs, £7 1*s*.

Paid [the] messenger to the trustees to give notice of the meeting on 7 November 1770, 3*s*. 6*d*.
Attended that meeting, £1 1*s*.
Paid my expenses, 5*s*. 6*d*.
The like for meeting 29 November [*rectius* December] following, £1 10*s*. 6*d*.
Expenses [of] my clerk, 3*s*.
The like for the bailiff of the manor of Huish, 1*s*. 6*d*.
Horse hire and expenses to pay the widows their four quarterly payments, 14*s*.
1 year's salary as receiver to Michaelmas 1770, £30

Holding Froxfield court after Michaelmas 1770, £1 1*s.*
To the servants there as usual, 2*s.*
The like at Huish, £1 3*s.*
Arrears outstanding for which the receiver craves an allowance. From William Holloway a desperate debt of long standing due before the late receiver's time, £222 16*s.* 6*d.*; William Munday, the like, £15
Receiver's journey to town to pass this account, £5 5*s.*
To the receiver's bill of costs of passing his account, £13 0*s.* 4*d.*
To the trustees' bill of costs for the like, £7 4*s.* 4*d.*
Total disbursements, £700 3*s.* 2*d.*
Due from receiver to balance this account, £1,921 4*s.* 2*d.*
[Total] £2,621 7*s.* 4*d.*
[*Signed*] P. Holford

Account of John Ward, receiver of the rents and profits of the estate belonging to the hospital, for the outstanding arrears allowed in the receiver's last account and for 1 year's rents and profits ending Michaelmas 1815 old style (from WSA 2037/27)

[*Charge*]
Arrears returned in last account
Edward Newman, £80
William Robbins, £400
Robert Fowler, £76 10*s.*
1 year's rent due Michaelmas 1815
[Froxfield]
William Sellwood, the farm, £210
Edward Newman, Smith's bargain, £40; Cripps's bargain, £41 10*s.*; Newman's cottage, £2; Tarrant's, £42
William Newbury, Cross Keys etc., £54; late Smith's arable, £35; west end of Horseshoe mead, £3 10*s.*
William Merriwether, east end of Horseshoe mead, £4; advance on rent he pays to Mr. Sellwood, £10 6*s.*; Froxfield coppices, £26
Joseph Drury, Little mead and Marsh ground, £3
Jonathan Trueman, Blue Lion, £7
Mary Kimber, late Andrews's, £6
1 year's conventionary rents, £19 5*s.* 6*d.*
[Huish]
William Robbins, Huish, £800
James Racey, new cottage, Midsummer 1815, £3
Thomas Marks, new cottage, Midsummer 1815, £3
William Jessitt, new cottage, Midsummer 1815, £3
1 year's conventionary rents, £37 1*s.*
James Warwick, Milton farm, £130

J. H. Penruddocke, Fyfield farm, £200
Robert Fowler, Oare, £155
Thomas Pyke, Clench, £60; Clench, £2
[Chirton]
W. and H. Hayward, Chirton, £230
1 year's conventionary rents, 4*s.*
Dividends on £2,600 Old South Sea annuities, £70 4*s.*
Dividends on £235 9*s.* 5*d.* Old South Sea annuities, £6 7*s.* 2*d.*
Dividends on £113 9*s.* 2*d.* Old South Sea annuities in trust for Huish rectory, £3 1*s.* 4*d.*
Casual receipts
1 year's property tax certificate to Lady day 1814, £167 7*s.* 9*d.*; the like to Lady day 1815, £193 0*s.* 7*d.*
Received of the treasurer of the Wells clerical fund 2 years' allowance for widow Mary Morgan for 1814 and 1815, £42. These funds are retained by the trust towards reimbursing the expense of Mrs. Morgan's maintenance at Brislington under Dr. Fox's care, who has also received 2 years' pension of £10 from the Corporation of the Sons of the Clergy for 1814 and 1815.
Received of Mr. Edward Newman the remainder of the debt due on note deducting an allowance explained in the agreement on his quitting, £33 1*s.*
[Total] £3,219 8*s.* 4*d.*
Balance due to the accountant, £758 6*s.* 4½*d.*
[Total] £3,977 14*s.* 8½*d.*
Discharge
Balance of last account, £784 19*s.* 6½*d.*
Widows' dividends
13 October 1815
Paid 44 widows a quarter's dividend at £8 each due this day, Elizabeth Phillips, Rebecca Lloyd, Mary Mony, Alice Rogers, Elizabeth Edwards, Mary Symonds, Elizabeth Price, Elizabeth Lancaster, Elizabeth Bailey, Sarah Jenkins, Elizabeth Ann Graves, Margaret Lowder, Elizabeth Hodge, Sarah Francis, Grace Atwood, Honor Morgan, Elizabeth Milne, Maria West, Mary Brown, Mary Lampard, Mary Maynard, Mary Hill, Sarah Biggs, Elizabeth Crewe, Mary Pewsey, Mary Palmer, Martha Holmes, Frances Berry, Mary Crook, Mary Godley, Jane Hopgood, Elizabeth Ridley, Martin Bailey, Hester Brackstone, Amy Rawlins, Elizabeth Trueman, Mary Pettit, Mary Habgood, Martha Godley, Gertrude Gordon, Sarah Bacon, Ann Mills, Jane Williams, Rosamond Cox, £352
Paid Elizabeth Graves, an absentee, by order, £8
Paid Mrs. Corlett one quarter to Michaelmas 1815, £8
Paid Mrs. Currie to time of quitting, as per order, £4 12*s.* 6*d.*

9 January 1816

Paid 43 widows a quarter's dividend at £8 each due this day, Elizabeth Phillips, Rebecca Lloyd, Mary Mony, Alice Rogers, Elizabeth Edwards, Mary Symonds, Elizabeth Price, Elizabeth Lancaster, Elizabeth Bailey, Sarah Jenkins, Hester Lewis, Elizabeth Ann Graves, Margaret Lowder, Elizabeth Hodge, Sarah Francis, Grace Atwood, Elizabeth Milne, Maria West, Mary Brown, Mary Lampard, Mary Maynard, Mary Hill, Sarah Biggs, Elizabeth Crewe, Christian Monk, Mary Pewsey, Mary Palmer, Martha Holmes, Frances Berry, Mary Godley, Jane Hopgood, Elizabeth Ridley, Martin Bailey, Hester Brackstone, Amy Rawlins, Elizabeth Trueman, Mary Pettit, Martha Godley, Gertrude Gordon, Ann Mills, Jane Williams, Rosamond Cox, Ann Holdstock, £344

Paid Christian Monk and Ann Holdstock one quarter each to Michaelmas 1815, £16

Paid S. Corlett one quarter to Christmas 1815, £8

Paid Mary Crook's representatives to the day of her decease, £6 19*s.*

Paid for her funeral, £1 1*s.*

9 February 1816

Paid Elizabeth Bailey's representatives to the day of her decease, £2 13*s.* 4*d.*

Paid Elizabeth Bailey's representatives for her funeral, £1 1*s.*

11 April 1816

Paid 43 widows a quarter's dividend at £8 each due at Lady day last, Elizabeth Phillips, Mary Mony, Alice Rogers, Elizabeth Edwards, Mary Symonds, Elizabeth Price, Elizabeth Lancaster, Sarah Jenkins, Hester Lewis, Elizabeth Ann Graves, Margaret Lowder, Elizabeth Hodge, Sarah Francis, Grace Atwood, Elizabeth Milne, Maria West, Mary Brown, Mary Lampard, Mary Maynard, Mary Hill, Sarah Biggs, Elizabeth Crewe, Christian Monk, Mary Pewsey, Mary Palmer, Martha Holmes, Frances Berry, Jane Cundell, Mary Godley, Jane Hopgood, Elizabeth Ridley, Martin Bailey, Hester Brackstone, Amy Rawlins, Elizabeth Trueman, Mary Pettit, Mary Habgood, Martha Godley, Gertrude Gordon, Ann Mills, Jane Williams, Rosamond Cox, Ann Holdstock, £344

Paid Mary Habgood one quarter to Christmas 1815, £8

Paid Mrs. Corlett one quarter to Lady day 1816, £8

Paid Mrs. Davies three quarters to Lady day 1816, £24

8 July 1816

Paid 44 widows a quarter's dividend at £8 each due the 6th instant, Mary Mony, Alice Rogers, Mary Symonds, Elizabeth Price, Elizabeth Lancaster, Sarah Jenkins, Hester Lewis, Elizabeth Ann Graves, Margaret Lowder, Elizabeth Hodge, Sarah Francis, Grace Atwood, Honor Morgan, Elizabeth Milne, Maria West, Mary

Brown, Elizabeth Davies, Mary Lampard, Mary Maynard, Mary Hill, Sarah Biggs, Elizabeth Crewe, Christian Monk, Mary Pewsey, Mary Palmer, Martha Holmes, Frances Berry, Jane Cundell, Mary Godley, Jane Hopgood, Elizabeth Ridley, Martin Bailey, Hester Brackstone, Amy Rawlins, Elizabeth Trueman, Mary Pettit, Mary Habgood, Martha Godley, Gertrude Gordon, Sarah Bacon, Ann Mills, Jane Williams, Rosamond Cox, Ann Holdstock, £352

Paid Mrs. Corlett one quarter to 6 July, £8

Paid nurses

At Michaelmas, £10 2*s.*

At Christmas, £10 16*s.*

At Lady day, £8 15*s.* 6*d.*

At Midsummer, £11 2*s.*

Insurance

Paid 1 year's insurance to Lady day 1817, £6 2*s.*

Rent of lifehold estates etc. taken in hand

Charles Stagg, 1 year to Michaelmas 1815, £24

William Rudman, 1 year to Michaelmas 1815, £24

William Rudman, to November 1815, when he died, £3

Mrs. White, to 3 August 1814, by order, £4 10*s.*

Mr. Pyke, 1 year to Michaelmas 1815, £3 5*s.* 6*d.*

Mr. Penruddocke, 1 year to Michaelmas 1815, £3 4*s.* 9*d.*

Thomas Hailstone, for rent of a cottage lost, £3

Property tax

William Robbins and Robert Fowler, half a year to Lady day 1815, £47 15*s.*; half a year to Michaelmas 1815, £49 15*s.*

John Stagg, half a year to Lady day 1815, £10; half a year to Michaelmas 1815, £10

William Sellwood, half a year to Lady day 1815, £10 10*s.*; half a year to Michaelmas 1815, £10 10*s.* 6*d.*

Messrs. Hayward, 1 year to Lady day 1815, £20

James Warwick, 1 year to Lady day 1815, £13

Edward Newman, 1 year to Lady day 1815, £10 1*s.* 4*d.*

William Newbury, 1 year to Lady day 1815, £7 9*s.* 10*d.*

T. Pyke, half a year to Lady day 1815, £3 2*s.*; half a year to Michaelmas 1815, £3 2*s.*

William Merriwether, 1 year to Lady day 1815, £3 2*s.*; on quit rent, 1 year to Lady day 1815, 12*s.*

John Banning, 1 year to Lady day 1815, £2

James Cannings, 1 year to Lady day 1815, £1 6*s.*

Joseph Drury, 1 year to Lady day 1815, 16*s.*

Jonathan Trueman, 1 year to Lady day 1815, 14*s.*

T. Banning, 1 year to Lady day 1815, 4*s.*

Repairs

Jere York, bricklayer, £33 19*s.*
James Pickett, glazier, £12 14*s.* 10*d.*
Robert Hawkins, brick, lime, etc., £12 2*s.* 5*d.*
James Wiltshire, carpenter, £7 13*s.*
William Arman, blacksmith, £7 11*s.* 4*d.*
Labour and sundries at the hospital
Edward Newman's account, including salary, £24 19*s.* 4*d.*
Balance of account of disbursements respecting the new lodge, deducting money received for timber, £186 18*s.* 8*d.*
Salaries
Revd. A. Meyrick, chaplain, 1 year to Lady day 1816, £50
Mr. Marsh, apothecary, 1 year to 1 June, £50
J. Ward, receiver, 1 year to Lady day, £50
Guy Warwick, bailiff, £4
Thomas Dobson, chapel clerk, £2 10*s.*
Casual payments
Mr. Merriwether, for reserves, £1 9*s.* 3*d.*
Dr. Fox, for Mrs. Morgan, £28 16*s.* 6*d.* [and] £21 13*s.* 3*d.*
Clerk's bill for holding courts, attending meetings, etc., £15 7*s.*; respecting exchange at Fyfield, £6 4*s.* 2*d.*
Interest on balance of account in advance to the trust, as by voucher, £37 15*s.* 6*d.*
Revd. C. Mayo, 2 years' dividend received for him with trust dividend to Michaelmas 1815, £6 2*s.* 8*d.*
Arrears
Robert Fowler, £77 10*s.*
William Robbins, £718 10*s.*
James Cannings, £11 14*s.*
Messrs. Hayward, £15
Total discharge £3,977 14*s.* 8½*d.*
Total charge £3,219 8*s.* 4*d.*
Balance £758 6*s.* 4½*d.*
7 August 1816. Examined and allowed, and the balance of £758 6*s.* 4½*d.* due to the accountant is to be carried to his next account.
[*Signed*] E. Goddard, William Northey

The account of Thomas Baverstock Merriman, receiver of the rents and profits of the estates belonging to the hospital, for the outstanding arrears allowed in the receiver's last account and for 1 year's rents and profits ending Michaelmas 1860 old style (from WSA 2037/28)

Charge
1 year's rents due Michaelmas 1860
Froxfield

Revd. T. G. P. Atwood, Kimber's, £6; small paddock, 10*s.*; 11 acres, part of Manor farm, £13 15*s.*; Bunce's copyhold, late Drury, £35
Nathan Aldridge, cottage, late Hawkins, 15*s.* (half year to Lady day)
John Talbot, cottage, late Hawkins, 15*s.* (half year to Michaelmas)
John Brown, cottage, late E. Newman's executors, £2 2*s.*
Richard Coombs, dwellinghouse, £30; part late Drury, £5 10*s.*; 1 acre, late J. Redman, £1 15*s.*
Richard Draper, cottage, late Hawkins, £2 12*s.*
Daniel Draper, cottage, late Pound, £3
John Francis, house, late Merriwether's, £15; 6 acres, part late Drury, £12 10*s.*
Alexander Francis (policeman), new cottage, formerly malthouse, £3
13 garden tenants, £4 8*s.* 6*d.*
29 garden tenants, new gardens, 6a. 3r. 2p., £14 12*s.*
John Giles, cottage, late Brown, £1 15*s.*
William C. Gooding, granary, late Hillary, £2 10*s.*; 5a. 2r. 23p., late J. Redman, £11
Alfred Gooding, new cottage, £3 3*s.*
Widow Hobbs, cottage, late Brown, £1 15*s.*
George Hart, cottage, late Dyson's, £3 10*s.*
Joseph Hedges, cottage, late Hawkins, £2 15*s.*
Mary Holmes, cottage, late Hawkins, £2 16*s.*
Henry Holmes, cottage, late Dobson's, £3
Alfred Holmes, new cottage, £1 11*s.* 6*d.* (half year to Lady day)
Richard Amor, new cottage, £1 11*s.* 6*d.* (half year to Michaelmas)
Thomas Holmes, new cottage, £3 3*s.*; carthouse, 5*s.*
Thomas Harris, cottage, late Hillary, £2
John James, cottage, late Hawkins, £2 12*s.*
John Kempfield, new cottage, £3 3*s.*
William Lewis (Rudge), part late Drury, 15*s.*
James Martin, Blue Lion, £25; 3 acres taken from Brewery farm, £4 10*s.*; 2a. 3r. 2p., late J. Redman, £6
William Naish, late Bettridge's, £15; woodhouse, part late Kimber's, 10*s.*
Thomas Hobbs, cottage and garden, remainder of late Kimber's, £5
James Pearse, cottage, late Dobson's, £1 15*s.*
John Pyke, new cottage, £3 3*s.*
John Redman, Manor and Brewery farms, £510; part late Drury, £74 10*s.*; cottage occupied by Joseph Stagg, £1 15*s.*; cottage occupied by Charles Dobson, £1 10*s.*
William Rider, cottage, late Hillary, £2
William Henry Rider, cottage, late E. Newman's executors, £2 12*s.*
Charles Shettle, cottage, late E. Newman's executors, £2 15*s.*; woodhouse, late Widow Day, £1

Stephen Snook, dwellinghouse and two meadows, £28; 4a. 3r. 7p., late J. Redman, £10
Widow Stroud, cottage, late Hawkins, £2 10*s.*
Edward Skeats, new cottage, £3 3*s.*
John Talbot, cottage, late Drury, £1 6*s.* (half year to Lady day)
Nathan Aldridge, cottage, late Drury, £1 6*s.* (half year to Michaelmas)
Widow Taylor, cottage, late Drury, £1 15*s.*
John Truckle, cottage, late A. Newman's executors, £3
Henry Withers, new cottage, formerly malthouse, £3
Thomas Waters, cottage, late Smith's, £2 12*s.*
William Wise, Cross Keys inn, £19 10*s.*; cottage, £3 3*s.*; 2a. 2r. 11p., near Cross Keys, deduct £1 for ground used for new cottages, £5
Joseph Westall, cottage, late Smith's, £2 5*s.*

Huish
Revd. W. Bleeck, garden opposite Vicarage, £1 1*s.*
Robert Cook, cottage, late Widow Alexander, £2 10*s.*
John Godding, new tenement, £4
Jacob Hailstone, house and carpenter's shop, £6 6*s.*
William Young, farm, £438; six new tenements, £15; two new cottages, £5; Fishlock's cottage, on the hill, ... [*rent not specified*]

Milton
Francis Church, farm, £218
Thomas Blackman, cottage, late Warwick, £3
James Stagg, cottage, late Warwick, £3
John Waite, cottage, late Warwick, £2 2*s.*

Little Salisbury, cottage gardens
Jesse Head, small piece now lying waste, 6*d.*
Edward Kimmer, 21 poles, 15*s.*
William Shipway, 21 poles, 15*s.*

Fyfield and Clench
George Amor (late Frippence), new cottage (Kingstone's lodge), £2 10*s.*
George Amor (late Yates), new cottage (Kingstone's lodge), £2 10*s.*
James Brewer, farm, late Ann Banning's, £78 10*s.*
James Joseph Kingstone, farm, £355 5*s.*

Milkhouse Water, cottage gardens
William Bailey, 16 poles, 8*s.*
George Clemence, 25 poles, 6*s.* 6*d.*
George Shipway, 31 poles, 15*s.* 9*d.*

Oare
Henry Edmonds, farm, £168

Chirton
Henry Hayward, farm, £207

Quit rents
1 year's quit rents in Froxfield, £7 13*s.*

1 year's quit rents in Chirton, 4*s*.
[Dividends]
1 year's dividends on £2,656 18*s*. 3*d*. 3 per cent consols in [the] names of Horatio Nelson Goddard and Francis Leyborne Popham, esqs., due 5 January 1861, £79 14*s*. 2*d*.
1 year's dividends on £128 19*s*. 3 per cent consols due 5 January 1861 [held] in trust for Huish rectory, £3 17*s*. 4*d*.
Casual receipts
Received of F. L. Popham, esq., for shooting over the lands at Froxfield 1860–1, £9
Received of Harry Hayward for shooting over the lands at Chirton 1860–1, £5
Received of William Young for shooting over the lands at Huish 1860–1, £7
Received of Jacob Hailstone for 164 faggots from Huish, £1 18*s*. 4*d*.
Received of William Young for 7 cwt. 3 qr. of bark from Huish, at £5 10*s*. a ton, £2 2*s*. 6*d*.
Received of W. C. Gooding for 450 faggots, at 14*s*. a hundred, sold at Froxfield, £3 3*s*.
Received of William Young for small oak trees and saplings in Coffer wood and on Huish Hill, £39
Received of C. and G. E. May for 1 ton 12 cwt. 3 qr. of bark from Froxfield, at £5 15*s*. a ton, £9 8*s*. 4*d*.
Arrears of rent returned in [the] last account
Jesse Head for garden at Milton, 3 years, 1*s*. 6*d*.
[Total] £2,624 16*s*. 5*d*.

Discharge
Widows' dividends
2 August 1860
Paid Catherine Carpenter's representatives to the time of her death on 24 July 1860, £1 16*s*.; allowance for funeral, £1 1*s*.; deduct for broken windows, 1*s*. 6*d*. [Total] £2 15*s*. 6*d*.
24 August 1860
Paid Elizabeth Cooke two quarter's dividends due 6 July 1860, £18; deduct amount declared by the trustees 12 July 1860 to be forfeited for absence without leave, £5; dividend from 6 July to 24 August 1860, the time of her resignation, £4 18*s*.; deduct for broken windows, 1*s*. 6*d*. [Total] £17 16*s*. 6*d*.
11 October 1860
Paid 45 widows a quarter's dividend at £9 each, due this day, £405
Paid Elizabeth Anne White from the time of her taking possession on 18 August to 11 October, £5 8*s*.
Paid Elizabeth Gough from the time of her taking possession on 15 August to 11 October, £5 14*s*.
Paid Betty Wride from 6 July to 13 August last, the time of her

resignation, £3 16*s*.; deduct for broken windows, 3*s*. 4*d*. [Total] £3 12*s*. 8*d*.

10 December 1860

Paid Catherine Caithness's representatives to the time of her death on 3 December, £5 6*s*.; allowance for funeral, £1 1*s*.; deduct for broken windows, 2*s*. 4*d*. [Total] £6 4*s*. 8*d*.

7 January 1861

Paid 43 widows a quarter's dividend at £9 each, due 6th instant, £387

Paid Jesse Augusta Martell one quarter's dividend due 11 October last when she was absent with leave, £9

1 February 1861

Paid Frances Hunter one quarter's dividend due 6 January 1861, £9; proportion of one quarter's dividend from 6 January to 25 January 1861, the time of her resignation, £1 18*s*.; deduct for broken windows, 8*d*. [Total] £10 17*s*. 4*d*.

6 April 1861

Paid 44 widows a quarter's dividend at £9 each, due this day, £396

Paid Maria Jacob one quarter's dividend due 6 January last, when she was absent with leave, £9

Paid Harriet Austin [likewise], £9

Paid Ann Gay [likewise], £9

Paid Sophia Ann Catherine Williams from the time of her taking possession on 25 February to 6 April 1861, £4 2*s*.

6 July 1861

Paid 44 widows a quarter's dividend at £9 each, due this day, £396

Paid Bridget Williams one quarter's dividend due 6 April last, when she was absent with leave, £9

Paid Mary Ann Clifton [likewise], £9

Paid Charlotte Monkhouse from the time of her taking possession on 17 April to 6 July 1861, £8 2*s*.

Paid nurses

At Michaelmas 1860, Christmas 1860, Lady day 1861, Midsummer 1861: [*no payment recorded*]

Insurance

Paid 1 year's insurance and duty in Sun Fire Office to Lady day 1862 for property at Froxfield, £20 1*s*. 4*d*.

[Likewise] for property at Milton, Chirton, Huish, etc., £18 12*s*.

Repairs etc. at hospital

W. C. Gooding, carpenter, [for] general repairs to widows' houses and porter's lodge, principally ordered at view meeting, £31 19*s*. 10*d*.

James Pickett, plumber and glazier, £5 16*s*. 2*d*.

John Humphreys, blacksmith, £1 1*s*. 6*d*.

William Naish, bricklayer, £6 1*s*. 1*d*.

T. S. Pearce for porter's call bell etc., £4 17*s*. 6*d*.

Repairs to houses etc.
Froxfield
House occupied by Stephen Snook. John Beard, bricks, lime, and sand, £8 1*s.* 6*d.*; T. S. Pearce for spouting, tenant paying for fixing it, £3 2*s.* 1*d.*
House occupied by William Naish. John Faithful for paving bricks etc., tenant finding labour, £6 17*s.*
House occupied by John Francis. John Redman, straw for shed, £3
Cottages. W. C. Gooding, carpenter, £12 7*s.* 9*d.*; William Naish, bricklayer, £5 8*s.* 1*d.*; John Beard, bricks and lime, £4 18*s.* 9*d.*; John Humphreys, blacksmith, 10*s.*; James Pickett, glazier, 2*s.* 9*d.* [Total] £23 7*s.* 4*d.*
Farm occupied by John Redman. W. C. Gooding, carpenter, £3 2*s.* 11*d.*; John Beard, bricks and lime used in water meadow, £3 0*s.* 9*d.*; William Shaw for draining pipes, £6 5*s.* [Total] £12 8*s.* 8*d.*
Broomsgrove farm, occupied by J. J. Kingstone
John Mitchell, further on account for building new stables and cattle shed, £50
John Mitchell, [likewise], £50
John Mitchell, balance, £11 17*s.*
Huish farm, occupied by William Young
William Young, bricks and lime for repairing wall at field barn, £5 18*s.*
Robbins, Lane, & Co., deals for barn's doors, £8 12*s.* 4*d.*
Cottages at Milton, Clench, etc.
James May, mason and carpenter, on account, £10; balance, £4 11*s.* 7*d.*
D. Unthank for straw, £4 10*s.*
John Head, thatcher, £2 13*s.* 4*d.*
James May, mason and carpenter, [for] building new end wall and part of front wall etc. to a cottage at Milton occupied by John Waite [and] damaged by the wind, and repairs to Blackman's cottage, £13 10*s.* 5*d.*
George Amor for repairs to his cottage, 9*s.*
Huish and Oare
Thomas Gale for sawing for cottages at Huish Hill [and] Huish, new privy and pigsties at cottages at Huish, and farmhouse at Oare, £10 9*s.* 9*d.*
Thomas Gale for sawing for farm at Oare [and] cottages at Huish, and for felling timber, barking, faggoting, etc., £3 12*s.* 6*d.*
Jacob Hailstone, carpenter, on account for work to cottages at Huish [and] Huish Hill, and farmhouse at Oare, £12
Henry Hailstone for ironwork to the cottages, £1 7*s.*
David Hammond, mason, on account for work at cottages at Huish and farmhouse at Oare, £8
Salaries
Revd. T. G. P. Atwood, officiating chaplain, half year to Michaelmas

1860, £25; half year to Lady day 1861, £25

R. H. Barker, surgeon, half year to Christmas 1860, £30; half year to Michaelmas 1861, £30

T. B. Merriman, receiver, 1 year to Lady day 1861, £90

Aaron Brown, chapel clerk, half year to Michaelmas 1860, £1 5*s*.; half year to Lady day 1861, £1 5*s*.

W. C. Gooding, porter, 1 year to Michaelmas 1861, £25

Casual payments

Joseph Drury. 1 year's rent to Michaelmas 1860 for land, part of his lifehold, let with cottages formerly malthouse, £3 3*s*.

Poor rates for almshouses, porter's house, and cottages at Froxfield, £12 3*s*. 2*d*.

Highway rate for almshouses, porter's house, and cottages at Froxfield, £1 10*s*. 5*d*.

Church rate for [those buildings], £1 0*s*. 3*d*.

Poor rate for cottages at Huish, £2 8*s*.

Poor rate for cottages at Milton, £1 5*s*.

Highway rate on woods in hand at Clench, 6*s*. 6*d*.

Half year's land tax on woods in hand at Clench, due Lady day 1861, 4*s*. 3*d*.

[To] J. P. Gilmore 1 year's tithe rent charge for gardens at Froxfield to 1 October 1860, £2 12*s*. 8*d*.

[To] Revd. J. H. Gale, vicar of Milton, 1 year's tithe rent charge for coppices in hand, due Michaelmas 1860, £1 1*s*.

[To] Revd. F. H. Buckerfield 1 year's subscription to Little Bedwyn schools to Michaelmas 1861, £3 3*s*.

[To] Marlborough and Great Bedwyn district Society for Promoting Christian Knowledge, £1 1*s*.

[To] W. C. Gooding for cutting timber, barking, faggoting, etc. at Froxfield, £5 7*s*. 10*d*.; for paid men assisting at fire at John Humphreys's at Froxfield, £1

Wine for chapel and sick widows, £1 5*s*.

[To] W. E. Baverstock for valuing timber in Coffer wood etc. sold to William Young for £39, £2

Paid for steward's, chaplain's, and officiating chaplain's dinners in July 1860, £2 6*s*. 6*d*.

Allowances to cottage and garden tenants on payment of their rents and expenses to court etc., £2 1*s*. 3*d*.

Paid for receipt and postage stamps, and stamps on cheques, 5*s*. 3*d*.

[To] Revd. W. Bleeck 1 year's dividends on £128 19*s*. 3 per cent consols due 5 January 1861, received *contra*, £3 17*s*. 4*d*.

[To] William Young for larch trees and planting them in Coffer wood, £3 14*s*.

[To] Thomas Gale for felling timber, barking, faggoting, etc. at Huish, £2

[To] Jacob Hailstone for marking trees, faggoting, etc. at Coffer wood,

£1 5s. 6d.

[To] Dawson & Sons [for] advertizing for a clergy widow in *The Times* newspaper and P[ost] O[ffice] O[rder], £1 1s. 3d.

Steward's bill and sundry payments, £11 15s. 10d.

Steward's bill re Chirton exchange, one moiety (the other paid by Mr. Hayward), £8 5s. 11d.

Arrears of rent

Jesse Head for garden at Milton, 4 years, 2s.

Balance of the receiver's last account, no. 20, due to him, £62 1s. 7d.

[Total] £2,411 7s. 1d.

Total charge £2,624 16s. 5d., total discharge £2,411 7s. 1d., [balance] £213 9s. 4d.

11 July 1861. Examined and allowed, and the balance of £213 9s. 4d. due from the receiver is to be carried to his next account

[*Signed*] Ailesbury, H. N. Goddard, Ernest Bruce, G. H. Walker Heneage, Shelburne, T. Sotheron Estcourt, G. W. Wroughton, J. L. Popham

ADMISSION PAPERS 1830–45

(from WSA 2037/80)

In each case there is a printed form by means of which a trustee directed the porter to admit his nominee to a vacant house. It gives the number of the house, the reason for it being vacant, and details of the nominee. Enclosed are certificates to prove the details of the nominee's marriage and of her husband's death.

8 April 1830

Order to admit Mary Fowler, widow, relict of Thomas Fowler late of Hammersmith, to no. 46, vacant by the death of Sarah Bacon; a lay widow, counties-at-large. Signed by John Pearse.

Marriage certificate of Thomas Fowler and Mary Richards, married in the church of St. George, Hanover Square, 17 April 1780, and both of that parish.

Burial certificate of Thomas Fowler, aged 67, of Grove Place, Hammersmith, buried 29 October 1824.

30 June 1830

Order to admit Ann Parker, widow, relict of the Revd. Marcus Aurelius Parker late of Wanborough, to no. 19, vacant by the death of Elizabeth Rook; a clergy widow, three-counties. Signed by John Awdry.

Marriage certificate of Marcus Aurelius Parker and Ann Early, both of Louth, married in Louth church 6 August 1805.

Burial certificate of Marcus Aurelius Parker, aged 50, of Wanborough, buried there 27 May 1830.

4 November 1830

Order to admit Eliza Maria Fowler, widow, relict of the Revd. John Fowler late of Walworth, to no. 12, vacant by the death of Hester Lewis; a clergy widow, Wiltshire, Berkshire, or Somerset. Signed by Edward William Leyborne Popham.

Marriage certificate of John Fowler of Easton in Gordano and Eliza Maria Chandler of Barnwood, married in Easton in Gordano church 3 November 1773.

Burial certificate of the Revd. John Fowler of St. John's chapel, West Lane (now West Street), Walworth, died 3 October 1817 and buried there 10 October 1817.

[Enclosed in these papers is a letter of 17 March 1827 from T. G. Bucknall Estcourt recommending Mrs. Fowler: he has no nomination and asks the steward for the names of those with the next three or four nominations so that he can arrange an exchange]

18 December 1830

Order to admit Hannah Phillips, widow, relict of John Phillips late of Bristol, to no. 30, vacant by the death of Mary Kimber; a manor widow. Signed by T. G. Bucknall Estcourt.

Marriage certificate of John Phillips and Hannah Baverstock, married at Clifton parish church 4 March 1794.

Burial certificate of John Phillips, buried at the parish church of St. Augustine, Bristol, 9 December 1800.

4 February 1832

Order to admit Elizabeth Scriven, widow, relict of Robert Scriven late of Little Hinton, to no. 40, vacant by the death of Mary Newman; a manor widow. Signed by [Lord] Ailesbury.

Marriage certificate of Robert Scriven of Wootton Rivers and Elizabeth Alder of Pewsey, married at Wootton Rivers 2 November 1801.

Burial certificate of Robert Scriven, aged 54, buried at Little Hinton 28 May 1831.

13 April 1832

Order to admit Elizabeth Slatter, widow, relict of the Revd. Thomas Slatter late of Shipton-on-Cherwell, to no. 18, vacant by the death of Hannah Thompson; a clergy widow, counties-at-large. Signed by E. Goddard.

Marriage certificate of Thomas Slatter and Elizabeth Strange, widow, both of St. George's parish, Bloomsbury, married in the parish church there 26 June 1811.

Burial certificate of Thomas Slatter, rector, of Shipton rectory, aged 45, buried 15 April [1831]

27 June 1832

Order to admit Harriet Compton, widow, relict of John Compton late of Chisenbury, farmer, to no. 25, vacant by the death of Mary Day; a lay widow, London or Westminster. Signed by John Awdry.

Marriage certificate of John Compton and Harriet Nicholas, both of Enford, married in Enford church 22 May 1794.

Burial certificate of John Compton, aged 51, of Chisenbury, buried at Enford 4 November 1813.

1 August 1832

Order to admit Ann Hay, widow, relict of the Revd. Richard John Hay late of Rotterdam, to no. 11, vacant by the resignation of Catherine Pyne; [a clergy widow], three-counties, Wiltshire, Berkshire, or Somerset. Signed by John Dugdale Astley.

Marriage certificate of Richard John Hay and Ann Goodenough, both of Codford St. Peter, married at the parish church there 29 August 1789.

Burial certificate of Richard John Hay, B.A., of University College, Oxford, nearly 17 years British chaplain of the Episcopal Church of England established in Rotterdam, died 22 January 1832, aged 63, and buried in the great church 26 January by Joseph Bosworth, British chaplain at Amsterdam. [The certificate bears a seal depicting the Anglican church at Rotterdam]

5 October 1832

Order to admit Mary Davies, widow, relict of the Revd. Richard Davies late of Wrington, to no. 12, vacant by the death of Eliza Maria Fowler; a clergy widow, Wiltshire, Berkshire, or Somerset. Signed by Thomas Vilett.

Marriage certificate of Richard Davies of Clifton and Mary Brown of Dulverton, married in Dulverton church 25 September 1794.

Burial certificate of Richard Davies, perpetual curate of Churchill and Puxton, of Wrington, aged 68, buried 11 August 1832 at Wrington.

1 March 1833

Order to admit Martha Skillman, widow, relict of William Skillman late of Deddington, to no. 26, vacant by the death of Sarah Biggs; a lay widow, counties-at-large. Signed by E. W. L. Popham.

Marriage certificate of William Skillman and Martha Butler, both of St. Giles's parish, Oxford, married in St. Giles's church 14 October 1799.

Burial certificate of William Skillman, aged 69, of Deddington, buried there 4 June 1828.

15 July 1833

Order to admit Elizabeth Vincent, widow, relict of William Vincent late of Tamworth, to no. 48, vacant by the death of Elizabeth Bradshaw; a lay widow, counties-at-large. Signed by T. G. Bucknall Estcourt.

Marriage certificate of William Vincent of Tamworth and Elizabeth Gilbert of the parish of St. Martin's, Birmingham, married in St. Martin's church 26 July 1784.

Burial certificate of William Vincent, aged 55, buried at Tamworth 29 August 1811.

2 August 1833

Order to admit Margaret Richardson, widow, relict of the Revd. J. Richardson late of Wath, to no. 14, vacant by the death of Margaret

Lowder; a clergy widow, counties-at-large. Signed by Ambrose Goddard.

Marriage certificate of John Richardson of St. Bees parish, gentleman, and Margaret Cannel of Kirk Braddan parish, married in the chapel of St. James in St. Bees parish 13 May 1821.

Burial certificate of John Richardson, aged 38, clerk, of Wath, buried 12 August 1832.

28 February 1834

Order to admit Delia Mary Cosens, widow, relict of the Revd. Reyner Cosens late of Mere, to no. 4, vacant by the death of Martha Pocock; a clergy widow, three-counties. Signed by Francis Warneford.

Marriage certificate of Reyner Cosens and Delia Mary Foote, both of Bruton parish, married there 7 September 1829.

Burial certificate of Reyner Cosens, aged 27, of Mere, buried there 4 February 1834.

5 June 1834

Order to admit Mary Slade, widow, relict of Hercules Wyborn Slade late of Bovingdon and since of Beaufort Buildings, to no. 28, vacant by the death of Ann Steer; a lay widow, counties-at-large. Signed by [Lord] Ailesbury.

Marriage certificate of Hercules Wyborn Slade and Mary Gregory, both of Inkpen, married there 17 June 1798.

Burial certificate of Hercules Wyborn Slade, aged 56, of 12 Beaufort Buildings, buried 18 May 1833 in the parish of St. Clement Danes.

20 January 1835

Order to admit Mary Oldfield, widow, relict of William Oldfield late of Brough, to no. 30, vacant by the death of Hannah Phillips; a manor widow. Signed by John Pearse.

Marriage certificate of William Oldfield and Mary Outram, both of Holy Trinity parish, Kingston-upon-Hull, married there 28 August 1805.

[Burial certificate lacking]

30 January 1835

Order to admit Mary Trusler, widow, relict of Dr. Trusler late of Bathwick, to no. 16, vacant by the death of Sarah Francis; a clergy widow, counties-at-large. Signed by E. W. L. Popham.

Marriage certificate of the Revd. John Trusler of St. John's [parish], Clerkenwell, and Mary Ann Frances Louisa Legoux of St. James's parish, Westminster, under licence from the archbishop of Canterbury, 6 January 1788.

Burial certificate of the Revd. John Trusler, D.D., aged 85, of Bathwick Villa, buried at Bathwick 23 June 1820.

9 February 1835

Order to admit Mary Edwards, widow, relict of Robert Edwards late of Broad Town, to no. 44, vacant by the death of Elizabeth Batt; a manor widow. Signed by John Awdry.

Marriage certificate of Robert Edwards, junior, grocer, and Mary Gale, both of Clyffe Pypard parish, married there 29 February 1796 by E. Goddard.

Burial certificate of Robert Edwards of Broad Town, aged 55, buried 12 November 1828 at Clyffe Pypard.

23 February 1835

Order to admit Jane Braim, widow, relict of the Revd. Thomas Braim late of West Wittering, to no. 15, vacant by the secession of Ellenora Martha Caddick; a clergy widow, London or Westminster. Signed by J. H. Penruddocke.

Marriage certificate of Thomas Braim, schoolmaster, and Jane Steele, both of Leeds parish, married there 25 December 1809.

Burial certificate of Thomas Braim of Lower Thornhaugh, St. Giles, aged 38, buried 31 August 1825 in the parish of St. James's, Westminster.

22 May 1835

Order to admit Ann Gray, late of Bristol, widow, relict of Henry Gray late of Westbury (Wilts.), to no. 46, vacant by the death of Mary Fowler; a lay widow, counties-at-large. Signed by John Dugdale Astley.

Marriage certificate of Henry Gray and Ann Pile, both of St. John's parish, Devizes, married there 12 September 1808.

Burial certificate of Henry Gray of Westbury, aged 43, buried there 29 July 1823.

Certificate that Mrs. Gray is now [living], and has for the last 2 months lived, in the house of Joshua Hague in West Street, Bristol, [an] out-parish of St. Philip and St. Jacob.

21 October 1835

Order to admit Eleanor Bailey, widow, relict of Benjamin Bailey late of Norfolk Street hospital, to no. 24, vacant by the death of Sarah Rickword; a lay widow, counties-at-large. Signed by Thomas Vilett.

Marriage certificate of Benjamin Bailey and Eleanor Noble, both of St. Marylebone parish, married there 24 February 1794.

Burial certicate of Benjamin Bailey, aged 50, of St. Marylebone, buried there 4 July 1815.

20 January 1836

Order to admit Catherine Breach, widow, relict of Walter Gaby Breach late of Middlesex, to no. 27, vacant by the death of Elizabeth Crewe; a lay widow, London or Westminster. Signed by E. Goddard.

Marriage certificate of Walter Gaby Breach and Catherine Bodman, both of Beanacre, married in Melksham church 6 September 1798.

Burial certificate of Walter Gaby Breach, aged 39, of Hilmarton, buried in Bromham parish 15 April 1817.

21 May 1836

Order to admit Charlotte Durnford, widow, relict of John Durnford late of Marlborough, to no. 39, vacant by the death of Jane Tarrant; a manor widow. Signed by [Lord] Ailesbury.

Marriage certificate of John Durnford and Charlotte Wooldridge, widow, both of St. Peter's parish, Marlborough, married there 27 August 1798.

Burial certificate of John Durnford, aged 56, of St. Peter's [parish], Marlborough, buried there 9 September 1825.

7 June 1836

Order to admit Mary Hemus, widow, relict of the Revd. John Edward Hemus late of Boughton, to no. 9, vacant by the death of Elizabeth Lancaster; a clergy widow, three-counties. Signed by T. G. Bucknall Estcourt.

Marriage certificate of John Edward Hemus of Padworth and Mary Wilkinson of Puttenham, married at Puttenham 26 June 1817.

Burial certificate of John Edward Hemus, aged 48, of Boughton, buried 8 November 1835.

6 August 1836

Order to admit Elizabeth Welch, widow, relict of Thomas Welch late of Shadwell, to no. 22, vacant by the marriage of Elizabeth Brind; a lay widow, counties-at-large. Signed by Ambrose Goddard.

Marriage certificate of Thomas Welch and Elizabeth Fowler, both of the parish of St. George's, Hanover Square, married there 17 September 1821.

Burial certificate of Thomas Welch, aged 36, of High Street, Shadwell, buried in the parish of St. Paul's, Shadwell, 5 March 1828.

16 September 1836

Order to admit Sarah Witt, widow, relict of the Revd. Edmund Witt, vicar of Wool, to no. 1, vacant by the death of Mary Morgan; a clergy widow, three-counties. Signed by E. Goddard.

Marriage certificate of Edmund Witt, clerk, of Wool and Sarah Taylor Simpson of Frome Selwood, a minor with the consent of her parent, married at Frome Selwood 17 September 1810.

Burial certificate of Edmund D. Witt, aged 48, of Stokeford, vicar of the parish, buried at Wool 15 January 1835.

22 April 1837

Order to admit Elizabeth Washbourne, widow, relict of Thomas Washbourne late of Standen Farm (Wilts.) and since of Hampshire, to no. 24, vacant by the death of Eleanor Bailey; a lay widow, counties-at-large. Signed by J. H. Penruddocke.

Marriage certificate of Thomas Washbourne of Wroughton and Elizabeth Vivash of Lydiard Tregoze, married at Lydiard Tregoze 26 November 1798.

Burial certificate of Thomas Washbourne, aged 39, [who] died by a fall from his horse, buried at Wroughton 7 June 1808.

10 October 1837

Order to admit Betty Wride of Froxfield, widow, relict of John Wride late of Taunton St. Mary Magdalen, to no. 32, vacant by the death of Frances Bray; a manor widow. Signed by Thomas Vilett.

Marriage certificate of John Wride of Taunton St. Mary and Betty Bartlett of Langport parish, married at Langport 5 October 1803.

Burial certificate of John Wride, aged 51, of East Street, Taunton St. Mary Magdalen, buried there 4 April 1824.

1 January 1838

Order to admit Anne Waldron, widow, relict of the Revd. Thomas Waldron late of Bath, to no. 5, vacant by the death of Frances Weales; a clergy widow, Wiltshire, Berkshire, or Somerset. Signed by J. Dugdale Astley.

Marriage certificate of Thomas Waldron and Anne Glover, both of Great Malvern, married there 7 September 1795.

Burial certificate of the Revd. Thomas Waldron, aged 64, of Malvern, buried there 18 November 1825.

3 August 1838

Order to admit Elizabeth Maylor Periam, widow, relict of George Periam late of Red Lion Street, to no. 47, vacant by the death of Jane Spanswick; a lay widow, London or Westminster. Signed by John Awdry.

Marriage certificate of George Periam and Elizabeth Maylor Rice, both of the parish of St. Stephen's, Coleman Street, London, married there 8 November 1796.

Burial certificate of George Periam, aged 42, of Red Lion Street, buried in the parish of Christchurch [Spitalfields] (Mdx.) 22 September 1805.

[The order to admit contains a letter from Thomas Merriman to Mrs. Periam: he was desired by Mr. Awdry to send to her the annexed nomination (*i.e.* order to admit) to a tenement and, in London in 10–14 days, offers to call on her and give information. The letter is dated 4 August and addressed to her at 28 Carey Street]

6 August 1838

Order to admit Maria Coombs, widow, relict of Richard Coombs late of Bishop's Cannings, to no. 42, vacant by the death of Elizabeth Wells; a lay widow, Wiltshire, Berkshire, or Somerset. Signed by E. W. L. Popham.

Marriage certificate of Richard Coombs of Berwick St. James and Maria Rowden of Compton [Chamberlayne], married at Compton 5 November 1807.

Burial certificate of Richard Coombs, aged 42, of the chapelry of Southbroom, buried there 5 December 1826.

2 February 1839

Order to admit Mary Ann Whitelock, widow, relict of Edward Whitelock late of Pentonville, to no. 28, vacant by the death of Mary Slade; a lay widow, counties-at-large. Signed by T. G. Bucknall Estcourt.

Marriage certificate of Edward Whitelock and Mary Ann Mullord, both of the parish of St. George's, Hanover Square, married there 13 October 1799.

Burial certificate of Edward Whitelock, aged 40, S.L., buried in the parish of Christ Church and St. Leonard, Foster [Lane], in the City of London 1 April 1808.

12 April 1839

Order to admit Sophia Owen, widow, relict of Owen Owen late of [the parish of] St. George's, Hanover Square, to no. 27, vacant by the death of Catherine Breach; a lay widow, London or Westminster. Signed by [Lord] Ailesbury.

Marriage certificate of Owen Owen of the parish of St. George's, Hanover Square, and Sophia Kingston of the parish of St. James's, Westminster, married in St. James's church 3 December 1815.

Burial certificate of Owen Owen, aged 80, of Royal Hill in Greenwich parish, buried 24 February 1837.

22 April 1839

Order to admit Frances Broughton, widow, relict of Brian Broughton, clerk, late of Long Ditton, to no. 19, vacant by the death of Ann Parker; a clergy widow, Wiltshire, Berkshire, or Somerset. Signed by Ambrose Goddard.

Marriage certificate of Brian Broughton, clerk, of Long Ditton and Frances Fagg of St. Marylebone, married in Long Ditton church 12 July 1825.

Burial certificate of Brian Broughton, aged 71, of Long Ditton, for 21 years rector of Long Ditton, buried there 15 January 1838.

3 May 1839

Order to admit Fanny Maria Hancock, widow, relict of John Hancock late of Ludgvan (*Ludgoon*), to no. 38, vacant by the death of Nanny Brinsden; a lay widow, London or Westminster. Signed by J. Dugdale Astley.

Marriage certificate of John Hancock and Fanny Maria Francis, both of the parish of St. George's, Hanover Square, married there 11 January 1815.

Burial certificate of John Hancock, aged 47, of Varfell (*Vorfill*), buried in Ludgvan parish 19 March 1835.

9 August 1839

Order to admit Sarah Painter, widow, relict of John Painter late of Froxfield, to no. 35, vacant by the death of Ann Dangerfield; a manor widow. Signed by J. H. Penruddocke.

Marriage certificate of John Painter of Kintbury and Sarah Smoaker of Hungerford, married in Hungerford church 15 October 1797.

Burial certificate of John Painter, aged 65, of Froxfield, buried there 10 June 1838.

11 March 1840

Order to admit Mary Pocock, widow, relict of Robert Pocock late of Reading, to no. 23, vacant by the death of Elizabeth Wells; a [lay] widow, counties-at-large. Signed by Thomas Vilett.

Marriage certificate of Robert Pocock of Warminster parish and Mary Crook of Newbury parish, married in Newbury church 7 May 1812.

Burial certificate of Robert Pocock, aged 48, of Albion Street, buried in the parish of St. Giles, Reading, 24 May 1837.

20 July 1840

Order to admit Mary Scotford, widow, relict of William Scotford late of

Swindon, to no. 29, vacant by the death of Mary Whitley; a lay widow, London or Wesminster. Signed by Ambrose Goddard.

Marriage certificate of William Scotford of Swindon parish and Mary Collins of Aynho parish, married in Aynho church 7 September 1809.

Burial certificate of William Scotford, aged 48, of Swindon, buried there 30 August 1826.

25 January 1841

Order to admit Sarah Brothers of Tottenham Park, widow, relict of John Brothers late of Marlborough, to no. 33, vacant by the death of Mary Willis; a lay widow, three-counties. Signed by [Lord] Bruce.

Marriage certificate of John Brothers and Sarah Martin, both of the parish of St. Leonard, Shoreditch, married in St. Leonard's church 1 January 1811.

Burial certificate of John Brothers, aged 44, of St. Peter's parish, Marlborough, buried there 5 March 1832.

16 February 1841

Order to admit Betty Gough, widow, relict of William Gough late of Bethnal Green, to no. 44, vacant by the death of Mary Edwards; a manor widow. Signed by John Awdry.

Marriage certificate of William Gough and Betty Bailey, both of Trowbridge, married there 11 April 1803.

Burial certificate of William Gough, aged 42, of Bethnal Green, buried in the Gibraltar burying ground there 23 March 1823.

26 April 1841

Order to admit Marian Godfrey, widow, relict of Charles Godfrey late of London, to no. 27, vacant by the death of Sophia Owen; a lay widow, London or Westminster. Signed by William Codrington.

Marriage certificate of Charles Godfrey and Marian Hendy, both of the parish of St. Martin in the Fields, married 21 June 1830.

Burial certificate of Charles Godfrey, aged 40, of Branch Place, buried in the district parish of St. John the Baptist 14 April 1839.

2 August 1841

Order to admit Jane Morris, widow, relict of the Revd. Elias Walker Morris late of Newbury, to no. 19, vacant by the resignation of Frances Broughton; a clergy widow, three-counties. Signed by E. W. L. Popham.

Marriage certificate of Elias Walker Morris of the parish of St. Giles, Oxford, and Jane Tustin of Combe (*Long Coombe*) parish, married in Combe church 12 July 1832.

Death certificate of Elias Walker Morris, aged 31, a minister of the Church of England, died of consumption at East Field, Victoria Place, Newbury, 10 April 1841.

17 February 1842

Order to admit Charlotte Prescott Bree, widow, relict of the Revd. Robert Francis Bree late of St. Michael's [*deleted*: College Street] [*added*: Royal] in the City of London, to no. 2, vacant by the death of Elizabeth Phillips;

a clergy widow, London or Westminster. Signed by T. G. Bucknall Estcourt.

Marriage certificate of Robert Francis Bree, clerk, widower, of St. Olave parish, Chichester, and Charlotte Maxwell of Hascombe, married in Hascombe church 14 June 1827.

Burial certificate of Robert Francis Bree, aged 66, of 23 Rockingham Row West, Old Kent Road, curate of the parish of St. Michael Royal in the City of London, buried in that parish 2 February 1842.

28 March 1842

Order to admit Ann Varrender, widow, relict of George Varrender, to no. 50, vacant by the death of Ann Geare; a lay widow, counties-at-large. Signed by John Awdry.

Marriage certificate of George Varrender of Blackland and Ann Homes of Box, married in Box church 8 June 1789.

Burial certificate of George Varrender, aged 56, of Blackland, buried there 23 April 1823.

3 September 1842

Order to admit Elizabeth Ann Belcher, widow, relict of Robert Belcher, to no. 48, vacant by the death of Elizabeth Vincent; a lay widow, counties-at-large. Signed by E. W. L. Popham.

Marriage certificate of Robert Belcher, widower, of the parish of St. Marylebone, and Elizabeth Ann Turrell, widow, of the parish of St. George, Hanover Square, married in St. George's church 21 January 1832.

Burial certificate of Robert Belcher, aged 71, of 28 Oxford Street, buried in the parish of St. Marylebone 31 January 1837.

27 October 1842

Order to admit Eleanor Heath, widow, relict of the Revd. William Heath late of East Grinstead, to no. 12, vacant by the death of Mary Davies; a clergy widow, three-counties. Signed by [Lord] Ailesbury.

Endorsed Afterwards declined accepting the tenement.

20 March 1843

Order to admit Eleanor Botham, widow, relict of George Botham late of Caversham, to no. 48, vacant by the resignation of Elizabeth Ann Belcher; a lay widow, counties-at-large. Signed by T. G. Bucknall Estcourt.

Marriage certificate of George Botham and Eleanor Frankland, both of the parish of St. Sepulchre, London, married in the church of St. Sepulchre 16 March 1788.

Burial certificate of George Botham, aged 65, of Speenhamland, buried in the parish of Speen 21 April 1827.

11 October 1843

Order to admit Sarah Brooks, widow, relict of Samuel Brooks late of Leicester, to no. 28, vacant by the resignation of Mary Ann Whitelock; a lay widow, counties-at-large. Signed by [Lord] Ailesbury.

Marriage certificate of Samuel Brooks, hosier, of St. Margaret's parish,

Leicester, and Sarah Outram of the parish of Holy Trinity, Kingston-upon-Hull, married 22 October 1807.

Burial certificate of Samuel Brooks, aged 32, buried in the parish of St. Martin, Leicester, 5 May 1811.

27 November 1843

Order to admit the Hon. Mrs. Barbara Bedford, widow, relict of the Revd. Thomas Bedford late of Wilshamstead, to no. 2, vacant by the death of Charlotte Prescott Bree; a clergy widow, London or Westminster. Signed by Thomas Vilett. *Endorsed* Took possession 30 November.

Marriage certificate of Thomas Bedford of the parish of St. Paul, Bedford, and Barbara St. John of the parish of Cardington, married in Cardington church 20 July 1813.

Burial certificate of Thomas Bedford, aged 28, of Tavistock Street, St. Giles in the Fields, buried in the parish of St. George, Bloomsbury, 16 March 1816.

16 March 1844

Order to admit Ann Applegate, widow, relict of Thomas Applegate late of Westbury (Wilts.), to no. 41, vacant by the death of Mary Read; a manor widow. Signed by Ambrose Goddard.

Marriage certificate of Thomas Applegate, widower, of Trowbridge, and Ann Bendy, widow, of Steeple Ashton parish, married in Semington chapel 4 May 1824.

Death certificate of Thomas Applegate, aged 53, ironmonger, died at Westbury of water on the chest 26 July 1838.

6 April 1844

Order to admit Elizabeth Kirby, widow, relict of the Revd. John Malsbury Kirby late of ... [*MS. blank*], Worcestershire, to no. 12, vacant by the death of Mary Davies; a clergy widow. Signed by [Lord] Ailesbury. *Endorsed* No. 12 is a clergy, three-counties, house but, no application having been made by a widow from that district within 12 months from advertisement, the marquess of Ailesbury nominates under rule 19 a clergy widow from a different district.

Marriage certificate of John Malsbury Kirby of the parish of Manchester, clerk, and Elizabeth Peell of the parish of St. Thomas, Winchester, married in St. Thomas's church 6 June 1823.

Burial certificate of the Revd. J. Malsbury Kirby, aged 45, of Stourbridge, buried in the parish of Old Swinford 8 December 1840.

2 July 1844

Order to admit Anna Maria Batt, widow, relict of George Batt late of Penton Mewsey, to no. 50, vacant by the death of Ann Varrender; a lay widow, counties-at-large. Signed by Henry Manvers Pierrepont.

Marriage certificate of George Batt of Idmiston and Anna Maria Batt of Grateley, married at Quarley 7 December 1815.

Burial certificate of George Batt, aged 58, of Penton Hill Farm, buried in

Weyhill parish 31 August 1838.

16 October 1844

Order to admit Susanna Bailes, widow, relict of the Revd. John Bailes late of Hilperton, to no. 4, vacant by the marriage of Delia Mary Cosens; a clergy widow, three-counties. Signed by [Lord] Bruce.

Marriage certificate of John Bailes, clerk, and Susanna Chapman, both of Hilperton parish, married there 7 January 1815.

Burial certificate of John Bailes, aged 69, clerk, of Hilperton, curate of Whaddon, buried at Whaddon 15 January 1842.

4 April 1845

Order to admit Anna Maria Duke, widow, relict of John Holloway Duke late of the colony of Demerara Essequibo, to no. 15, vacant by the death of Jane Braim; a clergy widow, London and Westminster. Signed by Henry Manvers Pierrepont. *Endorsed* Mrs. A. M. Duke took possession 1 May 1845.

There being no marriage certificate, the following letters were written.

Salston (*Saltstone*) House
8 April 1845
My Dear Madam

I have had the pleasure of receiving this morning your letter of the 5th instant and I would recommend you to lose no time in writing to Barbados for the required certificate of your marriage.

I am quite ready, however, in the absence of such certificate to bear my testimony both to the respectability of your character during the time that I knew you in the West Indies and to your having been the wife of one of my clergy, whom I very highly esteemed and whose premature death was very deeply regretted throughout the diocese. You are at liberty to make use of this letter.

And with my sincere wishes for your success I remain, my dear madam, very faithfully yours, W. H. Coleridge, late bishop of Barbados and the Leeward Islands.

P.S. I have written also by the post to the Rt. Hon. Mr. Pierrepont.

Sir

I have the honour to acknowledge the receipt of your letter this morning and beg to offer my grateful thanks for your kindness in dispensing at present with the necessity of my marriage certificate. On the receipt of your letter I have written to Barbados to forward it immediately but cannot expect an answer under 2 or 3 months as the packet will not sail before the 2nd of the next month. I sincerely hope they may be able to procure it, but after my marriage a severe storm desolated the island and the church was destroyed. Should the registers not have been saved (which, however, I trust they were) would an affidavit of persons present at my marriage be sufficient? One witness is now in England. The late bishop of Barbados can testify to the truth of my statement respecting the storm and destruction of Christ Church, and every effort shall be made to procure the certificate.

I feel much regret in trespassing so much on your kindness. My mind is much harrassed by the state of uncertainty I have been and am still in, and shall therefore feel relieved if you, Sir, will kindly favour me with an answer by return of post.

I remain, Sir, you most grateful and truly obliged servant, A. M. Duke.
17 April 1845
7 Pelham Crescent, Brompton.

Affidavits

I Anne Elizabeth Killikelly Green, wife of Mr. William Henry Green of the Ordnance Department, Chatham Lines, do hereby make oath and declare that I was present at the marriage of the late Revd. John Holloway Duke, afterwards rector of Trinity parish and rural dean of Essequibo, with Anna Maria Storey, and that it was solemnized at Christ Church in the island of Barbados in the West Indies 19 April 1827. Anne E. K. Green. *Endorsed* Sworn before me at Rochester this 3 May 1845, John Batten, J.P.

I do hereby certify under oath that the Revd. John Holloway Duke, late rector of Trinity parish, Essequibo, British Guiana, died 26 October 1841, and that the funeral solemnities were performed by me on the following day. [*Signed*] John Robinson, officiating minister, St. Swithun's, late curate of Trinity parish. Georgetown, Demerara, 2 December.
Endorsed 1842.

15 April 1845

Order to admit Grace Gale of Froxfield, widow, relict of William Gale late of Great Bedwyn, to no. 37, vacant by the death of Mary Exton; a manor widow. Signed by [Lord] Ailesbury. *Endorsed* Mrs. Gale took possession 18 April 1845.

Marriage certificate of William Gale, widower, and Grace Sadler, both of Great Bedwyn parish, married there 18 April 1805.

Burial certificate of William Gale, aged 62, of Great Bedwyn, buried there 14 August 1816.

29 April 1845

Order to admit Mary Trimmer, widow, relict of the Revd. Henry Trimmer late of Norwich, to no. 13, vacant by the death of Elizabeth Ann Graves; a clergy widow, counties-at-large. Signed by Ernest Bruce.

Marriage certificate of the Revd. Henry Trimmer of Newdigate and Mary Deacon of the parish of St. Pancras, married in the church of St. Pancras 5 June 1823.

Burial certificate of Henry Trimmer, aged 43, of St. Saviour's, Norwich, buried in the parish of St. George Tombland in the city and county of Norwich 27 July 1842.

23 May 1845

Order to admit Elizabeth Cooke, widow, relict of Henry Cooke late of Black Notley, to no. 13, vacant by the resignation of Mary Trimmer; a clergy widow, counties-at-large. Signed by G. W. Wroughton.

Marriage certificate of the Revd. Henry Cooke, widower, of the parish of St. Marylebone, and Elizabeth Cope Lodder of Hammersmith parish, married in Hammersmith church 25 September 1834.

Burial certificate of Henry Cooke, aged 72, of Picton Place, Picton Terrace, buried in St. Peter's parish in the county of the borough of Carmarthen 29 April 1842.

15 September 1845

Order to admit Mary Lee, widow, relict of Frederick Lee, rector of Easington, curate of Thame, to no. 16, vacant by the death of Mary Trusler; a clergy widow, counties-at-large. Signed by T. G. Bucknall Estcourt. *Endorsed* Mrs. Lee took possession 2 October 1845.

Marriage certificate of Frederick Lee, clerk, and Mary Ellis, both of Aylesbury, married there 10 February 1831.

Burial certificate of the Revd. Frederick Lee, aged 43, of Thame, buried there 11 November 1841.

22 December 1845

Order to admit Bridget Williams of New Street, Covent Garden, widow, relict of the Revd. Daniel Williams late of Llanfair, to no. 2, vacant by the resignation of the Hon. Barbara Bedford; a clergy widow, London or Westminster. Signed by H. N. Goddard.

Marriage certificate of the Revd. Daniel Williams and Bridget Vaughan, both of Llanllugan parish, married there 17 September 1813.

Burial certificate of the Revd. Daniel Williams, vicar of Llanfair Caereinion and perpetual curate of Llanllugan, buried 29 February 1836.

Attached

Covent Garden, 17 December 1845

T. B. Merriman, esq.

My Dear Sir

Many thanks for your obliging letter.

Mrs. Williams has resided in Northumberland Street, Strand, and in New Street, Covent Garden, for the last 3 years continuously.

She is the widow of the Revd. Daniel Williams, vicar of Llanfair in the county of Montgomery and diocese of St. Asaph, who died 22 February 1836. He had been in the church 60 years, the last 9 of which he was vicar of that parish, the 51 former curate of Llanllugan in the same county.

Mrs. Williams has one son in the clergy orphan school, a boy sadly afflicted and I fear not likely to grow up to man's estate.

Is there any form of petition for Froxfield? If so, I would take care to fill up all the particulars required according to the facts. As to the point of residence, she appears to be qualified by her having resided in her present abode, 13 New Street, Covent Garden, every day for above a year. Mrs. Williams was born in 1791.

Believe me my dear Sir
Most truly your
S. H. Bowers.

INDEX

WILTSHIRE RECORD SOCIETY
(AS AT OCTOBER 2013)

PRIVATE MEMBERS

ADAMS, MS S, 23 Rockcliffe Avenue, Bathwick, Bath BA2 6QP
ANDERSON, MR D M, 6 Keepers Mews, Munster Road, Teddington, Middlesex TW11 9NB
BADENI, COUNTESS JUNE, Garden Cottage, Norton, Malmesbury SN16 0JX
BAINBRIDGE, DR V, 60 Gloucester Road, Lower Swainswick, Bath BA1 7BN
BANKS, MR B H, 16 Velley Hill, Gastard, Corsham, SN13 9PU
BARNETT, MR B A, 3 The Orangery, Academy Drive, Corsham, SN13 0SF
BATHE, MR G, Byeley in Densome, Woodgreen, Fordingbridge, Hants SP6 2QU
BAYLIFFE, MR B G, 3 Green Street, Brockworth, Gloucester GL3 4LT
BENNETT, DR N, Hawthorn House, Main Street, Nocton, Lincoln LN4 2BH
BERRETT, MR A M, 10 Primrose Hill Road, London NW3 3AD
BERRY, MR C, 17 Fore Street, Hayle, Cornwall TR27 4DX
BLAKE, MR P A, 18 Rosevine Road, London SW20 8RB
BOX, MR S D, 73 Silverdale Road, Earley, Reading RG6 2NF
BRAND, DR P A, 155 Kennington Road, London SE11 6SF
BROWN, MR D A, 36 Empire Road, Salisbury SP2 9DF
BROWN, MR G R, 6 Canbury Close, Amesbury, Salisbury SP4 7QF
BROWNING, MR E, 58 Stratton Road, Swindon SN1 2PR
BRYSON, DR A, Humanities Research Institute, 34 Gell Street, Sheffield S3 7QW
CARRIER, MR S, 9 Highfield Road, Bradford on Avon BA15 1AS
CARTER, MR D, Docton Court, 2 Myrtle Street, Appledore, Bideford EX39 1PH
CAWTHORNE, MRS N, 45 London Road, Camberley, Surrey GU15 3UG
CHALMERS, MR D, Bay House West, Bay Hill, Ilminster, Somerset TA19 0AT
CHANDLER, DR J H, 3 Bermondsey Mews, Otley LS21 1SN
CHURCH, MR T S, 12 Cathedral View,

Winchester SO23 0PR
CLARK, MR G A, Highlands, 51a Brook Drive, Corsham SN13 9AX
CLARK, MRS V, 29 The Green, Marlborough SN8 1AW
COBERN, MISS A M, 4 Manton Close, Manton, Marlborough SN8 4HJ
COLCOMB, MR D M, 38 Roundway Park, Devizes SN10 2EO
COLES, MR H, Ebony House, 23 Lords Hill, Coleford, Glos GL16 8BG
COLLINS, MR A, 22 Innox Mill Close, Trowbridge BA14 9BA
COLLINS, MR A T, 36 Wasdale Close, Horndean, Waterlooville PO8 0DU
COLMAN, Mrs P, 37a Bath Road, Atworth, Melksham SN12 8JW
CONGLETON, LORD, West End Lodge, Ebbesbourne Wake, Salisbury SP5 5JW
COOMBES-LEWIS, MR R J, 45 Oakwood Park Road, Southgate, London N14 6QP
COOPER, MR S, 12 Victory Row, Royal Wootton Bassett, Swindon SN4 7BE
COWAN, MRS E, 24 Lower Street, Harnham, Salisbury SP2 8EY
CRAVEN, DR A, 17 Steamship House, Gasferry Road, Bristol BS1 1GL
CROOK, MR P H, Bradavon, 45 The Dales, Cottingham, E Yorks HU16 5JS
CROUCH, MR J W, 25 Biddesden Lane, Ludgershall, Andover SP11 5PJ
CROWLEY, DR D A, 7 Eversley Court, Wymering Road, Southwold IP18 6BF
CUNNINGTON, Ms J, 1177 Yonge Street, #214, Toronto, Ont. M4T 2Y4, Canada
DAKERS, PROF C, Ferneley Cottage, Water Street, Berwick St John, Shaftesbury SP7 0HS
D'ARCY, MR J N, The Old Vicarage, Edington, Westbury BA13 4QF
DAVIES, MRS A M, Barnside, Squires Lane, Old Clipstone, Mansfield NG21 9BP
DYSON, MRS L, 1 Dauntsey Ct, Duck St, West Lavington, Devizes SN10 4LR
EDE, DR M E, 12 Springfield Place, Lansdown, Bath BA1 5RA
EDWARDS, MR P C, 33 Longcroft Road, Devizes SN10 3AT
FIRMAGER, MRS G M, 72b High Street, Semington, Trowbridge BA14 6JR
FLOWER-ELLIS, DR J G, Kyrkogatan 2A, SE-815, 38 TIERP, Sweden
FOSTER, MR R E, Cothelstone, 24 Francis Way, Salisbury, SP2 8EF
FOWLER, MRS C, 10 Ullswater Road, Wimborne, Dorset, BH21 1QT
FOY, MR J D, 28 Penn Lea Road, Bath BA1 3RA
FROST, MR B C, Red Tiles, Cadley, Collingbourne Ducis, Marlborough SN8 3EA
GAISFORD, MR J, 8 Dudley Road, London NW6 6JX
GALE, MRS J, PO Box 1015, Spit Junction, NSW 2088, Australia
GHEY, MR J G, Little Shute, Walditch, Bridport DT6 4LQ
GODDARD, MR R G H, Sinton Meadow, Stokes Lane, Leigh Sinton, Malvern, Worcs WR13 5DY
GOSLING, REV DR J, 1 Wiley Terrace, Wilton, Salisbury SP2 0HN
GOUGH, MISS P M, 39 Whitford Road, Bromsgrove, Worcs B61 7ED
GRIFFIN, D, C J, School of Geography, Queen's University, Belfast BT7 1NW
GRIST, MR M, 38 Springfield, Bradford on Avon BA15 1BB
HARDEN, MRS J O, The Croft, Tisbury Road, Fovant, Salisbury SP3 5JU
HARE, DR J N, 7 Owens Road, Winchester, Hants SO22 6RU
HARTE, DR N, St Aldhelm's Cottage, 5 Stokes Road, Corsham SN13 9AA
HEATON, MR R J, 16 St Bernard's Crescent, Harlow Road, High Wycombe HP11 1BL
HELMHOLZ, PROF R W, Law School, 1111 East 60th Street, Chicago, Illinois 60637 USA
HENLY, MR C R G, 27 Harden's Close, Chippenham SN15 3AA
HERRON, MRS Pamela M, 25 Anvil Crescent, Broadstone, Dorset BH18 9DY
HICKMAN, MR M R, 184 Surrenden Road, Brighton BN1 6NN
HICKS, MR I, 153 Cornbrash Rise, Trowbridge BA14 7TU

HICKS, PROF M A, Department of History, University of Winchester SO22 4NR
HILLMAN, MR R B, 20 West Ashton Road, Trowbridge BA14 7BQ
HOBBS, MR S, 63 West End, Westbury BA13 3JQ
HORNBY, MISS E, 70 Archers Court, Castle Street, Salisbury SP1 3WE
HOWELLS, DR Jane, 7 St Mark's Rd, Salisbury SP1 3AY
HUMPHRIES, MR A G, Rustics, Blacksmith's Lane, Harmston, Lincoln LN5 9SW
INGRAM, DR M J, Brasenose College, Oxford OX1 4AJ
JAMES, MR & MRS C, 20 The Willows, Yate, Bristol, BS37 5XL
JEACOCK, MR D, 16 Church Street, Wootton Bassett, Swindon SN4 7BQ
JOHNSTON, MRS J M, Greystone House, 3 Trowbridge Road, Bradford on Avon BA15 1EE
KENT, MR T A, Rose Cottage, Isington, Alton, Hants GU34 4PN
KITE, MR P J, 13 Chestnut Avenue, Farnham GU9 8UL
KNEEBONE, MR W J R, Rose Cottage, Barbican Hill, Looe PL13 1BB
KNOWLES, MRS V A, New Woodland Cottage, Stanton St Bernard, Marlborough SN8 4LP
LANSDOWNE, MARQUIS OF, Bowood House, Calne SN11 0LZ
LAURENCE, MISS A, 1a Morreys Avenue, Oxford OX1 4ST
LAWES, MRS G, 48 Windsor Avenue, Leighton Buzzard LU7 1AP
LEE, DR J, 66 Kingshill Road, Bristol, BS4 2SN
LUSH, DR G J, 5 Braeside Road, West Moors, Ferndown, Dorset BH22 0JS
MARSH, REV R, 67 Hythe Crescent, Seaford, East Sussex BN25 3TZ
MARSHMAN, MR M J, 13 Regents Place, Bradford on Avon BA15 1ED
MARTIN, MS J, 21 Ashfield Road, Chippenham SN15 1QQ
MASLEN, MR A, 6 Whitestone Road, Frome BA11 2DN
MATHEWS, MR R, 57, Anthony Road, Denistone, NSW 2114, Australia
MOLES, MRS M I, 40 Wyke Road, Trowbridge BA14 7NP
MONTAGUE, MR M D, 115 Stuarts Road, Katoomba, NSW 2780, Australia
MOODY, MR R F, Fair Orchard, South Widcombe, East Harptree, Bristol BS40 6BL
MORIOKA, PROF K, 3-12, 4-chome, Sanno, Ota-ku, Tokyo, Japan
MORLAND, MRS N, 33 Shaftesbury Road, Wilton, Salisbury SP2 0DU
NAPPER, MR L R, 9 The Railway Terrace, Kemble, Cirencester GL7 6AU
NEWBURY, MR C COLES, 6 Leighton Green, Westbury BA13 3PN
NEWMAN, MRS R, Tanglewood, Laverstock Park, Salisbury SP1 1QJ
NICOLSON, MR A, Sissinghurst Castle, Cranbrook, Kent TN17 2AB
NOKES, MR P M A, 3 Rockleaze Avenue, Bristol BS9 1NG
OGBOURNE, MR J M V, 4 Aster Drive, Stafford ST16 1FH
OGBURN, MR D A, 110 Libby Lane, Galena, Missouri 65656, USA
OGBURN, SENIOR JUDGE R W, 303 West Hahn's Peak Avenue, Pueblo West, Colorado, 81007, USA
PARKER, DR P F, 45 Chitterne Road, Codford St Mary, Warminster BA12 0PG
PATIENCE, MR D C, 29 Priory Gardens, Stamford, Lincs PE9 2EG
PERRY, MR W A, 11 Buttercup Close, Salisbury SP2 8FA
POWELL, MRS N, 4 Verwood Drive, Bitton, Bristol BS15 6JP
PRICE, MR A J R, Littleton Mill, Littleton Pannell, Devizes SN10 4EP
PRIDGEON, DR E, 4 Williams Court, Park Street, Hungerford RG17 0DR
RAYBOULD, MISS F, 20 Radnor Road, Salisbury SP1 3PL
RAYMOND, MR S, 38 Princess Gardens, Trowbridge BA14 7PT
ROBERTS, MS M, 45 Spratts Barn, Royal Wootton Bassett, Swindon SN4 7JR
ROBINSON, MRS S, The Round House, 109 Chitterne, Warminster BA12 0LH

Rogers, Mr K H, Silverthorne House, East Town, West Ashton, Trowbridge BA14 6BE
Rolfe, Mr R C, 4 The Slade, Newton Longville, Milton Keynes MK17 0DR
Saunt, Mrs B A, The Retreat, Corton, Warminster, BA12 0SL
Sharman-Crawford, Mr T, One Mapledurham View, Tilehurst, Reading RG31 6LF
Sheldrake, Mr B, The Coach House, 4 Palmer Row, Weston super Mare, BS23 1RY
Shewring, Mr P, 73 Woodland Road, Beddau, Pontypridd, Mid-Glamorgan CF38 2SE
Singer, Mr J, 49 Bradwall Road, Sandbach, Cheshire CW11 1GH
Slocombe, Mr I, 11 Belcombe Place, Bradford on Avon BA15 1NA
Smith, Mr P J, 6 Nuthatch, Longfield, Kent DA3 7NS
Sneyd, Mr R H, Court Farm House, 22 Court Lane, Bratton, Westbury BA13 4RR
Spaeth, Dr D A, School of History and Archaeology, 1 University Gardens, University of Glasgow G12 8QQ
Stevenage, Mr M R, 49 Centre Drive, Epping, Essex CM16 4JF
Stone, Mr M J, 26 Awdry Close, Chippenham SN14 0TQ
Suter, Mrs C, 16 Swindon Road, Highworth, Swindon, SN6 7SL
Sutton, Mr A E, 22 Gravel Hill, Wimborne BH21 1RR
Tatton-Brown, Mr T, Fisherton Mill House, Mill Road, Salisbury, SP2 7RZ
Taylor, Mr C C, 11 High Street, Pampisford, Cambridge CB2 4ES
Taylor, Miss H, 14 Pampas Court, Warminster BA12 8RS
Thompson, Mr & Mrs J B, 1 Bedwyn Common, Great Bedwyn, Marlborough SN8 3HZ
Thomson, Mrs S M, Home Close, High St, Codford, Warminster BA12 0NB
Tighe, Mrs D, Strath Colin, Pettridge Lane, Mere, Warminster BA12 6DG
Vine, Mr R E, 11 Brocks Mount, Stoke sub Hamdon, Somerset, TA14 6PJ
Waite, Mr R E, 18a Lower Road, Chinnor, Oxford OX9 4DT
Warren, Mr P, 6 The Meadows, Milford Mill Road, Salisbury SP1 2SS
Williamson, B, 40 Florence Park, Bristol BS6 7LR
Wiltshire, Mr J, Cold Kitchen Cottage, Kingston Deverill, Warminster BA12 7HE
Wiltshire, Mrs P E, 23 Little Parks, Holt, Trowbridge BA14 6QR
Woodward, A S, 35 West Ridge Drive, Stittsville, Ontario K2S 1S4, Canada
Wright, Mr D P, Gerrans, Coast Road, Cley-next-the-Sea, Holt NR25 7RZ
Younger, Mr C, The Old Chapel, Burbage, Marlborough SN8 3AA

UNITED KINGDOM INSTITUTIONS

Aberystwyth
National Library of Wales
University College of Wales
Bath. Reference Library
Birmingham. University Library
Bristol
University of Bristol Library
University of the West of England
Cambridge. University Library
Cheltenham. Bristol and Gloucestershire Archaeological Society
Chippenham
Museum & Heritage Centre
Wiltshire and Swindon History Centre
Coventry. University of Warwick Library
Devizes
Wiltshire Archaeological & Natural History Society
Wiltshire Family History Society
Durham. University Library
Edinburgh
National Library of Scotland
University Library
Exeter. University Library

Glasgow. University Library
Leeds. University Library
Leicester. University Library
Liverpool. University Library
London
  British Library
  College of Arms
  Guildhall Library
  Inner Temple Library
  Institute of Historical Research
  London Library
  The National Archives
  Royal Historical Society
  Society of Antiquaries
  Society of Genealogists
Manchester. John Rylands Library
Marlborough
  Memorial Library, Marlborough College
  Merchant's House Trust
  Savernake Estate Office
Norwich. University of East Anglia Library
Nottingham. University Library
Oxford
  Bodleian Library
  Exeter College Library
Reading. University Library
St Andrews. University Library
Salisbury
  Bemerton Local History Society
  Bourne Valley Historical Society
  Cathedral Library
  Salisbury and South Wilts Museum
Southampton. University Library
Swansea. University College Library
Swindon
  English Heritage
  Swindon Borough Council
Taunton. Somerset Archaeological and Natural History Society
Trowbridge. Wiltshire Libraries and Heritage
Wetherby. British Library Document Supply Centre
York. University Library

INSTITUTIONS OVERSEAS

AUSTRALIA

Adelaide. University Library
Crawley. Reid Library, University of Western Australia
Melbourne. Victoria State Library

CANADA

Halifax. Killam Library, Dalhousie University
London, Ont. D.B.Weldon Library, University of Western Ontario
Ottawa, Ont. Carleton University Library
Toronto, Ont
  Pontifical Inst of Medieval Studies
  University of Toronto Library
Victoria, B.C. McPherson Library, University of Victoria

EIRE

Dublin. Trinity College Library

GERMANY

Gottingen. University Library

JAPAN

Sendai. Institute of Economic History, Tohoku University
Tokyo. Waseda University Library

NEW ZEALAND

Wellington. National Library of New Zealand

UNITED STATES OF AMERICA

Ann Arbor, Mich. Hatcher Library, University of Michigan
Athens, Ga. University of Georgia Libraries
Atlanta, Ga. The Robert W Woodruff Library, Emory University
Bloomington, Ind. Indiana University Library
Boston, Mass. New England Historic and Genealogical Society
Boulder, Colo. University of Colorado Library
Cambridge, Mass.
  Harvard College Library
  Harvard Law School Library
Charlottesville, Va. Alderman Library, University of Virginia
Chicago
  Newberry Library
  University of Chicago Library
Dallas, Texas. Public Library

Davis, Calif. University Library
East Lansing, Mich. Michigan State University Library
Evanston, Ill. United Libraries, Garrett/Evangelical, Seabury
Fort Wayne, Ind. Allen County Public Library
Houston, Texas. M.D. Anderson Library, University of Houston
Iowa City, Iowa. University of Iowa Libraries
Ithaca, NY. Cornell University Library
Los Angeles
  Public Library
  Young Research Library, University of California
Minneapolis, Minn. Wilson Library, University of Minnesota
New York
  Columbia University of the City of New York
Piscataway, N.J. Rutgers University Libraries
Princeton, N.J. Princeton University Libraries
Salt Lake City, Utah. Family History Library
San Marino, Calif. Henry E. Huntington Library
Santa Barbara, Calif. University of California Library
South Hadley, Mass. Williston Memorial Library, Mount Holyoke College
Urbana, Ill. University of Illinois Library
Washington. The Folger Shakespeare Library
Winston-Salem, N.C. Z.Smith Reynolds Library, Wake Forest University

LIST OF PUBLICATIONS

The Wiltshire Record Society was founded in 1937, as the Records Branch of the Wiltshire Archaeological and Natural History Society, to promote the publication of the documentary sources for the history of Wiltshire. The annual subscription is £15 for private and institutional members. In return, a member receives a volume each year. Prospective members should apply to the Hon. Secretary, c/o Wiltshire and Swindon History Centre, Cocklebury Road, Chippenham SN15 3QN. Many more members are needed.

The following volumes have been published. Price to members £15, and to non-members £20, postage extra. Most volumes up to 51 are still available from the Wiltshire and Swindon History Centre, Cocklebury Road, Chippenham SN15 3QN. Volumes 52-65 are available from Hobnob Press, 30c Deverill Road Trading Estate, Sutton Veny, Warminster BA12 7BZ

1. *Abstracts of feet of fines relating to Wiltshire for the reigns of Edward I and Edward II*, ed. R.B. Pugh, 1939
2. *Accounts of the parliamentary garrisons of Great Chalfield and Malmesbury, 1645–1646*, ed. J.H.P. Pafford, 1940
3. *Calendar of Antrobus deeds before 1625*, ed. R.B. Pugh, 1947
4. *Wiltshire county records: minutes of proceedings in sessions, 1563 and 1574 to 1592*, ed. H.C. Johnson, 1949
5. *List of Wiltshire boroughs records earlier in date than 1836*, ed. M.G. Rathbone, 1951
6. *The Trowbridge woollen industry as illustrated by the stock books of John and Thomas Clark, 1804–1824*, ed. R.P. Beckinsale, 1951
7. *Guild stewards' book of the borough of Calne, 1561–1688*, ed. A.W. Mabbs, 1953
8. *Andrews' and Dury's map of Wiltshire, 1773: a reduced facsimile*, ed. Elizabeth Crittall, 1952
9. *Surveys of the manors of Philip, earl of Pembroke and Montgomery, 1631–2*, ed. E. Kerridge, 1953
10. *Two sixteenth century taxations lists, 1545 and 1576*, ed. G.D. Ramsay, 1954
11. *Wiltshire quarter sessions and assizes, 1736*, ed. J.P.M. Fowle, 1955
12. *Collectanea*, ed. N.J. Williams, 1956
13. *Progress notes of Warden Woodward for the Wiltshire estates of New College, Oxford, 1659–1675*, ed. R.L. Rickard, 1957
14. *Accounts and surveys of the Wiltshire lands of Adam de Stratton*, ed. M.W. Farr, 1959
15. *Tradesmen in early-Stuart Wiltshire: a miscellany*, ed. N.J. Williams, 1960
16. *Crown pleas of the Wiltshire eyre, 1249*, ed. C.A.F. Meekings, 1961
17. *Wiltshire apprentices and their masters, 1710–1760*, ed. Christabel Dale, 1961
18. *Hemingby's register*, ed. Helena M. Chew, 1963
19. *Documents illustrating the Wiltshire textile trades in the eighteenth century*, ed. Julia de L. Mann, 1964
20. *The diary of Thomas Naish*, ed. Doreen Slatter, 1965

21–2. *The rolls of Highworth hundred, 1275–1287*, 2 parts, ed. Brenda Farr, 1966, 1968

23. *The earl of Hertford's lieutenancy papers, 1603–1612*, ed. W.P.D. Murphy, 1969
24. *Court rolls of the Wiltshire manors of Adam de Stratton*, ed. R.B. Pugh, 1970
25. *Abstracts of Wiltshire inclosure awards and agreements*, ed. R.E. Sandell, 1971
26. *Civil pleas of the Wiltshire eyre, 1249*, ed. M.T. Clanchy, 1971
27. *Wiltshire returns to the bishop's visitation queries, 1783*, ed. Mary Ransome, 1972
28. *Wiltshire extents for debts, Edward I – Elizabeth I*, ed. Angela Conyers, 1973
29. *Abstracts of feet of fines relating to Wiltshire for the reign of Edward III*, ed. C.R. Elrington, 1974
30. *Abstracts of Wiltshire tithe apportionments*, ed. R.E. Sandell, 1975

31. *Poverty in early-Stuart Salisbury*, ed. Paul Slack, 1975
32. *The subscription book of Bishops Tounson and Davenant, 1620–40*, ed. B. Williams, 1977
33. *Wiltshire gaol delivery and trailbaston trials, 1275–1306*, ed. R.B. Pugh, 1978
34. *Lacock abbey charters*, ed. K.H. Rogers, 1979
35. *The cartulary of Bradenstoke priory*, ed. Vera C.M. London, 1979
36. *Wiltshire coroners' bills, 1752–1796*, ed. R.F. Hunnisett, 1981
37. *The justicing notebook of William Hunt, 1744–1749*, ed. Elizabeth Crittall, 1982
38. *Two Elizabethan women: correspondence of Joan and Maria Thynne, 1575–1611*, ed. Alison D. Wall, 1983
39. *The register of John Chandler, dean of Salisbury, 1404–17*, ed. T.C.B. Timmins, 1984
40. *Wiltshire dissenters' meeting house certificates and registrations, 1689–1852*, ed. J.H. Chandler, 1985
41. *Abstracts of feet of fines relating to Wiltshire, 1377–1509*, ed. J.L. Kirby, 1986
42. *The Edington cartulary*, ed. Janet H. Stevenson, 1987
43. *The commonplace book of Sir Edward Bayntun of Bromham*, ed. Jane Freeman, 1988
44. *The diaries of Jeffery Whitaker, schoolmaster of Bratton, 1739–1741*, ed. Marjorie Reeves and Jean Morrison, 1989
45. *The Wiltshire tax list of 1332*, ed. D.A. Crowley, 1989
46. *Calendar of Bradford-on-Avon settlement examinations and removal orders, 1725–98*, ed. Phyllis Hembry, 1990
47. *Early trade directories of Wiltshire*, ed. K.H. Rogers and indexed by J.H. Chandler, 1992
48. *Star chamber suits of John and Thomas Warneford*, ed. F.E. Warneford, 1993
49. *The Hungerford Cartulary: a calendar of the earl of Radnor's cartulary of the Hungerford family*, ed. J.L. Kirby, 1994
50. *The Letters of John Peniston, Salisbury architect, Catholic, and Yeomanry Officer, 1823–1830*, ed. M. Cowan, 1996
51. *The Apprentice Registers of the Wiltshire Society, 1817– 1922*, ed. H. R. Henly, 1997
52. *Printed Maps of Wiltshire 1787–1844: a selection of topographical, road and canal maps in facsimile*, ed. John Chandler, 1998
53. *Monumental Inscriptions of Wiltshire: an edition, in facsimile, of Monumental Inscriptions in the County of Wilton, by Sir Thomas Phillipps*, ed. Peter Sherlock, 2000
54. *The First General Entry Book of the City of Salisbury, 1387–1452*, ed. David R. Carr, 2001
55. *Devizes Division income tax assessments, 1842–1860*, ed. Robert Colley, 2002
56. *Wiltshire Glebe Terriers, 1588–1827*, ed. Steven Hobbs, 2003
57. *Wiltshire Farming in the Seventeenth Century*, ed. Joseph Bettey, 2005
58. *Early Motor Vehicle Registration in Wiltshire, 1903–1914*, ed. Ian Hicks, 2006
59. *Marlborough Probate Inventories, 1591–1775*, ed. Lorelei Williams and Sally Thomson, 2007
60. *The Hungerford Cartulary, part 2: a calendar of the Hobhouse cartulary of the Hungerford family*, ed. J.L. Kirby, 2007
61. *The Court Records of Brinkworth and Charlton*, ed. Douglas Crowley, 2009
62. *The Diary of William Henry Tucker, 1825–1850*, ed. Helen Rogers, 2009
63. *Gleanings from Wiltshire Parish Registers*, ed. Steven Hobbs, 2010
64. *William Small's Cherished Memories and Associations*, ed. Jane Howells and Ruth Newman, 2011
65. *Crown Pleas of the Wiltshire Eyre, 1268*, ed. Brenda Farr and Christopher Elrington, rev. Henry Summerson, 2012

VOLUMES IN PREPARATION

Wiltshire papist returns and estate enrolments, 1705–87, edited by J.A. Williams; *The parish registers of Thomas Crockford, 1613–29*, edited by C.C. Newbury; *Wiltshire rural industry organiser surveys and reports, c. 1938 – c. 1957*, edited by Ian Hicks; *Public health in 19th-century Wiltshire*, edited by Negley Harte; *The churchwardens' accounts of St. Mary's, Devizes, 1600–1700*, edited by Alex Craven. *Wiltshire Quarter Sessions order book, 1642–52*, edited by Ivor Slocombe. The volumes will not necessarily appear in this order.

A leaflet giving full details may be obtained from the Hon. Secretary, c/o Wiltshire and Swindon History Centre, Cocklebury Road, Chippenham, Wilts. SN15 3QN.